The Oxfordshire Record Society
Volume 73

The Parish in Wartime

THE OXFORDSHIRE RECORD SOCIETY

The Society was founded in 1919. Its objectives are to publish transcripts, abstracts and lists of primary sources for the history of the county of Oxfordshire and to extend awareness and understanding of archives relating to Oxfordshire. The Society welcomes proposals for volumes for publication. There are no restrictions on time period or topic.

The publication programme of the Society is overseen by an Editorial Committee, established in 2017. Its members are:

Elizabeth Gemmill, BA, MA, PhD
Deborah Hayter, MA
Adrienne Rosen, MA, DPhil
Kate Tiller, OBE, DL, MA, PhD, FSA, FRHistS
Simon Townley, BA, PGCE, DPhil, FSA
Paul Gaskell (Secretary, ORS, *ex officio*)

Information about the Society, its publications and how to make a proposal for a publication may be found on its website:

http://www.oxfordshire-record-society.org.uk/

The Parish in Wartime

Bishop Gore's Visitations of Oxfordshire, 1914 and 1918

Edited by Mark Smith

The Boydell Press
Oxfordshire Record Society
Volume 73

© Oxfordshire Record Society 2019

All rights reserved. Except as permitted under current legislation
no part of this work may be photocopied, stored in a retrieval system,
published, performed in public, adapted, broadcast,
transmitted, recorded or reproduced in any form or by any means,
without the prior permission of the copyright owner

First published 2019

An Oxfordshire Record Society publication
Published by Boydell & Brewer Ltd
PO Box 9, Woodbridge, Suffolk IP12 3DF, UK
and Boydell & Brewer Inc.
668 Mt Hope Avenue, Rochester, NY 14620–2731, USA
website: www.boydellandbrewer.com

ISBN 978-0-902509-75-7

A CIP catalogue record for this book is available
from the British Library

The publisher has no responsibility for the continued existence or accuracy of
URLs for external or third-party internet websites referred to in this book, and
does not guarantee that any content on such websites is, or will remain, accurate
or appropriate

This publication is printed on acid-free paper

Printed and bound in Great Britain by
TJ International Ltd, Padstow, Cornwall

For Jane and Sarah
Without whom this project would not have been possible.
With whom it has been a pleasure.

Contents

Foreword	ix
Acknowledgements	xi
Editorial Conventions	xii
Introduction	1
The Visitation of 1914	65
The Visitation of 1918	337
Glossary	587
Select Bibliography	589
Index	591

Foreword

This latest volume of the Oxfordshire Record Society (ORS) series is published in the Society's centenary year and, fittingly, it presents a major source covering the whole county as it was a hundred years ago. The Oxfordshire visitations of 1914 and 1918 were framed by the questions which the bishop of Oxford, Charles Gore, put to his parish clergy. The resulting returns say much of the state of the Church, faith and religious practice in Oxfordshire on the eve of the First World War and again as the conflict was nearing its exhausting end. They also reflect the Established Church's ubiquitous presence and involvement in most aspects of local life. The visitations offer not a narrowly religious view of Oxfordshire life but something much broader, partly prompted by the bishop's choice of questions but also reflecting parish life on the ground and the vivid variety of Oxford clergy and their views, which shine through untrammelled by any questionnaire.

Ecclesiastical visitation returns have been a popular choice for publication by record societies. They are a source that is widespread, long-running, preserved in institutional archives, and which captures a key institution and its wide-ranging relationships with local communities. ORS has twice before ventured into this field, with volumes of the 1738 returns to bishop Secker (the first surviving visitation record for the Oxford diocese) and the 1854 returns to bishop Samuel Wilberforce. The latter, together with the Society's publications of Wilberforce's letter books and diocese books, shows how the county in the mid-nineteenth century experienced a reinvigoration of parish and diocesan life, in which resident clergy, new or restored churches, increased and varied worship, and active educational and social provision all featured prominently. The publication of the 1914 and 1918 returns enables us to see the results of that Victorian transformation in practice and how far it was being sustained into the early twentieth century.

By publishing twentieth-century visitations ORS has broken fresh ground, the fruits of which are soon apparent. A range of themes are illuminated, including the impact of rural depopulation, the relationship of competing traditions of High and Evangelical churchmanship, attitudes to nonconformity, the role of women in church life, class consciousness (witting and unwitting), and contrasting community experiences (from estate-dominated village societies like Heythrop to rapidly growing suburbs like Caversham). The 1914 and 1918 returns together open up the question of the impact of the war, a particular interest of bishop Gore who in 1918 asked clergy about its 'moral and spiritual effect on the different classes' in their parishes. The detail is rich – afternoon evensong to meet blackout restrictions from 1916, the reading of rolls of honour of names of parishioners on military service, and the effects of high wartime wages with clergy comment often directed to the young and female. (At Littlemore, girls' choice of munitions work was judged 'more often owing to high pay than patriotism'.) The returns also suggest broader historical trends and questions on which Mark Smith's expert introduction guides us. This centenary volume shows afresh the ongoing and developing value of the Society's work.

Kate Tiller, Chair, Oxfordshire Record Society

Acknowledgements

I wish to record my thanks to the Oxfordshire History Centre, the custodian of the records of the Oxford Diocese, for permission to publish my transcription of the visitation returns. Thanks are also due to Giles Darkes and the Oxfordshire Record Society, who gave permission for the re-publication of the Oxfordshire parish map first published by the Society in *An Historical Atlas of Oxfordshire*. No transcription project can ever be truly a solo effort and I am very happy to acknowledge the assistance of the editors of the Oxfordshire Record series: Dr William Whyte who first commissioned the project and Dr Kate Tiller who helped to bring it to completion. The project would not have been possible without the support of Mark Priddey and his colleagues at the Oxfordshire History Centre. They produced hundreds of documents on request with high professionalism and remarkable cheerfulness, given the excessive weight of the visitation volumes themselves. Their excellent coffee – a model for any record office – helped provide the stamina required for the intense struggle with clerical handwriting. I should also like to thank my consultants on Classical and New Testament Greek, Alison Samuels and Professor Peter Oakes, for their assistance in both translating and contextualising the forays of the clergy beyond the bounds of the English language. My academic colleagues and students listened patiently, on more occasions than they should have had to, to my preliminary conclusions on what might have been going on in the Oxfordshire parishes of 1914–18 and provided valuable commentary and encouragement. Most of all I should like to express my gratitude to my wife Jane and my daughter Sarah (already developing her skills as a budding historical researcher) who turned the project into a genuine family enterprise. They were involved in photographing the records so that they could be worked on outside History Centre hours, accompanying me on field trips to sample the churches recorded in the surveys, assisting at various stages of the transcription and finally providing the critique that ensured my own grammar and orthography would be a little more consistent than that of the early twentieth-century Oxfordshire clergy. Any and all remaining errors are, of course, entirely my own.

Mark Smith

Editorial Conventions

The Oxfordshire clergy whose returns to the bishop's visitation questionnaires provide the material for this volume displayed a glorious diversity in their use of the English (and occasionally Greek or Latin) language – particularly in grammar, spelling and mode of expression. This is part of the interest of the material and valuable evidence of the diversity of their backgrounds, experience and cast of mind. Their responses are thus presented in full and with only the lightest of editorial filters interposed to produce a readable text. I have kept editorial interventions to a minimum and have followed the convention of indicating them by the use of square brackets. Such interventions are of two kinds: editorial comments represented by *italic text* within square brackets and editorial interpolations represented by plain text within square brackets.

Comments generally indicate text which is indecipherable [*indeciph.*] or where my reconstruction is conjectural [*conj.*], both thankfully rare in this material. More frequently it represents the many ways in which the clergy indicated an inability (or refusal) to engage with one or more questions, finding a range of ways of striking it through or alternatively leaving the space for an answer blank: all these are indicated by [*No response*]. The word [*sic*], commonly used to indicate errors in spelling, grammar or sense, is employed sparsely and only where it seemed strictly necessary. In material produced over four years and by almost three hundred different writers there are inevitable variations in usage and spelling even of frequently used terms and so long as their meaning is clear I have not sought officiously to intervene between the reader and the text. I have, for example, made no attempt to arbitrate between the many Oxfordshire clergy who referred to the Prayer Book service of Morning Prayer as 'Matins' and the many others who preferred 'Mattins'. Similarly, I have allowed the many variations on Nonconformist, Non-Conformist, Non-conformist, non-conformist and nonconformist (referring principally to non-Anglican Protestants) which can be found sometimes within the same return and even within the same question, to engage the reader directly and without comment. It is often asserted that modern users of English have no idea of the correct use of the apostrophe. Even a brief exposure to the writings of the early twentieth-century Oxfordshire clergy amply demonstrates that this is far from being a recent phenomenon – at least among the university-educated classes. Here too I have adopted a policy of interfering as little as possible, changing or adding to punctuation only when absolutely necessary to maintain the sense intended by the author.

Editorial interpolations generally take the form of one or two letters inserted where they were clearly omitted inadvertently, as in the case of a reference to the

Rector's wif[e] at Midddleton Stoney in 1914. They are also used to repeat text where the original employed ditto marks in a list which cannot be accommodated within the format of the transcription. Additionally they indicate which element or elements of a multi-part question a given section of text is directed to, when, in the original, it is only represented by paragraphing or other formats which could not be reproduced in a transcribed volume. Thus text paragraphed to refer to sub-sections i–iii of question 4 in 1914 is introduced in answers to that question by [i–iii]. Most original abbreviations (e.g. H.C. for Holy Communion or St for Saint) are either in common usage or so plain in their meaning, in the context in which they appear, that it has been possible to leave them as they stand. Less familiar or accessible ones, together with details of some of the organisations (with their acronyms) and technical terms referred to in the returns, are explained in a Glossary (see pp. 587–8). The Oxfordshire clergy were nowhere more ingenious than in finding symbols for the word 'and'; with at least twenty, and probably more, variants to be found in the returns, I have adopted the simple expedient of expanding all of them to 'and', without drawing further attention to this choice.

The occasional use of Greek or Latin is presented in the text with a translation and explanation in a footnote, and some references to particular organisations or other features of parish life are also explained there. Otherwise footnotes are chiefly used to give supplementary information on the population of the parishes from the *Oxford Diocesan Calendar,* based on the 1911 census. Footnotes are also used to give a summary of the previous career of the clergyman completing the return, information having been drawn principally from the 1911 census and *Crockford's Clerical Directory.*

The visitation returns are presented here in the same order in which they are preserved. They were bound by the diocesan administrators in large volumes, in alphabetical order, by name of parish. The names were the official ones in use in 1914–18, printed annually in the *Oxford Diocesan Calendar* and used by the clergy (with minor variations) at the head of their returns. In the vast majority of cases, these names coincide with the modern usage, but there are a few examples where a reader searching for a particular parish may not find it in the expected alphabetical location. In particular, when the name was formed of two words the first of which is an adjective, the second was almost invariably used as the primary identifier. Thus, Little Tew will be found not under 'L' but under 'T', rendered as 'Tew, Little'; and perhaps more surprisingly, Hook Norton under 'N' as 'Norton, Hook'. However, a handful of parish names that in modern usage are formed of two words, in 1914 were written as one. Thus Brize Norton is not found under 'N' as 'Norton, Brize' but under 'B', rendered as 'Brizenorton'. In case of doubt the reader is advised to consult the index, which includes a full list of place names mentioned in the returns. The map represents the parishes of Oxfordshire as at 1850, and a handful of parishes in the 1914–18 returns are omitted (for example, Highfield and Leafield with Wychwood) because they were created in the second half of the nineteenth century. Their locations can readily be identified from a range of sources, especially www.achurchnearyou.com and www.visionofbritain.org.uk.

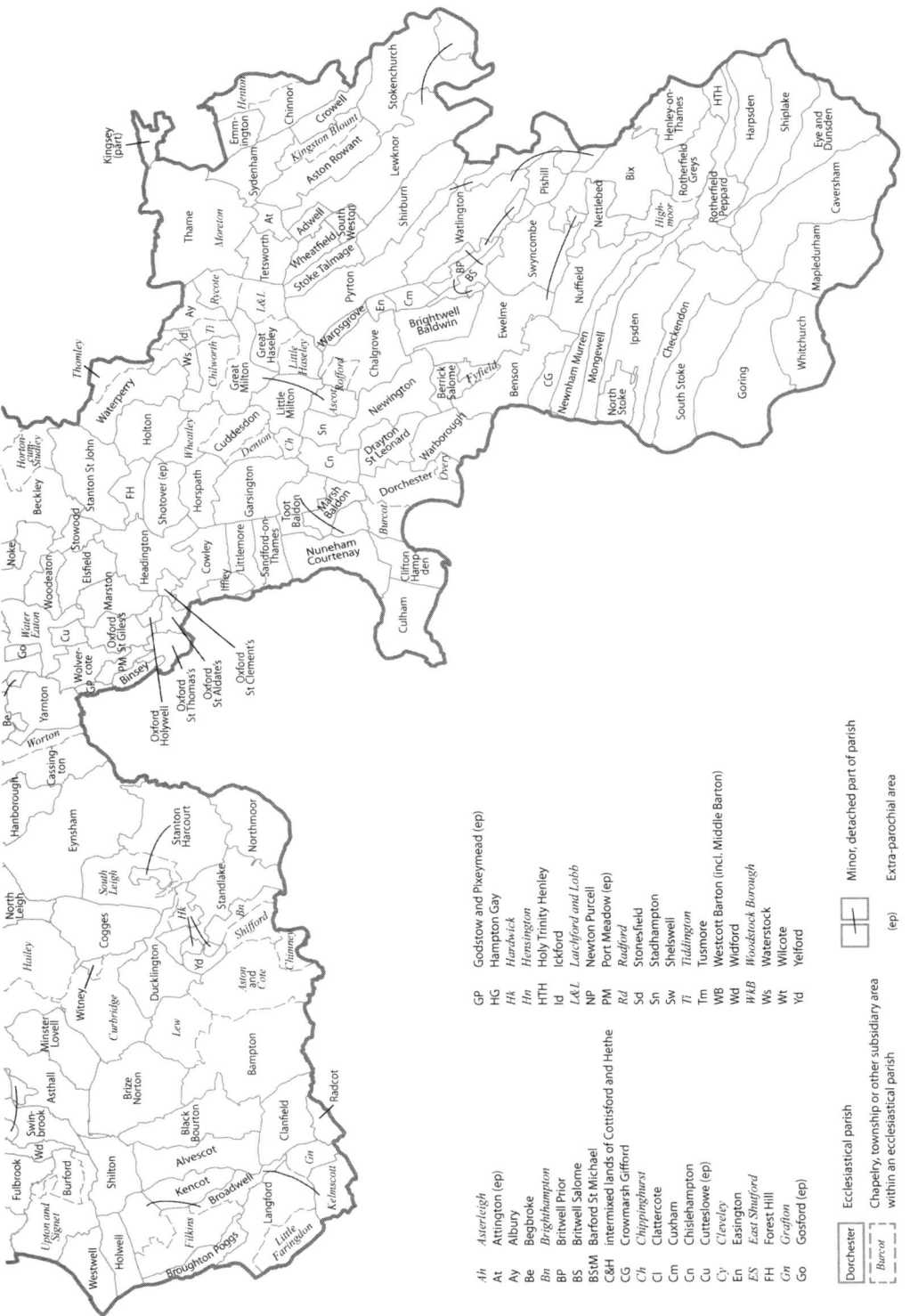

Introduction

The Visitation and the Returns

The visitation of a diocese, a tour by the bishop in person who would stop at major centres to meet the clergy and churchwardens from the surrounding parishes, was an ancient practice in the Church of England. It had, since the middle ages, been used for a range of purposes: disciplinary, administrative, financial and pastoral, with an increasing focus on the last of these from the beginning of the eighteenth century. In the conduct of his visitations, in the second decade of the twentieth century, bishop Gore clearly stood heir to this long tradition. In 1914, for example, he stopped in a total of twelve centres, those in Oxfordshire being Banbury, Oxford, Bicester, Wantage, and Witney.[1] However, the practice inherited by Gore of issuing a questionnaire to be completed by the clergy in advance of his visit was rather more recent. The introduction of such printed *pro forma* is usually attributed to bishop William Wake, who first used one in his visitation of the diocese of Lincoln in 1706, and developed it further over successive visitations. This process continued under Edmund Gibson, his successor at Lincoln, who in 1718 produced a pastorally focused survey widely regarded as a model. This encouraged the spread of visitation surveys more broadly so that by the middle of the eighteenth century printed *pro forma* addressed to the clergy were in use in almost every diocese in the church.[2] The Oxford diocese was a relatively early adopter, with its earliest surviving survey dating from 1738 – the primary visitation of bishop Thomas Secker – which contained twelve questions focused on a range of pastoral issues including the residence of the clergy, the presence of non-Anglicans or non-churchgoers in the parish and the existence of charitable

---

1   *Oxford Diocesan Magazine*, 9 (1914), p. 156. Gore also stopped at four centres in Buckinghamshire and three in Berkshire.
2   W. J. Sheils, 'Bishops and Their Dioceses: Reform of Visitation in the Anglican Church c.1680–c.1760', *CCEd Online Journal*, 1 (2007). http://www.theclergydatabase.org.uk/cce_a1/. J. Broad (ed.), Records of Social and Economic History: New Series, 49, *Bishop Wake's Summary of Visitation Returns from the Diocese of Lincoln, 1706–1715, Vol. 1 Lincolnshire* (Oxford, 2012), pp. xiv–xix.

institutions, especially schools.[3] Such surveys were developed further during the Victorian period and, in Oxford, particularly during the episcopate of Samuel Wilberforce (1845–69).[4] His 1854 articles of enquiry, for example, had grown to twenty-three questions, many with sub-sections, producing more than thirty individual queries. These again had a principally pastoral focus with attention on the presence of the clergy, the services they provided, the fabric of the church building, provision for education, and one more recent concern – the methods used to complete the returns for the Religious Census of 1851.[5]

Historians have made considerable use of both visitation returns and the summaries (often known as 'Specula') compiled from them, especially in the study of the eighteenth-century church[6] and to a lesser extent its Victorian successor.[7] The diocese of Oxford is particularly well suited to such a study owing to the exceptionally complete state of preservation of its visitation records. Altogether, at least some clergy returns have survived for a total of thirty-nine separate episcopal visitations between 1738 and 1899, with a further eleven taking the archive into the twentieth century as far as 1936. Partly because the study of the twentieth-century parish has hitherto attracted less historical attention than that of earlier periods, twentieth-century visitations have suffered comparative neglect.[8] The two visitations conducted by Charles Gore in 1914 and 1918, for example, have lain virtually

3   H. A. Lloyd-Jukes (ed.), *Articles of Enquiry Addressed to the Clergy of the Diocese of Oxford at the Primary Visitation of Dr Thomas Secker, 1738,* Oxfordshire Record Society, 38 (Oxford, 1957).
4   For the development of the episcopal visitation in the nineteenth century, see A. Burns, *The Diocesan Revival in the Church of England c. 1800–1870* (Oxford, 1999), pp. 23–40. For Wilberforce as a leading episcopal reformer, see A. Burns, 'Samuel Wilberforce', *ODNB*. https://ezproxyprd.bodleian.ox.ac.uk:4563/10.1093/ref:odnb/29385.
5   E. P. Baker (ed.), *Bishop Wilberforce's Visitation Returns for the Archdeaconry of Oxford in the Year 1854,* Oxfordshire Record Society, 35 (Oxford, 1954).
6   See, for example, W. R. Ward (ed.), *Parson and Parish in Eighteenth-Century Hampshire: Replies to Bishop's Visitations,* Hampshire Record Series, 13 (Winchester, 1995); J. Jago, *Aspects of the Georgian Church Visitation Studies of the Diocese of York 1761–1776* (London, 1997); J. Gregory (ed.), *The Speculum of Archbishop Thomas Secker,* Church of England Record Society, 2 (Woodbridge, 2003).
7   See V. A. Hatley (ed.), *The Church in Victorian Northampton: Visitation Records of Bishop Magee, 1872–1886,* Northamptonshire Record Society, 37 (Northampton, 1992); E. Royle and R. M. Larsen (eds), *Archbishop Thomson's Visitation Returns for the Diocese of York, 1865,* Borthwick Texts and Studies, 34 (York, 2008); R. Pugh and M. Pugh (eds), *The Diocese Books of Samuel Wilberforce Bishop of Oxford 1845–1869,* Oxfordshire Record Society, 66 (Oxford, 2008).
8   Thus far, only one volume based on early twentieth-century visitation material has been published, covering a visitation conducted between 1911 and 1915 in Derbyshire and Nottinghamshire and reproducing a set of summary returns published in the diocesan magazine. M. Austin (ed.), *Under the Heavy Clouds: The Church of England in Derbyshire and Nottinghamshire 1911–1915: The Parochial Visitation of Edwyn Hoskyns Bishop of Southwell* (Whitchurch, 2004).

unused, with the exception of a handful of citations in Pamela Horn's study of English rural life during the First World War[9] and a brief discussion by Clive Field in an article in *Southern History*.[10]

Charles Gore's 1914 survey, prepared for the first visitation since his appointment in 1911, can be seen very much as a continuation of the established tradition. Issued for completion in June 1914, it comprised eleven questions spread over four sides of foolscap, some with a number of sub-sections, to produce a total of twenty-one individual queries. As with its Victorian predecessors, the survey had a strong pastoral focus. The questions centred on the sacramental ministry of the Church, seeking information about the practice of both baptism and Holy Communion in the parishes, religious instruction for children and adults, provision for the children of nonconformist parents in church schools, and two new topics: the encouragement of interest in the work of the Church overseas, and arrangements for lay representation in the councils of the Church at both diocesan and parochial level.[11] Interestingly, however, Gore seems to have dropped a question, almost invariably asked by his predecessors, about the increase or decrease since the last visitation in the size of the general congregation. His focus was on provision made by the church rather than response to it.

A total of 226 Oxfordshire incumbents responded in full or in part to the 1914 survey which therefore provides an overview of the state of the Church of England in the Oxford archdeaconry in the last unclouded summer before the war. The 1918 survey was substantially different. Conducted in March 1918, just as the great German spring offensive was swinging into action on the western front and with no end to the war in sight, it broke with its predecessors in both form and content. It spread only six questions and eleven individual queries across four foolscap pages and posed two of them at the head of blank sheets inviting discursive answers – many incumbents duly obliged.[12] It retained the pastoral focus of the established tradition but with an entirely new emphasis on change – both change already accomplished as a result of the war and change anticipated at least partly as a consequence of the conflict. It was still interested in patterns of worship, but with a view to charting innovation under wartime conditions; its main question on education sought not so much information about school provision as to canvass the views of the clergy on impending changes to the system likely to be introduced after the war. The most significant question, however, aimed to get to the heart of the issues facing the parochial clergy, 'What can you report as to the moral and spiritual effect on the different classes in your parish' first of the war itself and then of the great Anglican initiative of 1916 – the National Mission of Repentance and Hope. The 229 returns

---

9   P. Horn, *Rural Life in England in the First World War* (Dublin, 1984).
10 C. D. Field, 'A Godly People? Aspects of Religious Practice in the Diocese of Oxford, 1738–1936', *Southern History*, 14 (1992), pp. 46–73.
11 Oxfordshire History Centre (OHC), MS Oxf. Dioc. c.377.
12 OHC, MS Oxf. Dioc. c.380.

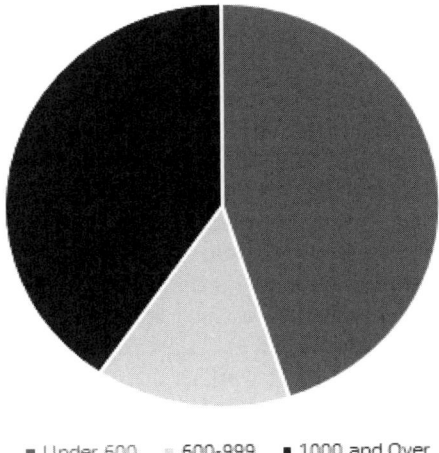

Figure 1: Church of England parishes by population
Source: A. Haig, *The Victorian Clergy* (Beckenham, 1984), p. 294,
based on an Anglican survey of the 1890s.

to the 1918 survey thus provide important insights into clerical attitudes to key issues facing the church. They also record clerical perceptions of the impact of war in their own localities, unaffected by the problems of hindsight which shape much other commentary on this period.[13]

However, as Figures 1 and 2 illustrate, Oxfordshire was not a representative sample of the church as a whole. Oxfordshire, overwhelmingly rural with only two substantial settlements (Banbury and Oxford itself) and a number of market towns such as Witney and Chipping Norton, was a county of small parishes. While 45 per cent of parishes in England and Wales had populations of fewer than 600, the corresponding figure in Oxfordshire was 70 per cent. Most of these were rural parishes, but they were supplemented by a handful of city parishes in central Oxford like All Saints or St Mary the Virgin. Its lack of extensive urbanisation meant that the county also had a far lower proportion of parishes with populations of 1,000 or more than did the church as a whole: 18 per cent in Oxfordshire compared with over 40 per cent nationally. Most of these were urban or suburban parishes like Cowley (the largest parish in Oxfordshire), with a population in 1911 of around 12,000, Henley, and also Caversham on the Oxfordshire side of the Thames opposite Reading.

---

13   For a brief discussion of this problem, see A. Gregory, *The Last Great War: British Society and the First World War* (Cambridge, 2008), pp. 1–8.

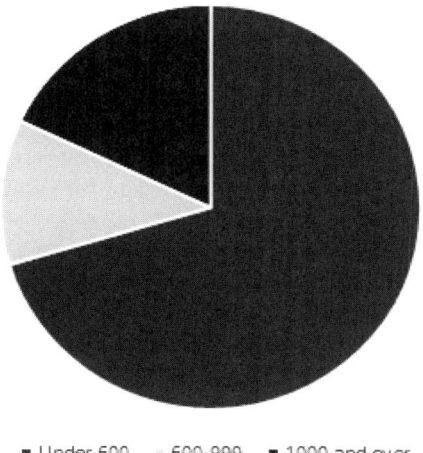

Figure 2: Oxfordshire parishes by population
Source: *Oxford Diocesan Calendar* (Oxford, 1914), pp. 92–127.

Early twentieth-century Oxfordshire therefore principally represented the rural world in which the Church of England was traditionally heavily invested and in which the ratio of Anglican incumbents to people was relatively high.

The Services of the Church

The information sought by the 1914 survey on church services related entirely to the provision made for the sacraments of baptism and Holy Communion. With respect to baptism the bishop sought information on whether the ceremony was incorporated into the regular round of services for Morning or Evening Prayer, as opposed to being administered privately either in the family home or in church outside regular service times. The former was the pattern envisaged in the Book of Common Prayer and an implementation of it had, as James Obelkevich has noted, been an objective of reforming bishops from the middle of the nineteenth century.[14] It was also widely supported by clergy, who wished to emphasise that baptism was an initiation into the church rather than simply a naming ceremony.[15] This campaign is often judged to have been a success but the results from Oxfordshire present a distinctly mixed picture. Of the 195 returns to give definitive information

---

14   J. Obelkevich, *Religion and Rural Society: South Lindsey 1825–1875* (Oxford, 1976), pp. 127–30.
15   F. Knight, *The Nineteenth-Century Church and English Society* (Cambridge, 1995), pp. 86–9.

on this point, only sixty-three, or less than one-third, indicated that local practice fell in line with reformist expectations, with the evening service being the usual choice.[16] Some clergy had clearly given considerable thought to ways of making the change acceptable to their congregations, and at Tadmarton, for example, the rector had responded to the potential objection that the introduction of a baptism would make evensong too lengthy by omitting the sermon on occasions when a baptism was conducted.[17] However, an almost identical number, sixty-four returns, answered no to this question, often citing practical objections such as the mother considering 6 pm too late for their children to be out, fear of the baby crying, or objections from the rest of the congregation.[18] There is also some evidence of a contrast between the urban and rural experience in relation to baptismal practice. Almost all the returns indicating Sunday Morning or Evening Prayer as the regular context for baptism came from rural parishes, where the frequency of baptisms would have been relatively low. In contrast, neither of the Banbury parishes and only a small minority of the Oxford parishes conducted baptisms during their evening service and even then on weekdays rather than Sundays when attendance would have been lower – a policy also adopted by the churches in Witney and Bicester.[19] At Ambroseden the vicar was clear that some parents would simply refuse to bring their children for Anglican baptism if he did not allow them to have the ceremony in the afternoon;[20] and the remaining returns demonstrate not only that this was a common preference in Oxfordshire but also that a large number of incumbents were willing to accommodate it. Some sixty-eight returns were explicit on this point[21] and the same practice may well be concealed behind many of those answering 'no' to the bishop's question or responding in an equivocal manner.

The Church of 1914 stood at the end of a major development in Anglican practice especially in rural parishes – the migration of the service of Evening Prayer from the afternoon (its normal position up to at least the middle of the nineteenth century)[22] to the early evening beginning at some time between 5.00 and 6.30 pm. This moved Anglican provision into a space hitherto the preserve of nonconformity and thus heightened the immediacy of competition between the churches, effectively demanding an exclusive commitment to one church or the other.[23] By 1914 the evening service seems to have become particularly popular with working-class

16 E.g. 1914 Begbroke; Waterstock.
17 1914 Tadmarton. See also 1914 Salford.
18 1914 Sarsden cum Churchill; Clifton Hampden; Claydon; Benson.
19 For Oxford examples see: 1914 Oxford, St Frideswide; Oxford, St Thomas.
20 1914 Ambroseden.
21 E.g. 1914 Bodicote; Nuffield; Souldern.
22 See K. Tiller, *Church and Chapel in Oxfordshire 1851*, Oxfordshire Record Society, 55 (Oxford, 1987) for the virtual ubiquity of afternoon service in mid-nineteenth-century Oxfordshire.
23 For a similar development in the diocese of Lincoln see Knight, *Nineteenth-Century Church*, pp. 34–6.

adults.[24] However, as the rector of Hook Norton noted, the migration of Evening Prayer from the afternoon to the evening had upset the traditional association of baptism with that service. In many parishes incumbents had taken advantage of the removal of Evening Prayer to introduce new forms of service in the afternoon. The development of special Sunday afternoon services for children, often associated with Sunday schools or catechism, which was well underway by 1914, seems in many parishes to have provided a natural home for baptisms which could thus be celebrated in a church context without disturbing regular adult congregations.[25]

The work of George Herring and Nigel Yates has shown that the Oxford diocese was an early stronghold of Anglo-Catholicism. Before 1870, only the diocese of London had more Tractarian incumbents than Oxford. By 1903 it was exceeded only by London, Canterbury and Truro in the percentage of its clergy adopting what were then regarded as ritualist practices.[26] The liturgical pattern revealed by clergy responses to the question about the availability of communion services in 1914 is suggestive of the pervasive influence of Anglo-Catholic ecclesiastical culture, though not necessarily Anglo-Catholic theology, in Oxfordshire. The clearest sign of this was the virtual ubiquity of early morning communion, usually at 8 am but sometimes at 7 or 8.30 am. In most churches the early celebration had become a regular feature of Sunday whether or not there was another communion service later in the day. In one hundred of the churches making a clear response to this question early communion happened every week; in a further forty-eight it was weekly with one exception each month for a later communion; and in another twenty-seven, early communion alternated with a communion later in the morning. Only twelve churches had no early communions at all and these were mostly places with very small populations, like Merton with 143 people and Rousham with 123.[27] The variation in practice seems to have been less a function of theological tradition than of the individual circumstances of the parish, as at Cottisford, whose return stated that early communion at 8.30 am was held only when sufficient communicants could be gathered – an understandable caveat since its population was only 167 at the 1911 census. In Oxford, where congregations could more easily be brought together, only two of the twenty churches did not provide early morning communion on a regular basis.[28]

A similar pattern is evident from the broader arrangements for the provision of communion services. In only thirty-six Oxfordshire churches was communion available at some point on Sunday less than once a week: eleven of these celebrated

---

24   1918 Whitchurch; South and New Hinksey.
25   E.g. 1914 Ascot-under-Wychwood; Bucknell; Chinnor; Ewelme. Cf. D. M. Thompson, *Baptism, Church and Society in Modern Britain* (Bletchley, 2005), p. 155.
26   G. Herring, *The Oxford Movement in Practice* (Oxford, 2016), pp. 50–1; N. Yates, *Anglican Ritualism in Victorian Britain 1830–1910* (Oxford, 1999), pp. 84, 280, 386–414.
27   1914 Merton; Rousham; Waterstock.
28   1914 Cottisford, Hardwick and Finmere; Oxford, St Matthew; Oxford, St Peter le Bailey.

it three times a month, seventeen twice a month and only eight retained what had a hundred years previously been the standard practice in many Anglican churches of a monthly communion. Again, these tended to be small rural parishes, from Wiggington with a population of 226 to Binsey with only 58 people.[29] In eighty-six parishes communion was available on a weekly basis, and in the remainder, it was more frequent still. This was not necessarily a badge of churchmanship since both Evangelical and High Church parishes might make similar provision: there were approximately eight services a month both at High Church Wolvercote and Evangelical Oxford, St Aldate, for example.[30] However, the most elaborate provision – more than ten communions in the average month – was restricted to churches clearly associated with the Anglo-Catholic tradition. Prominent among these were Oxford parishes like St Philip and St James, which had three communion services every Sunday morning and one on each weekday, with more elaborate provision on festivals, and St Barnabas, which provided four Sunday communions as well as two on regular weekdays.[31] Similar levels of provision could be found in a total of thirty-one parishes including ones on the edge of Oxford like Cowley St John and also Headington, whose incumbent Robert Townson was one of the most determined exponents of Anglo-Catholicism in the county, and other large centres of population like Banbury and Caversham.[32] However, where clergy were sufficiently committed, similar patterns of sacramental activity could be maintained even in small rural parishes. At Freeland, with its ideal Anglican grouping of church, vicarage and school designed by J. L. Pearson in the 1860s, but a population of only 181, there were six Sunday communion services in a four-week month and one on most weekdays, producing a total of thirty communions over twenty-eight days. Here the service records, meticulously kept by the incumbent Ernest Wilson, show that his sacramental provision, as would have been the case in other churches, formed just a part of the liturgical commitment: a pattern of twenty-two services every week, three a day Monday to Saturday and four on Sunday. He maintained this 1914 pattern throughout the war in all weathers and to congregations varying from one at early morning weekday Mattins to a couple of dozen at Sunday evensong.[33]

The one area of Anglo-Catholic sacramental enthusiasm which had struggled to make its way in Oxfordshire before 1914 was the introduction of a sung service. Less than 10 per cent of Oxfordshire churches managed choral communion

---

29   1914 Binsey; Holton; Holwell; Wiggington.
30   1914 Oxford, St Aldate; Wolvercote.
31   1914 Oxford, St Barnabas; Oxford, St Philip and St James. See other examples at Oxford, St Paul; Oxford, St Thomas.
32   1914 Banbury; Caversham; Cowley St John; Headington. See also 1914 Henley-on-Thames; Witney.
33   J. Sherwood and N. Pevsner, *The Buildings of England. Oxfordshire* (London, 1974), pp. 606–7. 1914 Freeland; OHC PAR 108/1/R7/10-11, Freeland Register of Services 1902–15, 1916–21.

services on a weekly basis and a similar number monthly. As might be expected, the majority of these were in significant population centres such as Oxford or Henley,[34] but, especially in a stripped-down form, they might also be found in smaller parishes like Barford or Brizenorton.[35] A further 15 per cent of Oxfordshire parishes managed a sung or partially sung communion a few times a year on great festivals, but almost 60 per cent had no choral services at all. Unlike the provision of said communion this was an area in which unaided clerical enthusiasm was insufficient. Some congregations were resistant and many rural parishes simply could not muster the necessary resources for an Anglo-Catholic sung service,[36] as the incumbent of Stoke Row reported: 'Choral service at present impracticable. Isolated country parish. Very poor organist and frequently Vicar has to play the Harmonium himself.'[37] Rural musicians and juvenile choirs had a constant problem of turnover and, especially in parishes subject to population decline, even if success was achieved there could be no assurance of continuity. Thus, the rector of Britwell Salome explained his lack of a choral service: 'I have one boy of suitable age for choir. Unfortunately no voice. I had a fine 4 part choir some years ago trained in both voice production and sight reading by myself but now have no material in this little parish.'[38]

Perhaps surprisingly, given the distractions and pressures of wartime, a comparison of the returns for 1914 and 1918 suggests that the period was one of considerable liturgical change in Oxfordshire. Some of the changes can be attributed straightforwardly to the dislocations produced by wartime conditions. Thus a handful of rural parishes had to reduce their provision of services or even began to hold services alternately in the morning and evening – a reversion to an early nineteenth-century practice and for the same reason – pluralism was creeping back into the church on the back of the manpower shortages produced by the conflict.[39] A more direct wartime effect was produced by the extended zeppelin attacks of 1916, supplemented the following year by Gotha bombers. Although the raids did relatively little damage, they provoked an extension into the midland counties of the blackouts already in force along the east coast – a measure that caused problems for evening services in the winter months. Around 10 per cent of parishes reported that they had made changes because of an inability to darken the church to the required standard. (This is almost certainly an underestimate because the return was completed after most churches had resumed their normal schedule.) In most cases, winter 'evensong' or 'evening prayer' was simply moved back into the afternoon – again a reversion to the schedule prevalent in the same parishes in

---

34   See, for example, 1914 Oxford, St Frideswide; Oxford, St Margaret; Henley, Holy Trinity.
35   1914 Barford St Michael; Brizenorton; Hampton Poyle.
36   1914 Tew, Little; Begbroke; Norton, Hook.
37   1914 Stoke Row. See also 1914 Newington.
38   1914 Britwell Salome with Britwell Prior.
39   See, for example, 1918 Beckley; Lewknor; Milcombe.

the 1850s – but clearly both unknown and unwelcome to early twentieth-century congregations. A few, like Ewelme, where the earlier service suited people living in outlying farms, found the change beneficial,[40] but the majority reported declining congregations, as at Rousham where essential farm work prevented attendance. Consequently, most incumbents expressed a determination to change back as soon as possible.[41]

In only a few cases do Oxfordshire clergy seem to have regarded the lighting restrictions as offering an opportunity to experiment. At Bucknell in central Oxfordshire, for example, the incumbent began an 'Evensong of a Mission character', in the schoolroom using a shortened form of the liturgy. The innovative liturgy and the practical benefits of a warmer meeting space in the school produced good congregations and what he described as 'very hearty' services.[42] At Holy Trinity in the slums of St Ebbes, the incumbent, Ernest Cox, secured the permission of the bishop to hold his evening service at 3 o'clock and to take advantage of the darkened church to hold a 'lantern service' at 6.30. For eight consecutive weeks, the church was crowded with a well-behaved congregation, but in the end the expense was too great to continue; and since the crowds did not attend when he resumed the normal service pattern, at the request of his established congregation, Cox felt his experiment had failed and decided not to attempt a second series of lantern services the following winter. Clearly, the pull of his core congregation and of liturgical continuity was an extremely strong one.[43]

Experiments like those at Bucknell and Holy Trinity Oxford may have been rare but the introduction of more mainstream liturgical practices related to the war was virtually ubiquitous in Oxfordshire. In August 1915, on the first anniversary of the war, bishop Gore published a letter in his diocesan magazine recommending a change in the conduct of Evening Prayer. After the third collect, instead of proceeding to read the state prayers the clergyman would lead the congregation in a series of war intercessions with a particular focus on local men in the army and navy.[44] Churches from all parts of the Anglican spectrum adopted this proposal with enthusiasm, including in the city of Oxford both the advanced Anglo-Catholic St Thomas the Martyr and St Andrew's, which had been founded ten years previously to provide an Evangelical alternative for the more Protestant inclined residents of north Oxford.[45] Such prayers might be liturgical or extempore and probably were commonly associated with the reading out of a 'Roll of Honour' listing all those from

---

40   1918 Ewelme. See also 1918 Holton; Nuneham Courtenay.
41   1918 Rousham. See also 1918 Nuffield.
42   1918 Bucknell. For similar experiments see 1918 Tew, Great; Stoke Row.
43   1918 Oxford, Holy Trinity.
44   *Oxford Diocesan Magazine,* 9 (1914), p. 115.
45   1918 Oxford, St Thomas; Oxford, St Andrew. M. Smith, 'Evangelicals in a "Catholic" Suburb: The Founding of St Andrew's North Oxford, 1899–1907', in C. Dyer et al. (eds), *New Directions in Local History since Hoskins* (Hatfield, 2011), pp. 216–30.

the parish away on military service. In populous parishes this was not an inconsiderable undertaking, and at Leafield, for example, the roll contained around 120 names. At Enstone, a substantial parish in the mixed farming region on the edge of the Cotswold escarpment, the incumbent reported that the prayers had both helped people anxious about their menfolk and increased the number of communicants. He had also experimented with using the Litany with greater frequency at evening services because its responsive form encouraged the more reticent among his parishioners to join audibly in the prayers.[46] This variation in the standard Anglican liturgical pattern seems to have been very welcome in the parishes of Oxfordshire. Clergy reported enthusiastically on the appreciation expressed by their congregations and their positive spiritual response to the prayers. At Highfield, for example, the vicar remarked that the changes had made 'the services more real, and less monotonous', while at Rotherfield Greys the incumbent was so enthusiastic about the opportunities that they presented that he used the occasion of the visitation to request that the liberty to make such changes be continued.[47]

In addition to the restructuring of their evening services many parishes also instituted further services of intercession. Sometimes these were held on Sundays, but more often on the evenings of weekdays, as with the Wednesday evening services held regularly since 1914 at Chinnor.[48] In most cases these seem to have been simple meetings for prayer, using authorised forms, held either in the church or the church school and again often featuring the reading out of a roll of parishioners serving in the forces. The Evangelical vicar of St Matthew's Oxford, who adopted this practice at his weekly service for men as well as a mid-week special intercession service for the war, found that, 'The effect has been decidedly good in the way of the better attention and devotion of the people to something they have not always been accustomed to; and in showing that the Church *can* adapt herself to varying needs and emergency.'[49] Other incumbents preferred more elaborate provision. St Thomas the Martyr, for example, read out the names of its servicemen every Sunday morning, which the incumbent reported gave 'a good deal of pleasure'. But he also held a day of prayer once a month and a weekly communion 'with special intention for sailors and soldiers'. Uniquely in the sample the church also celebrated a weekly communion 'with special intention for those fallen in the war',[50] perhaps employing the forms of prayer for the dead newly authorised by the Church of England in 1917 (though other churches may well have been using the same forms without drawing attention to them in the returns). Additional services were clearly more difficult to

---

46   1918 Leafield with Wychwood; Enstone.
47   1918 Hethe; Highfield; Iffley; Rotherfield Greys; Yarnton.
48   1918 Chinnor.
49   1918 Oxford, St Matthew. At the time of writing an excellent example of a handwritten 'Roll of Honour', much amended with details of men killed, wounded or taken prisoner during the war, hangs in a frame in the church of St Nicholas, Tadmarton.
50   1918, Oxford, St Thomas.

sustain than regular Sunday worship, given the exigencies of wartime; and while some parishes recorded that attendance was well sustained even in the fourth year of the war,[51] others noted a growing weariness and a falling off of attendance.[52] However, sometimes such special services could be very powerful occasions of the kind more commonly associated with Methodism, as the rector of St Clement in Oxford reported:

> On Palm Sunday 1918 there was a noticeable feeling of tension at all the services and later in the evening after the evening service the suggestion was made that an all night service of prayer for our army and navy should be held. This took place on Monday night March 25th. In spite of the shortness of notice about two hundred people assembled in church at 10 pm and the service of Prayer went on until after 4 am.[53]

Palm Sunday (24 March) 1918 marked the most dangerous phase of the German spring offensive as the advance of their forces threatened to drive the French and British armies apart, and on the 26th the allies were finally impelled by the depth of the crisis to appoint a single commander in chief to oversee the whole of the western front.

That some adaptation to the special conditions of wartime should be evident by 1918, even in quiet rural corners of the diocese, is perhaps not surprising. However, the returns also provide clear evidence that in parallel with the wartime innovations a substantial number of Oxfordshire incumbents were also determined to develop the sacramental teaching and practice of their parishes in ever more pervasive and elaborate forms during the war years. Given that it was already starting from a high base in 1914, it is striking that the move towards a more sacramental construction of Anglican parochial practice had been pushed even further by 1918 – a development strongly supported by bishop Gore.[54] Over a quarter of the parishes recorded voluntary changes to their patterns of worship since 1914 which represented an increase or an elaboration of sacramental provision and in many cases both. At St Cross in Oxford, for example, a 9.45 Eucharist was added to the menu of Sunday services, elaborated by the use of coloured vestments, and a daily Eucharistic celebration was begun in September 1915. The pattern at Adderbury near Banbury was similar except that the 9.45 choral communion was restricted to the fourth Sunday in the month.[55] Other parishes introduced communion later in the day on one or more Sundays in the month: 11.00, for example, at Charlbury, at Albury in central Oxfordshire and at Rotherfield Peppard in the Chilterns.[56] Given the high

---

51   E.g. 1918 Aston Rowant; Combe.
52   E.g. 1918 Brizenorton; Horspath.
53   1918 Oxford, St Clement.
54   *Oxford Diocesan Magazine*, 10 (1915), p. 148.
55   1918 Oxford, St Cross; Adderbury. For other examples see 1918 Clifton Hampden; Glympton.
56   1918 Charlbury with Chadlington; Albury; Rotherfield Peppard.

level of sacramental activity in which Oxfordshire parishes already engaged, many of those not reporting additional sacramental services probably had little scope for more. The incumbent of Chinnor, for example, reported that he already had 'a fairly full complement of services for a country parish'.[57] The direction of travel, however, was clear. In only two or three parishes was there any sign of a reduction in the number of communion services or the level of ceremonial with which they were celebrated.[58]

The reasons for the timing of this surge in activity are worth further investigation and may include both a conception of increased need for sacramental access during the conflict and the opportunities created by the absence or distraction of other key figures in the parochial community by wartime service. However, the principal objective of the innovations is clear – an attempt to change the character of mainstream worship in the diocese. Despite the ubiquity of early morning communions it was almost certainly the case in Oxfordshire, as in Robert Beaken's study of Colchester during the first world war, that either Morning or Evening Prayer remained, in the majority of churches, the service with the largest congregation, with the evening service particularly popular with agricultural labourers.[59] It was the purpose of the changes underway by 1918, as the incumbent of South Banbury put it, to make 'Sung Eucharist … the chief service on Sunday morning'.[60] This is a change in Anglican practice commonly associated by historians with the 'Parish Communion' movement of the 1950s,[61] and unless this view is mistaken, the Oxford diocese was some three decades ahead of other parts of the church both in introducing this pattern and in feeling its effects. Sometimes the returns provide evidence of careful preparation for this development. Albury's return, for example, noted that 'the people have had a good deal of teaching about it', while in other churches there was an air of experimentation. The incumbent of Bloxham, for example, reported that on the first Sunday in the month,

> the Head Master of All Saints has given us his High Celebration of the Holy Communion in the Parish church. This he has done, after consulting with the Wardens and in spite of the fact that this parish had no recent experience of vestments etc, and was rather in opposition, so far as I can judge … the reverence

---

57 1918 Chinnor.
58 Examples can be found at Southleigh and Headington – in both cases associated with the arrival of a new incumbent.
59 R. Beaken, *The Church of England and the Home Front 1914–1918* (Woodbridge, 2015), p. 126.
60 1918 Banbury, South. Making communion the main morning service had been urged by Gore at his 1914 visitation. C. Gore, *The War and the Church and Other Addresses Being the Charge delivered at his primary Visitation, 1914* (London, 1914), pp. 32–4.
61 For Parish Communion see, for example, J. Morris, 'Anglicanism in Britain and Ireland', in J. Morris (ed.), *The Oxford History of Anglicanism*, vol. 4: *Global Western Anglicanism c.1910–Present* (Oxford, 2017), p. 421.

and beauty of the service has cleared away many misconceptions … I hope it will be the normal service one Sunday in the month in term time.[62]

As this return suggests, the elaboration of Eucharistic celebration and the attempt to make it the main service of the day was principally a clerical enthusiasm rather than a response to demand. Those who consulted more widely tended to be deterred. The vicar of Northmoor, for example, reported that he had made several suggestions for changes to his parishioners but they had consistently rejected any innovations; while at Barton Westcot the vicar said that he had considered making Holy Communion the chief service but that 'It has not seemed possible to advocate to change the present arrangement.'[63] The majority of the clergy making such changes, however, seem to have relied principally on their own authority or powers of persuasion, and a number met with success, especially when the change was not wholesale. At Chipping Norton, for example, a Choral Eucharist was inserted before 11.00 Mattins and the regular sermon removed from the latter and attached to the former – enhancing its status as the main service. As a result, communicants had increased and the vicar felt a real need had been met.[64] This was far from a universal experience, however, and the returns also provide plentiful evidence of disquiet about the new prominence of sacramental worship. At Aston Rowant, for example, where the incumbent had started with Choral Eucharist every Sunday, he found 'old-fashioned and very regular parishioners simply could not understand the point', so he retreated to holding it once a month and adding a sermon.[65]

These incumbents were unusual in giving ground when members of their congregations objected to innovation. The vicar of St Frideswide's, in Oxford, reported that several people had left the choir and the church when he substituted Gregorian chant for Anglican – but there is not a hint in the return that he might consider relaxing his policy. A few expressed optimism that their changes would eventually be accepted, as at Sibford Gower, where the vicar noted a falling off of attendance in the weeks when he substituted Choral Eucharist as the principal service instead of Mattins, but concluded, 'those who come have expressed a real liking for the Service and I have little doubt that it will eventually win its way'. Similarly, the vicar of Swalcliffe thought that the issue was that 'country people move very slowly' but implied that persistence would eventually be rewarded.[66] In some cases, though, this hope was considerably deferred and rested less on the clergy's ability to win the support of their current adult congregations than on what the vicar of Spelsbury called 'the rising generation'.[67] Others reported parishioners voting with their

---

62   1918 Albury; Bloxham.
63   1918 Northmoor; Barton Westcot.
64   1918 Chipping Norton. See also 1918 Horton-cum-Studley; Watlington.
65   1918 Aston Rowant.
66   1918 Oxford, St Frideswide; Sibford Gower and Epwell; Swalcliffe with Shutford.
67   1918 Spelsbury. See also 1918 Glympton.

feet without comment, as at Adderbury – 'It is attended by about 30 who much appreciate it. But those who I thought would really be pleased practically ignore it altogether' – or else blamed the absentees for carelessness. At Sandford on Thames, where the incumbent had made a series of changes including the introduction of Choral Eucharist, he noted that the choir and some of the people had shown some interest and then added, 'The slackness in attendance at Public Worship is very distressing. The idea of <u>obligation</u> seems almost non-existent, and anything else is allowed as an excuse for not coming to Church.'[68]

Most revealing about the clerical drive towards a more sacramental construction of parochial Anglicanism, however, are the returns which justified liturgical change against a background of decline in attendance by emphasising an increase in the number of communicants, as in the case of the choral celebrations at Rotherfield Peppard.

> The change has not commended itself to the older members of the congregation who generally absent themselves from the service and the congregation at the Choral Celebration is considerably below average. The non-communicants cannot be persuaded to stay until the end of the service, in spite of continued appeals and they all depart after the sermon. On the other hand, the number of communicants at this service is far in excess of the numbers that used to attend when the H.C. was held as a separate service after Morning Prayer. The average numbers are now in the proportion of 30 under the new system to 15 under the old so from this point of view the time change would seem to be justified.[69]

Frances Knight has drawn attention to the tendency of the Anglo-Catholic emphasis on the construction of the parish as a Eucharistic community to drive a wedge into the larger parish community in the middle decades of the nineteenth century.[70] It is at least arguable that the returns show the same process at work in the liturgical innovations of the early twentieth century; and that some of the changes in English religion commonly associated with the war might in fact have been the consequence of those innovations. This is certainly suggested by the views of the rector of Holton – the only incumbent in the Oxford archdeaconry willing to use his return to challenge the sacramental reconstruction of the parish.

> If there should be in this question a reference to the unwarrantable disorganisation of Sunday Morning services which is taking place in so many churches at the present time, and which is alienating so many church people from their parish Church, I have to say that it does not obtain here. The order of the administration of the LORD's Supper is not, and never was intended, for general or universal use: and the present movement is a false error, and will do harm instead of good.[71]

---

68   1918 Adderbury; Sandford-on-Thames.
69   1918 Rotherfield Peppard.
70   Knight, *Nineteenth-Century Church*, pp. 202–3.
71   1918 Holton.

The Education of the People

Both sets of returns sought information on primary education in Oxfordshire parishes. This was an area in which the Church of England had, for more than a century, been a principal provider, especially via the charity school movement and the development of day schools, mostly in connection with the National Society for Promoting the Education of the Poor in the Principles of the Established Church, established in 1811.[72] In 1914 the main focus of the bishop's enquiry was on the level of provision, the involvement of the parish clergy in elementary schools and other forms of education for children, and whether they believed the results to be satisfactory. From this point of view, the returns suggested an Anglican educational enterprise in relatively good heart. Of the 226 parishes making a return, 195 recorded a school in operation, the vast majority being church schools, and only thirty-one recorded the absence of such provision. Almost all these were parishes with relatively small populations like All Saints and St Andrew's in Oxford, or Ardley and Fewcott, whose populations were 110 and 150 respectively and whose schools had been closed because of falling rolls (giving rise, in the case of Fewcott, to considerable local resentment).[73] Where the school was operated under the auspices of the National Society, the clergy had a straightforward right of entry and approximately half of Oxfordshire's incumbents took advantage of this to provide or supervise the religious education of their young parishioners on a regular basis, sometimes once a week and often more frequently. At St Paul's in Oxford, for example, the vicar taught in the local day schools every Tuesday and his assistant curate on Thursdays,[74] while at Upper Heyford the rector taught in the day school three days a week.[75] This figure rises to almost 60 per cent when more occasional involvement is taken into account.[76] However, clerical intervention was rather less straightforward when the school was provided by the County (or County Borough) Council, acting in its role, established by the 1902 Education Act, as the Local Education Authority. A number of clergy who were not active in their local schools tended to cite the Council control of the school as the reason for their absence,[77] and the rector of Claydon, an expert on education, reported his frustration at being banned

---

72   For the National Society see Lois Louden, *Distinctive and Inclusive The National Society and Church of England Schools 1811–2011* (London, 2012). For brief accounts of the development of primary education specifically in an Oxfordshire context, see P. Horn (ed.), *Village Education in Nineteenth-Century Oxfordshire*, Oxfordshire Record Society, 51 (Oxford, 1979), pp. xi–xlvii; K. Tiller, 'Education in the Nineteenth Century: Elementary Schools', in K. Tiller and G. Darkes (eds), *An Historical Atlas of Oxfordshire*, Oxfordshire Record Society, 67 (Oxford, 2010), pp. 128–9.
73   1914 Oxford, All Saints cum St Martins; Oxford, St Andrew; Ardley; Fewcott.
74   1914 Oxford, St Paul. See also 1914 Kirtlington.
75   1914 Heyford, Upper.
76   E.g. 1914 Ramsden.
77   E.g. 1914 Tew, Great; Stoke, South with Woodcote.

from teaching in the schools by the managers.[78] The 1902 Education Act had been a highly controversial piece of legislation because it introduced a system of local rate support for denominational schooling (mostly in the hands of Anglicans and Roman Catholics), creating a grievance for nonconformists who found themselves being taxed to support the propagation of religious views from which they conscientiously dissented.[79] This made Anglican clerical penetration of religiously neutral educational spaces particularly sensitive, especially when there was a significant nonconformist presence in the parish, as at Hanwell and Hook Norton, where the clergy were careful of local sensibilities.[80] However, not all Council schools were no-go areas for the Anglican clergy; at Stonesfield, for example, the rector was able to teach New Testament subjects with the permission of the local authority.[81] Neither was the form of school management the only reason given for a lack of clerical involvement. Some found themselves unable to teach because of illness or other infirmity,[82] while others felt themselves unequal to the task. The vicar of St Philip and St James in Oxford was particularly forthright on this point:

> The clergy never teach in the Day Schools – <u>they attend for the purpose of learning how to teach</u>, but it would be unfair for them to injure the reputation of the proper staff by mixing up their amateur incompetence with the skill and long experience of the properly qualified teachers.[83]

With only a few exceptions, notably at Little Tew where the exasperated vicar sought episcopal action to resolve what appears to have been a feud with the schoolmistress,[84] the clergy seem to have been broadly content with the teaching delivered in church schools especially.[85] This followed a syllabus devised by the diocese and was subject to regular inspection. The returns frequently cited good reports from the Diocesan Inspectors in support of their conclusions.[86] Moreover, this favourable judgement sometimes extended to the religious teaching at schools under Council control, as at Milton-under-Wychwood where the vicar judged the teaching to be 'well and conscientiously given'.[87]

---

78 1914 Claydon.
79 P. Chadwick, *Shifting Alliances: Church and State in English Education* (London, 1997), pp. 14–24; D. W. Bebbington, *The Nonconformist Conscience: Chapel and Politics, 1870–1914* (London, 1982), pp. 142–52; G. I. T. Machin, *Politics and the Churches in Great Britain 1869–1921* (Oxford, 1987), pp. 284–93.
80 1914 Hanwell; Norton, Hook.
81 1914 Stonesfield.
82 E.g. 1914 Mollington; Newington, South.
83 1914 Oxford, St Philip and St James.
84 1914 Tew, Little.
85 Though there was a tendency to add a qualifying adjective as in 'fairly satisfactory', 1914 Henley-on-Thames; or satisfied 'on the whole', 1914 Shenington with Alkerton.
86 E.g. 1914 Cassington; Newington, South; Swyncombe.
87 1914 Milton-under-Wychwood. See also 1914 Bix.

If the 1914 returns give an impression of an educational system in good heart laying firm foundations for the future, a rather different view emerges from an examination of the same subject on the evidence of the 1918 survey. This is partly a matter of perspective. The 1914 survey focused on the provision of elementary education; 1918 was concerned with the trends in the take up of that education and its prospects in the post-war period. Question 3 of the 1918 survey asked clergy to state the current number of children enrolled in day school as compared with the situation twenty, thirty or forty years previously. This was, it should be noticed, a somewhat ill-thought-out enquiry, since it asked for information which pre-dated the incumbencies of virtually all the respondents and seems to have left many of them scrabbling for the means to give an answer. Some clearly did have reliable sources to hand: the vicar of Burford triumphantly produced an unbroken series of statistics for Council elementary and infant schools for the two decades prior to the visitation, along with an incomplete accounting for the church school in Fulbrook.[88] However, complete answers were very rare,[89] and many incumbents failed to respond or explained that they could not obtain the necessary information,[90] while some could only give a very impressionistic response.[91] Others, determined to attempt a reply, sought information from former teachers,[92] consulted old log books,[93] and in the case of Middleton Stoney counted the faces in a photograph.[94] Even using their best efforts, most respondents who did essay a response could only manage a single data point over the previous forty years with which they could compare current school rolls; but despite the patchy data with which he was presented, the bishop would have been able to discern a clear pattern in the results. A total of 168 returns provided comparative information and the results, grouped by the size of the parish population, are shown in Figure 3.

In the first group, those with populations of 300 or less, parishes with rising rolls were a tiny minority and one of these had risen principally because of an amalgamation with a closing school in another part of the parish.[95] Although school attendance was particularly low in 1918 because of the early withdrawal of boys to engage in agricultural work,[96] the majority were in decline because they served communities that had themselves been losing population since the agricultural depression which began in the 1870s, by a process of out-migration that also tended

---

88   1918 Burford with Fulbrook.
89   Examples can be found at 1918 Albury; Leafield with Wychwood; Milton, Little; Somerton.
90   E.g. 1918 Alvescot; Bix; Islip.
91   1918 Fifield and Idbury.
92   1918 Kingham; Wardington.
93   1918 Henley-on-Thames; Oxford, St Clement; Shenington with Alkerton.
94   1918 Middleton Stoney.
95   1918 Bradwell with Kelmscot.
96   1918 Farringdon, Little.

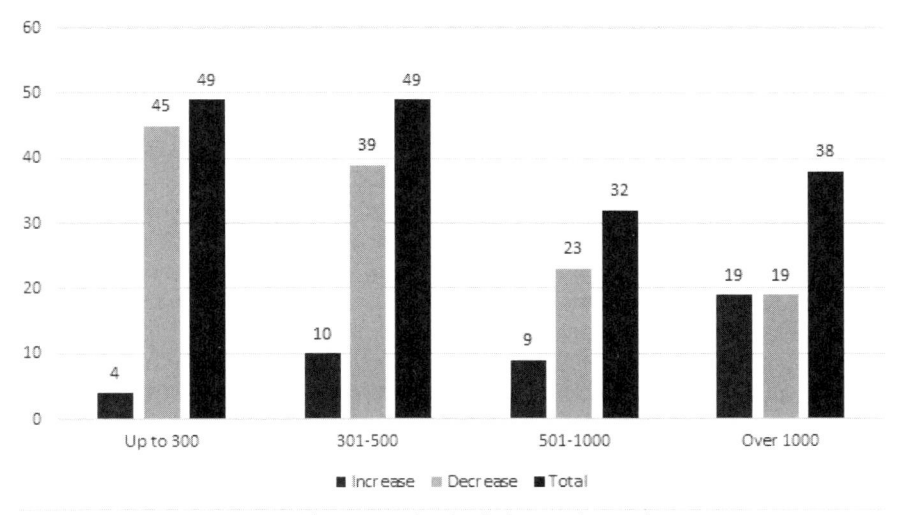

Figure 3: Change in school rolls by parish population

to produce an older population profile.[97] At North Aston, for example, school rolls had fallen to less than a quarter of 1891 levels by 1917. The larger rural parishes like Broughton and Stonesfield with populations between 301 and 500 fared only a little better, with declining schools outnumbering growing ones by almost four to one. The third group – parishes with populations between 501 and 1,000 – included some smaller urban parishes like St Cross in Oxford and parishes that had experienced population growth like Bodicote on the edge of Banbury and Shiplake in the far south of the county. Nonetheless, school rolls fell in the majority of these parishes too, and it was only in the final group of parishes, with populations in excess of 1,000, that significant numbers of expanding schools could be found. These were almost all in urban areas, where population had been on the rise in the early twentieth century, and the tendency towards withdrawing boys for work in the fields was less strongly felt.[98] Overall, as Figure 3 indicates, there were in 1918 126 parishes reporting falling school rolls and only forty-two reporting growing ones – a ratio of exactly 3:1. However great the hopes invested in Anglican elementary education and the commitment of the clergy to engagement with it, this was clearly a system under pressure.[99]

---

97 J. Nash, 'Population Change 1851–1901', in Tiller and Darkes (eds), *Historical Atlas of Oxfordshire*, pp. 138–9. 1918 Claydon.
98 1918 Banbury; Headington Quarry; Oxford, St Giles; Witney.
99 For similar conclusions about the pressures on Anglican education (and the parish system more generally) in the Buckinghamshire archdeaconry, see G. Masom, 'Parishes under Pressure – The Church of England in South Buckinghamshire 1913–1939', *Journal of Religious History*, 42 (2018), pp. 317–42.

The fourth question on the 1918 return was, as already noted, relatively unusual. Rather than seeking information it instead sought the views of the clergy on a response to the changes to the schools system contemplated in what would become the Fisher Education Act of 1918 and on possible ways of improving religious education in the generality of schools without reigniting the religious controversy that had followed the 1902 act. Gore had been intimately involved in consultations around the education proposals and made his own views public in a speech in the House of Lords subsequently published in the June 1917 number of the *Diocesan Magazine*.[100] He warmly supported the proposal to increase the school leaving age to 14 for all children and argued for restrictions on working hours between the ages of 14 and 18 to enable more working-class children to benefit from part-time secondary education. With respect to religious education, the bishop drew attention to what he regarded as the crucial issue of the proper training of the teachers who would be required to deliver that education, especially in Council schools. His question sought the approval of his clergy for a policy of concessions with respect to the management of church schools, specifically the admission of nonconformist managers, the opening up of headteacher positions to non-Anglicans and the provision of facilities for nonconformist religious teaching where the church school was the only school in the parish. The anticipated *quid pro quo* for such concessions was that Anglican clergy would be allowed entry to Council schools to provide religious education, for the children of Anglican parents, based on Anglican doctrine.

With respect to the admission of nonconformist ministers or other accredited teachers there was some division among the returns, with a handful of ministers, including some of the more pugnacious Anglo-Catholics, opposed to any form of compromise.[101] Some Anglican incumbents were clearly exasperated by this attitude and pointed to the growth of Anglo-Catholicism as problematic in achieving the sort of *modus vivendi* that seemed desirable in rural ministry, especially under wartime conditions.[102] In practice the majority were prepared to make this concession.[103] However, when it came to the issues of management and especially the appointment of headteachers, the spirit of compromise was much harder to find. The clerical commitment to the provision of what they often described as 'definite church teaching'[104] deterred them from supporting any step that might dilute the Anglican atmosphere of church schools or approximate to the 'undenominational' education to be found in Council schools or the nonconformist schools run by the British and Foreign Schools Society.[105] Such concerns were magnified by the hopes

---

100 *Oxford Diocesan Magazine*, 12 (1918), pp. 85–90.
101 E.g. 1918 Dorchester with Burcot.
102 E.g. 1918 Ducklington with Hardwick; Holton.
103 E.g. 1918 Duns Tew; Milton, Little; Stokenchurch.
104 E.g. 1918 Adderbury; Southleigh; Swalcliffe with Shutford.
105 1918 Chipping Norton; Claydon; North Hinksey. For British Schools in Oxfordshire see Tiller, 'Education', pp. 128–9.

for renewal that the clergy invested in the 'rising generation', as at Henley where the vicar of Holy Trinity saw his school as 'the invaluable nursery of the Church'.[106] Most of the parish clergy thus continued to place their faith in a continuation of church schools (with only minor concessions to nonconformist parents) despite the decline in numbers which so many of them had also identified. The bishop, in contrast, concerned about the future viability of the system in the light of the limited resources available to support it and the structural changes that the government had in mind, favoured root and branch reform. His 'charge' (the address he gave to his clergy as he toured the diocese in the course of the visitation) proposed that, in areas where the only elementary school was a church school, management should be handed over to the Local Education Authority and mainstream religious education undertaken by properly trained teachers on an inter-denominational basis (while retaining facilities for Anglican teaching where there was a demand).[107] It would be difficult to imagine a set of proposals less in line with the broad trend of clerical opinion expressed in the returns, and the bishop may perhaps have regretted his experiment in seeking them.[108]

The Anglican educational enterprise in early twentieth-century Oxfordshire extended far beyond provision of elementary schools, and most of the second half of the 1914 survey was concerned with exploring it. Question 6 sought information about the presence of secondary schools and the religious instruction given in them. With the exception of Oxford itself and a few of the market towns, like Chipping Norton and Thame, secondary education was poorly developed in Oxfordshire.[109] Some of the respondents felt the question was so incongruous in the context of their rural parishes that they embellished their negative answers with an exclamation mark![110] However, where secondary schools did exist, the clergy do seem to have attempted to engage with them, as at Aston, where the vicar gave instruction on the Prayer Book once a week in a training school for domestic servants;[111] although some schools also had their own chaplains or clerical headmasters[112] and others seem to have eschewed contact with the parish clergy.[113]

In contrast to the position of secondary schools, the great educational innovation of the late eighteenth century – the Sunday school – was virtually ubiquitous

---

106 1918 Henley, Holy Trinity. For a contrary view, see 1918 Rotherfield Peppard: a return which also sheds further light on the growing tendency to regard the creation of a body of regular communicants as the chief end of parish ministry.
107 C. Gore, *Dominant Ideas and Corrective Principles* (Oxford, 1918), pp. 52–68.
108 Further discussion of clerical attitudes and the bishop's response can be found in M. Smith, '"War to the Knife": The Anglican Clergy and Education at the End of the First World War', *Churches and Education, Studies in Church History*, 55 (2019) doi:10.1017/stc.2018.22.
109 Tiller, 'Education', p. 128.
110 E.g. 1914 Northmoor; Sandford-on-Thames; Stoke, South with Woodcote.
111 1914 Bampton Aston and Cote. See also 1914 Banbury; Oxford, St Philip and St James.
112 1918 Bloxham; Caversham; Cowley St John; Oxford, St Mary Magdalene; Thame.
113 1918 Henley-on-Thames.

in Oxfordshire parishes, with a total of 198 reporting their presence and only twenty-eight parishes being without them. In a couple of cases the returns give the impression of a temporary hiatus[114] but in the remaining twenty-six a range of reasons were cited. These included a lack of resources necessary to organise a school[115] and, especially in some parishes in the city of Oxford, a lack of children to teach.[116] Some churches had substituted a children's service for Sunday school, as at Hethe or Westwell,[117] and there is clear evidence in a handful of the more resolutely Anglo-Catholic parishes of a rejection of the Sunday school model altogether. At St Barnabas in Oxford, for example, where the vicar openly confessed to not believing in Sunday schools, catechism, on a Catholic pattern, was used instead – the advantage being that it removed teaching responsibilities from the hands of the laity and vested them entirely in those of the clergy.[118] In the large majority of parishes that did have Sunday schools, there was, as might be expected, a spectrum of size and degree of elaboration. This stretched from tiny schools in rural parishes like Shenington[119] which had only three children, to large urban parishes like Cowley where 300 children met in classes on Sunday.[120] The commitment required to maintain the Sunday school enterprise, especially among lay parishioners, was considerable. Not only was it necessary to find people with sufficient leisure to engage in the teaching, but they also required some form of training in order to make that teaching effective. In urban contexts this seems generally to have been sustainable: at Henley, for example, approximately 300 children were looked after by sixteen teachers who met every Friday to receive instruction on their lessons for the following Sunday. However, the tendency towards residential segregation of different social classes in early twentieth-century towns meant that some parishes were much better provided than others. In Oxford, parishes in middle-class areas reported no problems in finding teachers; and in the south of the city, St Ebbe's compensated for a lack of local talent by drawing in teachers from north Oxford and, in term time, from university undergraduates.[121] However, in the poorer area to the south of St Ebbe's, the incumbent of Holy Trinity, which was seeking to run a Sunday evening 'Ragged School' for girls from the poorest families as well as regular Sunday schools, reported that, 'If only we could get teachers our Sunday Schools could be immensely increased in number of children and in the efficiency

114 1914 Claydon; Farringdon, Little.
115 1914 Spelsbury.
116 1914 Oxford, All Saints; Oxford, St Mary the Virgin; Oxford, St Michael; Heythrop. Heythrop cited a lack of both – a problem exacerbated by the dispersed nature of settlement in the parish.
117 1914 Hethe; Highmore; Westwell.
118 1914 Oxford, St Barnabas. See also 1914 Headington.
119 1914 Shenington with Alkerton. See also 1914 Cornwell; Weston, South with Adwell.
120 1914 Cowley. See also 1914 Woodstock.
121 1914 Henley-on-Thames; Oxford, St Ebbe.

of instruction.'[122] Holy Trinity, a new parish created to help cope with the expanding population of the city in the mid-1840s, illustrates the difficulties that could ensue when such sub-division left new parishes without sufficient resources to undertake effective ministry.[123]

In an echo of the strains being experienced in the elementary school system, the problem of finding voluntary teachers to staff Sunday schools was even more acute in Oxfordshire's rural parishes. A number of returns commented on difficulties in this respect, and at Spelsbury, the vicar reported that he was unable to have a Sunday school because there was no one willing to teach in it.[124] In the nineteenth century, the principal families of a rural parish might be relied on for a broad engagement in charitable activity including Sunday schooling,[125] but there is little sign of such activity in early twentieth-century Oxfordshire. At Binsey, the Sunday school was taught by 'the daughter of a principal resident', and at Steeple Barton, the Sunday school was run by the squire; but these are the only examples visible in the returns, except for Middleton Stoney where Lady Jersey took a class for girls in her mansion at Middleton Park when she was in residence.[126] In the absence of substantial help from the gentry or the rural middle classes the clergy either taught the schools themselves, as at Barford,[127] or turned for assistance to the only other readily available pools of voluntary labour – the staff of the parish elementary school and their own families. Only one Oxfordshire incumbent felt it to be inappropriate to ask day school teachers to exercise their profession on Sundays as well[128] and they were very commonly to be found either in sole charge of a Sunday school or working alongside the parish clergy. At Asthall, for example, the Sunday school was conducted by the 'Assistant Mistress and Monitoress under supervision of the Vicar'.[129] It is difficult to be sure about the degree to which such activity was always entirely voluntary, especially given the influence exercised on the management of National Schools by local incumbents, and in a few cases it was thought appropriate, or necessary, to pay day school staff for their work in Sunday schools – transforming the schools from a voluntary into a professional endeavour.[130] However this was an unusual situation; and at Cadmore End the vicar attributed the success of his Sunday school, attended by every child in his parish, to

---

122 1914 Oxford, Holy Trinity.
123 For a similar difficulty see 1914 Banbury, South.
124 1914 Spelsbury; Brightwell Baldwin; Finstock and Fawler.
125 A sparkling account of the not always easy relationship between a clergyman and such a committed family can be found in W. O. Chadwick, *Victorian Miniature* (London, 1960). Such activity was sufficiently commonplace to be a reference point in novels like Charlotte Bronte's *Shirley*.
126 1914 Binsey; Barton, Steeple; Middleton Stoney.
127 1914 Barford St Michael. See also 1914 Nuffield; Wendlebury.
128 1914 Albury.
129 1914 Asthall. See also 1914 Ducklington with Hardwick; Haseley, Great.
130 1914 Henley, Holy Trinity; Middleton Stoney.

the outstanding commitment of the head and teachers of the day school, who had kept it going despite a series of vacancies in the living.[131]

The vicarage was the other main source of Sunday school labour in rural Oxfordshire and, given the tendency of clerical sons to be absent at school or university, this meant, in practice, the wives and daughters of the clergy. Many of the returns record their involvement. At Newington, for example, the rector, John Pendlebury, described a system in which he and his wife divided the school into two groups, with Mrs Pendlebury, an 'experienced and effective' teacher, taking the more senior role, while the tiny Sunday school at South Weston was simply described as 'Mrs Espinasse's S. School'.[132] Oxfordshire incumbents were often at pains to record their appreciation for the support they received from their families. The return from Holton noted, 'The S. S. teachers are my own daughters – one has Cambridge Diploma – another daughter who occasionally teaches also has Camb. Diploma – I am absolutely satisfied with results.'[133] Even warmer was the report from Mapledurham where the vicar believed that his daughter literally deserved a medal for twenty years' service almost single-handed in his Sunday school, and asked for the bishop's help in ensuring that she received it, adding, 'My daughter devotes a great deal of time and thought to the preparation of Sunday School, and the parents are very grateful to her as they have reason to be.'[134]

Clergy, anxious to ensure their Sunday schools were adequately staffed, often ended up with a mix of labourers, as at Marston, where the most efficient teachers were the headmaster of the school and an undergraduate, or Benson, where the vicar was able to call on the services of students at the Missionary College in Dorchester, one of the female day school teachers and 'some ladies of the parish'.[135] Even if they did not superintend the schools themselves, some clergy went to considerable lengths to support their voluntary teachers, encouraging them to link with wider diocesan resources, holding training sessions at which the forthcoming lessons were discussed,[136] or travelling to teachers' homes to deliver lesson plans and explain them.[137] A range of resources were available and used in Oxfordshire to support Sunday school work, from relatively traditional catechisms which operated by rote learning[138] to more modern systems that were based around stories or on visual images or where attendance **was** encouraged by the collection of coloured

---

131   1914 Cadmore End.
132   1914 Newington; Weston, South with Adwell. See also 1914 Lewknor; Stoke Talmage; Tadmarton.
133   1914 Holton.
134   1914 Mapledurham.
135   1914 Marston; Benson. See also 1914 Culham; Drayton.
136   1914 Bicester; Highfield; Islip; Thame.
137   1914 Ambroseden; Stonesfield.
138   1914 Burford with Fulbrook. For this method in operation see Oxford, St Thomas; Henley, Holy Trinity.

stamps.[139] At Broughton, the rector commented on the results, 'The Sunday School Teachers are given copies of "The Young Churchman" I find the lessons excite far more interest than former efforts, and the Sunday School has increased in size considerably these last few years.'[140] Naturally, the quality of teaching provided by volunteers could not always be relied upon, especially given the other demands on their time, particularly in the case of working people, and some clergy expressed concerns in this area.[141] Others commented on the limited reach of their schools – at Lewknor, for example, the schools were attended only by the children of the labourers, the farmers remaining aloof – or on difficulties with particular sections of the community.[142] However, these were a small minority of the returns and the vicar of Enstone may have spoken for many when he told the bishop, 'I have found the work with children in Sunday School and Catechising more encouraging than anything else, thanks to the kind and intelligent help of the teachers.'[143]

The Oxfordshire clergy rarely relied solely on day and Sunday schools for the Christian education of their flocks. Just under half the returns recorded the use of traditional catechetical methods of rote-learned question and response, at least on an occasional basis, and in more than seventy parishes it was undertaken weekly.[144] Only a few returns recorded reasons for desisting – at Tadmarton, for example, the rector thought it had effectively been superseded by Sunday schooling, while the vicar of Claydon had been unable to cope with the 'exceptional indocility … of the children'.[145] When it came to provision for older children and adults, which featured in questions 5 and 8 of the 1914 survey, there are signs of a relatively high level of activity in Oxfordshire parishes. Unsurprisingly, given the moves already underway towards a sacramental construction of parish life, preparation for communion played an important part. Confirmation classes were referred to in around 16 per cent of the returns,[146] but were, in practice, almost certainly virtually ubiquitous in Oxfordshire parishes and played a major part in clerical strategies for reaching young parishioners after they had left school.[147] Many parishes went further and established guilds, classes or special preparation services in order to encourage parishioners to become regular communicants. These were often serious endeavours. In rural Kencot, for example, the rector prescribed a course of reading for the month ahead and provided an exposition of it at each meeting

139 1914 Bampton Proper; Chinnor; Minster Lovell.
140 1914 Broughton. For a similar report in a day school context see 1914 Tackley.
141 1914 Charlton-on-Otmoor; Woodstock.
142 1914 Lewknor. For a Sunday school in trouble at least partly because of clerical unpopularity, see 1914 Filkins.
143 1914 Enstone. See also 1914 Heyford, Lower.
144 1914 Garsington; Milcombe; Oxford, St Philip and St James.
145 1914 Tadmarton; Claydon.
146 E.g. 1914 Barton Westcot; Cassington; Northleigh.
147 1914 Spelsbury; Tackley.

for the benefit of the members, while at suburban Summertown the 'young lads' and 'young women' were expected to attend a preparation service once a month, and at least one service on a Sunday, and to receive communion a minimum of once a month. In the market town of Thame, younger communicants were given 'spiritual stewards' who acted as mentors, encouraging them to attend meetings and to receive communion on a regular basis.[148] Some guilds at least were flourishing enterprises. At Cadmore End, for example, the guild had a membership of over eighty out of a parish population of 290, and its monthly meetings attracted as many men as women – a success the vicar put down partly to his teaching method, which allowed members to ask questions.[149]

Although guilds were common, perhaps especially in leading Anglo-Catholic parishes,[150] the most popular mode of seeking to develop the Christian education of parishioners of all ages post-Sunday School, so far as the evidence of the returns is concerned, was the Bible class. Classes for men were reported in over 33 per cent of parishes and for women in over 27 per cent. Classes were generally held on Sunday afternoons or weekdays and in rural parishes they were frequently seasonal, often held at times of the year when work on the land was less intensive.[151] In urban parishes, on the other hand, classes might be very extensive. At Banbury St Mary, for example, there were eight Bible classes – one each for men and women, two for girls and four for lads.[152] The clergy seem to have relied on such classes, which could combine time for instruction with opportunities for recreation,[153] as a means to engage with older boys and young men in particular.[154] They provided an opportunity to deepen the acquaintance of parishioners with the scriptures and Christian doctrine in a less formal setting than the regular church services, though the vicar of St Thomas noted that his young men's class preferred to go through the Gospels repeatedly – noting ingenuously that 'very possibly I did not make the Acts very interesting'![155] However, in some cases at least, confirmation was regarded as a sort of graduation from Anglican instruction and it was more difficult, especially in the case of boys, to get them to receive further teaching thereafter.[156]

Bible classes were sometimes supported with materials provided by national societies like the Bible Reading League or the Scripture Union,[157] and many similar

---

148   1914 Kencot; Summertown; Thame.
149   1914 Cadmore End. See also 1914 Henley-on-Thames.
150   E.g. 1914 Cowley St John; Oxford, St Frideswide. Though they could be found in Evangelical parishes too. See Oxford, St Clement.
151   1914 Charlton-on-Otmoor; Fewcott; Finstock and Fawler; Highmore.
152   1914 Banbury. See also 1914 Henley-on-Thames.
153   1914 Milton-under-Wychwood; Nuneham Courtenay.
154   1914 Caversham; Coggs; Ducklington with Hardwick; Kidlington.
155   1914 Oxford, St Thomas.
156   1914 Enstone; Goring; Mollington. Knight, *Nineteenth-Century Church*, pp. 92–8. J. Obelkevich, *Religion and Rural Society: South Lindsey 1825–1875* (Oxford, 1976), pp. 134–5.
157   1914 Drayton; Salford.

bodies were available to help clergy develop teaching opportunities allied with a range of activities for all their parishioners (usually disaggregated by both age and gender). Some of the most prominent Anglican organisations were surprisingly under-represented in the returns made by the Oxfordshire clergy. The presence of a branch of the Church Lads' Brigade, founded in 1891 and probably the leading Anglican male youth organisation before the first world war,[158] was reported in only four parishes in 1914,[159] and Boy Scouts in only two.[160] This may have been because these organisations were relatively thinly spread in predominantly rural Oxfordshire or, alternatively, because the clergy did not see them as particularly useful means of religious instruction.[161] Much the same can be said of the Band of Hope, reported in only four returns,[162] and the Church of England Temperance Society, which was absent altogether – a surprising result given the relatively high prominence of concern about the misuse of alcohol in church circles.[163] However, three Anglican organisations – the Girls Friendly Society, Mothers' Union and the Church of England Men's Society – were prominently represented across the whole range of Oxfordshire parishes.

The Girls Friendly Society (GFS), probably the first organisation run by and for lay Anglican women, was launched in 1874 and was almost certainly at the peak of its influence in the years immediately preceding the first world war. A social purity organisation for unmarried women, 'for the upholding of Christian maidenhood based upon the national Church', it operated through local branches run by 'associates' (usually from the upper and middle classes) who admitted 'members' from the working classes, often domestic servants but also shopworkers and other female occupations.[164] The distinction between two classes of members (in which honorary members contributed but did not directly benefit from the organisation) was a familiar structure in rural clubs and societies, though unlike the village clubs studied by Shaun Morley, in the GFS the associates remained firmly in control.[165] From the point of view of the clergy, the GFS was a significant part of the parish

---

158 M. Austin, 'Like A Swift Hurricane.' People, Clergy and Class in a Midlands Diocese, 1914–1919 (Chesterfield, 2014), pp. 129–36.
159 1914 Charlbury with Chadlington; Chipping Norton; Langford; Middleton Stoney.
160 1914 Marston; Pyrton.
161 They tended to be reported when a Bible class was held in connection with them. See 1914 Chipping Norton; Pyrton.
162 1914 Ardley; Crowmarsh Gifford; Ipsden with North Stoke; Tadmarton.
163 Gore, War and the Church, pp. 75–6. For a thorough review of the relationship between religion and alcohol in the Victorian period, see B. Harrison, Drink and the Victorians, 2nd edn (Keele, 1994), pp. 167–81.
164 B. Harrison, 'For Church, Queen and Family: The Girls' Friendly Society 1874–1920', Past and Present, 61 (1973), pp. 107–38. D. Doughan and P. Gordon, Women, Clubs and Associations in Britain (Abingdon, 2006), pp. 89–92.
165 S. Morley, Oxfordshire Friendly Societies 1750–1918, Oxfordshire Record Society, 68 (Oxford, 2011), p. 9.

machinery, bridging the gap between Sunday school and confirmation class and the parochial organisations for mothers and adult women;[166] and as Harrison has argued, the virtues of chastity and temperance which it sought to inculcate were perhaps of particular value in giving girls resources to help them navigate some of the perils of service occupations.[167] This may have been particularly important in rural Oxfordshire, many of whose young women departed their parishes for a spell in domestic service.[168] However, its principal attraction to girls, in the forty parishes that reported the local presence of the GFS, was probably the opportunities it offered for regular and respectable sociability, as in the case of Sarsden where it met weekly during the winter months.[169] A similar role, for married women, was played by the Mothers' Union (MU) whose presence was noted in approximately 10 per cent of the returns for 1914. Founded in 1885, in the Winchester diocese, partly to provide a home for GFS girls who had entered into marriage, the MU also grew rapidly in the years before the first world war[170] and its work to support Christian family life and parenting could be quite vigorous, even in small parishes. Wootton, for example, had an active branch with many members, while at Mapledurham, where one of the vicar's daughters was its leading mover, there were fortnightly meetings and also occasional addresses, either in church or at the vicarage, by specially invited speakers including 'ladies' and visiting clergy.[171] Other parishes had established Bible classes in connection with their Mothers' Union,[172] and at Broughton Pogis, the rector expressed appreciation for its contribution in leading 'parents to look after childrens spiritual life'.[173]

The last of the three organisations, the Church of England Men's Society (CEMS), was founded in 1899 by an amalgamation of three existing groups with a mission to work among men, and in some parishes at least, especially urban ones, was the backbone of work among adult male parishioners.[174] In Oxfordshire, a little over 10 per cent of the returns made reference to the presence of a branch, including larger parishes like Bloxham with a population of over 1,000,[175] small rural ones like Middleton Stoney, and tiny urban parishes like St Mary the Virgin and St Peter

---

166   See, for example, 1914 Cuddesdon.
167   Harrison, 'For Church', pp. 117–19. C. Moyse, *A History of the Mothers' Union: Women, Anglicanism and Globalisation, 1876–2008* (Woodbridge, 2009).
168   E.g. 1914 Chesterton.
169   1914 Sarsden cum Churchill; Headington Quarry. Though some met less frequently: 1914 Hanborough.
170   Harrison, 'For Church', pp. 109–11.
171   1914 Mapledurham; Wootton. See also 1914 Stadhampton.
172   1914 Ewelme; Littlemore.
173   1914 Broughton Pogis.
174   C. F. Garbett (ed.), *The Work of a Great Parish* (London, 1915), pp. 129–36.
175   1914 Bloxham. See also 1914 Caversham; Headington Quarry.

in the East in Oxford.[176] Some clergy used the CEMS to draw in older boys[177] and many made regular study arrangements for their local groups.[178] According to the vicar of Charlbury,

> Our Church of England Men's Society has met steadily once a month for 6 years for systematic study. Average attendance some years 35, some years 20. For past twelve months we have taken the services in the Prayer Book in succession.[179]

CEMS branches could supply a useful pool of assistants for the local clergy and in some parishes they developed further into a body that could be used as a sounding board by incumbents willing to try the experiment. At Marston, the vicar sought advice from his CEMS members over ways to reach out to previously neglected 15- to 18-year-olds, while at Charlbury the vicar reported that his CEMS branch had 'largely acted as a Church Council … Generally the work of the Parish has been carried on with full consultation and help of our laymen and they do a good share of work.'[180]

Important though the work of such national organisations was, the Oxfordshire clergy found many other ways to approach the Christian education and spiritual formation of their parishioners. Some sought to introduce them to Christian literature, like Robert Hunt who read *Pilgrim's Progress* to the men and lads of his tiny parish.[181] Quite frequently, classes were held on particular topics, as at Begbroke where the rector aimed to hold sessions on the Bible, the Prayer Book and Church History during the winter months.[182] Outside the structures of the national organisations, special services or additional meetings for particular groups, especially for men or mothers, were also a common feature of parish life and sometimes were significant undertakings. At Holy Trinity Henley, for example, there was a monthly men's service and three mothers' meetings a week in autumn, winter and spring.[183] Some clergy found tracts, leaflets or parish magazines delivered to every home a useful way of making contact with people who might be reluctant to come to meetings;[184] others sought to bring the meetings to the people by holding them in cottages or other informal surroundings away from the church.[185]

---

176   1914 Middleton Stoney; Ramsden; Oxford, St Mary the Virgin; Oxford, St Peter in the East.
177   1914 Rollright, Great; Pyrton.
178   Cuddesdon; Hanborough; Middleton Stoney.
179   1914 Charlbury with Chadlington.
180   1914 Marston; Charlbury with Chadlington.
181   1914 Albury; Oxford, St Frideswide.
182   1914 Begbroke. See 1914 Cadmore End; Oxford, St Philip and St James; and also Kidlington for a less successful attempt.
183   1914 Henley, Holy Trinity. See also 1914 Caversham; Rotherfield Greys; Sydenham; Oxford, St Michael.
184   1914 Cassington; Oxford, St Clement; Oxford, Holy Trinity.
185   1914 Claydon; Marston.

The subject of foreign missions was high on the agenda of the Church of England in the decade before the first world war with interest stirred not only by the progress of its own missionary endeavours but also by the great World Missionary Conference held in Edinburgh in 1910.[186] Consequently, the final question asked in 1914 by Gore on engagement with the education of parishioners, was on the subject of their interest in missions. As might be expected, this produced a range of responses; but the overall impression given by the returns is of a significant effort to encourage support for missions and mission organisations and a generally positive response to those efforts. Work in the field was principally coordinated by missionary societies, some linked to specific traditions in the church like the Universities Mission to Central Africa (UMCA) and the Oxford Mission to Calcutta, both representing the Anglo-Catholic tradition, or the Colonial and Continental Church Society and the Church Missionary Society (CMS), representing the Evangelical tradition. There were also more broad bench societies, like the Society for the Propagation of the Gospel (SPG), which might be supported by a range of opinion within the church.[187] Of the returns citing support for particular missionary societies, much the most popular was the SPG and its junior branch the King's Messengers, which were mentioned in approximately 25 per cent of the 1914 returns: most usually singly but also in combination with other societies including, in some cases, the UMCA[188] and in others the CMS.[189] The next most popular societies were the CMS or its supporters' organisation the Gleaners Union, which was referred to in twenty returns (around 8 per cent), and the UMCA, which was recorded in twelve (5 per cent). The strong links of these societies with individual traditions within Anglicanism make their presence a useful index of the churchmanship of their supporting parishes, especially where it was combined with support for other societies in the same tradition. Thus at St Thomas in Oxford, the congregation supported both the UMCA and the Anglo-Catholic Zanzibar mission which was linked to it, while the Evangelicalism of the parish of Swerford was signalled by its support for both the CMS and two inter-denominational Evangelical organisations, the British and Foreign Bible Society and the Evangelical Alliance.[190] However, this

---

186 B. Stanley, *The World Missionary Conference, Edinburgh 1910* (Grand Rapids, MI, 2009).
187 The literature on missions is vast but for useful recent work, especially on the relationship of missions and empire, see A. Porter, *Religion versus Empire: British Protestant Missionaries and Overseas Expansion, 1700–1914* (Manchester, 2004); H. M. Carey, *God's Empire: Religion and Colonialism in the British World c.1801–1908* (Cambridge, 2011); and for Anglo-Catholic missions, R. Strong, 'The Oxford Movement and Missions', in S. J. Brown, P. Nockles and J. Pereiro (eds), *The Oxford Handbook of the Oxford Movement* (Oxford, 2017), pp. 485–99.
188 E.g. 1914 Checkendon; Oxford, St Thomas.
189 E.g. 1914 Finstock and Fawler; Tetsworth.
190 1914 Oxford, St Thomas; Swerford. See also 1914 Kingham; Oxford, St Frideswide; Nettlebed.

method is not infallible and the returns also show some unlikely associations, most clearly in the parish of St Philip and St James in Oxford, a church undoubtedly in the Anglo-Catholic tradition which also had an annual collection for the CMS – an indication perhaps of the eirenic attitude of the vicar towards his Evangelical parishioners.[191]

Support for these societies, or missionary activity more generally, was part of the general weave of parish life in most places in Oxfordshire. In some cases, this was at a relatively low level, as at Hook Norton which had an annual sermon and missionary meeting, or Stoke Talmage which had occasional lectures and days of intercession.[192] However, in many places support for missions was clearly a more prominent feature of church-based activity. The major societies had developed considerable publicity machines over the course of the nineteenth century and many of their periodicals made their way into Oxfordshire homes, especially *The Church Abroad*, *The Mission Field* and the *Quarterly Intercession Paper* (all produced by the SPG) and the *Church Missionary Gleaner* (produced by the CMS).[193] Missionaries at home on leave might be called on to visit parishes in support of their missions:[194] the vicar of Mapledurham commented, 'I endeavour as often as I can to get preachers who can speak from their personal experience of work (in S. Africa N. Zealand etc)',[195] and in some cases the clergy had such experience themselves.[196] Such contacts made the parish church a conduit through which even relatively isolated Oxfordshire communities could be linked to and given a vision of the wider world. Sometimes this was explicitly linked to the duties of empire, as the vicar of Spelsbury put it (in terms painful to twenty-first-century sensibilities): 'I constantly refer to this subject in sermons, and exhort people to remember the obligations of their Country towards our own people in newly colonised lands and towards the subject Races under our Dominion.'[197]

However, in addition to any sense of obligation, the exoticism of the missionary enterprise almost certainly made it easier to stir interest in it, for example through the use of lantern lectures to promote both regular intercession and financial support.[198] Interest in missions nonetheless went far beyond entertainment. Some parishes established study circles, missionary guilds or parochial missionary associations to support the work.[199] Others developed personal links with individual

---

191 1914 Oxford, St Philip and St James. See also 1914 Hanborough. For Davey Biggs see Smith, 'Evangelicals in a "Catholic" Suburb', pp. 226–9.
192 1914 Norton, Hook; Stoke Talmage. See also 1914 Brightwell Baldwin; Whitchurch.
193 1914 Launton.
194 1914 Hanwell; Kencot. This activity was usually referred to as deputation work.
195 1914 Mapledurham.
196 1914 Drayton.
197 1914 Spelsbury.
198 E.g. 1914 Somerton; Stoke Row; Stokenchurch.
199 E.g. 1914 Broughton Pogis; Fritwell; Oxford, St Andrew; Oxford, St Margaret.

mission stations or particular parts of the world: the vicar of Chesterton reported that his parish had a particular interest in the Argentine – a link fostered by a visit from Edward Every, the recently consecrated Anglican bishop of Argentina. Holton's interest in India was focused by clergy in the parish or their family members going out as missionaries. Stonesfield showed the possibility of another kind of link, collecting regularly for the British Colombia Church Aid Association because a large number of people from the village had emigrated to British Colombia.[200] Only a handful of parishes reported difficulty in raising interest[201] and some displayed a good deal of activity and evident enthusiasm. At Highmore, for example, collecting boxes for the SPG were distributed and the parish took an active part in a missionary exhibition at Henley.[202] While at Highfield, for example, the vicar had annual sermons, visits by deputations from the CMS and SPG, meetings with missionary speakers, missionary addresses and sermons, and quarterly services for children.[203] As with many other aspects of the early twentieth-century parish, children were an important focus of attempts to promote support for missions. Fourteen of the returns mention the presence of the King's Messengers, the juvenile wing of the SPG, and others arranged special events or classes aimed at children.[204] Children might also be drawn in by missionary activity with which they could particularly identify, as at Marston where the vicar reported that the children had contributed towards the support of two boys in the CMS mission at Jabalpur, or at Sarsden where the Sunday school was providing for the education of a boy in Burma.[205] Some historians have followed one line of contemporary commentary in judging this kind of activity as a form of exploitation, especially where working-class children were contributing financially, and as a means of incorporating the working classes into an essentially elite project.[206] However, by encouraging children to consider themselves as givers rather than merely objects of charity it may also have reinforced a sense of dignity or even agency among the children, as at Highmore where the secretary of the juvenile branch was a 9-year-old boy who was responsible *inter alia* for forwarding the offertory at missionary children's services to the SPG.[207]

---

200 1914 Chesterton; Holton; Stonesfield. For other examples of particular links see 1914 Milcombe; Pyrton; Stanton Harcourt; Tackley.
201 E.g. 1914 Clanfield; Merton; Wardington.
202 1914 Highmore. For similar activity see 1914 Chastleton; Filkins; Kidmore End; Witney.
203 1914 Highfield.
204 H. P. Thompson, *Into All Lands: The History of the Society for the Propagation of the Gospel in Foreign Parts 1701–1950* (London, 1951), pp. 239–40. 1914 Banbury; Ewelme; Enstone.
205 1914 Marston; Sarsden cum Churchill; Oxford, St Thomas.
206 S. Thorne, *Congregational Missions and the Making of an Imperial Culture in 19th-Century England* (Stanford, CA, 1999), pp. 124–54. Though Thorne also recognises that missionary philanthropy could also have more egalitarian implications. E.g. ibid., pp. 160–1.
207 1914 Highmore.

INTRODUCTION

The multiplicity of services, activities and organisations recorded in the returns show parish life in the early twentieth century being maintained at the same intensity established in the late Victorian period, and, given the elaboration of sacramental services already underway, the tempo was, if anything, being raised even further. However, clearly not all was well in the parishes of rural Oxfordshire: the parochial model was threatened by the same economic and demographic forces that threatened the viability of the parish community itself. Some parishes had been losing population since the agricultural depression of the 1870s, and this process seems to have accelerated in the 1890s with an average loss of 20 per cent in the smallest towns and 13 per cent in villages as compared to their 1851 population.[208] Out-migration tended to skew the population distribution in these parishes, and at Taynton, for example, the vicar reported, 'This village is inhabited chiefly by old people', and consequently that, 'There are no young women able to attend classes.'[209] This process was reinforced by the economic opportunities that drew young people in particular away from their own parishes to work elsewhere. Many returns commented in particular on the tendency for young women to leave for domestic service as soon as they had finished school,[210] and in some parishes this applied to young men as well.[211] This made it difficult to recruit members of parish organisations and help with running them, since the most promising graduates from school and Sunday school were often among the first to leave.[212] It was also fatal for a parochial enterprise that invested so much stock in the promise of the 'rising generation'. As the vicar of Lewknor glumly reported,

> I consider the children to be well instructed in Religion at the time they leave School … Of the later result, I cannot judge. The boys leave the village for the towns, the girls for Service. The dull ones only remain. Confirmation at the age of 13 – 14 is the end of my influence as a rule.[213]

The Oxfordshire Clergy

The men sent out by the church to labour in the harvest fields of the parishes of Oxfordshire are revealed by the returns to be variegated in their character, priorities and attitudes; but they also shared a number of features in common. One of the most striking of these was their educational background. In the late Victorian period, the clerical profession remained one dominated by university graduates. However, there was an increasing number of non-graduate clergy, some trained

---

208 Nash, 'Population Change 1851–1901', pp. 138–9.
209 1914 Taynton.
210 E.g. 1914 Crowmarsh Gifford; Mollington; Swalcliffe with Shutford; Sydenham.
211 E.g. 1914 Barton, Steeple; Checkendon; Stoke, South with Woodcote. For a close analysis of the problem see 1914 Bampton Lew.
212 1914 Kidlington.
213 1914 Lewknor.

■ Oxford ■ Cambridge ✔ Other ■ None

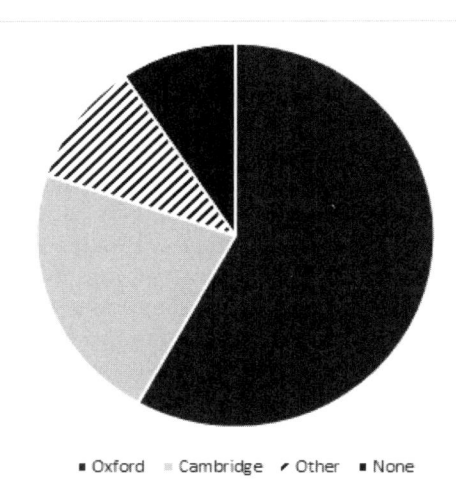

Figure 4: Higher education of the clergy

in colleges specially designed to facilitate their entry into the profession like St Bees, Lampeter and St Aidan's Birkenhead,[214] or as non-graduate trainees at colleges which like Cuddesdon or Wells accepted a mixed entry.[215] As a result, according to the research conducted by Kelsey Sterling, around 13 per cent of Anglican clergy were non-graduates in 1914.[216] However, such non-graduate clergy were under-represented in early twentieth-century Oxfordshire and of the 277 incumbents who served parishes responding to the surveys of 1914 and 1918 only 9 per cent were non-graduates (see Figure 4). Some of these were relatively late entries to the priesthood having previously pursued another vocation, like Lawrence Roberts, rector of Ardley, who was ordained in 1886 after a career as an officer in the Royal Navy.[217]

As Figure 4 illustrates, of those with university degrees the largest proportion, as might be expected, had graduated from their local institution, the University of Oxford. Oxford graduates made up some 58 per cent of Oxfordshire incumbents, compared with less than 30 per cent nationally, while 22 per cent had graduated

---

214 D. Dowland, *Nineteenth-Century Anglican Theological Training: The Redbrick Challenge* (Oxford, 1997). For Oxfordshire examples see 1914 Elsfield; Sandford St Martin.

215 1914 Wheatfield. For the later Victorian clergy see A. Haig, *The Victorian Clergy* (London, 1984); B. Heeney, *A Different Kind of Gentleman* (Hamden, CT, 1976); A. Russell, *The Clerical Profession* (London, 1980); K. Sterling, 'The Education of the Anglican Clergy, 1830–1914', PhD thesis, University of Leicester (1982).

216 Sterling, 'Anglican Clergy', p. 581. Sterling's conclusion was based on a sample of just under 3,500 clergymen recorded in the standard Anglican reference work *Crockford's Clerical Directory* for 1914.

217 1914 Ardley.

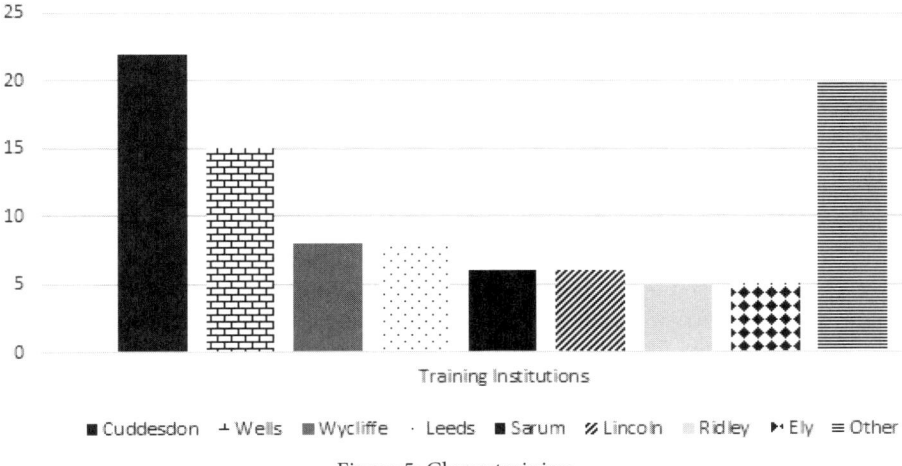

Figure 5: Clergy training

from Cambridge, a little less than the national proportion, again just under 30 per cent.[218] The remaining 10 per cent of Oxfordshire incumbents had graduated from other institutions. A few of these were unusual, like Simon Stephen, vicar of Steeple Barton, who held a PhD from the Sorbonne and who was ordained by the Roman Catholic bishop of Mardin before being received into the Church of England in 1901, or Robert Hudgell, who graduated from King's College, Windsor, Nova Scotia (Canada's first chartered university), though his Licence in Theology (L.Th.) might place him in a middle ground between graduates and non-graduates.[219] Most, however, came from other British or Irish universities, especially Durham, Trinity College Dublin and the University of London.[220]

If a large majority of Oxfordshire incumbents shared a similar educational background the same could not be said of their participation in the professional training offered by the new post-graduate clerical training colleges opened in increasing numbers from the mid-Victorian period. The first were at Chichester (1839) and Wells (1840), both associated with the High Church tradition.[221] The Oxford diocese opened its own at Cuddesdon in 1854, which rapidly acquired a

---

218 For national proportions see Haig, *Victorian Clergy*, p. 32.
219 1914 Barton, Steeple; 1918 Coggs. The same categorisation might be applied also to a handful of clergy whose chief qualification was the AKC awarded by King's College London. E.g. 1914 Oxford, St Barnabas; 1918 Whitchurch.
220 1914 Begbroke; Norton, Hook. 1918 Stanton Harcourt.
221 Haig, *Victorian Clergy*, p. 74.

reputation for particularly advanced High Churchmanship.[222] All three of these provided clergy, although Chichester was a relatively small contributor with only three Oxfordshire incumbents having trained there – all, at least initially, as non-graduates.[223] On the other hand, as illustrated in Figure 5, Wells and Cuddesdon were the most significant providers of college-trained incumbents in the diocese, contributing fifteen and twenty-two respectively.

However, if the existing incumbents in 1914 are compared with the new ones who arrived between the two surveys, it is clear that Cuddesdon, in particular, grew in importance, with ten of its contribution of twenty-two belonging to the new cohort.[224] This pattern was partially replicated, though on a smaller scale, by Wycliffe Hall, a college based in north Oxford and founded in the Evangelical tradition in 1877, suggesting that local contacts and networks became particularly important in finding incumbents for Oxfordshire parishes under wartime conditions. With the exception of Wycliffe, among the major providers only Ridley Hall in Cambridge, which supplied five Oxfordshire incumbents across the period, was a college firmly in the Evangelical camp. The other substantial contributors, such as Lincoln and the Leeds Clergy School, were High Church institutions,[225] further underpinning Anglo-Catholic influence in early twentieth-century Oxfordshire. The remaining incumbents with college training came from a range of institutions with varied theological characters, including Lichfield, Gloucester, the Church Missionary Society College in Islington and St Stephen's House in Oxford, but none of them supplied a large enough number of incumbents to be influential.[226] Moreover, while the proportion of college-trained clergy may have been on the rise in the three decades before the first world war, they still only represented around a third of a clerical body most of which had trodden a more traditional path to their incumbencies via a series of more junior appointments in the church or the closely allied profession of education.

With or without the benefit of college training the journey into an Oxfordshire rectory or vicarage was often a lengthy one. Figure 6 shows the number of years spent by the Oxfordshire incumbents of 1914–18 between their ordination as priests and their first appointment to an incumbency.

A small minority (around 22 per cent of the total) achieved their incumbencies relatively early in their careers, one to five years after their ordination.[227] About half

---

222 M. D. Chapman, *God's Holy Hill: A History of Christianity in Cuddesdon* (Charlbury, 2004), pp. 107–11; A. Atherstone, 'The Founding of Cuddesdon: Liddon, Ritualism and the Forces of Reaction', in M. D. Chapman (ed.), *Ambassadors of Christ* (Aldershot, 2004), pp. 23–50.
223 1914 Cropredy; Nuffield; Watlington.
224 E.g. 1918 Finstock and Fawler; North Hinksey; Kidmore End.
225 Haig, *Victorian Clergy*, pp. 86–8.
226 E.g. 1914 Brizenorton; Tew, Little; Shilton. 1918 Minster Lovell.
227 E.g. 1914 Kencot; Northleigh; 1918 Oxford, St Mary Magdalene.

■ 1 to 5   6 to 10   11 to 15   ■ 16 to 20   ▪ over 20

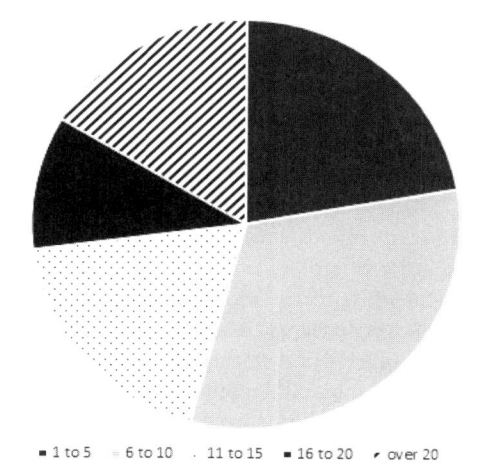

Figure 6: Years between ordination and first incumbency

waited between six and fifteen years;[228] but a substantial number waited even longer: 11 per cent for between sixteen and twenty years[229] and an even larger proportion (17 per cent) for more than twenty years.[230] As a number of historians have noted, the phenomenon of clergy having to wait a considerable length of time for their first incumbency was partly a question of supply and demand. From the mid-Victorian period, there was a surge in the numbers of young men entering the ministry. They were propelled by the combined enthusiasm of the Evangelical and High Church revivals in the Church of England. In the first few decades they were also attracted by a combination of rising prosperity, especially among rural clergy whose incomes were boosted by enclosure and a strong market for agricultural produce, and an increase in the number of benefices, as the Church expanded to serve the populations of the growing towns and cities. The total number of clergy rose from around 14,600 in 1841 to over 25,000 in 1901,[231] and the effect of the rise in ordinations combined with inadequate retirement arrangements for older clergy[232] led to a problem of over-supply and thus lengthening periods spent in assistant curacies waiting for a benefice to become vacant.[233]

Several of the Oxfordshire incumbents had career paths which support this interpretation. Andrew Hercules Gillmor, for example, a Trinity College Dublin graduate, served seven separate curacies over a period of sixteen years before his

---

228 E.g. 1914 Beckley; Hailey cum Crawley. 1918 North Hinksey; Oddington.
229 E.g. 1914 Charlton-on-Otmoor. 1918 Heythrop.
230 E.g. 1914 Bucknell; Fewcott. 1918 Harpsden; Mollington.
231 Haig, *Victorian Clergy*, p. 3.
232 Haig, *Victorian Clergy*, pp. 319–29.
233 Haig, *Victorian Clergy*, pp. 234–48.

first incumbency at Begbroke. Charles Frederic Girdlestone spent twenty-two years in curacies after his ordination as priest, before being appointed as vicar of Merton.[234] Some also followed other traditional routes, combining experience in one or more curacies with work as a schoolmaster or school chaplain. Benjamin Hamilton, for example, another Irish university graduate, was ordained priest in 1875 but did not become an incumbent until in 1913, at the age of 65, he was appointed to Fewcott. In the intervening thirty-three years he combined work in a series of curacies and chaplaincies with an appointment at Haberdashers' Aske's school. A somewhat grander version of the same career path was that of Francis St John Thackeray, a classical scholar from Merton College Oxford, who was ordained to the priesthood in 1867 and achieved his first incumbency at Mapledurham in 1883, having served for a quarter of a century as assistant master at Eton. He had already published on classical subjects during his school career and continued to do so for at least the first two decades of his parochial ministry.[235]

Oxfordshire incumbencies also continued to provide a destination for a few clergymen who had followed an academic vocation. Charles Augustus Whittuck, for example, ordained priest in 1879, spent thirteen years as Tutor and Vice-Principal of Brasenose College Oxford before moving into parish ministry, and was eventually appointed as vicar of the University Church in Oxford.[236] An alternative career route for an aspiring clergyman in previous centuries was to find a post, usually as a chaplain, in the household of a nobleman, who might reward this service with appointment to a benefice in his patronage.[237] Among the incumbents making returns to the 1914 and 1918 surveys, however, there was only one example of this phenomenon: Henry William Leycester O'Rorke, a graduate of Trinity College Cambridge and Wycliffe Hall, who after serving chaplaincies with the Missions to Seamen became, in 1908, Domestic Chaplain to the Duke of Devonshire, transferring in 1915 to a similar post with the Duke of Marlborough – which seems to have brought with it the rectory of Woodstock.[238]

A review of the careers of Oxfordshire incumbents of 1914–18 also reveals a different dynamic behind the relatively late entry into parochial ministry – not just a shortage of vacant benefices but also an expansion in the alternatives. This included the considerable growth in secondary education and specialist colleges in the Victorian period and the expansion of the army and navy, which created chaplaincy and other positions. Some of these were in new public schools: Frederic John Hall, for example, spent thirteen years as assistant master at Haileybury

---

234 1914 Begbroke; Merton. See also 1914 Finmere; 1918 Cassington.
235 1914 Fewcott; Mapledurham. See also 1914 Blechingdon; Farringdon, Little; 1918 Bucknell.
236 1914 Oxford, St Mary the Virgin. See also 1914 Harpsden; and for a mixed career involving a number of the above elements, 1914 Blechingdon.
237 W. Gibson, *A Social History of the Domestic Chaplain 1530–1840* (London, 1997).
238 1918 Woodstock.

– a new public school built on the foundation of the former East India Company college – and a further twenty years as headmaster of Northaw Preparatory School before accepting the vicarage of Shirburn.[239] Others were specialist institutions, like the Royal Military Academy in Gosport where Frederick Corden Nash taught mathematics for four years alongside his first curacy, or the Army School in Maidenhead and Imperial Service College in Windsor where Sidney Herbert Scott held chaplaincies *en route* to the rectory of Oddington.[240] Some were created by the Church itself, like the Missionary College in Dorchester or St Augustine's College Canterbury where Watkin Wynn Williams, the future rector of Drayton St Leonard, was employed as Vice-Principal of the former and fellow and Tutor of the latter for a total of sixteen years before his first incumbency.[241] In addition to those who took advantage of the expansion of educational positions, a few Oxfordshire incumbents had spent lengthy periods of time in naval or military chaplaincies. William Stuart Harris, for example, a Cambridge graduate ordained to the priesthood in 1877, spent twenty-six years as a chaplain in the navy, serving in action at the bombardment of Alexandria in 1882 and rising to become Chaplain of the Fleet and Archdeacon for the Royal Navy.[242]

In addition to the expansion of traditional non-parochial roles for clergy, the nineteenth century saw the development of new opportunities which had clearly proved attractive to future Oxfordshire incumbents. These sometimes took the form of organisational or other roles in Anglican or occasionally inter-denominational organisations in England. Ernest William Cox, for example, spent six of the nine years between his ordination as priest and his first incumbency at Holy Trinity Oxford as an organising secretary for the Church Missionary Society. Other incumbents had worked for organisations as diverse as Anglo-Catholic Sisterhoods, the High Church Additional Curates Society, the inter-denominational British and Foreign Bible Society and the ultra-Protestant Protestant Reform Society.[243] However, the largest growth in new opportunities arose from imperial expansion and the development of large-scale missionary activity in the nineteenth century. The development of British colonies in this period brought with it opportunities to work in chaplaincies or fully fledged colonial churches around the world. James Edward Bouverie Brine, for example, occupied a succession of chaplaincies in Ceylon for around fifteen years before returning to parochial ministry in England. Similarly, Whylock Pendavis served thirty-eight years in a series of posts in the church in Mauritius, ending as archdeacon and examining chaplain to the bishop, returning to England at the age of 56 as rector of Hethe.[244] A further

---

239 1914 Shirburn. See also 1914 Rotherfield Greys; Wood Eaton.
240 1914 Hailey cum Crawley; 1918 Oddington.
241 1918 Drayton St Leonard.
242 1914 Bucknell. See also 1918 Stonesfield.
243 1914 Oxford, Holy Trinity; 1918 Rotherfield Peppard; Freeland; 1914 Kingham; Ardley.
244 1914 Horton-cum-Studley; Hethe. See also 1914 Hampton Poyle.

large sphere for clerical activity was opened up by the expansion of the British missionary enterprise. Some future Oxfordshire incumbents occupied missionary posts at home, like Herbert Edwin Henshaw Coombes who worked at Penarth and Barry in Wales for the Missions to Seamen,[245] but the majority of such posts were overseas. William Spendlove spent the first fourteen years of his career as a CMS missionary in Canada before returning in his early fifties to look after the tiny parish of Drayton.[246] Similarly William Joseph Richards worked in a series of posts with the CMS in India for thirty-five years before his first incumbency at Shilton.[247]

Given the range of opportunities open to late Victorian clergymen, the incumbents of early twentieth-century Oxfordshire probably brought a wider range of experience to their parochial ministry than any previous generation. It is interesting, therefore, that the returns provide little or no evidence of reflection on the applicability of that experience in an Oxfordshire context.[248] However, a consequence of the lengthy journeys so many of the clergy took to their Oxfordshire parishes was that, as Figure 7 illustrates, they were, in terms of age, a distinctly mature group.

Figure 7 shows the age at each survey of the respondents, relying principally on their declared age at the 1911 census.[249] Already in 1914 younger incumbents were thin on the ground, with the distribution heavily skewed towards the over-fifties. The youngest respondent was the curate of St Frideswide, aged 29, and the youngest incumbent was Charles Aylen, aged 32 (but he belonged to a small group – only twelve incumbents, or 5 per cent of the total, were aged under 40).[250] The bulk of the incumbents might be thought of as middle-aged: ninety-nine, or 45 per cent, were aged between 45 and 59[251] but a substantial cohort were considerably older. Seventy-six, or almost 35 per cent, were aged 60 or over[252] and of these, twenty were aged 70 or more – almost twice as many as those aged under 40. This suggests that small parishes in rural Oxfordshire may have been particularly attractive as retirement positions.[253] Moreover, while these aged incumbents may have brought considerable experience to their roles, they were unlikely to be men who could invigorate parish life: some of them were clearly already finding the work too much.[254] This age profile was all the more important because the vast majority of Oxfordshire

---

245 1914 Ipsden with North Stoke.
246 1914 Drayton. See also 1914 Milton-under-Wychwood.
247 1914 Shilton. See also 1914 Cornwell; Oxford, St Andrew; 1918 Harpsden.
248 For a rare example see 1918 Tackley.
249 This was possible to establish for 219 respondents in 1914 and 210 in 1918.
250 E.g. 1914 Shiplake; Clanfield; Ducklington with Hardwick.
251 E.g. 1914 Aston Rowant; Kingham; Warborough.
252 E.g. 1914 Blechingdon; Dorchester with Burcot; Rotherfield Peppard.
253 This is certainly a plausible interpretation of William Richards's decision to take on the cure of the 201 souls in the parish of Shilton after his thirty-five-year career in India. 1914 Shilton. See also 1914 Drayton.
254 E.g. 1914 Middleton Stoney. A similar story may lie behind the very minimal return made by the 80-year-old Albert Smith at Duns Tew.

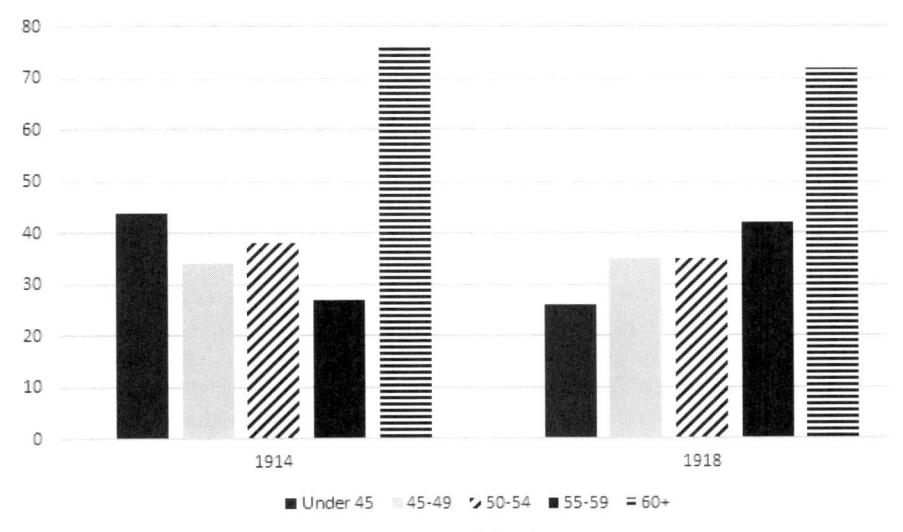

Figure 7: Age of the clergy

clergy were sole practitioners. Only thirty-three parishes had curates – almost all of them large parishes with populations approaching or exceeding 1,000. Eleven of these were in Oxford and the remainder mostly in town or suburban parishes like Cowley, Banbury, Bicester and Summertown.[255] Older clergy, who tended to be concentrated in small rural parishes, were thus left without clerical assistance, and some clearly felt the lack: 66-year-old Benjamin Hamilton feared that his capacity to teach was diminishing and ended his response on the subject of education with a heartfelt plea, 'Does Oxford not contain one son – who would for the Love of God – come and join me in teaching the Catholic faith in this hamlet?'[256]

As is clear from Figure 7, the war years saw an intensification of the tendency for Oxfordshire parishes to be staffed by older men. The younger group of incumbents under 45 had shrunk to twenty-six or only 12 per cent of the total. Although the middle group of clergy, aged between 45 and 59, had grown to 53 per cent of the total, it was now skewed towards the older end of this age band, with incumbents aged between 55 and 59 making up 37.5 per cent of the cohort, up from 30 per cent in 1914. The oldest group of incumbents, aged 60 or more, still made up almost 35 per cent of the total; but this group had also aged, with incumbents in their seventies now making up 34 per cent of the group compared with 26 per cent four years earlier. The respondents to the 1918 survey included six incumbents in their eighties, including the aptly named 83-year-old Charles

255 *Oxford Diocesan Calendar* (Oxford, 1914), pp. 92–127.
256 1914 Fewcott.

Henry Faithfull at Rousham, and William Wood, still ministering to the three hundred people of Rotherfield Greys at the age of 88.[257] This age profile suggests that younger clergy were either unable to acquire Oxfordshire livings because of the inability or unwillingness of their elders to retire, or that they were being siphoned off into other forms of service – for example as military chaplains.[258] Bearing in mind the slight difference in the identity of the parishes responding to the two surveys, the number of parishes in which the incumbent was supported by a curate remained the same. Curates continued to be concentrated in the larger parishes, though some of these, like Bicester and Headington Quarry, had lost theirs by 1918. However, a handful remained in the smaller rural parishes and one had been found, for example, to assist 85-year-old Francis St John Thackeray at Mapledurham.[259] The men who had to see their parishes through the war years, therefore, were not new recruits to the ministry but Victorian ordinands, reaching the priesthood in the 1870s and 1880s if not before. Their outlook and expectations were shaped by that background and it is against this that their response to the bishop's questionnaire should be read.

The ability to trace the clergy in the census of 1911 also provides an opportunity to identify their marital status and some information about the nature of their households. Despite a vogue for celibacy among some sections of the Anglo-Catholic wing of the Church[260] and the prominence of its influence within the Oxford diocese, in only around 18 per cent of the 257 clerical households successfully identified was the clergyman unmarried.[261] Given the maturity of the cohort under consideration this is not unexpected; and stage in the lifecycle may have been a more significant indicator of marital status than theological conviction, since some younger Evangelical incumbents, like Thomas Gilbert, were unmarried, while some of the most prominent Anglo-Catholic incumbents in the diocese, like Nathaniel Poyntz and Robert Townson, were married with substantial families.[262] Several of the clerical wives were artists or professionals in their own right: Mary Ellen Carew Hunt, married to the rector of Albury, was a medical doctor; Mary Jessie Hammond Skrine, the wife of the vicar of St Peter in the East in Oxford, was a novelist with several published titles to her name and continued publishing into the 1920s.[263] Particularly striking was the decision of Innes Elisabeth Paget to record

257 1918 Rousham; Rotherfield Greys. See also 1918 Duns Tew; Leafield with Wychwood; Middleton Stoney.
258 Though according to the Calendar only two Oxfordshire incumbents were doing duty as chaplains in that year. *Oxford Diocesan Calendar* (Oxford, 1917), pp. 192–206.
259 *Oxford Diocesan Calendar* (1917), pp. 110–11.
260 J. S. Reed, *Glorious Battle: The Cultural Politics of Victorian Anglo-Catholicism* (Nashville, TN, 1996), pp. 220–1.
261 E.g. 1914 Charlbury with Chadlington; Kidmore End; Oxford, St Mary Magdalene.
262 1914 Oxford, St Clement; Dorchester with Burcot; Headington.
263 Titles included *The World's Delight* (1902) and *A Step-Son of the Soil* (1910). 1914 Albury; Oxford, St Peter in the East.

`. 0  . 1  ■ 2  ■ 3    4+`

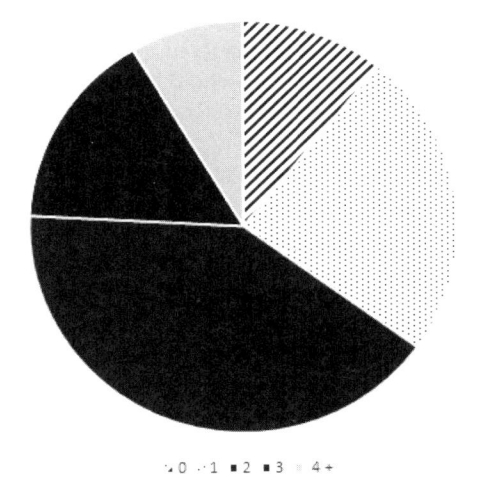

Figure 8: Resident servants in clerical households

her occupation in the 1911 census as 'Suffragist'.[264] It is perhaps more surprising, given the advanced age of many incumbents, that only ten of the households were headed by a clergyman recorded as 'widowed' in the 1911 census, though a number may have remarried.[265]

Figure 8 classifies incumbent households according to the number of resident servants at the 1911 census. Around 11 per cent had no resident servants at all[266] and a further 24 per cent had only one,[267] although they may have been assisted by non-resident servants doing jobs like cook or kitchen maid and coming in from the village. The majority had the two or three that might be expected in a respectable professional household[268] and a dozen of these added a governess to assist with the early education of the children.[269] There was, however, a minority (9 per cent) of rather grander households, some with four or five resident servants, like that of Philip Armitage whose twelve-person household included himself, his wife, four young children, their governess and a further five female servants.[270] A handful

---

264 1918 Cassington.
265 E.g. 1914 Bampton Lew. 1918 Freeland; Rotherfield Peppard. Robert Carew Hunt, for example, had been married to his current wife for one and a half years but had children aged between 9 and 20 from a previous marriage.
266 E.g. 1914 Begbroke; Chalgrove with Berrick Salome; Chastleton.
267 E.g. 1914 Asthall; Oxford, Holy Trinity; Sibford Gower and Epwell.
268 E.g. 1914 Duns Tew; Littlemore. 1918 South and New Hinksey. For a general discussion of middle-class servant keeping, see P. Horn, *The Rise and Fall of the Victorian Servant*, 2nd edn (Stroud, 2004), pp. 19–35.
269 E.g. 1914 Chipping Norton. 1918 Swalcliffe with Shutford.
270 1914 Nettlebed. See also 1914 Nuneham Courtenay; Oxford, St Giles.

were even more lavish, like that of Edmund Johnson, the rector of Sarsden, who together with his wife and daughter was catered for by six resident servants; and perhaps the most magnificent clerical household in Oxfordshire – that of the vicar of Chesterton, Charles Leslie Norris, whose household consisted of his wife and five servants: a cook, a maid, a housemaid, a kitchen maid and a butler.[271] This represented a status approximating to that of the gentry (with whom Norris clearly enjoyed a close relationship), and which would have been familiar to the richer clergymen of the previous century but which was becoming rarer with the contraction of agricultural profits from the 1870s.[272] Norris's support staff was not restricted to his household, though, as in 1914 he also had a curate to help him look after the 348 souls in his parish.[273]

For the vast majority of Oxfordshire clergy who did not have the assistance of a curate, the support of, especially female, members of their household – wives, daughters and sometimes sisters[274] – was often a crucial element of their ministry. This has already been noted with reference to Sunday schools, but in many parishes this activity was much more wide-ranging. They ran Bible classes for boys and girls, young men and women;[275] they took the lead in branches of the Girls Friendly Society; they instructed the Band of Hope and ran the Mothers' Union.[276] At Salford, the rector's wife played the organ at two services each Sunday as well as running the morning Sunday school, and at Mapledurham, one of the elderly vicar's unmarried daughters described herself in the 1911 census as 'Voluntary Sunday School Teacher and Parish Worker' and the other as 'Voluntary Organist Parish Worker and Housekeeper'.[277] In effect such women were playing the role of unpaid curates in support of their husbands and fathers, and much of the high tempo of activity maintained in many Oxfordshire parishes would have been impossible without them. At the 1911 census, Margaret Morris, who had been married for forty-one years to the vicar of Sydenham, probably spoke for many when she described her occupation as 'helping the vicar', and Julia Walford certainly played a quasi-curate's role when she filled in the 1918 visitation survey on behalf of her husband who was too ill to complete it.[278]

271 1914 Sarsden cum Churchill; Chesterton. See also 1918 Woodstock.
272 Haig, *Victorian Clergy*, pp. 297–9.
273 *Oxford Diocesan Calendar* (1914), p. 100.
274 For clergy whose unmarried sisters were members of the household see 1914 Deddington; 1918 Aston, North.
275 1914 Finstock and Fawler; Garsington; Hasley, Great; Middleton Stoney; Stanton St John.
276 1914 Aston Rowant; Tadmarton; Mapledurham.
277 1914 Salford; Mapledurham.
278 1914 Sydenham; 1918 Ascot-under-Wychwood. The parish role of clerical wives and particularly daughters is explored for the Victorian period in M. Yamaguchi, *Daughters of the Anglican Clergy: Religion, Gender and Identity in Victorian England* (Basingstoke, 2014).

The War and the National Mission

The innovative nature of Gore's question on education in the 1918 survey has already been noted and much the same could be said of question 3: 'What can you report as to the moral and spiritual effect on the different classes in your parish (a) of War time, (b) of the National Mission?' This was not a question that invited the Oxfordshire clergy to reflect theologically on the war[279] but rather to consider its impact on actual behaviour and attitudes in their parishes. Such views are sometimes described as 'through the vicarage window', but this almost certainly is to underestimate the incumbents' capacity for informed observation, as pastors engaged at many levels and in many contexts with their parishioners. William Palmer, for example, who had worked with the agricultural labourers in his parish for more than twenty years, first as curate and then as vicar, reported that, 'Men and lads converse freely with one as an old friend as to what belongs to their daily work and outlook.'[280]

Perhaps the most striking result from a survey of the clergy estimates of the moral and spiritual impact of the war is that no clear overall pattern emerges, but rather that they detected a wide range of responses in both rural and urban contexts. Interestingly, given the stress placed in much of the historiography on the first world war as a transformative event in the history of English religion,[281] in approximately 20 per cent of the sample – especially small villages but also large ones like Westwell and Wheatley – the clergy could detect no effect whatsoever.[282] In the remote seigneurial village of Asthall, for example, the incumbent reported that, 'For the most part, the parishioners live as if there was no war, or at any rate as if it did not concern themselves', and at Hampton Poyle the people seemed, 'quite unmoved'.[283] In a few cases, clergy reported that they had not been in the parish for long enough to come to a judgement or had insufficient information to work on[284] – though at Shipton-under-Wychwood the vicar had made up for his lack of acquaintance by consulting both the churchwardens and the local doctor, who 'are all agreed that they are unable to perceive any effect',[285] while at Cropredy, the incumbent, who had arrived during the course of the war, reported, 'examining one's common sense and power of observation, I should say that the "moral and spiritual effects" of [the war] "on the different classes in this parish" has been as nearly as possible Nil'.[286]

---

279 For a general disinclination to do this between 1914 and 1918 see S. Bell, *Faith in Conflict: The Impact of the Great War on the People of Britain* (Solihull, 2017), pp. 26–8.
280 1918 Enstone.
281 See, for example, R. Currie, A. Gilbert and L. Horsley, *Churches and Churchgoers: Patterns of Church Growth in the British Isles since 1700* (Oxford, 1977), p. 30.
282 E.g. 1918 Bucknell; Cropredy; Freeland; Westwell; Wheatley.
283 1918 Asthall; Hampton Poyle. See also 1918 Albury; Rotherfield Peppard.
284 E.g. 1918 Ardley; Emmington; Finstock and Fawler.
285 1918 Shipton-under-Wychwood.
286 1918 Cropredy.

Many of the returns did however raise alarm about the negative moral effects of the war on their parishioners. Those who commented on specific examples of wrongdoing, mostly located in urban or larger parishes, tended to regard the primary moral questions, in a manner with which their Victorian predecessors would have been entirely comfortable, as revolving around either drink or sexual conduct and not infrequently both. John Stansfield, vicar of St Ebbe's in Oxford, almost certainly had these in mind when he described the war as 'morally disastrous with a small section of the women',[287] and the vicar of St Mary's, Banbury, consciously linked them together when he remarked that, 'There have been many sad cases of unfaithfulness among soldiers' wives, and the downfall of some of them is directly traceable to drinking habits.'[288] However, some incumbents detected other specific moral failings. George Rodwell at Bampton, for example, was concerned about 'A considerable growth of the spirit of enmity and faction and want of consideration' in his parish.[289] Such sharply focused comments on the malfeasances of parishioners were extremely rare in the returns, occurring in only 5 per cent of cases. Much more common were more generalised but no less deeply felt expressions of concern about the consequences of the widespread social dislocation produced by wartime conditions.

The incumbents of small rural parishes, in particular, were worried by the large-scale movements of population brought about by the war which brought unprecedented disturbance to their settled communities. At Bletchingdon, for example, the vicar detected a generalised trend towards 'demoralisation; a tendency aggravated by the presence of bodies of troops in the neighbourhood and soldiers billeted in the village'.[290] At Drayton St Leonard, Watkin Williams was worried about the presence of incomers, reporting, 'The advent as workers on the land of women from the towns, eg shop girls from Harrods stores and Whiteley's, is a dangerous element. I have not come across any women at this work who lift the standard of thought and practice.'[291] Some urban incumbents also worried about the impact of new arrivals. This was a particular concern in Oxford, where colleges were in use for the training of officer cadets[292] who presented an obvious temptation for unwary parishioners. The vicar of the poverty-stricken parish of Holy Trinity reported:

> The girls of from about fifteen years upwards seem to have it as their aim in life to impress the cadets stationed in Oxford. This shows itself largely in the manner of dress (short skirts and transparent stockings etc) and in their forcing themselves upon the attention of the cadets.[293]

---

287 1918 Oxford, St Ebbe.
288 1918 Banbury. See also 1918 Launton; Thame.
289 1918 Bampton Proper. See also 1918 Godington.
290 1918 Bletchingdon.
291 1918 Drayton St Leonard.
292 M. Graham, *Oxford in the Great War* (Barnsley, 2014), pp. 47–9.
293 1918 Oxford, Holy Trinity. See also 1918 Aston, Steeple.

At Witney, the concern about unrestrained female sexuality was provoked by an even more exotic set of incomers – the workforce on the new aerodrome, three hundred of whom had been recruited from Portugal and who 'had a bad effect upon the girls especially those between 14 and 16'.[294] The wording of the question encouraged the expression of concern rather than a description of what might have been done to address it. Consequently, there is little evidence in the returns of churches acting to help their parishioners navigate these difficulties, though at St Michael at the North Gate in Oxford, Alfred Smith, the curate, dispensed fatherly counsel to the shop girls in his congregation:

> I advised them to make no friendships with officers or cadets, unless they took their friends to their own homes. Several of them I knew have done this and I know of no case in which even a flighty girl has fallen.

Again, partly because of the structure of the question, there was no reporting of concerns about equivalent moral dangers to the men of the villages who were away on active service or other war work, and instead a general tendency to emphasise examples of good behaviour.[295] However, there were concerns about girls and young women working away from home in hospitals or manufacturing munitions.[296] In the village of Glympton, the incumbent thought that, even if they stayed in the parish, the need for women and girls to work on the land tended to coarsen their character.[297]

A more frequent concern, explicitly registered in almost 10 per cent of the returns and underlying fears of moral decline in others, was the question of money. A combination of the shortage of labour (with at least 11 per cent of the agricultural labour force away on military service)[298] and the rising pressure to increase agricultural production[299] brought a brief burst of wartime prosperity to many rural Oxfordshire households. For families who had previously survived on a much lower standard of living derived from a notoriously poorly paid occupation[300] the difference could be significant, especially if to the government separation allowances were added the income of family members working at enhanced rates. Although the system took time to crank into action, by 1917 separation allowances were being regularly paid to the wives of private soldiers with a single child at the

---

294 1918 Witney. See also 1918 Swyncombe.
295 E.g. 1918 Littlemore.
296 E.g. 1918 Cowley.
297 1918 Glympton.
298 M. Daunton, *Wealth and Welfare: An Economic and Social History of Britain 1851–1951* (Oxford, 2007), p. 61.
299 For a brief account of the pressures on rural life in the war, see A. G. V. Simmonds, *Britain and World War One* (London, 2012), pp. 193–220.
300 Agricultural labour in Oxfordshire was particularly poorly paid by national standards with wages pitched around 15s a week. K. Tiller, 'Labouring Lives', in Tiller and Darkes (eds), *Atlas of Oxfordshire*, p. 116; Simmonds, *Britain and World War One*, p. 194.

rate of 23s a week[301] – on its own 50 per cent more in cash terms than the pre-war agricultural wage, and sufficiently attractive, in the view of some incumbents, for couples to marry in order to secure them.[302] Work at enhanced wages was available in a number of forms, including munitions work, especially for younger women and girls,[303] and agricultural work, especially for boys, whom the education authorities were increasingly willing to release early into this section of the labour force.[304] In 1917 the government set a minimum wage for agricultural labour of 25s a week, making agriculture a sector in which increased wages exceeded increases in the cost of living.[305] However, the incumbent of Cowley, for example, found that boys who before the war had earned 8s a week on the land at age sixteen were now receiving 35s.[306] If combined with a second wage or a separation allowance this would represent an unprecedented level of income for a labourer's family, and a sense of unusual prosperity was strongly reflected in the returns.[307] At Stoke Row, unprecedented agricultural wages meant that the vicar had great difficulty in finding anyone prepared to dig a grave for a reasonable fee,[308] while in the village of Salford the vicar reported, 'many there are who are far better off in a monetary point of view than they have ever been before in their lives, and they do not appear to be anxious that the war should come to an end'.[309]

The clergy worried about the moral impact of rising incomes on local communities. At Shipton-on-Cherwell, George Duncan noted a more serious disposition among his flock in the early stages of the war, but then, 'rapidly a more materialistic spirit arose in the people and the sudden prosperity began to lead to pleasure seeking'.[310] The same process could be seen in suburban Oxford where at St Matthew's the vicar reported, 'I fear that the many who have more money than they formerly were accustomed to are now going in for pleasure and luxuries to a larger extent than known before.'[311] At Drayton St Leonard, the incumbent felt that the great rise in wages was a danger since it emphasised the importance of material

301 Simmonds, *Britain and World War One*, p. 172.
302 1918 Chesterton.
303 J. Cotter, *Oxfordshire: Remembering 1914–18* (Stroud, 2014), pp. 67–9. Graham, *Oxford*, pp. 60–2; 1918 Cowley.
304 1918 South and New Hinksey; Aston, Steeple.
305 Daunton, *Wealth and Welfare*, pp. 61–2. Gregory, *Last Great War*, pp. 194–5.
306 1918 Cowley. See also 1918 Heyford, Lower.
307 E.g. 1918 Oxford, St Matthew; Stokenchurch; Wiggington. For a discussion of the general debate around working-class living standards during the war, see Gregory, *Last Great War*, pp. 187–208.
308 1918 Stoke Row.
309 1918 Salford.
310 1918 Shipton-on-Cherwell. Though he noted a greater earnestness had recently begun to return.
311 1918 Oxford, St Matthew. See also 1918 Hanwell where the rector thought farmers rather than labourers were given to unseemly gaiety.

things, as opposed to spiritual, out of all proportion and also tended to make his people lose their heads.[312]

The new availability of money intersected with and reinforced the most commonly reported form of social dislocation – noted in around 15 per cent of the returns – that of children getting out of hand. The ready availability of wages, the lack of the disciplinary presence of fathers and elder brothers absent in the army, and the distraction of mothers engaged in war work led, on the evidence of the returns, to a precocious independence, especially on the part of boys but also in some cases that of teenage girls.[313] Clergy clearly found this disturbing because it dislocated long-established social hierarchies in their parishes, and terms like 'wildness', 'unruliness and discourtesy' and 'out of hand' abound in the returns.[314] However, its significance for a church which invested so many of its hopes in the rising generation went far beyond temporary discomfort. It potentially represented long-term damage because it short-circuited traditional means for the moral formation and religious socialisation of the young. Alfred Bisdee at St Barnabas reported discouragement among the teachers over the indiscipline of children at day school;[315] 'our Sunday schools', lamented the vicar of Holy Trinity Oxford, 'are fallen away dreadfully';[316] while at Combe, the incumbent noted that the irregularity of the elder boys in attending Sunday school was reflected in poor church attendance – even among the choir boys.[317]

However, incumbents reporting moral declension as a result of the war often saw a mixed picture with improvements in other respects,[318] and more incumbents reported moral improvements in their parishes consequent on the war than had emphasised the problems. Around 5 per cent characterised the respect they had for the attitudes and determination of their parishioners using the language of sacrifice highlighted by Adrian Gregory as a major feature of the war years.[319] Thus at Sandford St Martin, 'there has been very little grumbling with regard to the sacrifices which the war has brought, whether in suffering or economy of food. An excellent example in all these respects has been set by the Squire.'[320] Similarly, at Little Farringdon, the vicar reported, 'There is an observable spirit of patience and submission to the restrictions imposed by the conditions of wartime, with recognition that all must contribute in service and sacrifice (as of son-soldiers) for

---

312   1918 Drayton St Leonard.
313   1918 Aston, Steeple; Banbury; Milton, Little.
314   1918 Watlington; Leafield with Wychwood; Bicester.
315   1918 Oxford, St Barnabas. See also 1918 Standlake with Yelford.
316   1918 Oxford, Holy Trinity.
317   1918 Combe.
318   E.g. 1918 Banbury; Shipton-on-Cherwell.
319   Gregory, *Last Great War*, *passim*.
320   1918 Sandford St Martin.

the sake of the country.'[321] Others stressed that the war had brought communities closer together, leading to greater sympathy and a sense of common interest between neighbours and sometimes across classes – the Home Front's equivalent of the oft-cited comradeship of the trenches.[322] According to the incumbent of St Peter in the East, Oxford, for example:

> What can be confidently certified is an increase of kindness, fellowship and service; greater sympathy, understanding and helpfulness between classes as between individuals. These are things which can be observed, and I find they are recognised by my parishioners as well as by myself.[323]

Many more reported growth in simple kindness between neighbours and generosity as a response to the stresses of war, as at Cassington, where the vicar was 'inclined to think that the effect of the war has been to draw all families together in neighbourliness and helpfulness to each other,'[324] and Banbury, where the war had 'provoked a very wonderful growth of the spirit of national service and there is an undeniable readiness of generosity which is evoked not only in response to war claims, but by almost any appeal of a charitable or religious nature.'[325] Others commented on the development of traditional virtues such as thrift and temperance – though there was a tendency to attribute the latter more to the rise in beer prices than a growth in virtue![326] To the clergy, however, the most noticeable examples of moral uplift lay in the practical efforts made by all classes of their parishioners in the common cause of the nation, the community and the men at the front. At Shipton-on-Cherwell, for example, the return commented that, 'Some of the women workers show their moral sense in the steady way they do work that cannot be altogether pleasant and needing great moral effort.'[327] At St Philip and St James in middle-class north Oxford, whose annual flower show, opened by the Duke of Marlborough, had been one of the great social occasions of the Edwardian suburb, the men were now busy growing vegetables as well as doing a variety of other war work, while the ladies were actively engaged as nurses or hospital visitors.[328] At neighbouring St Cross, the vicar reported, 'The women of the various classes are for the most part trying to do something. A party of middle-class women meets weekly at the Vicarage for needle-work, and with what they take home turn out an extraordinary amount of work.'[329]

---

321 1918 Farringdon, Little. See also 1918 Aston Rowant; Ducklington with Hardwick; Barton, Steeple.
322 Bell, *Faith in Conflict*, pp. 207–8.
323 1918 Oxford, St Peter in the East. See also 1918 Ipsden with North Stoke; Ramsden.
324 1918 Cassington. See also 1918 Henley-on-Thames; Tackley.
325 1918 Banbury. See also 1918 Fritwell; Somerton.
326 1918 Mapledurham; Stoke, South with Woodcote; Henley, Holy Trinity; Wytham.
327 1918 Shipton-on-Cherwell.
328 1918 Oxford, St Philip and St James. Smith, 'Evangelicals in a "Catholic" Suburb', p. 227.
329 1918 Oxford, St Cross.

A final moral change provoked a mixed response among incumbents – a sense of greater independence of mind or broadening of outlook among their parishioners. Some found this threatening, as it undermined the deferential relationships to which they were accustomed. As Charles Tywrhitt, the Anglo-Catholic rector of Barton Westcot, noted, 'There is sign of greater independence of spirit in some cases of persons who have for various reasons returned to the parish after absence for considerable periods. This has not perhaps made them easier to deal with.'[330] Others, by contrast, welcomed the change as promising for the future,[331] and at Drayton St Leonard, the rector even welcomed the presence of non-church-going socialist soldiers because they stirred the local population and gave them the courage to protest against poor housing conditions.[332] Comments like that of Tyrwhitt should be taken as confirmation of Callum Brown's view that, 'Much of what British churchmen at the time characterised as loss of faith was actually loss of Edwardian reverence for social authority – for obedience to the clergy.'[333] However, the alternative reaction of Tyrwhitt's colleagues suggests either that they were more confident in their own capacity to deal with the bracing air of post-war egalitarianism or that they believed that the Church would be better off if freed from its dependence on a deferential social order. For some clergy at least the loss of this sort of authority was not so much a 'crisis' as an opportunity.

The general issue of the relationship between the first world war and religion in England has attracted increasing interest in recent years. New research has allowed a reappraisal of older views that the war produced a fundamental disillusionment with the churches in general and especially the Church of England which had uncritically supported Britain's participation in the slaughter on the western front; while the horrors of war fatally undermined traditional Christian teaching on the goodness and omnipotence of God.[334] Stuart Bell, for example, has argued convincingly that the theological challenges were neither so prominent nor so serious as previously thought,[335] and there is a wide consensus that while the war had a disruptive impact on the churches it was not associated with any major collapse in organised religion.[336] As a result, the principal debate among historians is now

330 1918 Barton Westcot. See also 1918 Chesterton.
331 E.g. 1918 Cuddesdon; Enstone.
332 1918 Drayton St Leonard.
333 C. G. Brown, *Religion and Society in Twentieth-Century Britain* (Harlow, 2006), p. 112.
334 While characteristic of older historiography like A. Marwick, *The Deluge: British Society and the First World War*, 2nd edn (London, 1973), pp. 217–18, 297–9, and D. L. Edwards, *Christian England III: From the 18th Century to the First World War* (London, 1914), pp. 362–6, similar views can still be found in more modern writing, e.g. G. Robb, *British Culture and the First World War*, 2nd edn (London, 2015), pp. 137–40.
335 This is the main thesis of Bell, *Faith in Conflict*.
336 J. Wolfe, *God and Greater Britain: Religion and National Life in Britain and Ireland, 1843–1945* (London, 1994), pp. 236–7; Brown, *Religion and Society*, pp. 88–112; M. Snape, 'The Great War', in H. McLeod (ed.), *The Cambridge History of Christianity*, vol. 9: *World*

about whether the continued resilience of the churches in the succeeding decades is best understood as part of a period of relative prosperity prior to the onset of significant religious decline in the second half of the twentieth century or as a phase in a longer-term process of gradual recession accelerated in the 1960s.[337]

When it came to reporting on the spiritual effects of the war, the clergy were, understandably, somewhat reticent. 'Of spiritual as distinct from moral effect', noted John Skrine, 'it is less easy to speak with confidence. "It cometh not with observation."'[338] Indeed, for many, when it came to spiritual matters, the two parts of the bishop's question – the effects of the war and the effects of the National Mission – were not in practice distinguishable from each other. The 'National Mission of Repentance and Hope' of 1916 was the Church of England's major attempt to respond to the conditions of wartime. Its intention, at least from the point of view of the bishop of Oxford, was to put before the nation, and especially that part of it which considered itself to be attached to the Church of England, an ideal of a church and society based on Christian brotherhood and fellowship, and to promote repentance for whatever had hindered its development in the past.[339] Although initially sceptical about the project, Gore threw himself wholeheartedly behind it: organising retreats for the Oxfordshire clergy at Radley College and Queens College Oxford, to assist in their preparation;[340] appointing clerical missioners; and commissioning groups of lay people to visit parishes in support of the mission events which were timed for October and November 1916.[341] The mission is often judged to have been a failure,[342] and Adrian Gregory, reviewing the mission at a national level, has described the vision of its principal promoters as 'hubristic'.[343] However,

---

Christianities c.1914–c.2000 (Cambridge, 2006), pp. 144–7; C. Field, 'Keeping the Spiritual Home Fires Burning: Religious Belonging in Britain during the First World War', *War and Society*, 33 (2014), pp. 244–68; Gregory, *Last Great War*, pp. 152–86.

337 C. G. Brown, *The Death of Christian Britain* (London, 2001); S. Green, *The Passing of Protestant England: Secularisation and Social Change c.1920–1960* Cambridge, 2011), pp. 29–91; C. Field, 'Gradualist or Revolutionary Secularization? A Case Study of Religious Belonging in Inter-War Britain, 1918–1939', *Church History and Religious Culture*, 93 (2013), pp. 57–93.

338 1918 Oxford, St Peter in the East.

339 For the developing objectives of the National Mission, see D. M. Thompson, 'War, the Nation, and the Kingdom of God: The Origins of the National Mission of Repentance and Hope 1915–16', in W. J. Sheils (ed.), *The Church and War: Studies in Church History*, 20 (1983), pp. 337–50. For Gore's representation of the Mission to the diocese, see *Oxford Diocesan Magazine* (1916), pp. 19–20.

340 *Oxford Diocesan Magazine* (1916), pp. 35, 51; 1918 Milton-under-Wychwood.

341 Men engaged in the 'Pilgrimage of Witness' were organised via the diocesan CEMS, and women by a special committee set up for women's work. *Oxford Diocesan Magazine* (1916), pp. 106–7, 121. 1918 Combe; Rotherfield Greys.

342 A. Wilkinson, *The Church of England and the First World War* (London, 1978), pp. 72–9. Wolfe, *God and Greater Britain*, p. 240.

343 Gregory, *Last Great War*, p. 171.

the mission took a variety of forms in the parishes of Oxfordshire,[344] was pursued with varying degrees of enthusiasm, and some incumbents at least detected positive effects from the mission as well as from the war.

About 25 per cent of the returns reported little or no difference in the spiritual temperature of their parishes as a result of the war or the mission. Some of these expressed a level of concern about this state of affairs which clearly indicates an expectation that such a national emergency ought in itself to have provoked a spiritual response. At Minster Lovell, for example, Charles Farr lamented, 'The moral and spiritual effect of the War in this parish is most unsatisfactory. There is no marked increase of desire for spiritual things.'[345] Similarly Rawdon Willis was grieved that,

> The spiritual effect of the War on the people generally has not been encouraging. It has not touched and turned the hearts of the men to God, as I have hoped and prayed for: I mean that, so far as outward observation goes, the War has not got the mass out of the rut.[346]

However, for others this was simply a continuation of a happy situation from before the war, as at Pyrton: 'I notice very little if any change in the ordinary agricultural labourer: he was not adverse to religion before the War: he is not adverse now.'[347] Many clergy attributed the lack of change as much to the demands on time and energy of war work as to any other cause, as Maurice Jones explained:

> It should not be forgotten … that every person in the parish is so engrossed in work of some kind that very little leisure is left available for attendance at church services and religious exercises and I imagine that this has much to do with the apparent indifference to the claims of religion.[348]

Most such statements were relatively bland; but the incumbent of Barford, Alfred Highton, a former UMCA missionary, used his return to deliver a broadside against what he clearly perceived as unrealistic expectations:

> The people have the Incarnation, the Church and the Bible and Christian teaching in the Church Schools at any rate, if they are not converted by these means, it is not likely that war, pestilence or famine should convert them, nor if one rose from the dead, as one has indeed risen![349]

Around 20 per cent of the returns recorded spiritual decline, challenge or at least adversity as a result of the war. Perhaps half a dozen of these described spiritual

---

344   1918 Barford; Oxford, St Cross; Oxford, St Frideswide.
345   1918 Minster Lovell.
346   1918 Henley, Holy Trinity.
347   1918 Pyrton. See also 1918 Milton-under-Wychwood.
348   1918 Rotherfield Peppard. Similar remarks also came from urban parishes. 1918 Oxford, St Philip and St James.
349   1918 Barford St Michael.

unsettlement or theological challenge.[350] Charles Bayfield, at Ambroseden, for example, reported, 'I have to meet arguments "How can there be a good God with so much suffering permitted", and also, I fear, "Perhaps there is no truth revealed or no God at all."'[351] Similarly, at Ewelme, the rector explained,

> I think they are greatly puzzled and perplexed by what is happening and how it is to be reconciled with the Divine Government of the world? If God is on the side of right, why doesn't right win speedily and decisively? Can the Christian view of the world maintain itself against material force?

But he also reported that the people were 'ready to hear what the church had to say with reference to the events and conditions of the time'.[352] Some sensed future problems but perhaps couldn't quite believe in their emergence, as in the case of Shenington, whose vicar explained, 'I have heard one or two who have lost sons in the war complain at first of God allowing it to take place. But I doubt if they meant it actually.'[353] Three recorded a serious spiritual challenge. At Swerford, some people, mainly women, had told the vicar that the war had 'destroyed, or shaken, their belief in God'.[354] The other cases concerned upper-class parishioners, who may have been more articulate in expressing their views than the rest. At Beckley, among some of the wealthy, the incumbent detected 'a hardening and repelling effect as to the religious spirit';[355] while the vicar of Goring was disturbed to find that, 'Amongst the men of the upper classes there is an almost savage feeling of resentment against the enemy, and no response at all to the Gospel spirit in that regard.'[356] However, other incumbents found an increased interest in and acceptance of Christian doctrine, as at Stanton Harcourt where the curate Frederick Butler reported, 'Distinctive Christian doctrines and facts have increased influence: the Incarnation, the Cross, Forgiveness, the Triumph of Love, the new life.'[357]

The remaining reports of negative effects of the war concerned declining congregations. In several cases these recorded decline compared with the early months of the war, when there was a well-documented surge in attendances at both regular church services and special occasions for intercession.[358] Usually this was a popular

---

350 The relative scarcity of these comments tends to support Stuart Bell's argument, noted above, that such issues were infrequently articulated during the war.
351 1918 Ambroseden. See also 1918 Adderbury; Oxford, St Frideswide.
352 1918 Ewelme. See also 1918 Charlbury with Chadlington; Horley with Hornton.
353 1918 Shenington with Alkerton.
354 1918 Swerford.
355 1918 Beckley. Though the vicar felt the problem may have been exposed rather than caused by the war.
356 1918 Goring.
357 1918 Stanton Harcourt.
358 A. Gregory, 'Beliefs and Religion', in J. Winter (ed.), *The Cambridge History of the First World War*, vol. III (Cambridge, 2014), p. 420; Field, 'Home Fires', p. 250.

response to clerical initiatives[359] but at South Weston and Adwell the initiative was that of a layman:

> At the beginning of the war the moral and spiritual effect was distinctly good. A working man suggested a special service in church for the dismissal of our young men who joined up in September 1914 and I think hardly a man woman or child was absent from that service.[360]

This enthusiasm was often sustained into 1915. At Chipping Norton, for example, for the first six months to a year of the war, services saw increased attendances, with special intercession services for the men at the front particularly well supported – especially after the first shocks of death and the appearance of repatriated wounded. 'There was a "soberness and watching unto prayer", and a 'wonderful God-consciousness and dependence on God'. However, it seemed that as the war dragged on and the shocks became more routine, the spiritual effort was not maintained (though the vicar felt that the spirit of devotion remained strong among his female parishioners – especially the bereaved and those with sons and husbands still at the front).[361] Clearly, like the popular enthusiasm for enlistment, which seems to have accompanied the early months of the war,[362] the popular enthusiasm for intercession was unlikely to be maintained at such an unusually high pitch for an extended period of time, especially when the pressures of increased working hours and/or family responsibilities began to take their toll. Several of the returns commented on this phenomenon, not so much in relation to the regular intercessory services on Sundays, but to the additional services which had been established during the week. At Lewknor, the vicar reported,

> The saddest point is the fact that 'war weariness' had taken the form of neglect of united intercessions at the weekly intercession. On Sundays, however, good congregations attend and there is considerable interest taken to see that no names are omitted from the list of parishioners and friends which is read out each time.[363]

Where declining regular congregations were reported, the causes were not disillusionment but rather the dislocations of wartime. At Lower Heyford, for example, regular congregations were depleted by the absence of sixty-three men on military service out of a total parish population of four hundred; hard work, including work on construction of a new aerodrome at nearby Upper Heyford; and the displacement of the evening service into the afternoon because of lighting restrictions.[364]

---

359   1918 Blechingdon; Oxford, St Giles; Standlake with Yelford.
360   1918 Weston, South with Adwell.
361   1918 Chipping Norton.
362   Though for a qualification of the notion of enthusiasm for the war in 1914 see Gregory, *Last Great War*, pp. 9–39.
363   1918 Lewknor. See also 1918 Bix; Horspath; Sibford Gower and Epwell.
364   1918 Heyford, Lower. See also 1918 Brizenorton; Broughton Pogis; Glympton; Oxford, St Paul.

Recession in church attendance was far from being the normal experience in wartime Oxfordshire and there were more parishes reporting either sustained numbers[365] or modest growth at Sunday worship than those recording decline. This applied both to urban and rural parishes: Arthur Jones at Banbury had larger regular Sunday congregations in 1918 than he had experienced in the previous twelve years,[366] while Thomas Tanner at Spelsbury had a 'very great improvement' in attendance at both church and Sunday school though not at Holy Communion.[367] Some were buoyed up by their experience of the young men of the parish returning on leave from the front. At Charlbury, men coming home were regular in both church attendance and as communicants,[368] and according to the vicar of Newington,

> What pulls us together is the visit on leave of those serving in the War. One and all they are a joy – not only in their keenness about church (and communion) but in their extraordinary development of intelligence and wider outlook on general questions.[369]

While some found the National Mission to be a failure,[370] others attributed growing congregations to its effects. William Elphick thought it might account for the increasing numbers attending the 10 am sung Eucharist at Shiplake,[371] and at Dunsden there were prominent conversions which 'made a real stir in the place'.[372]

Nonetheless, by far the most common response to the question on the effects of the war and the mission, represented in around a third of the returns, was not to comment on an increase in the extent of religious practice, or at least in churchgoing, but rather to remark on an increase in its intensity. Some attributed this to their parishioners taken as a whole, thus, at Aston Rowant, 'the Spirit of Prayer is more fully realised in the parish. Parishioners come readily to any special services for prayer and feel what it means to be praying together.'[373] Similarly at Shirburn, the vicar, Frederic Hall, detected 'a more serious tone a greater inclination to turn to the comforting strength of religion especially when the grief at the loss of a dear relation is on them'.[374] The most frequent comments, however, separated the parish into those already firmly linked to the church before the war, whose faith had been

---

365 E.g. 1918 Combe; Emmington; Sandford St Martin; Woodstock.
366 1918 Banbury. See also 1918 Goring; Henley-on-Thames.
367 1918 Spelsbury. See also 1918 Ducklington with Hardwick; Finstock and Fawler; Wardington; Yarnton.
368 1918 Charlbury with Chadlington.
369 1918 Newington.
370 1918 Fringford; Standlake; Shipton-under-Wychwood.
371 1918 Shiplake.
372 1918 Dunsden.
373 1918 Aston Rowant. See also 1918 Oxford, St Peter in the East.
374 1918 Shirburn. See also 1918 Hanwell, where the rector detected a deepening of belief among the agricultural labourers who made up the vast majority of his parishioners.

deepened and whose practice had become more extensive, and those not previously attached, on whom there had been only a small effect and frequently none at all. Some measured this at least partially by participation in the sacraments, thus, at Chinnor,

> A few have undoubtedly been led to more regular worship and have attended our weekly intercession regularly. Of the young men who have gone to the front and who were communicants before they left, I find that they still come to communion when on leave. Most of those who were indifferent to religion before the war seem to remain the same in spite of their experience. I have about three cases of men who have taken a more thoughtful view of things and these I am in touch with and if they are not able to be presented for confirmation at the front, I shall hope to secure them on their return.[375]

In other parishes there was a more general commentary, as at Kidmore End:

> But my impression here is much the same as elsewhere – That those who were serious are more so: Those who thought – think more: Those who were religious are more so: Those who practised their religion do so rather more: The good are better. But those who didn't think, and those who didn't appear religious, and who didn't practice their religion – seem much the same. And yet – there does seem much more seriousness: and I am told the services are as well attended, in spite of numbers of regular attendants having gone![376]

Adjectives like 'serious', 'devout' and 'earnest' abound in the returns but almost always applied to people already connected to the church,[377] as at Coggs, where the National Mission had been a turning point, so that there had been 'a spirit of earnestness amongst the faithful ever since'.[378] Such changes were less easy to measure than changes in the number of communicants or attendance at particular services but they were significant for the character of the Church of England in the parishes nonetheless.

The Representation of the Laity

Both the 1914 and 1918 surveys contained enquiries about participation in new Anglican structures for the representation of the laity. In 1914, the questions related to people on the register to elect parochial representatives to Ruri-decanal conferences and whether Parochial Church Councils (PCCs) had been established – an option available on a voluntary basis since the 1870s and reinforced by Convocation in the 1890s.[379] In 1918, there was a single question about how many

---

375   1918 Chinnor. See also 1918 Mapledurham.
376   1918 Kidmore End.
377   1918 Banbury, South; Brizenorton; Burford with Fulbrook; Marston.
378   1918 Coggs. See also Milton, Little; Norton, Hook; Oxford, St Aldate.
379   O. Chadwick, *The Victorian Church, Part II* (Cambridge, 1970), pp. 193–202.

men and women had registered to vote in the Parochial Church Meetings which (under a modified scheme including all women for the first time)[380] would elect lay members directly to the Ruri-decanal conference, the Diocesan Conference and, where it was in operation, the PCC, and also conduct other necessary church business. Reviewing the response across the diocese at his 1914 visitation, Gore, a leading advocate of lay representation and church reform, expressed shock at the low take up of this process in his diocese. Only in 28 per cent of parishes in the diocese had anyone signed the declaration that entitled them to vote, and the total, Gore calculated, was less than 2 per cent of the Anglican communicants eligible to become electors. PCCs, moreover, existed in only 10 per cent of parishes, and he urged clergy to make progress in the construction of proper rolls of electors and where possible the election of PCCs, to the membership of which women were now to be admitted without restriction.[381]

If anything, the 1914 Oxfordshire returns show a rather poorer response than that of the diocese as a whole. Only a little over 23 per cent of parishes recorded figures for the number of registered electors[382] or provided an assurance that at least a few had signed the declaration required.[383] In almost all of these the numbers of electors were very small, rising above ten in only 6 per cent of parishes[384] and including women in only 3 per cent. Clearly Gore was right in believing that lay representation was at an early stage of development in Oxfordshire. Some incumbents reported a disinclination on the part of their parishioners to participate in the formal processes.[385] However, rather more did participate on a less formal basis, especially in small parishes where every qualified elector was known to the incumbent and the signing of forms was felt to be superfluous – a world of face to face rather than bureaucratic transactions.[386]

PCCs were very rare in 1914, being in place in less than 10 per cent of parishes and even in some of these not set up in the manner or with the scope envisaged by Convocation.[387] In explaining this lack of development, incumbents took refuge in the small size of their parishes or the disinclination of their parishioners,[388] though the disinclination may have been at least as strong among the clergy and Stafford Meredith Brown may have spoken for many when he answered the question about

---

380 The previous scheme had only admitted women who were also rate-payers.
381 Gore, *War and the Church*, pp. 86–92.
382 E.g. 1914 Beckley; Launton; Tetsworth.
383 E.g. 1914 Bampton Proper; Charlton-on-Otmoor; Marston.
384 These were mostly urban parishes or unusually large rural ones. See 1918 Banbury, South; Chipping Norton; Littlemore; Warborough.
385 E.g. 1914 Albury; Oxford, St Mary Magdalene.
386 1914 Crowell; Culham; Pyrton.
387 For Councils see 1914 Bicester; Chinnor; Oxford, St Andrew. For Councils formed on other than elected lines or with limited scope see 1918 Middleton Stoney; Summertown; Watlington.
388 1914 Benson; Mollington; Piddington.

whether his parish had a PCC, 'No and should not wish it.'[389] However, the returns also give evidence of informal mechanisms for consultation which may have been at least as effective – this was most frequently a matter of occasional or regular discussions with churchwardens and sometimes sidesmen, but could also be rather more extensive, as at Cassington where the vicar used a range of parish organisations as well as the regular round of church services as a means of canvassing the views of his parishioners.[390] By 1918, after four more years of advocacy by Gore, the position with respect to electors had improved somewhat, with the number of parishes where a roll was in operation having doubled to 47 per cent – though this would have still fallen short of the bishop's ambitions for church reform in this area. In the small majority of parishes where numbers were returned it is clear that there was some variation in effort or enthusiasm. At Enstone, for example, only eight names had been collected from a population of over 900 while at Holwell the rector had collected sixty-two names from a population of only 150.[391] Some of those who had not compiled a roll explained that it was thought best to delay it until after the end of the war when the men of the parish would have returned;[392] others were concerned about the limitation of the franchise to communicant or at least confirmed Anglicans – a limitation which was a matter of conviction for their bishop.[393] The most common reason given, however, was a concern about the capacity of their parishioners effectively to exercise their franchise: an indication perhaps of the prejudices of a predominantly university-educated clergy.[394] One clear result from a review of those returns where the number of electors was disaggregated by gender is a strong trend for women to outnumber men in a ratio of around 3:2[395] and often more.[396] While this is not unexpected from a demographic point of view, given the absence of men at war, it does mark a significant change in that the weight of female participation in Anglican activity could for the first time be reflected in elections to its representative bodies (though not necessarily on those bodies themselves)[397] – a development which the bishop certainly supported and which was some way in advance of the limited Parliamentary franchise offered to women in November 1918.[398]

389 1914 Fringford. For more widespread clerical scepticism about PCCs see *Oxford Diocesan Magazine*, 11 (1915), pp. 54–5.
390 1914 Banbury; Stoke Talmage; Cassington.
391 1918 Enstone; Holwell. See also 1918 Highfield; Farringdon, Little.
392 1918 Stokenchurch.
393 1918 Rotherfield Peppard; Gore, *Dominant Ideas*, pp. 28–9.
394 1918 Crowell; Emmington; Nuffield.
395 E.g. 1918 Yarnton.
396 E.g. 1918 Chipping Norton; Glympton; Whitchurch.
397 See 1918 Charlbury with Chadlington.
398 Gore, *Dominant Ideas*, pp. 30–3.

Roman Catholics in Oxfordshire

The final question in the 1918 survey, directed to Oxfordshire incumbents only, concerned the number of Roman Catholics resident in each parish. In the eighteenth century this was a common question provoked by concern about the possible political threat posed by the Catholic community.[399] In 1918, however, the question seems to have been principally antiquarian in nature, with numbers sought for comparison with historical records kept in the bishop's palace at Cuddesdon (presumably compiled from earlier visitations). The 1918 survey showed a relatively thinly spread Catholic community in Oxfordshire, recorded in 47 per cent of the returns, but in the vast majority of these numbers were small, often individuals[400] or one or at the most two families.[401] Larger communities were mostly limited to the towns, with the largest estimated at over 850 in Banbury,[402] but there were a few larger Catholic concentrations in rural Oxfordshire focused on Catholic 'big houses',[403] institutions,[404] or churches.[405] Usually good relations seem to have existed between the Anglican clergy and their Roman Catholic neighbours,[406] and only at Begbroke, where the former manor house had been converted into a Catholic priory, was tension apparent, with the incumbent finding the friars 'very unpleasant and undesirable neighbours', though for reasons that he did not choose to specify.[407] A few returns specified the nationality of the Catholic residents, with only three references to Irish Catholics[408] and one entry into the world of P. G. Wodehouse in the form of the French chef at Newington House.[409] The most common reference, however, was to Belgian refugees, who could still be found in 1918 not only in Oxford parishes[410] but also in six other parishes in the county including Lewknor where one had married a local farmer.[411]

---

399 Lloyd-Jukes (ed.), *Articles of Enquiry*.
400 E.g. 1918 Barton, Steeple; Drayton St Leonard; Stratton Audley.
401 E.g. 1918 Brizenorton; Ewelme; Tadmarton.
402 1918 Banbury. See also 1918 Bicester; Chipping Norton; Summertown.
403 1918 Mapledurham, Newington.
404 1918 Begbroke; Enstone; Oxford, St Cross.
405 1918 Hethe.
406 E.g. 1918 Cowley; Newington.
407 1918 Begbroke.
408 1918 Ambroseden; Cowley. However, it is likely that some of the larger town populations contained a substantial number with Irish birth or parentage.
409 1918 Newington.
410 1918 Oxford, St Margaret; Oxford, St Mary Magdalene. Graham, *Oxford*, pp. 107–9.
411 1918 Aston, North; Lewknor; Middleton Stoney; Stanton St John; Thame; Woodstock.

Conclusion

When it comes to an assessment of the health of the Church of England in the early twentieth century, the clergy returns to bishop Gore's two visitations reveal a complex picture. The church of the 1914 returns showed many traces of the vigour of Anglicanism at its late Victorian zenith. All the parishes in the survey were served by resident incumbents, sometimes with the assistance of curates, who maintained the tempo of parish life at an unmistakably high level. Whether measured by the frequency of services, their attempts to engage children and young people, the broad sweep of their educational initiatives for adults or their promotion of mission, there is little doubt that the Anglican parochial machinery was being operated in top gear. There was, as might be expected, a variety of views among the clergy about the results of all this effort – a variety produced perhaps at least as much by differences in character as by their parochial experience. Nonetheless, on the surface at least, the Church of England was both a busy and successful institution in Oxfordshire on the eve of the first world war.

At the same time, the returns provide a clear indication that all was not well with the Anglican model of parochial ministry. Some of the problems afflicting the church were evident at a structural level. The church's heavy investment in rural ministry paid dividends in the highly active parish evident in the returns, but even in rural Oxfordshire this investment was beginning to look unbalanced. A church that could maintain a ratio of clergy to people of 1:58 at Binsey and 1:3,265 at Blechingdon was in danger of failing the populations of its larger parishes. This was a problem that would get even worse with the post-war boom in the parts of the diocese closest to Greater London,[412] and given that the solution proposed by the bishop was not a reconstruction of the parish system but a somewhat romantic vision of the resettlement of the countryside[413] it was a problem unlikely seriously to be addressed. Moreover, the issues of clerical deployment were significantly exacerbated by the hollowing out of many of the communities that they served. Declining demand for agricultural labour and the gradual decay of employment provided by the 'big house' worsened the prospects for the rural economy and promoted a demographic slide. Falling school rolls and the departure of many young people for the towns not only undermined the health of local communities, it also undermined an Anglican parochial model that invested so many of its resources and so much of its hope in the 'rising generation'. Just like the communities it served, the clerical workforce also displayed signs of ageing; and while, in many cases, the incumbents of Oxfordshire parishes brought a wealth of experience

---

412 Masom, 'Parishes under Pressure'.
413 Gore, *Dominant Ideas*, p. 8.

to their parishes, it is doubtful that, as a body, they were the men to lead a vigorous response to a church under challenge.[414]

The war, as the 1918 returns make clear, certainly presented the church with such a challenge. It dislocated many aspects of the church's life, removing some of its keenest workers and supporters, pressurising involvement in religious activities by the alternative demands of war work, and disrupting its mechanisms for the religious socialisation of the young by removing them from school to work for the national war effort. From 1916, even church services – especially evening services, increasingly the cornerstone of church attendance for agricultural labourers – were disrupted by the imposition of lighting regulations in response to German bombing. To this extent, where congregations were falling in wartime Oxfordshire, they might more fairly be judged to be Missing in Action than Absent without Leave. However, not all the pressure on the extent of Anglican participation came from outside factors – some was also a product of the policies pursued by the church itself. In particular, the effort to make a Eucharistic service the main service of the day – a clear objective of both the bishop and many of his parochial clergy – could hardly have been more effective if it had been deliberately designed to bear down on popular participation. This was not only because it emphasised an aspect of the practice of worship which, as the incumbent of Glympton reported, many adults looked upon as 'strange and abnormal',[415] but also because such services were almost exclusively held in the morning – the time of worship least patronised by working men.[416] The full effects of this development were almost certainly not yet visible in 1918, although there were some early warning signs, and further research on the 1920s and 1930s would be necessary fully to gauge its effects. Moreover, it was perhaps inevitable that the preoccupation with the construction of the parish as a Eucharistic community should have led the clergy to view both connection with the church and spiritual improvement largely in terms of the extent and frequency of the reception of communion. This not only significantly influenced their liturgical priorities but may, in at least some cases, have led the clergy to overlook the less sacramental but no less deeply felt spirituality of some of their parishioners.

While, as already noted, the Oxfordshire returns present no clear picture of either growth or decline in the extent of religious practice among Anglicans during the war years, they do very strongly suggest that the war did, after all, exercise a powerful influence on Anglican religious life, providing the occasion for an increase, perhaps even a revival, in its intensity. Positive commentary on the deepening of spiritual life is the predominant theme in the clerical responses to the 1918 survey. However, only occasionally was this a verdict on the spirituality of parishioners in general.

---

414 Their conservatism over church schools, for example, certainly frustrated the bishop's hopes for a new path to reconstruction of primary education. *Oxford Diocesan Magazine*, 13 (1918), pp. 128–9.
415 1918 Glympton.
416 E.g. 1914 Salford.

More usually it was a commentary on a deeper attachment of those previously attached to the church, a greater devotion on the part of those already devout. This was contrasted with the reaction of those outside the sphere of regular practice who were either unaffected or drifted further away. Many of the Oxfordshire clergy were deeply impressed by the new energy and quality of spiritual life that they detected, but at the same time, they were drawing attention to a process of radicalisation – a deepening of the differences between the core and the periphery of their congregations. This development had potentially serious consequences for their post-war fortunes if it effectively raised the barriers to entry into the life of the church for the generality of parishioners – a phenomenon reinforced by and reinforcing the Eucharistic exclusivity with which it coincided. The clergy may have been mistaken about the depth of this revival of devotion, or it may not have persisted long beyond the end of the war, but it would be unwise to ignore its potential effects when investigating the fortunes of the church thereafter. In the 1920s and 1930s, just as it had during the war years, the Church of England sought to assert its role as the National Church. It adopted a baptismal rather than communicant franchise for its own representative institutions, providing the occasion for Charles Gore's resignation as bishop of Oxford in 1919.[417] It sanctified the local and national rituals of remembrance that emerged in the inter-war years and also took a lead in seeking to create what Matthew Grimley has described as 'a national moral community which reached far beyond the Anglican faithful'.[418] At the same time, however, its internal dynamics threatened to widen the distance between those same Anglican faithful and the wider parochial communities of which they were a part. While maintaining the rhetoric and public ritual of a National Church, Anglicanism, at least at parish level, may already have been moving increasingly swiftly along a path to becoming a gathered Church.

---

417 A. Wilkinson, 'Charles Gore', *ODNB*.
418 M. Grimley, *Citizenship, Community, and the Church of England* (Oxford, 2004), p. 12.

The Visitation of 1914

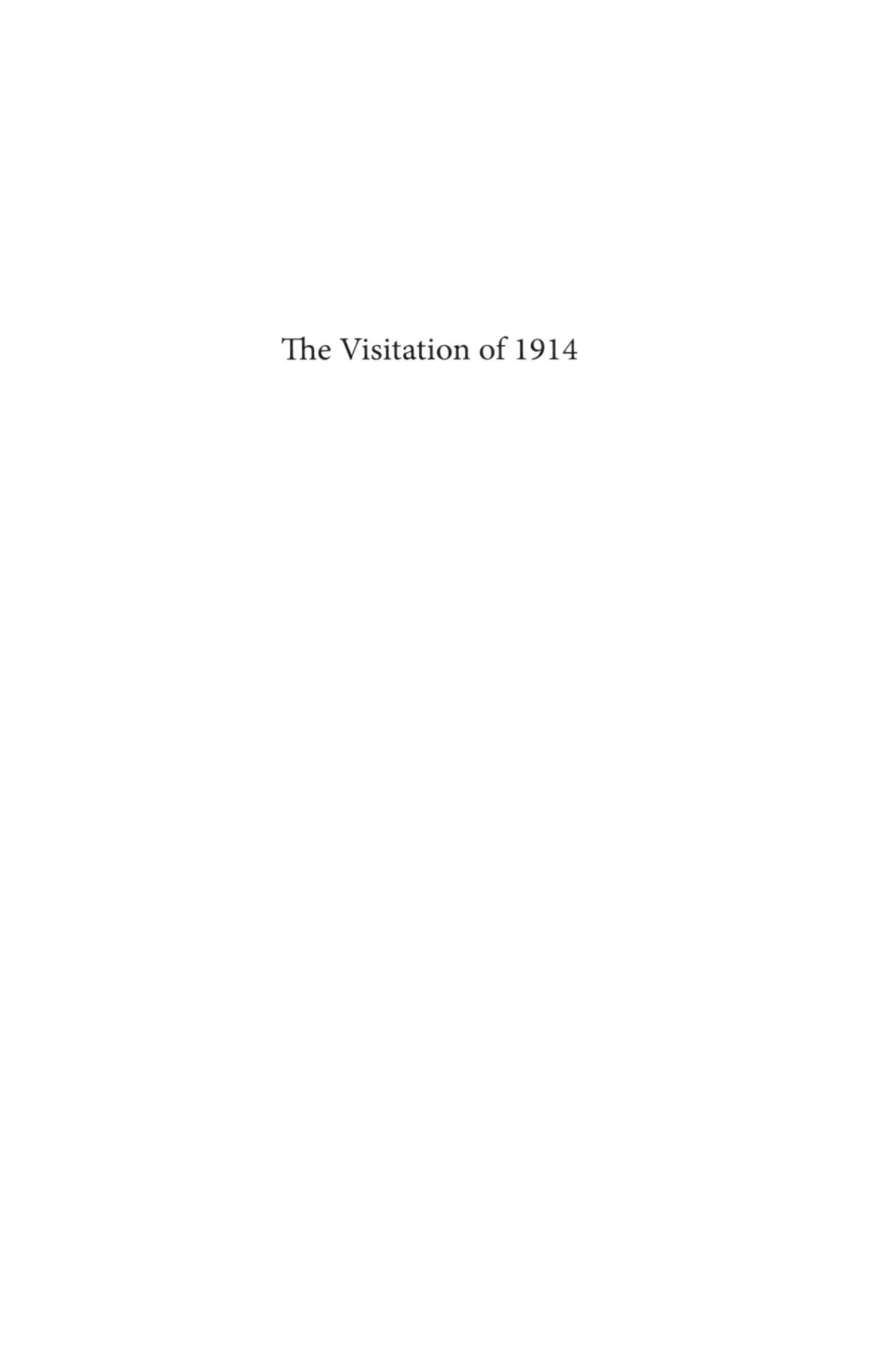

DIOCESE OF OXFORD
VISITATION, 1914

CUDDESDON,
June 13th, 1914.

MY DEAR BROTHER,

You know that I am to conduct a Visitation of the Diocese in the autumn. The list of centres and dates is in this month's Diocesan Magazine. The Summons will be issued in August to all beneficed and licensed Clergy and to the Churchwardens.

Full enquiries have been made through the Rural Deans on a number of matters concerning the churches and churchyards; but there are certain enquiries which I desire to make directly of the Incumbents; and I beg you to let me have answers to the following questions by June 30th.

Believe me to be
Yours very truly in our Lord
C. OXON:

Name of Parish: ....

QUESTIONS TO BE ANSWERED BY THE INCUMBENT OR BY THE OFFICIATING CLERGYMAN

1. Do you ever have an administration of Holy Baptism during the course of Morning or Evening Prayer, as directed in the Prayer-book?

2. At what hours is the Holy Communion celebrated in your parish,
    (a) each Sunday,
    (b) on Ascension Day,
    (c) on Saints-days
    (d) on ordinary week-days?

3. Is the service of Holy Communion ever a Sung Service?
    If so, at what hour?

4. What is done in your parish for the religious instruction of children (a) in Church (b) in Sunday-schools (c) in the Day-schools?
    Do the Clergy teach, and if so, how often, in the Day-schools?
    What is done for the religious instruction of the Sunday-school teachers?
    How far are you satisfied or dissatisfied with results attained?

5. What is done in your parish for the religious instruction of the lads and young women?

6. Is there any secondary school in your parish, and, if so, what religious instruction is given there?

7. If you have only a church school in your parish, is any provision made for the children of Nonconformist parents to receive the religious teaching acceptable to them?

8. Is anything done in your parish to promote systematic study of the principles of our religion among adults?

9. What is done to promote an intelligent interest among your parishioners in the work of the Church overseas, and to encourage them in systematic prayer for the evangelisation of the world?

In view of the work of the Archbishop's Committee on Church and State I want information on these heads.

10. How many (a) men, (b) women, in your parish have signed the declaration qualifying them, under the rules of the Representative Church Council, to vote for Ruridecanal representatives?

11. Have you a parochial Church Council? With what powers? How often has it met since last October?

(Signed)

Incumbent.

ADDERBURY[1]   Incumbent C. F. Cholmondeley[2]

1. Baptism at morning or evening prayer? Yes.

2. Communion times

a) Sunday 7. 8. or 11.

b) Ascension Day 6. 8. 11.

c) Saints Days 8.

d) Week-days? [*No response*].

3. Is Communion ever sung? Yes. 8, on great Festivals.

4. Religious teaching to children a) Church b) Sunday School and c) Day school? i) Clergy teach in Day schools? ii) Religious teaching to Sunday school teachers? iii) Satisfactory results?

[a] Daily religious instruction from 9.10–9.40. [b] Sunday Schools morning and afternoon. Catechising in Church monthly and on Ash Wednesday and Ascension Day. [i–iii] Clergyman teaches in Day School once a week. On the whole results are satisfactory.

5. Religious teaching to lads and young women? Bible Class on Sundays for lads. Bible Class on Week night for young men. Bible Class for young women.

6. Secondary school in Parish? No.

7. Teaching for Nonconformist children? There is no demand from Nonconformists.

8. Organised study for adults? [*No response*].

9. Interest in mission? There are intercessions in Church at intervals. Meetings arranged from time to time. Collections are made quarterly at houses.

10. Voters for Ruridecanal representatives a) men b) women? None that I am aware of.

11. PCC? No.

1. Population 650
2. Charles Fiennes Cholmondeley graduated from New College Oxford in 1887 and was ordained priest in 1890. He had been Vicar of Adderbury since 1913 having previously served two curacies and as Rector of Little Sampford in Essex. He was 50 years of age at the time of the 1914 Visitation and at the 1911 census his household consisted of his wife Katherine, and two female domestic servants.

ALBURY[1]   Incumbent R. W. C. Hunt[2]

1. Baptism at morning or evening prayer? No.

2. Communion times

a) **Sunday** 8. and also at 12 on first Sunday in the month.

b) **Ascension Day** Choral at 8.

c) **Saints Days** 8.

d) **Week-days?** On Thursdays in Advent and Lent and occasionally at other times.

3. Is Communion ever sung? Always on festivals at Eight o'clock. I began this two years ago and I find it to be greatly appreciated by the people.

4. Religious teaching to children a) Church b) Sunday School and c) Day school? i) Clergy teach in Day schools? ii) Religious teaching to Sunday school teachers? iii) Satisfactory results?

(a) The school children come for a special service to Church on Ascension Day, and on 10 other Days in the year. (b) The Sunday school is very small – as is the Day school. It is held on Sunday mostly and is taken by my Daughter. No other teachers are procurable, except the Day School teachers and I hold strongly that they should not be expected to teach on Sundays. (c) The Diocesan syllabus is followed. [i–iii] So far as my health has allowed I have taught in the Day School. The teaching given by the mistresses both in the mixed school and in the Infant School has been excellent and the results can be traced not only by examination at the hand of the Diocesan Inspectors, who gave us the "Excellent" award but in the remarkably high average both of communicants and of those who go regularly to church every Sunday and in the general behaviour of the children and young folk.

5. Religious teaching to lads and young women? The lads come very regularly to church and all through the Trinity season I give a course of instruction. In a tiny agricultural parish like this, it is very difficult to put the men and lads together, but I tried, with some success, the reading to them of the Pilgrim's Progress, over winter, and they liked that very much. The Young Worker course to G.F.S. meetings.

6. Secondary school in Parish? [*No response*].

7. Teaching for Nonconformist children? I have now no Nonconformist children.

8. Organised study for adults? Only by the lending of books to the more intelligent of the parishioners.

9. Interest in mission? References to mission work overseas are constantly being made in sermons and special missionary intercessions are made after Evensong on Wednesdays. I hope to give some illustrated lectures this winter.

10. Voters for Ruridecanal representatives a) men b) women? My folk abhor all meetings whether ecclesiastical or civil, and a quorum is only obtained for the Parish or other meetings, with great difficulty. Only five men have signed the declaration referred to.

11. PCC? No.

1. Population 183.
2. Robert Walter Carew Hunt graduated from Merton College Oxford in 1887 and was ordained priest in 1891. He had been Rector of Albury since 1911 having previously served as Curate of Littlemore and successively as incumbent of Hughenden and St Giles Reading. He was 49 in 1914 and at the 1911 census he shared a household with his wife, a medical doctor, three children and six unmarried female servants.

ALVESCOT[1] Incumbent W. Neate[2]

1. Baptism at morning or evening prayer? No – it is administered once a month at the Children's Service at 3 o'clock – a considerable number of adults being present.

2. Communion times

a) Sunday At 12 o'c. on the 1st in the month – at 8 o'c. other Sundays at 7.30 and 12 on High Festivals.

b) Ascension Day 8 o'c.

c) Saints Days At 8 o'c, but not on all Saint Days.

d) Week-days? Only special days of Intercession.

3. Is Communion ever sung? At 7.30 on Christmas Day, Easter Day, Whitsunday.

4. Religious teaching to children a) Church b) Sunday School and c) Day school? i) Clergy teach in Day schools? ii) Religious teaching to Sunday school teachers? iii) Satisfactory results?

(a) A Children's Service with Catechising at 8 o'c. on the first Sunday in the month. The children are taken to Church at 11 on Sunday, and as often as possible at 11.15 on Saints Days instead of the Scripture Lesson. (b) Sunday School at 10 o'c. and 2.15. (c) Religious instruction for the first 40 minutes every day. [i–iii] The Rector sets questions on the Syllabus and corrects the answers. They are supplied with lessons to teach. Satisfied.

5. Religious teaching to lads and young women? A Bible class through the winter for men and lads over 16 (10 attended regularly). A Bible class for girls over 13 – A missionary study circle (9).

6. Secondary school in Parish? None.

7. Teaching for Nonconformist children? There are no nonconformist children.

8. Organised study for adults? No.

9. Interest in mission? The Church Abroad is circulated with the Parish Magazine (50). A monthly short Intercession at the end of the evening service.

10. Voters for Ruridecanal representatives a) men b) women? None.

11. PCC? No.

1. Population 315.
2. Walter Neate graduated from New College Oxford in 1874 and was ordained priest in 1876. He had been Rector of Alvescot since 1878 having previously served as Curate of Aberford in Yorkshire. He was 61 in 1914 and at the 1911 census he shared a household with his wife, three unmarried adult children, three unmarried female servants and a married male assistant.

AMBROSEDEN[1]   Incumbent C. Bayfield[2]

1. Baptism at morning or evening prayer? Not of late years except very rarely. I am convinced that we should lose some children if I did not allow parents to have Baptism on Sunday afternoons. The Service is performed then, and shared in by Sunday School teachers and scholars.

2. Communion times

a) **Sunday** 8.30 am but on first Sunday in month midday. But some 8.30 communions are omitted.

b) **Ascension Day** Midday.

c) **Saints Days** None.

d) **Week-days?** None.

3. Is Communion ever sung? No.

4. Religious teaching to children a) Church b) Sunday School and c) Day school? i) Clergy teach in Day schools? ii) Religious teaching to Sunday school teachers? iii) Satisfactory results?

(b) 2. Sunday Schools. I superintend ours regularly, and do the same to the other occasionally. Children are taught the Church Catechism, and selected portions of Scripture. [i–iii] We have a Council School and I do not teach in it. For religious instruction of Sunday School teachers, I visit them and talk about the subjects taught, i.e., for the Sunday School 1 ½ mile distant. For Sunday School in Ambrosden village, I speak to my own family, who are the teachers. I think the results are satisfactory.

5. Religious teaching to lads and young women? Nothing special, beyond a Mothers' Union and G.F. Society, for the M. Union there being a meeting with address in Vicarage.

6. Secondary school in Parish? No.

7. Teaching for Nonconformist children? Provided (Council) School.

8. Organised study for adults? No.

9. Interest in mission? Only sermons for S.P.G and, especially when I take round the collecting boxes, I endeavour to make them in earnest about the work, dwelling upon our Lord's command that we should do it.

10. Voters for Ruridecanal representatives a) men b) women? None.

11. PCC? No.

1. Population 564
2. Charles Bayfield was a graduate of Cumbrae College, a theological college founded for the Episcopal Church in Scotland in 1851. He was ordained priest in 1883, and became Vicar of Ambroseden in 1884 having served a curacy at White Roding in Essex. He was 71 in 1914 and at the 1911 census he shared a household with his wife, a widowed sister-in-law, five unmarried daughters aged between 17 and 24 and two unmarried female servants.

ARDLEY[1]   Incumbent L. G. A. Roberts[2]

1. Baptism at morning or evening prayer? When convenient.

2. Communion times

a) Sunday 8 am 3rd Sunday, 11 am 1st Sunday.

b) Ascension Day 8 am.

c) Saints Days [*No response*].

d) Week-days? Christmas, Whitsunday 8 am and 11 am and in evening if anyone would come.

3. Is Communion ever sung? No, never.

4. Religious teaching to children a) Church b) Sunday School and c) Day school? i) Clergy teach in Day schools? ii) Religious teaching to Sunday school teachers? iii) Satisfactory results?

Children attend Sunday School every Sunday morning at 10 o'clock and come to church regularly every morning Service on Sunday and are taught in Church. They have also afternoon instruction. In the Day School, until closed, the Rector instructed Day School children once a week. My own family only do the teaching just now, as we have no Day School teachers. Schools closed. I don't think children anywhere are better up in their Bibles and Prayer book. The difficulty in a small village of only 110 is after Confirmation they think they are done with instruction. I think that Confirmation should not be administered too early.

5. Religious teaching to lads and young women? Bible Classes and Band of Hope.

6. Secondary school in Parish? No.

7. Teaching for Nonconformist children? No Nonconformists now, they attend church.

8. Organised study for adults? Bible instruction, without Sectarian bias, on principles of Protestant (Reformed) Prayer Book.

9. Interest in mission? Every opportunity is taken to inform them as to the Progress of God's Kingdom at Home and abroad, and prayer therefor during Lent and Advent. Our offertories are very good.

10. Voters for Ruridecanal representatives a) men b) women? Our Vestry declines to interfere in this under present system.

11. PCC? Our Vestry is the only channel, barring Election of Overseer, in which case Parish settles its non-secular affairs. This is found more satisfactory than Clergymen interfering, and is much appreciated.

1. Population 110.
2. Lawrence Graeme Allan Roberts was ordained as priest in 1889 in Montreal having previously been a gunnery officer in the Royal Navy. He served a number of parishes in Canada before moving to England in 1896 where after curacies in Somerset and London he became Rector of Lillington in 1900, moving to the Rectory of Ardley in 1908. A strong Protestant, he served as secretary of the Protestant Reform Society between 1896 and 1899. He was 70 in 1914 and at the 1911 census he shared a household with his wife, an unmarried son and two female unmarried servants.

ASCOT-UNDER-WYCHWOOD[1]   Incumbent C. Walford[2]

1. Baptism at morning or evening prayer? No. Baptisms are administered for the morning 'folk' at the Children's Services, at which adults also attend.

2. Communion times

a) **Sunday** At 8 am, except on last Sunday in month, when it is at midday.

b) **Ascension Day** 7.30 am.

c) **Saints Days** We have not hitherto had a Celebration.

d) **Week-days?** None.

3. Is Communion ever sung? No.

4. Religious teaching to children a) Church b) Sunday School and c) Day school? i) Clergy teach in Day schools? ii) Religious teaching to Sunday school teachers? iii) Satisfactory results?

(a) There is a Children's Service in the Church on the last Sunday in the month, at which an instruction is given. Also on Saints' Days (b) There is a Sunday School, morning and afternoon, except in the last Sunday in the month, when we have the Children's Service. The lessons in the morning followed the course of the Collect, Epistle, and Gospel, the Collect being learned. The afternoon lessons are taken from one of the lessons for the day. (c) The Religious Instruction in the Day School follows the course of the Diocesan Syllabus, except on the Saint's Days, when the children come to Church. (1) I do not teach regularly in the Day School as I have felt that the instruction was given more effectively by the trained teachers: perhaps I have been wrong here. I, however, take a class occasionally and in the absence of any of the Teachers. (2) The Day School Teachers help me with the Sunday School in the morning; and in the afternoon my wife and I take it between us with the help of one or two older scholars for the Infants. We have no Teachers meeting. (3) It would be a great gain if we had classes into which we might draft the older scholars but we have no teachers.

5. Religious teaching to lads and young women? There is a class for young girls in connection with the Girls Friendly Society and there is a Reading Room for lads, but there is no class for definite Religious Instruction.

6. Secondary school in Parish? No.

7. Teaching for Nonconformist children? There has been no demand on the part of the Nonconformists for leave to teach in our School; and I do not think that we should be justified in making provision for the dissemination of doctrines in the Church of England School other than the doctrines of the Church of England.

8. Organised study for adults? There has been nothing done.

9. Interest in mission? There are sermons once in the year upon Foreign Missionary Work, with a lecture usually by a Missionary. The Rogation Days have also been observed as days of special intercession for Missions.

10. Voters for Ruridecanal representatives a) men b) women? The papers have not been signed the election having been made by those who were known to me as Communicants of the Church of England.

11. PCC? There is no Parochial Church Council beyond the Vestry, which I have tried to make a reality. It is difficult to persuade our people to come to it.

1. Population 365.
2. Charles Walford graduated from St John's College Oxford in 1879 and was ordained priest in 1881. After serving five curacies, including Hanborough and Steeple Aston in Oxfordshire, he became Vicar of Ascot under Wychwood in 1893. He was 61 years of age in 1914. His

household was not found in the 1911 census. In 1901 he was sharing a household with his wife, two infant children, his mother and sister-in-law and two unmarried female servants.

ASTHALL[1]   Incumbent W. H. K. Ward[2]

1. Baptism at morning or evening prayer? Yes.

2. Communion times

a) Sunday 1st and 2nd after Matins 3rd 4th 5th at 8 am.

b) Ascension Day 8 a.m.

c) Saints Days Formerly 8 a.m. but had to be dropped, as the requisite number was not obtained.

d) Week-days? [*No response*].

3. Is Communion ever sung? At the great festivals. 8 o'clock. Partly sung at the Celebration on the 2nd Sunday.

4. Religious teaching to children a) Church b) Sunday School and c) Day school? i) Clergy teach in Day schools? ii) Religious teaching to Sunday school teachers? iii) Satisfactory results?

(a) Children's Service on afternoon of 3rd Sunday. (b) Sunday School at Asthall conducted by Assistant Mistress and Monitoress under supervision of the Vicar. At Asthall Leigh by a lady. (c) Daily 9.5 to 9.50 taking the Syllabus of Religious Instruction for use in the Diocese. [i–iii] The Vicar used to take the instruction in the Prayer Book, but having satisfactory teachers in the school he now takes a class once a week. So far I have had no cause to be dissatisfied.

5. Religious teaching to lads and young women? There are very few of either and the parish being very scattered it is almost impossible to form classes. I am hoping, however, shortly to have a Communicant's Guild.

6. Secondary school in Parish? No.

7. Teaching for Nonconformist children? No: the parents have always been satisfied that their children should receive the religious instruction given in the school. The only exception ever made was for children of Baptist parents, who not unnaturally objected to the teaching of the Church Catechism.

8. Organised study for adults? [*No response*].

9. Interest in mission? The parishioners are entering keenly into the Missionary Forward Movement, and I trust are remembering the work in their prayer, as they are constantly urged to do. The prayer for Overseas Missions is used regularly in the Churches.

10. Voters for Ruridecanal representatives a) men b) women? None.

11. PCC? There is no Council.

1. Population 313.
2. William Hallowes Kirwan Ward graduated from Trinity College Cambridge in 1880 and was ordained priest in 1904. After two brief curacies he became Vicar of Asthall with Astall Leigh in 1904. He was 57 in 1914 and at the 1911 census he shared a household with his wife and one unmarried female servant. Ward's son William was subsequently killed at Gallipoli in 1915.

ASTON, NORTH[1]   Incumbent H. R. A. Wilson[2]

1. Baptism at morning or evening prayer? Yes. It is the general rule here.

2. Communion times

a) Sunday 8 am except 1st Sunday in the month then 11 am.

b) Ascension Day 5 am and 11 am.

c) Saints Days 8 am generally – sometimes 11 am.

d) Week-days? [*No response*].

3. Is Communion ever sung? No.

4. Religious teaching to children a) Church b) Sunday School and c) Day school? i) Clergy teach in Day schools? ii) Religious teaching to Sunday school teachers? iii) Satisfactory results?

(a) Children of Day School attend Church at 9 am on Saints Days. (b) Sunday School in the afternoon each Sunday at 2.30 pm. Children are expected to attend Church in the morning. (c) The Children are well taught by the Day School Teachers. Results at Diocesan Inspection have been excellent. [i–iii] We give books to Sunday School Teachers. Besides the Vicar and his wife we have two Teachers so that a class for Teachers with so small a number would be difficult to keep going. We belong to Sunday School Teachers Association in the R.D. and attend its meetings. The Sunday School has only been started since last Advent, before this the Vicar had the children in Church each Sunday to Catechise. The difficulty was to Catechise a small number of children of varying ages from 3 to 14. So the Sunday School may be said to be experimental. It seems to be working well and is certainly better for the Infants. So far as the Religious Instruction goes I am quite satisfied with what is given in the Day School. So far as my personal influence goes I should like to teach myself in the Day School but I find it would be difficult without upsetting the sensibilities of the present Teacher. With regard to the Sunday School I hope to improve as time goes on.

5. Religious teaching to lads and young women? We have a weekly Bible Class for lads in the winter. We have a women's meeting in the winter – which consists of Bible Instruction and Hymns – as all our girls go out to service we have only a few unmarried women.

6. Secondary school in Parish? No.

7. Teaching for Nonconformist children? I think there is only one child in the school of Nonconformist parents. I do not think they object to the present religious instruction, so we do not make special provision.

8. Organised study for adults? No.

9. Interest in mission? We have an Annual Missionary Meeting. We have a certain number of Missionary boxes. We have an annual Sunday for Foreign Missions.

10. Voters for Ruridecanal representatives a) men b) women? I do not know of any.

11. PCC? No.

1. Population 221.
2. Henry Remington Allen Wilson graduated from Trinity College Cambridge in 1892 and then trained at the Leeds Clergy School. He was ordained priest in 1894 and then after three curacies became Rector of Marton in 1899 and Vicar of North Aston in 1912. He was 44 in 1914 and at the 1911 census he was sharing a household with his wife and one unmarried female servant.

ASTON, STEEPLE[1] Incumbent F. J. Brown[2]

1. Baptism at morning or evening prayer? No.

2. Communion times

a) **Sunday** 8 am on last Sunday at noon as well.

b) **Ascension Day** 8am.

c) **Saints Days** 8 am.

d) **Week-days?** [*No response*].

3. Is Communion ever sung? No.

4. Religious teaching to children a) Church b) Sunday School and c) Day school? i) Clergy teach in Day schools? ii) Religious teaching to Sunday school teachers? iii) Satisfactory results?

(a) On certain Holydays in Church. (b) On Sunday morning at 10 in afternoon at 2.15 (c) On all Days sanctioned by Time-Table in Day School. The Incumbent examines from time to time. The teaching is very well done by the School Staff as shown by reports of Diocesan Inspector that he is content. [i–iii] It is extremely difficult to get the Sunday School teachers together. One of them is a School Teacher at a distance and only comes home on Saturday evening; one is a laundress whose work is only done late on that evening; the others are Day School teachers. Children come most regularly up to a certain age.

5. Religious teaching to lads and young women? Bible class for lads also for girls.

6. Secondary school in Parish? None.

7. Teaching for Nonconformist children? One of the School Staff is a Dissenter.

8. Organised study for adults? Nothing systematic.

9. Interest in mission? 50 copies of SPG publications circulated each month. Sunday School children practically 'Kings Messengers'.

10. Voters for Ruridecanal representatives a) men b) women? 12 men is the largest number who attended a meeting for Election of Lay Representatives.

11. PCC? No.

1. Population 615.
2. Frederick John Brown graduated from Brasenose College Oxford in 1872 and was ordained priest in 1873. He was curate of St Philip and St James in Oxford from 1872 to 1886 and became Rector of Steeple Aston in 1896. He served as Rural Dean of Woodstock from 1900. He was 64 in 1914 and at the 1911 census he was single and sharing a household with two unmarried female servants.

ASTON ROWANT[1]   Incumbent F. N. Crowther[2]

1. Baptism at morning or evening prayer? No. Baptisms take place at the childrens service.

2. Communion times

a) Sunday 8.0 am every Sunday: and after morning service on the first Sunday in the month as well.

b) Ascension Day 8.0 a.m.

c) Saints Days At 8.0 am occasionally e.g. All Saints Day as a rule there is no congregation.

d) Week-days? Never.

3. Is Communion ever sung? No.

4. Religious teaching to children a) Church b) Sunday School and c) Day school? i) Clergy teach in Day schools? ii) Religious teaching to Sunday school teachers? iii) Satisfactory results?

(a) I have a service for children in church on the first Sunday in every month with catechisms. (b) There is a Sunday School every Sunday both in the morning and afternoon: I always open both and always take a class in the morning, all the winter months I have a Bible Class for the lads who have just left school in the afternoon: in the summer I supply the place of any Teacher who may be absent and so generally teach. (c) I read prayers and teach a class three days a week. [i–iii] I have found great difficulty in teaching the Sunday School Teachers: they are for the most part busy people and it is not easy for them to attend a class. When I first came here 10 years ago I began a class but the attendance soon declined and only one Teacher came; I thought it best then to discontinue: I then gave each Teacher a copy each month of the Church Sunday School Magazine so that they might teach the lesson given in it for each Sunday: the result was that the magazine was taken into School and the Teacher read out the lesson to the class. As this was far from satisfactory and I had in the meanwhile secured some Teachers whose time was more at their disposal I went back to a meeting. At the suggestion of the Archdeacon of Berkshire I held it after afternoon Sunday School; but the Teachers said it interfered with their Tea, so now I am trying a meeting every fortnight on a weekday at which the lessons for the two following Sundays are discussed: for the time being this seems fairly satisfactory, but when the winter comes I doubt if the Teachers will attend. I am not altogether without hope that during the last 10 years some small good may have been done, but the results are scarcely apparent. What does happen is this – I am known to take an interest in the School therefore that affords a way of putting pressure on me: so if I use any discipline over the children or offend the parents, the children are removed and sent to the Nonconformist Sunday School.

5. Religious teaching to lads and young women? I have a Bible Class for lads who have left School every Sunday afternoon (except the first Sunday in the month) from Harvest to Easter. My wife has a branch of the Girls Friendly Society but most of the girls as soon as they leave School go away as domestic Servants.

6. Secondary school in Parish? No.

7. Teaching for Nonconformist children? On receipt of a circular from the National Society some time ago, I spoke to a leading Nonconformist in the Parish and told him that if he would like to give religious teaching acceptable to himself in the School I would do what I could to make suitable arrangements. I have heard no more.

8. Organised study for adults? There is a branch of the C.E.M.S. but it does not prosper: in connection with it I have tried both a Bible Class and Missionary Study during winter months, but without success: all the common people are in their gardens and in the winter they do not care to come out into the wet and mud of the roads especially if they have been out in the cold and rain all the day. There is a branch of the Mothers Union; meetings are held every alternate week throughout the winter and instruction given.

9. Interest in mission? We have at least one Missionary Meeting during the winter, and sermons on one Sunday. I take some Foreign Mission as a subject for catechising from time to time.

10. Voters for Ruridecanal representatives a) men b) women? I called a meeting: hardly anybody attended: the two or three who did were churchwardens or sidesmen: regular communicants: they did not trouble to sign a declaration testifying to what was perfectly well known.

11. PCC? No.

1. Population 532.
2. Francis Nelson Crowther graduated from Corpus Christi College Oxford in 1881 and was ordained priest in 1882. After serving a curacy in Worcestershire he became Assistant Master at Richmond School in Yorkshire and then served as a chaplain at seven different locations in India between 1885 and 1904 and in 1902 was appointed as an Honorary Canon of Madras Cathedral. In 1904 he returned to England as Vicar of Aston Rowant. He was 56 in 1914 and at the 1911 census he shared a household with his wife, 19-year-old daughter and one unmarried female servant.

BALDON, MARSH WITH TOOT[1]   Incumbent H. A. Goodwin[2]

1. Baptism at morning or evening prayer? Generally. There have been exceptions.

2. Communion times

a) Sunday Twice a month at 8 am and twice at 11 am.

b) Ascension Day 8 am.

c) Saints Days [*No response*].

d) Week-days? [*No response*].

3. Is Communion ever sung? Once a year at Toot. 8 am.

4. Religious teaching to children a) Church b) Sunday School and c) Day school? i) Clergy teach in Day schools? ii) Religious teaching to Sunday school teachers? iii) Satisfactory results?

a. A month Childrens Service b. Sunday School, each Sunday in Marsh Baldon School. c. Very good instruction given by the Day School Teachers. [i–iii] The Clergy do not teach in the Day School. The results are quite satisfactory.

5. Religious teaching to lads and young women? No regular instruction is given. Most of the young men and women attend the Church Services.

6. Secondary school in Parish? No.

7. Teaching for Nonconformist children? Only a Church School. No nonconformists attend.

8. Organised study for adults? No.

9. Interest in mission? Only by means of sermons.

10. Voters for Ruridecanal representatives a) men b) women? None at present. No instructions have been received.

11. PCC? No.

1. Population 463.
2. Harry Arthur Goodwin graduated from St Catherine's College Cambridge in 1874 and was ordained priest in 1875. After a curacy in Sheffield he served as Chaplain of the South Yorkshire Asylum from 1878 to 1907 and as Perpetual Curate of Owlerton. He became Rector of Marsh Baldon and Vicar of Toot Baldon in 1912. He was 66 in 1914 and at the 1911 census he shared a household with his wife and two unmarried female servants.

BAMPTON PROPER[1]   Incumbent G. E. C. Rodwell[2]

1. Baptism at morning or evening prayer? I have done so.

2. Communion times

a) Sunday 8am, and midday after Matins, and 7am Great Festivals.

b) Ascension Day 8 am.

c) Saints Days 8 am.

d) Week-days? 8 am Lent and Advent.

3. Is Communion ever sung? No.

4. Religious teaching to children a) Church b) Sunday School and c) Day school? i) Clergy teach in Day schools? ii) Religious teaching to Sunday school teachers? iii) Satisfactory results?

(a) I catechize, Catechism and Marden manuals. (b) Marden manual taught. (c) Usual religious subjects taught after Prayers. [i–iii] The Clergy teach on Fri morning each week. Sunday School Teachers not regularly instructed on account of simplicity of book used. They meet occasionally.

    A very great improvement in <u>knowledge</u> is noticeable since the Marden system has been introduced: and an extraordinary improvement in attendance since the Stamp system has been started.

5. Religious teaching to lads and young women? Quarterly meetings for Prayer and address of the Communicants Guild.

6. Secondary school in Parish? <u>None</u>.

7. Teaching for Nonconformist children? None has ever been asked for. All the children, with one or two exceptions, come to the Ascension Day service. All, without exception, attend my religious instruction.

8. Organised study for adults? Only by lending books when people will read them.

9. Interest in mission? Quarterly addresses: days of Intercession: authorized prayer frequently used: House to House Visitation of Mission Committee.

10. Voters for Ruridecanal representatives a) men b) women? I do not know exactly. I think very few.

11. PCC? No.

1. Population 1,240.
2. George Edward Chippindall Rodwell graduated from Keble College Oxford in 1887 and was ordained priest in 1891. After serving three curacies he became Rector of Washford Pyne in 1902 and then Vicar of Bampton in 1906. In 1899 he published *New Testament Greek. A course for beginners, etc.* He was 48 in 1914 and at the 1911 census he shared a household with his wife, six children aged between 5 and 15, a nurse, a governess and two unmarried female servants.

BAMPTON ASTON AND COTE[1]   Incumbent N. Germon[2]

1. Baptism at morning or evening prayer? Yes, with the exception of the Children's Service, it is the time I have for Baptisms.

2. Communion times

a) Sunday at 8 a.m. with the exception of the second Sunday when it is at 11 a.m. Every 1st Sunday there is a Celebration at S. Mary's Shifford at 11 a.m.

b) Ascension Day at 8 a.m.

c) Saints Days at 8 a.m.

d) Week-days? [*No response*].

3. Is Communion ever sung? Yes. 11 a.m.

4. Religious teaching to children a) Church b) Sunday School and c) Day school? i) Clergy teach in Day schools? ii) Religious teaching to Sunday school teachers? iii) Satisfactory results?

(a) There is a Children's Service with catechising once a month. (b) The Children are instructed in a course of lessons: at the present time they are being taken in a course on the Catechism. (c) The Syllabus of Religious Instruction for use in the Diocese is taught. [i–iii] The Vicar teaches once a week in the Day-Schools. Besides the Vicar four out of the five Day-school Teachers help in the Sunday School and are the only Teachers, but they receive no special preparation. There has been an attempt made in the course of the past year to re-organise the Sunday School, but with what results it is a little early yet to judge. For the time being there is a falling off in numbers. One of the chief difficulties is the apparent want of interest on the part of the children.

5. Religious teaching to lads and young women? Nothing at present outside the ordinary Services of the Church.

6. Secondary school in Parish? There is a training School for Domestic Servants. Daily religious instruction is given, the syllabus in use in the Diocese being adopted. The Vicar gives instruction in the Prayer Book once a week.

7. Teaching for Nonconformist children? No.

8. Organised study for adults? No.

9. Interest in mission? Instruction was given in the winter to children attending the Sunday School, and there is a Quarterly Service of Intercession for Foreign Missions held in the Parish Church.

10. Voters for Ruridecanal representatives a) men b) women? I have not been able to ascertain that any signed the declaration in the former Vicar's time, and none have signed in the course of the last year and a half.

11. PCC? No.

1. Population 759.
2. Nicholas Germon graduated from St Mary Hall Oxford in 1881 and was ordained priest in 1884. After serving two curacies he was appointed Vicar of West Leigh in 1885, moving to be Vicar of Bampton Aston with Cote in 1912. He was 54 in 1914 and at the 1911 census he shared a household with his wife and two unmarried female servants.

BAMPTON LEW[1]   Incumbent J. Jackson[2]

1. Baptism at morning or evening prayer? Baptism is always administered after the Second Lesson at Evening Prayer.

2. Communion times

a) **Sunday** at 11 am.

b) **Ascension Day** at 11 am.

c) **Saints Days** [*No response*].

d) **Week-days?** [*No response*].

3. Is Communion ever sung? No.

4. Religious teaching to children a) Church b) Sunday School and c) Day school? i) Clergy teach in Day schools? ii) Religious teaching to Sunday school teachers? iii) Satisfactory results?

a. The children are sometimes catechised or specially addressed on Sundays at Evensong. b. Also, they are taught in Sunday School. c. The Vicar occasionally, and at regular intervals, teaches in the Day School at Times provided in Time Table. <u>N.B. Through no choice of his own, the Vicar has to reside 2 ½ miles away</u>. As to the last query, he is satisfied that he does what he can – not what he would. <u>The smallness of the population, and some circumstances affecting it, render some of these inquiries rather inapplicable</u>. The whole population of Lew, of which the great part is ever changing, is 115, contained in 25 dwellings. The scarcity of cottages keeps <u>down</u> the population. The young migrate or emigrate. Approximate analysis: 25 couples = 50 old and middle aged; Servants in great house, resident intermittently = 20; Of school age and under = 25; Rest, labourers of full age. Consequently, none that may be described as 'lads and young women' – amenable to special religious instruction – except perhaps such as one married woman whom I lately brought to confirmation.

5. Religious teaching to lads and young women? See account of population on preceding page.

6. Secondary school in Parish? No.

7. Teaching for Nonconformist children? The need has not arisen. All parents are satisfied with the School, which gives satisfaction to Government and Diocesan Inspectors. For over 20 years I have successfully struggled for the maintenance of the School in the parish – resisting projects of the L.E.A. for carting off the children to a County School elsewhere.

8. Organised study for adults? No, except what may be effected by methods described under article 4, and by ordinary sermons.

9. Interest in mission? The subject is not neglected in sermons.

10. Voters for Ruridecanal representatives a) men b) women? None.

11. PCC? No.

1. Population 116.
2. Joseph Jackson graduated from Trinity College Durham in 1862 and was ordained priest in 1883. He served six curacies before becoming Vicar of Shilton in Oxfordshire in 1883 and then Vicar of Bampton Lew in 1887. In 1882 he published as editor *Collects exemplified; being illustrations from the Old and New Testaments of the Collects for the Sundays after Trinity [With the text.] By the author of A commentary on the Epistles and Gospels in the Book of Common Prayer ... (E. F. S.)*. He was a widower aged 76 in 1914 and at the 1911 census he shared a household with his wife and one unmarried female servant.

BANBURY[1] Incumbent A. J. Jones[2]

1. Baptism at morning or evening prayer? No.

2. Communion times

a) Sunday 7. 8. 12.

b) Ascension Day 6, 7, 8, 12.

c) Saints Days 7.30; and 11 (occasionally).

d) Week-days? 7.30.

3. Is Communion ever sung? No.

4. Religious teaching to children a) Church b) Sunday School and c) Day school? i) Clergy teach in Day schools? ii) Religious teaching to Sunday school teachers? iii) Satisfactory results?

There are three services (graded) for children every Sunday afternoon in this Parish. The books used by the Teachers and clergy are: (i) Sunday School Lessons – J. P. Trevelyan (ii) Inter-diocesan Lessons – H. D. S. Sweetapple (iii) Catechising for Church and Sunday School – Potter and Sheard. The Vicar and his Senior assistant Priest teach in the day schools, twice a week each. The Vicar also gives instruction in the Private schools. The Sunday School Teachers meet for instruction every fortnight. The children assemble for Sunday School at 10 and 2.30 on Sundays. Occasionally some of the older children are taken to a special celebration of the Holy Communion – e.g. for the King's Messengers. I am far from being dissatisfied with the results obtained, on the whole. There is certainly a better spirit of reverence among the children, and they appear to be better instructed in matters of the faith than formerly. Many of the parents take a keen interest in their written work for the Sunday 'Catechism'. The Infants are given special instruction on Sunday evenings by one of the Day School staff on kindergarten lines.

5. Religious teaching to lads and young women? <u>Bible Classes</u>. One for men. One for women. Two for girls. Four for lads.

6. Secondary school in Parish? The Municipal or Technical School in Dr Burton's Parish. I am in constant touch with it, but he will doubtless answer this question.

7. Teaching for Nonconformist children? No difficulty of this kind in Banbury.

8. Organised study for adults? <u>Study circles</u>. (a) C.E.M.S. (b) Mothers' Union. Monthly instruction in a communicants' guild. Instruction for 'King's Messengers' fortnightly.

9. Interest in mission? (a) Distribution of missionary literature. (b) Missionary work Party. (c) Quarterly service of Intercession. (d) Monthly office for Missions. (e) Frequent sermons on missions.

10. Voters for Ruridecanal representatives a) men b) women? I am afraid that I have no record of the actual numbers.

11. PCC? We have no Parochial church council. But the churchwardens and the sidesmen meet under the chairmanship of the Vicar to discuss questions of importance every quarter. We have 5 churchwardens and 40 sidesmen for the two churches.

1. Population 6,131.
2. Arthur John Jones graduated from Lincoln College Oxford in 1893 and then trained at Cuddesdon. He was ordained priest in 1895 and served as Curate of Aylesbury from 1894 until he was appointed as Vicar of Banbury in 1906. He served as Rural Dean of Deddington from 1912. He was 43 in 1914 and at the 1911 census he was single and sharing a household with two unmarried female servants.

BANBURY, SOUTH[1]   Incumbent F. M. Burton[2]

1. Baptism at morning or evening prayer? No. But sometimes during the Sunday afternoon Childrens' Service.

2. Communion times

a) Sunday 7. 8. and mid-day.

b) Ascension Day 7. and 8.

c) Saints Days at 6. 7. or 8.

d) Week-days? at 8.

3. Is Communion ever sung? Christ ch. 1st Sunday in month at 8. S. Leonard's 3rd Sunday [in month at] 10.45. Sung Eucharist and Sermon following on matins plain at 10.15.

4. Religious teaching to children a) Church b) Sunday School and c) Day school? i) Clergy teach in Day schools? ii) Religious teaching to Sunday school teachers? iii) Satisfactory results?

(a) Christ ch. Catechising at 2.15. S. Leonards. The catechism at 2.40. (b) Regular teaching in both Sunday Schools. Ch.ch. This year and next "The Church and Her Services" national society. S. Leonard's. Dupanloup[3] (c) Diocesan syllabus. [i–iii] The Clergy teach on examin. standards 3 days a week. Sunday Sch. Teachers – monthly meeting to go through coming lessons. Ch.ch. we suffer from having no day schools at this end of the Parish, [but] we get an eclectic set of scholars. There is a perennial difficulty in getting adequate Teachers, as any better class people have pews in S. Mary's and teach there. S. Leonard's. The day school Teachers kindly and willingly help, so here all is well, no difficulty, and splendid results from the catechism.

5. Religious teaching to lads and young women? Two flourishing Bible classes for lads and young women at Ch.ch. and S. Leonards.

6. Secondary school in Parish? There are several large secondary schools in my Parish, but they all prefer S. Mary's as we cannot give them seats in our free and open churches.

7. Teaching for Nonconformist children? [*No response*].

8. Organised study for adults? At my men's service (by the request of the members) I comment on books of the Bible instead of giving sporadic addresses. We have been at the Book of the unveiling for the past 6 months. Next Sunday I hope to finish C. XI.

9. Interest in mission? We have meetings. C.E.M.S. (two branches). Kings Messengers. S.P.G. sermons. Special prayer every Sunday at mens' Service.

10. Voters for Ruridecanal representatives a) men b) women? (a) about 50 (b) about 30

11. PCC? No. We have 4 chwardens 35 sidesmen These meet 4 times a year and discuss the affairs of the Parish.

I am sorry that this paper is so long overdue.

1. Population 7,327.
2. Frederick Martin Burton graduated from Trinity Hall Cambridge in 1875 and was awarded the degrees of LLM in 1880 and LLD in 1887. He was elected FSA in 1893. Burton was ordained priest in 1882 and after serving two curacies he became Rector of Cowden in Kent in 1890, moving in 1896 to become Vicar of South Banbury. He also served as Domestic Chaplain to Lord De L'isle and Dudley 1894–97 and to the Duke of Marlborough 1900–08. He was aged 60 in 1914 and at the 1911 census he was living with his wife and one female servant.
3. See 1914 Oxford, St Barnabas, note 3.

BARFORD ST MICHAEL[1]   Incumbent A. C. Highton[2]

1. Baptism at morning or evening prayer? Sometimes at Evensong, usually at the 3 o'c. children's service.

2. Communion times

a) Sunday 8 o'c. 2nd 4th and 5th; 11 o'c. 1st and 3rd Sunday.

b) Ascension Day 7.30 a.m.

c) Saints Days [*No response*].

d) Week-days? Every Friday at 8 o'c.; if there is a Saint's Day in the week The Gospel and Epistle and Collect for it is then used.

3. Is Communion ever sung? At 11 o'c. hymns only, and Kyrie Eleison.

4. Religious teaching to children a) Church b) Sunday School and c) Day school? i) Clergy teach in Day schools? ii) Religious teaching to Sunday school teachers? iii) Satisfactory results?

I teach twice a week in the Day Schools and usually take Sacraments, and Prayer Book services, except with the Infants. I myself take all S.S. teaching at 10 o'c. am on Sundays, and at Children's services at 3 o'c. The children generally pass a good Examination at the Diocesan inspection. Those children who come to Sunday morning S.S. make good progress, and learn a good deal, and say what they have learned at the 3 o'c. service. I find a difficulty in getting boys for confirmation, there are only two coming on at present. They come to the boys and lads club and behave well, but I find a difficulty in getting them to treat their religion seriously, either in attending a Bible Class or in coming to confirmation.

5. Religious teaching to lads and young women? Nothing beyond confirmation classes.

6. Secondary school in Parish? No.

7. Teaching for Nonconformist children? If they ask for it Bible teaching is only to be given, but they very seldom do, none do at present and the dissenters make no objection to church teaching.

8. Organised study for adults? At 7 o'c. on Wednesday there is instruction and intercession.

9. Interest in mission? Every day at Evensong a collect is said for Foreign Missions and I have 24 Missionary boxes distributed in the parish and a monthly instruction at the Children's service.

10. Voters for Ruridecanal representatives a) men b) women? They do not at present trouble about it.

11. PCC? No, but we discuss matters at a yearly meeting of churchgoers at Easter.

1. Population 310.
2. Alfred Charles Highton graduated from Queen's College Oxford in 1875 and was ordained priest in 1882. Between 1881 and 1897 he occupied a series of seven curacies and also served as a missionary with UMCA at Mbweni, Zanzibar, 1887–89. He became Vicar of Great Barford (Barford St Michael) with Barford St John in 1898. He published *William de Winton* (1903). He was 61 years of age in 1914 and at the 1911 census he was single and the only other member of his household was his female housekeeper.

BARTON, STEEPLE[1]   Incumbent S. Stephen[2]

1. Baptism at morning or evening prayer? Yes.

2. Communion times

a) **Sunday** 8 a.m. (8.30 a.m. in winter). 11 a.m. Alternate Sundays.

b) **Ascension Day** After Mattins at 11.30.

c) **Saints Days** 8 a.m. (8.30 a.m. in winter).

d) Week-days? [*No response*].

3. Is Communion ever sung? [*No response*].

4. Religious teaching to children a) Church b) Sunday School and c) Day school? i) Clergy teach in Day schools? ii) Religious teaching to Sunday school teachers? iii) Satisfactory results?

In the Day-Schools the Diocesan Syllabus is faithfully carried out. The Sunday Schools are in charge of the Squire and are held in Church or at his house.

5. Religious teaching to lads and young women? They generally leave the village.

6. Secondary school in Parish? [*No response*].

7. Teaching for Nonconformist children? They are satisfied with the Church's teaching.

8. Organised study for adults? Long courses of sermons.

9. Interest in mission? Intercession, sermons, offertory.

10. Voters for Ruridecanal representatives a) men b) women? [*No response*].

11. PCC? [*No response*].

1. Population 665.
2. Simon Stephen was awarded a PhD at the Sorbonne in 1884 followed by a DD in 1888. He was ordained priest in 1888 by the Roman Catholic Bishop of Mardin and was received into the Church of England in 1901. After serving two curacies he became Vicar of Steeple Barton in 1904. He was aged 49 in 1914 and at the 1911 census he was recorded as single, the only other member of his household being a married female servant.

BARTON WESTCOT[1]   Incumbent C. R. Tyrwhitt[2]

1. Baptism at morning or evening prayer? [*No response*].

2. Communion times

a) Sunday 7 2nd Sunday; 8 other Sundays; 11 1st Sunday.

b) Ascension Day 8.

c) Saints Days 8.

d) Week-days? [*No response*].

3. Is Communion ever sung? 11 1st Sunday.

4. Religious teaching to children a) Church b) Sunday School and c) Day school? i) Clergy teach in Day schools? ii) Religious teaching to Sunday school teachers? iii) Satisfactory results?

Occasional Children's Service on Sundays. Sunday school 10 a.m. every Sunday. No Day School in parish. Manual given to Teachers in Sunday School. Sunday School attend Morning Service in Church. [i–iii] All the Church Children attend Sunday School very regularly. I cannot say that I am altogether satisfied with the results. They are however kept together. With my own personal work I am not satisfied.

5. Religious teaching to lads and young women? Confirmation classes each year since I have been here.

6. Secondary school in Parish? No.

7. Teaching for Nonconformist children? No.

8. Organised study for adults? Mothers' Meeting.

9. Interest in mission? A few missionary Magazines are circulated. Other Missionary intelligence by S.P.G Publications inserted in Parish magazine. A few Missionary boxes.

10. Voters for Ruridecanal representatives a) men b) women? [*No response*].

11. PCC? No.

1. Population 159.
2. Cecil Robert Tyrwhitt graduated from Christ Church Oxford in 1884 and was ordained priest in 1887. After an initial curacy he was appointed as Chaplain of Christ Church and Curate of Cowley St John in 1890. He served as a UMCA missionary in Zanzibar 1893–96 and then as Chaplain of St Augustine College Canterbury 1897–1902. He was appointed to the Rectory of Barton Westcote in 1911. He was 52 years of age in 1914. His household was not found in the 1911 census.

BECKLEY[1]   Incumbent P. V. Doyne[2]

1. Baptism at morning or evening prayer? Occasionally at Evensong.

2. Communion times

a) Sunday 8 am. 11.45 on the first Sunday of the month.

b) Ascension Day 7.45 am.

c) Saints Days 7.45 am.

d) Week-days? Occasionally at 7.45 am.

3. Is Communion ever sung? At 8 am on the Great Festivals.

4. Religious teaching to children a) Church b) Sunday School and c) Day school? i) Clergy teach in Day schools? ii) Religious teaching to Sunday school teachers? iii) Satisfactory results?

(a) Children attend daily at Matins. Sunday afternoon there is Children's Service at 3. with Catechizing. (b) Sunday School is held in the morning at 10 o'clock. (c) Diocesan Syllabus of Religious Instruction given each day from 9.20 to 9.55. Vicar teaches daily in Schools. [i–iii] For the time being the results seem fairly satisfactory but they only carry as far as Confirmation after which they leave the Parish both boys and girls with few exceptions.

5. Religious teaching to lads and young women? Communicants Classes and Guild.

6. Secondary school in Parish? No.

7. Teaching for Nonconformist children? We have only a Church School and speaking for the last 20 years no application has ever been made for teaching other than given according to the principles of the Church of England.

8. Organised study for adults? No.

9. Interest in mission? There is a Missionary Guild which has its Special Prayers for daily use, and there are quarterly meetings and occasionally Special Intercession Services.

10. Voters for Ruridecanal representatives a) men b) women? Five or six.

11. PCC? No.

1. Population 248.
2. Philip Valentine Doyne graduated from Clare College Cambridge in 1886 and was ordained priest in 1887. He served two curacies between 1886 and 1894, when he became Vicar of Beckley. He was aged 55 in 1914 and at the 1911 census he was living in a household with his wife and two sons, together with a married female servant.

BEGBROKE[1]   Incumbent A. H. Gillmor[2]

1. Baptism at morning or evening prayer? Nearly always after the Second Lesson at Evening Prayer on Sundays.

2. Communion times

a) Sunday 8 o'c. and 11 o'c. alternately. On Great Festivals at 8 o'c. and 11 o'c.

b) Ascension Day 8 o'c. At first I had celebration of the Holy Communion on Ascension Day at 8 o'c. and 11 o'c., but the communicants at 11 o'c. were not sufficient.

c) Saints Days 8 o'c.

d) Week-days? Not at present.

3. Is Communion ever sung? I regret not, as the people are not at present sufficiently musical, but hope it may be possible yet.

4. Religious teaching to children a) Church b) Sunday School and c) Day school? i) Clergy teach in Day schools? ii) Religious teaching to Sunday school teachers? iii) Satisfactory results?

I catechise each Sunday in Church, and take part in the teaching in the Sunday-school each Sunday. A copy of "Our Empire", a paper for Sunday-school children, published by the S.P.C.K. is distributed every Sunday to each child in the Sunday-school. It is a paper of excellent Church teaching and is helpful not only to the children, but also to the parents and others at home. [i–iii] There is no Day-school. The children attend Kidlington and other schools. I give some help to the Sunday-school teachers in preparation work each week. I am fairly satisfied with the result.

5. Religious teaching to lads and young women? I purpose having classes in the winter season in the Bible and Prayer Book and Church History.

6. Secondary school in Parish? No.

7. Teaching for Nonconformist children? With the exception of some Roman Catholics there are no Nonconformists in the parish.

8. Organised study for adults? A Communicants Class has been lately formed. Books are lent from time to time to some of the people. I have Matins and Evensong daily throughout the year, and the Litany on Wednesdays and Fridays as well as Sundays, and some of the adults come when they can on weekdays.

9. Interest in mission? The parishioners take an interest in the work of the S.P.G. Sermons are preached and there is an annual collection for the S.P.G. and Missionary Boxes are taken each year by some of the people. The amounts contributed are fair and a test of interest.

10. Voters for Ruridecanal representatives a) men b) women? Four men have signed the declaration.

11. PCC? No.

1. Population 93.
2. Andrew Hercules Gillmor graduated from Trinity College Dublin in 1887 and was ordained priest in 1893. He served a series of seven curacies both in England and Ireland between 1892 and 1909 when he was appointed Rector of Begbroke. He was aged 45 in 1914 and at the 1911 census he was single and living in a household with his unmarried sister.

BENSON[1]   Incumbent J. E. Field[2]

1. Baptism at morning or evening prayer? I have not done so for several years as people are unwilling to bring children at those hours and some would absent themselves if they expected a baptism.

2. Communion times

a) **Sunday** 8 on most Sundays (every Sunday in summer) – midday twice a month.

b) **Ascension Day** 8.

c) **Saints Days** 8 occasionally.

d) **Week-days?** only on exceptional occasions.

3. Is Communion ever sung? After 11 o'clock matins once a month and on the three chief festivals.

4. Religious teaching to children a) Church b) Sunday School and c) Day school? i) Clergy teach in Day schools? ii) Religious teaching to Sunday school teachers? iii) Satisfactory results?
There is a monthly Catechism in Church on the lesson taught in the Sunday School. The teachers in the Sunday School are (a) students from Dorchester College, one in morning another in afternoon (b) one of the women teachers in the Day School and occasionally more than one (c) some ladies of the parish. [i–iii] I teach the upper class in the Day School twice a week, usually undertaking the Acts of the Apostles and the Prayer Book lessons. All the teachers give religious instruction in their own divisions, following the Diocesan Syllabus. Some of the Sunday School teachers attend a fortnightly Bible Class at the Vicarage. I am by no means satisfied with the results, but trust they are fairly satisfactory.

5. Religious teaching to lads and young women? I have a Bible Class for lads, but cannot secure regular attendance. One for better instructed young women (school teachers and others) is held fortnightly, as a rule. One for the less instructed, monthly as a rule, is less successful.

6. Secondary school in Parish? No.

7. Teaching for Nonconformist children? There is a separate Nonconformist class once a week when the majority of children are taught the Prayer Book. A Nonconformist teacher has taught this class until lately and it is probable that his successor may do so. Otherwise one of the School staff takes it.

8. Organised study for adults? I know of no means of doing so except in the Bible Class already described, which is not confined to <u>young</u> women.

9. Interest in mission? The subject is kept constantly before them in sermons, and also in Bible Class.

10. Voters for Ruridecanal representatives a) men b) women? I fail entirely to create any interest in it, except with the two or three persons who attend the meeting and sign the declaration: but no record has been kept.

11. PCC? No. I have found no desire for such a council, and it would be very difficult to form one, or, if formed, to get it to meet.

1. Population 1,065.
2. John Edward Field graduated from Worcester College Oxford in 1862. He served a series of three curacies and two chaplaincies between 1864 and 1880 and was appointed Vicar of Benson in 1881. He was the author of *The Apostolic Liturgy and the Epistle to the Hebrews* (1881) and *St Berin the Apostle of Wessex* (1902). He was aged 73 in 1914 and at the 1911 census he was living in a household with his wife and an unmarried female servant.

BICESTER[1] Incumbent W. O'Reilly[2]

1. Baptism at morning or evening prayer? Yes, very often at week-day Evensongs.

2. Communion times

a) **Sunday** Every Sunday 8:0, also 1st Sun 12:15. 2nd Sun 7:0.

b) **Ascension Day** 7:30 and 11:00.

c) **Saints Days** 7:30 and 8:15.

d) **Week-days?** 7:30 am Black-letter Saints Days, and other days, by notice.

3. Is Communion ever sung? Yes. On Great Festivals at 11:0. On Saints Days at 8:15 or 9:0.

4. Religious teaching to children a) Church b) Sunday School and c) Day school? i) Clergy teach in Day schools? ii) Religious teaching to Sunday school teachers? iii) Satisfactory results?

Catechism in Church every Sunday. Systematic Instruction on the Faith in Sunday School morning and afternoon. Also in Day Schools. [i–iii] The Clergy teach in the Day Schools 3 or 4 times a week. A Teachers' Class is held weekly by the Clergy for Sunday School Teachers. A slow but gradual improvement is taking place all round, but there is still much to be desired.

5. Religious teaching to lads and young women? Bible Classes are held for each every week.

6. Secondary school in Parish? There is none.

7. Teaching for Nonconformist children? No provision is made: but if it were asked for I should be willing to make it.

8. Organised study for adults? Sermons bearing on Christian dogma are frequently preached.

9. Interest in mission? Yearly sermons: and often additional sermons. A Missionary Guild for work. A Children's Guild, with weekly sewing party, and monthly service of intercession. Missionary Boxes. A Missionary Sale of Work.

10. Voters for Ruridecanal representatives a) men b) women? I do not know. There is no interest taken in the matter. I should think about half a dozen signed the declaration.

11. PCC? Yes. It deals with most matters, except Dogma and Ritual. It has met twice since October.

1. Population 3,385.
2. Walter O'Reilly graduated from Corpus Christi College Cambridge in 1898 and was ordained priest in 1900. He served three curacies between 1899 and 1907 when he was appointed Vicar of Bicester and also Chaplain to the Union Workhouse in Bicester. He was aged 37 in 1914 and at the 1911 census he was living in a household with his wife, four children under 10, and two unmarried servants, a cook and a housemaid.

BINSEY[1]   Incumbent C. A. Heurtley[2]

1. Baptism at morning or **evening prayer?** Yes.

2. Communion times

a) **Sunday** at 11 a.m. on 1st Sunday in each month.

b) **Ascension Day** at 11 a.m.

c) **Saints Days** [*No response*].

d) **Week-days?** [*No response*].

3. Is Communion ever sung? No.

4. Religious teaching to children a) Church b) Sunday School and c) Day school? i) Clergy teach in Day schools? ii) Religious teaching to Sunday school teachers? iii) Satisfactory results?

There is no school – but the few children there are – and the numbers vary from 1 or 2 to 10 or 12 as the families come and go – are taught on Sunday afternoons by the daughter of a principal resident.

5. Religious teaching to lads and young women? There are but 2 or 3 of these, and nothing in the way of religious instruction is given them, beyond the service and sermon in the Parish Church.

6. Secondary school in Parish? No.

7. Teaching for Nonconformist children? There are no Nonconformists.

8. Organised study for adults? No.

9. Interest in mission? Nothing beyond the annual Sermons for S.P.G.

10. Voters for Ruridecanal representatives a) men b) women? None.

11. PCC? No.

1. Population 58.
2. Charles Abel Heurtley graduated from Oriel College Oxford in 1869 and was ordained priest in 1870. After serving two curacies he became Rector of Ashington in 1878 and Rural Dean of Storrington from 1905. He became Vicar of Binsey in 1911. He was aged 68 in 1914 and at the 1911 census he was living in a household with his wife and a female unmarried servant.

BIX[1]   Incumbent C. W. Formby[2]

1. Baptism at morning or evening prayer? No. This has not been carried out here for many years.

2. Communion times

a) **Sunday** 1st and 3rd Sunday after Midday Service, 2nd 4th and 5th at 8 a.m.

b) **Ascension Day** [*No response*].

c) **Saints Days** [*No response*].

d) **Week-days?** [*No response*].

3. Is Communion ever sung? No. Hymns are sung at the Great Festivals at 8. or 7.30 a.m.

4. Religious teaching to children a) Church b) Sunday School and c) Day school? i) Clergy teach in Day schools? ii) Religious teaching to Sunday school teachers? iii) Satisfactory results?

[i] No. <u>Teachers</u> are Rector his wife and two serv[ants] (a) A children's service is held in Church about 4 times a year on account of the scattered population. A more frequent service has been found difficult to maintain. Only a very [few] attending. I have tried it. (b) Sunday School every Sunday at 10 am (c) The religious instruction given in the Council School is very sound all teachers being Church people. Our reports [are] good compared with other parishes – large town parishes in which I have worked [–] the children here are I think considerably above the average in their religious knowledge. We aim at <u>in Sunday School</u> <u>Catechism</u> by memory top classes do explanation of catechism. <u>Bible lesson</u> based on stamp pictures. About ½ do Collects learned <u>over and over</u> again specially and given for use as prayer throughout life.

5. Religious teaching to lads and young women? Now that our Parish Room is completed I hope that a class of Elder lads on a weekday evening may be possible. For girls a flourishing Branch of G.F.S.

6. Secondary school in Parish? No.

7. Teaching for Nonconformist children? Council School. There is no nonconformist child in our school.

8. Organised study for adults? There is a good Branch of M.U. – but beyond this No not at present. We have this matter in view and hope to form a Branch of C.E.M.S from which some systematic Bible feeding may be possible. The Mothers Meeting have this advantage the population here being labourers mainly are not capable of much study.

9. Interest in mission? A Missionary Association is being formed. "The Church Abroad" is circulated. Special sermons describing the current conditions of missionary work are preached quarterly. S.P.G. Intercession Service is used periodically in Church. Collections every other month for S.P.G.

10. Voters for Ruridecanal representatives a) men b) women? I received no information on this matter from my predecessor. I can find no register.

11. PCC? No.

1. Population 400.
2. Charles Wykeham Formby graduated from Keble College Oxford in 1886 and was ordained priest in 1893. After serving two curacies he was Rector of Ravenstone 1903–08 and Barlborough between 1908 and 1911, when he was appointed as Rector of Bix. He was the author of *Education and Modern Secularism* (1896) and *Re-creation* (1907). He was aged 49 in 1914 and at the 1911 census he was living in a household with his wife and two female servants: a married cook and an unmarried housemaid.

BLACKBOURTON[1]   Incumbent H. O. Shore[2]

1. Baptism at morning or evening prayer? No.

2. Communion times

a) **Sunday** 8.0 also 12.0 on 1st Sunday.

b) **Ascension Day** 8.0.

c) **Saints Days** 8.0.

d) **Week-days?** [*No response*].

3. Is Communion ever sung? No.

4. Religious teaching to children a) Church b) Sunday School and c) Day school? i) Clergy teach in Day schools? ii) Religious teaching to Sunday school teachers? iii) Satisfactory results?

(a) Every Sunday afternoon there is a children's service in the Church. There is also Sunday School which is held in the Day School at 10 a.m. I teach once a week in the Day school.

5. Religious teaching to lads and young women? There are lectures in the school during the winter months on Temperance, Missions, etc.

6. Secondary school in Parish? No.

7. Teaching for Nonconformist children? No.

8. Organised study for adults? [*No response*].

9. Interest in mission? Lantern lectures, and Special Sermons are preached. Special prayers for missions are said every Sunday.

10. Voters for Ruridecanal representatives a) men b) women? [*No response*].

11. PCC? No.

1. Population about 600.
2. Harrington Offley Shore graduated from Emmanuel College Cambridge in 1896 and then trained at Ely College, being ordained priest in 1901. He served three curacies between 1893 and 1913, when he was appointed as Vicar of Black Bourton. He was 46 years of age in 1914 and according to the 1911 census summary books he was the only male in a six-person household.

BLETCHINGDON[1]   Incumbent C. J. Ball[2]

1. Baptism at morning or evening prayer? Rarely.

2. Communion times

a) Sunday 8 a.m. usually. After Mattins on 1st Sunday in month.

b) Ascension Day 8 a.m., and after Mattins.

c) Saints Days 8 a.m. occasionally.

d) Week-days? Never.

3. Is Communion ever sung? After Mattins always. 11.45.

4. Religious teaching to children a) Church b) Sunday School and c) Day school? i) Clergy teach in Day schools? ii) Religious teaching to Sunday school teachers? iii) Satisfactory results?

[i] No. [ii] Nothing special. All are instructed Commun[icants] [iii] Things are improving. The outlook is far from hopeless. (a) Sermon to children on certain days. Occasional catechising. (b) Sunday school before Mattins. (c) Daily Prayers and Hymns. Lessons by Teachers (all churchpe[ople]).

5. Religious teaching to lads and young women? Not many lads or young women (except the feeble minded) stay in this decaying village. The young people attend the services of the church better than their elders.

6. Secondary school in Parish? No.

7. Teaching for Nonconformist children? Nonconformity is hardly in evidence here. There are not six Dissenting families in the place, and not six children belonging to such in the School (which is not Church property but belongs to the Bletchingdon Charity). The question of specific religious teaching has never been raised so far as I am aware.

8. Organised study for adults? No. This is a purely agricultural parish, and no sort of study is popular.

9. Interest in mission? We have sermons for S.P.G etc. and collect what we can. The people are, for the most part, miserably poor.

10. Voters for Ruridecanal representatives a) men b) women? None that I know of.

11. PCC? No.

1. Population 488.
2. Charles James Ball graduated from Queen's College Oxford in 1872 and was awarded a DLitt in 1910. He was ordained priest in 1875 and occupied two curacies between 1874 and 1876, when he became a schoolmaster at Merchant Taylors' School. He was Censor and Chaplain of King's College London 1878–79 and of Lincoln's Inn 1880–1900. He was appointed Rector of Bletchingdon in 1899 and was also Lecturer in Assyriology at Oxford in 1906. He was 63 in 1914 and at the 1911 census he was living in a household with his wife and two servants: a cook who was a widow and an unmarried house parlourmaid.

BLOXHAM[1]   **Incumbent C. H. Verey**[2]

1. Baptism at morning or evening prayer? No.

2. Communion times

a) Sunday 8 am, also at 7am 1st Sunday and 12 noon 3rd Sunday.

b) Ascension Day 6 am and 8 am.

c) Saints Days 8 am.

d) Week-days? 8 am one day in the week during Lent and advent.

3. Is Communion ever sung? Occasionally. 8 am.

4. Religious teaching to children a) Church b) Sunday School and c) Day school? i) Clergy teach in Day schools? ii) Religious teaching to Sunday school teachers? iii) Satisfactory results?

(a) The children come to church on Ascension Day and every Sunday morning. There is a children's service with catechising every other Sunday afternoon. (b)

Sunday School every Sunday at 10 am every other Sunday. (c) The Diocesan Syllabus is taught every School morning from 9 am til 9.45 am

[i–iii] Yes. One day a week. A regular course is always taken in the Sunday School and the teachers are given books for their instruction. The results are fairly satisfactory, the chief cause of dissatisfaction is that the children leave the Sunday School as soon as they leave the Day School.

5. Religious teaching to lads and young women? Confirmation classes. Bible classes, Communicants preparation service.

6. Secondary school in Parish? All Saints School: (one of the Woodward schools) Catholic Church Teaching.

7. Teaching for Nonconformist children? No.

8. Organised study for adults? C.E.M.S. Prayer and Bible study during the winter months.

9. Interest in mission? Missionary Sermons, Meetings, Kings Messengers, Study Circle.

10. Voters for Ruridecanal representatives a) men b) women? No records have been kept.

11. PCC? No. Meetings of Churchwardens and Sidesmen take the place of it.

1. Population 1,335.
2. Cecil Henry Verey graduated from Trinity Hall Cambridge in 1896 and trained at Cuddesdon in 1897. He was ordained priest in 1900 and held two curacies between 1898 and 1908 when he was appointed as Vicar of Bloxham. He was aged 41 in 1914 and at the 1911 census he was living in a household with three unmarried female servants: a cook and two maids.

BODICOTE[1]   Incumbent H. N. Fowler[2]

1. Baptism at morning or evening prayer? Occasionally at Evening Prayer. Usually at a Children's Service.

2. Communion times

a) **Sunday** 7 a.m. and noon on 1st S. 8a.m. on 2nd, 4th, and 5th, noon on 3rd.

b) **Ascension Day** 7 a.m.

c) **Saints Days** 8 a.m. on some (not all) Saints' Days.

d) **Week-days?** None.

3. Is Communion ever sung? Yes. 8 a.m. on Great Festivals.

4. Religious teaching to children a) Church b) Sunday School and c) Day school? i) Clergy teach in Day schools? ii) Religious teaching to Sunday school teachers? iii) Satisfactory results?

1. (a) Children's Services at 2.30 p.m. on 1st and 3rd Sundays. (b) Sunday School at 10 and 2.30. (c) Daily at usual time i.e. till 9.45. 2. In Day Schools the Vicar takes a class regularly on Wednesdays: also at other times occasionally. 3. Very little. 4. I have not been here long enough to give directly an answer to this question. The School gets excellent reports from the Diocesan Inspector and their knowledge of Religious Subjects is decidedly above the average.

5. Religious teaching to lads and young women? Confirmation classes.

6. Secondary school in Parish? No.

7. Teaching for Nonconformist children? No: there would be no doubt, if required.

8. Organised study for adults? Mothers Union. Services and Meetings. C.E.F.S. Meetings etc.

9. Interest in mission? Sermons. Meetings on subject of Foreign and Home Missions. Distribution of leaflets etc. Subject brought before people at private visits.

10. Voters for Ruridecanal representatives a) men b) women? None, as far as I know.

11. PCC? No.

1. Population 657.
2. Hugh Newell Fowler graduated from New College Oxford in 1876 and was ordained priest in 1879. He was Assistant Master at Malvern College 1876–88 and Rector of Coryton 1904 to 1912, when he became Vicar of Bodicote. He was 60 in 1914 and at the 1911 census he was living in a household with his wife, a 23-year-old daughter and two unmarried female servants, a cook and a housemaid.

BOURTON, GREAT[1]   Incumbent S. R. Standage[2]

1. Baptism at morning or evening prayer? Have not had a case for some years now.

2. Communion times

a) Sunday On 1st and 3rd at midday, on 2nd, 4th and 5th at 8 am.

b) Ascension Day At 11.

c) Saints Days [*No response*].

d) Week-days? [*No response*].

3. Is Communion ever sung? No.

4. Religious teaching to children a) Church b) Sunday School and c) Day school? i) Clergy teach in Day schools? ii) Religious teaching to Sunday school teachers? iii) Satisfactory results?

There are occasionally Children's Services in Church but I do not find them as satisfactory as the normal Sunday School. We have always had Sunday School at 10 and 2 and for over 22 years I have always taught the Upper Group both M and A. [i–iii] In the Day School there is religious instruction for 40 min and I go and take it twice a week. Sunday School Teachers are at present confined to myself, wife and daughter, and I am fairly satisfied with the results.

5. Religious teaching to lads and young women? Nothing definitely.

6. Secondary school in Parish? No other School.

7. Teaching for Nonconformist children? I don't think so.

8. Organised study for adults? No.

9. Interest in mission? By Meetings and Sermons.

10. Voters for Ruridecanal representatives a) men b) women? None.

11. PCC? No.

1. Population 406.
2. Samuel Ray Standage was ordained priest in 1883. He was Assistant Master of Ardingley College Sussex 1881–85, Curate of Deddington 1885–88, and Steeple Aston 1888–91. He became Vicar of Claydon in 1891 and moved to be Vicar of Great Bourton in 1904. He was aged 58 in 1914 and at the 1911 census he was living in a household with his wife and four children: three daughters, aged between 10 and 15, and a 2-year-old son, together with an unmarried female servant.

BRADWELL WITH KELMSCOT[1]   Incumbent H. T. Adams[2]

1. Baptism at morning or evening prayer? What Baptisms I have had have been at the Children's Services.

2. Communion times

a) Sunday At Bradwell Alternate Sundays 8.30 am and 12 except 4th Sunday in month. At Kelmscott 1st Sunday in month.

b) Ascension Day 11.0 am at Bradwell.

c) Saints Days No Celebration.

d) Week-days? No Celebration.

3. Is Communion ever sung? No.

4. Religious teaching to children a) Church b) Sunday School and c) Day school? i) Clergy teach in Day schools? ii) Religious teaching to Sunday school teachers? iii) Satisfactory results?

At Bradwell there is Sunday School twice a Sundays, Children's Service on the 1st Sunday in the Month. At Kelmscott there is Sunday School once on the Sunday and Children's S. Service the 2nd Sunday in the month. [i–iii] I occasionally go to the Day School and take the Upper Division and hope to do this more regularly. The Sunday School Teachers prepare their own work. The Children at Bradwell are bright, intelligent and are getting on well with their work. The Children at Kelmscott are improving and there are intelligent ones among them. I use the Stamp system (Home Words Series) and in this, they all take a great interest.

5. Religious teaching to lads and young women? There is a branch of the Girls Friendly Society and Kings Messengers. A Bible Class for the young men of Bradwell and Kencot, held at Kencot.

6. Secondary school in Parish? No.

7. Teaching for Nonconformist children? No.

8. Organised study for adults? No.

9. Interest in mission? There is a Missionary meeting and Sermons are preached on the subject of Foreign and Home Missions.

10. Voters for Ruridecanal representatives a) men b) women? None.

11. PCC? No.

1. Also known as Broadwell. Population 98.
2. Henry Theophilus Adams trained at Sarum College in 1894 and occupied two curacies between 1896 and 1900 when he was appointed Vicar of Newbold Pacey. He moved in 1912 to become Vicar of Bradwell. He was aged 42 in 1914 and at the 1911 census he was living in a household with his wife, three children under 10, and two unmarried female servants.

BRIGHTWELL BALDWIN[1] Incumbent T. Hainsworth[2]

1. Baptism at morning or evening prayer? Holy Baptism is usually administered during Evening Prayer on Sundays.

2. Communion times

a) Sunday at 8.0 a.m. 1st Sunday in the Month 11.00 a.m.

b) Ascension Day 7.30 and 10.0 a.m.

c) Saints Days 7.30 a.m.

d) Week-days? [*No response*].

3. Is Communion ever sung? [*No response*].

4. Religious teaching to children a) Church b) Sunday School and c) Day school? i) Clergy teach in Day schools? ii) Religious teaching to Sunday school teachers? iii) Satisfactory results?

b. Sunday School each Sunday 10 o'clock to 11 o'clock c. Religious instruction in day school every morning 9.0 to 9.45 which is taken by me each Friday morning. There are no Sunday School Teachers.

5. Religious teaching to lads and young women? Mens Bible Class Sunday Afternoons 2.0 to 3.0 Confirmation Classes.

6. Secondary school in Parish? None.

7. Teaching for Nonconformist children? The School is a Council School.

8. Organised study for adults? [*No response*].

9. Interest in mission? Missionary Sermons and Meeting.

10. Voters for Ruridecanal representatives a) men b) women? [*No response*].

11. PCC? Business of the Church conducted by Rector and Church wardens.

1. Population 187.
2. Thomas Hainsworth trained at the Dorchester Missionary College and was ordained priest in 1892. He was a missionary in southern Africa 1892–1901, Priest in Charge of Lorenco Marques 1901–07, and then held curacies in Barnsley 1907–10 and in Raistrick between 1910 and 1913 when he became Rector of Brightwell Baldwin.

BRITWELL SALOME WITH BRITWELL PRIOR[1]   Incumbent J. C. Mansfield[2]

1. Baptism at morning or evening prayer? Always after 2nd Lesson and Evening Prayer <u>is the rule</u>.

2. Communion times

a) **Sunday** at Morning Prayer on 1st, 3rd 4th and 5th Sundays. At 8 am on the 2nd Sunday.

b) **Ascension Day** at 8 am.

c) **Saints Days** on some at 8 am.

d) **Week-days?** none on week days.

3. Is Communion ever sung? No. I have one boy of suitable age for choir. Unfortunately no voice. I had a fine 4 part choir some years ago trained in both voice production and sight reading by myself – but now have no material in this little parish.

4. Religious teaching to children a) Church b) Sunday School and c) Day school? i) Clergy teach in Day schools? ii) Religious teaching to Sunday school teachers? iii) Satisfactory results?

The sum total of children in three parishes from 14 to 5 is not above 20. (a) Sunday School from 10.15 to 10.45 on Sundays. (b) There is no Day School. The children attend Brightwell Baldwin Schools. (c) There are no Sunday School teachers to be got. I have to do what teaching is to be done. I have a class for children in the Parish Room on weekdays in the winter and also on Sunday Evenings where children with others are taught religious instruction and [singing].

5. Religious teaching to lads and young women? There are no unmarried young women. They leave this parish for situations at 14 years – There are as a rule no more than 4 or 5 lads on the farms. No other industry.

6. Secondary school in Parish? No.

7. Teaching for Nonconformist children? No school of any kind.

8. Organised study for adults? No special classes. All the Church people here are poor labourers on the farms. The farmer is a dissenter.

9. Interest in mission? No special meetings.

10. Voters for Ruridecanal representatives a) men b) women? [*No response*].

11. PCC? No.

1. Population 126.
2. Joseph Charles Mansfield graduated from the Royal University of Ireland in 1888 and was awarded AKC in 1890. He was ordained priest in 1891 and occupied three curacies until his appointment as Rector of Britwell Salome in 1898. He was aged 52 in 1914 and at the 1911 census he was living in a household with his wife, three pupils and two unmarried female servants: a cook and a housemaid, both 14 years of age.

BRIZENORTON[1]   Incumbent T. W. Sturgiss[2]

1. Baptism at morning or evening prayer? No. Taken at Children's Service in afternoon.

2. Communion times

a) Sunday 8 am Except 3rd Sunday and then at 11.0.

b) Ascension Day 8 am.

c) Saints Days 8 am.

d) **Week-days?** None.

3. Is Communion ever sung? 11 am service. Not to a Set Service, but a Hymn during celebration and at Cleansing of Vessels and Nunc Dim on leaving.

4. Religious teaching to children a) Church b) Sunday School and c) Day school? i) Clergy teach in Day schools? ii) Religious teaching to Sunday school teachers? iii) Satisfactory results?

In Church on 3rd Sunday I catechise Sunday Schools every Sunday afternoon. We have a Council School and I do not teach there. The teachers are good and well instructed persons. The teaching is chiefly on the prayer book. It is good but not entirely satisfactory. We greatly miss regular religious teaching which I have for nearly 40 years given in the day schools before I came here. There is little foundation of Bible history to build upon.

5. Religious teaching to lads and young women? Nothing beyond sermons.

6. Secondary school in Parish? No.

7. Teaching for Nonconformist children? This has been a Council School since 1875.

8. Organised study for adults? Not regularly. I have Communicant Classes during Lent.

9. Interest in mission? Prayers for Missions are said in Church and copies of prayers are given to Communicants. We had a Mission Study Circle last winter when 10 persons attended.

10. Voters for Ruridecanal representatives a) men b) women? None so far as I know.

11. PCC? No. We have periodical meetings of the 2 wardens and four sidesmen to discuss parish financial affairs.

1. Population 511.
2. Thomas William Sturgiss trained at Lichfield College in 1875 and was ordained priest in 1878. He was awarded a BA by Trinity College Dublin in 1887. He occupied two curacies between 1877 and 1887, when he was appointed Vicar of Marston, moving in 1912 to become Vicar of Brize Norton. He was the author of *The Poultry Manual* (1909). He was aged 60 in 1914 and at the 1911 census he was living in a household with his wife and an unmarried female servant.

BROUGHTON[1]   Incumbent B. W. Bradford[2]

1. Baptism at morning or evening prayer? Very occasionally.

2. Communion times

a) **Sunday** 11a.m 1st S. in month, 8 a.m. 3rd S. in month.

b) **Ascension Day** 8. am.

c) **Saints Days** [*No response*].

d) **Week-days?** [*No response*].

3. Is Communion ever sung? No.

4. Religious teaching to children a) Church b) Sunday School and c) Day school? i) Clergy teach in Day schools? ii) Religious teaching to Sunday school teachers? iii) Satisfactory results?

(a) Nothing in Church (b) After the teaching for the Day a lesson is given based on 'The Young Churchman' published by Home Words Ltd (c) I teach in the N. Newington School each Monday morning. The Headmaster and Mistress are both excellent Church people. The Sunday School Teachers are given copies of 'The Young Churchman' I find the lessons excite far more interest than former efforts, and the Sunday School has increased in size considerably these last few years. Of the after results it is difficult to speak with certainty. I find that almost all old Sunday Scholars present themselves for Confirmation.

5. Religious teaching to lads and young women? Nothing.

6. Secondary school in Parish? No.

7. Teaching for Nonconformist children? It has never been asked for. The Bishop's prize has twice in the last 14 years been won by children of the chief Dissenter in the Parish.

8. Organised study for adults? No.

9. Interest in mission? Missionary Meetings are held.

10. Voters for Ruridecanal representatives a) men b) women? I cannot state numbers. Not many attended the meeting at which they were requested to sign.

11. PCC? No.

1. Population 499.
2. Basil Wyatt Bradford graduated from Brasenose College Oxford in 1892 and then trained at Sarum College. He was ordained priest in 1894 and occupied a curacy between 1893 and 1896 when he was appointed Assistant Master at Elstree School. He was appointed Curate of Broughton in 1900 and then as Rector of the same parish in 1906. He was aged 44 in 1914 and at the 1911 census he lived in a household with a widowed cook and two unmarried female servants.

BROUGHTON POGIS[1]   Incumbent W. P. Roberts[2]

1. Baptism at morning or evening prayer? Yes and I prefer these times.

2. Communion times

a) Sunday 1st Sunday in month after M.P. 3rd S. at 8 am.

b) Ascension Day 8 am.

c) Saints Days Not usual unless for special purpose.

d) Week-days? Not at all.

3. Is Communion ever sung? No.

4. Religious teaching to children a) Church b) Sunday School and c) Day school? i) Clergy teach in Day schools? ii) Religious teaching to Sunday school teachers? iii) Satisfactory results?

We have a Sunday School in the Parish which is well attended for the size of this place. My wife and a lady helper take this S. School. I teach in the Broughton-cum-Filkins Day School once a week – this is not in our own Parish but in Filkins – The majority of the Children who attend come from Filkins and the Vicar of Filkins has more to do with the Supervision of the Day School than myself as it is in his Parish.

5. Religious teaching to lads and young women? We have a Missionary Meeting for young people once a week – where they make baskets etc in aid of Missions – and have lectures about S.P.G. work. This is during the winter months. This helps to support an Indian Child. There is a G.F.S. Branch – Mothers Union Branch which causes parents to look after childrens spiritual life.

6. Secondary school in Parish? No.

7. Teaching for Nonconformist children? Our school is in Filkins.

8. Organised study for adults? Our Parish is very small 82 last Census – We do what we can but of course under the circumstances elaborate organisations are out of the question.

9. Interest in mission? I lay special stress in preaching on this point.

10. Voters for Ruridecanal representatives a) men b) women? None.

11. PCC? No.

[*Signed*] Your Lordship's faithful and obedient servant in Christ.

1. Population 86.
2. William Prowting Roberts trained at Sarum College in 1898 and was ordained priest in 1901 having previously served as a Captain in the Hampshire Regiment. He was Curate of Egremont 1900–02 and Vicar of Dunkeswell Abbey from 1903 to 1909, when he became Rector of Broughton Pogis. He was aged 49 in 1914 and at the 1911 census he lived in a household with his wife and three unmarried female servants.

BUCKNELL[1]   Incumbent W. S. Harris[2]

1. Baptism at morning or evening prayer? In afternoon – Sunday Catechism. All the children are present and a number of adults.

2. Communion times

a) **Sunday** 8.30 + 11.0 (sung) on 1st Sunday in month.

b) **Ascension Day** 8.30.

c) **Saints Days** 9.0.

d) **Week-days?** 8.30.

3. Is Communion ever sung? Yes. (i) On the 1st Sunday in each month at 11.0 (ii) On the Great Festivals at 8.30. (iii) On all the Holy Days at 9.0 – when the school children are present.

4. Religious teaching to children a) Church b) Sunday School and c) Day school? i) Clergy teach in Day schools? ii) Religious teaching to Sunday school teachers? iii) Satisfactory results?

(a.) 'Catechism' by the Rector every Sunday afternoon. Holy Eucharist on Saints Days. All the children in the parish attend. (b.) No Sunday School. (c.) Daily Instruction in Day Schools from 9 to 9.40. [i–iii] The teaching in the Day School is very carefully and conscientiously carried out [by the] Head and Assistant Teachers.

5. Religious teaching to lads and young women? Nothing special – Confirmation classes and Instruction in Advent and Lent.

6. Secondary school in Parish? No.

7. Teaching for Nonconformist children? There are no Nonconformists.

8. Organised study for adults? Nothing special.

9. Interest in mission? Sermons, addresses and Lectures (Lantern etc) upon Missionary Work.

10. Voters for Ruridecanal representatives a) men b) women? I have no information.

11. PCC? No.

1. Population 221.
2. William Stuart Harris graduated from Trinity College Cambridge in 1876 and was awarded an honorary DD by the University of Aberdeen in 1903. He was ordained priest in 1877 and then served as a chaplain in the Royal Navy between 1879 and 1900. He was present at the bombardment of Alexandria in 1882, and after chaplaincies in various ships he was appointed Chaplain of the Fleet 1901–06 and Archdeacon for the Royal Navy 1902–06. Between 1902 and 1910 he was Honorary Chaplain to King Edward VII. He was Rector of

Dene 1906–10 and then Vicar of Etwall between 1910 and 1913 when he was appointed as Rector of Bucknell. He was 60 years of age in 1914 and at the 1911 census lived in a household with his wife, a son and a daughter in their early twenties, and two unmarried female servants.

BURFORD WITH FULBROOK[1]   Incumbent W. C. Emeris[2]

1. Baptism at morning or evening prayer? Occasionally at Evensong on weekdays.

2. Communion times

a) Sunday 8 am.

b) Ascension Day 6 am and 8 am.

c) Saints Days 8 am.

d) Week-days? Burford Wednesdays 8 am. Fulbrook Fridays 8 am.

3. Is Communion ever sung? Yes. On the Greater Festivals after Matins (one Service) at 10.30 am. On First Sunday in each month (separate Service) at 11 am.

4. Religious teaching to children a) Church b) Sunday School and c) Day school? i) Clergy teach in Day schools? ii) Religious teaching to Sunday school teachers? iii) Satisfactory results?

(a) There is a Children's Service each Sunday afternoon except on the first Sunday in the month. This Service I take myself and Catechise the children on the Lesson they have been taught in the Morning School. We also have Special Services for Children on Ash Wednesday, Good Friday, Ascension Day and occasionally on other week days at 5 pm. At Fulbrook there is a Children's Service in the afternoon on the 3rd Sunday in each month and 4 times in the year the children come to Church for a short Service instead of receiving Religious Instruction in School. (b) Sunday School is held every Sunday at 10 am and on the first Sunday in the month at 2.30 pm also. At Fulbrook Sunday School is held every Sunday at 10.00 except as stated above on the 3rd Sunday in the month. Potter and Sheard's Catechizings for Church Sunday Schools are used. (c) At Burford there are Council Schools and therefore only the County Council Syllabus can be taught. I have reason to believe that the Instruction is good.

At Fulbrook the Diocesan Syllabus is followed in the Church School there and the Reports of the Diocesan Inspectors have always been excellent. [i–iii] The Vicar teaches at Fulbrook School every Friday morning and the Curate generally on Tuesdays. Occasional classes are held for the Instruction of the Sunday School Teachers. On the whole the Results are encouraging. It is very difficult to keep the older boys and girls in the Sunday School[s] up to the time when they are confirmed.

5. Religious teaching to lads and young women? A class is held by the Rev A L Gutch for older lads on Sunday afternoons. A class for young women and older girls has been held at the Vicarage until the last two months. The lady who took the class has now left the town and other arrangements will have to be made.

6. Secondary school in Parish? Yes. The boys are given Bible Lessons and those whose Parents wish it are taught the Church Catechism by the Headmaster. When boys come to me to be prepared for Confirmation I find them well grounded in religious knowledge and they generally know their Catechism well. The boys attend Church regularly twice each Sunday and also on Ash Wednesday and Ascension Day at 11 a.m.

7. Teaching for Nonconformist children? [*No response*].

8. Organised study for adults? I have been thinking of starting a class for this purpose.

9. Interest in mission? We have a parochial Missionary Committee. The Church Abroad is circulated with the Deanery Magazine. There are Missionary Sermons and Meetings from time to time. Missionary Intercessions are offered after Evensong on Saturday evenings, occasionally on Sunday evenings and during Lent a short Service of Intercession at Noon was held once a week. Study Circles have been held. There is a Missionary Library.

10. Voters for Ruridecanal representatives a) men b) women? About 25.

11. PCC? No.

1. Population 1,591.
2. William Charles Emeris graduated from New College Oxford in 1886 and was ordained priest in 1889. After serving two curacies 1888–96 he was Vicar of Taynton and Great Barrington in Gloucestershire 1896–1907. In 1907 he was appointed as Vicar of Burford. He was 50 years old in 1914 and at the 1911 census he lived in a household with his elder sister and three female servants, one a widow and two unmarried.

CADMORE END[1]   Incumbent H. F. P. Davson[2]

1. Baptism at morning or evening prayer? We always endeavour to have one each year but most people prefer 3.30 pm.

2. Communion times

a) Sunday First in month 11.45. Second 8.0 am. Third 11.45. Fourth 8.0 am.

b) Ascension Day 8.0 am.

c) Saints Days [*No response*].

d) Week-days? None.

Easter Sunday, Christmas Day, Whitsunday and Harvest Festival 7.0 am 8.0 am and 11.45.

3. Is Communion ever sung? Yes. First Sunday in the month. 11.45.

4. Religious teaching to children a) Church b) Sunday School and c) Day school? i) Clergy teach in Day schools? ii) Religious teaching to Sunday school teachers? iii) Satisfactory results?

No. We attend meetings of the Wycombe Deanery Sunday School [Association]. Well satisfied. (a) Catechising on the great Festivals (See Note below.) (b) Sunday School is held on every Sunday at ten o'clock and Instruction is given by myself with the Day School Teachers. The latter are excellent churchwomen and during many vacancies in the Living in the course of the last 20 years the Head Teacher has kept the Sunday School together and never allowed the work to flag. Sunday School is attended by every child in the parish and the attendance is most regular. (c) The Religious Instruction is given by the Day School Teacher to whom reference has been made above. The School is well reported on by the Diocesan Inspectors. One of the great difficulties in this parish is to get people of any age to turn out for classes or services in the afternoon; many live across the common some miles and if they come morning and evening are reluctant to turn out in the afternoon and though I have tried regular Childrens' Services they are never successful as it is seldom possible to get more than half a dozen children. The same remark applies to classes, the young men saying they think if they come to church morning and evening they ought to have the afternoon free. The Morning and Evening Services are always well attended the children coming straight from Sunday School in the morning and the adults attending Morning and Evening in large numbers.

5. Religious teaching to lads and young women? Great stress is laid on confirmation preparation and the Communicants Guild monthly meetings are a great help in this respect especially the provision made for the asking of questions. This Guild now has a membership of over 80. I enclose a copy of the Rules[3] for your Lordship's perusal and information as I think [it] explains the objects of the Guild and the methods of its working more clearly than I could do in this space. The Guild numbers as many men as women and nearly all the young men.

6. Secondary school in Parish? No.

7. Teaching for Nonconformist children? There is only one Nonconformist family in the parish and they are satisfied with the religious instruction given. Should the question ever be raised I feel sure the Managers would raise no objection to any Nonconformist giving teaching to children of their own denomination, but it would be difficult to find a person qualified to do so.

8. Organised study for adults? Church History Classes have been held and much Church Defence Work has been done in the parish in the past year with very encouraging results.

9. Interest in mission? We take our part in the work of the Missionary Forward Movement of the Wycombe Deanery, Meetings are held from time to time in the parish at which addresses are given and constant pulpit references are made to this important subject.

10. Voters for Ruridecanal representatives a) men b) women? Eight.

11. PCC? No.

1. Population 290.
2. Herman Francis Prideaux Davson graduated from Pembroke College Oxford in 1892 after a distinguished undergraduate career in which he was awarded four university prizes. In 1895 he was awarded AKC First Class: a BD followed in 1908. He was ordained priest in 1896 and after serving a curacy at Brill he became Vicar of Worminghall in 1900. He was appointed as Vicar of Cadmore End in 1910. He was 41 in 1914 and at the 1911 census he lived in a household with his wife and one unmarried female servant.
3. This document is not preserved with the returns.

CASSINGTON[1]   Incumbent G. W. C. Ward[2]

1. Baptism at morning or evening prayer? Not at present. But all the scholars and 10 to 30 adults always present.

2. Communion times

a) Sunday 8am except 1st Sun. when 11. Holy days 8 and 11.

b) Ascension Day 8 am.

c) Saints Days not at present excep. annunc. at 9.30.

d) Week-days? No.

3. Is Communion ever sung? Not yet. (Hymns used).

4. Religious teaching to children a) Church b) Sunday School and c) Day school? i) Clergy teach in Day schools? ii) Religious teaching to Sunday school teachers? iii) Satisfactory results?

In church there is a little catechism every Sunday at 3.15 pm and occasionally at 11 a.m. on Sunday, also on Wednesday and Ascension Day at 11 a.m. In Sunday School there is always a little talk to all with questions by clergy or teachers at 10 a.m. and 2.30. There are 6 classes, two with one teacher, 4 with a teacher at 10 and another teacher at 2.30 pm. [i–iii] In the Day schools there are 3 classes from 9.10 (after the authorised little services) till 9.45. The vicar took the 1st class 5 times a week for 4 years, for the last years 4 times a week. Very occasionally the Sunday School Teachers attend a R. Decanal Lecture on Model Lesson. The Diocesan Inspector's Report this {year month} [sic] and usually was T.S. (Thoroughly Satisfactory). I myself think, till the scholars leave day school (nearly always at 13 years) there is a good religious and moral tone a moderate amount of religious knowledge with a considerable degree of intelligence. Out and out backsliders afterwards are not numerous.

5. Religious teaching to lads and young women? Several of the lads and girls stay on at Sunday School after they leave the day school. Occasionally lads attend the mens' meeting (at 1.30 on Sunday winter and summer.) Besides this, annual confirmation courses (8 weeks or 10) there is not much actual instruction outside church sermons.

6. Secondary school in Parish? No secondary school.

7. Teaching for Nonconformist children? There is only one family of nonconformist children. I myself always recognise their tenets in my teaching and they attend our morning Sunday School. The only other "provision" made is that if there were any to teach them they would be heartily welcome.

8. Organised study for adults? Books recommended and lent. There is in winter every week or fortnight a mutual Improvement Lecture for both sexes wh. sometimes teaches some of the principles more or less indirectly. Tracts or leaflets delivered on special subjects occasionally delivered and at every house. Mothers Union Quarterly circulated.

9. Interest in mission? The S.P.G "monthly" "Church Abroad" is sent to every home and given and explained to every Sunday Scholar. Foreign Missions are touched on in the Day School Teaching; sermons sometimes. Authorised days of prayer observed.

10. Voters for Ruridecanal representatives a) men b) women? 8 men – no women yet.

11. PCC? No. We talk things over at the Easter vestry meeting, men's meeting, mothers' meeting. Nothing of any sort is ever done without being fully explained morning and evening on Sunday from the pulpit and one or more weeks allowed for anyone, as invited, to criticise. If any individual makes a suggestion it has always been possible (for 5 years of my incumbency) to carry it out.

1. Population 296.
2. George William Crofts Ward graduated from St John's College Cambridge in 1883 and was ordained priest in 1885. He served three curacies and also a year as Vicar of Albrighton between 1884 and 1900, when he was appointed Vicar of Carsington Derbys. He moved to become Vicar of Cassington in 1909. He was 59 years old in 1914 and at the 1911 census he lived in a household with his wife and two female domestic servants.

CAVERSHAM[1]   Incumbent C. W. E. Cleaver[2]

1. Baptism at morning or evening prayer? Very occasionally on a weekday. It is administered at the Children's Service.

2. Communion times

a) Sunday (1) 7 and 8 and on 1st S. 8 and 12.15 (2) 7, 8, 9.30, 11 (3) 8 and 10 (4) 8 and on 1st S. 12 as well.[3]

b) Ascension Day (1) 6 and 8, and in the other churches at various times (early).

c) Saints Days 8 in all churches.

d) Week-days? Parish Church Tues 7 and Thurs 8. In two of the other Churches daily.

3. Is Communion ever sung? St John's Every Sunday at 9.30 and 11 am. St Andrew's (Every Sunday) at 10 am.

4. Religious teaching to children a) Church b) Sunday School and c) Day school? i) Clergy teach in Day schools? ii) Religious teaching to Sunday school teachers? iii) Satisfactory results?

(a) Catechising every Sunday in all our churches. (b) Sunday School classes in all four districts every Sunday. (c) Religious Instruction given daily in our Day Schools which are three in number. [i–iii] Each of the clergy as a rule teach twice a week. Preparation classes for Sunday School Teachers are held fortnightly by myself. The results obtained by our Sunday School Teachers are only fair owing to the very serious difficulty of securing men and women of education.

5. Religious teaching to lads and young women? Bible Classes and Guilds are provided. Lads leaving Sunday School are being well looked after from then until they reach the age of 18 and even after that age.

6. Secondary school in Parish? No excepting Queen Anne's School which has its own Chaplain.

7. Teaching for Nonconformist children? The Clergy are not permitted to give instruction in the one Council School in Caversham.

8. Organised study for adults? Yes among members of C.E.M.S. Three sisters of the Community of St Peter Kilburn[4] now hold several classes for women and elder girls weekly. There are also, during the winter, Mission Services with Instruction weekly.

9. Interest in mission? We have a Missionary Union which holds quarterly meetings and has an annual Sale of Work. Missionary Magazines and Monthly Intercession Papers are distributed. Quarterly deputation from Individual Missions S.P.G. We have regular meetings every week for Kings Messengers S.P.G.

10. Voters for Ruridecanal representatives a) men b) women? Nothing has been done as yet.

11. PCC? Mr Brancker priest in charge of St Andrew's has a Church Council. It is simply advisory. It has met several times since last October.

1. Population 10,000.
2. Charles William Euseby Cleaver graduated from Christ Church Oxford in 1885 and was ordained priest in 1887. He served two curacies between 1886 and 1898, when he

was appointed Vicar of Caversham. He was 52 in 1914 and at the 1911 census he lived in a household with his wife, a female friend and three unmarried female domestic servants.

3. Caversham had four churches and the numbers in brackets probably refer in numerical order to St Peter's (the parish church), St Andrew's, St John's Lower Caversham and St Barnabas Emmer Green.

4. One of a series of Anglo-Catholic Sisterhoods founded in the mid-nineteenth century, in 1861.

CHALGROVE WITH BERRICK SALOME[1]   Incumbent T. O. Floyd[2]

1. Baptism at morning or evening prayer? Yes: during evening prayer.

2. Communion times

a) Sunday At <u>Chalgrove</u> 1st S. in month 12.0. 2nd and 4th at 8.0 3rd at 7.0. At <u>Berrick</u> 3rd and 5th S. at 8.30.

b) Ascension Day At <u>Ber.</u> 8.30 at <u>Ch.</u> 10.0.

c) Saints Days At <u>Ber.</u> 8.30 or 10.0.

d) Week-days? at <u>Ch.</u> 10.0 on Wedn: in Lent and Adv.

3. Is Communion ever sung? Yes on festivals at 7.30 at Chalgrove. Sometimes with hymns at Berrick.

4. Religious teaching to children a) Church b) Sunday School and c) Day school? i) Clergy teach in Day schools? ii) Religious teaching to Sunday school teachers? iii) Satisfactory results?

The day school is a council school, in which the Vicar has no rights: on six days of the year the managers allow the children to attend church but three of these days usually come in the holidays. There is no catechising of the children in church. With two churches to serve it is impossible to arrange for a special childrens service: I believe my predecessor used to catechize at evensong occasionally instead of preaching: but the adult members of the congregation much objected to it. [i–iii] The teachers in the Sunday school are provided with courses of lessons: one of the courses published by the national society each year. I think that the results are not unsatisfactory on the whole.

5. Religious teaching to lads and young women? Nothing beyond the ordinary services in church.

6. Secondary school in Parish? No.

7. Teaching for Nonconformist children? There is no church school.

8. Organised study for adults? Nothing beyond the services in church.

9. Interest in mission? Occasional sermons and collections for foreign missions. A few parishioners have missionary boxes.

10. Voters for Ruridecanal representatives a) men b) women? None, so far as I know.

11. PCC? No.

1. Population 401.
2. Thomas Owen Floyd graduated from Keble College Oxford in 1894 and was ordained priest in 1897. He served as curate at St Mary Magdalen Oxford between 1896 and 1912 when he was appointed Vicar of Chalgrove. He was 41 in 1914 and at the 1911 census he lived in a single-person household.

CHARLBURY WITH CHADLINGTON[1]   Incumbent J. D. Payne[2]

1. Baptism at morning or evening prayer? At Charlbury at the close of the Children's Service. So at Chadlington. At Shorthampton after Second Lesson at Evensong.

2. Communion times

a) Sunday 8 am every Sunday at Charlbury and Chad. 11 am 1st and 3rd Sunday.

b) Ascension Day 6.30 am and 8 am.

c) Saints Days 8 am.

d) Week-days? 8 am.

3. Is Communion ever sung? No.

4. Religious teaching to children a) Church b) Sunday School and c) Day school? i) Clergy teach in Day schools? ii) Religious teaching to Sunday school teachers? iii) Satisfactory results?

(a) in church: Children's Service Charlbury 1st and 3rd, Chadlington 2nd and 4th Sundays in month. At Shorthampton short instruction each Sunday afternoon. (b) At Charlbury and Chadlington good staff of teachers (numerically). At Charlbury for several years a weekly class for Teachers at Vicarage. But at present each teacher is following a book viz at Charlbury Robinson's Church Catechism Explained. At Chadlington Potter and Sheard's course. (c) The only Church day school is at Chadlington, where Rev T.P. Field (assist. Curate) teaches regularly. At Charlbury the Children's Service reaches 100 out of the 160 of the Council School. At Chilson (tho' a Council School) the Diocesan Inspector is permitted by the Managers. [i–iii] As to results. The Children's Service is the main opportunity. Our teachers, though numerous, and with a real interest in the children, find the work onerous. We have a Deanery Sunday School Teachers Association which meets quarterly for Lectures – average attendance 70 teachers.

5. Religious teaching to lads and young women? We have a Church Lads' Brigade numbering 25. The main work among lads is at Confirmation Classes. But they attend Church well every Sunday (at each Church). There is a Class of about 30 young women taught by a lady at Charlbury, at Chadlington G.F.S. class.

6. Secondary school in Parish? None.

7. Teaching for Nonconformist children? At Chadlington the Nonconformist children do Scripture work only while the majority also do Prayer Book instruction. But all are examined by Diocesan Inspector. Curiously enough the best examination results are often obtained by Children whose parents are "anything or nothing".

8. Organised study for adults? Yes. Our Church of England Men's Society has met steadily once a month for 6 years for systematic study. Average attendance some years 35, some years 20. For past twelve months we have taken the services in the Prayer Book in succession: Mattins, Evensong, Litany, Holy Communion, Holy Baptism, Confirmation, Marriage.

9. Interest in mission? We have a Church Guild for Foreign Missions. One year C.E.M.S. took a book on Islam. We have King's Messengers branch and instruction. We had a Candidate from this Parish training at Warminster doing very well, but he died suddenly of rheumatic fever last year.

10. Voters for Ruridecanal representatives a) men b) women? About 20 men on last occasion. No women. Our Ruridecanal representatives have attended well.

11. PCC? Our Church of England Men's Society has largely acted as a Church Council. But our Churchwardens and Sidesmen (numbering 12) meet when occasion demands. For instance, they met this week to organize a Church Fete for our Church Roof Fund. Generally the work of the Parish has been carried on with full consultation and help of our laymen and they do a good share of work. Vestry meetings well attended.

1. Population 2,114.
2. Julius Delmege Payne graduated from St John's College Oxford in 1893 and was ordained priest in 1895. He served two curacies between 1894 and 1903 when he was appointed as Vicar of Charlbury. He was the author of *An Historical Survey of the English Bible* (1911). He was 43 in 1914 and at the 1911 census he lived in a household with his elder sister, younger brother and two unmarried female servants.

CHARLTON-ON-OTMOOR[1]   Incumbent C. E. Prior[2]

1. Baptism at morning or evening prayer? (I baptise a few gipsy children) For parishioners almost invariably: I think in 10 years that, except private baptisms, there have been only 2 or 3 cases of Holy Baptism otherwise than in the service.

2. Communion times

a) **Sunday** 1st and 3rd S after Mg. Prayer, 2nd and 4th at 8 am. On the first Sunday of the month the H.C. is celebrated at Murcott 9 am.

b) **Ascension Day** 8 am.

c) **Saints Days** 8 am All Saints Day (and Ash Wednesday).

d) **Week-days?** Not at all.

3. Is Communion ever sung? No.

4. Religious teaching to children a) Church b) Sunday School and c) Day school? i) Clergy teach in Day schools? ii) Religious teaching to Sunday school teachers? iii) Satisfactory results?

Sunday School. There are Sunday schools here and at Murcott. The no. of children altogether is about 57, 37 here and 20 at Murcott Day School. Instruction follows the Syllabus of the Diocese. [i–iii] I teach at least once in the week. Sunday School Teachers are grown people, and would not find time to come to a Class. I have offered it more than once. The results are moderately satisfactory. The teachers come from working families, (there are hardly any others here), and are prevented from being regular by domestic circumstances in some cases. At Murcott (1 ¾ m away) the Sunday School serves as a morning service for the children, and they would not come up here, if they had no Sunday School.

5. Religious teaching to lads and young women? I have had a Bible Class once a week for lads and young men during the winter months (Oct to Easter), and get about 10. I started a class of the same kind for young women, but it rapidly dwindled: they are too much occupied.

6. Secondary school in Parish? No.

7. Teaching for Nonconformist children? Some parents a few years ago claimed exemption for their children under the Act of 1871. Their children do some Scripture work while the other receive Church and Prayer Book Instruction. There are children of nonconformists who say the Catechism with the rest. It is rather unreal, but I do not know that I should object, if their parents do not.

8. Organised study for adults? No, except what is done under no. 5.

9. Interest in mission? Very little, except on special occasions. There is a small class of children who are instructed on Missionary subjects by a lady resident at Murcott. We supply a few copies of the 'Mission Field'.

10. Voters for Ruridecanal representatives a) men b) women? Very few have actually signed the papers, as I know who are "qualified persons."

11. PCC? No.

1. Population 423.

2. Charles Edward Prior graduated from Queen's College Oxford in 1872 and was ordained priest in 1877. He served a curacy 1877–79 and was Lecturer at St Magnus London Bridge 1880–83 while pursuing a career as a teacher. He was Assistant Master at Bradfield College 1873–75 and then at Merchant Taylors' School 1875–95. He was appointed as Rector of Charlton in 1895 and as Rural Dean of Islip in 1899. He was 64 in 1914 and at the 1911 census he lived in a household with his young nephew and two unmarried female servants.

CHASTLETON[1]   Incumbent J. A. Burnley[2]

1. Baptism at morning or evening prayer? Yes.

2. Communion times

a) Sunday 1st and 3rd at 8.30 am and 11 am all Sundays.

b) Ascension Day 8.30 am.

c) Saints Days 8.30 am not started.

d) Week-days? 8.30 am once a week [not started].

3. Is Communion ever sung? Choir working up for a choral Holy Communion 1st Sunday in month at 11 am.

4. Religious teaching to children a) Church b) Sunday School and c) Day school? i) Clergy teach in Day schools? ii) Religious teaching to Sunday school teachers? iii) Satisfactory results?

(a) Service in Church. (b) Sunday Schools in Day School. (c) Inspected by the Diocesan Inspector.

5. Religious teaching to lads and young women? They attend Church Sunday.

6. Secondary school in Parish? Small Church day School.

7. Teaching for Nonconformist children? Very few Nonconformists.

8. Organised study for adults? [*No response*].

9. Interest in mission? [*No response*].

10. Voters for Ruridecanal representatives a) men b) women? [*No response*].

11. PCC? Small parochial Church Council. Viz. 2 churchwardens 4 sidesmen.

1. Population 184.
2. James Albert Burnley graduated from Queens' College Cambridge in 1894 and trained at Ridley Hall Cambridge in 1895. He was ordained priest in 1897 and served six curacies between 1896 and 1908, when he accepted an appointment as a workhouse chaplain. He also spent a year as Acting Chaplain to the Forces in South Africa 1901–02. He was appointed as Rector of Chastleton in 1914. He was 41 in 1914 and at the 1911 census he shared a household with his wife and 7-year-old daughter.

CHECKENDON[1]   Incumbent J. T. Munn[2]

1. Baptism at morning or evening prayer? No but I usually administer the Sacrament at the afternoon childrens Service.

2. Communion times

a) **Sunday** 8 am except 1st S. in month at midday (on great festivals at both and 7 am as well).

b) **Ascension Day** 8.

c) **Saints Days** 8 am.

d) **Week-days?** occasionally 8 am.

3. Is Communion ever sung? On great festivals after Mattins (11 am) or to begin at 11 as a separate service, Mattins having been said previously at 10.15.

4. Religious teaching to children a) Church b) Sunday School and c) Day school? i) Clergy teach in Day schools? ii) Religious teaching to Sunday school teachers? iii) Satisfactory results?

1. Childrens Service and catechizing at 3 every Sunday afternoon, except 1st Sunday in month. 2. Sunday School in the morning at 10 am. 3. Instruction given by teacher. [i–iii] I only give instruction on special occasions. On Ascension Day and Ash Wednesday the Day School children are brought to Church either before or after Secular instruction. The result is fairly satisfactory, the children answer generally quite intelligently.

5. Religious teaching to lads and young women? I have periodical (quarterly or oftener) instructions and preparation services for communicants – to which I especially invite those recently confirmed. Very frequently the Girls and Boys leave the Parish at the age of 15 or 16.

6. Secondary school in Parish? No.

7. Teaching for Nonconformist children? There is no chapel in the Parish and practically no dissent. I don't think there are any children of Nonconformist parents attending our school, certainly none who make any grievance of having to receive the ordinary teaching.

8. Organised study for adults? Nothing but such teaching as they get from one in Church.

9. Interest in mission? Annual missionary meeting for S.P.G. [Annual missionary] Sunday with special Sermons. Occasional talks on missy subjects and collections on Saints Days for S.P.G. and U.M.C.A. Intercession Services sometimes (e.g. Rogation days).

10. Voters for Ruridecanal representatives a) men b) women? Only 3 or 4 men have qualified though at the last election I made it widely known. I intend to make an effort to obtain a good many more signatures this year in view of the new financial scheme. I should be very glad to send round a form for signature to every parishioner if such a form could be obtained.

11. PCC? No.

1. Population 435.
2. John Turner Munn graduated from University College Oxford in 1886 and then trained at Wells Theological College, being ordained as priest in 1888. He served two curacies 1887–95 and then as Vicar of Waterfoot between 1896 and 1908, when he was appointed to the Rectory of Checkendon. He was aged 50 in 1914 and at the 1911 census he shared a household with his wife, two school-aged children, a nursery governess and two other unmarried female servants.

CHESTERTON[1]   Incumbent C. L. Norris[2]

1. Baptism at morning or evening prayer? It is always administered at the Children's Service.

2. Communion times

a) Sunday 8.30. midday 1st Sunday.

b) Ascension Day 8.30.

c) Saints Days On certain at 8.30.

d) Week-days? [*No response*].

3. Is Communion ever sung? Semi-choral at 8.30 on Festivals.

4. Religious teaching to children a) Church b) Sunday School and c) Day school? i) Clergy teach in Day schools? ii) Religious teaching to Sunday school teachers? iii) Satisfactory results? Children's Service around Sunday School.

5. Religious teaching to lads and young women? Bible Class for lads and also for members of the G.F.S.

6. Secondary school in Parish? No.

7. Teaching for Nonconformist children? No chapel in Parish – practically no Dissenters. No question as to separate religious teaching has ever arisen.

8. Organised study for adults? [*No response*].

9. Interest in mission? The Parish is specially interested in work in the Argentine and Bishop Every has himself been to stimulate their interest in his Diocese.

10. Voters for Ruridecanal representatives a) men b) women? [*No response*].

11. PCC? Answer to 10 and 11. The Parish is small and distinctly Church of England. It may be termed almost medieval in its characteristics. It is practically "run" by the 2 landowners both loyal and most generous Churchmen. Rightly or wrongly, I have considered it best during my incumbency to allow things to go on as they have for many years past. In my opinion they cannot be bettered as things, at present stand. I have always conscientiously considered that to upset the present happy condition of affairs in any way, would show a great want of tact.

1. Population 348.
2. Charles Leslie Norris graduated from New College Oxford in 1884 and was ordained priest in 1886. He served curacies 1885–92, was Rector of Cliffe Lewis 1892–1900, then Vicar of Swalcliffe with Shutford 1900–03. He occupied the Rectory of Newton Longville between 1903 and 1907, when he was appointed as Vicar of Chesterton. He was aged 51 in 1914. At the 1911 census he shared a household with his wife and five unmarried servants: a cook, a maid, a housemaid, a kitchen maid and a butler.

CHINNOR[1] Incumbent L. Baldwyn[2]

1. Baptism at morning or evening prayer? Occasionally at Evensong. Regular Baptisms take place at Children's Services 1st and 3rd Sundays in month.

2. Communion times

a) Sunday 8 am also 7 am on Great Festivals and 11 am on 1st Sunday in month.

b) Ascension Day 8 am.

c) Saints Days 8 am.

d) Week-days? [*No response*].

3. Is Communion ever sung? Yes. At 8 am, on all Great Festivals.

4. Religious teaching to children a) Church b) Sunday School and c) Day school? i) Clergy teach in Day schools? ii) Religious teaching to Sunday school teachers? iii) Satisfactory results?

Children's Service with catechising on two Sundays in the month at 3 pm. Sunday School at 10 am and 2.30 pm. Infants are taught in new methods which work very well – on two Sundays expression lessons are used in large Schools – This works very well too. Sunday School Teachers meet occasionally at Rectory for instruction – usually a manual of instruction is followed for each year. The results seem quite satisfactory.

5. Religious teaching to lads and young women? Classes for lads and young women, but some difficulty is found in procuring satisfactory teachers for young men.

6. Secondary school in Parish? [*No response*].

7. Teaching for Nonconformist children? Children of Nonconformists are given separate teaching when parents request it.

8. Organised study for adults? Manuals on church principles and history are circulated by the Rector amongst those who can be induced to read a little in the winter months.

9. Interest in mission? Special sermons for S.P.G. and a well-attended Lecture in School Room – The interest in Foreign Missions has been well sustained in this parish for many years. There are over 50 boxes out and an average of £10 – £12 is sent to the Society every year on St Andrew's Day or the eve of St Andrew's.

10. Voters for Ruridecanal representatives a) men b) women? [*No response*].

11. PCC? The Church Council is elected at the Easter Vestry and its powers are chiefly those of meeting to consult with the Rector in all matters concerning church work and the parish. There have been 4 meetings since last Oct.

1. Population 1,000.
2. Leonard Baldwyn graduated from Exeter College Oxford in 1887 and trained at Sarum College 1888, being ordained priest in 1890. He served two curacies between 1889 and 1902, when he was appointed as Rector of Chinnor. He was aged 55 in 1914 and at the 1911 census he shared a household with his wife, his 19-year-old son and two unmarried female servants.

CHIPPING NORTON[1]   Incumbent G. A. Littledale[2]

1. Baptism at morning or evening prayer? Yes. Many baptisms take place after 2nd Less. at weekday Evensong, but more generally <u>after</u> the Sunday afternoon Catechism.

2. Communion times

a) Sunday 8 am.

b) Ascension Day 6 am and 8 am.

c) Saints Days 8 am.

d) Week-days? Occasionally.

3. Is Communion ever sung? Yes on Greater Festival and Harvest Fest – sometimes 8 am [sometimes] 11 am.

4. Religious teaching to children a) Church b) Sunday School and c) Day school? i) Clergy teach in Day schools? ii) Religious teaching to Sunday school teachers? iii) Satisfactory results?

(a) <u>In Church</u>: "The Catechism" each Sun. afternoon Standards IV – VII and Ex. Stands. (b) <u>Sunday morn and afternoon</u> – 10 am and 2.30 am for Stands. I, II, III. Infants 10 am, simple teaching. Infants 2.30, Kindergarten S.S. (c) The clergy teach on three mornings in the week in Boys and Girls Sch. in Preparation for Dioc. Inspection. [i–iii] <u>Sunday School Teachers</u>. Each a manual given for their guidance. All my attempts to get them to a Teachers class on week days end with very few attending. The Teachers have every evening of the week engaged; and as there are 3 Grades of Lessons (i. Catechism; ii. Standards I – III; and iii Infants) it is not easy to take a subject which will suit all. <u>Fairly satisfied</u> with results – several Day School Teachers help on Sundays – but <u>not satisfied</u> with Teachers Meetings for instruction. The clergy cannot undertake a class on Sundays. The Teachers cannot come regular on a week night. We have a weekly Bible Class for CLB and also a Sunday BC for men (Lay Evangelist's work). A Sunday class for Y. women / a Lady's work.

5. Religious teaching to lads and young women? 1. CLB bible class each Tuesday. 2. Y. Women's BC each Sun. afternoon (see above). 3. Confirmation classes.

6. Secondary school in Parish? Yes, 'St Margaret's School' is recognized by the Education Authority and has a C. of E. Mistress at the head of it. There is also a Primitive Methodist v. cheap school for young people; and a Wesleyan cripples home – nominally "undenominational"; but all go to the Wesleyan Chapel on Sunday.

7. Teaching for Nonconformist children? We have 1. Ch. of England 2. Council 3. R.C.: day schools

8. Organised study for adults? Only the adult Bible classes and Sermons.

9. Interest in mission? There is a small Foreign Missionary Working Party of Ladies; and the Quarterly Intercession Paper is distributed.

10. Voters for Ruridecanal representatives a) men b) women? 33 men, 7 women.

11. PCC? No Ch. Council; when advice is wanted I consult with the Ch. wardens and occasionally with the sidesmen and 16 Lay Representatives of the R. D. Conference.

1. Population 4,315.
2. Godfrey Armytage Littledale graduated from Brasenose College Oxford in 1877, trained at Leeds Clergy School 1878, and was ordained priest in 1880. He served two curacies between 1879 and 1886, when he was appointed as Vicar of Chipping Norton. He also served as Rural Dean of Chipping Norton 1903–05. He was aged 60 in 1914 and at the 1911 census he shared a household with his wife and two daughters, aged 21 and 14, together with a governess and three other unmarried female servants.

CLANFIELD[1]   Incumbent W. Bryant[2]

1. Baptism at morning or evening prayer? [*No response*].

2. Communion times

a) **Sunday** 8.am but on 1st S. in month 11 am.

b) **Ascension Day** before 8 am.

c) **Saints Days** occasionally at 7.30 am.

d) **Week-days?** [*No response*].

3. Is Communion ever sung? 1st Sunday in month at 11 am and on Great Festivals at 11 am when Service is also read at 7 am and 8 am.

4. Religious teaching to children a) Church b) Sunday School and c) Day school? i) Clergy teach in Day schools? ii) Religious teaching to Sunday school teachers? iii) Satisfactory results?

(a) Children's Service 1st Sun month and Great Festivals at 3 pm. Ash Wednesday and Ascension Day at 11.15 am (b) Sunday School mornings at 10 am Afternoons at 2.30 pm except when there is Children's Service in Church. (c) Day School from 9 am – 9.50 am. [i–iii] I teach in Day School three times a week occasionally more often. Sunday Sch. Teachers have been persuaded to attend Diocesan Course, last year three went to Wantage. The results attained seem fairly satisfactory.

5. Religious teaching to lads and young women? At present time – nothing. It is hoped soon that it may be possible to start Bible Class for lads.

6. Secondary school in Parish? No.

7. Teaching for Nonconformist children? No.

8. Organised study for adults? Nothing beyond ordinary Church Services.

9. Interest in mission? Annual Sermons and Meeting.

10. Voters for Ruridecanal representatives a) men b) women? [*No response*].

11. PCC? Yes – Two Churchwardens, four Sidesmen. It has met once since last October.

1. Population 530.
2. William Bryant graduated from Exeter College Oxford in 1896 and trained at the Chancellor's School Lincoln in 1897, being ordained priest in 1899. He held curacies at Kidlington and Deddington between 1898 and 1908, when he became Vicar of Clanfield. He was aged 38 in 1914 and at the 1911 census he shared a household with his wife and one unmarried female servant.

CLAYDON[1]   Incumbent A. C. Hoggins[2]

1. Baptism at morning or evening prayer? Only 3 or 4 Baptisms usually in year – always try to get them at Evening Prayer but have only once or twice succeeded – excuses too late for babies and congregation strongly object – morning too early – not dressed.

2. Communion times

a) **Sunday** 8 and 10.

b) Ascension Day 7.15 and 11.

c) Saints Days 7.15.

d) Week-days? 7.15 except in absence of Vicar.

3. Is Communion ever sung? Sundays at 10. Ascension Day at 11 Xmas Day at Midnight and 11 am. On five other days attempt is made to sing the service at 7.15 – not always successful – last time S George's Day.

4. Religious teaching to children a) Church b) Sunday School and c) Day school? i) Clergy teach in Day schools? ii) Religious teaching to Sunday school teachers? iii) Satisfactory results?

a. An address is always given to the children at the 10 am Sung Eucharist on Sundays – and any other time that offers. b. An address is actually given in the afternoon – but it has to take the form of a story or no one will come to it and even then only those under 13 or 14 will attend it. Catechism was tried for about a year and was fairly successful for about three months – then irregularity of attendance and the exceptional indocility (due to the condition of the village) of the children gradually destroyed it. The Vicar can get no help of any value and the formal Sunday School is at present in suspense. c. The Day School has been "Council" for some thirty years. The "Scripture" lessons are carefully divested of any trace of religious teaching – to please the Dissenting Managers – and the teacher was informed before the arrival of the present Vicar that the Managers object to the Vicar of the Parish as such being allowed even to enter the School. (As Manager I visit the School frequently and am the only Manager to do so but to avoid friction I never speak to the children on any subject. As I have all my life been accustomed to visit and teach in the schools almost daily, as I have been an Inspector and as at the present moment I lecture frequently on teaching etc it can be understood how galling the position is to me.) It is scarcely necessary to say that I am dissatisfied with the results of this condition of things – almost to despair.

5. Religious teaching to lads and young women? Everything is regulated by "what has been done in Claydon". The custom is for the child to leave school on the earliest day on which it is permitted and at the same time to leave Sunday School and regular Church attendance. As a result very few of the so called "Church people" are confirmed.

6. Secondary school in Parish? [*No response*].

7. Teaching for Nonconformist children? [*No response*].

8. Organised study for adults? When I first came I attempted Cottage Meetings: one was held and attended by 4 persons two of whom were Dissenters – I have so far found it impossible to arrange another.

9. Interest in mission? Collections are made – frequent instruction is given – and deputations are invited – one year there were two – but results very unsatisfactory – prayer (for any purpose) is not yet understood. I, who have been so much in the Mission field, find it very hard to ask the people here to contribute towards the evangelisation of those who have so much more sense of religion than themselves.

10. Voters for Ruridecanal representatives a) men b) women? As our only adult male communicant in the village is People's Churchwarden and therefore already a member of the Church Council it seemed more than unnecessary to hold a meeting at which he could be the only candidate for election.

11. PCC? We elect annually a Church Council and meetings are summoned monthly: they usually fall through from lack of attendance: I think five may have been held since last October.

1. Population 215.
2. Albany Charles Hoggins graduated from Trinity College Cambridge in 1869 and was ordained priest in 1873. He occupied a series of livings including vicarages in Guiana, Australia and New Zealand and from 1909 in London, moving to become Vicar of Claydon in 1911. He was also in 1911 Chaplain of the Sisterhood of St Thomas in Oxford. The 1911 census found him living in the Warden's Lodge in St Thomas Oxford.

CLIFTON HAMPDEN[1]   Incumbent R. Gibbs[2]

1. Baptism at morning or evening prayer? Yes. I generally suggest it and have had just I think 7 at Mattins in 16 years. The fear of the baby crying usually deters – The Catechizing service the usual time.

2. Communion times

a) **Sunday** 8.am. 1st Sunday at 7 am also – and last 12 noon.

b) **Ascension Day** 6 am and 9 am.

c) **Saints Days** 8 am or 9 am.

d) **Week-days?** 2 days in week or 1 day – 7.45 am.

3. Is Communion ever sung? Partly with Hymns On special occasions at 11 am – Mattins being <u>said</u> before.

4. Religious teaching to children a) Church b) Sunday School and c) Day school? i) Clergy teach in Day schools? ii) Religious teaching to Sunday school teachers? iii) Satisfactory results?

(a) Catechizing every Sunday – Service every Saints Day. Present[ly] at the H.C. with Hymns for the time of year. (b) No Sunday School. I aim at teaching twice a week in the school. (c) Regular teaching Oxford syllabus. [i–iii] As we have no chapel I continue with the regular teaching in Day School with the Catechizing on Sunday without Sunday School seems sufficient.

5. Religious teaching to lads and young women? Beyond an attempt to keep those lately confirmed and a quarterly preparation class nothing special.

6. Secondary school in Parish? No.

7. Teaching for Nonconformist children? Only a Church School. No demand for other than Church teaching.

8. Organised study for adults? No nothing beyond the 2 sermons on Sundays.

9. Interest in mission? 6 have Quarterly Intercession paper. The Collect allowed by Convocation used at the Celebration every 3rd Sunday. Mission prayer at Childrens Service every Sunday. Missionary Magazine circulated among C.E.M.S. members and a few others.

10. Voters for Ruridecanal representatives a) men b) women? I do not remember receiving any such declaration.

11. PCC? No.

1. Population 306.
2. Reginald Gibbs graduated from Keble College Oxford in 1891 and trained at Cuddesdon, being ordained priest in 1893. He served two curacies in Devon between 1892 and 1897 and became Vicar of Clifton in 1898. He was aged 46 in 1914 and at the 1911 census he shared a household with his wife, four young children, and three unmarried female servants.

COGGS[1] Incumbent E. J. U. Payne[2]

1. Baptism at morning or evening prayer? I used to do so frequently – recently the wish has been expressed against it.

2. Communion times

a) **Sunday** 8 am 3rd Sunday, noon 1st S. in month.

b) **Ascension Day** 8.15 am.

c) **Saints Days** No.

d) **Week-days?** No.

3. Is Communion ever sung? No.

4. Religious teaching to children a) Church b) Sunday School and c) Day school? i) Clergy teach in Day schools? ii) Religious teaching to Sunday school teachers? iii) Satisfactory results?

I do not teach any class in the Day School. The Day School children come to Church from the School about 8 times in the year. It is hard to find Sunday School teachers other than the Day Sch. teachers or out of ones own family. Just now I have one or two who work in factory, they can only be helped by books. The results are, I think, hopeful. The work of the Sunday School has improved lately.

5. Religious teaching to lads and young women? A quite large class of lads up to the age of 17 or 18 come to this house. Mrs Payne has them in a Bible Class. There are some Girls belonging to the G.F.S. who meet in Witney.

6. Secondary school in Parish? No.

7. Teaching for Nonconformist children? There is a Teacher appointed who belongs to a well known family of Nonconformists in the Parish.

8. Organised study for adults? Only such as comes from membership of the C.E.M.S.

9. Interest in mission? We have a meeting for S.P.G.

10. Voters for Ruridecanal representatives a) men b) women? Perhaps 8 men, no women.

11. PCC? No.

1. Population 888.
2. Edward James Undy Payne graduated AKC in 1882 and was ordained priest in 1883. He was curate of Kilburn 1882–83 and of Coggs between 1883 and 1884, when he succeeded to the Vicarage. He was also Chaplain of the Witney Union Workhouse in 1883. He was 63 in 1914 and at the 1911 census he shared a household with his wife, 23-year-old daughter, school-age son and one unmarried female servant.

COMBE[1]   Incumbent S. S. Pearce[2]

1. Baptism at morning or evening prayer? No, it is generally celebrated at 3pm on 1st Sunday of month.

2. Communion times

a) Sunday 8 am except on 1st S. of month when at noon.

b) Ascension Day 7.30 am.

c) Saints Days at 10 am as a rule.

d) Week-days? On Greater Festival and Sunday in octave of St Lawrence (Dedication) and Harvest Festival at 8 am and 12 noon. On Easter Day at 7 am 8 am and 12 noon.

3. Is Communion ever sung? Yes. At 8 am on Greater Feasts Easter, Whitsunday and Christmas Day and Feast Sunday (S. after 10 Aug) and Harvest Festival (1st week in October).

4. Religious teaching to children a) Church b) Sunday School and c) Day school? i) Clergy teach in Day schools? ii) Religious teaching to Sunday school teachers? iii) Satisfactory results?

In Church: in order to enable the children above the Infants class to register their own attendance at church on Sundays and Holy Days I have employed the Faith Society's system of stamps which answers its purpose fairly well since the Blank places in their stamp albums disclose the fact of their omission to worship to the child in a plain unmistakeable way; the blanks spoiling the appearance of the page where they occur. In order to help the young people to become familiar with the Holy Communion service before Confirmation Age I have required their presence at the Choral celebrations – that is to say those boys and girls who are singers in the choir. On the 4th Sunday of the month at 2.30 pm there is a short childrens service at which there is a catechizing or instruction by Question and answer. On Ash Wednesday and Ascension Day it is customary for the whole school (except the Infants) to attend the morning service at the Parish Church at which there is an address to suit the children. [i–iii] In School: I take the upper standards in the united school at the Prayer Book subjects following the syllabus children of nonconformist parents are taught with the children of church parents – there is no religious difficulty in this parish – though about nearly ½ the children are Wesleyans of a kind and do not belong to the Church S. School. I have never met with an opposition, though I have always made it known at the first lesson after each vacation that I understand some of the children to be chapel children and others church children. I wish the children to go to the place of worship which their parents desire. Very often the nonconformist children get Bishop's Prayer Bk after inspection.

5. Religious teaching to lads and young women? The only religious instruction for lads takes place at the time of preparation for confirmation. In the winter months there is a class taken by my wife for young women and girls who have left school. Occasionally I have had a pupil teacher under my instruction for the Oxford Locals and other examinations as I have at the present moment.

6. Secondary school in Parish? No. None.

7. Teaching for Nonconformist children? No special provision is made though there is only a Church school here and there is no one competent to give it.

8. Organised study for adults? I am afraid there are no adult Bible classes.

9. Interest in mission? The duty of supporting the work of Evangelisation of the World I have persistently pressed upon the parishioners and I think I may say is fairly responded to. We have a system of missionary boxes out – 21 at present moment. A meeting once a year at the school in autumn and 2 Sundays in the year Advent S and Whitsunday are wholly devoted to this cause in offerings and sermons.

10. Voters for Ruridecanal representatives a) men b) women? 4 or 5 men.

11. PCC? No.

N.B. Combe parish is entirely one of country labouring class with no gentry and four farmers.

1. Population 427.
2. Stephen Spencer Pearce graduated from Exeter College Oxford in 1882 and trained at Wells Theological College in 1883, being ordained priest in 1885. He held a series of four curacies between 1884 and 1891, when he became Vicar of Combe. He was 53 in 1914 and at the 1911 census he shared a household with his wife, 9-year-old son and two unmarried female servants.

CORNWELL[1]   Incumbent R. P. Burnett[2]

1. Baptism at morning or evening prayer? Yes 1st Sunday in month 3 pm.

2. Communion times

a) Sunday 1st and 3rd Sundays at Morning Prayer 11 am. All other Sundays 8 am.

b) Ascension Day 8 am.

c) Saints Days [*No response*].

d) Week-days? [*No response*].

We had 42 Communicants on Easter Day.

3. Is Communion ever sung? No.

4. Religious teaching to children a) Church b) Sunday School and c) Day school? i) Clergy teach in Day schools? ii) Religious teaching to Sunday school teachers? iii) Satisfactory results?

We have no Day-School. We have a Children's Service with instruction in Church Sunday afternoon. The <u>Rector</u> takes <u>all</u> the elder Children in Sunday-School every Sunday. The infants are taken by a young friend. We only have about 17 children altogether. They attend regularly and always seem interested and attentive. The results so far are, I think, satisfactory. Our total population is only between 70 and 80.

5. Religious teaching to lads and young women? We have only a few and they attend Church pretty regularly. We have a juvenile branch of the C.E.F.S.

6. Secondary school in Parish? No.

7. Teaching for Nonconformist children? We have no Day School in our parish. The children attend Churchill School.

8. Organised study for adults? [*No response*].

9. Interest in mission? We have meetings for S.P.G. and S.P.C.K. Special Sermons etc in Advent.

10. Voters for Ruridecanal representatives a) men b) women? [*No response*].

11. PCC? No.

1. Population 79.
2. Richard Parry Burnett graduated from St John's College Cambridge in 1875 and was ordained priest in 1877. Between 1876 and 1880 he served curacies in England and then spent twenty years as a chaplain in India including a period as a domestic chaplain to the Bishop of Madras 1882–93. In 1900 he returned to England as Rector of Cornwell. He was appointed Honorary Diocesan Inspector of Schools in 1907. He was aged 60 in 1914 and at the 1911 census he was described as a widower and shared a household with two unmarried female servants.

COTTISFORD, HARDWICK AND FINMERE[1]   Incumbent S. M. Statham[2]

1. Baptism at morning or evening prayer? Yes – otherwise is the exception.

2. Communion times

a) Sunday <u>Cottisford</u> 12 noon 1st and 3rd Sundays Summer months <u>Hardwick</u> 12 1st Sunday in month, 8.30 if sufficient numbers.

b) Ascension Day 8.30 Cottisford 12.00 Hardwick.

c) Saints Days 8.30 if numbers ante Comm. otherwise

d) Week-days? [*No response*].

3. Is Communion ever sung? No. Only a hymn at Christmas, Easter and Whitsun.

4. Religious teaching to children a) Church b) Sunday School and c) Day school? i) Clergy teach in Day schools? ii) Religious teaching to Sunday school teachers? iii) Satisfactory results?

a. 2.0pm Children Harvest to Easter; 3.0 pm Children Easter to Harvest. b. Catechism and Bible instruction. c. Catechism and Bible. Rector teaches occasionally in Day School.

5. Religious teaching to lads and young women? G.F.S. Church Service – special Advent and Lent with sermons on Wednesday Evenings.

6. Secondary school in Parish? No.

7. Teaching for Nonconformist children? No dissent in Cottisford. Two R.C. families in Hardwick and one dissent but the children attend church.

8. Organised study for adults? [*No response*].

9. Interest in mission? Foreign Mission service and sermon.

10. Voters for Ruridecanal representatives a) men b) women? [*No response*].

11. PCC? No.

1. Population 167.
2. Sherard Montagu Statham graduated from Queens' College Cambridge in 1880 and was subsequently awarded LLD by Trinity College Dublin in 1903. He was ordained priest in 1883 and after serving an initial curacy was Vicar of Stowupland 1889–90, Rector of Elworthy 1890–91, Vicar of River with Guston 1891–1907 and Chaplain to the military prison at Dover. He was Vicar of All Saints Hatcham Park between 1907 and 1911 when he became Rector of Cottisford. He was 55 in 1914 and at the 1911 census he shared a household with his wife and one unmarried female servant.

COWLEY[1]   Incumbent G. Moore[2]

1. Baptism at morning or evening prayer? We take the Baptisms at 3 o'clock services.

2. Communion times

a) Sunday 8 am and 11 am in the first Sunday in the month.

b) Ascension Day Yes.

c) Saints Days Yes.

d) Week-days? [*No response*].

3. Is Communion ever sung? No.

4. Religious teaching to children a) Church b) Sunday School and c) Day school? i) Clergy teach in Day schools? ii) Religious teaching to Sunday school teachers? iii) Satisfactory results?

a. See other side. b. 300, children attend our Sunday schools and are brought to Church and catechised every Sunday. c. My opinion is that the <u>Teachers</u> in our Day Schools will be the difficulty in the future, many of them never go to a place of worship and take no interest in the welfare of the children. G.M.

5. Religious teaching to lads and young women? We have a Guild for young men and women.

6. Secondary school in Parish? <u>No.</u>

7. Teaching for Nonconformist children? We have 475 children daily in our 3 Schools Boys Girls and Infants, I am in the Schools every morning taking the Scriptures till 9.45. We have never had a complaint from a parent or a child withdrawn from religious instruction.

8. Organised study for adults? [*No response*].

9. Interest in mission? [*No response*].

10. Voters for Ruridecanal representatives a) men b) women? [*No response*].

11. PCC? [*No response*].

1. Population 2,600.
2. George Moore graduated from Jesus College Oxford in 1873 and was ordained priest in 1874. He served a curacy at St Mary Magdalen Oxford between 1873 and 1875, when he became Vicar of Cowley. He was aged 71 in 1914. He was described as a widower at the 1911 census when he shared a household with two unmarried female servants.

COWLEY ST JOHN[1] Incumbent A. C. Scott[2]

1. Baptism at morning or evening prayer? Yes. At Evensong on Thursdays.

2. Communion times

a) Sunday 7. 8. 9.30 and 11 at Parish Ch. 7.30 and 9.30 at St Albans.

b) Ascension Day 5. 6. 7. 8. 9 and 11 at Parish Ch. 6.30 at St Albans.

c) Saints Days 7. 8. 9 and 11 at Parish Ch. 7.30 at St Albans.

d) Week-days? 7 and 8 at Parish Ch. Wed: 9.30 Thursday 5 or 6. Various at St Albans. At the Church of S. John Evangelist HC is celebrated daily at 6. 7. 8 also; on Saints Days at 9. And on Sundays at 9.30 and 11. Daily at St John's Hospital. 6.45 am; S. Basil's Home 7 a.m.; Fairacres Court 7.15.

3. Is Communion ever sung? Parish Church 9.30 and 11; St Alban's 9.30; St John Evangelist 9.30 and 11.

4. Religious teaching to children a) Church b) Sunday School and c) Day school? i) Clergy teach in Day schools? ii) Religious teaching to Sunday school teachers? iii) Satisfactory results?

(a) There is a "Catechism" on Sunday afternoons at Parish Ch. S. Albans, S. John Evan. and at Cowley Rd Mission. Childrens' Eucharist at Parish Ch. S Albans and S John Evan. (b) Short Sunday School before Catechism in the Schools. (c) Day Schools. Each school comes to Church once a month for children's Eucharist and weekly in Lent. During Holy Week daily for special service. The Diocesan Scheme of Religious Instruction is followed in the schools. [i–iii] The Vicar and three assistant Clergy each teach twice a week in the Schools. The Sunday School Teachers are only required to teach the set questions and a short Bible story bearing on the subject of the Catechism, their work is to get to know and influence the children, they sit with them at the Eucharist and at Catechism. The Infants on Sundays are under a duly qualified Teacher. The Pupil Teachers have religious instruction given to them by a lady who has a good Birmingham degree. How far are you satisfied? I am not at all satisfied. I find Oxford children were far more difficult than Birmingham children. They seem more shallow and so far, few of the teachers have got the true hold on them, that so many of my Birmingham teachers had on theirs. This is where great improvement ought to come.

5. Religious teaching to lads and young women? Guilds and classes conducted by Clergy, Sisters and ladies.

6. Secondary school in Parish? Milham Ford School. Very Protestant. We have a special "religious" class for pupil teachers who go there.

7. Teaching for Nonconformist children? There is a large Council School in addition to the parochial schools and schools of the society of S. John Evan.[3]

8. Organised study for adults? Church Reading Society lectures.

9. Interest in mission? A Parochial Missionary Union with Missionary Meetings and Intercession Services in Church.

10. Voters for Ruridecanal representatives a) men b) women? I have heard nothing of it since I have been in the Parish.

11. PCC? No. The churchwardens and Sidesmen meet occasionally.

1. Population 12,000.
2. Alfred Cecil Scott graduated from St John's College Cambridge in 1882 and trained in the Leeds Clerical School in 1883, being ordained priest in 1885. He was Curate at St John's Upper Norwood 1884–94, Vicar of Headcorn Kent 1894 to 1900, and of St Alban Bordesley, Birmingham 1900–10. He was also an Honorary Canon of Birmingham between 1907 and 1910, when he became Vicar of Cowley St John. He was aged 52 in 1914 and at the 1911 census he shared a household with his wife and two unmarried female servants.
3. The society of St John the Evangelist, popularly known as the Cowley Fathers, was the first Anglican religious order for men, founded by Richard Benson in 1866. Its headquarters were in Cowley and its members engaged in extensive pastoral work in the parish.

CROPREDY[1]   Incumbent M. Maltby[2]

1. Baptism at morning or evening prayer? Yes – Evening Prayer but not always.

2. Communion times

a) Sunday 8 am 1st S. in Month at 12.

b) Ascension Day 7 am 8 am and 11 am.

c) **Saints Days** 8 am.

d) **Week-days?** Lent and Advent Thursdays 8am.

3. Is Communion ever sung? 8 am on the Great Festivals.

4. Religious teaching to children a) Church b) Sunday School and c) Day school? i) Clergy teach in Day schools? ii) Religious teaching to Sunday school teachers? iii) Satisfactory results?

(a) Occasional services in Church for Children. (b) Sunday Mornings. (c) Weekly. I think generally speaking the teaching in Day School and S. School satisfactory.

5. Religious teaching to lads and young women? Instructions given.

6. Secondary school in Parish? No.

7. Teaching for Nonconformist children? No.

8. Organised study for adults? By communicants instruction.

9. Interest in mission? By Literature. Parochial Collections. Special Intercessions. Sermons.

10. Voters for Ruridecanal representatives a) men b) women? Very few.

11. PCC? No, not a Council, but on all matters of Parochial Interest the Church Wardens, Sidesmen and Communicants are called together for Consultation.

1. Population 405.
2. Maurice Maltby trained at Chichester College in 1891 and was ordained priest in 1893. He served three curacies between 1892 and 1907, when he was appointed Vicar of Cropredy. He was 51 in 1914 and at the 1911 census he shared a household with his wife and one unmarried female servant.

CROWELL[1]   Incumbent F. N. Davis[2]

1. Baptism at morning or evening prayer? Always in the course of evening prayer – after 2nd lesson.

2. Communion times

a) **Sunday** Alternate Sundays at 8 am.

b) **Ascension Day** 8am.

c) **Saints Days** 8 am.

d) **Week-days?** Only on special occasions – then at 8am.

3. Is Communion ever sung? No.

4. Religious teaching to children a) Church b) Sunday School and c) Day school? i) Clergy teach in Day schools? ii) Religious teaching to Sunday school teachers? iii) Satisfactory results?

The children go to day school in Chinnor – the rector of Crowell is a manager of this school and frequently visits it. The rector's wife is very interested in the Sunday School which meets for 2 separate hours on Sunday. There are no other teachers. The teacher has attended several "Teachers Training Weeks". In so small a parish one cannot see that matters could be much improved. The children receive no special religious instruction in church – they attend the services.

5. Religious teaching to lads and young women? During the winter there are weekly classes for (1) lads and (2) girls.

6. Secondary school in Parish? [*No response*].

7. Teaching for Nonconformist children? [*No response*].

8. Organised study for adults? No, but the rector is careful to make his sermons vehicles of definite church teaching and he believes that his congregation have a fairly intelligent grasp of Christian doctrine.

9. Interest in mission? Only one sermon a year.

10. Voters for Ruridecanal representatives a) men b) women? None; the antecedents and status of the people are so well known as to make formal action unnecessary.

11. PCC? No.

1. Population 83.
2. Francis Neville Davis graduated from Pembroke College Oxford in 1894 and was ordained priest in 1895. He served two curacies between 1894 and 1902, when he became Rector of Crowell. He was 46 in 1914 and at the 1911 census he shared a household with his wife, 11-year-old daughter and one unmarried female servant.

CROWMARSH GIFFORD[1]   Incumbent H. W. Fulford[2]

1. Baptism at morning or evening prayer? I always have it at the afternoon (children's) service in the presence of a congregation.

2. Communion times

a) **Sunday** 7 or 8 – once a month at the 11 Service.

b) **Ascension Day** 7.

c) **Saints Days** 7.30.

d) **Week-days?** As a rule there is no celebration.

3. Is Communion ever sung? Never.

4. Religious teaching to children a) Church b) Sunday School and c) Day school? i) Clergy teach in Day schools? ii) Religious teaching to Sunday school teachers? iii) Satisfactory results?

The children are carefully taught in the day school. There is 'Catechism' every Sunday in Church. [i–iii] I teach, as a general rule, once a week in the day school. The Sunday School teachers have the opportunity of hearing lectures on method at Wallingford and elsewhere. One of them attended the last course regularly. I am fairly satisfied that the children are carefully instructed in elementary Church doctrine and Scripture. I am not altogether satisfied with the Sunday School. It is, in a village like this, very difficult to get competent teachers, and, owing to the habit of lying in bed late on Sundays, it is hard to get parents to send their children to morning Sunday School. They come well to afternoon Catechism.

5. Religious teaching to lads and young women? Bible Class every Sunday during the winter months (six) for lads and Girls Friendly Society (classes for probationers and meetings for members). (There are very few young women in the Parish. They usually leave the village for domestic service elsewhere).

6. Secondary school in Parish? No.

7. Teaching for Nonconformist children? They are taught Scripture. If there were any desire on the part of parents that a nonconformist minister should teach (e.g. once a week), the managers would be prepared to make the necessary arrangements. The number of withdrawals from Church teaching is considerable, but every child receives instruction in the Old and New Testaments. The Church teaching is given once a week.

8. Organised study for adults? I have given a short course of sermons on the cardinal doctrines of the Faith, and another on the main facts of the History of the English Church. In a small village it is difficult to do much.

9. Interest in mission? Missionary Meetings and sermons, and addresses (once a fortnight in the winter) to the Band of Hope.

10. Voters for Ruridecanal representatives a) men b) women? At present, none, so far as I am aware. My predecessor may know better than I. There will be about 40 entitled to vote, all of whom would probably sign when an election was pending.

11. PCC? The Churchwardens and Sidesmen form a parochial Church Council. I am hoping to arrange for a meeting soon but hitherto there have been no regular meetings.

1. Population 277.
2. Henry William Fulford graduated from Clare College Cambridge in 1887 and was ordained priest in 1888. He began his clerical career with curacies in Cambridge, also serving as Junior Proctor and Senior Proctor in the University and as Librarian of Clare College.

He was Dean of Clare between 1884 and 1907 and became Rector of Crowmarsh Gifford in 1912. He was the author of *Epistle of St James (Churchmen's Bible)* (1901), *Epistles to Galatians and Romans* (1908), *Epistles to the Thessalonians and Pastoral Epistles* (1911) and contributor to *Hastings Dictionary to Christ and the Gospels* (1906) and *Hastings Encyclopaedia of Religion and Ethics* (1908). He was 59 in 1914 and at the 1911 census he shared a household with his wife, 27-year-old daughter and three unmarried female servants.

CUDDESDON[1]   Incumbent J. B. Seaton[2]

1. Baptism at morning or evening prayer? Not since I came: there have only been two Baptisms.

2. Communion times

a) **Sunday** On two Sundays 8 and 12 – on the other Sundays 7, 8 and 10.

b) **Ascension Day** 6 and 7.45.

c) **Saints Days** 7.45.

d) **Week-days?** On Wednesdays and Fridays at 7.45.

3. Is Communion ever sung? Yes. At 10 o'clock.

4. Religious teaching to children a) Church b) Sunday School and c) Day school? i) Clergy teach in Day schools? ii) Religious teaching to Sunday school teachers? iii) Satisfactory results?

There is an afternoon service for children every Sunday in Church. On Sunday mornings there is a Sunday School taught by the assistant Curate, [and] an experienced lady who also instructs the younger of the other two Sunday School teachers. The children seem to be well taught, but I have been in charge of the parish for too short a time to enable me to enquire sufficiently into the results attained.

5. Religious teaching to lads and young women? Nothing as yet for the lads: the young women are taught through the G.F.S. associate.

6. Secondary school in Parish? No.

7. Teaching for Nonconformist children? I doubt if we have any children of Nonconformist parents but will inquire.

8. Organised study for adults? Not as yet – except through a small Bible Class for women on Sunday afternoons and a monthly class for men in connexion with CEMS.

9. Interest in mission? There is a fortnightly intercession in Church – and the Q.I.P is circulated amongst a few people. I am hoping to organise the parish for this work.

10. Voters for Ruridecanal representatives a) men b) women? Two (Mr Gale and Mr Ryman) appear to have been elected to represent the parish, but as far as I can make out, no declaration has been signed. [*inscribed in a different hand and signed*: R.W. Sutcliffe].

11. PCC? No.

1. Population 443.
2. James Buchanan Seaton graduated from Christ Church Oxford in 1890 and was ordained priest in 1893. After an initial curacy he was Vice Principal of the Leeds Clergy School 1896–1900, Curate of Leeds 1896–1905 and Secretary of the Leeds Church Extension Society 1899–1905. He served as Perpetual Curate of Armley between 1905 and 1909 and then moved to South Africa where he was Rector of St Mary's Johannesburg and Archdeacon of Johannesburg until 1913 when he returned to England and became Vicar of Cuddesdon. He was 46 years of age in 1914. Not in the UK in 1911, at the 1901 census he was recorded as single, sharing a household with one unmarried female servant.

CULHAM[1]   **Incumbent W. J. Oldfield**[2]

1. Baptism at morning or evening prayer? Always.

2. Communion times

a) Sunday 8 and 11 alternately.

b) Ascension Day 8.

c) Saints Days None.

d) Week-days None.

3. Is Communion ever sung? No.

4. Religious teaching to children a) Church b) Sunday School and c) Day school? i) Clergy teach in Day schools? ii) Religious teaching to Sunday school teachers? iii) Satisfactory results?

(a) When I came here I tried monthly catechising in Church. But it was a complete failure. (b) Sunday School every Sunday morning. (c) Daily from 9.15 – 9.50. I teach and set papers twice a week. The teachers are the headmaster of the day school, my wife and a farmer's daughter who is training for a teacher. To the latter I supply notes of lessons. I think the present system fairly satisfies the present conditions, but I look forward to a time when more intelligent help can be secured from some lay parishioner in Sunday School and Bible Class.

5. Religious teaching to lads and young women? Nothing, except in preparation for Confirmation.

6. Secondary school in Parish? None.

7. Teaching for Nonconformist children? No child is withdrawn from the regular religious instruction given.

8. Organised study for adults? No.

9. Interest in mission? Missionary boxes, literature, intercession, frequent sermons, annual meeting.

10. Voters for Ruridecanal representatives a) men b) women? None. Only well known qualified persons have attended the meetings, so that there has been no need to put the signing of the forms into requisition.

11. PCC? No. Until the Church is disestablished I see no hope of getting Church Councils in these small agricultural parishes, where a quorum cannot be got for a statutory Parish Meeting and hardly for a Parish Council.

1. Population 341.
2. William John Oldfield graduated from Christ Church Oxford in 1879 and was subsequently awarded a DD in 1907. He was ordained priest in 1881. He had a varied clerical career, including a series of curacies in England, being Rector of St Mary Belize and Commissary for Honduras, Principal of St Paul's Missionary College, Burgh, Lincolnshire, 1890–96, and a Prebendary of Lincoln 1894. He undertook work among the Copts in Eygpt between 1900 and 1904 and then returned to England as Curate of Stanton Harcourt. He became Vicar of Culham in 1911 and Editor of the *Oxford Diocesan Calendar* in 1913. He was the author of *A Primer of Religion*, 1906. He was 56 in 1914 and at the 1911 census he shared a household with his wife and one unmarried female servant.

CUXHAM[1]   Incumbent L. P. Fedden[2]

1. Baptism at morning or evening prayer? I make it the rule with a few rare exceptions.

2. Communion times

a) Sunday On the 1st and 3rd at noon 2nd, 4th and 5th 8 am.

b) Ascension Day 8am.

c) Saints Days No celebrations – no communicants came when I had services.

d) Week-days? No celebration in the week.

3. Is Communion sung? No – I wish it were possible.

4. Religious teaching to children a) Church b) Sunday School and c) Day school? i) Clergy teach in Day schools? ii) Religious teaching to Sunday school teachers? iii) Satisfactory results?

Weekly catechising of the children in Church at 3 pm on Sunday. Sunday School in the morning. Church Day Schools. Occasionally. None possible. Report of Diocesan Inspector Summary Mark T.S. (Thoroughly Satisfactory). "I was truly pleased to see this little school once more. It continues to be skilfully taught and admirably influenced. Beyond the few suggestions which I made at the time to the

Head Teacher, I have nothing to add to the Summary Mark, which well describes the condition of the school as regards Religious Knowledge."

5. Religious teaching to lads and young women? Nothing extraordinary.

6. Secondary school in Parish? No.

7. Teaching for Nonconformist children? There are no nonconformists. If there were, I should gladly allow teaching by an authorised teacher in the classroom.

8. Organised study for adults? No.

9. Interest in mission? A working party held at the Rectory for the Universities' Mission to Central Africa and sermons.

10. Voters for Ruridecanal representatives a) men b) women? None.

11. PCC? No.

1. Population 127.
2. Lorenzo Player Fedden graduated from Merton College Oxford in 1885 and was ordained priest in 1886. He served six curacies 1885–1900 and as Vicar of Corston between 1900 and 1902, when he was appointed as Rector of Cuxham. He was 54 in 1914 and at the 1911 census he shared a household with his wife.

DEDDINGTON[1]   Incumbent T. Boniface[2]

1. Baptism at morning or evening prayer? [*No response*].

2. Communion times

a) **Sunday** at 8am except 1st Sunday in the month at mid-day.

b) **Ascension Day** at 8am.

c) **Saints Days** Chiefly after Mattins at 11am.

d) **Week-days?** None.

3. Is Communion ever sung? Semi choral on the Greater Festival at 8 am. Kyries, Offertory Sentences, Sanctus, Gloria in Excelsis and Hymns are sung. Choir present.

4. Religious teaching to children a) Church b) Sunday School and c) Day school? i) Clergy teach in Day schools? ii) Religious teaching to Sunday school teachers? iii) Satisfactory results?

(a) Catechising once a month. (b) Sunday School twice on each Sunday except Catechising Sunday and then only once. (c) Each day for half an hour. One of the Clergy the Assistant Curate teaches in Clifton School every Wednesday morning. The Sunday School teachers are supplied with the Lesson Books but there is no weekly Class for them. I don't consider the results very satisfactory, but it is a great help in keeping children attached to the Church.

5. Religious teaching to lads and young women? There is a Class for lads during the winter months on Sunday afternoons taken by myself.

6. Secondary school in Parish? None in connection with the church or kept by Church people.

7. Teaching for Nonconformist children? No provision made for Nonconformists children – if they object to the Catechism they would not be compelled to learn it; but as a fact I believe there are very few objectors.

8. Organised study for adults? Nothing.

9. Interest in mission? Meetings and Sermons from time to time. Day of Intercession for Foreign Missions Kings Messengers and Forward Movement effort.

10. Voters for Ruridecanal representatives a) men b) women? 12 men.

11. PCC? No.

1. Population 1,466.
2. Thomas Boniface graduated from Jesus College Cambridge in 1866 and was ordained priest in 1868. He served four curacies between 1867 and 1878, when he was appointed as Vicar of Deddington with Clifton and Hempton. He was 70 in 1914 and at the 1911 census he shared a household with his two unmarried sisters and one unmarried female servant.

DORCHESTER WITH BURCOT[1]   Incumbent N. C. S. Poyntz[2]

1. Baptism at morning or evening prayer? Never in Parish church. Always in Hamlet Chapel.

2. Communion times

a) **Sunday** 8 and 9.30 am.

b) **Ascension Day** 8.30 am Sung.

c) **Saints Days** 8.30 am [Sung].

d) **Week-days?** 8 am.

3. Is Communion ever sung? Yes 9.30 am on ordinary Sundays. 9.15 on Great Festivals.

4. Religious teaching to children a) Church b) Sunday School and c) Day school? i) Clergy teach in Day schools? ii) Religious teaching to Sunday school teachers? iii) Satisfactory results?

(a) Catechism occasionally on Sundays. Catechism once a week in Lent. (b) Religious Instruction, excepting when there is catechism in Church. (c) Religious instruction every day. Clergy teach 5 days in the week. Notes of lessons prepared in many cases. On the whole I think good is done.

5. Religious teaching to lads and young women? Bible Class for lads.

6. Secondary school in Parish? No.

7. Teaching for Nonconformist children? Church Association has a meeting house, and the agent holds classes there for the Dissenters.[3]

8. Organised study for adults? Adults can attend the Bible Class and we try in sermons to promote the principles of religion.

9. Interest in mission? A missionary work Party. The presence and work of the Missionary College.[4] The observance of Day of Intercession. Sermon and Collections for S.P.G.

10. Voters for Ruridecanal representatives a) men b) women? None.

11. PCC? No.

Only just returned from the Continent. July 4 14.

1. Population 965.
2. Nathaniel Castleton Stephen Poyntz graduated from Pembroke College Oxford in 1868 and was ordained priest in 1870. He served five curacies between 1869 and 1886, when he was appointed as Vicar of Dorchester with Burcot. He was 67 in 1914. His household was absent from the 1911 census but in 1901 it contained his wife, two sons and three unmarried female servants.
3. The Church Association, an Anglican society, was founded in 1865 to combat the spread of ritualism in the Church of England. Although regarded as somewhat extreme in its Protestantism by the beginning of the twentieth century, Poyntz was being polemical in classifying its meetings as nonconformist.
4. The Saints Peter and Paul Theological College was intended to train candidates for the Anglican ministry overseas. It was founded in Dorchester in 1878 largely through the efforts of Poyntz's predecessor as Vicar of Dorchester, W. C. Macfarlane.

DRAYTON[1]   Incumbent W. Spendlove[2]

1. Baptism at morning or evening prayer? Not actually at M and E Service, but I have had <u>special services</u> for baptisms in consequence of slackness re. it.

2. Communion times

a) Sunday HC is celebrated at 12.15 first Sunday in month. Also at 9.30 on Festive days.

b) Ascension Day [*No response*].

c) **Saints Days** [*No response*].

d) **Week-days?** Not on week days, being a small parish of poor working class people.

3. Is Communion ever sung? No. HC Service is said in natural voice, as are all the services, but a mixed choir sing the responses, Canticles creeds and Psalms are recited.

4. Religious teaching to children a) Church b) Sunday School and c) Day school? i) Clergy teach in Day schools? ii) Religious teaching to Sunday school teachers? iii) Satisfactory results?

Religious instruction for children is carefully attended to in Church by occasional services in Church, in Sunday School by myself, my wife and the school master and mistress twice on Sunday with average attendance of 30 out of 40 on day Register, in Day School by Headmaster and Mistress with occasional visits by me. [i–iii] I am satisfied by the results attained as attested by Diocesan Inspection but dissatisfied with some parents of Nonconformist connection who discourage their Children's attendance at S. School. There is no Chapel in this small village. I consider the so-called Nonconformist persons in this village to be lacking in desire for any Religious instruction and certainly they have no Religious Faith. It is this class which is causing disturbance and political strife in rural life – they are most bitter – but offer me no personal resentment.

5. Religious teaching to lads and young women? There are practically no young women here, they leave for service when School ends. There are only 5 or 6 young lads. For these and some parents there is a Bible Reading League, about thirty members and they meet occasionally. Also a HC Class for new communicants.

6. Secondary school in Parish? No. The children make good attendances and get away from home at 13 or 14 getting employment at Banbury 2 miles distant.

7. Teaching for Nonconformist children? No special provision is made for Non Cons, I have tried a prayer meeting and Bible Class, fixed up a parish room in Rectory, but they would not attend. The only school or religious teaching in this parish is the Church of England, consequently we are a happy family.

8. Organised study for adults? Not apart from Church Services except the Bible Reading League and instruction imparted at Mothers Meeting numbers about 25.

9. Interest in mission? I have Sermons and Lantern Lectures and get special Preachers. Having been a Foreign Missionary, Northern Canada, I give information continually in and out of Church and these few poor people (Pop 160) give £15 to oversea work annually.

10. Voters for Ruridecanal representatives a) men b) women? Two men.

11. PCC? We have a Parochial Church Committee which meets occasionally. It is responsible for funds for parochial and extra-parochial needs. It met 3 times since Oct and is not [sic] getting up a Sale of Work for Home and Foreign Missions.

1. Population 165.
2. William Spendlove was ordained priest in 1883 and served as a CMS missionary at four stations in Canada 1881–1905. He was also Diocesan Registrar for Mackenzie River between 1886 and 1905, when he became Rector of Drayton. He was 60 in 1914 and at the 1911 census he shared a household with his wife and 21-year-old son, who was recorded as a confirmed invalid.

DUCKLINGTON WITH HARDWICK[1]   Incumbent C. Tristram[2]

1. Baptism at morning or evening prayer? No: but Holy Baptism is sometimes administered during (but always in the afternoon) a children's service.

2. Communion times

a) Sunday at 12.0 and 8.0 am.

b) Ascension Day 8 am.

c) Saints Days [*No response*].

d) Week-days? [*No response*].

3. Is Communion ever sung? No.

4. Religious teaching to children a) Church b) Sunday School and c) Day school? i) Clergy teach in Day schools? ii) Religious teaching to Sunday school teachers? iii) Satisfactory results?

There is a Children's Service once a month, on other Sundays. I am obliged to go to the second church at Hardwick at 3 pm, which prevents attention on Sundays to men and children. There are two Sunday Schools, at which the Day School Teachers and others attend. The religious instruction in the Day School is well given by the Teachers. I teach once or twice a week. The Sunday School is well attended and the results are good.

5. Religious teaching to lads and young women? There is a Bible Class for lads fairly well attended. A sewing class for girls which may lead to formation of GFS. Two good meetings for Mothers at Ducklington and Hardwick.

6. Secondary school in Parish? There is no secondary school here.

7. Teaching for Nonconformist children? I should be very pleased for the Nonconformist Minister to teach his children in the school, but he lives a long way from the Parish.

8. Organised study for adults? There is a Bible Class for young men and a Bible reading at the class held for girls.

9. Interest in mission? There have been the usual Missionary Meetings in the Parish, and an Intercession for foreign missions at the end of Evening Prayer.

10. Voters for Ruridecanal representatives a) men b) women? Four men.

11. PCC? I have only been here one year. There has never been a Parochial Church Council: but I am very willing to start one.

1. Population 450.
2. Christopher Tristram graduated from Magdalen College Oxford in 1898 and trained at the Bishop's Hostel Farnham. He was ordained priest in 1902 and served two curacies between 1900 and 1912, when he became Rector of Ducklington. He was aged 37 in 1914 and at the 1911 census he was unmarried and sharing a household with an unmarried housekeeper.

DUNS TEW[1]   Incumbent A. Smith[2]

1. Baptism at morning or evening prayer? Not as a rule – only very occasionally.

2. Communion times

a) **Sunday** 8 and 11 (twice in the month).

b) **Ascension Day** 8 am.

c) **Saints Days** 8 am.

d) **Week-days?** [*No response*].

3. Is Communion ever sung? No.

4. Religious teaching to children a) Church b) Sunday School and c) Day school? i) Clergy teach in Day schools? ii) Religious teaching to Sunday school teachers? iii) Satisfactory results?

(a) In church an occasional children's service with Catechizing (b) Regular Sunday Sch. Instruction (c) Regular Church teaching. [i] Once a week.

5. Religious teaching to lads and young women? [*No response*].

6. Secondary school in Parish? No.

7. Teaching for Nonconformist children? No, but there has not been any demand for it.

8. Organised study for adults? No.

9. Interest in mission? [*No response*].

10. Voters for Ruridecanal representatives a) men b) women? a. 2.

11. PCC? No.

1. Population 233.
2. Albert Smith graduated from Lincoln College Oxford in 1856 and was ordained priest in 1858. He was Assistant Master at King Edward's School Birmingham, 1856–63, Headmaster of Sutton Coldfield Grammar School and Curate of Canwell between 1863 and 1902, when he became Vicar of Duns Tew. He was aged 80 in 1914 and at the 1911 census he was sharing a household with his wife, unmarried daughter and an unmarried theological student who was boarding with the family, together with two unmarried female servants.

ELSFIELD[1]   Incumbent W. H. Elkington[2]

1. Baptism at morning or evening prayer? At the close of Evening Prayer. Or any day or time to suit the convenience of the Parents.

2. Communion times

a) Sunday Alternate Sundays 8.30 and Mid-day.

b) Ascension Day [*No response*].

c) Saints Days [*No response*].

d) Week-days? [*No response*].

3. Is Communion ever sung? Never.

4. Religious teaching to children a) Church b) Sunday School and c) Day school? i) Clergy teach in Day schools? ii) Religious teaching to Sunday school teachers? iii) Satisfactory results?

The Vicar teaches frequently in the Day School. The Vicar is solely responsible for the Sunday School which is taken in the Church and is only occasionally assisted by the School Teacher. No other help available.

5. Religious teaching to lads and young women? Members of the G.F.S. meet occasionally at the Vicarage. In Advent and Lent, at the special services Instruction is given – and the men and lads have the opportunity of coming – which they do. Classes in small villages do not take.

6. Secondary school in Parish? No.

7. Teaching for Nonconformist children? No Nonconformists in the Parish. No Chapel.

8. Organised study for adults? [*No response*].

9. Interest in mission? 2 Sundays in the year devoted to mission work at Home and abroad with collections. Other days for intercession.

10. Voters for Ruridecanal representatives a) men b) women? 2 representatives.

11. PCC? No.

1. Population 163.
2. William Hardwick Elkington trained at St Bees College and was ordained priest in 1890. He served five curacies between 1888 and 1898 and in 1899 was appointed Vicar of Elsfield. He seems to have been absent from home at the 1911 census, but his household comprised his wife, two children and two unmarried female servants.

ENSTONE[1]   Incumbent W. J. Palmer[2]

1. Baptism at morning or evening prayer? Yes; the last two occasions being Whitsun Day and Trinity Sunday.

2. Communion times

a) Sunday 8 am and after 11 o'clock Matins on 1st Sunday in the month and on Great Festivals. On Easter Day also at 6.30 am.

b) Ascension Day 7, 7.30 or 8am and 10.30 or 11.

c) Saints Days 7.30 or 8 am.

d) Week-days? [*No response*].

3. Is Communion ever sung? No.

4. Religious teaching to children a) Church b) Sunday School and c) Day school? i) Clergy teach in Day schools? ii) Religious teaching to Sunday school teachers? iii) Satisfactory results?

(a) The children are Catechised in Church every Sunday, Good Friday, Ascension Day and Xmas Day – the exceptions have been the few Sundays the Vicar has been away for holiday. (b) Every Sunday at 10 am is Sunday School. (c) According to the County Council Syllabus – four out of five teachers are communicants. [i–iii] Three teachers in Sunday School are day school teachers of experience. Other helpers are young girls who have been in the school and have been confirmed. All teachers work according to Vicar's request. Classes have been held, but not recently for the younger teachers. The Deanery Sunday School Association is a help to the teachers in many ways. Nearly every Sunday morning I take some or other of the children myself, as well as superintend and one's first aim is to teach the Collects, the Catechism and the Gospels. I have found the work with children in Sunday School and Catechising more encouraging than anything else, thanks to the kind and intelligent help of the teachers. One finds the work tell as the children grow up, in the influence it gives one with them. I have been here since early in 1898 and came to the Benefice in 1904. It helps one get at the adults in the homes. I won't say I am satisfied, but have much to be thankful for in this matter. I try to follow the Church plan and remember what the Bishop of Lincoln used to say – I mean Dr King.

5. Religious teaching to lads and young women? One tries to make the utmost use of the classes for Confirmation. They come well to church on Sunday evenings, when instructions rather than sermons are given. There are very few girls at home. Lads will come to catechising after leaving day school, until confirmation.

6. Secondary school in Parish? None.

7. Teaching for Nonconformist children? The schools were taken over by the secular authorities 40 years ago.

8. Organised study for adults? No meetings or classes are held for this purpose. The magazine (The Sign) has a good circulation. One recommends the popular editions of theological books; especially those published for your Lordship at 6d. Opportunity is taken for courses of addresses and instructions in Lent and Advent.

9. Interest in mission? Ever since I have been Vicar here I have held classes for children and have presented them for examination in the Diocesan Missionary Study. This the children love. Through them missionary boxes and leaflets circulate in the homes of the parish.

10. Voters for Ruridecanal representatives a) men b) women? None. The voting for Ruridecanal representatives always follows immediately after the Easter Vestry business. Those present have always been qualified to vote.

11. PCC? No.

1. Population 932.
2. William Jackson Palmer graduated from the University of Oxford in 1891 and was ordained priest in 1897. He served three curacies between 1895 and 1904, the last of these, from 1898, at Enstone where he was appointed Vicar in 1904. He was 42 in 1914 and at the 1911 census he shared a household with his wife and one unmarried female servant.

EWELME[1]   Incumbent J. A. Dodd[2]

1. Baptism at morning or evening prayer? No. Baptism is administered at an afternoon service for children when there is usually a fair number of adults present, as well as children.

2. Communion times

a) Sunday 1st Sunday in month at noon; other Sundays at 8 am.

b) Ascension Day at 8am.

c) Saints Days at 8 am.

d) Week-days? [*No response*].

3. Is Communion ever sung? The first part of the Communion Service is sung at the noon celebration on the 1st Sunday in the month.

4. Religious teaching to children a) Church b) Sunday School and c) Day school? i) Clergy teach in Day schools? ii) Religious teaching to Sunday school teachers? iii) Satisfactory results?

There is Children's Service and Catechising in Church once a month. Sunday School at 10 and 2.30 every Sunday. In the Day School, the teaching is given under the Diocesan Syllabus. [i–iii] The Clergy do not teach in the Day School. In the Sunday School, the lessons are given according to the Diocesan syllabus, published by the C. of E. Sunday School Institute. Each Teacher is supplied with a copy and is expected to prepare the lesson from it. I find that the teachers carry this out very well. I should not say that the teaching is very effective – that of amateurs never is – but a great deal of good is done indirectly by the connection which is established between the teacher and the children

5. Religious teaching to lads and young women? There is a Bible Class for elder girls, and another for members of the Mothers' Union. There are confirmation classes every year. The lads and young women attend Church very well on Sunday evenings, and the teaching they are given is aimed chiefly at them.

6. Secondary school in Parish? No.

7. Teaching for Nonconformist children? No provision is made for nonconformist teaching as none has been asked for. I do not think that any real demand for it exists, or should be quite ready to see that it is provided.

8. Organised study for adults? I hope something is done in the Sunday sermons – but nothing is specially undertaken.

9. Interest in mission? Kings Messengers Class. Missionary meetings and sermons in church.

10. Voters for Ruridecanal representatives a) men b) women? The number attending the meeting held for this purpose was small. I do not remember how many were men and how many women – all had previously signed the declaration.

11. PCC? No.

1. Population 489.
2. Joseph Arthur Dodd graduated from Corpus Christi College Oxford in 1883 and was ordained priest in 1888. Between 1886 and 1893 he served London curacies at St George in the East and St Botolph Aldgate. He was appointed Rector of Lower Heyford in 1893 and then of South Hackney in 1897. He moved to become Rector of Ewelme in 1911. He was 53 in 1914 and at the 1911 census he was single, sharing a household with three unmarried female servants.

EYNSHAM[1]   Incumbent W. N. Bricknell[2]

1. Baptism at morning or evening prayer? No.

2. Communion times

a) **Sunday** 8 am and at 12. The first Sunday in the month.

b) **Ascension Day** 6 am 8am and 11-30 am.

c) **Saints Days** at 8 am and 11 am for Invalids.

d) **Week-days?** No.

3. Is Communion ever sung? No.

4. Religious teaching to children a) Church b) Sunday School and c) Day school? i) Clergy teach in Day schools? ii) Religious teaching to Sunday school teachers? iii) Satisfactory results?

a. Childrens Service in Church 1st Sunday in the month. B. Sund. School twice on a Sunday. C. Schools are Provided Schools. The Sunday School Teachers are all well educated and thoroughly well instructed in the Principles of Religion. [iii] I am quite satisfied.

5. Religious teaching to lads and young women? Classes are held for mutual improvement.

6. Secondary school in Parish? No.

7. Teaching for Nonconformist children? All parochial schools.

8. Organised study for adults? No.

9. Interest in mission? Sermons and Lectures with Lantern.

10. Voters for Ruridecanal representatives a) men b) women? [*No response*].

11. PCC? No.

1. Population 1,502.
2. William Nash Bricknell graduated from Merton College Oxford in 1886 and went on to train at the Leeds Clergy School, being ordained priest in 1889. He served two curacies between 1887 and 1893, when he was appointed as Vicar of Eynsham. He was 51 in 1914 and at the 1911 census he shared a household with his wife, 16-year-old niece and two unmarried female servants.

FARRINGDON, LITTLE[1]   Incumbent J. H. Kirkby[2]

1. Baptism at morning or evening prayer? No opportunity as yet.

2. Communion times

a) **Sunday** 8 am 12 noon 1st and 3rd Sunday.

b) **Ascension Day** 5.30 am 7.30am.

c) **Saints Days** 8 am.

d) **Week-days?** [*No response*].

3. Is Communion ever sung? No.

4. Religious teaching to children a) Church b) Sunday School and c) Day school? i) Clergy teach in Day schools? ii) Religious teaching to Sunday school teachers? iii) Satisfactory results?

(a) by Children's Services (b) Regular Sunday School to be started (c) School begins every day with ¾ hour religious instruction. [i–iii] Vicar takes the lesson twice a week. Monitress preparing for Oxford Local Exam. in which Divinity and Religious History a subject. We are fortunate in having an excellent School Mistress in Mrs Clark, and monitress (Norah Bayliff).

5. Religious teaching to lads and young women? Miss Marion Kirkby has just joined me, and we hope to have classes and to take other opportunities when there is less pressure of work out doors.

6. Secondary school in Parish? No.

7. Teaching for Nonconformist children? No nonconformist families.

8. Organised study for adults? Branch of Church of England Men's Society to be started.

9. Interest in mission? Organisation of C.E.M.S. to be utilized.

10. Voters for Ruridecanal representatives a) men b) women? None.

11. PCC? No.

1. Population 127.
2. John Henry Kirkby graduated from University College Oxford in 1876 and was ordained priest in 1881. He was Assistant Chaplain of St Peter's College Radley 1879–1914 and Sub-Warden from 1909 to 1914, when he became Vicar of Little Farringdon. He was 58 in 1914 and at the 1911 census he was unmarried and living in a combined household at Radley College.

FEWCOTT[1]   Incumbent B. Hamilton[2]

1. Baptism at morning or evening prayer? I have not been able to do so hitherto.

2. Communion times

a) **Sunday** 8 am or after the 11 o'clock M.P.

b) **Ascension Day** 8 and 11.

c) **Saints Days** 11 usually.

d) Week-days? None.

3. Is Communion ever sung? No. There is no regular organist and no choir.

4. Religious teaching to children a) Church b) Sunday School and c) Day school? i) Clergy teach in Day schools? ii) Religious teaching to Sunday school teachers? iii) Satisfactory results?

a) Instruction every Sunday afternoon* I teach the older children – Mrs Hamilton with the occasional help of a parishioner takes the Infants in the Vicarage. *It is then that children are baptized. There is no day-school or teachers. The day-school in this parish was closed some years ago – and the children were sent to Ardley and Fritwell. Ardley was closed some months ago – and two most excellent women – devout and faithful – sent away. This line of action was most keenly resented, I understand, by all concerned – £40 per an. is paid to the Carrier. This parish Church was closed for 7 or 8 years four – six months before I came the only service was held at 3 pm. Is it any wonder that the spiritual life of the people is at a low ebb. I sadly want a like minded brother – a priest if possible. You do not know, my Lord, how unwilling I am to write what must only add to the heavy burden of your work and thought. I do not intend to let things go on as they are – but before I take any steps wh. – under God – must lead to success – I want your mind and wishes – I am not keen for having anything to do with any Board of Education – State Control I abhor. But I cannot get the children without the machinery to move them to come – I am still in possession of long tried powers of teaching elementary, secondary – and collegiate – but they will soon leave me. Does Oxford not contain one son – who would for the Love of God – come and join me in teaching the Catholic faith in this hamlet?

5. Religious teaching to lads and young women? I conducted a Bible Class for lads last winter and spring.

6. Secondary school in Parish? No school.

7. Teaching for Nonconformist children? [*No response*].

8. Organised study for adults? No.

9. Interest in mission? Nothing beyond addresses and exhortations in Church.

10. Voters for Ruridecanal representatives a) men b) women? None.

11. PCC? No.

1. Population 150.
2. Benjamin Hamilton graduated from the Queen's University (Cork) in 1867 and received an MA from Trinity College Dublin in 1885. He was ordained priest in 1875. He served a number of chaplaincies and curacies 1874–1913 in addition to acting as Assistant Master at Haberdashers' Aske's school between 1882 and 1913, when he became Perpetual Curate of Fewcott. He was 66 in 1914 and at the 1911 census he shared a household with his wife, a boarding scholar and one unmarried female servant.

FIFIELD AND IDBURY[1]   Incumbent G. E. Mann[2]

1. Baptism at morning or evening prayer? Occasionally.

2. Communion times

a) **Sunday** 7 or 8 or 9.30.

b) **Ascension Day** 8 or 9.

c) **Saints Days** occasionally at 8.0 or 9.0.

d) **Week-days?** 0.

3. Is Communion ever sung? On alternate Sundays at Fifield at 9.30 and on high festivals at 8.0 On high festivals at Idbury at 10.30. Occasionally on Holy days at Fifield or Idbury at 9.0.

4. Religious teaching to children a) Church b) Sunday School and c) Day school? i) Clergy teach in Day schools? ii) Religious teaching to Sunday school teachers? iii) Satisfactory results?

(a) Catechising in Church at Fifield on alternate Sundays. (b) Sunday School at Fifield on alternate Sundays. At Idbury every Sunday. (c) Religious instruction according to the diocesan syllabus in the Parish School at Idbury. [i–iii] The Rector teaches in day school once a week. The classes for Sunday School teachers are at present suspended. The Rector found the candidates for Confirmation exceeding well instructed.

5. Religious teaching to lads and young women? A class for members of the G.F.S. is held during the winter. It is hoped that newly confirmed will continue in their classes.

6. Secondary school in Parish? No.

7. Teaching for Nonconformist children? There is a Church School, but no special teaching is desired. The parents send their children to the teaching provided.

8. Organised study for adults? A class for members of the Mothers' Union is held during the winter at Fifield and Idbury in alternate weeks.

9. Interest in mission? A S.P.G. lecture is occasionally given.

10. Voters for Ruridecanal representatives a) men b) women? None as far as I know.

11. PCC? No.

1. Population 377.
2. Gother Edward Mann trained at the Chancellor's School Truro in 1888 and was ordained priest in 1891. After a series of curacies and chaplaincies he became Vicar of St Matthew's Guernsey 1897–1903, Chaplain to the Sisters of Bethany Orphanage Bournemouth 1903–08

and was Rector of Glympton, Oxfordshire between 1908 and 1910, when he became Rector of Fifield. He was 46 in 1914 and at the 1911 census he and his wife shared a household with their butler Percy Weston and his wife Caroline who was employed as the cook.

FILKINS[1]   Incumbent W. C. Parr[2]

1. Baptism at morning or evening prayer? Not on Sunday.

2. Communion times

a) Sunday 8am.

b) Ascension Day 7.30 am and perhaps at 10 am.

c) Saints Days 7.30 am or 8 am – or 10 am.

d) Week-days? No daily celebration.

3. Is Communion ever sung? No.

4. Religious teaching to children a) Church b) Sunday School and c) Day school? i) Clergy teach in Day schools? ii) Religious teaching to Sunday school teachers? iii) Satisfactory results?

a. In Church we have a childrens service on Sunday at 3 pm. We use the color Stamps of the Society of Faith. I catechize generally on the Lesson of the Stamp. b. In the Sunday school at 10 am we use Lessons for the Church's children: adapted for the classes for the children. c. The Diocesan syllabus is followed and the teaching given by our professional staff is sound and good throughout the school. [i–iii] I teach 2 mornings a week and as a rule take the Catechism – Mr Roberts also attends as Rector of Broughton for we have a joint school for the two villages. I am afraid that we neither of us are as successful in our instruction as the staff teachers: but speaking for myself I hope that perhaps it is a good thing for me to go to the school, even if I am not very successful, as I obtain some knowledge of the children, tho I cannot say I am able to attract them. It is hardly possible in such a small school and with our teachers to have a class for instruction: it is not really necessary. Our Filkins Sunday school has improved of late. At the end of my second year I told those who were openly mutinous I thought they had better go; and since then there has not been much to complain of – The results attained are still unsatisfactory – nearly all the children leave the day they leave the day school – it is the "custom". I do not think any lad ever kneels for prayer after he leaves the Sunday school and Choir. (There are 2 exceptions to this statement) Most of the mutinous people who left behave badly in Church – it is the "Custom" – a good many of the girls cause me a good deal of anxiety – There has not been time for the new order to make its mark. I am not popular and I interfere as little as possible.

5. Religious teaching to lads and young women? We had a Sunday class for lads for a couple of winters conducted by Mrs Russell – when our Institute is open it may be possible to restore something of the kind: but I am very doubtful as to the success either on Sunday or weekday. I have already spoken to you of my difficulties with the young people.

6. Secondary school in Parish? No.

7. Teaching for Nonconformist children? Arrangements would be made if necessary but I do not think that anyone really feels aggrieved at the character of our teaching.

8. Organised study for adults? No.

9. Interest in mission? We distribute missionary leaflets with our magazine. We have endeavoured also to add to our missionary contributions by subscriptions and boxes. We have an Intercession once a month at our children's service and we collect for the support of a child in a Mission Home at Delhi from our children. We took part in the Missionary Exhibition at Witney last October.

10. Voters for Ruridecanal representatives a) men b) women? None. There is not the very smallest interest in the matter.

11. PCC? No.

1. Population 420.
2. Willoughby Chase Parr graduated from Magdalen College Oxford in 1875 and was ordained priest in 1877. Between 1876 and 1888 he served three curacies before accepting an appointment as Chaplain to the Forces, where he served in six stations including Malta and Standerton, South Africa, before returning in 1909 to become Vicar of Filkins. He was 60 in 1914 and at the 1911 census he shared a household with his wife and two unmarried female servants.

FINMERE[1]   Incumbent H. W. Trower[2]

1. Baptism at morning or evening prayer? Yes.

2. Communion times

a) Sunday 1st Sunday in month at 8 am 3rd Sunday at midday.

b) Ascension Day 8.

c) Saints Days [*No response*].

d) Week-days? [*No response*].

3. Is Communion ever sung? No.

4. Religious teaching to children a) Church b) Sunday School and c) Day school? i) Clergy teach in Day schools? ii) Religious teaching to Sunday school teachers? iii) Satisfactory results?

School twice on Sunday. The usual hours are observed for religious instruction in the Day School. [i–iii] The Rector teaches in the Day School as a rule twice a week. Nothing is done for the Instruction of Sunday School teachers – there is only one Volunteer who comes when she is able. I am not satisfied with results. The knowledge is sufficient – as testified to by the annual Diocesan Inspection reports but obedience and order is not to my satisfaction.

5. Religious teaching to lads and young women? Nothing special.

6. Secondary school in Parish? No.

7. Teaching for Nonconformist children? We have no professed nonconformists.

8. Organised study for adults? No.

9. Interest in mission? The subject is kept before them in sermons. One Sunday in the year is specially devoted to the subject and Missionary Boxes and literature are in use.

10. Voters for Ruridecanal representatives a) men b) women? I do not know.

11. PCC? No.

1. Population 222.
2. Henry William Trower graduated from Jesus College Oxford in 1866 and was ordained priest in 1869. After a succession of curacies he became Rector of Finmere in 1902. He was 69 in 1914 and at the 1911 census he was single and sharing a household with two unmarried female servants.

FINSTOCK AND FAWLER[1]   Incumbent A. C. Elwes[2]

1. Baptism at morning or evening prayer? No.

2. Communion times

a) **Sunday** 8.15 or mid-day.

b) **Ascension Day** 8.15 or mid-day.

c) **Saints Days** none

d) **Week-days?** None.

3. Is Communion ever sung? No.

4. Religious teaching to children a) Church b) Sunday School and c) Day school? i) Clergy teach in Day schools? ii) Religious teaching to Sunday school teachers? iii) Satisfactory results?

(a) Children's Service once a month. (b) Courses of lessons such as Potter and Sheard. (c) Diocesan Syllabus. [i–iii] No. Nothing. Very hard to get teachers at all. Children attend Sunday School but difficult to say with what result. Probably not much.

5. Religious teaching to lads and young women? Lads Bible Class is held on Sunday afternoons conducted by Mrs Elwes. Closed during summer. For the Girls there is a branch of the G.F.S.

6. Secondary school in Parish? No.

7. Teaching for Nonconformist children? The Managers of the School have offered facilities to the Nonconformists but no advantage has so far been taken of the offer.

8. Organised study for adults? No.

9. Interest in mission? Nothing. A few take missionary boxes. We have annual collections for CMS SPG and Diocesan Missionary Candidates Association.

10. Voters for Ruridecanal representatives a) men b) women? None.

11. PCC? No.

1. Population 500.
2. Albert Carey Elwes graduated from St John's College Oxford in 1895 and was ordained priest in 1898. He served two curacies between 1897 and 1901, becoming Vicar of Finstock in 1902. He was 46 years of age in 1914 and according to the 1911 census summary books shared a household with one other male and two females.

FOREST HILL[1]   Incumbent A. E. Negus[2]

1. Baptism at morning or evening prayer? Very occasionally at Evensong.

2. Communion times

a) Sunday on most at 8.5 am (and at midday 1st S. in month).

b) Ascension Day 7 am.

c) Saints Days 8.5 am.

d) Week-days? [*No response*].

3. Is Communion ever sung? No.

4. Religious teaching to children a) Church b) Sunday School and c) Day school? i) Clergy teach in Day schools? ii) Religious teaching to Sunday school teachers? iii) Satisfactory results?

(a) Children's Service at Church once a month. (b) Morning and afternoon School. (c) Diocesan syllabus followed. Clergy teach in Day School once a week. As regards results, it is difficult to say.

5. Religious teaching to lads and young women? They are gathered together in classes at Confirmation times.

6. Secondary school in Parish? No.

7. Teaching for Nonconformist children? Forest Hill children attend the Stanton St John School.

8. Organised study for adults? No.

9. Interest in mission? Sermons on behalf of S.P.G. and C.M.S. "Churches Abroad" presented with each copy of the Parish Magazine.

10. Voters for Ruridecanal representatives a) men b) women? None.

11. PCC? No.

1. Population 399.
2. Albert Edward Negus graduated from Lincoln College Oxford in 1892 and went on to train at Wycliffe Hall in 1897. He was ordained priest in 1898 having served chaplaincies at Magdalen and New College Oxford. He served two curacies between 1897 and 1902, when he became a Minor Canon of Bristol. He was Rector of Tubney from 1903 and became Vicar of Forest Hill in 1904. He was 45 in 1914 and at the 1911 census he shared a household with his wife, five young children, his brother-in-law (an unmarried chartered accountant) and two unmarried female servants.

FREELAND[1]   Incumbent E. W. Wilson[2]

1. Baptism at morning or evening prayer? Yes after second Lesson in Evening Prayer on Sundays.

2. Communion times

a) Sunday (1st) 6, 8 and 10.45 (2,3,4,5) 7.30.

b) Ascension Day 5, Church 7 St Marys House 9, Church.

c) Saints Days 7 and 9.

d) Week-days? 7 on Mon and Fri 7.30 on Tuesday, Thursday and Sat 7 on Wed in S. Mary's House.

3. Is Communion ever sung? Every Sunday at 10.45. Every Red letter Saint Day at 9.

4. Religious teaching to children a) Church b) Sunday School and c) Day school? i) Clergy teach in Day schools? ii) Religious teaching to Sunday school teachers? iii) Satisfactory results?

(a) They attend the Sung Mass every Red Letter Saints Day and every Sunday. [They attend] Sunday School in Church every other Sunday afternoon. (b) [They attend] Sunday School in School every other Sunday afternoon. [They attend] Church every Tuesday in Lent for instruction and every day in Holy Week except Holy Saturday. (c) [They attend] Religious instruction in school every day from 9.10 – 9.45. [i–iii] The Vicar goes into school most days for opening school and supervises the instruction and occasionally allows children to ask any questions they like which he answers. The Sunday School Teachers are given their lesson to teach in School. I am satisfied in so far as they all come forward for Confirmation and become Communicants.

5. Religious teaching to lads and young women? The Catechism which is held every Sunday afternoon at 3 in Church consists of all the Communicant Girls and Boys up to 17 or 18 years of age and several female adults come to the Catechism.

6. Secondary school in Parish? No.

7. Teaching for Nonconformist children? There is only a Church School. No provision is made for the children of Nonconf.

8. Organised study for adults? Catechism.

9. Interest in mission? A Bazaar is held every year for the Oxford Mission to Calcutta and we have frequent intercession in Church and one day a year is given to a continuous chain of prayer in Church.

10. Voters for Ruridecanal representatives a) men b) women? Two.

11. PCC? No.

1. Population 181.
2. Ernest William Wilson graduated from the University of Oxford in 1894 and trained at Cuddesdon, being ordained priest in 1896. He served two curacies between 1894 and 1904, when he became Vicar of Caversfield. In 1907 he moved to be Curate of St Mary and St John Cowley, before becoming Vicar of Freeland in 1909. He was 44 in 1914 and at the 1911 census he shared a household with his wife and two unmarried female servants.

FRINGFORD[1]   Incumbent S. Meredith Brown[2]

1. Baptism at morning or evening prayer? [*No response*].

2. Communion times

a) Sunday 1st in Month at Noon other Sundays at 8.

b) Ascension Day 8

c) Saints Days 8

d) Week-days? [*No response*].

3. Is Communion ever sung? No

4. Religious teaching to children a) Church b) Sunday School and c) Day school? i) Clergy teach in Day schools? ii) Religious teaching to Sunday school teachers? iii) Satisfactory results?

The children are catechised once a month in Church. I and my daughter run the Sunday School of practically whole parish. I take the Scripture each Wednesday. Used to teach daily, but found it too much. I have no Sunday School teacher beyond my child.

5. Religious teaching to lads and young women? I regret to say that Mr Chinnerys Class has ceased owing to his unfortunate illness and we have not been able to replace him.

6. Secondary school in Parish? No.

7. Teaching for Nonconformist children? There is no demand for Dissent here.

8. Organised study for adults? Not beyond usual Services.

9. Interest in mission? Missionary services and boxes.

10. Voters for Ruridecanal representatives a) men b) women? I don't know.

11. PCC? No and should not wish it.

1. Population 333.
2. Stafford Meredith Brown (formerly Brown) trained at Lichfield Theological College in 1878 and was ordained priest in 1882. He served two curacies 1880–88 and became Vicar of Horsey, Norfolk, in 1889, moving in 1910 to be Rector of Fringford. He was 60 in 1914 and at the 1911 census he shared a household with his wife, three unmarried children aged between 17 and 22 and two unmarried female servants.

FRITWELL[1] Incumbent J. L. Meredith[2]

1. Baptism at morning or evening prayer? Yes during the course of Evening Prayer on Sundays. Baptisms in this parish generally take place then.

2. Communion times

a) **Sunday** 1st Sund in month 6 am, 8am. Other Sundays 8 am 11 am.*

b) **Ascension Day** 6am* 8am.

c) **Saints Days** 7. 30 am 9am.*

d) **Week-days?** 7.30 am Tuesdays and Thursdays.

3. Is Communion ever sung? Those mark with * in answer to Question 2.

4. Religious teaching to children a) Church b) Sunday School and c) Day school? i) Clergy teach in Day schools? ii) Religious teaching to Sunday school teachers? iii) Satisfactory results?

(a) Catechism at 3 pm each Sunday except during holidays. Children come and sing their own service at the 9 am Celebration on Red Letter Saints Days. (b) Sunday School each Sunday at 10 am except during holidays. (c) Religious Instruction from

9.5 am – 9.45 am each day the Day Schools are open. [i–iii] I supervise the Religious Instruction though not teaching personally but I "coach" the PT's for the Diocesan Examinations in which they generally get a 1st Class. The Sunday School being small and therefore only 2 teachers being needed I do not hold a class. They use Haslock and Potter's books which I supply. Am quite satisfied with the results. The Day Schools obtained the highest mark for Religious Knowledge the last 3 years, and I find my candidates for Confirmation have a really good hold of the Catholic Faith at any rate so far as knowledge goes when they come to me for preparation.

5. Religious teaching to lads and young women? There is a Communicants Guild but beyond this I rely upon teaching from the pulpit.

6. Secondary school in Parish? Only a "night" school in winter in which of course there is no religious instruction.

7. Teaching for Nonconformist children? It has been offered but they do not seem to wish for it. In fact the children with very few exceptions come to church with the others for the 9 a.m. Celebration on Red Letter Saints Days.

8. Organised study for adults? No.

9. Interest in mission? A Missionary Guild, also a missionary meeting once a year. Also sermons at intervals on missions etc.

10. Voters for Ruridecanal representatives a) men b) women? None.

11. PCC? Yes. With advisory powers. It meets on the second Monday in March, June, September and December. It has been a great help to me in many ways and keeps up the interest of those really keen on the work of the Church in this parish.

1. Population 455.
2. John Llewellyn Meredith graduated from Worcester College Oxford in 1890 and went on to train at Ely College, being ordained priest in 1893. He served two curacies between 1892 and 1895, when he became Vicar of Fritwell. He was 46 in 1914 and at the 1911 census he shared a household with his wife and one unmarried female servant.

GARSINGTON[1]   Incumbent E. H. Horne[2]

1. Baptism at morning or evening prayer? Sometimes, at the Service in the afternoon.

2. Communion times

a) **Sunday** sometimes 8am sometimes 12 noon.

b) **Ascension Day** [*No response*].

c) **Saints Days** [*No response*].

d) **Week-days?** [*No response*].

3. Is Communion ever sung? No.

4. Religious teaching to children a) Church b) Sunday School and c) Day school? i) Clergy teach in Day schools? ii) Religious teaching to Sunday school teachers? iii) Satisfactory results?

In Day School, the teachers instruct the children according to the Diocesan Syllabus of Religious Instruction, and the children are inspected annually. There is only one Sunday-school teacher in addition to the Headmaster of the day school. The Infants are taught on Sunday morning and afternoon, in School; with some elders in the morning. I take the elders (boys and girls) in church each Sunday afternoon, by Catechising. My short experience of this parish justifies a continuation of this plan.

5. Religious teaching to lads and young women? For lads, a Bible Class taken by myself during the six months of winter. For young women, a Bible Class when my wife is able to take it.

6. Secondary school in Parish? No.

7. Teaching for Nonconformist children? No: there has been no question raised.

8. Organised study for adults? No: only one or two have the leisure for the systematic study of anything.

9. Interest in mission? The subject is regularly dealt with in the pulpit.

10. Voters for Ruridecanal representatives a) men b) women? None: there is no one of leisure to be a representative, and the parishioners are not organised enough to understand the electing of electors.

11. PCC? No.

1. Population 579.
2. Edward Hastings Horne graduated from Trinity College Oxford in 1887 and was ordained priest in 1890. He served four curacies between 1889 and 1900 including that of St Peter le Bailey in 1892. In 1900 he became Rector of Stanford Dingley, moving in 1912 to become Rector of Garsington. He was 51 in 1914 and at the 1911 census he shared a household with his wife, her 81-year-old aunt and two unmarried female servants.

GLYMPTON[1]   Incumbent H. W. Sawyer[2]

1. Baptism at morning or evening prayer? Yes – during Evening Prayer on Sundays.

2. Communion times

a) Sunday First Sunday in month at noon. Other Sundays at 8.

b) Ascension Day 8 and 11.45.

c) Saints Days 8.

d) Week-days? [*No response*].

3. Is Communion ever sung? No.

4. Religious teaching to children a) Church b) Sunday School and c) Day school? i) Clergy teach in Day schools? ii) Religious teaching to Sunday school teachers? iii) Satisfactory results?

There is a Sunday School on Sunday afternoons. There is definite Religious Instruction each morning in the Day School. The Clergyman teaches once a week in the Day School. The population is shifting and it is difficult to see much result from the religious instruction.

5. Religious teaching to lads and young women? Bible Classes are held in the winter months.

6. Secondary school in Parish? No.

7. Teaching for Nonconformist children? No. But no question ever arises on this point.

8. Organised study for adults? No.

9. Interest in mission? [*No response*].

10. Voters for Ruridecanal representatives a) men b) women? None.

11. PCC? No.

1. Population 167.
2. Herbert William Sawyer graduated from Trinity College Cambridge in 1896 and went on to train at Wells Theological College, being ordained priest in 1898. He served two curacies between 1897 and 1906, when he became Vicar of Fawley, moving in 1912 to become Rector of Glympton. He was 40 in 1914 and at the 1911 census he shared a household with his wife, 2-year-old son and two unmarried female servants.

GORING[1]   Incumbent A. E. Dams[2]

1. Baptism at morning or evening prayer? Not in the Parish Church, but we have done so in the Mission Room.

2. Communion times

a) Sunday 1st, 8 and midday, 2nd 6.15 and 8, 3rd 8 and midday, 4th 8, 5th 8.

b) Ascension Day 6.15, 8 and 11 am.

c) Saints Days 8 am.

d) Week-days? Thursdays 7.30 am.

3. Is Communion ever sung? On the Sunday after Christmas, Easter, Whitsuntide and the Dedication Festival, after Morning Prayer at 11 am.

4. Religious teaching to children a) Church b) Sunday School and c) Day school? i) Clergy teach in Day schools? ii) Religious teaching to Sunday school teachers? iii) Satisfactory results?

(a) There is a Children's Service every Sunday at 2.30, at which the children are catechised and instructed. This is very well attended. (b) There are Sunday Schools for Boys, Girls and Infants every Sunday at 10 am. The Boys and Girls go on to Church. The Infants have a service of their own in the School room. (c) The Clergy teach once a week each at least in the Day School. The Curate takes a fixed class and subject. The Vicar goes from Class to Class. [ii–iii] The Sunday School Teachers have a Meeting every fortnight, at which the lessons for the two following Sundays (prepared and sent round beforehand[)] by the Vicar, are explained and discussed. On the whole the arrangements for the Religious Instruction of the children work well, but the great difficulty is to carry it on beyond the school age.

5. Religious teaching to lads and young women? I cannot say that anything has yet been successfully attempted in this way. Classes have been tried and have failed. Something is done by means of monthly meetings of the Communicants' Guild, but these are not well attended by the younger people, and hardly at all by the lads.

6. Secondary school in Parish? There is no secondary school in the Parish.

7. Teaching for Nonconformist children? The Children of Nonconformist parents have the choice of an alternative when Catechism or Prayer Book subjects are being taught. But practically all prefer the Diocesan Syllabus, and there is no special class for Nonconformists.

8. Organised study for adults? Not yet. A good deal of definite instruction is given in sermons, and in other ways. But there has not so far been any provision for systematic study.

9. Interest in mission? As much as possible by that means is done through the Kings Messengers, S.P.G. Intercession is made every Friday at Evensong, and on two Sundays in the year. There is very little real interest in the parish in Church work overseas, but I think progress is being made.

10. Voters for Ruridecanal representatives a) men b) women? About 12 men only, and no women.

11. PCC? No, but this is about to be formed in connection with the Finance Scheme. It was not thought to be desirable in this parish to form a Church Council until the Finance Scheme was ready to be adopted. The Churchwardens and Sidesmen have acted as a Council when required.

1. Population 1,600.
2. Allen Edward Dams graduated from Trinity College Dublin in 1889 and was ordained priest in 1891. He served three curacies between 1890 and 1898, when he became Rector of Crowmarsh Gifford, moving in 1909 to become Vicar of Goring. He was 46 in 1914 and at

the 1911 census he shared a household with his wife, three young children, their governess and two unmarried female servants.

HAILEY CUM CRAWLEY[1]   Incumbent F. C. Nash[2]

1. Baptism at morning or evening prayer? Occasionally during Evening Prayer.

2. Communion times

a) Sunday 8 am or 11.30 am or both.

b) Ascension Day 5.30 am 8am and after Matins at 10 am.

c) Saints Days After Matins at 10 am.

d) Week-days? [*No response*].

3. Is Communion ever sung? On Great Festivals 11.30 am.

4. Religious teaching to children a) Church b) Sunday School and c) Day school? i) Clergy teach in Day schools? ii) Religious teaching to Sunday school teachers? iii) Satisfactory results?

(a) A Children's Service with Catechizing is held monthly in each Church. (b) There is a Sunday School for Hailey Children and one for Crawley Children. (c) The Headmaster of our Day School and his staff are most zealous in giving religious instruction and excellent results are shown. [i–iii] I supervise the teaching in the Day School and occasionally examine the classes. I have not found it possible to give instruction to the Sunday School Teachers, owing to the difficulty of getting them together for a class. Many of them work until late. It is very difficult to estimate results. Several who were scholars a few years ago are now Teachers. I feel that it would be a distinct loss to the religious life of the Parish if we had no Sunday Schools.

5. Religious teaching to lads and young women? A Bible Class for Boys and Girls after the Sunday School age.

6. Secondary school in Parish? No Secondary School.

7. Teaching for Nonconformist children? There is only a Church School. No provision is made in it for special instruction to the children of Nonconformist parents. The children of keen Nonconformists are usually sent to the Wesleyan School at Witney.

8. Organised study for adults? Nothing beyond teaching from the Pulpit, and that given at C.E.M.S. meetings.

9. Interest in mission? A Sermon on Missionary work quarterly. Circulation of literature. Intercession for missionary work weekly. Branch of Kings Messengers.

10. Voters for Ruridecanal representatives a) men b) women? About 15.

11. PCC? One has recently been formed. Its work is scarcely defined at present. It is intended that among other things it should undertake the Church Finance Scheme.

1. Population 1,019.
2. Frederick Corden Nash graduated from St Catherine's College Cambridge in 1876 and was ordained priest in 1880. He was mathematics master at the Royal Military Academy Gosport 1877–81 and then served two curacies between 1879 and 1891 before becoming Vicar of Berden in Essex. In 1899 he became Organizing Secretary of the Oxford Diocesan Church of England Temperance Society, until 1905, when he became Vicar of Hailey. He was 60 in 1914 and at the 1911 census he shared a household with his wife, 3-year-old nephew and one unmarried female servant.

HAMPTON POYLE[1]   Incumbent S. T. Gwilliam[2]

1. Baptism at morning or evening prayer? Yes, always. If ever I have to take a Baptism in a week day I read a shortened form of evening prayer.

2. Communion times

a) Sunday 8 am or 11 am.

b) Ascension Day [8 am or 11 am].

c) Saints Days Not usually.

d) Week-days? Never.

3. Is Communion ever sung? Yes at 11 o'clock. I have recently made that rather a feature of my work here and I find the choir likes it.

4. Religious teaching to children a) Church b) Sunday School and c) Day school? i) Clergy teach in Day schools? ii) Religious teaching to Sunday school teachers? iii) Satisfactory results?

No Day Schools in the parish.

5. Religious teaching to lads and young women? [*No response*].

6. Secondary school in Parish? None.

7. Teaching for Nonconformist children? [*No response*].

8. Organised study for adults? [*No response*].

9. Interest in mission? Yes. We have collections for S.P.G. and S.P.C.K. of which I am the representative in this deanery, with a parish missionary meeting on the lawn some Sunday evening in summer.

10. Voters for Ruridecanal representatives a) men b) women? [*No response*].

11. PCC? [*No response*].

1. Population 116.
2. Samuel Thorn Gwilliam graduated from King's College London in 1892 having been ordained priest in 1876. He served a curacy in Jamaica from 1875 to 1880 and a chaplaincy at Leipzig between 1881 and 1883 and three curacies in England between 1884 and 1891. He became Rector of Hampton Poyle in 1897. He was 61 in 1914 and at the 1911 census he shared a household with his wife, 15-year-old son and one unmarried female servant.

HANBOROUGH[1] Incumbent R. C. S. Bailey[2]

1. Baptism at morning or evening prayer? No. Holy Baptism is administered at the Children's Service, held every Sunday afternoon and attended by many adults.

2. Communion times

a) Sunday 8 am (and 12.15 am each first Sunday in the month).

b) Ascension Day 6 am and 8 am and 10 am.

c) Saints Days 7.45 am, or 8am or 10 am.

d) Week-days? [*No response*].

On some of the greatest Festivals Holy Communion is celebrated at 6am, 7am, 8am, 12.15 am.

3. Is Communion ever sung? Yes as far as the Prayer for the Church Militant. 12.15 am.

4. Religious teaching to children a) Church b) Sunday School and c) Day school? i) Clergy teach in Day schools? ii) Religious teaching to Sunday school teachers? iii) Satisfactory results?

(a) There is a Children's Service every Sunday afternoon with a course of addresses on Bible Subjects, generally Old Testament subjects. The Children are taken to Church on Ash Wednesday in Holy Week and on Ascension Day. (b) There is a Sunday School at 10 am on Sunday mornings both at Church Hanborough and Long Hanborough. The Collects are learned by heart, and also the Parables. Instruction is given on New Testament subjects. (c) The Diocesan Syllabus is followed in the Religious instruction; Hymns and Psalms are learned. [i–iii] I teach in School three times a week (twice, the elder children; once the Infants). I see nothing to boast about but at the same time I see much to encourage in the results attained. The ideal system, to my thinking, would be for the Parents to teach the Bible to their Children at home, and for the Clergy to supplement this teaching on Sundays. Teaching the Bible in School for Examination purposes tends to dullness and a lack of reverence; but as this ideal system is unattainable, I do not see how the present system can be improved upon.

5. Religious teaching to lads and young women? There is a Young Men's Bible-Class in the Autumn, Winter and Spring. There is a Communicants' Service of Preparation twice a year. There is a branch of the G.F.S., which meets at the Rectory once a quarter, and to which an address is given twice a year.

6. Secondary school in Parish? No.

7. Teaching for Nonconformist children? No child is withdrawn from the existing instruction and we conclude that this is not unacceptable to Nonconformist parents. So far as I can judge, Nonconformity is the result of tradition in this village or a preference for a Nonconformist type of Service. The Nonconformists have rarely any thought-out system.

8. Organised study for adults? Courses of Sermons are given in Advent and Lent, and occasionally at other times. A definitely doctrinal subject is preached about from time to time. Addresses are regularly given to the members of the C.E.M.S. and of the Mothers' Union.

9. Interest in mission? Sermons on missionary work are preached. Our people give, by means of Offertories, Free-Will Offerings, boxes, etc, to S.P.G: C.M.S.: U.M.C.A.: Oxford Mission to Calcutta: Mission to Madagascar: the Bible Society.

10. Voters for Ruridecanal representatives a) men b) women? I think, none: but those who vote are known to be Churchmen.

11. PCC? No.

1. Population 853.
2. Robert Cuthbert Steele Bailey graduated from St John's College Oxford in 1903 and then trained at Wells Theological College. He was ordained priest in 1905 and then served curacies in Woolwich 1904–08 and Burford between 1908 and 1911, when he became Rector of Hanborough. He was 33 in 1914 and at the 1911 census he shared a household with his wife and one unmarried female servant.

HANWELL[1] Incumbent J. P. Morgan[2]

1. Baptism at morning or evening prayer? Yes.

2. Communion times

a) **Sunday** at 8.30 am, except 1st Sunday in month and then after Mattins.

b) **Ascension Day** at 8.30 am.

c) **Saints Days** at 8.30 am.

d) **Week-days?** [*No response*].

3. Is Communion ever sung? No.

4. Religious teaching to children a) Church b) Sunday School and c) Day school? i) Clergy teach in Day schools? ii) Religious teaching to Sunday school teachers? iii) Satisfactory results?

(a) We have a children's service, using the form supplied by the S.P.C.K. – it has the Bishop's Sanction, we understand – and the Rector catechises the children, explaining to them the truths of the Faith. This Service which is attended by an average of 25 children and about 5 adults, is held regularly on the 1st Sunday in the month at 3.0 pm in the Church. (b) The Rector superintends the Sunday School himself and takes the senior class. He has not been absent on any Sunday in the year so far. The children are expected to be present at Mattins and a mark is given them for so doing at Sunday School which is held at 3.0 pm. The average attendance at Sunday School is 23: at the Day School 30. (c) The Day is a C.C. School. The form for religious instruction is that prescribed by the C.C. [i–iii] The Rector does not teach in the Day School, nor under existing circumstances would it be practicable. Though the population is so small, 197, there is a chapel and when the present Rector came to the Parish, Feb. 1913, out of five farmers four were nonconformist. Now three of the farmers attend Church. There is no hostility but in view of the political feeling the Rector does not think it wise at present to get on the School Committee, – that is, supposing a movement was made in that direction. Neither of his immediate predecessors was on it. Fortunately both the Day School Teachers are faithful Church women and invaluable to the clergyman. (d) They are instructed in the lessons appointed in the Form in use. All are ex-Sunday School scholars, and perhaps have as much influence for good as most others would have.

5. Religious teaching to lads and young women? There are few lads in proportion in the Parish: they mostly go away to the towns, mainly Banbury, of course. The church lads, perhaps half a dozen, chime the bells, five in number, for Mattins and Evensong, and usually remain for the Service. Indirectly in the Rifle Club and the Reading Room the Rector gets into touch with them. This winter the Rector hopes to start a Class: this will be his second winter here only. The G.F.S. is working successfully in this Parish: also the Mothers Union.

6. Secondary school in Parish? No.

7. Teaching for Nonconformist children? There is a C.C. School only.

8. Organised study for adults? The Rector is of opinion that the only feasible plan at present to promote this systematic study among our handful of farmers and labourers is to start a Bible Class. The Church people in this Parish are faithful; there were 36 communicants on Easter Day: the average at the 8.30 Celebration is 6. At the 11'oclock, monthly, 20.

9. Interest in mission? We have the usual Intercessory Service: special sermons on one Sunday in the year at Mattins and Evensong. There is also an annual meeting addressed by a deputation and four missionary boxes are distributed in the parish.

10. Voters for Ruridecanal representatives a) men b) women? None, I am sorry to say.

11. PCC? No.

1. Population 197.
2. John Percy Morgan graduated from Keble College Oxford in 1884 and in 1886 trained at Wells Theological College. He was ordained priest in 1888 and served four curacies until 1905, when he became Vicar of Stainfield between 1905 and 1907 then Vicar of Waterperry 1907–12 and Rector of Hanwell in 1913. He was 50 in 1914 and at the 1911 census he shared a household with his wife and two unmarried female servants.

HARPSDEN[1]   Incumbent J. W. Nutt[2]

1. Baptism at morning or evening prayer? Yes: at Evening Prayer.

2. Communion times

a) Sunday 1st and 3rd Sunday at noon: all others at 8.

b) Ascension Day noon.

c) Saints Days It is seldom during the week: difficult to get a congregation.

d) Week-days? [It is seldom during the week: difficult to get a congregation.]

3. Is Communion ever sung? When at noon it is choral to end of Creed, and a hymn is sung during the ablutions.

4. Religious teaching to children a) Church b) Sunday School and c) Day school? i) Clergy teach in Day schools? ii) Religious teaching to Sunday school teachers? iii) Satisfactory results?

(a) They are Catechised in Church on certain days. (b) and (c) I do not teach myself in the Sunday or Day Schools as I do not think it necessary, with two excellent teachers I have there, but I visit both and listen to what is going on. We always have excellent reports from the Dioc. Inspectors.

5. Religious teaching to lads and young women? [*No response*].

6. Secondary school in Parish? No.

7. Teaching for Nonconformist children? Such teaching has never been asked for.

8. Organised study for adults? [*No response*].

9. Interest in mission? Advent Sunday is always observed as a day of Special Intercession for Missions.

10. Voters for Ruridecanal representatives a) men b) women? None.

11. PCC? No.

1. Population 313.
2. John William Nutt graduated from Corpus Christi College Oxford in 1856 and was elected to a Fellowship at All Souls which he held between 1858 and 1875. He served as an Inspector of Schools 1860–67 and was ordained priest in 1868. He was Sub-Librarian of the Bodleian 1867–79 and an examiner in the School of Theology on nine occasions 1875–91. He was Rector of Harrietsham 1879–88, Rural Dean of Sutton 1886–88, Rector of Chelsfield 1888–92 and Examining Chaplain for the Bishop of London 1887–92. He became Rector of Harpsden in 1892. A scholar of eastern languages, he published a range of works including *Fragments of a Samaritan Targum with Preface* (1874) and *The Book of Proverbs in the O.T. Commentary for English Readers*. He was 80 in 1914 and at the 1911 census he shared a household with his wife and four unmarried female servants.

HASELEY, GREAT[1]   Incumbent W. G. Edwards[2]

1. Baptism at morning or evening prayer? Holy Baptism is administered at a Children's Service on the 2nd Sun in the month.

2. Communion times

a) Sunday at 8am except on the 1st Sunday in the month when it is celebrated at the 11 o'clock service. On Great Festivals at 7 am 8am and 11am.

b) Ascension Day at 8am.

c) Saints Days at 8am.

d) Week-days? It would be celebrated naturally at 8am.

3. Is Communion ever sung? Not as a complete service.

4. Religious teaching to children a) Church b) Sunday School and c) Day school? i) Clergy teach in Day schools? ii) Religious teaching to Sunday school teachers? iii) Satisfactory results?

(a) There is a children's service every Sunday at which the children are catechised on the instruction given the Sunday before. We use the stamp album system. (b) There is Sunday School at 10 am. The Head Teacher of the Day School takes the Senior children – the School being opened by the Rector. The Infants are taught by one of the Infant Teachers, the Rector giving them a short catechetical address. [i–iii] The Rector teaches the Senior children twice a week, taking definite portions of the Diocesan Syllabus in preparation for the Diocesan Inspection. The Sunday-School teachers are qualified to teach: and I think there is no need for special instruction in this case. Sunday Schools necessarily in country parishes with a dearth of people qualified to keep order and give instruction entail considerable watchfulness. I have no reason to be dissatisfied with the result, but wish better results could be obtained with less output [*sic*] of various kinds.

5. Religious teaching to lads and young women? The class for lads has been for some time discontinued owing to the resignation, partly through ill-health and partly from absence, of the lady who kindly managed it. The Mothers Union and the Girls Friendly Society are at work in the parish: and in addition until a month or two ago when my daughter left home, there was a Sunday Class for young women in particular. Mrs Edwards has 3 classes for women without restriction of age, but they are chiefly mothers in various parts of the parish.

6. Secondary school in Parish? There is none.

7. Teaching for Nonconformist children? The Nonconformists know that they can withdraw their children: but no child has ever been withdrawn: and I believe that there is no wish on their part that their children should have special teaching: but, if it were required, there would be no difficulty put in the way of making arrangements for the provision of religious teaching acceptable to them.

8. Organised study for adults? One of the aims of my sermons is to induce among the adults a personal at home study of Holy Scripture. It is known my library is at their service.

9. Interest in mission? The evangelisation of the world is a subject often brought forward in sermons. The S.P.G. has a branch here. C.M.S. is also supported. Intercessions at Holy Communion, as today – S. Peter's Day. Some of the parishioners read the Quarterly Intercession Paper. Special intercession services failed to attract.

10. Voters for Ruridecanal representatives a) men b) women? 13 men. No women.

11. PCC? No.

1. Population 517.
2. William Gilbert Edwards graduated from Christ Church Oxford in 1868 and was ordained priest in 1871. Between 1868 and 1873 he was Second Master of Twyford school, then after a year's curacy he occupied Minor Canonries at Chester and Windsor until 1894, when he became Rector of Great Haseley. He was 68 in 1914 and at the 1911 census he shared a household with his wife, two unmarried daughters aged 32 and 29, and three unmarried servants: two female and one male.

HEADINGTON[1]   Incumbent R. W. Townson[2]

1. Baptism at morning or evening prayer? [*No response*].

2. Communion times

a) **Sunday** 8 o'clock and 11 o'clock. On Great Festivals 7.15, 8 and 11 o'clock.

b) **Ascension Day** 8 o'clock.

c) **Saints Days** 8 o'clock.

d) **Week-days?** 8 o'clock.

3. Is Communion ever sung? Yes every Sunday at 11.

4. Religious teaching to children a) Church b) Sunday School and c) Day school? i) Clergy teach in Day schools? ii) Religious teaching to Sunday school teachers? iii) Satisfactory results?

[i] No. There is no instruction by Sunday School Teachers. The children all come to church twice each Sunday: they assemble there themselves and all the teaching is given by the parish priest.

5. Religious teaching to lads and young women? Classes are held for these as opportunity offers.

6. Secondary school in Parish? There is a Council School. I have no idea what religious instruction is given or if any.

7. Teaching for Nonconformist children? [*No response*].

8. Organised study for adults? The congregation and all who are willing to learn are systematically taught the Faith.

9. Interest in mission? They are taught as far as possible to realise their duties as members of the Catholic Church and all the responsibilities involved in their membership.

10. Voters for Ruridecanal representatives a) men b) women? None – to my knowledge.

11. PCC? No.

1. Population 1,352
2. Robert Walter Townson graduated from St John's College Oxford in 1889 and was ordained priest in 1891. He served three curacies between 1889 and 1897 and then became Chaplain to the Sisters of Bethany Bournemouth in 1898, becoming Vicar of Headington in 1899. A determined Anglo-Catholic, Townson's liturgical practices were cited before the Royal Commission on Ecclesiastical Discipline in 1905. He was 49 in 1914 and at the 1911 census he shared a household with his wife, three daughters, their cousin, a governess and two unmarried female servants.

HEADINGTON QUARRY[1]   Incumbent C. F. H. Johnston[2]

1. Baptism at morning or evening prayer? The usual Baptisms are during the 3pm Sunday service (shortened E P and catechizing) but Baptism is occasional administered during the 6.15 Evensong on Sunday (not on weekdays).

2. Communion times

a) Sunday 8 am: also 2nd S. at 7 am 1st and 3rd S. 11am.

b) Ascension Day 1892 4.15 and 11; 1893 4.15 and 9; 1894 11; 1895 4.15 and 11; 1896 4.15 and 9.30.

c) Saints Days 7.30 am.

d) Week-days? Thursday 7.30.

Ascension Day [Service times] 1897, 98 99 (4.15 9); 1900 (4.30 9); 1901, 2,3,4,5 (5 9); 1906, 7,8,9 (9); 1910 (7 8); 1911, 12 (7.30); 1913 (7.30 9); 1914 (7 9).

3. Is Communion ever sung? Not of late years one or twice at the 2nd of 3 celebrations on a great festival: <u>not</u> at 11

4. Religious teaching to children a) Church b) Sunday School and c) Day school? i) Clergy teach in Day schools? ii) Religious teaching to Sunday school teachers? iii) Satisfactory results?

(a) Catechizing every Sunday at 3: at 11 the older Infants and the younger classes of the boys and girls go out before the sermon during the singing of a hymn. The older ones remain for the sermon. (b) Sunday School for all at 10 am: the younger Infants finish their teaching with a short service in the Infant School. (c) Daily instruction according to the Diocesan Syllabus from 9 to 9.45 am. [i–iii] The clergy teach 4 times a week, once in each group. They have always been provided with graded Manuals, year by year eg St Paul's manuals; Catechism in Scripture Story; Potter and Sheard's; Nat. Soc.: New Methods: etc. I do not see any better methods than those which we try to carry out: and I could not point to any reason or result for dissatisfaction: we have very little assistance in the work from any one beyond those of the Day School teachers who help either in Sunday School, or at the Catechizing. The others are at present (June 1914) two working men and Mrs Johnston and Sister Alice.

5. Religious teaching to lads and young women? Sister Alice has a Bible Class on Sunday evening (early) for lads. G.F.S. girls attend the Vicarage Sunday morning class at 10. We are going to have a weekday Bible study for men which used to be held on Sundays.

6. Secondary school in Parish? No secondary School.

7. Teaching for Nonconformist children? I believe that the teaching in the Day School is quite acceptable to the Nonconformist parents. The Wesleyan minister (Rev. C. Pengelly) is not at all disposed to encourage dissatisfaction, nor have I any reason to suppose that any exists. A council school is within the bounds of the parish, but I have no reason to think that Nonconformist children are sent there in any number on the grounds of acceptable religious teaching. I am on the Board of Management.

8. Organised study for adults? Not at present beyond what is sometimes attempted at meetings of the C.E.M.S.

9. Interest in mission? Monthly intercessions in Church, after Sunday evensong. Collecting boxes in some houses for Home and Foreign Mission. A fortnightly meeting of boys and girls as King's Messengers, with the usual encouragements from Headquarters. Occasional visits from Missionaries.

10. Voters for Ruridecanal representatives a) men b) women? When we elected R.D. representatives 2 years ago, no one attended who needed to sign the declaration, all being communicants of full age, and known to one another as such.

11. PCC? We have not a parochial Church Council as yet. There have always been two church wardens and four or six sidesmen. For the current year we are meeting the requirements of Diocesan Finance by offertories, but we are contemplating the raising of funds by the method which will involve the forming of a parochial Church Council.

1. Population 2,362
2. Charles Francis Harding Johnston graduated from Christ's College Cambridge in 1867 and was ordained priest in 1868. Between 1868 and 1884 he occupied a series of teaching posts in schools and chaplaincies including one in Bombay. He served as Curate of Kidlington from 1884 to 1885 but then returned to India and was Archdeacon of Bombay between 1888 and 1890. He briefly occupied a curacy at All Saints' Oxford before becoming Vicar of Headington Quarry in 1902. He was the editor of *St Basil on the Holy Spirit, Revised text with notes and introduction* (1892). Johnston was 71 in 1914 and at the 1911 census he shared a household with his wife and two unmarried female servants.

HENLEY-ON-THAMES[1]   Incumbent J. F. Maul[2]

1. Baptism at morning or evening prayer? No.

2. Communion times

a) **Sunday** 1st and 3rd 8 and 12. Last 7 and 8 (sung) Gt Festivals 6.7.8.12.

b) **Ascension Day** 7 and 8.

c) **Saints Days** at 8.

d) **Week-days?** Wednesdays at 8 Fridays at 7.

3. Is Communion ever sung? At 8am last Sunday of Month.

4. Religious teaching to children a) Church b) Sunday School and c) Day school? i) Clergy teach in Day schools? ii) Religious teaching to Sunday school teachers? iii) Satisfactory results?

The two assistant Clergy each teach twice a week the Rector occasionally. There are about 300 children in the Sunday School and sixteen teachers. The teachers meet every Friday for instruction in the lesson for the following Sunday. The lesson is given to the children in School on Sunday morning, and in the afternoon it forms the subject of the catechising in the Church. I should mention that on Good Friday and Ascension Day all the 500 children in the National Schools come to Church for a special Service at 9.15 am. On Good Friday the Service consists of seven short addresses on the words from the Cross; interspersed with hymns. The results on the whole are, I think, fairly satisfactory from the number of children who annually present themselves for Confirmation.

5. Religious teaching to lads and young women? There are three classes for lads every Sunday independent of the Sunday School – between the ages of 15 and 23. There are over 80 in regular attendance. There are two Communicant classes for lads which meet once a month and before the great festivals. Into these classes the newly confirmed are drafted. Not so much is done for the Girls but there is the Guild of Mary the Virgin for Communicants with over 50 members – they meet once a month. There is also a Bible class every Sunday.

6. Secondary school in Parish? There is a secondary Boys' School, the religious teaching of which is by the scheme required to be that of the Church of England. This however, is evaded. The Catechism is not taught to any of the boys, and the Clergy are not invited to teach. The School is on the point of being placed under the authority of the Board of Education, and will cease to be a Church School.

7. Teaching for Nonconformist children? There is a safety-valve for Nonconformists in the shape of a British School, not in this Parish but in the Town.

8. Organised study for adults? There is a Mens Scripture study class which meets once a week as a rule. There is also a Communicants Association for men and women adults, which meets once a month for instruction and prayer.

9. Interest in mission? There is a Missionary Association for the support of the S.P.G. and U.M.C.A. The free-will offering scheme is in vogue, there is a large body of collectors there is also a branch of King's Messengers for the children, and an intercessory service once a month after Sunday evensong.

10. Voters for Ruridecanal representatives a) men b) women? None. It is unnecessary in the case of those who attend and are all well known to me.

11. PCC? No.

1. Population 3,200
2. John Fredric Maul graduated from Christ Church Oxford in 1872 and then trained at Cuddesdon. He was ordained priest in 1875 and after serving a curacy he became Vicar of St Paul Chichester and Chaplain to the Chichester Infirmary in 1879, moving to become Rector of Henley in 1883. He served as Rural Dean of Henley from 1901 to 1914 and was appointed an Honorary Canon of Christ Church in 1906. He was 64 in 1914 and at the 1911 census he was unmarried and shared a household with four unmarried female servants.

HENLEY, HOLY TRINITY (ROTHERFIELD GREYS)[1]

Incumbent R. M. Willis[2]

1. Baptism at morning or evening prayer? No.

2. Communion times

a) **Sunday** <u>8 am</u> every Sunday, also <u>7 am</u> 1st Sunday in month and also <u>noon</u> 1st and 3rd [Sunday in the month].

b) **Ascension Day** <u>7 am</u>, <u>8 am</u> and <u>Noon.</u>

c) **Saints Days** 8am.

d) **Week-days?** 8 am Thursdays in Advent and Lent.

3. Is Communion ever sung? Yes 8 am on High Festivals and at 8 am on the last Sunday in the month. The sung service was begun a year ago and has proved acceptable to the people.

4. Religious teaching to children a) Church b) Sunday School and c) Day school? i) Clergy teach in Day schools? ii) Religious teaching to Sunday school teachers? iii) Satisfactory results?

(a) Children's Service and Catechizing every Sunday at 3pm in the Church. (b) The Sunday-School Teachers are provided with copies of "Lessons for the Church's Children" by Potter and Sheard. Each course of lessons lasts one year. The Children are taught in accordance with Potter and Sheard's "Questions and Answers" system. The Head Mistress of the Day School is the Superintendent of the Boys' and Girls' (mixed) Sunday-School, and is paid for so being. (c) "The Syllabus of Religious Instruction for use in the Diocese of Oxford" is the basis of the daily teaching. [i–iii] The Vicar and the Assistant Curate both teach once a week in the Day School. Sunday-School Teachers' Meetings are held from time to time and taken by the Vicar. I think the Sunday- School is doing good work.

5. Religious teaching to lads and young women? A monthly Communicants' Class for lads. A weekly Bible Class for lads. A weekly Bible Class for boys. A monthly Communicants' Class for young women. A weekly Bible Class for girls who are too old for Sunday School. A branch of the G.F.S.

6. Secondary school in Parish? No secondary School.

7. Teaching for Nonconformist children? There is a British School in the Parish.

8. Organised study for adults? A branch of the C.E.M.S. A monthly Men's Service. A branch of the Mothers' Union. Three Mothers' Meetings each week during the Autumn, Winter and Spring.

9. Interest in mission? Deputations and Sermons each year for S.P.G. and C.M.S. A Missionary Association and Quarterly Intercession Services. Study-circles. Missionary Work Party.

10. Voters for Ruridecanal representatives a) men b) women? Not known.

11. PCC? No.

1. Population 3,776
2. Rawdon Marwood Willis graduated from St John's College Oxford in 1875 and trained at Leeds Clergy School in 1876, being ordained priest in 1888. He served two curacies between 1887 and 1907, when he was appointed Vicar of Highmore, moving in 1912 to become Perpetual Curate of Holy Trinity Henley (Rotherfield Greys). He was 49 in 1914 and at the 1911 census he shared a household with his wife and two unmarried female servants.

HETHE[1]   Incumbent W. Pendavis[2]

1. Baptism at morning or evening prayer? No – always during the Afternoon Service –which is the Children's service.

2. Communion times

a) Sunday 8 am and 11am on 1st S. in month and Festivals.

b) Ascension Day 8 am.

c) Saints Days 8 am.

d) Week-days? [*No response*].

3. Is Communion ever sung? No.

4. Religious teaching to children a) Church b) Sunday School and c) Day school? i) Clergy teach in Day schools? ii) Religious teaching to Sunday school teachers? iii) Satisfactory results?

(a) Catechizing in Church every Sunday afternoon with Instruction. (b) The Afternoon Childrens' Service with Catechizing and Teaching takes the place of Sunday School. (c) The Diocesan Syllabus of Instruction is followed. [i–iii] Yes – and is often present when the School Mistress teaches. In this small parish with but a small School the School Mistress is the only S.S. Teacher needed – and she is elderly and most capable.

5. Religious teaching to lads and young women? There are but few lads and young women. As soon as they are about 14 or 15 years of age – the lads find work as under-footmen – the girls also go into domestic service.

6. Secondary school in Parish? No.

7. Teaching for Nonconformist children? The children of Nonconformist parents are taught with the rest. There are but few of these: no objection has ever been made to Church teaching. There is a Roman Catholic Church and a Resident Priest in this Parish – and several R.C. families. The children of such families have consequently their own Rel. Instruction.

8. Organised study for adults? During Advent and Lent a series of Addresses is given.

9. Interest in mission? Church expansion in the dominions overseas – as well as Missionary work is often the subject of a sermon: beyond that there is little that can be done in a parish such as this.

10. Voters for Ruridecanal representatives a) men b) women? None.

11. PCC? No.

1. Population 284.
2. Whylock Pendavis graduated from Trinity College Dublin in 1874 and was ordained priest in 1876. After serving two curacies between 1875 and 1881 he went on to serve the majority of his career in Mauritius, ending as Honorary Canon, Sub-Dean, Archdeacon and Examining Chaplain to the Bishop of Mauritius. He returned to England to take up his appointment as Rector of Hethe in 1909. He was 61 in 1914 and at the 1911 census he shared a household with his wife, 14-year-old daughter and two unmarried female servants.

HEYFORD, LOWER[1] Incumbent V. R. Lennard[2]

1. Baptism at morning or evening prayer? [*No response*].

2. Communion times

a) Sunday Fortnightly on 1st Sun at midday on 3rd Sun at 8.30 am.

b) Ascension Day at 10 am.

c) Saints Days Only on Xmas day (2 celebrations) Ascension Day, Ash Wednesday and Harvest Festival.

d) Week-days? None.

3. Is Communion ever sung? No.

4. Religious teaching to children a) Church b) Sunday School and c) Day school? i) Clergy teach in Day schools? ii) Religious teaching to Sunday school teachers? iii) Satisfactory results?

(b) Sunday School each Sunday F 10.15 – 11 am and 2.30 – 3.20 pm (Curate teaching). Children's Service instead on 4th Sun. (a) A Children's Service and S. School. (c) Rector used to teach 4 days a week. Lately has discontinued, but there is a good and efficient School staff and we always get an excellent report F Diocesan Inspector. (3) No special instruction or classes. (4) The S. School is one of the most successful Institutions in the parish. Its History is interesting. A Sun-School was opened <u>in the</u>

Church for Reading and Writing in 1801. It was carried on for some 70 years. The number then dwindling, it was closed about 1870 and for 27 years until my appt. in 1897, there was no Church Sun. School only one at the Wesle[y]an Chapel. The Children were at Church at the evening Service. In 1898, I opened a Sun. with 60 children (greatly to our surprise). The Sun. School has been well attended since, and welcomed by the people. For some years my wife had a most successful Bible Class in connection with the School, for young men, but the numbers are now so small (both sexes leaving the parish early for occupations in the towns) that there are no grown up Scholars in the School.

5. Religious teaching to lads and young women? No special classes some Confirmation Classes. There is a Girls' club in the village.

6. Secondary school in Parish? No.

7. Teaching for Nonconformist children? No. No objections are heard.

8. Organised study for adults? No.

9. Interest in mission? Nothing beyond the teaching given in Church on the work and duty of missions.

10. Voters for Ruridecanal representatives a) men b) women? Three men and one woman.

11. PCC? No.

1. Population 455.
2. Vivian Rodwell Lennard graduated from Corpus Christi College Cambridge in 1872 and was ordained priest in 1881. After serving two curacies he served as Vicar of Lightcliffe (Yorks.) 1883–88, Astley (Warks.) 1888–90, and Rector of South Hackney between 1890 and 1897, when he moved to become Rector of Lower Heyford. He was the author of *Woman, Her Power, Influence and Mission* (1910), *The Longer Lent* (1911) and *Our Ideals* (1913). He was 66 in 1914 and at the 1911 census he shared a household with his wife, 24-year-old daughter and two unmarried female servants.

HEYFORD, UPPER[1]   Incumbent S. Cooper[2]

1. Baptism at morning or evening prayer? Yes.

2. Communion times

a) Sunday 11.30, 8 ,7, 8 on 1st 2nd 3rd and 4th Sundays respectively.

b) Ascension Day 8.30.

c) Saints Days 9.

d) Week-days? Wednesdays 8.10.

3. Is Communion sung? 8, 8.30, 9.

4. Religious teaching to children a) Church b) Sunday School and c) Day school? i) Clergy teach in Day schools? ii) Religious teaching to Sunday school teachers? iii) Satisfactory results?

1. In Church – Catechism every Sunday in Sunday School, preparation for Catechism in Day school first ¾ hour every morning. 2. The Rector teaches 3 days a week in the Day school. 3. Notes supplied. 4. Fairly satisfied. The Diocesan Inspector quite satisfied.

5. Religious teaching to lads and young women? Bible Class for young women on Sunday afternoon.

6. Secondary school in Parish? None.

7. Teaching for Nonconformist children? The Dissenters have their own Sunday School.

8. Organised study for adults? Two sermons preached every Sunday.

9. Interest in mission? A branch of the Kings Messengers instructed by the Rector. Day of Intercession. Annual missionary meeting. Occasional sermons and intercessions.

10. Voters for Ruridecanal representatives a) men b) women? I have written to my predecessor for information as I cannot find such a list. Reply enclosed. June 29[th.] 'I am sorry to say I have no record. I was ill when we elected. I did not know that a record had to be kept. As far as I remember, we used to get all the available people together, make them sign the paper, and then hold the election.'

11. PCC? Yes. Consultative. Oct 6 and 3 times since 1913.

1. Population 314.
2. Sydney Cooper graduated from New College Oxford in 1884 and trained at Cuddesdon College, being ordained priest in 1887. After serving two curacies between 1886 and 1894 he became Vicar of Christ Church Frome Selwood, moving to become Rector of Upper Heyford in 1912. He was 52 in 1914 and at the 1911 census he was described as married and shared a household with his 20-year-old daughter, four other children aged between 3 and 9, and two unmarried female servants.

HEYTHROP[1]   Incumbent C. G. Moon[2]

1. Baptism at morning or evening prayer? Only at Children's service.

2. Communion times

a) Sunday 8.30, 11 o'clock first Sunday. Festivals 7, 8.30 and 11.

b) Ascension Day 8.

c) Saints Days [*No response*].

d) **Week-days?** [*No response*].

3. Is Communion ever sung? [*No response*].

4. Religious teaching to children a) Church b) Sunday School and c) Day school? i) Clergy teach in Day schools? ii) Religious teaching to Sunday school teachers? iii) Satisfactory results?

a. I hold a childrens service which is well attended practically all the day children come and a great many others from a distance, we usually have about 80 – 90, and about 15 or 20 mothers. The children take a keen interest in the course of instruction and catechising. b. Sunday School as there is childrens service is not practicable owing to the great distance children have to come and the absolute lack of people suitable for teaching. c. In Day Schools. [i–iii] I attend regularly and at times take the instruction but mostly in the infant room to help the mistress in there, as in the other part the teaching is excellent. The religious instruction in Day School is now giving a good result and will shortly be better as the new Teachers get a greater hold over the children. The children at childrens service take a greater interest each year and I much regret leaving them and their service.

5. Religious teaching to lads and young women? I had a Bible Class on a weekday two years ago but, those lads have all gone, and the actual fact was the centre of this village is destitute of lads and young women.

6. Secondary school in Parish? [*No response*].

7. Teaching for Nonconformist children? [*No response*].

8. Organised study for adults? [*No response*].

9. Interest in mission? Yearly sermons and addresses in Lent.

10. Voters for Ruridecanal representatives a) men b) women? None that I know of.

11. PCC? [*No response*].

1. Population 246.
2. Cecil Graham Moon graduated from Magdalen College Oxford in 1890 and trained at Cuddesdon College, being ordained priest in 1893. After serving two curacies between 1891 and 1898 he became Rector of Westcote, moving to become Rector of Heythrop in 1906. He was 46 years old in 1914. His household was not found in the 1911 census but in 1901 he was sharing a household with his wife and two unmarried female servants.

HIGHFIELD[1]   Incumbent F. T. Colson[2]

1. Baptism at morning or evening prayer? Only for adults.

2. Communion times

a) **Sunday** 8 am and also midday 1st and 3rd Sunday in the month.

b) **Ascension Day** 7.30 am. 9.30am and midday.

c) **Saints Days** 8am or 11am.

d) **Week-days?** Occasionally at 8 or 9am.

3. Is Communion ever sung? No, the choir is not good enough.

4. Religious teaching to children a) Church b) Sunday School and c) Day school? i) Clergy teach in Day schools? ii) Religious teaching to Sunday school teachers? iii) Satisfactory results?

The Children are instructed in Church on the 2nd, 4th and 5th Sundays in the month. Sunday School is held every Sunday at 10 am and 2.45 pm. [i–iii] There are no Day Schools in the Parish. Meetings are held once a month for Sunday School Teachers. On the whole, considering that this is a small Parish, and nothing had been done for the Children till it was created 4 years ago, I think the results are very good indeed.

5. Religious teaching to lads and young women? Bible Classes are held on Sundays for Lads and Young Women.

6. Secondary school in Parish? No.

7. Teaching for Nonconformist children? There are no Day Schools in the Parish. The children go either to S. Andrew's Schools, Headington, or Headington Council School, or to Oxford.

8. Organised study for adults? No, however hope ere long to have Study Bands.

9. Interest in mission? Annual Sermons are preached Colls for the S.P.G. and the C.M.S. by deputations from those societies, and frequent reference is made to the subject in ordinary sermons. Meetings with Missionary speakers are held from time to time. Quarterly Missionary Services for Children are held in Church and Missionary Addresses and Sermons are given in Sunday School. Monthly Services are held for Intercessions for Foreign Missions and on the third Sunday in the month, special prayer for the work of the Church overseas is asked for at the 8 am Celebration. All members of the Communicants Prayer Union pray for Missions each Monday.

10. Voters for Ruridecanal representatives a) men b) women? None. At the two meetings which have been held to vote for Ruridecanal representatives all those present were known to me to be actual Communicants so I did not ask them to sign the forms of declaration.

11. PCC? No, but I consult the Churchwardens and Sidesmen (8) about matters connected with the Parish Church. A meeting will be held in July for this purpose.

1. Population 1,636. Highfield was a new parish formally constituted in 1910 to serve the growing population of New Headington, though an Anglican chapel had been in place there since 1870.

2. Francis Tovey Colson graduated from Corpus Christi College Cambridge in 1881 and trained at Ridley Hall, being ordained priest in 1882. After an initial curacy 1881–88 he was Vicar of Warley (Essex) 1888–92 and St John with St Stephen Reading between 1892 and 1909, when he became Vicar of Highfield. He became an Honorary Canon of Christ Church in 1903. He was 55 in 1914 and at the 1911 census he shared a household with his wife, their unmarried son, who was studying for Holy Orders, and two unmarried female servants.

HIGHMORE[1]   Incumbent J. Hughes[2]

1. Baptism at morning or evening prayer? No. Holy Baptism administered at the Children's Service.

2. Communion times

a) Sunday 8 am.

b) Ascension Day 8am.

c) Saints Days 8am.

d) Week-days? [*No response*].

3. Is Communion ever sung? Yes at noon 1st Sunday in the month and on Great Festivals.

4. Religious teaching to children a) Church b) Sunday School and c) Day school? i) Clergy teach in Day schools? ii) Religious teaching to Sunday school teachers? iii) Satisfactory results?

(a) Children's Service every Sunday at 3 pm. For the last nine months the Gospel for the Day has been considered. Collects are recited by the children. The Church Catechism is repeated at certain intervals. (c) The Diocesan Syllabus is taught. [i–iii] It has been the custom in the parish for the parish priest to give one lesson a week at the Day-Schools. I am satisfied that there is a recognised improvement in the intelligence of the children.

5. Religious teaching to lads and young women? Throughout the winter until Easter there was a Bible Class for lads between ages 14 and 21 every Monday night at 7.30. For young women a class on Fridays at 4.30 pm.

6. Secondary school in Parish? No.

7. Teaching for Nonconformist children? No objections on behalf of Nonconformist parents have been made and so no provision is required.

8. Organised study for adults? Yes. Last winter a class was held for men every Friday night at 7.30. Subject – The Apostles' Creed. This class has formed itself recently into a branch of the C.E.M.S.

9. Interest in mission? Last year the parish took an active part in the Henley Exhibition and intercessory services were held in Church. S.P.G. Boxes are distributed in the parish. The offertory for the 1st Sunday in the month at the children's service is given to the S.P.G. A boy of 9 acts as secretary and forwards the offertory to headquarters.

10. Voters for Ruridecanal representatives a) men b) women? [*No response*].

11. PCC? No.

1. Population 289.
2. John Hughes graduated from Lampeter College in 1901 and Jesus College Oxford in 1912. He was ordained priest in 1902 and after serving curacies in Wales became Welsh Chaplain at Jesus College Oxford in 1909 and also Curate of St Philip and St James Oxford in 1911. He moved from both these posts to become Vicar of Highmore in 1913. He was 40 in 1914 and at the 1911 census he shared a household with his wife, a widowed female relative and three unmarried female servants.

HOLTON[1]   Incumbent A. Langdale-Smith[2]

1. Baptism at morning or evening prayer? Occasionally, but not usually.

2. Communion times

a) Sunday 8.30 on third Sunday in month. 11.0 1st Sunday in month.

b) Ascension Day [*No response*].

c) Saints Days [*No response*].

d) Week-days? [*No response*].

3. Is Communion ever sung? No.

4. Religious teaching to children a) Church b) Sunday School and c) Day school? i) Clergy teach in Day schools? ii) Religious teaching to Sunday school teachers? iii) Satisfactory results?

[i–iii] Occasionally. The S.S. teachers are my own daughters – one has Cambridge Diploma – another daughter who occasionally teaches also has Camb. Diploma – I am absolutely satisfied with results.

5. Religious teaching to lads and young women? An open Bible Class during autumn and winter months discontinued in summer.

6. Secondary school in Parish? No.

7. Teaching for Nonconformist children? There is no trouble about this whatever – that I have ever heard.

8. Organised study for adults? I don't quite understand the question. I conclude the answer should be in the negative.

9. Interest in mission? Direct Sermons, constant allusions in sermons, meetings and lectures from time to time. Intercessions from time to time, missionary literature. And the fact that 2 have gone from the village as foreign missionaries. The Rev C. E. Tyndale – Diocese of Kashmir, Rev E. Langdale-Smith – Madras, and Miss E.D. Langdale-Smith will shortly be going (D.V.) as a missionary probably in India.

10. Voters for Ruridecanal representatives a) men b) women? None.

11. PCC? None.

1. Population 201.
2. Arthur Langdale-Smith (formerly Arthur Langdale Smith) graduated from Worcester College Oxford in 1875 and trained at the London College of Divinity, being ordained priest in 1878. He served two curacies between 1877 and 1884, was Vicar of Steeple Claydon 1884–88 and then of St Paul Birmingham between 1888 and 1891, when he moved to the Rectory of Holton. He was 61 in 1914 and at the 1911 census he shared a household with his wife, two sons and two daughters aged between 16 and 23, together with three unmarried female servants.

HOLWELL[1]   Incumbent J. B. Rainey[2]

1. Baptism at morning or evening prayer? Yes – in the course of Evening Prayer from March to September; otherwise at a special afternoon service.

2. Communion times

a) **Sunday** Holy Communion is administered once a month and at Xmas, Easter, Whitsunday and Trinity Sunday.

b) **Ascension Day** [*No response*].

c) **Saints Days** [*No response*].

d) **Week-days?** [*No response*].

3. Is Communion ever sung? No.

4. Religious teaching to children a) Church b) Sunday School and c) Day school? i) Clergy teach in Day schools? ii) Religious teaching to Sunday school teachers? iii) Satisfactory results?

A Sunday School is held morning and afternoon. I teach in the Sunday School together with my wife and daughter, and the Head Mistress. The Head Mistress and Supplementary Teacher give instruction in the Day School; and I give the higher groups a paper of questions once a week. The Report of the Diocesan Inspector last year was most satisfactory.

5. Religious teaching to lads and young women? After the preparation of the elder boys and girls for Confirmation and Holy Communion it would be difficult to form classes for religious instruction in so small a parish.

6. Secondary school in Parish? There is no secondary School.

7. Teaching for Nonconformist children? No parents have withdrawn their children from religious instruction nor have they expressed a wish that they should receive other than is given.

8. Organised study for adults? No.

9. Interest in mission? Sermons are preached on Missionary subjects. An address is given by a Missionary Deputation at the Annual Missionary Meeting; and several different Missionary Magazines are circulated in the Parish.

10. Voters for Ruridecanal representatives a) men b) women? The declaration has not been signed.

11. PCC? No.

1. Population 150.
2. James Bryant Rainey graduated from Pembroke College Oxford in 1874 and was ordained priest in 1876. He served two curacies between 1874 and 1884, when he became Rector of Holwell. He was 66 in 1914 and at the 1911 census he shared a household with his wife, two unmarried children (a daughter aged 33 and a son aged 32) and two unmarried female servants.

HORTON-CUM-STUDLEY[1]   Incumbent J. E. B. Brine[2]

1. Baptism at morning or evening prayer? No.

2. Communion times

a) Sunday 1st and 3rd 11.50 am. 2nd, 4th and 5th at 8 am.

b) Ascension Day 8 am.

c) Saints Days The Circumcision, Epiphany, Annunciation, S. Barnabas and All Saints at 8 am.

d) Week-days? No celebration

3. Is Communion ever sung? No

4. Religious teaching to children a) Church b) Sunday School and c) Day school? i) Clergy teach in Day schools? ii) Religious teaching to Sunday school teachers? iii) Satisfactory results?

(a) Weekly Catechizing on Sundays. (b) No Sunday School. (c) Daily 9.10 am to 9.45 am. [i–iii] The clergy teach in Day School twice a week. Not satisfied: there seems generally, especially with the lads, a great falling off when they leave school.

5. Religious teaching to lads and young women? Nothing.

6. Secondary school in Parish? No.

7. Teaching for Nonconformist children? Church School but no nonconformist children.

8. Organised study for adults? No.

9. Interest in mission? The usual Missionary Sunday, occasionally a missionary meeting. (These however seem to have fallen into abeyance in the Rural Deanery) and the annual intercession in Church.

10. Voters for Ruridecanal representatives a) men b) women? None that I am aware of. No interest is shown in the election of ruridecanal representatives which is generally done at the Easter Vestry. The attendance at this Vestry is on the average 4, including the Churchwardens and the Vicar.

11. PCC? No.

1. Population 298.
2. James Edward Bouverie Brine graduated from Christ Church Oxford in 1877 and trained at Cuddesdon College 1878–79, being ordained priest in 1880. After a trio of curacies between 1879 and 1887, one at St Thomas the Martyr in Oxford, he served a series of chaplaincies in Ceylon. He returned to England in 1902 as Curate of Hungerford and then was appointed Vicar of Cadmore End in 1904, moving in 1909 to become Vicar of Horton-cum-Studley. He was 58 in 1914 and at the 1911 census he shared a household with his wife, their 11-year-old daughter and two unmarried female servants.

IFFLEY[1]   Incumbent O. S. E. Clarendon[2]

1. Baptism at morning or evening prayer? Sometimes on weekdays.

2. Communion times

a) **Sunday** 8.15 (1st Sun in Month 8.15 and Noon, 2nd Sun 7.15 and 8.15).

b) **Ascension Day** 6.0, 8.0 and 11.0.

c) **Saints Days** 8.0.

d) **Week-days?** Weekly on Wed at 8.

3. Is Communion ever sung? No.

4. Religious teaching to children a) Church b) Sunday School and c) Day school? i) Clergy teach in Day schools? ii) Religious teaching to Sunday school teachers? iii) Satisfactory results?

(a) Children's service each Sunday at 3.0. School children come to Church for Religious Instruction on Holy Days at 9.0. (b) Sunday School each Sunday at 10.0. [i–iii] I teach in School twice a week. As regards Day School results are excellent. Sunday School – not nearly as good. But the School is a very small one.

5. Religious teaching to lads and young women? Occasional Communicant Class. G.F.S.

6. Secondary school in Parish? No.

7. Teaching for Nonconformist children? None is required.

8. Organised study for adults? Being close to Oxford, the Parish has the advantage of Lectures and Meetings there.

9. Interest in mission? Monthly Intercession for Foreign Missions. Yearly observance of Day of Intercessions. Many collections and sermons for various Missions. Missionary Working Parties. King's Messengers. Distribution of Missionary Literature Monthly.

10. Voters for Ruridecanal representatives a) men b) women? Only a few.

11. PCC? No.

1. Population about 1,100.
2. Owen Samuel Edward Clarendon graduated from Trinity College Dublin in 1895 and was ordained priest in 1897. He served three curacies between 1896 and 1910, when he was appointed as Vicar of Iffley. He was 41 in 1914 and at the 1911 census he shared a household with his wife, their 8-year-old daughter and two unmarried female servants.

IPSDEN WITH NORTH STOKE[1]   Incumbent H. E. H. Coombes[2]

1. Baptism at morning or evening prayer? No.

2. Communion times

a) Sunday at North Stoke twice at 8.30 and once Midday; at Ipsden twice at 8 and once midday in each month.

b) Ascension Day In forenoon at each Church.

c) Saints Days None.

d) Week-days? None.

3. Is Communion ever sung? No.

4. Religious teaching to children a) Church b) Sunday School and c) Day school? i) Clergy teach in Day schools? ii) Religious teaching to Sunday school teachers? iii) Satisfactory results?

Catechising once a month in each church. One Sunday School session in each parish each Sunday except when Catechising in Church. [i–iii] The Vicar teaches as a rule once a week in Day School. Occasional meetings are held for Sunday School teachers. The Sunday Schools are fairly satisfactory.

5. Religious teaching to lads and young women? The small population and other causes has prevented anything more than preparation classes for Confirmation.

6. Secondary school in Parish? No.

7. Teaching for Nonconformist children? There has been no request, and would probably be no one to undertake it, if offered.

8. Organised study for adults? No special organization.

9. Interest in mission? Occasional sermons and meetings. Instruction to Children in Sunday Schools. Band of Hope and Catechising.

10. Voters for Ruridecanal representatives a) men b) women? 5 men, 2 women.

11. PCC? No.

1. Population 401.
2. Herbert Edwin Henshaw Coombes graduated from St John's College Cambridge in 1889 and trained at the Cambridge Clergy Training School, being ordained priest in 1891. He served two curacies between 1890 and 1895, when he was appointed as Vicar of Houghton. He left to serve as Chaplain to the Mission to Seamen for the Bristol Channel at Penarth and Barry in 1901, where he remained until his appointment as Vicar of North Stoke with Ipsden in 1908. He was 46 in 1914 and at the 1911 census he shared a household with his wife, their three children aged between 1 and 7, their nurse and two unmarried female servants.

ISLIP[1]   Incumbent J. H. Carter[2]

1. Baptism at morning or evening prayer? Not recently.

2. Communion times

a) Sunday 8 but on the first Sunday after mattins also.

b) Ascension Day 7.0 (Choral) and 10.30.

c) Saints Days at 8 or 10.30.

d) Week-days? On Thursdays at 7.30.

3. Is Communion ever sung? Yes on all Great Festivals 11 o'clock except on Ascension Day when it is at 7.

4. Religious teaching to children a) Church b) Sunday School and c) Day school? i) Clergy teach in Day schools? ii) Religious teaching to Sunday school teachers? iii) Satisfactory results?

(a) The Children attend Mattins and Sermon on Sundays and Evensong on Saints Days when they are catechised. There is Catechising also on the first Sunday afternoon in each month. Sunday School – morning and afternoon all other Sundays. One hour is given to Religious Instruction each day in the Day School. [i–iii] I teach on Wednesdays and Fridays. The S.S. teachers attend a preparation class each Friday. I think the children in this parish are fairly well grounded in the knowledge of the Faith.

5. Religious teaching to lads and young women? Bible-class for lads on Sunday afternoon during the winter. Very difficult to keep up the attendance. There is also a Bible-class for the young women and girls but we have very few living in the parish. Nearly all go out to service at 14.

6. Secondary school in Parish? No.

7. Teaching for Nonconformist children? No special teaching is given to these. There seems to be no demand. We have no resident Nonconformist Minister or any one free to give it.

8. Organised study for adults? Nothing systematic. They listen to sermons very well and we try and teach them their religion by that means.

9. Interest in mission? Quarterly envelopes are distributed to each person over 16 as called for. We use a litany for Foreign Missions from time to time in Church we distribute about 20 copies of the Q.I.P.

10. Voters for Ruridecanal representatives a) men b) women? None.

11. PCC? Yes. To advise the Rector and Wardens. Twice.

1. Population 562
2. James Holderness Carter graduated from Exeter College Oxford in 1887 and was ordained priest in 1888. After an initial curacy in Dorset 1887–90 he served principally in South Africa including a period as Acting Chaplain to the Forces 1900–02 during the Boer War. He returned to England in 1905 to take up an appointment as Vicar of Burcombe, which he left in 1910 for the Rectory of Islip. He was 52 in in 1914 and at the 1911 census he shared a household with his wife, two teenage sons and three unmarried female servants.

KENCOT[1]   Incumbent H. E. Cooper[2]

1. Baptism at morning or evening prayer? At Children's service on Sunday afternoon.

2. Communion times

a) **Sunday** 8.30 or 11.

b) **Ascension Day** 8.

c) **Saints Days** 10.

d) Week-days? [*No response*].

3. Is Communion ever sung? No.

4. Religious teaching to children a) Church b) Sunday School and c) Day school? i) Clergy teach in Day schools? ii) Religious teaching to Sunday school teachers? iii) Satisfactory results?

(a) Sunday School attends Morning Service as a corporate whole. Quarterly Children's Service at 3 pm. (b) Sunday School 3 pm to 3.50. (c) No Day Schools: children attend Bradwell School. [ii] S.S. teachers meet weekly for instruction during the winter months.

5. Religious teaching to lads and young women? Bible Class for men Tuesday evening Sept. to April. Bible Class lads Sunday afternoon [Sept. to April]. G.F.S. Preparatory Class.

6. Secondary school in Parish? No.

7. Teaching for Nonconformist children? [*No response*].

8. Organised study for adults? At monthly meeting of Communicants' Guild a course of reading is prescribed for ensuing month an exposition of it given.

9. Interest in mission? 1. Missionary Working Party (with prayer and reading). 2. Distribution of Missionary Literature in house to house visitation. 3.Occasional meetings addressed by missionaries on furlough.

10. Voters for Ruridecanal representatives a) men b) women? [*No response*].

11. PCC? No Church Council.

1. Population 149.
2. Herbert Edward Cooper graduated from Peterhouse Cambridge in 1903 and was ordained priest in 1912. After serving an initial curacy between 1910 and 1912 he was appointed as Rector of Kencot in 1913. He was 42 in 1914 and at the 1911 census he was unmarried and living in a single-person household.

KIDDINGTON[1]   Incumbent A. F. Bellman[2]

The school, houses and all the parish <u>belongs</u> to the Squire population under 244, with exception of Church, Rectory and Glebe.

1. Baptism at morning or evening prayer? Taken on 1st Sunday in the month 3 o'c.

2. Communion times

a) Sunday 8 except 1st Sunday in month midday. Chief Festivals 6 or 7, 8 and midday.

b) Ascension Day 8 am.

c) Saints Days 7.45.

d) Week-days? [*No response*].

3. Is Communion ever sung? No.

4. Religious teaching to children a) Church b) Sunday School and c) Day school? i) Clergy teach in Day schools? ii) Religious teaching to Sunday school teachers? iii) Satisfactory results?

Service in Church 1st Sunday in Month at 3 o'c. Sunday School from 10 am to 10.40. [i–iii] The Rector teaches in the Sunday School and occasionally in the weekday, but the Squire runs the whole school. The results are on the whole satisfactory.

5. Religious teaching to lads and young women? Classes in the winter.

6. Secondary school in Parish? No.

7. Teaching for Nonconformist children? [*No response*].

8. Organised study for adults? Meetings of GFS and Mothers Union. Readings at Mothers Meeting.

9. Interest in mission? Intercession Service in church. Meetings in the school. Information in the Magazine, prayers given in it. Boxes for collection.

10. Voters for Ruridecanal representatives a) men b) women? [*No response*].

11. PCC? No.

1. Population 244.
2. Arthur Frederick Bellman graduated from St John's College Cambridge in 1875 and was ordained priest in 1878. He served a series of six curacies between 1876 and 1889 and then as Vicar of Staplefield until 1909 when he accepted the Rectory of Kiddington. He was 63 in 1914 and at the 1911 census he shared a household with his wife, two unmarried sons, aged 18 and 20, and two unmarried female servants.

KIDLINGTON[1]   Incumbent A. C. R. Freeborn[2]

1. Baptism at morning or evening prayer? Yes – but more usually at the afternoon service for Children on Sundays.

2. Communion times

a) Sunday 8 am and Noon on the 1st Sunday in each month.

b) Ascension Day 8 am.

c) Saints Days 8 am and sometimes at noon.

d) Week-days? [*No response*].

3. Is Communion ever sung? No

4. Religious teaching to children a) Church b) Sunday School and c) Day school? i) Clergy teach in Day schools? ii) Religious teaching to Sunday school teachers? iii) Satisfactory results?

(a) The Children are Catechised in Church on Sunday afternoons. They are taken to service every Sunday morning: and on certain Holy Days. (b) The arrangement of the Children is the same in the Sunday Schools as in the Day Schools. There is a different staff of Teachers in the afternoons from that of the mornings. The Lesson for each Sunday is drawn up by the Incumbent and a copy sent to every Teacher early in the week before the Sunday in question. This Lesson is taught in the morning and catechised upon in the afternoon. (c) In the Day-Schools, religious instruction is given to all the children from 9 am to 9.45 am. [i–iii] The clergy teach two mornings a week, the highest group of Children: and occasionally test the Children in Lower Groups and in the Infant Department. According to statistics, and to the Head Diocesan Inspectors Report, we have cause for thankfulness and reason for hopefulness: but with regard to our many manifest imperfections we have serious grounds for dissatisfaction.

5. Religious teaching to lads and young women? Beyond the instruction given in Church there is a good Bible Class for girls and young women. Similar classes have been started again and again for lads: and those who join them are just the very people who strike out for themselves and leave the Parish. However, the men and lads of Kidlington do attend church in greater numbers than women and girls.

6. Secondary school in Parish? No.

7. Teaching for Nonconformist children? The Managers of Kidlington Church Schools are prepared to grant the right of entry to a Nonconformist Teacher for the instruction of Nonconformist Children whose parents desire such instruction to be given. No application for such teaching has ever been made: and I do not believe that any real objection exists to the religious teaching given in our Schools.

8. Organised study for adults? Church History Lectures have been given by experts from outside the Parish – but they have never been well attended, despite strong efforts to arouse interest in the subject.

9. Interest in mission? There are Meetings held and Sermons preached every year on behalf of the SPG: Missionary Boxes are in circulation. There are separate funds raised for the Central African Universities Mission, the Women's SPG and a considerable number of people in Kidlington subscribe to other societies. Services for intercession for missionary work are held.

10. Voters for Ruridecanal representatives a) men b) women? I do not think that any men or women in Kidlington have signed the declaration in question. The matter was brought before the last meeting held in Kidlington in connection with the appointment of persons to vote for Lay Representatives for the Diocesan Conference but none of those present seemed willing to sign the declaration.

11. PCC? We have no Parochial Church Council.

1. Population 1,433.
2. Albert Corsellis Richard Freeborn graduated from Christ Church Oxford in 1882 and trained at Cuddesdon College in 1883, being ordained priest in 1885. He served curacies at Hungerford 1884–86, and at Kidlington between 1886 and 1887, when he succeeded to the Vicarage. Freeborn also served as Curate of Hampton Poyle 1892–97. He was 54 in 1914 and at the 1911 census he shared a household with his wife and one unmarried female servant.

KIDMORE END[1] Incumbent H. E. Robson[2]

1. Baptism at morning or evening prayer? Occasionally evensong for teaching purposes usually after a children's service.

2. Communion times

a) Sunday 8 every Sunday 12, 1st,3rd, 4th Sunday, 7 second Sunday.

b) Ascension Day 6,7,8 and 11.30.

c) Saints Days 7.30 and 11.30.

d) Week-days? Occasionally 7.30.

3. Is Communion ever sung? Yes 12 4th Sunday of Month. Christmas Eve 11.45 pm. Other Festivals 9.30 am.

4. Religious teaching to children a) Church b) Sunday School and c) Day school? i) Clergy teach in Day schools? ii) Religious teaching to Sunday school teachers? iii) Satisfactory results?

(a) In Church every Sunday afternoon except infants, who do kindergarten work. (b) Sunday School every Sunday morning. (c) Religious teaching in Day-School daily. [i–iii] The clergy do not teach in the Day-School. The Sunday Schools teachers are instructed once a month. I am satisfied with the work and progress of the Sunday School.

5. Religious teaching to lads and young women? A Bible Class of Lads. There is no class at present for young women.

6. Secondary school in Parish? No. Secondary School boys go to the Kendrick School in Reading.

7. Teaching for Nonconformist children? There is a Council School in the parish. The 'religious difficulty' is not known here.

8. Organised study for adults? I am accustomed to give courses of lectures in the winter and there is a very fair attendance. They had to be omitted this last winter owing to my illness.

9. Interest in mission? Intercessions once a month. Meetings with special speakers occasionally – a Guild of Box holders. This work is not strongly developed here.

10. Voters for Ruridecanal representatives a) men b) women? (a) about 10 (b) no women.

11. PCC? No. The Churchwardens and Sidesmen meet when necessary. It is not practical to have a Church Council here yet, but the way is being paved for it.

1. Population 1,330 (but probably about 1,600)
2. Herbert Eric Robson graduated from Queens' College Cambridge in 1900 and was awarded a BD from the University of Durham in 1911. After two curacies 1900–07 he was Rector of West Woodhay between 1907 and 1909, when he was appointed as Vicar of Kidmore End. He was 36 in 1914 and at the 1911 census he was single, sharing a household with his widowed housekeeper and one unmarried female servant.

KINGHAM[1] Incumbent W. Fisher[2]

1. Baptism at morning or evening prayer? It has not been the practise in Kingham Church.

2. Communion times

a) Sunday Midday on the first Sunday 8.30 am 2nd and 4th evening on the 3rd.

b) Ascension Day 8.30am.

c) Saints Days [*No response*].

d) Week-days? [*No response*].

3. Is Communion ever sung? No

4. Religious teaching to children a) Church b) Sunday School and c) Day school? i) Clergy teach in Day schools? ii) Religious teaching to Sunday school teachers? iii) Satisfactory results?

In Church there is a monthly Service. Lessons are given in Sunday School on Sunday afternoon. The Day School is a Council School. [ii–iii] A teachers' meeting is not at present practicable with the teaching staff that such a village as this provides. One has to be contented very much with being able to keep the School going.

5. Religious teaching to lads and young women? There is a Lads' Bible Class on Sunday afternoon but few attend it. I have no one to undertake a young women's class.

6. Secondary school in Parish? No.

7. Teaching for Nonconformist children? [*No response*].

8. Organised study for adults? Beyond the Sunday Services there is at present no opening for such an effort.

9. Interest in mission? Sermons and meetings are arranged in connection with the Church Missionary Society, the British and Foreign Bible Society and other Societies.

10. Voters for Ruridecanal representatives a) men b) women? None.

11. PCC? There is scarcely occasion here for a Church Council. Church matters are dealt with by the 2 Churchwardens and 4 Sidesmen.

1. Population 876.
2. William Fisher graduated from St John's College Cambridge in 1883 having been ordained priest in 1881. After serving two curacies 1880–93 he worked as a District Secretary for the British and Foreign Bible Society between 1893 and 1912, when he became Rector of Kingham. He was 58 years of age in 1914. At the 1911 census he was recorded as married but was staying as a visitor in a clerical household in Guildford.

KIRTLINGTON[1]   Incumbent G. C. May[2]

1. Baptism at morning or evening prayer? Not as yet. In previous Parish have done so.

2. Communion times

a) Sunday 8 am.

b) Ascension Day 7 and 8am.

c) Saints Days 7 am.

d) Week-days? [*No response*].

3. Is Communion ever sung? Yes. 11am one Sunday in month.

4. Religious teaching to children a) Church b) Sunday School and c) Day school? i) Clergy teach in Day schools? ii) Religious teaching to Sunday school teachers? iii) Satisfactory results?

[i] Yes weekly at least. [ii] Nothing. (a) Monthly (at present) Catechising. (b) The Catechism with the weeks Collect, Epistle, Gospel. (c) Diocesan Syllabus. The religious teaching and influence in the Day School is so good that the Sunday School is less unsatisfactory than it properly ought to be.

5. Religious teaching to lads and young women? Guild of S. Mary for young women.

6. Secondary school in Parish? No.

7. Teaching for Nonconformist children? Church School only. No provision. No request for Nonconformist teaching has been made since 1879.

8. Organised study for adults? No.

9. Interest in mission? Quarterly (at least) Instruction Sermons. H.M.A. Intercession Paper.

10. Voters for Ruridecanal representatives a) men b) women? I am told, none have signed.

11. PCC? No.

1. Population 600.
2. George Charles May graduated from St John's College Oxford in 1890 and trained at Wells Theological College in 1892, being ordained priest in 1894. After two curacies 1893–1901 he moved to South Africa, first as a chaplain with the South Africa Railway Mission and then in parish ministry. He returned to England in 1907 and served as Curate of St Andrew Catford until 1913, when he became Vicar of Kirtlington. He was 46 years of age in 1914. At the 1911 census he was recorded as single and sharing a household with his unmarried housekeeper.

LANGFORD[1]   Incumbent A. E. Jerram[2]

1. Baptism at morning or evening prayer? No.

2. Communion times

a) Sunday 8.30 1st Sun in month midday.

b) Ascension Day 8.0am.

c) Saints Days 8.0am.

d) Week-days? [*No response*].

3. Is Communion ever sung? No.

4. Religious teaching to children a) Church b) Sunday School and c) Day school? i) Clergy teach in Day schools? ii) Religious teaching to Sunday school teachers? iii) Satisfactory results?

I usually go into School and open with the Prayers. Sunday School – held every Sunday. Childrens' service in Church the 1st Sunday in each month.

5. Religious teaching to lads and young women? C Lads Bg. GFS Bible Class.

6. Secondary school in Parish? No.

7. Teaching for Nonconformist children? No.

8. Organised study for adults? Nothing more than systematic teaching in Church.

9. Interest in mission? Daily Intercessions and 1st Sun each month instead of a Sermon some special mission explained and 3 or 4 Intercessions summing up the whole asked for from the congregation. Kneeling and rising again between each Intercession.

10. Voters for Ruridecanal representatives a) men b) women? [*No response*].

11. PCC? I started one when I first came here but all the men work for large Farmers in the Parish. Those who were most capable and were asked to act refused. A small Council however exists consisting of the Wardens and a leading Farmer. We meet for discussion when anything important takes place.

1. Population 422.
2. Arnold Escombe Jerram graduated from Trinity College Cambridge in 1891 and trained at the Leeds Clergy School, being ordained priest in 1893. After initial curacies 1892–94 he was Vicar of Bradley (Yorks.) 1895–1906 and then Vicar of Thurstonland between 1906 and 1910, when he moved to become Vicar of Langford. He was 46 in 1914 and at the 1911 census he shared a household with his wife, four young children, their governess and two unmarried female servants.

LAUNTON[1]   Incumbent W. M. Miller[2]

1. Baptism at morning or evening prayer? [*No response*].

2. Communion times

a) Sunday 8 am. 1st Sunday also noon 3rd S. also 7 am.

b) Ascension Day 8am and noon.

c) Saints Days 8am.

d) Week-days? [*No response*].

3. Is Communion ever sung? Yes 8 am on Christmas, Easter and Whitsunday.

4. Religious teaching to children a) Church b) Sunday School and c) Day school? i) Clergy teach in Day schools? ii) Religious teaching to Sunday school teachers? iii) Satisfactory results?

(a) Children's Service 2.30 on Sundays. (b) Sunday School at 10 am. (c) The Diocesan Syllabus is taught in its entirety. [i–iii] The Rector teaches on three days in the week. The Sunday School Teachers are provided with notes of lessons which they teach on the morning of Sundays and which form the basis of the teaching at the Childrens Service. The Diocesan Inspectors report is <u>satisfactory</u>. I am satisfied that the children are well taught in faith and duty.

5. Religious teaching to lads and young women? A Bible Class for young women is held <u>regularly</u>. Classes for Confirmation are held in the winter. Lads who have been confirmed meet from time to time for preparation for Holy Communion.

6. Secondary school in Parish? [*No response*].

7. Teaching for Nonconformist children? The Managers have informed the parents of nonconformist children of their readiness to make such provision. It has also been made known to the Nonconformist Minister of Bicester, who is responsible for the service at Launton Chapel, that he can have the use of a classroom. The Parents do not avail themselves of this offer.

8. Organised study for adults? [*No response*].

9. Interest in mission? Meetings are held for instruction and for Intercession about four times in the year. Literature is circulated. Many copies of the Mission Field are taken.

10. Voters for Ruridecanal representatives a) men b) women? No women have signed the declaration. Only the few men (5 or 6 in number) attending the meeting for the election of the Ruridecenal Representatives have done so.

11. PCC? We have not a parochial Church Council.

1. Population 544.
2. William Montague Miller graduated from Hertford College Oxford in 1882 having been ordained priest in 1879. He was Curate of Witney 1877–85 and Vicar of Stony Stratford from 1885 to 1895, when he became Rector of Launton. He also served as Organising Secretary for the S.P.G. in the Buckinghamshire Archdeaconry 1895–1906, Diocesan Inspector of Schools for Oxford 1902–06 and as Rural Dean of Bicester from 1912. He was 64 in 1914 and at the 1911 census he shared a household with his wife, two daughters aged 33 and 28, and four unmarried female servants.

LEAFIELD WITH WYCHWOOD[1]   Incumbent T. W. Lee[2]

1. Baptism at morning or evening prayer? No. But at afternoon Children's Service, when adults are also present.

2. Communion times

a) Sunday 1st in month 12.15 pm other Sundays 8 am.

b) Ascension Day 8 am.

c) Saints Days 8 am on occasional Saints' days.

d) Week-days? [*No response*].

3. Is Communion ever sung? No.

4. Religious teaching to children a) Church b) Sunday School and c) Day school? i) Clergy teach in Day schools? ii) Religious teaching to Sunday school teachers? iii) Satisfactory results?

I (a) Catechising on the 3rd Sunday afternoon in the month. (b) 10 am and 2.30 pm for ¾ of an hour each time. (c) 9 – 9.45 daily by teachers. II Vicar teaches on Tuesdays and has papers sent him for correction on Fridays. III Fortnightly meetings at Vicarage, and three Deanery meetings annually at various centers [*sic*]. IV Very good results in Day School as to knowledge. In Sunday School the elder children leave too early.

5. Religious teaching to lads and young women? There are no classes at present, but these were maintained for many years. At Confirmation times attendance is good.

6. Secondary school in Parish? No.

7. Teaching for Nonconformist children? The Church School seems to satisfy the Nonconformists, who are few in number.

8. Organised study for adults? There are no adult classes held.

9. Interest in mission? There are more than 40 who hold S.P.G. Boxes. At the Children's Monthly Service the Collection is for S.P.G. A very good working party is held for S.P.G. Sermons and meetings for S.P.G. and C.M.S. in July and Nov. S.P.G. Collect is used monthly at 8 am Celebration and literature is distributed.

10. Voters for Ruridecanal representatives a) men b) women? None.

11. PCC? No.

1. Population 868.
2. Thomas William Lee graduated from Trinity College Cambridge in 1857 and was ordained priest in 1861. He was Assistant Master at Marlborough College 1859–63 and became Vicar of Leafield in 1875. He was 79 in 1914 and at the 1911 census he shared a household with his wife, two unmarried daughters aged 39 and 34 (the eldest described as a 'lecturer'), an unmarried female 'assistant' and three unmarried female servants.

LEWKNOR[1]   Incumbent J. C. F. Wimberley[2]

1. Baptism at morning or evening prayer? Yes, at Evening Prayer.

2. Communion times

a) Sunday 8.30 am or after Morning Prayer alternately.

b) Ascension Day I find 12 noon to be the most generally convenient hour.

c) Saints Days [I find 12 noon to be the most generally convenient hour.]

d) Week-days? [I find 12 noon to be the most generally convenient hour.]

3. Is Communion ever sung? No.

4. Religious teaching to children a) Church b) Sunday School and c) Day school? i) Clergy teach in Day schools? ii) Religious teaching to Sunday school teachers? iii) Satisfactory results?

(a) Children's Service with catechising – Sunday afternoon. This, when there are enough children. With a small population the number of children in the village of School age varies very considerably. (b) Sunday Schools – Infants and mixed – 10 am on Sunday mornings. Here again the numbers vary greatly. Nearly all the children of the labourers in the village attend, but children of farmers never. This seems to be a tradition of the village. (c) I teach once a week and the Rector of Adwell once a week. The Day School has children from 5 or 6 surrounding villages and hamlets. [ii–iii] Sunday School Teachers Meeting. That is, I go through the lessons with my wife and the two young women who assist her, at the Vicarage each week. I consider the children to be well instructed in Religion at the time they leave School and would like to give much of the credit for this to the Day School Master and Mistress – both sound church-people. Of the later result, I cannot judge. The boys leave the village for the towns, the girls for Service. The dull ones only remain. Confirmation at the age of 13 – 14 is the end of my influence as a rule.

5. Religious teaching to lads and young women? Young people of both sexes attend church well as a rule; when this is the case I do not hold special classes.

6. Secondary school in Parish? No.

7. Teaching for Nonconformist children? During the nine years of my incumbency no objections have been raised by parents to their children receiving the ordinary religious instruction.

8. Organised study for adults? No. Perhaps I may say that I frequently make the Sunday Evening Sermon an 'Instruction' rather than the Exhortation which commonly passes under the name of a 'sermon'.

9. Interest in mission? Missionary Meeting – a visit by an S.P.G. deputation in the autumn. Missionary boxes.

10. Voters for Ruridecanal representatives a) men b) women? I think three men and two women. For some reason there were very few at the meeting – at present very little interest is taken in the matter.

11. PCC? No.

1. Population 381.
2. John Conrad Fasham Wimberley graduated from Trinity Hall Cambridge in 1895 and trained at the Cambridge Clergy Training School, being ordained priest in 1898. He served four curacies between 1897 and 1905, when he became Vicar of Lewknor. He was 40 in 1914 and at the 1911 census he shared a household with his wife, their young son and daughter, a nurse and two unmarried female servants.

LITTLEMORE[1]   Incumbent G. J. Champion[2]

1. Baptism at morning or evening prayer? At Evening Prayer on week days occasionally.

2. Communion times

a) **Sunday** 1st and 3rd, 7 and 8: 2nd, 8: 4th 8. and 9.45.

b) **Ascension Day** 6 and 8.

c) **Saints Days** 8.

d) **Week-days?** Wednesday and Friday 7.15 also Vigils Ember Days 7 or 8. Tuesday and Thursday 8.0.

3. Is Communion ever sung? At 8 on 3rd Sunday and great Fests.

4. Religious teaching to children a) Church b) Sunday School and c) Day school? i) Clergy teach in Day schools? ii) Religious teaching to Sunday school teachers? iii) Satisfactory results?

(a) Children's Service Sundays at 3. Saints' Days and Sats in holidays. (b) Sunday School, 10. (c) Definite Church Teaching. [i–iii] I visit the Schools every day and read prayers. The Diocesan Inspector has lately been here, and given excellent reports of both schools. The Sunday School is steadily increasing in numbers, and, I think, in efficiency.

5. Religious teaching to lads and young women? For young women at the G.F.S. meetings.

6. Secondary school in Parish? No.

7. Teaching for Nonconformist children? During the 7 ½ years I have been here only 2 children have been withdrawn from the church teaching.

8. Organised study for adults? There is a Bible Class for the Mothers' Union. Addresses at Mothers' Meeting.

9. Interest in mission? Regular intercessions in Church, occasionally after Evensong on Sundays. Distribution of Quarterly Intercession Papers and of various Missionary Magazines. Collections for 7 or 8 Missions each year and once a month at Children's Service.

10. Voters for Ruridecanal representatives a) men b) women? About 25 men.

11. PCC? No.

1. Population 1,950 (including asylum).
2. George James Champion graduated from the University of London in 1891 and subsequently from Oriel College Oxford in 1904. He was ordained priest in 1894 and served three curacies 1893–1907, the last being at Cowley, St John between 1900 and 1907, when he

became Vicar of Littlemore. He was 47 in 1914 and at the 1911 census he shared a household with his wife and two unmarried female servants.

MAPLEDURHAM[1]   Incumbent F. St J. Thackeray[2]

1. Baptism at morning or evening prayer? Yes, during Evening Prayer.

2. Communion times

a) **Sunday** 8am on Easter, Whitsunday and second Sundays in the month occasionally 12.15 after Morning Prayer alternate Sundays.

b) **Ascension Day** On the Sunday after Ascension Day 12.15.

c) **Saints Days** None.

d) **Week-days?** None except on Xmas Day when it is at 8 am.

3. Is Communion ever sung? No.

4. Religious teaching to children a) Church b) Sunday School and c) Day school? i) Clergy teach in Day schools? ii) Religious teaching to Sunday school teachers? iii) Satisfactory results?

(a) Addresses are given in Church from time [to] time specially to the Children. (b) My daughter <u>Miss E.K. Thackeray</u> has undertaken for a very long period the Sunday School Teaching. She very rarely can obtain any help, and has to do it single-handed. The Subjects are chiefly those from the Church <u>Stamps</u>. From Advent to Trinity they follow the Church year, a course usually from the Old Testament and History. <u>N.B.</u> Some 2 years ago she was promised a <u>Medal</u> for over 20 years service in Sunday School work, but there was difficulty at the time, and it was never received. – I should be glad if it could be forwarded. (c) The School is situated 1¼ miles from the Vicarage and up a steep hill. This causes a good deal of difficulty. [i–iii] I have taken Classes in their religious lessons but I cannot do so as often as I would otherwise. The Schoolmistress is a good Church woman. The course of instruction during the last half-year has comprised Exodus to the death of Joshua, the latter part of the Life of Christ, – a selection of Parables and Miracles, the whole of the Catechism, Repetition of Psalms, Hymns, and some Parables. <u>Sunday School Teachers</u>. My daughter gets some of my Clerical Helpers to address the children on Special Subjects, and I do so myself occasionally. I may say that the Reports of the Diocesan Inspector are excellent. <u>Results</u>. Considering the great distance of many of the children's homes, I think the results are very fair on the whole. – My daughter devotes a great deal of time and thought to the preparation of Sunday School, and the parents are very grateful to her as they have reason to be. – More help is wanted, but one cannot see how it is obtainable.

5. Religious teaching to lads and young women? After their preparation for Confirmation, classes are held for lads and young women (separately) with instruction on the Holy Communion. Meetings of the Mothers Union are held by Miss Thackeray fortnightly, and from time to time special addresses are given both in Church and at the Vicarage by Clergy invited from outside the place, and by Ladies.

6. Secondary school in Parish? There is none.

7. Teaching for Nonconformist children? Not for children of Nonconformists. There are not many of them, and there has never been any request for it. – Permission is made for the Children of Roman Catholics (there are seven at present,) who are separately instructed by their Priest in the Class Room. This has worked well, and without any friction since 1894.

8. Organised study for adults? I frequently take subjects such as Prayer, – the Apostles Creed the Litany, the Beatitudes for a Course of Sermons extending over several weeks. I also give a course of Lectures in Lent, at the Vicarage this year it was on the Epistles. – The attendance is not large, but if I live, I purpose continuing it another year.

9. Interest in mission? There are always Sermons preached for the S.P.G., and I endeavour as often as I can to get preachers who can speak from their personal experience of work (in S. Africa N. Zealand etc) like my friend Archdeacon Harper and others.

10. Voters for Ruridecanal representatives a) men b) women? Some few years ago I conferred with my Churchwardens, and went into the question of the desirability or feasibility of a Representative Church Council – but we came to the conclusion that in such a Parish as this the population of which consists in the main of Farmers and their Labourers, it was not practicable.

11. PCC? We have no parochial Church Council.

*There are some special difficulties and hindrances connected with the Parish of Mapledurham. I. Local It is a very scattered village. There is only one part of it with as many as 15 or 16 houses together. Many Cottages stand quite alone, the distances are considerable, and some remote hamlets in the midst of the woods are almost inaccessible in the Winter months. There is no Parish Room and Meetings have to be held at the Vicarage, where also we have attempted Evening Classes for Manual Work – Reciting, Amusements, etc, but have had to discontinue them. The Squire is a Roman Catholic and an absentee. The Tenant of Mapledurham House, Mr Mills, is really very kind to the sick and the poor, but his interests are divided, as he has another house at Shipton, and lives there for many months in the Autumn and Winter. II. Financial A large House and Garden is very expensive to keep up – heavy repairs every year. There is a rooted impression that it is a rich living, because it used to have a Eton Fellowship attached to it. This ended when I came here and my coming also synchronized with the fall in Tithe. – I can raise very little money to help me in my Clerical Fund. People look at the gross value of the Living, while the average Nett value of the last 3 years is only £387. 18. 6-.

1. Population 547.
2. Francis St John Thackeray graduated from Merton College Oxford in 1854 and was ordained priest in 1867. He was elected FSA in 1884 and FGS in 1901. He was a Fellow of Lincoln College 1857–61 and Assistant Master of Eton College between 1858 and 1883, when he became Vicar of Mapledurham. He published as editor *Anthologia Latina*, 8th edition (1900) and *Anthologia Graeca*, 7th edition (1900). He was the author of *Eton College Library* (1881), *Guide to the Roman Coins at Eton College* (1882), *Translations from Prudentius into English Verse with Introduction and Notes* (1890), *Memoir of Dr Hawtrey* (1896), *Sermons preached in Eton College Chapel* (1897) and *Christian Biographies through Eighteen Centuries* (1908). He also edited jointly with Rev. E. D. Stone, *Florolegium Latinum*, vol. i (1899) and vol. ii (1902). He was 81 in 1914 and at the 1911 census he shared a household with two unmarried daughters in their forties, one described as 'Voluntary organist Parish Worker and Housekeeper' and the other as 'Voluntary Sunday School Teacher and Parish Worker', together with three unmarried female servants.

MARSTON[1]   Incumbent J. H. Mortimer[2]

1. Baptism at morning or evening prayer? No, I usually have it in the middle of the monthly Childrens Service.

2. Communion times

a) Sunday Early Celebration each Sunday in New Marston, early and midday celebration alternately in Parish Church.

b) Ascension Day 8 and 9.30.

c) Saints Days All-Saints Day only 8am.

d) Week-days? [*No response*].

3. Is Communion ever sung? Occasionally 9.30.

4. Religious teaching to children a) Church b) Sunday School and c) Day school? i) Clergy teach in Day schools? ii) Religious teaching to Sunday school teachers? iii) Satisfactory results?

(a) Monthly Children's Service in afternoon in Old Marston: each Sunday in New Marston. (b) Sunday School morning and afternoon in Old Marston. Morning in New Marston. (c) Religious Instruction every day from 9.15 to 10 am. [i–iii] I teach in the Day-School twice a week. I have lately revived a monthly Sunday-School Teachers' meeting. I am absolutely satisfied with the teaching in the Day-School – the head-master and his wife (who is also mistress) are both excellent Christians and Church-people. I am fairly well satisfied with that in the Sunday School in Old Marston. My head-master (who teaches and superintends in the morning) and an undergraduate who takes a boys' class in the afternoon are the only really efficient teachers. However, the teaching in New Marston Sunday School is first-rate. The attendance is good in both places, especially so in New Marston.

5. Religious teaching to lads and young women? There is a class for Boy Scouts in New Marston, but with that exception the lads of from 15 to 18 have been rather neglected I am sorry to say. However, I have talked the matter over with my C.E.M.S. members and we have a plan in hand for getting them together on Sunday evenings. I have occasional services for members of the G.F.S. The younger members attend a class on Sundays.

6. Secondary school in Parish? No.

7. Teaching for Nonconformist children? No. Nonconformity is practically dead in Old Marston. The Chapel is closed. Services are occasionally held in the Chapel at New Marston but the New Marston children, generally speaking, attend S. Clements School.

8. Organised study for adults? No – with the exception of a Bible-reading union. I have a cottage meeting for adults on Sundays.

9. Interest in mission? Regular missionary services at certain intervals, and monthly collections in Church. Occasional lantern meetings in the winter. Children have "supported" (to a certain extent) two native boys in C.M.S. Mission at Jabalpur.

10. Voters for Ruridecanal representatives a) men b) women? Very few: but I have not been all round the parish for signatures – I had forgotten all about the declaration.

11. PCC? Yes – in New Marston. It has no defined powers, but everything connected with the work of the Mission is laid before it. It has met about 7 times since October.

1. Population 716.
2. John Hamilton Mortimer graduated from Magdalen College Oxford in 1894 and trained at Wells Theological College in 1897, being ordained priest in 1899. He was Curate of Spitalfields 1898–99 and then of St Clement Oxford between 1899 and 1905, when he became Vicar of Marston. He was 42 years of age in 1914. At the 1911 census he was recorded as single and was visiting a fellow clergyman.

MERTON[1] Incumbent C. F. Girdlestone[2]

1. Baptism at morning or evening prayer? No – we have no Baptisms.

2. Communion times

a) **Sunday** 11 am alternate Sundays.

b) **Ascension Day** [*No response*].

c) **Saints Days** [*No response*].

d) Week-days? [*No response*].

3. Is Communion ever sung? No.

4. Religious teaching to children a) Church b) Sunday School and c) Day school? i) Clergy teach in Day schools? ii) Religious teaching to Sunday school teachers? iii) Satisfactory results?

Nothing. No School. Nothing.

5. Religious teaching to lads and young women? Nothing.

6. Secondary school in Parish? None.

7. Teaching for Nonconformist children? No school.

8. Organised study for adults? A great deal by sermons.

9. Interest in mission? Practically nothing. There is not interest, Enough to pay Church Expenses.

10. Voters for Ruridecanal representatives a) men b) women? I know of none.

11. PCC? We are feebly trying this experiment. It has met twice.

1. Population 143.
2. Charles Frederic Girdlestone graduated AKC 1899 and was ordained priest in 1890. He occupied a succession of seven curacies between 1889 and 1912 before being appointed Vicar of Merton in 1913. He was absent from home at the 1911 census but his household comprised his wife, his married son, also a clergyman, a single daughter and one unmarried female servant.

MIDDLETON STONEY[1] Incumbent W. H. Draper[2]

1. Baptism at morning or evening prayer? Sometimes but rarely – generally at Children's Service.

2. Communion times

a) Sunday 8.30 excluding 1st Sunday in month 11.45.

b) Ascension Day 8.

c) Saints Days Only "Missa Sicca" 10.15.

d) Week-days? 8 Thursday and Holy week.

3. Is Communion ever sung? No but on 4 occasions we have Celebrations with Hymn at 8 Christmas Day Easter Day Whitsunday Harvest Festival Sunday. NB Used to have a simple Choral celebration for those occasions but it broke down and I then fell back on hymns.

4. Religious teaching to children a) Church b) Sunday School and c) Day school? i) Clergy teach in Day schools? ii) Religious teaching to Sunday school teachers? iii) Satisfactory results?

[i] Once a week Boys. Once a week Girls. (a) <u>In Church</u> Monthly Children's service with Catechising in afternoon Sunday (small reward books given). (b) In <u>Sunday Schools</u> <u>Boys</u> morning before Church Short school. Afternoon given up the <u>idea</u> being that most of the boys being in choir attend Church twice some coming from a distance. <u>Girls</u> morning before church Short school. Afternoon School. (c) <u>Day Schools</u> Daily Boys Girls and Infants. The Rector once a week Boys once a week Girls. [ii–iii] Re <u>Teachers and Sunday Schools</u>. The Head Master and Mistress both very good and competent Church Teachers. (They are paid a little extra for this) Lady Jersey when at home takes Story Class of girls in the morning at the Park. One of my daughters teaches younger girls in afternoon. Rewards given. Fairly satisfied but no room for boasting! W.D.

5. Religious teaching to lads and young women? Confirmation Classes. An <u>Occasional</u> Communicant class girls. CEMS meetings with Bible Readings. Ch Brigade Lads "talks". Rectors wif[e] a Bible Class Sunday afternoons when the young women will come. Rector occasional Sunday afternoon address and prayers to servants at Middleton Park (N[ote] Crippled arm and 3 services make this <u>rare)</u>. Try to "get hold" of lads but as yet not much success. Church HC Addresses with Prayers at Sunday Evensong before Gt Festivals.

6. Secondary school in Parish? No.

7. Teaching for Nonconformist children? Made a beginning by formally asking the <u>pronounced</u> Dissenter of Parish whether he wished anything special. He is a nice good intelligent and independent man so regarded him as typical. His reply was I have thought it over and feel sure "my boy wd. get nothing but good from your Teacher". Have got leave to poach in neighbouring parishes to ask parents of children attending our school what their wish is but as yet have taken no step. Qy is it advisable to go into other parishes on this mission? I should like the Bishop's advice.

8. Organised study for adults? Ask them to give me subjects to treat in sermons.

9. Interest in mission? We have long had a Parish Missionary Association for Home and Foreign Missions. Our programme re F Missions is an Annual Sunday for Sermon and Offertories with address and meeting all Day of Intercession for FM. Monthly Working Party with prayers at Girls School. Village Club Evening. Adult Working Party (at their own homes preferred) with 1 or 2 meetings at Village Club Room for Intercession and Address. Boxes in many houses.

10. Voters for Ruridecanal representatives a) men b) women? [*No response*].

11. PCC? Yes. Membership now of all "Communicants" of full age Male and Female. Powers advisory. Met once since last October.

1. Population 273.
2. William Henry Draper graduated from Worcester College Oxford in 1859 and was ordained priest in 1861. After an initial curacy 1860–68, he was Rector of Edgcott (Bucks.) until 1874, when he became Rector of Middleton Stoney. He also served as Rural Dean of Bicester 1895–1911. He was 77 in 1914 and at the 1911 census he shared a household with his wife, two unmarried daughters, aged 38 and 23, and two unmarried female servants.

MILCOMBE[1]   Incumbent A. Goldring[2]

1. Baptism at morning or evening prayer? I have had three baptisms in eight years during Catechism to suit convenience of parents.

2. Communion times

a) Sunday Yes if possible.

b) Ascension Day Yes if possible.

c) Saints Days No.

d) Week-days? No.

3. Is Communion ever sung? Yes at 11 am on the first Sunday in every month and on the gt Festivals.

4. Religious teaching to children a) Church b) Sunday School and c) Day school? i) Clergy teach in Day schools? ii) Religious teaching to Sunday school teachers? iii) Satisfactory results?

I Catechise the children every Sunday afternoon. There is Sunday School every Sunday morning and religious instruction daily in the Day Schools.

5. Religious teaching to lads and young women? Nothing: there are practically none to instruct. Most of the young fellows are in the choir. The rest are dissenters.

6. Secondary school in Parish? No.

7. Teaching for Nonconformist children? The difficulty does not arise.

8. Organised study for adults? No: the more intelligent of my little flock are recommended books which I believe they read.

9. Interest in mission? We support the Lebombo Mission.

10. Voters for Ruridecanal representatives a) men b) women? I cannot give this information.

11. PCC? No.

1. Population 126.
2. Arthur Goldring graduated from Pembroke College Cambridge in 1881 and trained at the Chancellor's School Lincoln in 1883, being ordained priest in 1885. He served five curacies 1884–93 and was then Rector of Bury (Hunts.) 1893–97, Rector of Halwill (Devon) 1879–99 and then Rector of Paget with Warwick in Bermuda between 1899 and 1906, when he accepted an appointment as Vicar of Milcombe. He was 52 in 1914 and at the 1911 census he shared a household with his wife, 19-year-old daughter, 11-year-old son and one unmarried female servant.

MILTON, GREAT[1] Incumbent J. T. Fox[2]

1. Baptism at morning or evening prayer? No.

2. Communion times

a) **Sunday** 8 am or 8.30 am <u>and</u> noon on 1st Sunday in the month.

b) **Ascension Day** 8 am.

c) **Saints Days** 8am or 8.20 am.

d) **Week-days?** Only on special days.

3. Is Communion ever sung? No.

4. Religious teaching to children a) Church b) Sunday School and c) Day school? i) Clergy teach in Day schools? ii) Religious teaching to Sunday school teachers? iii) Satisfactory results?

The Sunday School meets each Sunday at 10 am. The children attend Matins on Sundays at 11 am. A children's Service is held every Sunday at 3 pm to 3.45 pm. [i–iii] At the present time I am not teaching in the Day School.

5. Religious teaching to lads and young women? A Communicants Class is held monthly. A Bible Class for Big Lads was held on Sunday mornings last year but is now discontinued.

6. Secondary school in Parish? No.

7. Teaching for Nonconformist children? No.

8. Organised study for adults? [*No response*].

9. Interest in mission? Missionary addresses (meetings) ditto church. Special appeal. Collection for S.P.G. and Oxford Mission to Calcutta. Missionary Boxes.

10. Voters for Ruridecanal representatives a) men b) women? [*No response*].

11. PCC? No.

1. Population 528.

2. John Thomas Fox graduated from Corpus Christi College Cambridge in 1882 and was ordained priest in 1886. He occupied four curacies between 1885 and 1902, when he became Vicar of Great Milton. He was 53 in 1914 and at the 1911 census he shared a household with his wife, 11-year-old daughter, her governess and two unmarried female servants.

MILTON, LITTLE[1]   Incumbent G. H. Fathers[2]

1. Baptism at morning or evening prayer? No.

2. Communion times

a) **Sunday** daily 8.15 and mid-day monthly.

b) **Ascension Day** 8.15.

c) **Saints Days** 8.15.

d) **Week-days?** [*No response*].

3. Is Communion ever sung? No.

4. Religious teaching to children a) Church b) Sunday School and c) Day school? i) Clergy teach in Day schools? ii) Religious teaching to Sunday school teachers? iii) Satisfactory results?

(a) On Sundays at 3.0 children are catechised in Church (b) Sunday School with Sermons at 10.0 am. (c) Children are taught according to the Diocesan Syllabus. [i–iii] No. Nothing. I am not satisfied.

5. Religious teaching to lads and young women? The lads are mostly at work and the young women at service away.

6. Secondary school in Parish? No.

7. Teaching for Nonconformist children? No.

8. Organised study for adults? No.

9. Interest in mission? Sermons are preached yearly, and boxes and a collection is taken; amount last year £4-9-0.

10. Voters for Ruridecanal representatives a) men b) women? None.

11. PCC? No.

1. Population 279.
2. George Henry Fathers graduated from the University of Oxford in 1888 and was ordained priest in 1894. He was Vice-Principal of Culham College between 1893 and 1907, when he became Vicar of Little Milton with Ascot. He was 52 in 1914 and at the 1911 census he was single and sharing a household with his widowed mother and two unmarried female servants.

MILTON-UNDER-WYCHWOOD[1] Incumbent A. Shildrick[2]

1. Baptism at morning or evening prayer? Occasionally but not generally.

2. Communion times

a) **Sunday** 8 am and after Mattins on first Sunday of the month.

b) **Ascension Day** either 8 am or 11 am.

c) **Saints Days** 8 am.

d) **Week-days?** None.

3. Is Communion ever sung? No.

4. Religious teaching to children a) Church b) Sunday School and c) Day school? i) Clergy teach in Day schools? ii) Religious teaching to Sunday school teachers? iii) Satisfactory results?

The only work being done is by the Sunday School which is not very satisfactory. The difficulty being to get teachers, duly qualified. There is no catechising on Sunday as there is no one to act as catechist at Milton. At Lyneham, till an accident happened to me, I always held a Children's Service before the usual Evensong at 3 o'clock. [i–iii] There is nothing done in the Day Schools by the Clergy, but the teaching faculty give half an hour each day to religious instruction and the work is well and conscientiously given. The school in our parish is a Council school. Sunday School Teachers Classes were held weekly till some time ago. They were not well attended and the skeleton lesson prepared by the Instructor was seldom clothed by the Teacher. I felt that many had work to do that prevented them giving the time to the preparation needed and amongst some of the most willing were those most incapable. I consider our Sunday School system an absolute failure.

5. Religious teaching to lads and young women? A young mans class is held on Sunday, and instruction given once during the week: they meet for instruction and recreation.

6. Secondary school in Parish? No.

7. Teaching for Nonconformist children? Ours is Council school.

8. Organised study for adults? No, except by constantly urging it from the pulpit.

9. Interest in mission? Preaching, and meetings and continuous conversation on missions at all times when opportunity occurs.

10. Voters for Ruridecanal representatives a) men b) women? None.

11. PCC? No.

1. Population 1,003.

2. Alfred Shildrick was ordained priest in 1882 in the diocese of Columbia in western Canada. After serving a succession of cures in Canada he became Curate of Milton-under-Wychwood between 1888 and 1890. He returned to British Colombia as an SPG missionary and then served as Rector of the New Westminster Cathedral between 1894 and 1909, when he returned to Milton-under-Wychwood, first as curate and then in 1911 he was appointed as Vicar. He was 58 in 1914 and at the 1911 census he shared a household with his wife and 18-year-old son.

MINSTER LOVELL[1]   Incumbent J. K. Smith[2]

1. Baptism at morning or evening prayer? No. The people have been urged to bring the children then: but will not. The late Vicar did. The afternoon. Baptising has increased annual average from 8 to 11–12.

2. Communion times

a) Sunday 8 am.

b) Ascension Day 5.30 or 7 am.

c) Saints Days 7.30 am.

d) Week-days? [*No response*].

3. Is Communion ever sung? On festivals at 8am. On Ascension Day at 7.30 am.

4. Religious teaching to children a) Church b) Sunday School and c) Day school? i) Clergy teach in Day schools? ii) Religious teaching to Sunday school teachers? iii) Satisfactory results?

Children taught in S. School and Catechised in Church by the Vicar. [i–iii] Yes: once a week. Senior Division. There are only 2 teachers beside Vicar. Numbers small owing to several reasons. Teachers provided with Lessons (Faith Press. Childrens and Stamp Lessons – which under circumstances are sufficient. Children and teachers present at Mattins when Vicar always uses the Sunday School Lesson (Gospel) as basis of his address. Satisfied as far as results can go with the small number of children. These proceed to Confirmation naturally and without pressure: and have been trained in the teaching concerning this and H. Communion. The small numbers are unsatisfactory but these are due to nonconformist parentage and distance. (The "Estate" difficulty).[3]

5. Religious teaching to lads and young women? We have very few. Girls go to service. Lads are mainly of nonconformist parentage. Have tried an evening class: but without results.

6. Secondary school in Parish? No.

7. Teaching for Nonconformist children? It has been offered and not desired. No children are withdrawn.

8. Organised study for adults? No: nor is possible beyond the following: the C.E.M.S. does this as far as possible with the men. Occasional Meetings of Communicants.

9. Interest in mission? Meetings: addresses at intervals: intercession service as a Sermon at Evensong.

10. Voters for Ruridecanal representatives a) men b) women? No. Not asked, as their communicant status is known. Several attended election meeting of R.D. representatives 2 ½ years ago: but there was no need of electing as but the 2 representatives were nominated.

11. PCC? No.

1. Population 445.
2. John Kinchin Smith graduated from Christ's College Cambridge in 1882 and was ordained priest in 1884. He was Second Master at St John's College, Hurstpierpoint 1883–88, SPG Chaplain at Spezia and Sorrento 1888–89 and then, returning to England, he served a succession of three curacies between 1890 and his appointment as Vicar of Minster Lovell in 1903. He was 53 in 1914 and at the 1911 census he shared a household with his wife, teenage son and daughter, and two boarding male pupils as well as two unmarried female servants.
3. This somewhat obscure comment may refer to the adjacent settlement of Charterville, established in the mid-nineteenth century by the Chartists and with a rather different and more independent character than that of the original village.

MIXBURY[1]   Incumbent B. A. Patten[2]

1. Baptism at morning or evening prayer? No. But generally in the Children's service.

2. Communion times

a) Sunday 8.15 am and midday alternately.

b) Ascension Day 8.15 am.

c) Saints Days [*No response*].

d) Week-days? [*No response*].

3. Is Communion ever sung? Yes, quarterly after matins at midday.

4. Religious teaching to children a) Church b) Sunday School and c) Day school? i) Clergy teach in Day schools? ii) Religious teaching to Sunday school teachers? iii) Satisfactory results?

(a) Catechising at monthly Children's service. (b) in afternoon Sunday School. (c) Daily for half an hour in Day School. [i–iii] Rector teaches once a week in the Day School. There are only 2 Sunday School Teachers with fairly good results.

5. Religious teaching to lads and young women? Girls Bible Class discontinued owing to lack of numbers. No lads Bible Class at present owing to difficulty of securing attendance and a suitable Teacher.

6. Secondary school in Parish? No.

7. Teaching for Nonconformist children? Not required, as there are no children of Nonconformist parents.

8. Organised study for adults? No, unless it be by an occasional course of sermons.

9. Interest in mission? Annual sermon for S.P.G. and a Lantern Lecture observance of Day of Intercession for Foreign Missions.

10. Voters for Ruridecanal representatives a) men b) women? Only six men.

11. PCC? No.

1. Population 244.
2. Basil Arthur Patten graduated from Pembroke College Cambridge in 1892 and was ordained priest in 1895. After two curacies he was Vicar of Hartwell 1901–03 and of Whittlebury with Silverstone between 1903 and 1908, when he was appointed Rector of Mixbury. He was 43 in 1914 and at the 1911 census he shared a household with his wife, 13-year-old daughter and three unmarried female servants.

MOLLINGTON[1]   Incumbent G. H. Purdue[2]

1. Baptism at morning or evening prayer? No.

2. Communion times

a) Sunday 8am once a month 12 once a month 8 and 12 on Chief Festivals.

b) Ascension Day 8am.

c) Saints Days [*No response*].

d) Week-days? [*No response*].

3. Is Communion ever sung? No.

4. Religious teaching to children a) Church b) Sunday School and c) Day school? i) Clergy teach in Day schools? ii) Religious teaching to Sunday school teachers? iii) Satisfactory results?

(a) – (b) Sunday School is held at 10.15 am every Sunday and in the winter the children come to the Vicarage for an hour in the afternoon. They also have a small library and take books home on Sunday. (c) This is a Church Day School and the children are taught the Subjects required for the Diocesan Inspection and do well. [i–iii] I have taught in Day School regularly every week (one-day-in the week) for 25 years – but cannot do it now. There are only 23 children in the school and we have two teachers. I advise my daughter who is our Sunday School Teacher. The children are quite well up in Religious Knowledge and come regularly to Church on Sunday mornings.

5. Religious teaching to lads and young women? The young girls leave home and go to service elsewhere as soon as they leave school. There is only one young woman whom I prepared for Confirmation and Communion. The lads are nearly all in the Choir – this keeps them to Church twice a Sunday and Choir Practice. They come to Confirmation Class when old enough. I fear they would not attend any other class – if there was one. They are all labourers and have little time to themselves.

6. Secondary school in Parish? No.

7. Teaching for Nonconformist children? No but it is not required. No children are withdrawn from our Church teaching.

8. Organised study for adults? Nothing more than 2 Sermons every Sunday which I honestly think is as much as they can well assimilate, with private interviews and regular visiting.

9. Interest in mission? We have a meeting for Foreign Missions which is well attended and 2 Sermons each year and I make frequent references to Missionary work in my Sermons.

10. Voters for Ruridecanal representatives a) men b) women? I have no precise information. I do not think any record has been kept.

11. PCC? No. This is a very small parish and I do not think there is a real want for it.

1. Population 176.
2. George Henry Purdue graduated from Keble College Oxford in 1877 and trained at Cuddesdon College, being ordained priest in 1878. After serving two curacies 1877–84 he was Vicar of Shottermill 1884–1904. He became Vicar of Mollington in 1911. He was 59 years old in 1914. His household was not found in the 1911 census but in 1901 he was sharing a household with his wife, their young son and daughter and their governess together with an unmarried female servant.

MONGEWELL[1]   Incumbent T. Hughes[2]

1. Baptism at morning or evening prayer? No.

2. Communion times

a) Sunday After the Morning Service.

b) Ascension Day No celebration.

c) Saints Days [No celebration].

d) Week-days? [No celebration].

3. Is Communion ever sung? No.

4. Religious teaching to children a) Church b) Sunday School and c) Day school? i) Clergy teach in Day schools? ii) Religious teaching to Sunday school teachers? iii) Satisfactory results?

Day School in North Stoke Parish. Religious Instruction by the Rector Mr Coombes. Other religious instruction given from the pulpit.

5. Religious teaching to lads and young women? Addresses from the pulpit.

6. Secondary school in Parish? No school in the parish.

7. Teaching for Nonconformist children? [*No response*].

8. Organised study for adults? Addresses from the pulpit.

9. Interest in mission? Same as no. 8.

10. Voters for Ruridecanal representatives a) men b) women? None.

11. PCC? No Council.

1. Population 117.
2. Thomas Hughes graduated from Trinity College Dublin in 1870 and was awarded LLD in 1875 and DD in 1890. He was ordained priest in 1870 and after serving three curacies 1870–90 and a chaplaincy in Rotterdam 1890–92 he was appointed Rector of Mongewell in 1893. He was 59 in 1914 and at the 1911 census he shared a household with his wife and five children aged between 8 and 21.

NETTLEBED[1] Incumbent P. Armitage[2]

1. Baptism at morning or evening prayer? No.

2. Communion times

a) Sunday 1st 12, 2nd 8 am, 3rd 12, 5th 8 am.

b) Ascension Day 12.

c) Saints Days Ash Wednesday 12.

d) Week-days? [*No response*].

3. Is Communion ever sung? No.

4. Religious teaching to children a) Church b) Sunday School and c) Day school? i) Clergy teach in Day schools? ii) Religious teaching to Sunday school teachers? iii) Satisfactory results?

No. Children's Service in Church 4th Sunday. Sunday School Morning and Afternoon not very satisfactory as far as teaching is concerned run by an old lady for the last

25 years or so. Things are improving: a good man has come lately to the village and is running a class for older boys very well.

5. Religious teaching to lads and young women? A branch of Y.W.C.A. is run well by lady in parish, who keeps well in touch with old members when they go out to service. For lads class see [4]

6. Secondary school in Parish? No.

7. Teaching for Nonconformist children? No Church School.

8. Organised study for adults? Only in sermons.

9. Interest in mission? Sermons for CMS and Colonial and Continental Church Society. A missionary meeting. Various other gatherings. Sowing party[3] for Medical Missions during Lent, with occasional talks on Missions. Small gatherings and sales for Missions run by children etc.

10. Voters for Ruridecanal representatives a) men b) women? None.

11. PCC? No.

1. Population 552.
2. Philip Armitage graduated from Trinity College Cambridge in 1892 and trained at Ridley Hall in 1893, being ordained priest in 1896. He was curate of Holy Trinity Cambridge 1895–1904 with the exception of a year as a missionary at Allahabad 1900–01. He was Vicar of Birling (Kent) between 1904 and 1908, when he was appointed as Vicar of Nettlebed. He was 43 in 1914 and at the 1911 census he shared a household with his wife, four young children, their governess and five unmarried female servants.
3. This may be a mistake for 'sewing party'. Alternatively, given the missionary societies supported in the parish it is a reference to an event for the junior supporters of the CMS known as the Sowers band.

NEWINGTON[1] Incumbent J. R. Pendlebury[2]

1. Baptism at morning or evening prayer? No – usually with hymns at the <u>children's</u> service.

2. Communion times

a) Sunday Always at 8.30 am (Festivals also 7.30 and noon).

b) Ascension Day 8.30 am.

c) Saints Days 8.30 am.

d) Week-days? Thursdays in Lent 8.30 am.

3. Is Communion ever sung? No. Want of <u>capacity to sing</u> is the difficulty. The 4 Ringers who alone are singers, are very poorly educated. Only hymns and the plainest chants are possible. Hymns at the early Eucharist monthly, have been tried, but given up.

4. Religious teaching to children a) Church b) Sunday School and c) Day school? i) Clergy teach in Day schools? ii) Religious teaching to Sunday school teachers? iii) Satisfactory results?

(a) <u>Children's service in Church</u> every Sunday afternoon except August with definite teaching on Creed and Sacraments, which supplies the deficiency of a County School (Stadhampton) in the week, as regards the express teaching of churchmanship. The Church Catechism always kept in the forefront. One third of the parish (Brookhampton) is a <u>compact</u> population with Stadhampton 1½ miles from the centre of Newington. All children there fall naturally into the Stadhampton arrangements. Exactly similarly another ⅓ of the parish (Berrick Prior) – 2 miles from here – regards itself <u>practically as one place</u> with Berrick Salome (attached to Chalgrove, – with church and Sunday class) – The <u>centre</u> of this Parish – which is alone the effective and responsive parish – consists of only 80 people. But all the children without exception (21) are under church instruction on Sundays – even including the 3 RC children of the French 'chef' of the Big House. This afternoon service is the one helpful and hopeful thing of the Rectors work. Not however that it builds up a new generation to live on in the place – (See answer 5) (b) There is <u>Sunday School</u> – (almost coincident with the above children) every Sunday morning – ie without the older ones. (c) There is <u>no Day School</u>. [i–iii] <u>Sunday School Teachers</u>. There is absolutely no possibility of such – except the Rector and his wife, – who divide the scholars into 2 groups. The latter is experienced and effective and takes the upper group. With the small number this is adequate.

5. Religious teaching to lads and young women? There is a remarkable <u>absence</u> of young people. We have children of school age and then, after a considerable gap, married people. Usually those confirmed have all gone away before the next (triennial) confirmation. This feature is very marked.

6. Secondary school in Parish? No.

7. Teaching for Nonconformist children? <u>No</u> day school at all.

8. Organised study for adults? No – not for 'study' as an act of their own – of which the <u>lower grade</u> of labourer such as we have here is incapable. An attempt is made to supply it in sermons of a teaching character.

9. Interest in mission? Only the Missionary Sunday.

10. Voters for Ruridecanal representatives a) men b) women? After due notice of a <u>meeting after Sunday Service</u> for this purpose – 4 men. One representative was then elected, and the matter not pursued further.

11. PCC? No.

1. Population 235.
2. John Roger Pendlebury graduated from Brasenose College Oxford in 1883 and was ordained priest in 1885. He served curacies at Burford, Cuddesdon and Prestwich 1884–95 and was Chaplain of the Clewer House of Mercy between 1895 and 1900, when he was appointed Rector of Newington. He was 52 in 1914 and at the 1911 census he shared a household with his wife, their 3-year-old daughter and two unmarried female servants.

NEWINGTON, SOUTH[1]   Incumbent C. J. Whitehead[2]

1. Baptism at morning or evening prayer? I think, with one exception, every Baptism here in the last 20 years has been after the 2nd lesson at Evening Prayer.

2. Communion times

a) **Sunday** Midday 1st Sunday in month 10 am, 3rd Sunday 8 am other Sundays.

b) **Ascension Day** 8 am.

c) **Saints Days** [*No response*].

d) **Week-days?** [*No response*].

3. Is Communion sung? No.

4. Religious teaching to children a) Church b) Sunday School and c) Day school? i) Clergy teach in Day schools? ii) Religious teaching to Sunday school teachers? iii) Satisfactory results?

(a) the children attend the service; we have our annual King's Messengers' Festival. (b) The Vicar, his daughter (who has just had a term at St Christopher's College Blackheath) and a devoted teacher with 16 years' experience teach in Sunday School. The Vicar takes the upper class in Church History in the summer months and the KM Syllabus in the winter. (c) The Diocesan Syllabus is taught by the regular staff and extremely well. [i–iii] The Vicar used to teach when possible on Tuesdays and Thursdays, but in recent years has been unable to do so at all regularly. I cannot estimate results: doubtless they might be better: what is needed is the example of parents.

5. Religious teaching to lads and young women? Only Confirmation Classes.

6. Secondary school in Parish? No.

7. Teaching for Nonconformist children? The Managers offered to give facilities, but we have very few bona fide Nonconformists, and the Nonconformist Manager considered that no change was needed. Once certainly a daughter of a Nonconformist farmer won the Diocesan Prize, and was very pleased to do so.

8. Organised study for adults? At one time we had a Communicants' Meeting once a month in the winter: we are now hoping next autumn to start a Branch of the Mothers' Union.

9. Interest in mission? We have several missionary meetings in the year: a number of Missionary Magazines are distributed, and we have a very keen Branch of King's Messengers. The Quarterly Intercession Paper is distributed.

10. Voters for Ruridecanal representatives a) men b) women? None have actually signed. Only a few actual Communicants known to me to be such attend meetings to elect their parochial representatives.

11. PCC? No. Sometimes I invite some of the regular Communicants to discuss Church Matters.

1. Population 222.
2. Christopher John Whitehead graduated from Exeter College Oxford in 1883 and was ordained priest in 1890. After an initial curacy 1889–93 he was appointed Vicar of South Newington. He was 56 in 1914 and at the 1911 census he shared a household with his wife, two sons (who were undergraduates at Exeter College), two unmarried daughters, aged 20 and 16, and two unmarried female servants.

NEWTON PURCELL AND SHELSWELL[1]   Incumbent A. St Q. Armstrong[2]

1. Baptism at morning or evening prayer? On occasion.

2. Communion times

a) Sunday Midday 1st Sunday in month.

b) Ascension Day 8 am.

c) Saints Days [*No response*].

d) Week-days? [*No response*].

3. Is Communion ever sung? No.

4. Religious teaching to children a) Church b) Sunday School and c) Day school? i) Clergy teach in Day schools? ii) Religious teaching to Sunday school teachers? iii) Satisfactory results?

(b) Sunday School 10.15 am, by Rector. (c) Supervision.

5. Religious teaching to lads and young women? [*No response*].

6. Secondary school in Parish? No.

7. Teaching for Nonconformist children? None.

8. Organised study for adults? [*No response*].

9. Interest in mission? Occasional sermon.

10. Voters for Ruridecanal representatives a) men b) women? (a) 3.

11. PCC? [*No response*].

1. Population 173.
2. Arthur St Quentin Armstrong graduated from Caius College Cambridge in 1892 and was ordained priest in 1896. He served a single curacy between 1894 and 1897, when he was appointed Rector of Newton Purcell. He was 44 in 1914 and at the 1911 census he shared a household with his wife, 21-year-old stepdaughter and four unmarried female servants.

NOKE[1]   Incumbent H. Thorp[2]

1. Baptism at morning or evening prayer? Evening Prayer.

2. Communion times

a) Sunday 1st Sunday in month at 11am 3rd [Sunday in the month] at 9am.

b) Ascension Day [*No response*].

c) Saints Days [*No response*].

d) Week-days? [*No response*].

3. Is Communion ever sung? No.

4. Religious teaching to children a) Church b) Sunday School and c) Day school? i) Clergy teach in Day schools? ii) Religious teaching to Sunday school teachers? iii) Satisfactory results?

In the Day School.

5. Religious teaching to lads and young women? Only church services and visiting.

6. Secondary school in Parish? [*No response*].

7. Teaching for Nonconformist children? No.

8. Organised study for adults? Teaching from pulpit only.

9. Interest in mission? Sermons on the subject.

10. Voters for Ruridecanal representatives a) men b) women? None.

11. PCC? We have not one.

1. Population 108.
2. Henry Thorp graduated from Hertford College Oxford in 1877 and was ordained priest in 1878. He served three curacies between 1877 and 1883, when he was appointed Rector of Noke. He was 70 in 1914 and at the 1911 census he was a widower sharing a household with a widowed relative by marriage, her young son and one unmarried female servant.

NORTHLEIGH[1] Incumbent W. J. H. Wright[2]

1. Baptism at morning or evening prayer? No.

2. Communion times

a) Sunday 8.30 am and after morning service alternately.

b) Ascension Day 6 am and 10 am.

c) Saints Days None.

d) Week-days? None.

3. Is Communion ever sung? No.

4. Religious teaching to children a) Church b) Sunday School and c) Day school? i) Clergy teach in Day schools? ii) Religious teaching to Sunday school teachers? iii) Satisfactory results?

(a) <u>In Church</u>. Children's Service on Ash Wednesday, Ascension Day, Easter and Whitsun. (b) <u>In Sunday School</u>. There was no Sunday School held for some ten years before I came to the parish. Our numbers are in consequence somewhat low as other denominations had gained a great hold. Number on books at present time 25. The lessons are graduated well to suit the age of the children. (c) <u>Day School</u>. Religious instruction given for ¾ hour each morning. [i–iii] I do not teach in the Day School. I found the teaching done there very thorough and the Head Master (who has been here 25 years) taking special interest in the work, that I decided to let things go on as they are until a change occurs. The highest mark Excellent has been awarded by the examiners each year since I have been here. <u>Sunday School Teachers</u>. The staff consists of myself, my wife and two other lady teachers – one a trained Infant mistress. They are of mature age and competent. I have every chance of judging the soundness of their teaching and the way it is given, which to my mind, as a former Public School Master is equally important as the knowledge. When the school grows as I hope it will and I have to fall back on the less competent assistance of younger teachers – they will be instructed in what they teach and how to teach it, as far as I can help them. I am only dissatisfied with the small numbers of our Sunday School.

5. Religious teaching to lads and young women? Confirmation Classes have been held each year.

6. Secondary school in Parish? No.

7. Teaching for Nonconformist children? No.

8. Organised study for adults? Yes in connection with the C.E.M.S.

9. Interest in mission? Six weeks ago last Sunday I told the people from the pulpit that so far we had concentrated our efforts towards our own church and its affairs, which needed so much, but the time had come when we must do something to show we realized the wider sphere of the church and that this year, having cleared off the debt on Church Expenses, we must contribute to the funds needed for evangelization. I have often asked the congregation to pray for those engaged in the work and for those among whom they labour.

10. Voters for Ruridecanal representatives a) men b) women? None.

11. PCC? Yes. All matters relating to the Church Restoration and boundaries are laid before them – plans specifications and estimates discussed and settled, ways and means of raising necessary funds. Three times.

1. Population 650
2. Walter John Hornagold Wright graduated from St Edmund Hall Oxford in 1908 and trained at Wycliffe Hall Oxford, being ordained priest in 1910. He served two curacies between 1908 and 1911 and was appointed as Vicar of North Leigh in 1912. He was 36 in 1914 but was not found in the 1911 census.

NORTHMOOR[1] Incumbent J. J. Turner[2]

1. Baptism at morning or evening prayer? We have our Baptisms after Children's Service on Sunday afternoon – children attend.

2. Communion times

a) Sunday 8 o'clock am.

b) Ascension Day 8 o'clock.

c) Saints Days 8 o'clock.

d) Week-days? [*No response*].

3. Is Communion ever sung? Yes! 1st Sunday in the month after shortened matins 11 o'clock.

4. Religious teaching to children a) Church b) Sunday School and c) Day school? i) Clergy teach in Day schools? ii) Religious teaching to Sunday school teachers? iii) Satisfactory results?

(a) At 10.15 I take the children in Church, in the Collect and Gospel, specially the Teaching of the Day. (b) On Sunday afternoon in Church I have the bigger boys and girls and we take ordinary Bible Teaching – and my Daughter teaches the younger children. Up to a few months ago I had Catechizing according to "Potter and Sheard" but it seemed to be unsatisfactory and they wanted a change. I may take it again soon. (c) I take the elder children in Day School when nearing an examination (scripture) and other times occasionally. [iii] By having the Children (about 30) in Church I think they are learning more reverence for the church than they used to have.

5. Religious teaching to lads and young women? As there are so few, and they are chiefly in the choir, I get a little talk in sometimes both individually and collectively at the practices.

6. Secondary school in Parish? No!

7. Teaching for Nonconformist children? The children of Nonconformist parents receive the same religious instruction as the rest.

8. Organised study for adults? No!

9. Interest in mission? Missionary Magazines are distributed and Lantern Lectures occasionally.

10. Voters for Ruridecanal representatives a) men b) women? None – so far.

11. PCC? No. Two Churchwardens.

1. Population 212
2. Joseph John Turner graduated from the University of Oxford in 1900 and was ordained priest in 1903. He served six curacies between 1901 and 1912, when he became Vicar of Northmoor. He was 54 in 1914 and at the 1911 census he shared a household with his wife, three school-age daughters and one unmarried female servant.

NORTON, HOOK[1]   Incumbent E. C. Freeman[2]

1. Baptism at morning or evening prayer? Sometimes on week days. I should like to see the old practice restored, but the transference of Evensong to the Evening appears to be the fact which has upset the ancient use.

2. Communion times

a) **Sunday** 8 am and <u>also</u> twice after Mattins during the month.

b) **Ascension Day** 8 am and 10.30 am.

c) **Saints Days** sometimes 8am and sometimes 10.30am.

d) **Week-days?** [*No response*].

3. Is Communion ever sung? Only practically, when there is a Celebration after Mattins. This is a matter of great grief to me.

4. Religious teaching to children a) Church b) Sunday School and c) Day school? i) Clergy teach in Day schools? ii) Religious teaching to Sunday school teachers? iii) Satisfactory results?

I catechise the Children every Sunday afternoon, and teach in the morning in Sunday School. Church Teaching is given in the Day Schools, and a few children avail themselves of the conscience clause when the lesson is on the Catechism. [i–iii] I abstain from motives of policy from teaching myself in the Day Schools, owing to the presence of a large proportion of Wesleyans, Baptists and Particular Baptists. The Day School always gets an excellent report from the Diocesan Inspector, but I am not satisfied at all with the results as far as they issue in the real training of the children in the faith and worship and system of the Church. The Sunday School Teachers are provided with Potter and Sheard's books.

5. Religious teaching to lads and young women? There is no organised system.

6. Secondary school in Parish? No.

7. Teaching for Nonconformist children? No.

8. Organised study for adults? No.

9. Interest in mission? Missionary meeting and sermons annually.

10. Voters for Ruridecanal representatives a) men b) women? None.

11. PCC? No.

1. Population 1,350.
2. Earnest Charles Freeman graduated from the University of Durham in 1892 and was ordained priest in 1894. He served two curacies 1893–99 and then spent five years as Rector of Gladstone in Queensland, returning to England in 1904 as Vicar of Claydon where he served until his appointment as Rector of Hook Norton in 1907. He was 44 in 1914 and at the 1911 census he was unmarried and sharing a household with two unmarried female servants.

NUFFIELD[1] Incumbent V. D. Browne[2]

1. Baptism at morning or evening prayer? The women in this parish find it most convenient to bring their Children to baptism on Sunday afternoon – but we occasionally use the service at Evensong which is at 6.30. We have no afternoon service.

2. Communion times

a) Sunday Communion is celebrated here once a month after morning prayer also at Easter, Whitsuntide and at Xmas at 8 am or Midday.

b) Ascension Day [*No response*].

c) Saints Days [*No response*].

d) Week-days? [*No response*].

3. Is Communion ever sung? No.

4. Religious teaching to children a) Church b) Sunday School and c) Day school?
i) Clergy teach in Day schools? ii) Religious teaching to Sunday school teachers?
iii) Satisfactory results?

Sunday School is held in the church every Sunday at 10 am. The Rector is the only Teacher no other person in this small agricultural hamlet being competent to teach. We have a County Council Day School and the Head Teacher is a Nonconformist his wife and daughter assisting him.

5. Religious teaching to lads and young women? I rely on plain speaking from the pulpit and the young lads in the village attend the Evening Service fairly well.

6. Secondary school in Parish? No.

7. Teaching for Nonconformist children? No Ch. School.

8. Organised study for adults? I do not understand the purport of this question but it seems inapplicable to such a parish as this.

9. Interest in mission? We have no Missionary Society in this parish.

10. Voters for Ruridecanal representatives a) men b) women? None.

11. PCC? We have no parochial Ch. Council.

1. Population 203.
2. Valentine Denis Browne trained at Chichester College in 1867 and was ordained priest in 1869, having formerly been an officer in the Royal Fusiliers. He served a series of six curacies including one at St Barnabas Pimlico between 1868 and 1887, punctuated by a three-year term as a chaplain on HMS *Swiftsure*. He became Vicar of Flamstead in 1887 where he ministered until appointed Rector of Nuffield in 1897. He was 70 in 1914 and at the 1911 census he was described as married but the enumeration listed no other members of his household.

NUNEHAM COURTENAY[1]   Incumbent H. T. G. Alington[2]

1. Baptism at morning or evening prayer? I have done so <u>once</u> when the Parents were willing, but they much prefer a separate service when there is always a good congregation.

2. Communion times

a) Sunday 8 am 2nd 4th and 5th; 12 noon 1st and 3rd Sundays.

b) Ascension Day 11.30 am.

c) Saints Days [*No response*].

d) Week-days? [*No response*].

3. Is Communion ever sung? Hymns are sung at 8am on Festivals.

4. Religious teaching to children a) Church b) Sunday School and c) Day school? i) Clergy teach in Day schools? ii) Religious teaching to Sunday school teachers? iii) Satisfactory results?

(a) Children attend the Morning Service after Sunday School, most of them voluntarily in the evening. Hymns chosen to suit them and attempts are made to interest them in the Sermons, and they have Flower Services. (b) Voluntary Teachers all Communicants and competent to teach in the Sunday School. (c) I teach on Wed. and Fri. each week and supervise the whole work. [iii] Upon the whole I think the Religious Instruction of children is distinctly satisfactory.

5. Religious teaching to lads and young women? They are prepared for Confirmation and attend church well. Separate classes are held in winter months at the Rectory (but more for amusement than for religious instruction) both for lads and young women.

6. Secondary school in Parish? No.

7. Teaching for Nonconformist children? There are very few and these are apparently quite content with our religious teaching.

8. Organised study for adults? Indirectly through the Mothers' Union.

9. Interest in mission? Sermons and offertories on behalf of both SPG and CMS. Many have boxes and special Litanies are said from time to time in Lent and Advent at Evening Services.

10. Voters for Ruridecanal representatives a) men b) women? (a) About 5.

11. PCC? No.

1. Population 304.
2. Hildebrand Thomas Giles Alington graduated from Magdalen College Oxford in 1890 and was ordained priest in 1897. He served a single curacy between 1896 and 1907, when he became Rector of Standlake, moving to the Rectory of Nuneham Courtenay in 1908. He was 47 in 1914 and at the 1911 census he shared a household with his wife and 10-year-old daughter, a male pupil and five unmarried servants – four female and one teenaged male gardener.

ODDINGTON[1]   Incumbent T. L. T. Fitzjohn[2]

1. Baptism at morning or evening prayer? Yes as often as required.

2. Communion times

a) **Sunday** Every other Sunday at 8 or 11 am.

b) **Ascension Day** 8 am.

c) **Saints Days** [*No response*].

d) **Week-days?** [*No response*].

3. Is Communion ever sung? No.

4. Religious teaching to children a) Church b) Sunday School and c) Day school? i) Clergy teach in Day schools? ii) Religious teaching to Sunday school teachers? iii) Satisfactory results?

Sunday classes. No day school.

5. Religious teaching to lads and young women? G.F.S.

6. Secondary school in Parish? [*No response*].

7. Teaching for Nonconformist children? [*No response*].

8. Organised study for adults? [*No response*].

9. Interest in mission? [*No response*].

10. Voters for Ruridecanal representatives a) men b) women? (a) Two.

11. PCC? No.

1. Population 131
2. Thomas Lechmere Tudor Fitzjohn graduated from Gonville and Caius College Cambridge in 1871 and was ordained priest in 1875. He served two curacies between 1874 and 1883, when he was appointed Vicar of Cardington, and he also served on the Shropshire bench as a JP from 1905. He was appointed as Rector of Oddington in 1906. He was aged 66 in 1914 and at the 1911 census he shared a household with his wife and two unmarried female servants.

OXFORD ALL SAINTS CUM ST MARTINS[1]   Incumbent A. J. Carlyle[2]

1. Baptism at morning or evening prayer? No.

2. Communion times

a) Sunday 8 am and 11 am.

b) Ascension Day 8 am.

c) Saints Days 8 am.

d) Week-days? [*No response*].

3. Is Communion ever sung? We have a Choral Celebration on certain great festivals at 8 am.

4. Religious teaching to children a) Church b) Sunday School and c) Day school? i) Clergy teach in Day schools? ii) Religious teaching to Sunday school teachers? iii) Satisfactory results?

We have no Day Schools, and there are so few children in the parish that I have not th[ought] it worthwhile to have a Sunday School.

5. Religious teaching to lads and young women? We have at various times had special meeting for young women.

6. Secondary school in Parish? No.

7. Teaching for Nonconformist children? We have no Church School.

8. Organised study for adults? I have during the winter months meetings on alternate weeks for men and women to consider and discuss religious questions.

9. Interest in mission? We do something in the way of meetings regularly for the C.M.S.

10. Voters for Ruridecanal representatives a) men b) women? We have not yet found any truly qualified person but annual meeting of the canonical numbers entitled to vote.

11. PCC? No. We do all the church business at the vestry.

1. Population 321
2. Alexander James Carlyle graduated from the University of Glasgow in 1876 and from Exeter College Oxford in 1886. He was awarded the degree of DLitt in 1910. He was ordained priest in 1889 and served a curacy at St Stephen's Westminster 1888–90, was Secretary of the Society for Promoting Christian Knowledge (SPCK) 1890–91, and Fellow of University College Oxford between 1893 and 1895, when he was appointed as Rector of Oxford All Saints with St Martin. He additionally served as Examining Chaplain to the bishop of Worcester 1897–1901. He was aged 52 in 1914 and at the 1911 census he shared a household with his wife, 10-year-old daughter and two unmarried female servants.

OXFORD ST ALDATE[1]   Incumbent T. W. Ketchlee[2]

1. Baptism at morning or evening prayer? [*No response*].

2. Communion times

a) **Sunday** 8.0 am every Sunday, Midday 2nd and 4th Sunday, Evening 1st and 3rd Sundays.

b) **Ascension Day** 8 am and 12 noon.

c) **Saints Days** 12 noon.

d) **Week-days?** [*No response*].

3. Is Communion ever sung? No.

4. Religious teaching to children a) Church b) Sunday School and c) Day school? i) Clergy teach in Day schools? ii) Religious teaching to Sunday school teachers? iii) Satisfactory results?

(a) The Day School comes to Church 12 times in the year. There is a monthly Children's Service in Church. The Morning Sunday School attends Morning Prayer. (b) There are morning and afternoon Sunday Schools. Nothing is done for the religious instruction of the Sunday School Teachers. (c) The Clergy have occasionally taught in the Day School.

5. Religious teaching to lads and young women? There is a Young Men's Bible Class – for those over 16. There is a Lads' Bible Class for those under 16. There is a Young Women's Bible Class.

6. Secondary school in Parish? No.

7. Teaching for Nonconformist children? There is a Council School as well as the Church School.

8. Organised study for adults? No.

9. Interest in mission? At present there are only the Sermons in Church on behalf of various Missionary Societies.

10. Voters for Ruridecanal representatives a) men b) women? As far as I can ascertain there has been no election of Ruridecanal Representatives since 1909: and I can find no record of those who voted.

11. PCC? Yes. Its powers seem to be mainly consultative. It met last in October 1913. It has not met since on account of the Vacancy in the Living. It usually meets once a quarter.

1. Population 3,355 (including Grandpont).
2. Thomas Wild Ketchlee graduated from Exeter College Oxford in 1894 and trained at Wycliffe Hall Oxford, being ordained priest in 1895. He served three curacies between 1894 and 1901, when he became Principal of the Bishop's Hostel in Liverpool and then Vicar of St Mark's, St Helen's 1903–11 and Commissary to the Bishop of Sierra Leone 1904–13. He was appointed as Rector of Oxford St Aldate in 1914. He was aged 46 in 1914 and at the 1911 census he was single and lived in a household with five boarders, two of whom were other Anglican clergy, and two unmarried female servants.

OXFORD ST ANDREW[1] Incumbent J. A. Harriss[2]

1. Baptism at morning or evening prayer? No.

2. Communion times

a) **Sunday** 8 am; 2nd and 4th Sundays 9.45 1st and 3rd Midday.

b) **Ascension Day** 8 am and Midday.

c) **Saints Days** 11 am.

d) **Week-days?** No celebrations arranged for ordinary weekdays.

3. Is Communion ever sung? No.

4. Religious teaching to children a) Church b) Sunday School and c) Day school? i) Clergy teach in Day schools? ii) Religious teaching to Sunday school teachers? iii) Satisfactory results?

There are neither Sunday Schools nor Day School in connexion with St Andrew's Church; nor are there now Services for Children in Church as formerly. They were dropped owing to the unsatisfactory attendance.

5. Religious teaching to lads and young women? Occasional classes and services are held for those who have been Confirmed from St Andrew's.

6. Secondary school in Parish? No.

7. Teaching for Nonconformist children? There is no school of this sort in the parish.

8. Organised study for adults? Certain classes and study circles do exist which I think can be said to fulfil this end.

9. Interest in mission? Classes are held and a parochial Missionary Association exists, one of the conditions of membership being an undertaking to pray for the Evangelization of the world. A monthly service of Missionary Intercession is held in the Church.

10. Voters for Ruridecanal representatives a) men b) women? I do not think any have done this.

11. PCC? Yes. Consultative and advisory. Four times.

1. Population 544.
2. James Adolphus Harriss graduated from Worcester College Oxford in 1881 and was ordained priest in 1883. After curacies in Plymouth and at St Peter le Bailey 1882–86, he served as a CMS missionary in India, returning to Britain in 1894 as Curate of Swansea. He was then successively Vicar of Holy Trinity Swansea 1897–1902 and Christ Church High Wycombe between 1902 and 1906, when he was appointed as the first Vicar of the new parish of Oxford St Andrew. He was aged 55 in 1914 and at the 1911 census he shared a household with his wife and three daughters, aged between 12 and 15 years, together with one unmarried female servant.

OXFORD ST BARNABAS[1]   Incumbent H. C. Frith[2]

1. Baptism at morning or evening prayer? We have not done so hitherto.

2. Communion times

a) **Sunday** 7. 8. 9. 11.

b) **Ascension Day** 5. 6. 7. 8. 11.

c) **Saints Days** 7. 8. 9.

d) **Week-days?** 7. 8.

3. Is Communion ever sung? Every Sunday and Holy Day. Sundays 9 and 11 Holy Days 9 (or 11).

4. Religious teaching to children a) Church b) Sunday School and c) Day school? i) Clergy teach in Day schools? ii) Religious teaching to Sunday school teachers? iii) Satisfactory results?

The Clergy do not teach regularly in the Days. But at least one of us in there during the week. We have a particularly good Headmaster and Head Mistress who are keen Catholics. On Sundays we have the Saint Sulpice method of Catechism,[3] so that all the teaching is in the hands of the Clergy. We have no Sunday School except for Infants. On the whole I am satisfied with the results attained.

5. Religious teaching to lads and young women? We have two Bible Classes every Sunday for lads. The elder girls remain as hon members of the Catechism in some cases up to the age of 21 or more: and there is also a monthly Bible Class for them.

6. Secondary school in Parish? No.

7. Teaching for Nonconformist children? There is practically no case of any parent objecting to the religious teaching given altho' they know it to be definitely church teaching.

8. Organised study for adults? No.

9. Interest in mission? We have a litany of intercession for Foreign Missions once a week, and the Poona Mission office once a month.

10. Voters for Ruridecanal representatives a) men b) women? I don't know that anyone has signed the declaration. I don't remember having seen a form since I came here.

11. PCC? No.

1. Population 2,410.
2. Herbert Charles Frith graduated AKC in 1897 and was ordained priest in 1898. After an initial curacy 1897–1904 he was Vicar of Holy Redeemer Clerkenwell between 1904 and 1911, when he became Vicar of Oxford St Barnabas. He was aged 42 in 1914 and at the 1911 census he shared a household in Clerkenwell with two other clergy, and three servants: a married couple and an unmarried female servant.
3. A highly structured catechetical method popularised in England by the translation of bishop Felix Dupanloup's lectures on the subject into English in 1890 and Spencer Jones's adaptation for Anglican use published as *The Clergy and the Catechism* (1895).

OXFORD ST CLEMENT[1]   Incumbent T. W. Gilbert[2]

1. Baptism at morning or evening prayer? No – only after the Children's service on Sunday afternoon.

2. Communion times

a) **Sunday** 8am every Sunday and also once a month at 11 am, 3. 45 pm and 6-30 pm.

b) **Ascension Day** 8 am.

c) **Saints Days** 8 am.

d) **Week-days?** None.

3. Is Communion ever sung? We sing nothing beyond the Kyrie.

4. Religious teaching to children a) Church b) Sunday School and c) Day school? i) Clergy teach in Day schools? ii) Religious teaching to Sunday school teachers? iii) Satisfactory results?

(a) We have the children in Church once a month for a service of their own. (b) We have Sunday Schools every Sunday at 10 am and 2.45 and use the graded instruction books. (c) We take the Diocesan Syllabus in all the Day Schools. [i–iii] The clergy teach three mornings every week in the Day School. The Sunday School Teachers have periodical meetings for Instruction and hints are also given by a trained Day School Mistress. I am satisfied that the instruction given by the older teachers is very sound, but the younger teachers need a lot of careful training before their work can be considered satisfactory.

5. Religious teaching to lads and young women? We have Bible Classes for lads and men and women and I have also commenced monthly Communicant Guilds for instruction purposes.

6. Secondary school in Parish? There is no secondary school in the parish.

7. Teaching for Nonconformist children? There is only our own church school in the parish but practically all the children of Nonconformist parents prefer to be present for the ordinary religious instructions. There is also a Council School not far away to which Nonconformists can send their children if they wish to avoid the Church School.

8. Organised study for adults? Nothing beyond recommendations from the pulpit and through the Parish magazine. I have a men's meeting every week but this touches mainly non church goers.

9. Interest in mission? We take an active share in C.M.S. and other branches of missionary work and have a working party every week for one or other societies: we have a 'missionary' sermon about once a month, a sale of work in the summer and one in the winter for missions.

10. Voters for Ruridecanal representatives a) men b) women? I have only been Incumbent here for a year and have not yet had any papers relative to Ruridecanal Conference.

11. PCC? Yes. I formed one last autumn: its powers have not been formally defined but they are of a general consultative nature. The Council here met every two months since its inception and by its rules is to meet at least quarterly.

1. Population 3,309.
2. Thomas Walter Gilbert graduated from Balliol College Oxford in 1905 and was awarded a BD in 1912. He trained at Wycliffe Hall Oxford in 1905 and was ordained priest in 1907. He served a curacy at Oxford St Clement 1906–08, going on to be Vicar of St Nicholas with St Runwald Colchester in 1908 before returning to St Clement's as Rector in 1913. He was aged 37 in 1914 and at the 1911 census he was unmarried and living in a single-person household.

OXFORD ST CROSS[1]   Incumbent O. D. Watkins[2]

1. Baptism at morning or evening prayer? Baptism at Holywell is usually administered in the shortened Evensong used on Sunday afternoons as a Children's Service and attended by some adults.

2. Communion times

a) Sunday 8 am. Also on 1st and 3rd Sundays 12.15. Also on 1st Sunday 7.

b) Ascension Day 8.

c) Saints Days 8.

d) Week-days? Thursdays and many other days 8.

3. Is Communion ever sung? At the Great festivals at 11.

4. Religious teaching to children a) Church b) Sunday School and c) Day school? i) Clergy teach in Day schools? ii) Religious teaching to Sunday school teachers? iii) Satisfactory results?

(a) Children's Service with Catechising every Sunday at 3.30 (b) Sunday School every Sunday at 10.15 and 3 (System at present in use – the Faith Press system) (c) Daily by teachers in Day school. [i–iii] Vicar teaches every Tuesday in Day-school. The teachers at Holywell are all of superior class and the detailed lessons printed by the Faith Press are found sufficient. Satisfied. The Head Mistress of the Day School, Miss V.E. Lyan is a devoted and excellent Church woman whose work as regards religious instruction could hardly be improved. The Sunday School is also at present in excellent hands.

5. Religious teaching to lads and young women? Very few lads, except choir – who receive instruction on Sundays. Elder lads not numerous enough for any organisation. Girls well looked after in Girls' Club and Bible Class.

6. Secondary school in Parish? No secondary school.

7. Teaching for Nonconformist children? No demand. Hardly any Nonconformist parents in parish.

8. Organised study for adults? Organisations for this purpose are not well suited to the size and character of the Holywell parish.

9. Interest in mission? Various missions are brought before the congregation with some frequency and the days of intercession observed. The children also have some instruction. But here again special parish organisations do not seem to be desirable.

10. Voters for Ruridecanal representatives a) men b) women? Hardly any. Voting usually after due notice given by qualified persons who have been present at a Vestry.

11. PCC? No.

1. Population 670.
2. Oscar Dan Watkins graduated from Merton College Oxford in 1873 and was ordained priest in 1874. After a curacy in Croydon 1873–76, he served a series of chaplaincies in northern India and was appointed as Archdeacon of Lucknow in 1897. He returned to England in 1902 as Rector of St Martin Colchester and was appointed Vicar of Oxford St Cross in 1907. He was the author of *Holy Matrimony, a Treatise on the Divine Laws of Marriage* (1895) and *The Divine Providence* (1904). He was aged 65 in 1914 and at the 1911 census he shared a household with his wife and two unmarried female servants.

OXFORD ST EBBE[1]   Incumbent J. S. Stansfield[2]

1. Baptism at morning or evening prayer? [*No response*].

2. Communion times

a) Sunday 8 am Noon 8 pm (last Sunday in month).

b) Ascension Day 6 am 7 am 11 am.

c) Saints Days [*No response*].

d) Week-days? Very seldom.

3. Is Communion sung? No.

4. Religious teaching to children a) Church b) Sunday School and c) Day school? i) Clergy teach in Day schools? ii) Religious teaching to Sunday school teachers? iii) Satisfactory results?

(a) Occasional Children's lesson in Church. (b) We teach about 180 Children in our Sunday Schools. (c) We have only an Infants' Day School in this parish the religious teaching is very good. [i–iii] I take prayers nearly every day in the Day-school. The Sunday School teachers are nearly all from the north of Oxford and the University. No regular teaching is given to the teachers but we meet occasionally. I am most dissatisfied with the results attained. We are commencing the "System of the Catechism" in September.

5. Religious teaching to lads and young women? For many months we have had two Bible Classes for lads on Sunday afternoon, and one for young women.

6. Secondary school in Parish? No.

7. Teaching for Nonconformist children? No. No wish has ever been expressed for separate religious teaching.

8. Organised study for adults? This is attempted every Wednesday evening.

9. Interest in mission? Missionary subjects are regularly taught and prayed for.

10. Voters for Ruridecanal representatives a) men b) women? I am not sure.

11. PCC? Yes. They give advice in every branch of church work. Power is very limited but advice frequently accepted. Six times.

1. Population 2,130.
2. John Stedwell Stansfield graduated from Exeter College Oxford in 1889 and became MRCS and LRCP in 1897. He trained at Wycliffe Hall Oxford in 1890 and was ordained priest in 1910. He was Chaplain to the Oxford Medical Mission in Bermondsey 1909–10 and Vicar of St Anne's Bermondsey between 1910 and 1912, when he moved to become Rector of Oxford St Ebbe. He was 58 in 1914 and at the 1911 census he was described as married and was sharing a household with his young son and daughter and two unmarried female servants.

OXFORD ST FRIDESWIDE[1]   Incumbent F. Young[2]

1. Baptism at morning or evening prayer? Very occasionally at Evensong on weekdays and only by special arrangement.

2. Communion times

a) Sunday 7, 8, the 1st and 3rd Sundays, 8 the 2nd and 4th Sunday.

b) Ascension Day 5.30, 7 sung at 9.

c) Saints Days 7 and 9 (sung) usually, sometimes 7 and 8.

d) Week-days? 7 o'clock and 9.30 Monday, 8 Wednesday and Thursday in addition. 7 and 8 during Lent and Advent and feasts with Octaves (usually).

3. Is Communion sung? Always at 11 o'clock on Sundays at 9.00 most Saints days.

4. Religious teaching to children a) Church b) Sunday School and c) Day school? i) Clergy teach in Day schools? ii) Religious teaching to Sunday school teachers? iii) Satisfactory results?

(a) Catechism every Sunday afternoon at 3 o'clock by children in church. Little Catechism (boys and girls) in the Boys' school. (b) Sunday School every Sunday morning at 10 o'clock for boys and girls. (c) In the Boys' School our only Church School I go in two mornings a week, Tuesday and Thursday. On other days the teachers teach the Diocesan Syllabus every morning 9 – 10. [i–iii] The Vicar used to go one morning a week in both girls and boys school. With regard to the Sunday School teachers, they are mostly young people who have been through our catechisms. There is a monthly meeting for them in which the next month's lessons are explained and notes taken by them. On the whole the results are good. The children are regular and many are very painstaking in answering at Catechism. Of course there are some slack children among them. Most of the teachers are keen and very regular and good Church people, all regular Communicants.

5. Religious teaching to lads and young women? There is a Bible Class for girls who have left the Catechism. I used to have a Lads' Bible Class, but it did not answer very well. The great majority of lads and young women come to Mass on Sunday mornings and many (especially girls) belong to their Communicants Guilds. Of course there are many failures.

6. Secondary school in Parish? No.

7. Teaching for Nonconformist children? None. We have never received any notice that non conformist children desire their own religion.

8. Organised study for adults? a. There are monthly Communicant Guild meetings for grown up people when the attendance is good. b. A small weekly prayer meeting every Friday. c. A course of Instruction after Evensong during Lent and Advent. d. Books provided in a book rack which many read and I think also books for Lenten reading.

9. Interest in mission? Prayer meeting for missions once a month. Quarterly papers for Lebombo, North Queensland, U.M.C.A. put on the table at the end of the church. Continual Intercession for mission on one day during the year. The children have a Coral League meeting and support a U.M.C.A. child.

10. Voters for Ruridecanal representatives a) men b) women? Two men, as far as I know.

11. PCC? <u>No.</u>

1. Population 2,794 (the Curate noted: 'there is clearly some error in the estimation of the population in respect of this parish and the mother parish of St Thomas the Martyr').
2. The curate rather than the incumbent, Frank Young graduated from St Edmund Hall Oxford in 1908 and trained at the Leeds Clerical School, being ordained priest in 1909. He served a curacy in Lambeth between 1908 and 1910, when he moved to Oxford as Curate of St Frideswide. He was aged 29 in 1914 and at the 1911 census he was living as a boarder with Arthur Smith, an insurance agent, and his wife Elizabeth.

OXFORD ST GILES[1]   Incumbent C. C. Inge[2]

1. Baptism at morning or evening prayer? No.

2. Communion times

a) **Sunday** 8 and 9.45. Also at 7 (monthly) and midday (fortnightly).

b) **Ascension Day** 6, 8, 11.45.

c) **Saints Days** 8 and sometimes 12.

d) **Week-days?** Thursdays at 8.

3. Is Communion ever sung? On 3rd Sunday in the month at midday.

4. Religious teaching to children a) Church b) Sunday School and c) Day school? i) Clergy teach in Day schools? ii) Religious teaching to Sunday school teachers? iii) Satisfactory results?

(a) The children are instructed on Sunday afternoons in Church. (b) Sunday School on Sunday mornings. (c) Religious Instruction every School day 9 to 9.45. [i–iii] Two of the clergy teach in School one day each. There is no class for Sunday School teachers. The religious teaching in day school seems to be well given; I am not equally satisfied with some sections of the Sunday School: we have a different set of children to a large extent on Sundays, the Day School being for girls and infants only, and attracting children from all parts of Oxford. It is very difficult to test the results of Sunday School teaching; they may very likely be better than I think.

5. Religious teaching to lads and young women? A lad's class has been attempted and failed. There are very few lads in the parish and most of them belong to clubs etc in other parishes and attend Sunday classes there. I am considering the possibility of cooperating with Y.M.C.A. in the care of our lads. We have no parochial class for young women, but some attend a G.F.S. Bible Class.

6. Secondary school in Parish? No.

7. Teaching for Nonconformist children? No. There are very few nonconformists, and separate treatment is not desired.

8. Organised study for adults? No.

9. Interest in mission? There is a Parochial Missionary Association: Quarterly Intercession Services are held, followed by an address on some department of missionary work.

10. Voters for Ruridecanal representatives a) men b) women? None, so far as I can ascertain.

11. PCC? No.

1. Population 2,110.
2. Charles Cuthbert Inge graduated from Magdalen College Oxford in 1891, studied at the British School in Athens, and trained at Ely College, being ordained priest in 1895. He served curacies 1894–1906 and was then Vicar of Holmwood until 1913, when he moved to Oxford as Vicar of St Giles. He was aged 45 in 1914 and at the 1911 census he was living in a household with his wife, three children under 5, his elderly mother, his unmarried sister and five unmarried female servants.

OXFORD ST MARGARET[1]   Incumbent E. W. Pullan[2]

1. Baptism at morning or evening prayer? No.

2. Communion times

a) Sunday 7, 8 (9 on 1st Sun) and 11.30.

b) Ascension Day 7, 8, 11.

c) Saints Days 7, 7.45, 10.

d) Week-days? 7. 45.

3. Is Communion ever sung? Yes 11.30 on Sundays, 11 on Great Feasts e.g. Ascension Day.

4. Religious teaching to children a) Church b) Sunday School and c) Day school? i) Clergy teach in Day schools? ii) Religious teaching to Sunday school teachers? iii) Satisfactory results?

(a) Catechism at Sundays at 3 pm. (b) Sunday School 10.30 – 11.30 am. (c) There are no Day Schools attached to the Parish. [i–iii] Sunday School Teachers are instructed on Thursday evenings for the following Sunday lesson. I am not satisfied and I am making inquiries with a view to improving our present system.

5. Religious teaching to lads and young women? S. Francis' Guild for Boys. S. Margaret's Guild for Girls. S. Agnes' Guild for Girls.

6. Secondary school in Parish? No.

7. Teaching for Nonconformist children? No school.

8. Organised study for adults? No.

9. Interest in mission? Intercession in Church on Wednesday evenings. Parochial Missionary Association – Every house is visited with a view to getting subscriptions for foreign missions. Study Circles are arranged from time to time. Missionary meetings and Sermons.

10. Voters for Ruridecanal representatives a) men b) women? At a meeting held on March 18, 1912 only a few well-known communicants were present: so that no declaration was signed as none was needed.

11. PCC? Yes. The Church Wardens and Sidesmen form the Council. It deals with Finance and with any other business of Parochial interests. It has not met since October as there has been no occasion for calling a meeting.

1. Population 1,748.
2. Edward Wilfred Pullan graduated from St John's College Oxford in 1899 and was ordained priest in 1901. He was Curate of Summertown from 1900 until 1906, when he became Vicar

of Oxford St Margaret. He was aged 41 in 1914 and at the 1911 census he was single and shared a household with another clergyman and two unmarried female servants.

OXFORD ST MARY MAGDALEN[1] Incumbent H. E. Clayton[2]

1. Baptism at morning or evening prayer? Occasionally – not very rarely – the last occasion was an Adult Baptism.

2. Communion times

a) **Sunday** 7am and 8am every Sunday – and at Midday (12.20) (1st and 3rd).

b) **Ascension Day** 7 am and 8 am.

c) **Saints Days** 7.45 am.

d) **Week-days?** On Wednesdays at 8 am. Sometimes on Fridays at 8am On Greater Feasts 6am, 7am, 8am(sung) and midday (12.20).

3. Is Communion ever sung? Yes – once a month and on Great Feasts at 8 am.

4. Religious teaching to children a) Church b) Sunday School and c) Day school? i) Clergy teach in Day schools? ii) Religious teaching to Sunday school teachers? iii) Satisfactory results?

(a) Catechizing or a simple Address (on Festivals) at 3 pm every Sunday. (b) Sunday School Lesson at 10.15 till 10.45 am on the Subject to be Catechized upon. Once a month the Church Catechism is repeated in Church. The Collect is learned and said every Sunday. Lessons drawn up for London Diocesan S. Sch. Assn now being used. (c) Day School. Lessons on Dioc. Syllabus every day from 9.15 to 9.50. [i–iii] The Vicar teaches on Monday (Boys) and Friday (Girls). Mr Gwillim teaches on Tuesday and Thursday. At present no lessons are being given to the Sunday School Teachers, as they are all skilled teachers (some certificated – others experienced in teaching). In past years regular instruction has been given by myself. On the whole I am fairly well satisfied with the instruction that is given to the Children – it comes out in the Catechising – and the Children who do not attend Church Schools make good progress in the Sunday School. The Confirmation results are good.

5. Religious teaching to lads and young women? No classes are being held at present for young lads and young women – but there are Bible classes held at centres, such as G.F.S. Lodge, to which some of the girls go. There are no young persons in my parish (beside those who teach in the Sunday School) who could take such classes. A Bible Class for Lads would be valuable if it could be managed as have had them from time to time but cannot do so at present.

6. Secondary school in Parish? Yes! The High School for Boys is in my parish, where Mr Cave, the headmaster, and the Rev H.R. Hall give regular and definite teaching to the Pupil Teachers who are sent by the LEA to the school. Other scholars are taught Scripture only – but it is well taught.

7. Teaching for Nonconformist children? The Central School for Boys (Council) stands alongside of St Mary Magdalene Boys' School. No children are withdrawn in the Boys' School – but there are three Jewesses in the Girls' School, who are taught Old Testament only, and have other lessons in Scripture apart. Their parents are well satisfied. No Nonconformist children are withdrawn from the Church Teaching.

8. Organised study for adults? Nothing special.

9. Interest in mission? Prayers are said monthly for UMCA and Holy Communion is celebrated at intervals (each Term at least). Sermons are preached Quarterly for Foreign Missions often by those who are working abroad. Missionary Literature is distributed among those who have Boxes and to the children.

10. Voters for Ruridecanal representatives a) men b) women? Not many – about eight on the last occasion – there is great reluctance in signing – though the number known to be qualified is quite large.

11. PCC? No.

1. Population 1,212.
2. Horace Evelyn Clayton graduated from Brasenose College Oxford in 1875 and was ordained priest in 1877. He was Curate of Oxford St Mary Magdalen 1876–80, Chaplain of New College 1879–85, and Divinity Lecturer at Magdalen College 1884–93. He was appointed as Vicar of Oxford St Mary Magdalen in 1894, Rural Dean of Oxford in 1896 and Honorary Canon of Christ Church in 1903. He was aged 61 in 1914 and at the 1911 census he was single and shared a household with a widowed housekeeper and one unmarried female servant.

OXFORD ST MARY THE VIRGIN[1]   Incumbent C. A. Whittuck[2]

1. Baptism at morning or evening prayer? No.

2. Communion times

a) Sunday 8am every Sunday and on first Sunday in month after 11am morning prayer.

b) Ascension Day 8 am.

c) Saints Days 8 am.

d) Week-days? Daily at 7.15 am during the academical term available for parishioners though not primarily intended for them.

3. Is Communion ever sung? No.

4. Religious teaching to children a) Church b) Sunday School and c) Day school? i) Clergy teach in Day schools? ii) Religious teaching to Sunday school teachers? iii) Satisfactory results?

No Day or Sunday Schools in the Parish. Very few children in the Parish, several who would be there being obliged to be boarded out owing to the requirements of the University Lodging House Delegacy.

5. Religious teaching to lads and young women? There is a small CEMS and GFS following. Members of the latter receive some biblical instruction. The lads and young women attending the Church (of whom there are a large number) do not for the most part belong to the Parish.

6. Secondary school in Parish? No.

7. Teaching for Nonconformist children? [*No response*].

8. Organised study for adults? No, not apart from the ordinary ministrations including lectures and addresses.

9. Interest in mission? No: there is nothing of this nature which is distinctively parochial apart from Missionary Sermons for various objects, an "all day" of continuous intercession in November, and the Jamaica Church dioc Association with which St Mary's has for many years been connected and in which a considerable proportion of the parishioners are enrolled (meetings of the same well supported).

10. Voters for Ruridecanal representatives a) men b) women? Some six or seven men. The declaration is usually signed at the annual Vestry.

11. PCC? No!

1. Population 152.
2. Charles Augustus Whittuck graduated from Oriel College Oxford in 1873 and was ordained priest in 1879. He was a Fellow of Brasenose College 1873–91 and between 1873 and 1886 was also Vice-Principal and Tutor. He moved to become Rector of Great Shefford 1887–96 and then Rector of Bearwood between 1896 and 1905, when he was appointed as Vicar of Oxford St Mary the Virgin. He was the author of *The Church of England and recent Religious Thought* (1893), *Learning and Working (Sermons on Practical Subjects)* (1889) and *The Good Man of the Eighteenth Century* (1901) and was also a contributor to *Hastings' Encyclopaedia of Religion and Ethics*. He was aged 64 in 1914 and at the 1911 census he shared a household with his wife, his unmarried nephew (a law student) and three unmarried female servants.

OXFORD ST MATTHEW[1]   Incumbent W. A. Williamson[2]

1. Baptism at morning or evening prayer? Not hitherto.

2. Communion times

a) **Sunday** 8am (3 times a month) noon (once) 7.30 pm (once).

b) **Ascension Day** 8 am.

c) **Saints Days** 8 am.

d) **Week-days?** None, so far.

3. Is Communion ever sung? No.

4. Religious teaching to children a) Church b) Sunday School and c) Day school? i) Clergy teach in Day schools? ii) Religious teaching to Sunday school teachers? iii) Satisfactory results?

(a) Children's Service with Catechizing 2 pm once a month. (b) Sunday School each Sunday 10 am and 2 pm (c) Only <u>Infants</u> Day School in parish. Books of instruction are given to teachers in S. Sch.

5. Religious teaching to lads and young women? Bible Class for Young men every Sunday at 2.15. Bible Class for Young women every Sunday at 3.0.

6. Secondary school in Parish? No secondary school.

7. Teaching for Nonconformist children? Boys and Girls School in St Aldates parish.

8. Organised study for adults? C.E.M.S. monthly meeting, and weekly men's service. Womens' instruction service every week.

9. Interest in mission? Sowers' Band and Gleaners' Union, with occasional missionary meetings. Prayer-meeting every week.

10. Voters for Ruridecanal representatives a) men b) women? I believe only 3 men.

11. PCC? No.

1. Population reckoned in St Aldate 3,335. New district about 2,500.
2. Wilfred Alexander Williamson trained at the London College of Divinity in 1883 and graduated from University College Durham in 1887. (He also received the degree of BA from the University of New Zealand in 1909.) He was ordained priest in 1889 and served five curacies 1888–1905. He was appointed Vicar of the new district of Oxford St Matthew in 1914. His household was not found in the 1911 census, possibly because he was in New Zealand.

OXFORD ST MICHAEL[1]   Incumbent W. M. Merry[2]

1. Baptism at morning or evening prayer? No: but always (so far as possible) make Baptism an integral part of a largely-attended Children's service.

2. Communion times

a) **Sunday** 8am: 2nd and 4th Sundays, noon, as well.

b) **Ascension Day** 8 am.

c) **Saints Days** 8 am: with occasionally, another Celebrations: at 11 am e.g. All Saints and Dedicat. Festival on Michaelmas Day.

d) **Week-days?** [*No response*].

3. Is Communion ever sung? No.

4. Religious teaching to children a) Church b) Sunday School and c) Day school? i) Clergy teach in Day schools? ii) Religious teaching to Sunday school teachers? iii) Satisfactory results?

I have only about two dozen children in my Parish; and have no Day or Sunday Schools. There is a Children's Guild (on a congregational basis) which has a monthly service on the first S of the month at 3 pm. The children of the Parish of a "Sunday School" age attend the Schools (both Day and Sunday) in other adjacent Parishes.

5. Religious teaching to lads and young women? A Bible-Class for Boys is held once a week during the months October – April. A largely attended service is held each Wednesday night (October – May), at the end of which an instructional and practical address is given by myself. Nominally on the Book of Psalms (Psalms being taken verse by verse and in order) but including in its scope any doctrinal questions that suggest themselves as well as more definitely spiritual teaching. This service is attended both by the younger folk and their elders.

6. Secondary school in Parish? No!

7. Teaching for Nonconformist children? [*No response*].

8. Organised study for adults? See answer to (5).

9. Interest in mission? Nothing other than annual missionary sermons, and a regular observance of the Day of Intercession with an address.

10. Voters for Ruridecanal representatives a) men b) women? I have no statistics at this point.

11. PCC? No.

1. Population 399.
2. Walter Mansell Merry graduated from Exeter College Oxford in 1885 and trained at Ely College in 1886, being ordained priest in 1888. He was Domestic Chaplain to the bishop of Ripon 1887–88, then served two curacies between 1888 and 1897, when he was appointed as Vicar of St Michael at the Northgate. He was aged 50 in 1914 and at the 1911 census he shared a household with his wife, two teenage daughters and three unmarried female servants.

OXFORD ST PAUL[1]   Incumbent B. J. Kidd[2]

1. Baptism at morning or evening prayer? Yes: Baptisms are advertised as to take place any day at evensong: and they generally do: though occasionally on Sundays at Catechism also.

2. Communion times

a) **Sunday** 8 and 11 (sung) on ordinary Sundays; 1st in month at 7 also.

b) **Ascension Day** 6; 6.25; and 8.

c) **Saints Days** 7 and 8.

d) **Week-days?** Daily: W. F at 8; other days at 7.30.

3. Is Communion ever sung? Yes Every Sunday at 11am.

4. Religious teaching to children a) Church b) Sunday School and c) Day school? i) Clergy teach in Day schools? ii) Religious teaching to Sunday school teachers? iii) Satisfactory results?

(a) Children are instructed every Sunday at the Sung Eucharist, 11 am, at Catechism, 2.45 pm. (b) Sunday School is held at 10.15 am, before they come to the Sung Eucharist at 11 am. There is no Sunday School in the afternoon, nor are the children brought to church "en masse". But each comes on his own account to Catechism in Church and they are all there. We find this system works much better because: a. it enables us to be independent of teachers who are hard to get: marking etc is done by monitors and monitresses. b. It makes the children responsible. (c) In Day-Schools. We only have a Boys School: our girls go to St Giles', the Convent or St Barnabas: in fact to St Giles and St Barnabas. It is a great weakness to have no infants. Church life is thin at the top because it is not fed from beneath. (d) The clergy teach in the Day Schools: Vicar on Tuesday and the Assistant-Curate on Thursdays. On Holy Days also the whole school comes to church 9 – 9.40 and is taught then. (e) Such Sunday-school teachers as we have are not taught in class but supplied with Q. and A. to teach: but we do not rely on Sunday School teachers. They are untrained and increasingly hard to get. Save that we have Sister Elizabeth (a certificated Mistress) at the head – a host in herself. (f) I do not believe in Sunday Schools: but in the Catechism and in teaching by the Clergy, in Day School, in Church, and in 'preparation for Confirmation'. Of course, if we had very large numbers and few clergy, then our system would need supplementing.

5. Religious teaching to lads and young women? We have Communicants' Guilds: for each.

6. Secondary school in Parish? None.

7. Teaching for Nonconformist children? The difficulty does not arise in Oxford where there is a sufficient choice of schools. Should any demand be made of us by Dissenting parents, I should be quite willing to meet it: and so I think would our Managers. We would do as we would be done by.

8. Organised study for adults? No: save for such teaching as we can give in church on Sundays. They are all at work from early morning to late at night: there is no educated person among them. But on Sunday, at sermon, they do listen and try to learn as well as they are capable of it. But "study" would be beyond them.

9. Interest in mission? We circulate the "Mission Field" and the S.P.G. Intercession Paper among a few grown up people. The children support U.M.C.A.; use "African Tidings": and are taught about it, on the first Sunday of each month.

10. Voters for Ruridecanal representatives a) men b) women? None.

11. PCC? No.

1. Population 2,320.
2. Beresford James Kidd graduated from Keble College Oxford in 1886 and was awarded the degrees of BD in 1898 and DD in 1904. He was ordained priest in 1888 and served a curacy at St Philip and St James 1887–1900. He was Chaplain and Divinity Lecturer at Pembroke College 1894–96, Theology Examiner for the University of Oxford 1902–04 and Theology Tutor at Pembroke College between 1902 and 1911. He also became Vicar of Oxford St Paul in 1904. He was the author of *The Thirty-nine Articles* (2 vols) (1899), *The Continental Reformation* (1902), *The Later Mediaeval Doctrine of the Eucharistic Sacrifice* (1898) and *Documents Illustrative of the Continental Reformation* (1911). He was 50 years old in 1914 and at the 1911 census he shared a household with his wife and two unmarried female servants.

OXFORD ST PETER LE BAILEY[1] Incumbent J. G. Watson[2]

1. Baptism at morning or evening prayer? No.

2. Communion times

a) **Sunday** 1st 11 am 2nd 8 am 3rd 6.30 4th 8 am.

b) **Ascension Day** 11.30 am.

c) **Saints Days** 8 am.

d) **Week-days?** [*No response*].

3. Is Communion ever sung? No.

4. Religious teaching to children a) Church b) Sunday School and c) Day school? i) Clergy teach in Day schools? ii) Religious teaching to Sunday school teachers? iii) Satisfactory results?

[*No response*].

5. Religious teaching to lads and young women? A Bible Class for Lads on Sundays. A Bible Class for Young Women Sunday afternoon.

6. Secondary school in Parish? No.

7. Teaching for Nonconformist children? There is only a mixed School in the Parish. There is also a Wesleyan Day School.

8. Organised study for adults? A Mens Bible Class Sunday Afternoons.

9. Interest in mission? Meetings from time to time giving accounts of the work of different missionaries.

10. Voters for Ruridecanal representatives a) men b) women? [*No response*].

11. PCC? Sidesmen are elected at Easter and they meet from time to time.

N.B. As I am only in charge of St Peter le Bailey, the answers I have given apply as far as I have been able to ascertain, to the position in the Parish up to the resignation of the late Rector.

1. Population 546 (diminishing).
2. James George Watson graduated from Worcester College Oxford in 1870 and was ordained priest in 1880. After an initial curacy he was Minister of St John the Evangelist, Spark Hill, Birmingham 1881–85, and Associate Secretary of the CMS for Buckinghamshire, Oxfordshire and the diocese of Peterborough 1885–1900. He served as Rector of Devizes between 1900 and 1909, when he became Rector of St Ebbe's until 1912. In 1914 he was in charge of St Peter le Bailey. He was 65 in 1914 and at the 1911 census he shared a household with his wife and three unmarried female servants.

OXFORD ST PETER IN THE EAST[1]   Incumbent J. H. Skrine[2]

1. Baptism at morning or evening prayer? No.

2. Communion times

a) Sunday 8am and on 2nd and 4th Sunday in month also at 11 am.

b) Ascension Day 8 am.

c) Saints Days 8 am (but only on a few Saints days).

d) Week-days? [*No response*].

3. Is Communion ever sung? Yes At 11am (on the greater festivals).

4. Religious teaching to children a) Church b) Sunday School and c) Day school? i) Clergy teach in Day schools? ii) Religious teaching to Sunday school teachers? iii) Satisfactory results?

(a) The children of the School (who are with few exceptions not parishioners) are instructed in church at 11.15 am on all Saints Days. (b) There is no Sunday School, the parish having hardly any children those there are the Holywell School provides for. (c) Religious Instruction is given daily in the Day School. [i–iii] The Clergy teach twice a week the older half of the School. Sunday School teachers. We have none (See under (b)) The results as tested by the Diocesan Inspectors are pronounced very satisfactory. My own experience is that the children are decidedly bright and easy to interest. (They are of a somewhat superior (social) class for the most part as fees are charged.)

5. Religious teaching to lads and young women? The lads of the parish hardly exist, but a small group of lads connected with the congregation is taught yearly in a Confirmation Class. A much larger class of girls is also taught so. A class for young women is held at the Vicarage on Sundays by the Vicar's wife. A system of services for younger Communicants has been started.

6. Secondary school in Parish? No. But the School of Magdalen College and of Queen's College (kept however in the New College School in Holywell) are within the parish bounds. These are extra-parochial.

7. Teaching for Nonconformist children? No provision is made. At present there are no children of such parents.

8. Organised study for adults? Meetings in church or elsewhere of the CEMS, and services with addresses for the Women's Guild are all that can be named as opportunities used for this.

9. Interest in mission? Sermons on behalf of the Societies and Services of Intercession.

10. Voters for Ruridecanal representatives a) men b) women? (a) men 2 (b) women 1. Note: These were only the persons who actually recorded a vote at the Election, first signing the declaration.

11. PCC? No.

1. Population 382 (including St John the Baptist).
2. John Huntley Skrine graduated from Corpus Christi College Oxford in 1871 and was awarded DD in 1912. He was ordained priest in 1876 and held a fellowship at Merton College between 1871 and 1879. He worked as Assistant Master at Uppingham School, 1873–87, Warden of Trinity College Glenalmond 1888–1902 and was Vicar of Itchen Stoke between 1903 and 1908, when he was appointed as Vicar of Oxford St Peter in the East. A prolific author, his published works included a drama, *Joan the Maid* (1895), work on education – *A Memory of Edward Thring* (1889), *Public School Hymns* (1899) – and several works of pastoral theology including *Pastor Ovium* (1909). He was 65 in 1914 and at the 1911 census he shared a household with his wife (a novelist) and four unmarried female servants.

OXFORD ST PHILIP AND ST JAMES[1]   Incumbent C. R. Davey Biggs[2]

1. Baptism at morning or evening prayer? Only on Easter Eve as a rule; but we have, when parents consent to it, Baptisms during Evensong.

2. Communion times

a) **Sunday** 7, 8,11.40.

b) **Ascension Day** 6.15, 7, 7.45, and 11. At 11 there is also a Sermon.

c) **Saints Days** 7, 7.45, 11.

d) Week-days? 8 everyday; also at 11, about once a fortnight, for invalids, in Lent there are additional celebrations at 7 and 11 each once a week.

3. Is Communion ever sung? Yes, always on Sundays and on Festivals such as Xmas and the Ascension and All Saints. We also have a Sung Communion on November 2nd, and when any public calamity calls for a general pleading for the Departed. On Sundays at 11.40 – without sermon. On Xmas day at 11.40 – without sermon. On Ascension Day at 11 with sermon. On all Saints at 7.30 am. On November 2nd at 10am.

4. Religious teaching to children a) Church b) Sunday School and c) Day school? i) Clergy teach in Day schools? ii) Religious teaching to Sunday school teachers? iii) Satisfactory results?

The children of the parish belong to too many different social grades for any net to be manufactured which would catch them all. There is catechising in Church every Sunday afternoon at 3 attended by all whose parents care to send or bring them and on Holy Days at 9 attended by the Day School. The Sunday Schools are very small and are held half an hour before Mattins and the Catechising for which the teachers bring the Scholars to Church so that they always hear a Sermon every Sunday at Mattins, and at the Catechising. They repeat Collects, Gospels, and (when they come) the Proper Prefaces, by heart. Nothing is done for the religious instruction of the Sunday School Teachers as such; they come to Church for the ordinary services, come to the Bible Classes in the winter months, and to the Guild Meetings and more than that is unnecessary. [i–iii] The clergy never teach in the Day Schools – <u>they attend for the purpose of learning how to teach</u>, but it would be unfair for them to injure the reputation of the proper staff by mixing up their amateur incompetence with the skill and long experience of the properly qualified teachers: N.B. <u>where promotion may depend on a Diocesan Inspector's Report, the report ought to be on work done by the Staff and the Staff only</u>. A poor teacher ought not to win credit from a good priest's teaching and a good teacher ought not to be embarrassed by an incompetent priest. For the results. There is no need to do more than quote the words of Mr Nixon the Diocesan Inspector yesterday that he had never been better pleased with any school in the diocese and that he wished our prayers had been in his hands before a new set were approved for the diocese. All the teachers are communicants and the five male teachers each serve the altar one day a week, the choir boys are drawn from the School in which the choirmaster teaches music and are passed to be Servers when their voices break. It would be hard to find a School where there was more support and sympathy for the Church. The Head Teacher has for some years past been engaged to give instruction in method etc to the Students at Cuddesdon.

5. Religious teaching to lads and young women? There are too many social strata for it to be possible to group 'the lads' and 'the young women'. They have their own opportunities of coming to church, and in church two sermons are preached every

Sunday: and their aim is – strange as it may seem from such a question as this being asked – to give religious instruction. There are also Classes of preparation for Confirmation and Bible Classes, but the Prayer Book says "ye shall call upon him to hear Sermons" and so we preach sermons.

6. Secondary school in Parish? There are a number of Secondary schools in the parish: one is managed by the Convent of the Holy Trinity and on occasion I go and help the teachers by taking a subject through the term for them. The others are by tradition opposed to having any dealings with the parish priest.

7. Teaching for Nonconformist children? We have only a Church School, and the Nonconformists who attend are perfectly satisfied to have the teaching which is given them, and it is a particular satisfaction to me, in my turn, when the Diocesan Inspector's choice for the Bishop's prize turns out to be a Nonconformist: they are told they can have another book instead of the Prayer Book, but always prefer the Prayer Book.

8. Organised study for adults? Generally, in the autumn there is a course of sermons on doctrine supplementary to the Confirmation Classes. From time to time courses of lectures are given in connection with the Church History Society: and at the beginning of the New Year books are recommended for reading during Lent.

9. Interest in mission? Sermons are preached every year and collections made for S.P.G. and C.M.S.: also for other Missionary Associations as need may be. A Litany for Missions is said on the first Friday of each month at 3 pm and at the Children's Service at 3 pm on the first Sunday in each month a "King's Messengers" service is used and instruction given on some part of the work and the Church overseas.

10. Voters for Ruridecanal representatives a) men b) women? The men and women do not take any interest in it.

11. PCC? No. Everything goes on most happily under the joint managership of 'Curate' and 'Churchwardens'; and when we have made experiments in the direction of a Church Council people felt it was fuss for the sake of it.

1. Population 3,201.
2. Charles Richard Davey Biggs graduated from St John's College Oxford in 1886 and was awarded BD in 1896 and DD in 1900. Biggs was ordained priest in 1889 and was then Vice-Principal of the Theological College of the Scottish Church in Edinburgh 1890–92, Chaplain to the Bishop of Jerusalem 1892–93 and a Fellow of St Augustine's College Canterbury 1893–95. He served a curacy at All Hallows Barking between 1897 and 1900, when he was appointed Vicar of Oxford St Philip and St James. He also held a Fellowship at St John's from 1891 to 1902 and was the author of *Six Months in Jerusalem* (1896) and *Public Worship in Book of Common Prayer* (1907). He was 48 in 1914 and at the 1911 census he shared a household with his wife and three unmarried female servants.

OXFORD ST THOMAS[1] Incumbent B. S. Hack[2]

1. Baptism at morning or evening prayer? Yes, on Wednesday evenings.

2. Communion times

a) **Sunday** 7, 8, 11.

b) **Ascension Day** 5, 6, 7, 8, 11.

c) **Saints Days** 7, 8, 9 or 6, 6.45, 8.

d) **Week-days?** 7. Also on Monday at 9.30 and on Thursday and Friday at 8.

3. Is Communion ever sung? Sundays at 11. All Holy Days at either 6.45 or 9 (Epiphany, Christmas Day, Ascension Day, S Thomas the Martyr, All Saints, and Michaelmas at 11 with Sermon.) (Holy Days immediately after Christmas, Easter and Whitsun Day at 9.30.).

4. Religious teaching to children a) Church b) Sunday School and c) Day school? i) Clergy teach in Day schools? ii) Religious teaching to Sunday school teachers? iii) Satisfactory results?

(a) Great Catechism every Sunday in church at 2.30 pm. Children's Service and Catechizing every Sunday at 3.30 pm. (Infants attend the first part only.) (b) Sunday School for boys, girls and infants at 10.30 am. Boys and Girls brought on to the 11 o'clock service in church. Infants remain longer with their teachers. (c) Religious instruction every morning at 9 am in School according to the Syllabus. But I have omitted some of this – the Acts of the Apostles sometimes and Morning Prayer and Litany. (i) Clergy teach three days a week normally. Sometimes this is not done, sometimes I go twice, so that there are four days. (ii) None. They teach the children the set questions for the afternoon. The Infant teachers are very good. (iii) It might all be much better, but I suppose it would be considered pretty fair. I wonder sometimes at the ignorance of the Gospel history and I venture to think that the Acts might be left for Bible Classes. Oddly enough my young men's Bible Class prefer to go through the Gospels again and again; very possibly I did not make the Acts very interesting.

5. Religious teaching to lads and young women? Two Bible Classes for lads and young men. Two Bible Classes for young women and girls.

6. Secondary school in Parish? None.

7. Teaching for Nonconformist children? No provision made. But I do not know of any single case now where a child has been withdrawn from the ordinary religious instruction. How far this is due to indifference on the part of dissenters or to the innocuous nature of our teaching I cannot say. I am definite enough. I think that it is due mostly to the fact that the zealous dissenters send their children to the Wesleyan School. Some women who will send children to the Baptist Mission Hall in the Parish on Sundays are quite content to leave matters alone on weekdays, save for a Band of Hope which I have rather broken up this year by means of a rival attraction.

8. Organised study for adults? An instruction is given after Evensong every Sunday in Lent and is popular. Once it was done in Advent. Bible Class for men on Mondays except in summer. Bible Class for women on Sunday afternoons.

9. Interest in mission? There is no system of study or instruction. Sermons are preached for U.M.C.A. and S.P.G. Also an occasional meeting. There is a Dorcas Meeting to provide garments for the natives in Zanzibar Diocese, and letters from Archdeacon Birley are sent to this meeting and are sometimes printed in the Parish Magazine. The children make toys and things for a Sale this next month. They support an Indian boy at Poona. If the Poona people would write more about it the children might be more interested. Intercessions in church once a month. Day of Continuous Prayer on the Vigil of S. Andrew.

10. Voters for Ruridecanal representatives a) men b) women? None.

11. PCC? No. The Offertory Fund is managed by the Vicar and Churchwardens. I am treasurer and pay the bills. The accounts are audited and passed by the Easter Vestry. The Vicar also controls the Poor Fund and some smaller funds. Assistant Clergy Fund and Sunday School Fund managed by the People's Churchwarden. The Parish Accounts are at the Old Bank, my own private account at London County and Westminster so that the risk of confusion is avoided.

1. Population 2,713.
2. Bartle Starmer Hack graduated from Christ Church Oxford in 1894 and trained at Ely College in 1895, being ordained priest in 1897. He was a curate at Witney 1896–1903 and then served at the Christ Church Mission in Poplar before being appointed as Vicar of Oxford St Thomas the Martyr in 1908. He was also appointed as Chaplain to Oxford Prison in 1909. He was 42 in 1914 and at the 1911 census he was single and sharing a household with his housekeeper and one other unmarried female servant.

OXFORD HOLY TRINITY[1]   Incumbent E. W. Cox[2]

1. Baptism at morning or evening prayer? No, only immediately before or after a service

2. Communion times

a) **Sunday** Every Sunday at 8.0; 2nd Sunday after Morning Service; 4th Sunday after Evening service.

b) **Ascension Day** at 7.45 am.

c) **Saints Days** Not at all.

d) **Week-days?** [Not at all.]

3. Is Communion ever sung? No.

4. Religious teaching to children a) Church b) Sunday School and c) Day school? i) Clergy teach in Day schools? ii) Religious teaching to Sunday school teachers? iii) Satisfactory results?

(a) (i) The Boys and Girls of the Sunday School attend the 11.0 am Service every Sunday and the Girls (only) remain for the Sermon which is sometimes more particularly addressed to them. (ii) We have a Children's Service in Church in the afternoon on the first Sunday of every month. All the Sunday School Children attend this. (iii) The girls of our Elementary Day Schools (for Girls only) attend Church on the first four week days in Holy Week and also on nine Saint's Days – these being so selected as to secure the Girls being taken to Church as nearly as possible once a month during the School Terms. (b) The Sunday Schools (Boys, Girls, and Infants) meet every Sunday morning and afternoon. We have also every Sunday night (except in the summer months) a "Ragged School" for the Religious Instruction of the poorest children (girls only). If we could only get teachers our Sunday Schools could be immensely increased in number of children and in the efficiency of instruction. (c) We have a Girls' Day School (Elementary) only. Here there is religious instruction every morning in every class. [i–iii] Both the Vicar and the Curate teach in the Day School one morning each week. A Class for the Instruction of our youngest Sunday Schools is held. These young teachers were children in the Sunday Schools. As stated above the results of our Sunday School teaching would be greater and wider if we could get teachers. We are now aiming at instructing our children both in Day and Sunday Schools more definitely in such matters as "Character", "Conscience", and "Purity of thought". I cannot help feeling that there has been an over emphasis on "head-knowledge" and not enough of such teaching as will touch the heart, character, conscience and thoughts. This applies more particularly to the Day School and also partly to the Sunday School.

5. Religious teaching to lads and young women? We have every Sunday afternoon a Bible Class for lads and one also for young women.

6. Secondary school in Parish? No such school.

7. Teaching for Nonconformist children? There is a Council School on the outskirts of the parish. No child has been withdrawn from Religious Instruction and no separate arrangements are made for Nonconformists.

8. Organised study for adults? Indications are given in the Parish Magazine and occasionally from the pulpit of books etc which should be read but the people here are all of the poorest class.

9. Interest in mission? In the Autumn and Winter months a missionary meeting is held every month. Reference is also made in the Parish Magazine and Pulpit and a number take in the "Church Missionary Gleaner".

10. Voters for Ruridecanal representatives a) men b) women? We had ten Parochial Lay Representatives elected in 1912 to the Ruri-decanal Conference. These were all men, and as far as I remember these ten were the only ones who signed the declaration. It was a case of electing each other on to the Conference. Of these three have now removed from us.

11. PCC? We have no such Council.

1. Population 2,765.
2. Ernest William Cox graduated from the University of Oxford in 1899 and was ordained priest in 1901. He was Curate at Holy Trinity 1901–02 and at Ewell from 1902 to 1904, when he moved to become Organising Secretary of the CMS for the dioceses of Liverpool and Sodor and Man and the archdeaconry of Chester 1904–06 and then Assistant Secretary of the CMS and Organising Secretary of its Medical Mission Auxiliary 1906–09. He returned to Oxford Holy Trinity as Vicar in 1910. He was 41 in 1914 and at the 1911 census he shared a household with his wife and one unmarried female servant.

PIDDINGTON[1]   Incumbent G. R. Tidmarsh[2]

1. Baptism at morning or evening prayer? No (There has been only one Baptism since I have been here and that was administered at the Children's service).

2. Communion times

a) Sunday after Mattins 1st S. in Month, 8am other Sundays.

b) Ascension Day 8am.

c) Saints Days [*No response*].

d) Week-days? [*No response*].

3. Is Communion ever sung? No.

4. Religious teaching to children a) Church b) Sunday School and c) Day school? i) Clergy teach in Day schools? ii) Religious teaching to Sunday school teachers? iii) Satisfactory results?

(As there was no Sunday School for ten years previous to my Incumbency, practically all the children go to the Dissenting Sunday School, and I have only two who come to me.) (a) Children's Service every Sunday 3 pm. (b) Sunday School 10 am. (c) 9.00 – 9.50 am each morning. [i–iii] I go into the Day School twice a week. There are no Sunday School teachers except myself. I can hardly say at present.

5. Religious teaching to lads and young women? Nothing at present. There are very few of either.

6. Secondary school in Parish? No.

7. Teaching for Nonconformist children? The School Mistress teaches those who are "withdrawn".

8. Organised study for adults? Last winter I gave lectures on "The Faith" in Church on Sundays after Evensong Service. They were very well attended. I propose to do the same again this winter.

9. Interest in mission? Nothing at present.

10. Voters for Ruridecanal representatives a) men b) women? None as far as I know.

11. PCC? There is no scope for one here.

1. Population 191.
2. George Reginald Tidmarsh graduated from Oxford University in 1896. He served a series of curacies at Willenhall 1906–09, Arundel 1909–10 and Littlehampton 1910–13. He was also Assistant Chaplain at the Royal Naval School Eltham 1901–03 and Loretto School 1904–06. He became Vicar of Piddington in 1913. He was 39 in 1914 and at the 1911 census he shared a household with his wife, their young son and one unmarried female servant.

PISHILL[1]   Incumbent G. M. J. Hall[2]

1. Baptism at morning or evening prayer? Yes, in the course of Evening Prayer.

2. Communion times

a) Sunday At 8 am or Midday.

b) Ascension Day At 8 am when the number is sufficient.

c) Saints Days None.

d) Week-days? [None.]

3. Is Communion ever sung? No.

4. Religious teaching to children a) Church b) Sunday School and c) Day school? i) Clergy teach in Day schools? ii) Religious teaching to Sunday school teachers? iii) Satisfactory results?

There is no separate religious instruction of children in church. In Sunday School there is an hour devoted to it in the mornings. In the Day School the first hour of every day. [i–iii] The Vicar teaches once a week in the Day School. He and his wife and his son (when he is at home for his holidays as a school-master) give the instruction in the Sunday School. The results appear to be satisfactory.

5. Religious teaching to lads and young women? Nothing at present. There are hardly any left in the parish.

6. Secondary school in Parish? No.

7. Teaching for Nonconformist children? There has never been any demand for such a thing. There is also a Roman Catholic School about a mile from ours in this parish.

8. Organised study for adults? The adults are farmers and farm labourers who in these days of scarce money and scarce hands have no time, if they had the inclination, for systematic study.

9. Interest in mission? An occasional sermon on the subject is preached and when finances will allow it an offertory is collected.

10. Voters for Ruridecanal representatives a) men b) women? None.

11. PCC? No.

1. Population 398.
2. George Mellish James Hall trained at the London College of Divinity in 1869 and subsequently graduated from Exeter College Oxford in 1887. He was ordained priest in 1872 and served a series of curacies between 1871 and 1888 (the last one being at All Saints Oxford), when he became Vicar of Pishill. He was 65 in 1914 and at the 1911 census he shared a household with his wife and unmarried son, aged 24, and two unmarried female servants.

PYRTON[1]   Incumbent J. W. B. Bell[2]

1. Baptism at morning or evening prayer? No. Parents almost universally try to stipulate for Sunday Afternoon.

2. Communion times

a) Sunday 8 am, 11.0 1st Sunday in month (early celebrations of late interrupted by illness).

b) Ascension Day 8 am and 11.0 am.

c) Saints Days None.

d) Week-days? None.

3. Is Communion ever sung? No.

4. Religious teaching to children a) Church b) Sunday School and c) Day school? i) Clergy teach in Day schools? ii) Religious teaching to Sunday school teachers? iii) Satisfactory results?

Sunday School every Sunday 10–11 am [i–iii] One morning each week. Manuals provided. I am satisfied influence of the teachers (voluntary) lasts beyond the School age.

5. Religious teaching to lads and young women? Sunday morning class at Vicarage chiefly for Scouts but other lads attend. G.F.S. classes at intervals held by the Parish Associate. Meetings of CEMS open to elder lads.

6. Secondary school in Parish? No school.

7. Teaching for Nonconformist children? Offered but not asked for. Only one professed nonconformist family resident in Parish and that nearer to another school. 4 children baptised in the Roman Church attend the School. The Father is a professed churchman and the Mother does not ask for special teaching.

8. Organised study for adults? There is a fair number of members of the CEMS.

9. Interest in mission? Annual Meetings on behalf of the S.P.G. Annual Sermons on behalf of the Maritzburg Mission of which a small branch was founded in the Parish some years ago, by a Parishioner who went out to work under the Bishop, and literature in connection with it circulated.

10. Voters for Ruridecanal representatives a) men b) women? Members attending meetings summoned for such election purposes invariably on the Communicants Roll of the Church – known by the Vicar to be qualified – they also knowing that he is quite aware of their qualification – facts which appear to make it somewhat invidious to press signatures upon them.

11. PCC? No.

1. Population 299.
2. John William Bussey Bell graduated from Magdalen Hall Oxford in 1863 and was ordained priest in 1872. He served two curacies 1871–80 and was Vicar of Bampton Lew 1880–86. He became Vicar of Pyrton in 1890. He was 71 in 1914 and at the 1911 census he was on holiday in Sidmouth with his wife and two unmarried children – a 34-year-old daughter and 21-year-old son.

RAMSDEN[1]   Incumbent H. R. Hall[2]

1. Baptism at morning or evening prayer? Yes: Evening Prayer.

2. Communion times

a) **Sunday** alternately 8.30am, after Morning Prayer.

b) **Ascension Day** 6am.

c) **Saints Days** none.

d) **Week-days?** none.

3. Is Communion ever sung? No.

4. Religious teaching to children a) Church b) Sunday School and c) Day school? i) Clergy teach in Day schools? ii) Religious teaching to Sunday school teachers? iii) Satisfactory results?

Sunday School children attend Church. Small classes in Sunday School: the basis of teaching Collect, Epistle, and Gospel for the day. [i–iii] I conduct the Morning School. The School Master the Aftn [School]. No special class is held for S.S.

teachers. All works happily, and the children come on regularly to Confirmation. The Day School work includes that of the Syllabus for the Diocesan Inspection. I visit the Day School only occasionally to give instruction.

5. Religious teaching to lads and young women? Nothing beyond Sunday services. I have had successful Bible Classes for Lads, and for Young Women, but these are just now in abeyance, owing to poor attendances.

6. Secondary school in Parish? No.

7. Teaching for Nonconformist children? Nonconformist children attend the Church School, and are taught the same subjects as the rest. No distinction has ever been demanded.

8. Organised study for adults? A branch of the C.E.M.S. studies religious principles weekly in the winter months. A women's Bible Class is held weekly through the year with the exception of two months in the Summer.

9. Interest in mission? Nothing outside the ordinary appeals for missions at certain seasons.

10. Voters for Ruridecanal representatives a) men b) women? None.

11. PCC? Yes: Powers limited to Vicar and Churchwardens: three times.

1. Population 358.
2. Henry Robert Hall graduated from Pembroke College Oxford in 1885 and was ordained priest in 1888. He was Curate at St Peter le Bailey in Oxford 1886–1904 and was also Sub-Librarian at the Oxford University Museum 1884–90 and Assistant Master at Oxford High School in 1890. He became Vicar of Ramsden in 1904. He was 52 years old in 1914 and at the 1911 census he shared a household with his wife, two unmarried daughters, aged 16 and 20, and his 8-year-old nephew.

ROLLRIGHT, GREAT[1] Incumbent S. W. B. Holbrooke[2]

1. Baptism at morning or evening prayer? Always at the Children's service on the 1st Sunday in the month.

2. Communion times

a) **Sunday** 8.30 am except on 1st Sunday in month.

b) **Ascension Day** 8 am.

c) **Saints Days** 8 am.

d) **Week-days?** [*No response*].

3. Is Communion ever sung? No.

4. Religious teaching to children a) Church b) Sunday School and c) Day school? i) Clergy teach in Day schools? ii) Religious teaching to Sunday school teachers? iii) Satisfactory results?

Catechising on 1st Sunday in month. Sunday School here each Sunday save 1st Sunday afternoon in the month when the service is in the Church. [i–iii] Day Schools twice per week from 9 to 9.40. Nothing is done for Sunday School Teachers. The attention given to the children in the afternoon lessons and reproduced at the service in Church has been very satisfactory.

5. Religious teaching to lads and young women? At present there is no lads class, but at 17 years of age we receive them into the CEMS. We have classes for smaller boys and girls who belong to the Kings Messengers. There is also a branch of the Mothers Union, to this several young belong.

6. Secondary school in Parish? No.

7. Teaching for Nonconformist children? Nothing is done for these because nothing has ever been asked for.

8. Organised study for adults? We have a branch of the CEMS. We have a Communicants Guild and other organisations alluded to above.

9. Interest in mission? We have an S.P.G. Sunday. S. Andrew's Day is observed as a day of intercession for missions.

10. Voters for Ruridecanal representatives a) men b) women? Two men.

11. PCC? No.

1. Population 310.
2. Sydney William Briscoe Holbrooke graduated from Wadham College Oxford in 1896 and was subsequently awarded BD in 1907 and DD in 1913. He was ordained priest in 1899 and after an initial curacy was Vicar of Chearsley 1901–08 and Chaplain to the Buckinghamshire Asylum between 1906 and 1908, when he became Rector of Great Rollright. He was 40 in 1914 and at the 1911 census he shared a household with his wife, a pupil and two unmarried female servants.

ROTHERFIELD GREYS[1]   Incumbent W. Wood[2]

1. Baptism at morning or evening prayer? Sometimes.

2. Communion times

a) **Sunday** 1st S. in month after matins at 11. 3rd S. at 8.30, one other S. – 8.30.

b) **Ascension Day** 8.30.

c) **Saints Days** 8.30 (but not on every S. Day).

d) **Week-days?** [*No response*].

3. Is Communion ever sung? No.

4. Religious teaching to children a) Church b) Sunday School and c) Day school? i) Clergy teach in Day schools? ii) Religious teaching to Sunday school teachers? iii) Satisfactory results?

(a) Occasionally they are addressed in Church. (b) Regularly in Sunday School by Trained and Voluntary Trs. (c) [Regularly in] Day School by (a) Trained Trs (daily) (b) Rector – once every week. The Head Tr is present at the Rector's lesson. As compared with other Parishes of which I have had charge and from my own past experience as Assist. Inspr. (Dioc'n.), I am well satisfied: still we fall far short of an ideal Parish.

5. Religious teaching to lads and young women? The Parish is too small for any organized instruction except in preparation for Confirmation – but the Mothers' Union meets periodically for Worship and Instruction: and (during the Winter months) there has been a "Mothers Meeting" addressed regularly once a week by the Rector.

6. Secondary school in Parish? No.

7. Teaching for Nonconformist children? We have no Nonconformists – and all the children, without exception, attend the Religious Teaching and the Catechism.

8. Organised study for adults? No.

9. Interest in mission? The work of the Church overseas is constantly brought before the people in sermons etc. The alms every Fifth Sunday being devoted to the S.P.G. and collections made at other times for different Societies.

10. Voters for Ruridecanal representatives a) men b) women? No signatures have been required. The population is altogether only 300.

11. PCC? No.

1. Population 301.
2. William Wood graduated from Trinity College Oxford in 1851 and was awarded BD and DD in 1868. He was ordained priest in 1853 and held a Fellowship at Trinity 1851–63, and was successively Sub-Warden of Radley College 1853–63, Perpetual Curate of Prestwood 1864–66, Warden of Radley 1866–70 and Vicar of Radley 1866–70, Vicar of Cropredy 1870–98, Diocesan Inspector for Oxford 1877–88, Rural Dean of Deddington 1881–98 and Rector of Monks Risborough 1898–1901, finally becoming Rector of Rotherfield Greys in 1902. He was 84 in 1914 and at the 1911 census he shared a household with his wife, 39-year-old daughter, and three unmarried female servants.

ROTHERFIELD PEPPARD[1] Incumbent C. E. Adams[2]

1. Baptism at morning or evening prayer? Sometimes but rarely.

2. Communion times

a) Sunday 8 and on 1st and 3rd Sundays of month 12 noon also at 7am on gt Festivals.

b) Ascension Day 8 and 12 noon.

c) Saints Days 8 am.

d) Week-days? Once a month at 8 generally on Thursday.

3. Is Communion ever sung? Yes at 12 noon on Great Festivals.

4. Religious teaching to children a) Church b) Sunday School and c) Day school? i) Clergy teach in Day schools? ii) Religious teaching to Sunday school teachers? iii) Satisfactory results?

Clergy teach in Day Schools once or twice a week. Instruction given to Sunday School Teachers generally on Saturday. It is almost impossible to get Sunday School Teachers here. Two or three ladies teach and occasionally the Day School Teachers. The Religious Instruction given in the Day School is most satisfactory.

5. Religious teaching to lads and young women? There is a Class for women and girls on Sunday afternoon. Several classes for lads have been started but I have found it very difficult to keep them together – owing to the very scattered nature of the Parish.

6. Secondary school in Parish? No.

7. Teaching for Nonconformist children? There is a dissenting School in the Parish.

8. Organised study for adults? No.

9. Interest in mission? There are Missionary Sermons, and each year one or two Missionary Meetings. Last year a series of meetings were held in connection with the Missionary Exhibition at Henley.

10. Voters for Ruridecanal representatives a) men b) women? None.

11. PCC? No.

1. Population 497.
2. Charles Edward Adams graduated from Sidney Sussex College Cambridge in 1872 and was ordained priest in 1873. After two initial curacies he was Vicar of Caton 1876–78 and Ellel Grange 1878–84, and a Diocesan Inspector of Schools in the Manchester diocese. He served the same role in the diocese of Oxford 1884–97, was Vicar of Binsey 1891–97 and Vicar of Earley between 1897 and 1904, when he became Rector of Rotherfield Peppard. He was 64 in 1914 and at the 1911 census he shared a household with his 22-year-old daughter and two unmarried female servants.

ROUSHAM[1] Incumbent C. H. Faithfull[2]

1. Baptism at morning or evening prayer? No.

2. Communion times

a) **Sunday** monthly at Midday.

b) **Ascension Day** 8.30 also 1st Sunday in the year, Easter day, Trinity Sunday and Harvest Thanksgiving.

c) **Saints Days** [*No response*].

d) **Week-days?** [*No response*].

3. Is Communion ever sung? No.

4. Religious teaching to children a) Church b) Sunday School and c) Day school? i) Clergy teach in Day schools? ii) Religious teaching to Sunday school teachers? iii) Satisfactory results?

Sunday School Day School (i) No. (ii) Only one Teacher.

5. Religious teaching to lads and young women? Population too small for classes of young people.

6. Secondary school in Parish? No.

7. Teaching for Nonconformist children? No. None of the Children withdrawn from religious instruction in School.

8. Organised study for adults? No.

9. Interest in mission? Services on Day of Intercession.

10. Voters for Ruridecanal representatives a) men b) women? None.

11. PCC? No.

1. Population 123.
2. Charles Henry Faithfull graduated from Lincoln College Oxford in 1856 and was ordained priest in 1858. After serving two curacies in the diocese of Oxford he was Vicar of Preston-Deanery (Northants.) between 1867 and 1873, when he became Rector of Rousham. He was 79 in 1914 and at the 1911 census he was unmarried and sharing a household with two unmarried female servants.

SALFORD[1] Incumbent T. J. Miller[2]

1. Baptism at morning or evening prayer? I have had during evening prayer – I like it but the people would not come to church if they knew. They complained of length of Service. I certainly think the Baptismal Service too long for mother and baby. What baptisms there are I generally take during the afternoon of the second Sunday in the month. I am sorry to say one never or very seldom sees a full complement of Godparents.

2. Communion times

a) Sunday alternately 8 and after M. prayer.

b) Ascension Day 8 am.

c) Saints Days [*No response*].

d) Week-days? [*No response*].

3. Is Communion ever sung? No.

4. Religious teaching to children a) Church b) Sunday School and c) Day school? i) Clergy teach in Day schools? ii) Religious teaching to Sunday school teachers? iii) Satisfactory results?

(a) Generally talk to children at morning service. No one else comes. (b) Sunday School held in morning at 10 am by my wife and daughter. Had Sunday School, afternoon, in the Schoolroom. Conducted by one of the masters from Kingham Homes.[3] Unfortunately he has left and I am unable to secure the services of any competent person in the neighbourhood and since my wife takes morning school and plays the organ at the two services I feel I cannot expect more from her.

5. Religious teaching to lads and young women? Bible Classes with poor results. Scripture Union.

6. Secondary school in Parish? [*No response*].

7. Teaching for Nonconformist children? County Council School.

8. Organised study for adults? Bible Class during Lent, no men but few women.

9. Interest in mission? Addresses. Lantern lectures.

10. Voters for Ruridecanal representatives a) men b) women? This is such a poor parish, there is not a man or woman who would interest themselves in the matter. I may add that I am not indifferent to these questions but this parish is the refuge of the undesirables of this neighbourhood.

11. PCC? [*No response*].

1. Population 339.
2. Thomas James Miller graduated from Downing College Cambridge in 1885 and was ordained priest in 1892. He served a series of four curacies, mostly in Yorkshire, 1888–95 and as Vicar of South Cave between 1895 and 1905, when he became Rector of Salford. He was absent from home on census night 1911 but his household consisted of his wife, 7-year-old daughter, and two unmarried female servants.
3. A reference to the nearby Kingham Hill school – an Evangelical foundation which took children into boarding houses and provided basic education together with training in a trade.

SANDFORD ST MARTIN[1]   Incumbent J. E. C. Williams[2]

1. Baptism at morning or evening prayer? Occasionally but as a rule at the Children's service on Sunday afternoon.

2. Communion times

a) Sunday 8 am (and midday on 1st Sunday in month).

b) Ascension Day 8 am.

c) Saints Days 8 am.

d) Week-days? [*No response*].

3. Is Communion ever sung? No, unless the chanting of the Kyrie, Responses, Gloria and Thanks may be counted as such. Midday – 1st Sunday in month.

4. Religious teaching to children a) Church b) Sunday School and c) Day school? i) Clergy teach in Day schools? ii) Religious teaching to Sunday school teachers? iii) Satisfactory results?

<u>In church</u>:- Catechizing of Sunday School children with an address at 2 pm on the 1st Sunday in each month. <u>In Sunday School</u>:- a selected portion of the Bible is studied by the Senior Boys Class (regularly taught by the Vicar in the afternoon, and by the Head Master in the morning) and by the Girls Class (regularly taught by Miss Norton, a thoroughly intelligent and competent Teacher) and Infants are taught the Catechism, the outlines of Early Bible History and the chief events in our LORD'S Life by Mrs Butler, and another experienced Woman-Teacher. [i–iii] <u>In the Day school</u> the Diocesan Scripture Syllabus is taken up from 9.10 to 9.45 am daily, by the Head Master and his wife (assistant) and the Vicar generally teaches twice weekly. The Vicar has no Sunday School <u>Teachers</u> Instruction Classes; but he regards the general results of Teaching in the Day and Sunday Schools as fairly satisfactory. For the last 3 years the Diocesan Report has been "Thoroughly Satisfactory".

5. Religious teaching to lads and young women? So far nothing has been done for the very few young women that could with difficulty avail themselves of any class – further than the Confirmation Class, and during the six winter months the Vicar has a Bible Class for men associated with the Young Men's Club and Reading Room.

6. Secondary school in Parish? No.

7. Teaching for Nonconformist children? There seems to be no need of enquiry by the Vicar on this point as no exception has been taken by any Nonconformist to the Church Teaching given, nor has a desire for any other teaching ever been voiced.

8. Organised study for adults? Nothing more than would naturally be associated with a Men's Bible Class.

9. Interest in mission? The claims of the S.P.G. are annually pressed upon the Congregation, Mission Field Literature is distributed, special sermons preached, and collections made.

10. Voters for Ruridecanal representatives a) men b) women? So far, none.

11. PCC? No.

1. Population 329.
2. John Ellis Cardigan Williams trained at St Aidan's College in 1885 and served an unusually long diaconate, not being ordained priest until 1904. He served six curacies 1887–1910, three of them in Wales. He was Vicar of Northmoor between 1910 and 1912, when he became Vicar of Sandford St Martin. He was 51 in 1914 and at the 1911 census he was described as married but the only other persons present on census night were two unmarried female servants.

SANDFORD-ON-THAMES[1]   Incumbent W. I. D. S. Read[2]

1. Baptism at morning or evening prayer? No. Baptisms are during the Children's Service on Sunday afternoon.

2. Communion times

a) Sunday at 8 (also 9.30 on the first Sunday in the month) and at 7,8 and 9.30 on the great festivals.

b) Ascension Day at 7 or 8.

c) Saints Days at 7 or 8.

d) Week-days? Seldom – if at all at 7 or 8.

3. Is Communion ever sung? Not at present.

4. Religious teaching to children a) Church b) Sunday School and c) Day school? i) Clergy teach in Day schools? ii) Religious teaching to Sunday school teachers? iii) Satisfactory results?

(a) A form of "The Catechism" is in use every Sunday. (b) Sunday School every Sunday at 10.10 am afternoon at 2.45. (c) The instruction is in the hands of the teachers. The Teachers use the "Eldernote Review"[3] for the purpose of their lessons for Sunday School, and the children are catechised and instructed on the same lesson in Church in the afternoon.

5. Religious teaching to lads and young women? There is a Class every Sunday morning in the Vestry for the Choir boys and any other lads who will attend. The young women who are members of G.F.S. have classes once a month or oftener.

6. Secondary school in Parish? No!

7. Teaching for Nonconformist children? There are only 2 families of professing Nonconformists in the Parish. The parents have not to my knowledge made any objection to their children being taught with the others.

8. Organised study for adults? Not otherwise than in Sermons.

9. Interest in mission? The alms at our Patronal Festival (S. Andrew) are given yearly to U.M.C.A. and the preaching then bears on the work of the Mission.

10. Voters for Ruridecanal representatives a) men b) women? Not any.

11. PCC? No.

1. Population 360.
2. William Inskip Digby Shuttleworth Read graduated from Exeter College Oxford in 1894 and was ordained priest in 1896. He served two curacies in Ealing and Norwood between 1895 and 1902, combining these posts with that of Assistant Master at St Paul's Preparatory School. He was a Licensed Preacher in the diocese of Oxford and Chaplain of Magdalen College School between 1902 and 1910, when he became Vicar of Sandford on Thames. He was 42 in 1914 and at the 1911 census he shared a household with his wife, two teenage sons and two female unmarried servants.
3. A specialist Sunday school publication.

SARSDEN CUM CHURCHILL[1] Incumbent E. J. F. Johnson[2]

1. Baptism at morning or evening prayer? Yes. Once at Sarsden during Evensong at 3 pm in 1913. Evening Prayer at 6 pm is considered by mothers to be an unsuitable hour for a very young child to be out of doors.

2. Communion times

a) Sunday 8am except 1st Sunday in month when it is after morning service.

b) Ascension Day 7.45 am.

c) Saints Days [*No response*].

d) Week-days? [*No response*].

3. Is Communion sung? No.

4. Religious teaching to children a) Church b) Sunday School and c) Day school? i) Clergy teach in Day schools? ii) Religious teaching to Sunday school teachers? iii) Satisfactory results?

(b) Sunday School Superintendent Mr W Anson Lay Reader, 10.15–10.45 am, 2 pm–2.30 pm. (c) Day Schools Diocesan Syllabus taught from 9.15 am to 9.45 am daily Mixed School. 11.30 to 12 noon daily Infants School. [i–iii] I do not teach but I am present once a week at prayers and listen to the teaching in the various standards and I am satisfied with it. (b) Once a month there is a missionary address with collections. Morning instruction the Collect for the week. Afternoon the life of Our Lord, S Luke's Gospel.

5. Religious teaching to lads and young women? There has been for some years a Bible Class for lads – which older men have attended. The difficulty has been to get the attendance of the lads. Unfortunately, the teacher left the Parish last November – since which time this class has been in abeyance. There is a Candidates Class for young women connected with G.F.S. carried on weekly during the winter months.

6. Secondary school in Parish? No.

7. Teaching for Nonconformist children? No provision has been asked for – and no objection is taken to the teaching of the Church Catechism.

8. Organised study for adults? No.

9. Interest in mission? Sermons for Church Missionary Society. Boxes. Literature circulated with reference to the Bible Society. The education of a Boy in school at Burma provided for by the Sunday School children. Intercession service at Advent for foreign missions.

10. Voters for Ruridecanal representatives a) men b) women? None.

11. PCC? No.

1. Population 691.
2. Edmund Joseph Francis Johnson graduated from St John's College Cambridge in 1879 and was ordained priest in 1882. After an initial curacy he was Vicar of two Gloucestershire parishes, Elmore 1883–88 and Hillesley between 1888 and 1903, when he became Rector of Sarsden. He was 54 in 1914 and at the 1911 census he shared a household with his wife, an unmarried daughter and six unmarried servants: a cook, a footman, a kitchen maid, a laundry maid, a housemaid and a visiting parlourmaid.

SHENINGTON WITH ALKERTON[1]   Incumbent A. Blytheman[2]

1. Baptism at morning or evening prayer? Usually have it in the afternoon with the Litany.

2. Communion times

a) **Sunday** 8.30 am on 2 Sundays in the month, or 3., and at 11am service on 2.

b) **Ascension Day** 7.45 am.

c) **Saints Days** none.

d) **Week-days?** None.

3. Is Communion sung? No.

4. Religious teaching to children a) Church b) Sunday School and c) Day school? i) Clergy teach in Day schools? ii) Religious teaching to Sunday school teachers? iii) Satisfactory results?

(a) Having 2 churches to serve there is no instruction in Church; it is done entirely in (b) by in the morning the Day School Teachers who volunteer for the work; in the afternoon by other voluntary workers. The teachers do not receive special instruction but are capable persons. On the whole I am satisfied; and the children generally have good reports in the Diocesan examinations. There are not many scholars in Sunday School after they once begin regular work in the fields. In fact just now only 3.

5. Religious teaching to lads and young women? Nothing. After Confirmation it is difficult to get hold of them in the country.

6. Secondary school in Parish? No.

7. Teaching for Nonconformist children? There never has been any demand for it. If there was, it would be met.

8. Organised study for adults? No.

9. Interest in mission? We have a Branch of King's Messengers. Annual meeting for S.P.G. and sermon for same. Intercession Service annually.

10. Voters for Ruridecanal representatives a) men b) women? I do not think at present any have. It is generally done at the Easter Vestry.

11. PCC? No.

1. Population 362.
2. Arthur Blytheman graduated from Balliol College Oxford in 1866 and was ordained priest in 1868. After an initial curacy, he became Rector of Shenington in 1869 and then of the combined parish of Shenington with Alkerton in 1900. He was 73 in 1914. His household was not found in the 1911 census.

SHILTON[1]   Incumbent W. J. Richards[2]

1. Baptism at morning or evening prayer? In the very few instances of Baptism I have been unable to do so.

2. Communion times

a) **Sunday** 7. 8 and at 11 mattins.

b) **Ascension Day** 7.

c) **Saints Days** [*No response*].

d) **Week-days?** [*No response*].

3. Is Communion sung? No.

4. Religious teaching to children a) Church b) Sunday School and c) Day school? i) Clergy teach in Day schools? ii) Religious teaching to Sunday school teachers? iii) Satisfactory results?

(a) There are so few children available, nothing. I had a children's service on Ascension Day. (b) We have a Sunday School which has increased from 6 children to 21 on the books. There are only two teachers and they do not need instruction. (c) There is daily religious teaching according to the Syllabus of the Diocese. [i–iii] The vicar teaches one day a week.

5. Religious teaching to lads and young women? It seems impossible to get them to attend as the lads are all engaged in farm work on Sundays and there are only one or two young women in service.

6. Secondary school in Parish? No.

7. Teaching for Nonconformist children? No demand has been made but the Nonconformists have a Sunday school.

8. Organised study for adults? [*No response*].

9. Interest in mission? There have been missionary meetings and sermons, and lantern lectures.

10. Voters for Ruridecanal representatives a) men b) women? I have not heard of the Rules.

11. PCC? Yes. Power to advise the Vicar. It has met twice since last October. It should be remembered that there are only about one hundred Church folk in the parish out of 200.

1. Population 201.
2. William Joseph Richards trained at the Church Missionary Society College in Islington in 1868 and was subsequently awarded a DD by the Archbishop of Canterbury in 1899. He was ordained priest in 1872 and served a series of CMS chaplaincy and college posts in India between 1871 and 1906, when he returned to England, serving as a Licensed Preacher in the Chichester diocese and then serving two curacies between 1910 and 1912, when he became Vicar of Shilton. He was the author of *The Indian Christians of St Thomas* (1908). He was 66 in 1914 and at the 1911 census he shared a household with his wife, an unmarried son aged 27, a married son and daughter-in-law, and two unmarried female servants.

SHIPLAKE[1]   Incumbent C. A. W. Aylen[2]

1. Baptism at morning or evening prayer? Yes: I have tried to persuade parishioners that other times are the exception.

2. Communion times

a) **Sunday** 8 am, 9.55 am. 1st Sunday 6.30 am, 8, 9.55 am.

b) **Ascension Day** 5 am, 7.30 am, 10 am.

c) **Saints Days** 8 am.

d) **Week-days?** 8 am Wednesdays.

3. Is Communion sung? Yes: Every Sunday at 9.55 am with Sermon.

4. Religious teaching to children a) Church b) Sunday School and c) Day school? i) Clergy teach in Day schools? ii) Religious teaching to Sunday school teachers? iii) Satisfactory results?

(a) 1. Children attend the Sung Eucharist every Sunday in the Parish Church in the morning. There is no compulsion. They come by themselves or with parents. 2. In the afternoon. i. The Catechism is held in the Parish Church every Sunday. ii. A Sunday School is held at the Mission Church for Infants. (b) There are no Sunday Schools in the strict sense and no teachers except for the Infants Class. The Sunday Instruction is given by the Clergy except in the case of the Infants. (c) The Diocesan Syllabus is used. [i–iii] I teach twice every week in the Day School. I think in regard to the Sunday teaching of the children the plan adopted is the best possible one in view of the scattered nature of this parish. There are considerably more children on the books for the Catechism and Infants Class than on that of the Day School and the attendance is good. I feel that the attendance of the children without being brought is a distinct advantage as they gain the habit of going to Church by themselves. I am bound to say that the order is very good. I think where there is Church Day School, Sunday morning should be given over to Worship rather than instruction. Our plan secures this.

5. Religious teaching to lads and young women? At present only a Communicants guild. One for lads one for young women. They meet separately in the parish church for Prayer and Instruction monthly. There is a Bible Class for women. I hope later on to form a class in the week for men and lads.

6. Secondary school in Parish? No.

7. Teaching for Nonconformist children? It has not been required. The few children who are dissenters receive Church instruction quite willingly. I have only heard of one parent who objects.

8. Organised study for adults? There has been a Study Circle.

9. Interest in mission? There is a Missionary Guild. It meets in Church for Intercession. Members hold collecting boxes. The sums collected are given to S.P.G.

10. Voters for Ruridecanal representatives a) men b) women? Not any.

11. PCC? No.

1. Population 960
2. Charles Arthur William Aylen graduated from Keble College Oxford in 1904 and went on to train at Cuddesdon College, being ordained priest in 1906. He served a curacy at Henley between 1905 and 1912, becoming Vicar of Shiplake in 1913. He was 32 in 1914 and at the 1911 census he was unmarried and a boarder in the household of a carman.

SHIPTON-UNDER-WYCHWOOD[1] Incumbent W. C. Carter[2]

1. Baptism at morning or evening prayer? I am always ready to have it and have had it at Morning Prayer but people prefer to bring babes to the afternoon service.

2. Communion times

a) Sunday 8 am (on First Sundays and Great Festivals also after Morning Prayer).

b) Ascension Day 8 am.

c) Saints Days 8 am.

d) Week-days? Only on special occasions.

3. Is Communion sung? On Christmas Day, Easter Day, Whitsunday: choral at 8 am.

4. Religious teaching to children a) Church b) Sunday School and c) Day school? i) Clergy teach in Day schools? ii) Religious teaching to Sunday school teachers? iii) Satisfactory results?

(a) Catechizing or addresses every Sunday of the year at which the children attend (with their teachers) on the subjects at Morning Prayer. (b) Sunday School 10 am at the School, after which the Children brought to the 11 o'clock Service. S. Michael Home children have instruction at the home and attend their service, each Sunday – and attend on Holy Days. (c) The Diocesan Syllabus is used and also the Children learn texts and are instructed in the week on the subjects for the catechizing for the following Sunday and learn the Collect. [i–iii] The Vicar teaches the First Division twice a week and S. Michael Home School[3] twice a week. The ages of the Teachers render this difficult. Teachers mtg given for arrangement of classes. I think the Church attendance is good, and the Children have their Church, and feel quite at home there.

5. Religious teaching to lads and young women? There are guilds by which we keep in touch with the young. Teaching by Ladies. Not definite Classes for religious instruction except for monitors and candidates for confirmation. The County Council night school has taken the place of Vicars evening classes.

6. Secondary school in Parish? No.

7. Teaching for Nonconformist children? No. The school has trust deed – at the present we have no exemption class.

8. Organised study for adults? We have mothers meeting.

9. Interest in mission? Some take in "The Mission Field". Copies of "The Church Abroad" are placed at the church door each month – appertaining to special intercession each month.

10. Voters for Ruridecanal representatives a) men b) women? I can only find 4 men sign [*sic*]. The two churchwardens are generally elected to vote for the Deanery representatives.

11. PCC? No.

1. Population 699.
2. William Collingwood Carter graduated from Christ Church Oxford in 1876 and trained at Sarum College 1876–77, being ordained priest in 1878. After an initial curacy he was Vicar of Little Tew 1880–89 and then Rector of Cornwell between 1889 and 1899. He became Vicar of Shipton-under-Wychwood in 1900. He was 61 in 1914 and at the 1911 census was recorded as a widower sharing a household with his 14-year-old daughter, her governess and three unmarried female servants.
3. A home and industrial school for girls aged between 6 and 14 opened in Shipton in 1900 under Anglican auspices with capacity for thirty girls.

SHIRBURN[1]   Incumbent F. J. Hall[2]

1. Baptism at morning or evening prayer? No. There are so few that I generally suit the convenience of the people.

2. Communion times

a) Sunday on the first Sunday in the month at 8 am on the third at noon.

b) Ascension Day at 8 am.

c) Saints Days No.

d) Week-days? No.

3. Is Communion sung? No.

4. Religious teaching to children a) Church b) Sunday School and c) Day school? i) Clergy teach in Day schools? ii) Religious teaching to Sunday school teachers? iii) Satisfactory results?

The Children are taught in Sunday Schools by my daughter and the School-Mistress, and the usual hour in the Day School and the result is satisfactory.

5. Religious teaching to lads and young women? Nothing.

6. Secondary school in Parish? No.

7. Teaching for Nonconformist children? There is no special provision, but they come naturally and without objection to Sunday School and morning lesson.

8. Organised study for adults? No.

9. Interest in mission? Sermons for the Great Societies.

10. Voters for Ruridecanal representatives a) men b) women? I have not received any such declaration.

11. PCC? No. The parish is too small.

1. Population 250.
2. Frederic John Hall graduated from Clare College Cambridge in 1869 and was ordained priest in 1872. He was Assistant Master at Haileybury College 1869–82, Vicar of Little Wymondley (Herts.) 1890–91 and then Headmaster of Northaw Preparatory School in Hertfordshire. He became Vicar of Shirburn in 1912. He was 67 in 1914 and at the 1911 census he shared a household with his wife, three unmarried children, a married daughter and his son-in-law, together with a large staff.

SIBFORD GOWER AND EPWELL[1]　　　　　　　　　Incumbent L. Moxon[2]

1. Baptism at morning or evening prayer? A General Rule to do so.

2. Communion times

a) **Sunday** 8am or 7.30. 12 noon 1st Sunday.

b) **Ascension Day** 9 am.

c) **Saints Days** 9am or 7.15.

d) **Week-days?** Thursdays 7.15 or 10 am.

3. Is Communion sung? Once a month 9am at Epwell.

4. Religious teaching to children a) Church b) Sunday School and c) Day school? i) Clergy teach in Day schools? ii) Religious teaching to Sunday school teachers? iii) Satisfactory results?

(a) Children are catechized in School by Vicar before going into church. (b) The Sunday School teachers take their lesson from the Vicar and then give the same to the children one Sunday on Doctrine and one on the narrative of Holy Scripture. (c) In the Day-Schools the Oxford Diocesan Syllabus is used. [i–iii] The Vicar teaches 2 mornings in the week.

5. Religious teaching to lads and young women? For lads, there is a Bible Class on Sunday afternoon. For girls, a Bible Class once a fortnight in the winter. There is a strong branch of the K.Ms.

6. Secondary school in Parish? No.

7. Teaching for Nonconformist children? This has never been asked for during my Incumbency. If so, the Managers would certainly consider it.

8. Organised study for adults? By Sermons and as much as possible by individual intercourse.

9. Interest in mission? Services of Intercession on Friday evenings. Annual Sermons and Meetings. Distribution of "Church Abroad" and Missionary boxes.

10. Voters for Ruridecanal representatives a) men b) women? None.

11. PCC? No.

1. Population 820
2. Leonard Moxon was ordained priest in South Africa in 1900. He served a series of curacies, then held the Vicarage of Cathcart in Cape Colony between 1906 and 1910, when he came to England as Vicar of Sibford Gower with Epwell. He was 39 in 1914 and at the 1911 census he shared a household with his widowed mother, unmarried sister and one unmarried female servant.

SOMERTON[1]   Incumbent G. E. Barnes[2]

1. Baptism at morning or evening prayer? No.

2. Communion times

a) Sunday 1st Sunday in month at Midday; 3rd Sunday at 8am.

b) Ascension Day at 8am

c) Saints Days [*No response*].

d) Week-days? [*No response*].

3. Is Communion sung? Yes on the Great Festivals at 8am.

4. Religious teaching to children a) Church b) Sunday School and c) Day school? i) Clergy teach in Day schools? ii) Religious teaching to Sunday school teachers? iii) Satisfactory results?

(a) The children are instructed at Sunday School in Church. (b) "Sunday School" in morning and afternoon. (c) The children are taught according to Syllabus during the religious hour. [i] No. [ii] The teachers are Mrs Barnes and the Day School Teacher [iii] Generally speaking results are satisfactory, but our children are not so bright a lot this year, perhaps, as usual.

5. Religious teaching to lads and young women? Confirmation Classes – and subsequently Communicant Classes.

6. Secondary school in Parish? No.

7. Teaching for Nonconformist children? No objection has ever been made to the religious teaching in the Church School.

8. Organised study for adults? [*No response*].

9. Interest in mission? S.P.G Meeting (Lantern Slides) Sermons and Collection for S.P.G.

10. Voters for Ruridecanal representatives a) men b) women? None.

11. PCC? No.

1. Population 272.
2. George Edward Barnes graduated from Trinity College Cambridge in 1869 and was ordained priest in 1872. He served two curacies between 1871 and 1875, when he was appointed as Rector of Somerton. He was 67 in 1914 and at the 1911 census he shared a household with his wife and five unmarried female servants.

SOULDERN[1]   **Incumbent E. J. S. Rudd**[2]

1. Baptism at morning or evening prayer? Not in my present Parish. The Baptisms are usually during the Children's service in the afternoon.

2. Communion times

a) Sunday Midday on first Sunday in the month: 8.15 on all other Sundays.

b) Ascension Day 8.15 am.

c) Saints Days Sometimes: then at 8.15 am.

d) Week-days? [*No response*].

3. Is Communion sung? No.

4. Religious teaching to children a) Church b) Sunday School and c) Day school? i) Clergy teach in Day schools? ii) Religious teaching to Sunday school teachers? iii) Satisfactory results?

(a) Catechising at the Children's Service on Sunday. About 20 such services during the last year: also on some Saints Days. (b) Sunday School every Sunday morning at 10.15 am and on Sunday afternoon when there is no Children's Service (c) The children are taught by the regular Teachers according to the Syllabus and exam' by the Diocn Inspectors. [i–iii] I have not taught in the Day School – Mr Leathley went into the School once a week at my request. No such instruction given – The Sunday School Teachers are well qualified. I do not see my way to answer this question.

5. Religious teaching to lads and young women? We try to keep a hold over our young people, and bring them to Confirmation, if the children of Church Parents.

There are no regular classes for them. We visit regularly at their homes and they come to church fairly well. Few young women remain in the Village.

6. Secondary school in Parish? No such school.

7. Teaching for Nonconformist children? No provision made: though I have more than once lately discussed the matter with the Master. No general objection is made to the teaching – only 3 or 4 (from one family) have been withdrawn from Catechism and Prayer Book.

8. Organised study for adults? No. (Books lent or given in a few individual cases).

9. Interest in mission? S.P.G., C.M.S., Bible Soc are all supported in this Parish and there is a Meeting held in behalf of each. Day of Intercession for Missions duly observed.

10. Voters for Ruridecanal representatives a) men b) women? I think none. As far as I remember only a few, all communicants, attended the meeting.

11. PCC? No Parochial Council.

1. Population 396.
2. Eric John Sutherland Rudd graduated from St John's College Cambridge in 1863 and was ordained priest in 1865. He held a fellowship at St John's 1867–88 and school posts at Sheffield Collegiate School and Malvern College before becoming Headmaster of the Cathedral School in Hereford 1869–75. He was Rector of St Florence (Pembs.) 1878–84, Vicar of Horningsey (Cambs.) 1884–87, Rector of Freshwater (IOW) 1887–91 and then Rector of Barrow (Suff.) between 1891 and 1901, when he became Rector of Souldern. He was 72 in 1914 and at the 1911 census he shared a household with his wife, two teenage children, two boarding pupils and two unmarried female servants.

SOUTHLEIGH[1]   Incumbent R. Wynter[2]

1. Baptism at morning or evening prayer? No.

2. Communion times

a) **Sunday** 8 am and 11 am.

b) **Ascension Day** 5.30 am and 9.0 am.

c) **Saints Days** 9.0 am.

d) **Week-days?** Daily 8.0 am.

3. Is Communion sung? Yes. Every Sunday 11 am. Saints Days 9 am.

4. Religious teaching to children a) Church b) Sunday School and c) Day school? i) Clergy teach in Day schools? ii) Religious teaching to Sunday school teachers? iii) Satisfactory results?

(a) Catechism every Sunday afternoon. (b) Catechism takes the place of Sunday School. (c) Religious instruction daily. (d) I teach at least twice weekly. (e) No Sunday

School teachers: one Superintendent. (f) It is difficult to be satisfied with the results of the Sunday School system as a whole. The children know what their Religion is, I think, fairly well. But as soon as they have the Catechism, it is a constant difficulty to get them to observe what they have been taught: e.g. in observance of the Lord's Day. In the case of the majority, any real conception of the worship of God as the chief object of life, and as a matter of obligation, is very faint, in spite of all the teaching the children receive. I believe some of the children here are beginning to grasp the idea of duty in their Religion, apart from feeling or likes and dislikes. And this I believe to be due to the fact that the Holy Communion is the chief Sunday Service, and as such is their act of Sunday worship. I do not think that any amount of Sunday School without this would effect much.

5. Religious teaching to lads and young women? Only the regular sermons and instructions. I am hoping to form 2 Bible Classes.

6. Secondary school in Parish? No.

7. Teaching for Nonconformist children? Nonconformist parents seem quite satisfied with the teaching of the Church for their children, and I have never heard any desire for any other. Very few Nonconformists here.

8. Organised study for adults? Only constant instruction in Church, and a table of books and tracts, on Christian doctrine etc, which have had a large sale. This has been very valuable.

9. Interest in mission? Collections are made and boxes distributed. We help a Parish in Central Africa.

10. Voters for Ruridecanal representatives a) men b) women? None, as far as I am aware.

11. PCC? No.

1. Population 305.
2. Reginald Wynter graduated AKC in 1901 and was ordained priest in 1902. After serving two curacies he was Rector of Pentridge 1907–09, Curate of Hawarden 1909–11 and Vicar of St Luke Clay Hill, Enfield between 1911 and 1912, when he became Vicar of Southleigh. He was 36 in 1914 and at the 1911 census he shared a household with his wife, their 1-year-old daughter and one unmarried female servant.

SPELSBURY[1]   Incumbent J. F. Rowley[2]

1. Baptism at morning or evening prayer? Baptism always administered at Morning or Evening Prayer on Sundays (as the Prayer Book directs) "when the most number of people come together" I have twice made an exception to the Prayer Book rule, viz the administering of Baptism to 2 adults – both of them ladies – who perhaps not unnaturally, asked that they might be baptised at week-day Matins, to avoid publicity I think: they had both been brought up as Quakers.

2. Communion times

a) **Sunday** either at 8am or 11.45 (alternate Sundays).

b) **Ascension Day** at 10 am.

c) **Saints Days** at 10am.

d) **Week-days?** Never.

3. Is Communion sung? The Service is sung once every month at 11.45 am.

4. Religious teaching to children a) Church b) Sunday School and c) Day school? i) Clergy teach in Day schools? ii) Religious teaching to Sunday school teachers? iii) Satisfactory results?

(a) I catechize all children sent to me every Sunday before Matins. (b) There is no Sunday-school, as there is nobody willing to teach. (c) This is a Council-school.

5. Religious teaching to lads and young women? They will not attend classes – with the exception of Confirmation Classes: then they are carefully instructed: nor are they forgotten in the Sunday Sermon.

6. Secondary school in Parish? No secondary school.

7. Teaching for Nonconformist children? We have only a Council School.

8. Organised study for adults? Nothing beyond constant and careful reference to the foundation truths of the Faith in Sermons.

9. Interest in mission? I constantly refer to this subject in sermons, and exhort people to remember the obligations of their Country towards our own people in newly colonised lands and towards the subject Races under our Dominion.

10. Voters for Ruridecanal representatives a) men b) women? I fear that little or no interest is taken by parishioners in this matter.

11. PCC? There is no Church Council.

1. Population 438.
2. James Farmer Rowley trained at the Chancellors School Lincoln in 1885 and was ordained priest in 1888. He served three curacies 1887–95 and was Vicar of Bramhope (Yorks.) between 1895 and 1898, when he became Vicar of Spelsbury. He was also Chaplain to Viscount Dillon in 1904. He was 49 in 1914 and at the 1911 census he shared a household with his wife, two young daughters and two unmarried female servants.

STADHAMPTON[1]   Incumbent A. A. D. Harding[2]

1. Baptism at morning or evening prayer? If I can persuade the parents: I have once since I came here. Usually it is inconvenient – the morning for household reasons, the evening as godparents from a distance have to return home. Half an hour before evening prayer secures a congregation here and is a time chosen if there is no children's service in the afternoon.

2. Communion times

a) Sunday Midday on 1st and 3rd Sundays, special Sundays on Harvest Festival; Advent 3rd Sunday early 8 am.

b) Ascension Day 7am for first time in parish.

c) Saints Days only S. John the Baptist (dedication of Stadhampton) 7.30am since I came.

d) Week-days? None.

3. Is Communion sung? No.

4. Religious teaching to children a) Church b) Sunday School and c) Day school? i) Clergy teach in Day schools? ii) Religious teaching to Sunday school teachers? iii) Satisfactory results?

1. The Day school is a Council school. 2. Sunday school is held on the 1st and 3rd Sundays of the month. Children's service with Catechizing or address on the subject taught the Sunday before on the 2nd and 4th Sundays. On the 5th Sunday a Children's service with a talk on Missionary work. 3. Hitherto there has been no sufficient help. The withdrawal of the Headmaster of the Council school has left the clergyman as the only efficient teacher. I have roughly a senior and junior school. I teach the senior school of girls and boys myself. The junior school I divided into classes which are taught by two maiden ladies and a couple of elder scholars, or rather three now. 4. I hold every fortnight a class of instruction for these elder scholars to teach them the lesson which in general outline the idea they will seek to impart. The difficulty is that elder scholars too often go away unexpectedly. There is very little sense of the importance of this Sunday School instruction in those who should teach or on the part of the parents of those who should come to be taught. 5. I am satisfied with the way things are moving but there has been no time for real results. The lads are most difficult to hold. The Sunday School has been so linked to the day school for years that when they leave one they leave the other. I hope to correct this by a Lad's Club, and other week day efforts as time goes on. Various circumstances keep the average attendance low. But between 60 and 70 names on the books is an encouraging response! Children not at Sunday school or children's service are generally at morning or evening service to both or either of which a good many children come.

5. Religious teaching to lads and young women? A few young women attend the Children's Services but save attendance at the Sunday Services there is nothing else at present. A good many attend fairly regularly on Sundays. I hope presently a Branch of the G.F.S. may be helpful.

6. Secondary school in Parish? No.

7. Teaching for Nonconformist children? [*No response*].

8. Organised study for adults? Not at present. A branch of the Mother's Union has been started and it proposes to have a definite Bible Instruction chiefly for the members but open to anyone else.

9. Interest in mission? Nothing beyond a magic lantern address once or twice a year.

10. Voters for Ruridecanal representatives a) men b) women? None that I know of. I must plead guilty to ignorance of this declaration. I asked the Easter Vestry to vote for and appoint R.D. representatives but no-one would serve.

11. PCC? (1) Yes. (2) Advisory in all financial matters, as to changes in church for external objects; changes in mode of conducting service. My object is to educate: also to bring home to the laity a sense of their place in the finance of the church under the new scheme of Finance. To give them any real power would be to stereotype Church life in this village. (3) We have met once since last October but shall meet again once before next October. Once or twice a year is considered enough. The Churchwardens I think are not cordial. They regard such a body as limiting their power of control. For instance in the work of repairing the church floor the work went to the best tender, not to the tender favoured, as the general mind, thought by the Churchwardens.

1. Population 381.
2. Alfred Arthur Duffield Harding graduated AKC in 1884 and then with a BA from the University of London in 1885. He was ordained priest in 1889 and served as Assistant Master at Queen's College Basingstoke 1886–89 and then a series of eight curacies, mostly in London, between 1889 and 1912, when he became Vicar of Chislehampton with Stadhampton. He was 48 years old in 1914 and at the 1911 census he shared a household with his wife, five sons aged between 3 and 11 and one unmarried female servant.

STANDLAKE WITH YELFORD[1]   Incumbent T. Lovett[2]

1. Baptism at morning or evening prayer? No.

2. Communion times

a) Sunday at 8 am – first Sunday also at 12 am.

b) Ascension Day 10 am.

c) Saints Days 10 am – but seldom.

d) Week-days? None.

3. Is Communion sung? No.

4. Religious teaching to children a) Church b) Sunday School and c) Day school? i) Clergy teach in Day schools? ii) Religious teaching to Sunday school teachers? iii) Satisfactory results?

Children instructed in Church on first Sunday at Childrens Service – also during Lent weekly in Church – and catechized. Sunday School held twice a Sunday throughout the year. Children taught according to Diocesan Syllabus in day schools. [i–iii] Clergy teach in Day Schools as a rule daily. Sunday School teachers have books of instruction but no weekly classes are held for them. The results attained are not very satisfactory as the children leave School when old enough to leave the Day School and do not seem to take further interest in the Sunday instruction.

5. Religious teaching to lads and young women? A class of instruction was started not long ago but did not made much headway as nothing of the kind had been heard of before. Some young men form the Bible Class with the more adult parishioners.

6. Secondary school in Parish? None.

7. Teaching for Nonconformist children? There is only a Church School and the parents of Nonconformist Scholars seem to accept willingly the ordinary Bible teaching of the school.

8. Organised study for adults? A Bible Class is held during the seven winter months chiefly for the purpose of studying these principles.

9. Interest in mission? SPG meeting is held during each year and sermons are also preached for the same object. Special days for intercession are also observed.

10. Voters for Ruridecanal representatives a) men b) women? The list has been mislaid but I believe about 12 men and the same number of women.

11. PCC? None.

1. Population 501 (1908). Yelford 11.
2. Thomas Lovett graduated from Magdalen College Oxford in 1887 and trained at Wells Theological College, being ordained priest in 1891. He served two curacies in Yorkshire between 1889 and 1908, when he became Rector of Standlake. In 1912 he was also appointed Rector of Yelford. He was 48 in 1914 and at the 1911 census he was unmarried and sharing a household with two unmarried female servants.

STANTON HARCOURT[1]   Incumbent F. Symes-Thompson[2]

1. Baptism at morning or evening prayer? No: but Godparents are invited to bring children to H. Baptism at evensong on Sundays.

2. Communion times

a) **Sunday** at 8am except on 1st Sunday then at 12.

b) **Ascension Day** at 7 and 8.

c) **Saints Days** at 8.

d) **Week-days?** [*No response*].

3. Is Communion sung? Yes at 11 o'c on the Great Festivals.

4. Religious teaching to children a) Church b) Sunday School and c) Day school? i) Clergy teach in Day schools? ii) Religious teaching to Sunday school teachers? iii) Satisfactory results?

(a) Catechising on 1st and 3rd Sundays. (b) Sunday school before church each Sunday (c) regular Bible and Prayer Book teaching each morning given by the staff. [i–iii] I teach the Catechism and Prayer Book the first 5 standards one morning in the week. I am preparing two teachers for the pupil teachers Diocesan Exam to be held on Dec 5 1914. I am dissatisfied with Sunday School, as I am unable to get adult teachers to take classes regularly.

5. Religious teaching to lads and young women? There is a fortnightly class for young women.

6. Secondary school in Parish? No.

7. Teaching for Nonconformist children? No: the school buildings are not very suitable.

8. Organised study for adults? The Parish Magazine containing the Sign is taken in by over 90 people and the winter session of C.E.M.S. is of value in this respect.

9. Interest in mission? The first Sunday in the month is generally the occasion for "Missionary" sermon; the Sunday school has "Missionary" Lesson. 10 children take in King's Messenger Mag. Several people have Boxes for S.P.G. we have a branch of the Borneo Association and the Quarterly Intercession Paper is distributed. Constantly before preaching at Evensong I allude to some overseas work and call on people to pray to or thank God.

10. Voters for Ruridecanal representatives a) men b) women? It is so difficult in a small place to get Ruridecanal representatives that the machinery is not used.

11. PCC? No.

1. Population 473.
2. Francis Symes-Thompson graduated from Christ Church Oxford in 1898 and trained at Cuddesdon College, being ordained priest in 1900. He served three curacies in the Oxford diocese between 1899 and 1906 and then spent a year as Priest in Charge of Colesberg, Cape Colony, returning to England as Vicar of Claydon between 1907 and 1911, when he became Vicar of Stanton Harcourt. His household was not found in the 1911 census.

STANTON ST JOHN[1]   Incumbent L. Davidson[2]

1. Baptism at morning or evening prayer? For many years Holy Baptism was taken at the afternoon services. These having given way to evening service – I must answer never at present.

2. Communion times

a) **Sunday** twice a month 1st S: at noon – 2nd S: at 8 am.

b) **Ascension Day** 7.30 am.

c) **Saints Days** Christmas day 8 and 12.

d) **Week-days?** No.

3. Is Communion sung? No.

4. Religious teaching to children a) Church b) Sunday School and c) Day school? i) Clergy teach in Day schools? ii) Religious teaching to Sunday school teachers? iii) Satisfactory results?

(a) The fortnightly aft: service for children has been discontinued – the few children left preferred the classes in Sunday school. (b) Sunday School at present: 3 morning classes at 10 am; 2 afternoon classes. (c) The diocesan syllabus is fully taught in the Day school – which serves this parish and Foresthill. [i–iii] The Rector takes the upper division every Tuesday throughout the year 9 – 9.45 am. Mr Negus takes the upper division every Friday throughout the year. Considering we have only 24 children (10 boys and 14 girls) left in the Sunday school – I do not think much can be done. Mr Nixon, diocesan Inspector, was pleased with day school on his visit. We have about half the number of children that we had 15 yrs ago. Sunday School teachers – the organist (lady), one school teacher, Rector's wife and daughters. They need no special class.

5. Religious teaching to lads and young women? The girls Bible class – teacher Miss Ward, lady organist has collapsed for want of members and Mrs Davidson's lads class, 5 pm on Sunday – suffered a like end, after the Confirmation in the Cathedral – last spring.

6. Secondary school in Parish? No.

7. Teaching for Nonconformist children? There is no demand. In Stanton St John there are no children of Nonconformist parents left. The few from Foresthill are contented with the Diocesan syllabus. Not one asked leave from the church service on Ascension Day – though told they might.

8. Organised study for adults? We have not any material here for such study.

9. Interest in mission? We hold meetings for the Zenana Society. Some of our younger people have at times joined "study circles".

10. Voters for Ruridecanal representatives a) men b) women? None – 4 or 5 qualified men attended the first meeting but they did not sign.

11. PCC? No.

1. Population 397.
2. Lionel Davidson graduated from New College Oxford in 1872 and was ordained priest in 1874. He served two curacies 1873–85 and was Rector of Chedburgh (Suff.) between 1885 and 1890, when he became Rector of Stanton St John. He was 65 in 1914 and at the 1911 census he shared a household with his wife, five unmarried children aged between 12 and 26, and two unmarried female servants.

STOKE ROW[1]   Incumbent T. W. Hutchinson[2]

1. Baptism at morning or evening prayer? No. Baptisms on any Sunday at times most convenient to Parent.

2. Communion times

a) Sunday 1st in month 8.30 am. 3rd [in month] after morning prayer.

b) Ascension Day No celebration.

c) Saints Days [No celebration.]

d) Week-days? [No celebration.]

3. Is Communion sung? No. Choral service at present impracticable. Isolated country Parish. Very poor organist and frequently Vicar has to play the Harmonium himself.

4. Religious teaching to children a) Church b) Sunday School and c) Day school? i) Clergy teach in Day schools? ii) Religious teaching to Sunday school teachers? iii) Satisfactory results?

(a) Children's Service each Sunday afternoon 2.45 pm. (b) Sunday School in morning. (c) Church Day School regularly inspected by Dio Ins. [i–iii] Since the Kenyon-Slaney clause[3] came into operation I have discontinued giving religious instruction in Day School. I teach myself in the Sunday School and Mrs Hutchinson assists. The influence of the Nuffield Golf Links etc extends to this Parish.

5. Religious teaching to lads and young women? I hold a "Church Club" free for the young men in the Institute several nights each week during the Winter months and Church Socials for the young women at intervals during the winter.

6. Secondary school in Parish? No.

7. Teaching for Nonconformist children? No children are withdrawn.

8. Organised study for adults? No.

9. Interest in mission? Lectures and Lantern (entertainments) held.

10. Voters for Ruridecanal representatives a) men b) women? [*No response*].

11. PCC? No. I am starting a branch of the CEMS, out of this a Parochial Church Council may grow.

1. Population 512.
2. Thomas William Hutchinson graduated from St John's College Cambridge in 1873 and was ordained priest in 1886. After two short curacies he was Vicar of New Buckenham (Norf.) 1888–96 and then Vicar of Great Wilbraham between 1896 and 1911, when he became Vicar of Stoke Row. He was 62 years old in 1914 and at the 1911 census he shared a household with his wife, his 30-year-old son and one unmarried female servant.
3. The Kenyon-Slaney clause (named after Conservative MP William Kenyon-Slaney) in the Education Act of 1902 gave control of religious education in non-provided schools to the managers as a whole rather than just the clergyman or the foundation managers appointed by the Church.

STOKE, SOUTH WITH WOODCOTE[1]   Incumbent H. G. Nind[2]

1. Baptism at morning or evening prayer? Yes! During the course of Morning Prayer.

2. Communion times

a) Sunday at 8 am and post matins.

b) Ascension Day at 8am and 11.15 am.

c) Saints Days [*No response*].

d) Week-days? [*No response*].

3. Is Communion sung? No.

4. Religious teaching to children a) Church b) Sunday School and c) Day school? i) Clergy teach in Day schools? ii) Religious teaching to Sunday school teachers? iii) Satisfactory results?

The children receive religious instruction in Church in children's Services. In morning and afternoon Sunday School when the Clergy teach as well as the teachers but not in the Day Schools, which are "provided". I help the teachers, as far as I can, by controlling the lines on which they are to teach. So far I am fairly satisfied with the results attained.

5. Religious teaching to lads and young women? Being an agricultural parish the lads and girls as soon as they leave School, go away into service. So there are but a few lads whom I try and influence through the various Clubs which I control.

6. Secondary school in Parish? No!

7. Teaching for Nonconformist children? [*No response*].

8. Organised study for adults? Yes! By bible classes.

9. Interest in mission? This is always brought before them during one week for missions at home and abroad each year.

10. Voters for Ruridecanal representatives a) men b) women? Not any, that I am aware of.

11. PCC? Not at present.

1. Population 928.
2. Hubert George Nind graduated from University College Oxford in 1868 and was ordained priest in 1876. He was Curate of Woodcote between 1869 and 1887, when he succeeded as Vicar of South Stoke with Woodcote. He was 68 years old in 1914 and at the 1911 census he was listed as a widower, sharing a household with his widowed sister, three unmarried daughters aged between 19 and 35, and three unmarried female servants.

STOKE TALMAGE[1]   Incumbent E. Davenport[2]

1. Baptism at morning or evening prayer? Yes.

2. Communion times

a) Sunday 8 o'clock – first Sunday of the month – mid-day.

b) Ascension Day 8 o'clock.

c) Saints Days 8 o'clock – when celebrated.

d) Week-days? [*No response*].

3. Is Communion sung? No.

4. Religious teaching to children a) Church b) Sunday School and c) Day school? i) Clergy teach in Day schools? ii) Religious teaching to Sunday school teachers? iii) Satisfactory results?

(a) In church on first Sunday of the month "Childrens Service" with short address and catechizing. (b) Every Sunday X [10].15 am – XI [11] o'Clock. (c) Scripture Lesson or Catechism 9–9.45 am every day. [i–iii] I take a class every morning with few exceptions. I consider the results satisfactory. I teach myself in Sunday School and Mrs Davenport and my daughter assist me. There are no Sunday School Teachers in the village. We teach mainly on the lines of the School Guardian but the Collect, Epistle and Gospel are either repeated by heart or read by the first class and explained, each Sunday.

5. Religious teaching to lads and young women? A Bible Class in the winter (evenings). School girls (King's Messenger) are taught on Sunday afternoons.

6. Secondary school in Parish? No.

7. Teaching for Nonconformist children? No. Nonconformist parents sanction their children being taught with the Church of England children. They also come to church with them.

8. Organised study for adults? Not more than when opportunity occurs in a Bible Class.

9. Interest in mission? Occasional Lectures and Sermons and Days of Intercession.

10. Voters for Ruridecanal representatives a) men b) women? (a) None. (b) None.

11. PCC? No. I advise with my Churchwardens. The people seem to prefer this. It is very difficult to get any others to any meeting.

1. Population 93.
2. Edward Davenport graduated from Trinity College Oxford in 1866 and was ordained priest in 1870. He was Assistant Master and Tutor at Wellington College between 1868 and 1904, when he was appointed as Rector of Stoke Talmage. He was 70 years old in 1914 and at the 1911 census he shared a household with his wife, three unmarried children aged between 13 and 23, and three unmarried female servants.

STOKENCHURCH[1]   Incumbent F. C. Load[2]

1. Baptism at morning or evening prayer? As a rule No. Occasionally on week days at Evensong: parents in every case have refused on Sundays.

2. Communion times

a) Sunday 8; 1st Sunday in month 8 and sung Eucharist 11.

b) Ascension Day 4.30 and 8.

c) Saints Days always 8 and 10.30 (by notice).

d) Week-days? Monday and Tuesday after Great Festivals as appointed; special days e.g. of Intercession etc not otherwise.

3. Is Communion sung? Yes 11.

4. Religious teaching to children a) Church b) Sunday School and c) Day school? i) Clergy teach in Day schools? ii) Religious teaching to Sunday school teachers? iii) Satisfactory results?

(a) Catechising on two Sundays in month and on all Great Festivals. The children also attend every Sunday morning Service at 11; all except infants (who go out before sermon) attending through every Eucharist First Sunday in month and other times when at 11. (Failed to get attendance of children at any service on weekdays) (b) All Children attend every Sunday for 10 and 2 school: also at 10 Good Friday and Christmas Day. Infants taught by pictures etc. Girls and Boys <u>one</u> lesson from

Messrs Potter and Sheards Second course of Sunday School Lessons; in the other gradually through year Catechism and Collects are said by heart and teaching from O.T. and N.T. given. Cards with Morning and Evening Prayer and other prayers given to each Child. (c) Council Schools – no teaching. [i–iii] Failed to get attendance of Teachers at a monthly meeting so above books were instituted and teachers desired to get up each lesson of Course. Under existing conditions of life of parish and its standard of education these methods, unsatisfactory as they may seem in themselves as a whole, seem to promise to augur a change for the better in the future.

5. Religious teaching to lads and young women? Bible Classes for both and further opportunities are taken afforded through work of G.F.S.

6. Secondary school in Parish? No.

7. Teaching for Nonconformist children? Council School.

8. Organised study for adults? Not at present; attempt through C.E.M.S. not successful yet.

9. Interest in mission? Sermon and visits from deputations. Lantern Lecture in winter special Sunday evening Intercession services.

10. Voters for Ruridecanal representatives a) men b) women? (a) 14) signed (b) none).

11. PCC? No.

1. Population 1,592.
2. Frederic Crawford Load graduated from University College Durham in 1893 and was ordained priest in 1903. He served three curacies 1902–08 and was Curate in Charge of Frieth Hambleden between 1908 and 1911, when he became Vicar of Stokenchurch. He was 44 in 1914 and at the 1911 census he was unmarried, sharing a household with his elderly parents, two older sisters and one unmarried female servant.

STONESFIELD[1]   Incumbent J. S. Barford[2]

1. Baptism at morning or evening prayer? Holy Baptism is administered in the middle of the <u>Children's Service</u> (2.30pm) Choristers proceed to the font. <u>Notice</u> is given during Matins, and some adults are usually present at the afternoon service. <u>Publicity</u> is, so far, ensured. But, hitherto, I have not baptised during Matins or Evensong.

2. Communion times

a) Sunday 8 all Sundays, save the last in the month when it is at 10 a.m. On Easter Day, etc, both at 8 and at 10.

b) Ascension Day Ascension 5.30 am and 7.30 am.

c) Saints Days 7.30 am: on S. James's Day (dedication) <u>also</u> at 5.30am.

d) Week-days? No regular celebration: an <u>occasional</u> celebration, for mourners (before a burial), or for invalid, at some morning hour convenient to recipients.

3. Is Communion ever sung? At 8am on Christmas Day, Easter Day, Whitsunday.

4. Religious teaching to children a) Church b) Sunday School and c) Day school? i) Clergy teach in Day schools? ii) Religious teaching to Sunday school teachers? iii) Satisfactory results?

a and b Children's service at 2.30 pm every Sunday: Sunday School at 10 am and at 2 pm (children proceed to Church just before 3.30). At the Childrens' Service I catechise on the lesson given in School, from notes prepared by myself. I visit teachers individually on Saturday, giving them a written copy of my notes and explaining such notes in detail. (There are 2 exceptions to this rule: my daughter – with a class of boys uses a <u>printed course</u> of lessons: and one other teacher, a communicant teacher in Day-School gives a short lesson of her <u>own</u> to the elder girls.) Except the <u>youngest</u> children, every child – this year – has a copy of the Church Catechism separately printed (SPCK), and is expected to learn a selected answer therefrom each week. (c) Day School, unfortunately a Council School, transferred to the County some 10 years ago. [i–iii] But the Education Committee allow me to teach myself twice a week, and I do so very gladly – taking the New Testament subjects (set forth in the syllabus of the Education Committee) with Standards IV, V, and VI. The Day School staff is <u>good</u>: all teachers are church folk and give their religious instruction reverently. We had an excellent report from the Chief Diocesan Inspector last year. "This School is being most effectively taught on quite the right lines..." Summary mark T.S. = Thoroughly Satisfactory. (I mention this, because by some strange error – the Diocesan Calendar notes our school as not being under Diocesan inspection! I am pointing this error out to Dr Oldfield.) I do not know how, in this village, to improve on present methods. Of course there is the difficulty – at Children's Service – of having "all ages" present together. But, with a small Sunday School, it is impossible to differentiate as I have done in larger parishes. In cases where we have moral support in <u>the homes</u> (parents' example and parents' tone, etc) I think that results are fairly encouraging. But all my experience urges that the <u>home</u> is the ultimate centre of influence, and the results of our teaching are necessarily affected thereby.

5. Religious teaching to lads and young women? (Apart from classes in preparation for confirmation) I have at present no organised instruction, save that given to <u>Kings Messengers</u> (confirmees under 21 years of age) we meet, as a rule, <u>weekly</u> … prayers and instruction. Originally, this was to be a mixed class, lads and girls together. But the lads failed; and I have not yet seen my way to arrange anything separate for them.

6. Secondary school in Parish? [*No response*].

7. Teaching for Nonconformist children? [*No response*].

8. Organised study for adults We have no study-circle, or corresponding organisation. I have tried a <u>course of instruction</u> (on Prayer Book) after weekday Evensong and there are "courses" of sermons from time to time. I hope that the series of articles, on Prayer Book, Church History, etc, in the monthly Magazine (SPCK) are studied by our people ... I distribute about 80 copies.

9. Interest in mission? Here again I hope that the <u>Magazine</u> is useful. I have mentioned the Kings Messengers above. S.P.G. report is circulated among the few whose "boxes" contribute the requisite sum. Annual meeting in school, and special Intercession in Church. Reference in ordinary Sermons. An occasional missionary story to the children. A large number of our Stonesfield folk have emigrated to British Columbia, and on several occasions we have given the Evening Collection to the British Columbia Church Aid Association: and on these occasions I have used a Collect for Missions before the Prayer for All Conditions of men.

10. Voters for Ruridecanal representatives a) men b) women? I have no record of those who have signed. Very few attended the meeting for electing representatives on the last occasion. I infer from the question that it is desirable to register a list of those who sign, and I purpose to have this done in future.

11. PCC? We have no Constituted Church Council. And I rather hesitate to call one into being until I can stir a more <u>real</u> and practical interest in our corporate Church life. I whole-heartedly desire a more intelligent and a more active co-operation on the part of the laity e.g. I have the Vestry meeting in the evening (contrary to former custom here) – when the workmen can attend. Apart from conference with the Churchwardens, from time to time, I invite our Church "generally" (notice in Church and in the Magazine) to assemble in the School, when such matters as the inception of the Diocesan Fund, or any particular need in parochial finance, give special opportunities for mutual Counsel. But, so far, such experiment has not been encouraging. People – with few exceptions – "don't come". After one such meeting, I wrote in our Magazine "We had intended, if this meeting had been well attended, to suggest that similar meetings should be held from time to time <u>at regular intervals</u>. Perhaps this suggestion may still be carried out" These words express my present attitude and my hope. I feel that a formally constituted Council should be the <u>outcome</u> of lay-feeling <u>already existing</u>, and that if the Council is formed in order to <u>create</u> the lay-interest there is danger – if not of failure – of a certain unreality. There are parishes, no doubt, where it is otherwise. But I think I know parishes (I am not thinking of this Diocese) where it has been so. And I do not feel that, in this village, we are yet ripe for the Council.

1. Population 494.
2. John Sheldon Barford graduated from St Catherine's College Cambridge in 1879 and was ordained priest in 1880. He served two curacies 1879–84 and was Vicar of Battersea 1883–84 and then of Sheringham between 1891 and 1909, when he became Rector of Stonesfield. He

was 58 years old in 1914 and at the 1911 census he shared a household with his wife and two unmarried female servants.

SUMMERTOWN[1]   Incumbent C. J. Burrough[2]

1. Baptism at morning or evening prayer? We are having one in a few weeks for the first time and hope to do so from time to time.

2. Communion times

a) **Sunday** 7, 8 and Choral at 10. Or 11.15.

b) **Ascension Day** 5.30 6.30 7.30 and after Matins at 10 am.

c) **Saints Days** 7.30 and after Matins at 10.

d) **Week-days?** Wed: and Fridays 7.30 and during Lent Tuesdays and Thursdays in addition also Rogation and Ember Days.

3. Is Communion ever sung? 10 am as a rule. But on Festivals and 1st Sunday in the month at 11.15 with sermon.

4. Religious teaching to children a) Church b) Sunday School and c) Day school? i) Clergy teach in Day schools? ii) Religious teaching to Sunday school teachers? iii) Satisfactory results?

a) Children's Service every Sunday at 3, and on Saints' Days at 9.5 am. b) The Sunday School is being worked on the Reformed lines. 3 divisions Infants – Primary – and Ordinary. c) Religious Instruction every day i.e. at Mon – Fri: inclusive for the first hour. [i–iii] The Clergy teach 3 times a week Sunday School teachers attend "Teachers classes". Results while children are of school age are satisfactory but difficult to keep in touch with them after.

5. Religious teaching to lads and young women? Bible Class for lads and one for young women on Sundays. There is also a Lads and Girls Communicants Guild with preparation service once a month – members are expected to attend this – one service at least on Sunday and to communicate at least once a month.

6. Secondary school in Parish? No.

7. Teaching for Nonconformist children? No provision is made. When taking "The Catechism" no child of nonconformist parents is expected to attend but joins another class where Old Testament or some simple Bible teaching is being given. In a conversation with Congregational Minister some time ago I expressed willingness to let him come and teach his children if I could have facilities to teach mine who attend the Central Council School. But I am not averse to allowing him to teach in our schools even without our quid pro quo.

8. Organised study for adults? Both in the CEMS and Womens' Guild subjects under the above head always form a large part in our year's work.

9. Interest in mission? A Parochial Missionary Association has been formed and been in existence for 2 years. We study by means of lectures and books (a library is provided) certain parts of mission field e.g. we have had four consecutive lectures on OMCA[3] 6 on India 4 + 1 on our colonies. Next session we hope to hear about China. Some of our younger members entered for Diocesan exam on China at Easter. An Intercession Service is held after Evensong on alternate Fridays and also after Evensong on the last Sunday in the month.

10. Voters for Ruridecanal representatives a) men b) women? All who attended the Easter Vestry expressed their willingness to sign the declaration – but very few women attend as a rule.

11. PCC? Yes. The Parochial Church Council which is composed of the Vicar 2 Churchwardens, 22 Sidesmen meet on first Monday of every month. All matters of Church interest are fully discussed and no action has been taken which has not been supported by a considerable majority of the Council, eg wafer bread was adopted by unanimous vote of the Council.

1. Population 4,300.
2. Charles James Burrough trained at Lichfield College in 1893 and was ordained priest in 1896. He subsequently graduated from St John's College Oxford in 1906. He served three curacies between 1895 and 1903, the last being at St Philip and St James in Oxford. He was then Reader at St John's College between 1903 and 1908, when he became Vicar of Summertown. He was 39 in 1914 and at the 1911 census he shared a household with his wife, four young children and four unmarried female servants.
3. Probably the UMCA is meant here.

SWALCLIFFE WITH SHUTFORD[1] Incumbent M. M. Knowles[2]

1. Baptism at morning or evening prayer? They are held during afternoon service, after 2nd lesson.

2. Communion times

a) **Sunday** 8am or 11 am, or both.

b) **Ascension Day** 11 am.

c) **Saints Days** 11am.

d) **Week-days?** [*No response*].

3. Is Communion sung? Yes Mid-day; after 11am shortened Mattins.

4. Religious teaching to children a) Church b) Sunday School and c) Day school? i) Clergy teach in Day schools? ii) Religious teaching to Sunday school teachers? iii) Satisfactory results?

With either 4 or 5 services each Sunday it is not possible to get in a Children's Service in Church – but they are taught regularly each Sunday in both parishes both morning and afternoon in Sunday School. [i–iii] Religious instruction in both Day Schools from 9 to 10 a.m. each day. Occasionally. We only occasionally get helpers in the Sunday School; we have no regular teachers. Have been too short a time to say.

5. Religious teaching to lads and young women? There is a Lads' Club and Bible Class. There practically are no young women in the parish, as they go out to Service as soon as they leave School.

6. Secondary school in Parish? No.

7. Teaching for Nonconformist children? No – all receive the church teaching in Day Schools.

8. Organised study for adults? By Sermons. Also – Special Service of preparation for Holy Communion, and instruction generally, will (D.V.) be held next winter.

9. Interest in mission? Children's and weekly meetings in winter months, and Entertainment. Special Intercessions in church. Lectures and Meetings.

10. Voters for Ruridecanal representatives a) men b) women? None.

11. PCC? No.

1. Population 534.
2. Maurice Mason Knowles graduated from Christ Church Oxford in 1889 and was ordained priest in 1893. After an initial curacy he was Curate in Charge of Bawdsey Ferry 1894–95 and then Headmaster of Eversley School between 1895 and 1912, when he became Vicar of Swalcliffe with Shutford. He was 50 years of age in 1914. His household was not found in the 1911 census.

SWERFORD[1]   Incumbent C. J. Shebbeare[2]

1. Baptism at morning or evening prayer? Only during shortened evensong on Sunday afternoon.

2. Communion times

a) Sunday 8am except on first Sunday in each month when it is at noon: and on Easter Day and Whitsun Day when it is celebrated twice.

b) Ascension Day Noon.

c) Saints Days Never on Saints days <u>as such</u>.

d) Week-days? Occasionally when required for any persons who are for some reason unable to be present on Sunday: then the hour has generally been 9 am.

3. Is Communion sung? No singing after the non-communicants have retired.

4. Religious teaching to children a) Church b) Sunday School and c) Day school? i) Clergy teach in Day schools? ii) Religious teaching to Sunday school teachers? iii) Satisfactory results?

(a) I talk to the children at afternoon service once a month except during holidays: and adopt the method of question and answer. (b) A Sunday School meets in the Rectory, every Sunday morning except during holidays, one hour before morning prayer. The younger children are taught by the Infant Schoolmistress, the elder children by me. (c) Religious instruction is given by the Schoolmaster during the religious hour. [i–iii] On one morning of the week I give this instruction to the elder children myself. With regard to the Sunday School teacher of the Infant Class, the position is perhaps a little unusual. She has been under 'High Anglican' influences, and her religious point of view is different from that of most people in this village. She is having, I feel sure, an excellent effect on the children and I have pursued the method of giving her a free hand and at the same time I have tried to encourage her to read. I think the teaching, under all these headings, has had some good effects. The Schoolmaster is a good and capable man: and it seems to me that the children here have, in rather unusual degree, been taught to think. The great difficulty which I find is that, in the effort to keep the children's minds alert, and to prevent their becoming restless and inattentive the 'spirituality' of the teaching is apt to evaporate: and I fancy the other teachers find a somewhat similar difficulty. Some of the children listen surprisingly well to sermons: and I think that possibly their attendance at Church does more for them than the religious instruction which they receive in Sunday School. The whole question is a very difficult one: and I am very far from saying that I am satisfied.

5. Religious teaching to lads and young women? Before the Easter and Christmas Communions, and sometimes at other times of year, I have invited the younger communicants (young men and young women separately) to a meeting of preparation. There has been no difficulty making them listen, and generally, in reply to questions, they are willing to talk pretty freely and frankly themselves. I do not believe that classes held more frequently would be better. Indeed I believe that the best means of instructing young people like ours is by very careful preaching in Church.

6. Secondary school in Parish? No secondary school.

7. Teaching for Nonconformist children? The Nonconformists are in cordial agreement with the teaching given.

8. Organised study for adults? A weekly Prayer-meeting is held on a weekday evening, preceded by a brief discussion of the passages appointed to be read during the week by the 'International Bible-Reading Union'. The Prayer meeting and Bible Class has continued for some 16 or 17 years. It was in existence when I came here: and was in the fairly recent past a source of great and evident blessing to the parish. Recently, except for three or four people who never fail to attend (two of them men) the meetings have been disappointing. A similar, but less systematic, meeting is held on Sunday afternoon and has a much larger and pretty regular attendance. Both are 'inter-denominational'.

9. Interest in mission? We have meetings of S.P.G. C.M.S. and the Bible Society. Some special missionary instruction has been given to children by means of a Study Scheme. For several years the 'Week of Prayer' of the 'Evangelical Alliance' has been observed in January. The meetings are held in the School, and have been generally well-attended. I am thankful to say that the meeting has shown a truly spiritual and an increasingly intelligent conception among our people of the value of prayer. A clerical neighbour, not an 'Evangelical', has given most valuable help.

10. Voters for Ruridecanal representatives a) men b) women? No men, no women.

11. PCC? No parochial Church Council.

In some respects Swerford might be described as an 'old world' parish. Its circumstances are in many ways peculiar. This, I think, has to be borne in mind in any discussion of the methods of work which are appropriate here.

1. Population 297.
2. Charles John Shebbeare graduated from Christ Church Oxford in 1888 and was ordained priest in 1889. He served two curacies between 1888 and 1898, when he was appointed as Rector of Swerford. He was the author of *Religion in an Age of Doubt* (1914). He was 48 in 1914 and at the 1911 census he was unmarried and living in a single-person household.

SWINBROOK AND WIDFORD[1]   Incumbent F. E. Foster[2]

1. Baptism at morning or evening prayer? Occasionally.

2. Communion times

a) Sunday 1st Sunday in month mid-day. 3rd and 5th 8.15.

b) Ascension Day 8.15 am or 11 am.

c) Saints Days Only one or two in the year 11 am.

d) Week-days? [*No response*].

3. Is Communion ever sung? No.

4. Religious teaching to children a) Church b) Sunday School and c) Day school? i) Clergy teach in Day schools? ii) Religious teaching to Sunday school teachers? iii) Satisfactory results?

(a) Catechizing every Sunday afternoon. (b) Every Sunday morning 10. (c) Diocesan Syllabus followed. [i–iii] I teach sometimes often and sometimes occasionally according as I think the children are progressing.

5. Religious teaching to lads and young women? C.E.M.S. G.F.S. members class, candidates class.

6. Secondary school in Parish? No.

7. Teaching for Nonconformist children? No.

8. Organised study for adults? No.

9. Interest in mission? We have two or three missionary meetings with lantern during winter. Missionary boxes. Every 2nd Sunday evening in month, after short sermon (generally on missionary work) we have silent prayer, one minute each, for various missionary work – work explained.

10. Voters for Ruridecanal representatives a) men b) women? No one lately – I think some did a few years back.

11. PCC? No.

1. Population 175
2. Francis Edward Foster graduated from St Mary Hall and Oriel College Oxford in 1894 and was ordained priest in 1897. He served an initial curacy in Liverpool between 1896 and 1898, when he became Rector of Swinbrook. He was appointed Diocesan Inspector for the Witney Deanery in 1907. He was 48 years of age in 1914 and at the 1911 census he shared a household with his wife, unmarried sister and one unmarried female servant.

SWYNCOMBE[1] Incumbent C. A. K. Irwin[2]

1. Baptism at morning or evening prayer? Occasionally – during Evening Prayer.

2. Communion times

a) Sunday 8.0 am 1st Sunday 11.45 am.

b) Ascension Day 8.0 am.

c) Saints Days 8.0 am.

d) Week-days? [*No response*].

3. Is Communion sung? No.

4. Religious teaching to children a) Church b) Sunday School and c) Day school? i) Clergy teach in Day schools? ii) Religious teaching to Sunday school teachers? iii) Satisfactory results?

(a) The Day School Children attend special services on Ash Wednesday, Good Friday and Ascension Day. The distance is too great and the hamlets too scattered for regular assembly in Church. (b) The Sunday Schools are entirely conducted by and have no other teachers but the Rector. (c) Diocesan Report May 29 1914. "I was particularly pleased with all I saw in this school today … It has today thoroughly earned the summary mark of Excellent. i. By the written work – distinctly above the average. Not a single bad paper. ii. By the very level of general answering. Group I Commended: All; Group II Commended: The Whole Class; Infants Commended: All. [i–iii] The Rector assists occasionally in Revision of work and took Prayer Book subjects in past year. There are no Sunday School Teachers. The Rector conducts morning and afternoon Sunday Schools for different sets of children. Results elusive – except for supply of Confirmation Candidates.

5. Religious teaching to lads and young women? Too few and too scattered for organization. The only opportunity is personal interviews with individuals.

6. Secondary school in Parish? No.

7. Teaching for Nonconformist children? Free entry offered but no desire to take advantage of it. Bishop's Prize frequently gained by Nonconformists.

8. Organised study for adults? ? No association of individuals except Mothers' Union.

9. Interest in mission? Literature and appeals for work of various Mission and Evangelizing Societies.

10. Voters for Ruridecanal representatives a) men b) women? ?

11. PCC? No.

1. Population 314
2. Charles Alfred Kemble Irwin graduated from Merton College Oxford in 1884 and was ordained priest in 1889. After an initial curacy served between 1888 and 1892 he was appointed as Rector of Swyncombe. He was 54 in 1914 and at the 1911 census he shared a household with his wife, unmarried brother and two unmarried female servants.

SYDENHAM[1] Incumbent W. Morris[2]

1. Baptism at morning or evening prayer? No.

2. Communion times

a) Sunday 1st Sunday at Morning Prayer 3rd Sunday at 8 am.

b) Ascension Day 8 am.

c) Saints Days [*No response*].

d) Week-days? [*No response*].

3. Is Communion sung? No.

4. Religious teaching to children a) Church b) Sunday School and c) Day school? i) Clergy teach in Day schools? ii) Religious teaching to Sunday school teachers? iii) Satisfactory results?

Sunday School every Sunday at 10 a.m., 2 p.m. Daily Scripture lesson in the Day School. Yes, I teach 3 times a week. One is never satisfied, but the results reach an average measure of success according to my experience.

5. Religious teaching to lads and young women? We have had from time to time a youth's Bible Class. Our young women usually leave the village quite young to go into service.

6. Secondary school in Parish? None.

7. Teaching for Nonconformist children? We have only a Church School in which all the children attend the religious instruction without any difficulty.

8. Organised study for adults? We have a Mother's Meeting always with a Bible Address; and a Men's Bible Class: these are held during the winter months.

9. Interest in mission? We have a monthly Missionary Address in the Sunday School and a Missionary Working Party held fortnightly, during which suitable missionary literature is read. There is a garden missionary sale in the summer.

10. Voters for Ruridecanal representatives a) men b) women? None.

11. PCC? No.

1. Population 239.
2. William Morris graduated from Sidney Sussex College Cambridge in 1869 and after serving two curacies 1869–79 was Vicar of St Olave Ramsey (IOM) 1879–96 and then Minister of St James Clifton between 1900 and 1903. He became Vicar of Sydenham in 1905. He was 67 in 1914 and at the 1911 census he shared a household with his wife (whose occupation was described as 'Helping the Vicar') and two unmarried female servants.

TACKLEY[1] Incumbent G. Perry Gore[2]

1. Baptism at morning or evening prayer? Have not done so here yet but found the custom of administering at the quarterly catechising of children when some adults are present.

2. Communion times

a) **Sunday** 8 am.

b) **Ascension Day** 6 am and 8 am.

c) **Saints Days** 8 am or 10 am.

d) **Week-days?** 8 am.

3. Is Communion sung? Not at present.

4. Religious teaching to children a) Church b) Sunday School and c) Day school? i) Clergy teach in Day schools? ii) Religious teaching to Sunday school teachers? iii) Satisfactory results?

(a) Monthly Catechising. (b) A regular Course of Instruction. The Sunday Services. O. Test. for two senior classes. N. Test. for junior classes. (c) The Diocesan syllabus, taught by the Teachers. This teaching has much improved under a young new Head Teacher and the last two reports have been quite satisfactory. [i–iii] I have not taught at present in the Schools – but during the last two terms have taken the religious instruction at a public service in the Church every Wednesday and this year added Ascension Day. Only a very few are withdrawn and have found some parents and nurses brought children not attending the day schools. I was much concerned about how best to help the teachers and after a good deal of search and inquiry fixed upon the <u>Marden</u> Series with their <u>sequence of pictures</u> and so far I am most gratified with the results. Both teachers and children are keener and they enforce an easy and simple preparation on the part of the teachers. And best of all they err if at all on the side of simplicity and don't attempt too much. The only hindrance being they are expensive for a small country school.

5. Religious teaching to lads and young women? There are really very few: but I hope to help them chiefly through prolonged instruction and preparation for Confirmation and First Communion. I spent over 3 months on the eight who came this year.

6. Secondary school in Parish? No.

7. Teaching for Nonconformist children? There is no provision for the Nonconformist children but I am trying to make the parents feel we shall take no undue advantage of our position. I have already visited their Sunday School and made the acquaintance of the teachers and invited them to join us in school festival and began last year this they considered but declined for the present.

8. Organised study for adults? I am following on the plan of teaching definite courses of Instruction in <u>Advent</u> and <u>Lent</u> both morning and evening. I found the office for Induction supplied an excellent subject for the first 3 <u>months</u> of the Incumbency.

9. Interest in mission? Have begun with twice weekly intercessions in Advent and Lent. Savings this year to be given to James Nash's S. John's School, Johannesburg.

10. Voters for Ruridecanal representatives a) men b) women? I must enquire about this. No list has been given to me.

11. PCC? No.

1. Population 451.
2. George Perry Gore trained at the Chancellor's School Lincoln in 1877 and was ordained priest in 1880. He served three curacies between 1879 and 1892, was Vicar of St Matthias Sneinton 1890–92 and was then Vicar of St Mary's Oldham between 1892 and 1912, when he became Rector of Tackley. He was 61 in 1914 and at the 1911 census he shared a household with his wife, three young children and their governess together with two unmarried female servants.

TADMARTON[1]   Incumbent A. E. Riddle[2]

1. Baptism at morning or evening prayer? It has been my rule ever since I came here in 1886, to administer the rite of Holy Baptism after the 2nd lesson at Sunday Evensong in accordance with the Rubric. The exceptions to this rule have been very rare. It has also been my custom to omit the Sermon whenever there is a Baptism.

2. Communion times

a) Sunday On the 1st Sunday in the month after 11 am Matins. On the 3rd and 5th Sundays at 8am. On Xmas Day, Easter Day and Whitsun Day at 8 am.

b) Ascension Day On Ascension Day at 8am.

c) Saints Days There is no Celebration on Saints Days.

d) Week-days? Nor on ordinary days.

3. Is Communion sung? Not now. For many years I had it so, but for various reasons have felt it best to discontinue the practice. I have sung it and had it sung at 11 a.m. on the 1st Sunday in the month Matins having been previously said at 10.30. I had a Choral Celebration for many years at Xmas, Easter, and Whitsuntide.

4. Religious teaching to children a) Church b) Sunday School and c) Day school? i) Clergy teach in Day schools? ii) Religious teaching to Sunday school teachers? iii) Satisfactory results?

The religious instruction of the children practically takes place entirely in the School, the spirit of the Rubric about Catechizing appearing to me to be thus more than sufficiently observed, Church Schools not being in existence when the Rubric was compiled. This instruction takes place both on Sundays and on all other days of the week except Saturdays. [i–iii] I myself take a class of the elder boys on Sunday mornings and on Mondays take the upper standards of the School. The only two other teachers in the Sunday School are my two daughters and I think it best to leave them to pursue their own methods which appear entirely satisfactory. My boys used to help me but now they are gone out into the world. From time to time I have received help from various parishioners. I think the results attained are on the whole excellent. There is a Branch of the Band of Hope and meetings are held every fortnight at which religious instruction bearing principally on a specific subject are given by my daughter, the Schoolmistress, myself and others.

5. Religious teaching to lads and young women? Band of Hope. G.F.S. I have attempted a Sunday Bible Class for the elder lads and Communicants' Classes, but the result has been not such as to lead me to fully endorse what Canon Skrine says of village lads in his Pastor Ovium.

6. Secondary school in Parish? No.

7. Teaching for Nonconformist children? Entirely unnecessary. The parents are all perfectly satisfied with the teaching as ordinarily given. There are only 2 children of Nonconformist parents in the School. The latter do not withdraw their children and have made no complaint.

8. Organised study for adults? No, except so far as these principles are inculcated by Sermons.

9. Interest in mission? An annual meeting, an annual special sermon, and references in other sermons. The distribution of 25 copies of "The Church Abroad" amongst the adults 1 copy of Kings Messengers. Every 1st Sunday in the month I read something to [*section trimmed from the manuscript*] pass round the box to which several contribute their pence and halfpence.

10. Voters for Ruridecanal representatives a) men b) women? None, to my knowledge.

11. PCC? No.

1. Population 318.
2. Arthur Esmond Riddle graduated from Worcester College Oxford in 1875 and was ordained priest in 1876. He served two curacies 1878–80 and was Perpetual Curate of Rydal (Westmd.) between 1880 and 1886, when he became Rector of Tadmarton. He was 61 in 1914 and at the 1911 census he was a widower sharing a household with five unmarried children aged between 14 and 27, together with three unmarried female servants.

TAYNTON[1]   Incumbent H. G. Hensley[2]

1. Baptism at morning or evening prayer? Not of recent years.

2. Communion times

a) Sunday 8 am twice in the month and after the 11.30 am Morning Service once in the month.

b) Ascension Day At 8 am.

c) Saints Days When I can get sufficient communicants.

d) Week-days? [*No response*].

3. Is Communion ever sung? No.

4. Religious teaching to children a) Church b) Sunday School and c) Day school? i) Clergy teach in Day schools? ii) Religious teaching to Sunday school teachers? iii) Satisfactory results?

We have a Childrens Service occasionally but not often as we have very few children in the Parish and find it more satisfactory to teach them as a Sunday School Class which we hold every Sunday. Religious instruction is given in the Day School by the School Master, who is a good teacher and the School is examined each year by the Diocesan Inspector. I teach in the Day School occasionally but not regularly. In this village the families change considerably, the agricultural labourers frequently leaving at Michaelmas, so that the school suffers from the constant changing of the children, otherwise I think the teaching is good, and the results satisfactory.

5. Religious teaching to lads and young women? We have had a Bible Class for youths on Sundays until recently, but the last few winters it has been difficult to get them together as the members leave when they reach 17 years thinking themselves too old, and just now in our small village there are no boys of an age to take their places. There are no young women able to attend classes. This village is inhabited chiefly by old people.

6. Secondary school in Parish? No.

7. Teaching for Nonconformist children? No. There are no parents, at present, who object to our Church teaching.

8. Organised study for adults? No.

9. Interest in mission? We have occasional meetings and services, a fortnightly working party and a children's evening connected with a candidates class of the G.F.S.

10. Voters for Ruridecanal representatives a) men b) women? None.

11. PCC? No.

1. Population 205
2. Henry Gabriel Hensley graduated from Corpus Christi College Cambridge in 1875 and was ordained priest in 1878. He served four curacies 1877–86 and was Vicar of St Paul Warwick between 1887 and 1908, when he became Vicar of Taynton. He was aged 60 in 1914 and at the 1911 census he shared a household with his wife, 18-year-old daughter and one unmarried female servant.

TETSWORTH[1]   Incumbent P. O. Potter[2]

1. Baptism at morning or evening prayer? As yet I have not been able to prevail upon any mother to bring her child either to the morning or evening service for Holy Baptism because contrary to the tradition of the Parish, but I do not despair. Sunday afternoon is the understood time for Holy Baptism immediately after the Catechising of the children.

2. Communion times

a) **Sunday** at 8.30 am on third Sunday at 12 o'c on first Sunday.

b) **Ascension Day** at 8.30 am.

c) **Saints Days** at 8.30 am. On Easter Day and Whitsunday two celebrations Xmas Day two celebrations.

d) Week-days? [*No response*].

3. Is Communion ever sung? No. Except on Easter morning at 8.30 when the service begins with singing.

4. Religious teaching to children a) Church b) Sunday School and c) Day school? i) Clergy teach in Day schools? ii) Religious teaching to Sunday school teachers? iii) Satisfactory results?

In the Church religious instruction is given to the children at 3.p.m. every Sunday by the Vicar and others. The teachers are kept in as close a touch as possible with the Diocesan Sunday School teachers association and also with the Vicar. Our Day Schools are Council schools and the nonconformist spirit is quite strong amongst us the Vicar therefore does not teach in the Day School. We try hard and results perhaps are fair.

5. Religious teaching to lads and young women? The elder lads and young women are invited and encouraged to be present at 3 pm in the Church when one endeavours to give suitable religious instruction.

6. Secondary school in Parish? No secondary school.

7. Teaching for Nonconformist children? No church school.

8. Organised study for adults? The aim of our work on Sunday is largely this. Books are lent and interviews are sought with this object in view.

9. Interest in mission? Missionary Boxes S.P.G. and C.M.S. are distributed, and literature likewise, sermons preached and lectures sometimes given.

10. Voters for Ruridecanal representatives a) men b) women? My Churchwardens with three or four others. No women.

11. PCC? No parochial Church Council.

1. Population 336.
2. Pearson Owen Potter trained at the London College of Divinity in 1890 and was ordained priest in 1892. He served as a missionary for the London Diocesan Home Mission 1891–94 and served a curacy in Southwark between 1894 and 1899, when he became Vicar of Tetsworth. He was 63 in 1914 and his household was not found in the 1911 census. At the 1901 census he was listed as unmarried and sharing a household with one unmarried male servant – a groom.

TEW, GREAT[1]   **Incumbent J. P. Malleson**[2]

1. Baptism at morning or evening prayer? Not for some years. Usually at Children's Service.

2. Communion times

a) Sunday 8 am each Sunday. 11 am first S. in month, 12 on 3rd S.

b) **Ascension Day** 8 am.

c) **Saints Days** 8 am.

d) **Week-days?** Not.

3. **Is Communion ever sung?** Yes. 11 am on 1st Sunday in month.

4. **Religious teaching to children a) Church b) Sunday School and c) Day school? i) Clergy teach in Day schools? ii) Religious teaching to Sunday school teachers? iii) Satisfactory results?**

(a) Once a month, afternoon Children's Service with address and catechising, by the Vicar. The Church children attend Church on Sunday morning including the Sung Eucharist once a month. Special instruction is given from time to time to enable them to understand and join in that Service. (b) Sunday School 10 am Collects learned and Collects and Gospel and Epistle explained. 2:30 p.m. (except when Service in Church) – Short Service at School and instruction mainly on Catechism. Occasionally on the Eucharist and for 5 or 6 weeks in the year on Foreign Missions. (c) Day School is a Council School. [i–iii] I do not teach there. The teachers give as full teaching as the law and the County Council permits. Sunday School Teachers are practically all trained day-school teachers (and myself). I do not give them special instruction. I miss the opportunity of giving Church Teaching in day-school. It is hard to make Sunday School take its place.

5. **Religious teaching to lads and young women?** I have from time to time managed to get together a class for young women, but not of lads. The number available is always small.

6. **Secondary school in Parish?** No.

7. **Teaching for Nonconformist children?** [*No response*].

8. **Organised study for adults?** We have a Communicants Guild. The special services and addresses fell off in attendance and were stopped. I intend to recommence this autumn.

9. **Interest in mission?** King's Messengers. (Boys and Girls). Parochial Missionary Association (S.P.G.). About 15 collecting boxes out. 12 copies of Quarterly Intercession Paper taken and distributed. Occasional Intercession Services. Annual Meeting and Sermons. Frequent allusion to the work in Sermons. (S.P.G.) "Church Abroad" distributed with the Parish Magazine.

10. **Voters for Ruridecanal representatives a) men b) women?** Only one or two, who attended a meeting for that purpose.

11. **PCC?** No.

1. Population 369.

2. John Philip Malleson graduated from Trinity College Cambridge in 1887 and was ordained priest in 1893. He was Curate of Great and Little Tew between 1892 and 1895, when he became Vicar of Great Tew. He was also Organising Secretary for the SPG 1895–1913. He was 49 in 1914 and at the 1911 census he was recorded as unmarried, sharing a household with his elderly parents and four unmarried female servants.

TEW, LITTLE[1]   Incumbent W. S. Hulme[2]

1. Baptism at morning or evening prayer? No. The Custom has been by former vicar to have it at the children's service. I have taken it at Evensong one Weekday.

2. Communion times

a) Sunday 1st Sunday at 7 and 8 and 12, 3d Sunday 8 and 12. Other Sundays at 8.

b) Ascension Day at 7 and 8 and at 12.

c) Saints Days at 8 am.

d) Week-days? On Thursdays in Advent and Lent.

3. Is Communion ever sung? No. Never – the congregation would not approve of it.

4. Religious teaching to children a) Church b) Sunday School and c) Day school? i) Clergy teach in Day schools? ii) Religious teaching to Sunday school teachers? iii) Satisfactory results?

Religious Instruction of children in church. Every Sunday afternoon a service for children unless I am prevented by ill-health. Have only 10 children. In Sunday Schools – there is none – and no one to help in the teaching but my wife. In the Day School – Whatever religious instruction is given by the Schoolmistress and her assistant alone and the Vicar is not allowed to go into the School and he considers it a great shame. I consider that Mrs Woolgrove[3] should be asked by your Lordship to state what instruction is given to all the children in that school. There are 23 children in that school whom I know were all baptized in the Church of England and belong to church parents but are quite wrongly sent by their parents to the Baptist chapel on Sundays for their school teaching and therefore I have no possible chance of giving them instruction in church principles. I have only 5 out of that 23 that I have any control over. I am not at all satisfied with the present conditions in Little Tew Schools and never shall be until something is done to compel parents who have their children baptized at church to send them to church so that they may be brought up in church principles and also have religious instruction in the school. Cannot your Lordship as patron of the Living do something in this direction? Or cannot your Lordship or the Archdeacon of Oxford inspect the School and the children or preach in church on the subject of Religious Instruction.

5. Religious teaching to lads and young women? This being an agricultural parish I do not see any possible opening for this work of instructing lads and young women.

6. Secondary school in Parish? None that I am aware of.

7. Teaching for Nonconformist children? There is no provision made for these children except what is given by the Baptist minister on Sunday.

8. Organised study for adults? Nothing is done in this direction except in connexion with confirmation classes.

9. Interest in mission? Some of our parishioners have boxes for S.P.G. and a lecture is given once a year for this Society – but I cannot get my people to attend intercessory services for foreign missions.

10. Voters for Ruridecanal representatives a) men b) women? I cannot give any information on this subject.

11. PCC? There is no parochial church council. There is only a parish meeting about charities and allotments with a chairman appointed every year.

1. Population 186.
2. Walter Saunders Hulme trained at Gloucester College in 1875 and was ordained priest in 1880. He served eight curacies 1878–1905 and was Chaplain of the Maidenhead Workhouse 1908–10. He became Vicar of Little Tew in 1912. He was 58 in 1914 and at the 1911 census he shared a household with his wife and one unmarried female servant.
3. Kate Woolgrove was the schoolmistress at Little Tew.

THAME[1]   Incumbent G. C. Bowring[2]

1. Baptism at morning or evening prayer? Sometimes at Children's Service.

2. Communion times

a) Sunday 8 am. (11 am 2 a month; 7.45 pm 1 [a month]).

b) Ascension Day 7 am, 8 am.

c) Saints Days 8 am or 7.30 am Great Festivals 4 times.

d) Week-days? No.

3. Is Communion ever sung? Not entirely. Partially Easter Sunday 8 am.

4. Religious teaching to children a) Church b) Sunday School and c) Day school? i) Clergy teach in Day schools? ii) Religious teaching to Sunday school teachers? iii) Satisfactory results?

(a) Monthly Service on 4th Sunday. (b) Carefully selected Text Books on Bible and P.B. are always in use by the teachers. (c) Diocesan Syllabus and Diocesan Inspection. [i–iii] Yes Weekly. Young teachers are instructed individually by the Clergy. Regular meetings are held throughout the winter. Results fairly satisfactory. The great need is more money for more perfect equipment of teachers e.g. a museum illustrating Scripture. This we hope to get now that the main part of the New Church Hall is finished and the work is more centralised. It was too scattered before to do much of this.

5. Religious teaching to lads and young women? A class is held every Sunday for (i) lads and (ii) young women at which systematic instruction is given in the Bible and Prayer Book. Young people are specially encouraged to join the Communicants' union which meets monthly (Oct-June). The younger communicants are placed under spiritual stewards who encourage them to regular attendance at their meetings and at the Holy Communion.

6. Secondary school in Parish? Yes. Two. Lord Williams Grammar School (Boys) and Thame Girl's Grammar School. Neither are church schools. Excellent Biblical Instruction is given in both. Good Church Teaching is given in the Boys School: the Principal being a Clergyman. The Boys attend the Parish Church on S. mgs and have their own School Services in the Evenings. Seven eighths of the girls are church girls and attend Parish Church both S. mg and Evng. A goodly number are annually prepared for Confirmation and these are our most regular members of the Comts Union.

7. Teaching for Nonconformist children? (1) Church and (2) British, now called the John Hampden School.

8. Organised study for adults? This subject is constantly dealt with at C.E.M.S. and M.U. meetings and in the Church itself on and around the Great Festivals.

9. Interest in mission? Branches of the Gleaners Union Young People's Union and Sowers, all of which have the above objects specially in view, have been formed and are all three doing a good work. A Study Circle among young men was held last winter.

10. Voters for Ruridecanal representatives a) men b) women? (a) 6, (b) 1. It has been the hardest thing possible to persuade the people of the reality of the thing so long as we can point to no real power as flowing from the whole plan. Prove to them that there is real power and things will form quickly enough. I will however try again.

11. PCC? No. Whenever any thing arises requiring special deliberation we find that the Clergy, Churchwardens and Sides-men (12) make an excellent body for the purpose.

1. Population 2,957.
2. Godfray Charles Bowring graduated from Hertford College Oxford in 1878 and was ordained priest in 1880. He served two curacies 1879–85 and was Vicar of Holy Trinity Oxford between 1885 and 1905, when he became Vicar of Thame. He was 58 in 1914 and at the 1911 census he shared a household with his wife, 24-year-old daughter and two unmarried female servants.

WARBOROUGH[1]   Incumbent A. H. Caldicott[2]

1. Baptism at morning or evening prayer? Generally at Children's Service in afternoon.

2. Communion times

a) **Sunday** 8 am.

b) **Ascension Day** 7 am and 8 am.

c) **Saints Days** 8 am.

d) **Week-days?** [*No response*].

3. Is Communion ever sung? No.

4. Religious teaching to children a) Church b) Sunday School and c) Day school? i) Clergy teach in Day schools? ii) Religious teaching to Sunday school teachers? iii) Satisfactory results?

(a) The elder children are catechised in Church each Sunday all the children about 5 times a year. (b) Morning and afternoon School. (c) Daily instruction. [i–iii] The Clergy do not teach but attend the School everyday for Prayers and to see that the Diocesan Syllabus is adhered to. A Teachers class is held once a month. On the whole the work is satisfactory. It is hampered by the early age at wh. children leave school.

5. Religious teaching to lads and young women? A bible class is held on Sunday for girls who have left School: nothing is done for the lads.

6. Secondary school in Parish? No.

7. Teaching for Nonconformist children? Practically every child in the Day School is also a member of the Sunday School. Those who are not are attendants at Church and children of parents who think a Sunday School rather beneath them.

8. Organised study for adults? No.

9. Interest in mission? A monthly intercession is held for foreign missions and mission literature is circulated. It is very sparsely attended.

10. Voters for Ruridecanal representatives a) men b) women? 14 men.

11. PCC? Yes. Consultative. Twice.

1. Population 608.
2. Arthur Henry Caldicott graduated from Corpus Christi College Oxford in 1890 and was ordained priest in 1892. He served two curacies 1891–95 and was Assistant Master at Elstree School (Herts.) between 1895 and 1896, when he became Vicar of Warborough. He was 46 in 1914 and at the 1911 census he shared a household with his wife and daughter, his elderly mother and 9-year-old niece, together with five unmarried female servants.

WARDINGTON[1]   Incumbent M. Kirkby[2]

1. Baptism at morning or evening prayer? No. No occasion, and the people would object. Holy Baptism every Sunday afternoon at the 3 pm Service.

2. Communion times

a) **Sunday** 8 am also 12 pm once a month and 10 am once a month.

b) **Ascension Day** 7 am, 8 am and 10 am Sung Service.

c) **Saints Days** 8 am, often 7 am as well.

d) **Week-days?** Thursday at 8 am always, generally twice if not three times a week.

3. Is Communion ever sung? Yes. 10 am once a month. Well attended. All the children come as it takes the place of their Sunday Sch.

4. Religious teaching to children a) Church b) Sunday School and c) Day school? i) Clergy teach in Day schools? ii) Religious teaching to Sunday school teachers? iii) Satisfactory results?

(a) Missa Cantata made especially with a first view to children once a month. (b) Other Sundays Sunday School at 10 am to 10.40. 3 pm. every Sunday Catechising. (c) Religious teaching every Schoolday from 9.5 – 9.45 under the teachers who are Communicants (One a Sidesman. The other a member of the guild). [i–iii] I go in constantly and supervise but do not teach as it is unnecessary and no child is withdrawn from Church teaching as it is. I am well satisfied with the results so far. I use the pulpit more for teaching than preaching and use the guild services for instructing the elder one.

5. Religious teaching to lads and young women? <u>No parish room</u>. No room of any kind to use. So do the best I conscientiously, can otherwise. Many young men and women come to the catechising.

6. Secondary school in Parish? [*No response*].

7. Teaching for Nonconformist children? Nonconformists don't hurt. A good Sunday School. They have a splendid room and as far as I can see they have no objection to our teaching having no definite faith here of their own.

8. Organised study for adults? I try, but the people do not wish for holy books. They say they have their bibles.

9. Interest in mission? Mission prayers etc after 3rd Collect at Evensong. Addresses, meeting and so on. But any suggestion of undertaking some definite work for "Beyond the seas" is met with a prop. to postpone the discussion "sine die".

10. Voters for Ruridecanal representatives a) men b) women? "Not ready".

11. PCC? (a) Yes. The guild of Communicants. All parochial matters discussed and decided. (b) Three or four times as occasion arose.

I have answered to the best of my powers.

1. Population 594.
2. Marsh Kirkby graduated from St Mary Hall Oxford in 1883 and was ordained priest in 1884. He held a series of eleven curacies 1883–1913, interrupted by a period as an assistant chaplain in Singapore between 1908 and 1910. He became Vicar of Wardington in 1913. He was 60 in 1914 and at the 1911 census he shared a household with his wife, three young daughters and one unmarried female servant.

WATERPERRY[1]   Incumbent T. J. Evans-Pritchard[2]

1. Baptism at morning or evening prayer? I point out to my people the directions in the Prayer Book; but in 4 cases out of 5 I have met their convenience by taking the baptism after Evening Prayer – in the 5th case during the course of Evening Prayer.

2. Communion times

a) **Sunday** 1st and 3rd Sunday mid-day, the other Sundays at 8 am.

b) **Ascension Day** 8 am.

c) **Saints Days** 8 am. On the Annunciation – for Mothers' Union at 10 am.

d) **Week-days?** On the Great festivals – 2 Celebrations – at 7 am and mid-day.

3. Is Communion ever sung? No.

4. Religious teaching to children a) Church b) Sunday School and c) Day school? i) Clergy teach in Day schools? ii) Religious teaching to Sunday school teachers? iii) Satisfactory results?

(a) Nothing beyond the usual Services. (b) For 5 months when Evensong is at 6 p.m., I hold a childrens service in the School at 2.15 each Sunday. This coming winter I propose holding, as an experiment, a Sunday Evensong once a month at 6 p.m. instead of 3 pm on that Sunday the children will have their little service at 2.15 p.m. (c) The children are taught on the lines of the Diocesan Syllabus.[i–iii] I teach in the Day-school twice a week. I find the work with the children most interesting. The children are keen and I have no reason to be dis-satisfied. I have no Sunday-school teachers.

5. Religious teaching to lads and young women? Nothing particular. What I hope for is that our young fellows will as a whole become regular in the attendance at church to begin with. In our small parish there are but a handful of them. Three of our lads were confirmed in Holy Week last. Practically all our young women are regular Communicants.

6. Secondary school in Parish? No.

7. Teaching for Nonconformist children? Strictly speaking I don't know that we have got any. Certainly I have heard no objections to the teaching given.

8. Organised study for adults? Beyond instruction imparted in sermons, No.

9. Interest in mission? We have special sermons on occasions, and we contribute towards the funds of S.P.C.K.; S.P.G.; and C.M.S. We are promised a Lantern.

10. Voters for Ruridecanal representatives a) men b) women? We have one Ruridecanal Representative; and he is elected at the Annual Vestry Meeting.

11. PCC? No.

1. Population 163.
2. Thomas John Evans-Pritchard graduated from Hertford College Oxford in 1886 and was ordained priest in 1888. He held four curacies and served two periods as a Licenced Preacher in the diocese of Chichester between 1887 and 1913, when he became Vicar of Waterperry. He was 56 in 1914 and at the 1911 census he shared a household with his wife and one unmarried female servant.

WATERSTOCK[1]   Incumbent B. L. Carr[2]

1. Baptism at morning or evening prayer? Yes.

2. Communion times

a) Sunday at 11.0 am 1st Sunday in the month at 8 am 3rd [Sunday in the month].

b) Ascension Day 8.0 am.

c) Saints Days [*No response*].

d) Week-days? [*No response*].

3. Is Communion ever sung? No.

4. Religious teaching to children a) Church b) Sunday School and c) Day school? i) Clergy teach in Day schools? ii) Religious teaching to Sunday school teachers? iii) Satisfactory results?

The Rector teaches the Sunday School in the morning and afternoon on Sunday. There are no Sunday School teachers the Rector being helped by his wife. Clergy teach twice a week in Day School.

5. Religious teaching to lads and young women? [*No response*].

6. Secondary school in Parish? No.

7. Teaching for Nonconformist children? There are not any Nonconformists.

8. Organised study for adults? [*No response*].

9. Interest in mission? [*No response*].

10. Voters for Ruridecanal representatives a) men b) women? [*No response*].

11. PCC? No.

1. Population 149.
2. Benjamin Lund Carr graduated from the University of Oxford in 1889 and was ordained priest in 1893. He served two curacies at Lancaster and Newlands 1891–94 and held the Vicarage at the latter between 1894 and 1913, when he became Rector of Waterstock. He was 58 in 1914 and at the 1911 census he shared a household with his wife, two young daughters and their governess and one unmarried female servant.

WATLINGTON[1] Incumbent S. C. Saunders[2]

1. Baptism at morning or evening prayer? No, except on Weekdays at Evensong. On Sunday, it is at 3 o'c Service.

2. Communion times

a) Sunday on the 1st at 8 and 12. 2, 3, 4 at 8. Last Sunday in the month 7.

b) Ascension Day 4.30, 7 and 10 am.

c) Saints Days 8.

d) Week-days? Thursday at 8.

3. Is Communion ever sung? Yes. On the first Sunday at 8. On Ascension Day at 4.30. On the Great Festivals at 8.

4. Religious teaching to children a) Church b) Sunday School and c) Day school? i) Clergy teach in Day schools? ii) Religious teaching to Sunday school teachers? iii) Satisfactory results?

(a) The children are catechised every Sunday afternoon at 3 pm. (b) There is Sunday School every Sunday from 10 to 10 45 am and from 2.15 to 2.30 pm. (c) Religious instruction is given every morning. [i–iii] This is a County school but the Clergy teach in it 3 times a week. There is a class weekly for Sunday School teachers. Satisfied on the whole but would like the power to teach more fully Church teaching in the day School.

5. Religious teaching to lads and young women? There is a Parish Class in the winter (1) for lads (2) for girls.

6. Secondary school in Parish? No.

7. Teaching for Nonconformist children? County School, the nonconformist minister is allowed to teach once a week in the School but he never does.

8. Organised study for adults? No.

9. Interest in mission? [*No response*].

10. Voters for Ruridecanal representatives a) men b) women? So far as I know none.

11. PCC? We have a finance Council which meet 4 times a year and at other times where needed. They decide about collection and examine and pass all accounts.

1. Population 1,474.
2. Sidney Charles Saunders trained at Chichester College in 1877 and subsequently graduated from Exeter College Oxford in 1895. He was ordained priest in 1880. He served three curacies 1879–90 and was Vicar of Cadmore End between 1890 and 1895, when he became Vicar of Watlington. He was 56 in 1914 and at the 1911 census he shared a household with his wife and three unmarried female servants.

WENDLEBURY[1]   Incumbent H. W. Gresswell[2]

1. Baptism at morning or evening prayer? Yes during Morn or Even Service – except when asked specially to take the Baptism separately in the afternoon.

2. Communion times

a) **Sunday** 8.30 am and after the Morning Service twice a month.

b) **Ascension Day** 8.30 am.

c) **Saints Days** None.

d) **Week-days?** None.

3. Is Communion ever sung? No.

4. Religious teaching to children a) Church b) Sunday School and c) Day school? i) Clergy teach in Day schools? ii) Religious teaching to Sunday school teachers? iii) Satisfactory results?

I take the Sunday School myself and Catechise the children in Church every Sunday morning before Morning Service at 10 o'clock. We have 21 Children in the Day School and they all attend the Sunday School. The Clergymen teach once a week in the Day School.

5. Religious teaching to lads and young women? During the winter months classes for young men and young women are held with a view to Confirmation.

6. Secondary school in Parish? No. There is no Secondary School.

7. Teaching for Nonconformist children? No: but if there were any Nonconformists at any time then provision would be made for them.

8. Organised study for adults? In the Sermons in Church.

9. Interest in mission? Sermons and Collection in Church once a year, and occasionally Lectures by Deputations with Collections – on behalf of the S.P.G.

10. Voters for Ruridecanal representatives a) men b) women? Two men.

11. PCC? No.

1. Population 177.
2. Henry William Gresswell graduated from Hertford College Oxford in 1874 and was ordained priest in 1877. He served a series of nine curacies between 1876 and 1902, when he became Rector of Wendlebury. He was the author of *Prayer and Temptation* (1900) and *Religion in Many Aspects* (1912). He was 62 in 1914 and at the 1911 census he shared a household with his wife and 2-year-old son.

WESTON, SOUTH WITH ADWELL[1] Incumbent R. T. Espinasse[2]

1. Baptism at morning or evening prayer? Practically always.

2. Communion times

a) Sunday After mat: except one Sunday each month. Every Sunday at S Weston. Once a month at Adwell.

b) Ascension Day 10.30.

c) Saints Days [10.30] Not on all Saints' Days.

d) Week-days? [10.30] on certain special occasions.

3. Is Communion ever sung? No.

4. Religious teaching to children a) Church b) Sunday School and c) Day school? i) Clergy teach in Day schools? ii) Religious teaching to Sunday school teachers? iii) Satisfactory results?

Four S Weston children (all that is) attend Mrs Espinasse's S. School. Mrs Birch Reynardson has few children at Adwell. Two (ie all of school age) S Weston children and two Adwell attend Lewknor. [i–iii] I go once a week and the Vicar of Lewknor once a week to give instruction. I am as satisfied as one can be considering the ridiculous smallness of numbers and the consequent impossibility of any reasonable organization. The result is at any rate an excellent understanding between the Rectory and the children and their parents.

5. Religious teaching to lads and young women? There are only two young women. The lads are about six in number and are keenly interested in Choir through which I am able to be in close personal touch with them without instruction otherwise than sermons and informal talks.

6. Secondary school in Parish? No.

7. Teaching for Nonconformist children? No school.

8. Organised study for adults? No.

9. Interest in mission? I speak as strongly as possible in and out of church and ask for intercessions for all Missionary undertakings, especially on days when we have special Communion Services with that particular intention.

10. Voters for Ruridecanal representatives a) men b) women? I am afraid that I can't quite understand this question. I have never succeeded in collecting together for Vestry meeting and such like more than the Churchwardens and possibly the clerk if I have specially urged him to attend. There are about 40 Communicants or rather more.

11. PCC? No. The smallness of population and the class of people make parochial organisation impossible and all I can do is to keep up such zeal and loyalty as I can by close personal friendship with my little flock.

1. Population 135.
2. Richard Talbot Espinasse graduated from Brasenose College Oxford in 1884 and was ordained priest in 1886. He was Assistant Master at Ardingly College 1884–90 and held a series of curacies and chaplaincies 1890–98. He held the Rectory of Oldcastle (Mon.) together with the Vicarage of Walterstone (Herefs.) between 1898 and 1900, when he became Rector of Adwell with South Weston. He was 51 in 1914 and at the 1911 census he shared a household with his wife, three children aged between 6 and 18, and one unmarried female servant.

WESTWELL[1]   Incumbent W. R. Sharpe[2]

1. Baptism at morning or evening prayer? Constantly in the Evening.

2. Communion times

a) Sunday at 8 am except on first S. in month.

b) Ascension Day 8 am.

c) Saints Days 8 am.

d) Week-days? On few occasions but at same time.

3. Is Communion ever sung? No.

4. Religious teaching to children a) Church b) Sunday School and c) Day school? i) Clergy teach in Day schools? ii) Religious teaching to Sunday school teachers? iii) Satisfactory results?

A Childrens' Service each Sunday. No Sunday School. The syllabus put forth for the Diocesan Inspector. The Clergy teach 2 or 3 times per week. No Sunday school teachers to instruct.

5. Religious teaching to lads and young women? Nothing special there are but 2 or 3 lads and no young women living in the place.

6. Secondary school in Parish? No.

7. Teaching for Nonconformist children? No. No demand for it.

8. Organised study for adults? No.

9. Interest in mission? A Missionary Meeting with lecture once or twice per annum a service of Intercession for Foreign Missions also Missionary Sermon once per annum 2. Collections 1 for general purpose and 1 for Missionary Student Fund.

10. Voters for Ruridecanal representatives a) men b) women? None.

11. PCC? No Parochial Church Council.

1. Population 92.
2. William Robert Sharpe graduated from Keble College Oxford in 1874 and was ordained priest in 1878. He served two curacies between 1875 and 1881, when he became Rector of Westwell. He was 63 in 1914 and at the 1911 census he shared a household with his wife and two unmarried female servants.

WHEATFIELD[1] Incumbent D. H. Davys[2]

1. Baptism at morning or evening prayer? Yes.

2. Communion times

a) **Sunday** 12 o'clock once a month.

b) **Ascension Day** [*No response*].

c) **Saints Days** 8 o'clock and 12 o'clock on the greater festivals.

d) **Week-days?** [*No response*].

3. Is Communion ever sung? No.

4. Religious teaching to children a) Church b) Sunday School and c) Day school? i) Clergy teach in Day schools? ii) Religious teaching to Sunday school teachers? iii) Satisfactory results?

Population 75. No day School. Instruction given in church to children on the occasion of an Infant Baptism on certain occasions when there is an afternoon service. Rector takes Sunday school 3 o'clock every Sunday. No other Sunday school teachers.

5. Religious teaching to lads and young women? Instruction given when preparing candidates for confirmation. Not enough to form a regular class – religious books lent.

6. Secondary school in Parish? No.

7. Teaching for Nonconformist children? No Church School.

8. Organised study for adults? Sermons in church. Monthly religious Magazine given away.

9. Interest in mission? Occasional Missionary Sermons. Missionary literature distributed.

10. Voters for Ruridecanal representatives a) men b) women? One.

11. PCC? No.

1. Population 72.
2. Douglas Henry Davys trained at Wells Theological College in 1883 and was ordained priest in 1886. He served two curacies 1885–90 and became Rector of Wheatfield in 1898. He was 52 in 1914 and at the 1911 census he was unmarried and sharing a household with two unmarried female servants.

WHEATLEY[1] Incumbent W. D. B. Curry[2]

1. Baptism at morning or evening prayer? Yes.

2. Communion times

a) **Sunday** 8 o'c or 7 o'c after Matins once a month.

b) **Ascension Day** 5.30 and 8 o'c.

c) **Saints Days** 8 o'c.

d) **Week-days?** Thursdays 8 o'c.

3. Is Communion ever sung? Yes. 8 am on Festivals.

4. Religious teaching to children a) Church b) Sunday School and c) Day school? i) Clergy teach in Day schools? ii) Religious teaching to Sunday school teachers? iii) Satisfactory results?

Every Sunday afternoon I have a Childrens service in which I instruct and catechize. I have classes for my Sunday School teachers. I do not teach in the Day Schools as owing to the "Merry Bell" schism[3] Bishop Paget advised me not to, but possibly soon I may be able to do so. I have though thoroughly loyal day school teachers and I go in and hear them teaching. I am not satisfied with the Sunday School teaching as I have at present to depend greatly on my Day School teachers for help.

5. Religious teaching to lads and young women? Classes for both are held.

6. Secondary school in Parish? No.

7. Teaching for Nonconformist children? I offered some four years ago a room in the school to the nonconformist minister to come and teach. This was refused as he felt unable to do it and moreover he said he doubted whether the people would wish it. Very often a nonconformist child gets the Bishop's prize.

8. Organised study for adults? A class was commenced last winter. Small results at present.

9. Interest in mission? Intercessions at Church on Fridays from 3–4 and I also read to the congregation extracts from various books bearing on the different places we are praying for. Quarterly intercession paper is distributed and a reading circle is being started. Once a month on Sundays after Evensong the congregation is also invited to stay for special intercessions for the Ch. abroad.

10. Voters for Ruridecanal representatives a) men b) women? None.

11. PCC? No.

1. Population 966.
2. William Dixon Blatchford Curry graduated from Exeter College Oxford in 1885 and trained at Wells Theological College, being ordained priest in 1874. After serving an initial curacy 1885–91 he was Vicar of South Hinksey with New Hinksey between 1891 and 1907, when he became Vicar of Wheatley. He was 53 in 1914 and at the 1911 census he shared a household with his wife, three daughters aged between 6 and 14, and two unmarried female servants.
3. The Merry Bells was a coffee house, meeting space and Temperance Hotel with club house and reading room opened in Wheatley in 1888 with financial support from the Miller family of Shotover. It was intended to be operated on inter-denominational lines and the 'schism' probably refers to some tension between the local Anglicans and nonconformists (probably the Congregationalists in this case) over the enterprise.

WHITCHURCH[1] Incumbent H. E. Trotter[2]

1. Baptism at morning or evening prayer? No.

2. Communion times

a) Sunday 8 am and 12 on first Sunday in the month.

b) Ascension Day 8 am.

c) Saints Days 8 am.

d) Week-days? [*No response*].

3. Is Communion ever sung? No owing to the difficulty of getting a choir in such a scattered parish as Whitchurch competent to sing the service.

4. Religious teaching to children a) Church b) Sunday School and c) Day school? i) Clergy teach in Day schools? ii) Religious teaching to Sunday school teachers? iii) Satisfactory results?

No. Books selected by the Rector are given the teachers and children, catechising each month. [i–iii] As regards the Day School very good reports are always received from the Diocesan Inspector. All the teachers in the Sunday School are teachers who have considerable experience in teaching – and I have no reason to be dissatisfied with the results.

5. Religious teaching to lads and young women? Bible Classes have been tried for lads – but not with much success.

6. Secondary school in Parish? No.

7. Teaching for Nonconformist children? The Managers have been asked to provide religious teaching for children of Nonconformist parents other than given to the other children. Only one child has been withdrawn from the religious teaching since I have been Rector and that only on the mornings when the Catechism was the subject.

8. Organised study for adults? No.

9. Interest in mission? A meeting in connection with the S.P.G. is occasionally held and annual sermons are preached and collections made on behalf of Foreign Missions.

10. Voters for Ruridecanal representatives a) men b) women? Unable to state. I have found it difficult to get people to take any interest in the election of Representatives. I summoned a meeting for the purpose and only a very few attended.

11. PCC? No.

1. Population 876.
2. Henry Eden Trotter graduated from Christ Church Oxford in 1868 and was ordained priest in 1870. He served two curacies 1869–73, was Vicar of Northam (Hants.) 1873–83 and of Ardington (Berks.) between 1884 and 1899, when he became Rector of Whitchurch. He was appointed Rural Dean of Henley in 1913. He was 69 in 1914 and at the 1911 census he shared a household with his wife, four unmarried children aged between 20 and 32, together with a footman and five unmarried female servants.

WIGGINGTON[1]   Incumbent H. J. Riddelsdell[2]

1. Baptism at morning or evening prayer? I propose to do so.

2. Communion times

a) Sunday 8 am (midday once a month).

b) Ascension Day 7 am this year.

c) Saints Days 8 am (as at present proposed).

d) Week-days? None.

3. Is Communion ever sung? Not yet.

4. Religious teaching to children a) Church b) Sunday School and c) Day school? i) Clergy teach in Day schools? ii) Religious teaching to Sunday school teachers? iii) Satisfactory results?

Once a week has been the custom. Nothing special I believe. No means of judging yet. Children's Service once a month has, I believe, been customary. Sunday Schools mg and aft. Day Schools – use Diocesan Syllabus.

5. Religious teaching to lads and young women? Nothing as far as I know.

6. Secondary school in Parish? No.

7. Teaching for Nonconformist children? I do not think so.

8. Organised study for adults? I believe not.

9. Interest in mission? Sermon once a year: collecting boxes etc. Systematic teaching is intended in the future, and missionary prayer meetings.

10. Voters for Ruridecanal representatives a) men b) women? I do not know.

11. PCC? No.

(Note: I have only just come to the Parish.)

1. Population 226
2. Harry Joseph Riddelsdell graduated from Jesus College Oxford in 1892 and was ordained priest in 1895. After an initial curacy in Leeds 1894–97, he served as Sub-Warden of St Michael's College Llandaff between 1897 and 1913, when he was appointed as Rector of Wiggington. He was 47 in 1914 and at the 1911 census he shared a household with his wife, elderly mother and two unmarried female servants.

WITNEY[1]　　　　　　　　　　　　　　Incumbent P. P. Goldingham[2]

1. Baptism at morning or evening prayer? Always at Evening Prayer on Fridays at one church and on Saturdays at the other. Never at Morning Prayer.

2. Communion times

a) **Sunday** 8 am also 7 am and noon on certain Sundays in the month.

b) **Ascension Day** 5 am, 7 am, 8 am, 11 am. (2 churches).

c) **Saints Days** 7. 30 am at one church and 8 am at the other.

d) **Week-days?** Wednesdays 8 am Thursdays 11 am.

3. Is Communion ever sung? Yes at chief festivals 8 am at one church, noon at the other.

4. Religious teaching to children a) Church b) Sunday School and c) Day school? i) Clergy teach in Day schools? ii) Religious teaching to Sunday school teachers? iii) Satisfactory results?

(a) Catechising weekly. (b) by Sunday School Teachers in classes. (c) Religious teaching is given in Day Schools from 9.15 am – 9.45 am daily. [i–iii] The clergy do teach in the Day Schools four mornings a week. Sunday School Teachers are given a book to use in their Sunday School teaching. Special classes for S. S. Teachers are very difficult to arrange here as everybody leads a busy life and our teachers have long hours of work and their evenings are mostly engaged in other things. In this town where Church and Nonconformity are so mixed it is difficult to speak of "results attained". It is a great problem how far church teaching given in the Day school has any result where the children come from Nonconformist homes, and are not asked to put their teaching in practise by attending the parish church on any weekday in the year. Nonconformist children can carry off the "Bishop's Prize" with no intention of putting the Church Catechism into force as far as membership in the Ch. of England is concerned.

5. Religious teaching to lads and young women? There is a lads class conducted by a layman on Sunday mornings. There are various classes for young women.

6. Secondary school in Parish? Yes. I have no means of knowing what the religious instruction is as far as the school goes. Some of the pupils attend the parish church and I prepare the candidates for confirmation, when there are any.

7. Teaching for Nonconformist children? There is a Church Day School and a Wesleyan Day School in Witney. Children seem to go to which is most convenient as far as their homes are concerned.

8. Organised study for adults? There are monthly Bible Addresses in addition to the various classes. There is no "study circle".

9. Interest in mission? Much work was done in preparation for the Missionary Exhibition. There is a monthly Intercession lead from the pulpit preceded by a very short sermon or Prayer. A lady prepares the Intercessions and the Rector leads the people in prayer for work overseas.

10. Voters for Ruridecanal representatives a) men b) women? 19 men.

11. PCC? No.

1. Population 4,610.
2. Philip Procter Goldingham trained at the Chancellor's School Lincoln in 1883 and was ordained priest in 1886. He served two curacies 1885–99 and was Vicar of Buckingham 1899–1911. He also served as Rural Dean of Buckingham between 1907 and 1911, when he became Rector of Witney. He was 53 in 1914 and at the 1911 census he shared a household with his wife, his curate as a boarder, and two unmarried female servants.

WOLVERCOTE[1]   Incumbent E. A. Sydenham[2]

1. Baptism at morning or evening prayer? Yes.

2. Communion times

a) Sunday 7.30. High Festivals 11. Occasionally at 9.

b) Ascension Day 4.45, 6.30, 7.30.

c) Saints Days 7.30.

d) Week-days? Thursdays 7.30.

3. Is Communion ever sung? Yes. 11 am.

4. Religious teaching to children a) Church b) Sunday School and c) Day school? i) Clergy teach in Day schools? ii) Religious teaching to Sunday school teachers? iii) Satisfactory results?

There is a children's Service, with Catechism and Address every Sunday at 2.30. Sunday School (in preparation for afternoon Service) every Sunday morning at 10.15. The School children are always present at Morning Prayer or Choral Eucharist on Sundays. [i–iii] No religious instruction given by Clergy in Day school. The numbers of the Sunday School shew an increase in the past year.

5. Religious teaching to lads and young women? There is a Bible Class for elder girls, also religious work is done through the G.F.S. I have not been very successful with the lads.

6. Secondary school in Parish? No.

7. Teaching for Nonconformist children? Ours is a Council School.

8. Organised study for adults? No. I have made several efforts in this direction without much result.

9. Interest in mission? There is the Wolvercote Missionary Society. Lectures on Missionary Subjects are given generally during the winter. The work of the U.M.C.A. receives special attention.

10. Voters for Ruridecanal representatives a) men b) women? [*No response*].

11. PCC? No.

1. Population 1,311
2. Edward Allen Sydenham graduated from Merton College Oxford in 1896 and trained at Wells Theological College, being ordained priest in 1898. He served three curacies between 1897 and 1910, when he became Vicar of Wolvercote. He was 40 in 1914 and at the 1911 census he was single and sharing a household with his unmarried housekeeper.

WOOD EATON[1]   Incumbent R. Hutchison[2]

1. Baptism at morning or evening prayer? Yes – as a rule.

2. Communion times

a) Sunday 8 am except 1st Sund. in month. Also 2nd Cel. on Xmas Easter and Whitsunday.

b) Ascension Day 8 am.

c) Saints Days 8 am.

d) Week-days? [*No response*].

3. Is Communion ever sung? [*No response*].

4. Religious teaching to children a) Church b) Sunday School and c) Day school? i) Clergy teach in Day schools? ii) Religious teaching to Sunday school teachers? iii) Satisfactory results?

The children are taught in Church on Sundays at 2.30 and 3.

5. Religious teaching to lads and young women? They are prepared for Confirmation.

6. Secondary school in Parish? [*No response*].

7. Teaching for Nonconformist children? My parish is joined with Noke for education. No such provision is made.

8. Organised study for adults? [*No response*].

9. Interest in mission? [*No response*].

10. Voters for Ruridecanal representatives a) men b) women? None.

11. PCC? No.

1. Population 80.
2. Robert Hutchison graduated from Exeter College Oxford in 1868 and was ordained priest in 1872. He was Assistant Master at St Edward's School, Summertown 1873–75, Curate of Beckley 1874–78, organising Secretary of the Church of England Incumbents' Sustentation Fund 1878–79, and then Curate of Upton cum Chalvey between 1879 and 1881, when he was appointed Rector of Wood Eaton. He was 68 in 1914 and at the 1911 census he shared a household with his wife, mother-in-law, unmarried 26-year-old daughter and two unmarried female servants.

WOODSTOCK[1]   Incumbent C. H. Minchin[2]

1. Baptism at morning or evening prayer? Yes sometimes in Evening prayer on weekdays and on Sundays in the course of Childrens Service.

2. Communion times

a) **Sunday** at 8; and at midday on 1st and 3rd Sundays in month.

b) **Ascension Day** at 8.

c) **Saints Days** at 8 or 11.

d) **Week-days?** [*No response*].

3. Is Communion ever sung? No.

4. Religious teaching to children a) Church b) Sunday School and c) Day school? i) Clergy teach in Day schools? ii) Religious teaching to Sunday school teachers? iii) Satisfactory results?

(a) There is monthly Childrens Service and an extra one on some Festivals in both Churches. (b) There are Sunday Schools in Woodstock Boys, Girls, and Infants, Bladon Mixed, Old Woodstock Infants. These six schools have their Superintendents and there is a sufficient staff of Teachers – including Supernumerary teachers we number 25. [i–iii] There is a monthly meeting of Sunday School Teachers at which the lessons for the month are reviewed and instruction given. There is much esprit de corps among the Supts and teachers and the Parents support the work and shew interest in their childrens progress. The difficulty is in the <u>stuff</u> of the Teaching Staff. The Clergy teach twice a week at least in the Day Schools. The teachers who are all Church people second their efforts, and give the religious instruction with good results, judging by the Inspectors Reports.

5. Religious teaching to lads and young women? We have one Strong class of lads under religious instruction every week. There are also classes for young women. The G.F.S. has failed to attract and is at present suspended. The C.E.M.S. is useful.

6. Secondary school in Parish? No.

7. Teaching for Nonconformist children? They receive such teaching in fundamentals in the Day School; and they have their own Sunday Schools.

8. Organised study for adults? Yes under the C.E.M.S. in winter sessions we have services lectures and efforts unto this end.

9. Interest in mission? The S.P.G. is so used.

10. Voters for Ruridecanal representatives a) men b) women? This has not been done.

11. PCC? I call the Churchwardens, Sidesmen and Lay Reps. together from time to time. There is no parochial Church Council.

Memo: May I be allowed to alter my answer to the question on page 4 "This has not been done" to "This has been done to this extent only: the persons who attended the meeting to elect representatives signed the declaration before voting"?

1. Population 2,271.
2. Charles Humphry Minchin graduated from St Mary Hall Oxford in 1876 and was ordained priest in 1880. He served three curacies 1878–87 and was Rector of Castle Combe (Wilts.) 1888–93. He then served three chaplaincies at Rotterdam, Neuilly and Pau 1893–1904 and as Rector of Rendlesham between 1904 and 1905, when he was appointed as Rector of Woodstock. He was 58 in 1914 and at the 1911 census he shared a household with his wife and two unmarried female servants.

WOOTTON[1] Incumbent F. R. Marriot[2]

1. Baptism at morning or evening prayer? No. (During the 'Afternoon' Service for children and others.)

2. Communion times

a) **Sunday** 8.15 or 11.0.

b) **Ascension Day** 8.0.

c) **Saints Days** No regular celebration.

d) **Week-days?** [*No response*].

3. Is Communion ever sung? No.

4. Religious teaching to children a) Church b) Sunday School and c) Day school? i) Clergy teach in Day schools? ii) Religious teaching to Sunday school teachers? iii) Satisfactory results?

(a) Regularly on Saints' Days. (b) once every Sunday (c) daily according to the Diocesan Syllabus. [i–iii] The Rector teaches in Day School occasionally. The Sunday School teachers do not receive instruction. Fairly satisfied.

5. Religious teaching to lads and young women? A course of instruction before Confirmation. Those confirmed are called together before the Great Festivals for instruction. There is a good class for the younger lads "Scripture and Prayer Union", meeting regularly. Up to a short time ago, there was a regular Bible Class on Sunday for lads. It became unsatisfactory, so was discontinued. But it is hoped to make a fresh start.

6. Secondary school in Parish? No.

7. Teaching for Nonconformist children? No. Evidence was provided some time ago that the present teaching was in no way unacceptable.

8. Organised study for adults? Not systematic. C.E.M.S. meets during winter – subject various. Mother's Union is active – with many members.

9. Interest in mission? I hope that the Church congregation do take an intelligent interest in this. They certainly respond keenly and generously. The subject is often brought before them.

10. Voters for Ruridecanal representatives a) men b) women? Some men had received the papers when first they were issued – but I cannot remember that any were given in signed.

11. PCC? No.

1. Population 610.
2. Frank Ransome Marriot graduated from New College Oxford in 1884 and was ordained priest in 1886. He was Chaplain to the bishop of Rochester 1887–89 and Curate of Warlingham with Chelsam from 1888 to 1890, when he became Vicar of the same benefice. He served in this position until 1900, when he was appointed as Rector of Wootton. He was 52 in 1914 and at the 1911 census he shared a household with his wife, 9-year-old daughter, her governess and five unmarried female servants.

WORTON, OVER AND NETHER[1] Incumbent H. A. W. Buss[2]

1. Baptism at morning or evening prayer? There have been only two Baptisms since I came here. One was an adult and there was special service. The other took place just before Evening Service when Congregation was assembled.

2. Communion times

a) **Sunday** either 8 am or noon.

b) **Ascension Day** [*No response*].

c) **Saints Days** 8 am All Saints Day.

d) **Week-days?** [*No response*].

3. Is Communion ever sung? No.

4. Religious teaching to children a) Church b) Sunday School and c) Day school? i) Clergy teach in Day schools? ii) Religious teaching to Sunday school teachers? iii) Satisfactory results?

The juvenile population is small. I take most of them on Sunday afternoons. There has been a Bible Class for Elder Girls, at present the Teacher has left, and I am trying to find another. The religious instruction in the Day School is given by the Master who seems to impart a good general knowledge to the Children. I have been here hardly long enough to judge of results.

5. Religious teaching to lads and young women? We have had classes.

6. Secondary school in Parish? No.

7. Teaching for Nonconformist children? No, as this question has never arisen.

8. Organised study for adults? I urge the people to read, but as they are mainly agricultural labourers, I cannot say with what result as to knowledge gained.

9. Interest in mission? Intercessions and an Annual Lecture also Sermons on Missionary Work.

10. Voters for Ruridecanal representatives a) men b) women? As far as I know, none. While I have been here no form of declaration has been sent.

11. PCC? No.

1. Population 119.
2. Harold Alfred Woodward Buss graduated from Emmanuel College Cambridge in 1902 and trained at Ridley Hall, being ordained priest in 1904. He served five curacies between 1903 and 1913, when he became Rector of Over Worton. He was 43 in 1914 and at the 1911 census he was unmarried and living in a single-person household.

WROXTON WITH BALSCOTE[1]   Incumbent A. Haig[2]

1. Baptism at morning or evening prayer? Always at Balscote, not at Wroxton.

2. Communion times

a) Sunday 8 am and in addition 10.30 am once a month.

b) Ascension Day 8 am.

c) Saints Days 8 am.

d) Week-days? None.

3. Is Communion ever sung? At 10.30 am once a month.

4. Religious teaching to children a) Church b) Sunday School and c) Day school? i) Clergy teach in Day schools? ii) Religious teaching to Sunday school teachers? iii) Satisfactory results?

I catechise the children twice a month on Sunday afternoon at Wroxton in Church. Sunday School is held twice a Sunday for the instruction of the children and to take them to Church. Mrs Haig superintends and teaches, but the other teachers are uneducated and inefficient and there is no better material to draw upon. At Balscote the School mistress teaches. I teach in the Day School at Wroxton twice a week.

5. Religious teaching to lads and young women? Nothing.

6. Secondary school in Parish? There is no such School.

7. Teaching for Nonconformist children? No such provision is made.

8. Organised study for adults? No.

9. Interest in mission? Nothing as yet beyond the Annual S.P.G. meeting, Sermons in Church, and Addresses to members of the C.E.M.S. I had made up my mind to start a Prayer Meeting on alternate weeks in the two villages, but ill health since

Xmas made me postpone it. I hope to do this on return from my holiday. I forgot the King's Messengers, something is done there.

10. Voters for Ruridecanal representatives a) men b) women? I am uncertain about this, and, being away from home, I cannot ascertain.

11. PCC? I have no parochial Church Council.

1. Population 569.
2. Arthur Haig graduated from Pembroke College Cambridge in 1881 and was ordained priest in 1882. He served two curacies 1881–83 and was then a missionary with the SPG and Cambridge University Mission at Delhi 1883–91 and Karnal in the Punjab 1891–98. He returned to England and was Rector of St Martin Bedford between 1900 and 1907, when he was appointed as Vicar of Wroxton. He was 56 in 1914 and at the 1911 census he shared a household with his wife and two unmarried female servants.

YARNTON[1]   Incumbent B. Parsons[2]

1. Baptism at morning or evening prayer? No.

2. Communion times

a) Sunday 8 am; and midday on 1st S. in month.

b) Ascension Day 8 am.

c) Saints Days 10 am.

d) Week-days? [*No response*].

3. Is Communion ever sung? No.

4. Religious teaching to children a) Church b) Sunday School and c) Day school? i) Clergy teach in Day schools? ii) Religious teaching to Sunday school teachers? iii) Satisfactory results?

Childrens Service with Catechising every Sunday afternoon. Vicar teaches Prayer Book and Catechism in Day School on Wednesdays. No Sunday School Teachers.

5. Religious teaching to lads and young women? [*No response*].

6. Secondary school in Parish? No.

7. Teaching for Nonconformist children? No provision is made as there is no request or desire for the same.

8. Organised study for adults? No.

9. Interest in mission? Special sermons. Service of Intercession. Missionary boxes.

10. Voters for Ruridecanal representatives a) men b) women? Two men.

11. PCC? No.

1. Population 312.
2. Bertram Parsons graduated from All Souls College Oxford in 1901 and was ordained priest in 1902. He served three curacies between 1901 and 1910, when he became Vicar of Yarnton. He was 40 years old in 1914 and at the 1911 census he shared a household with his wife and one unmarried female servant.

The Visitation of 1918

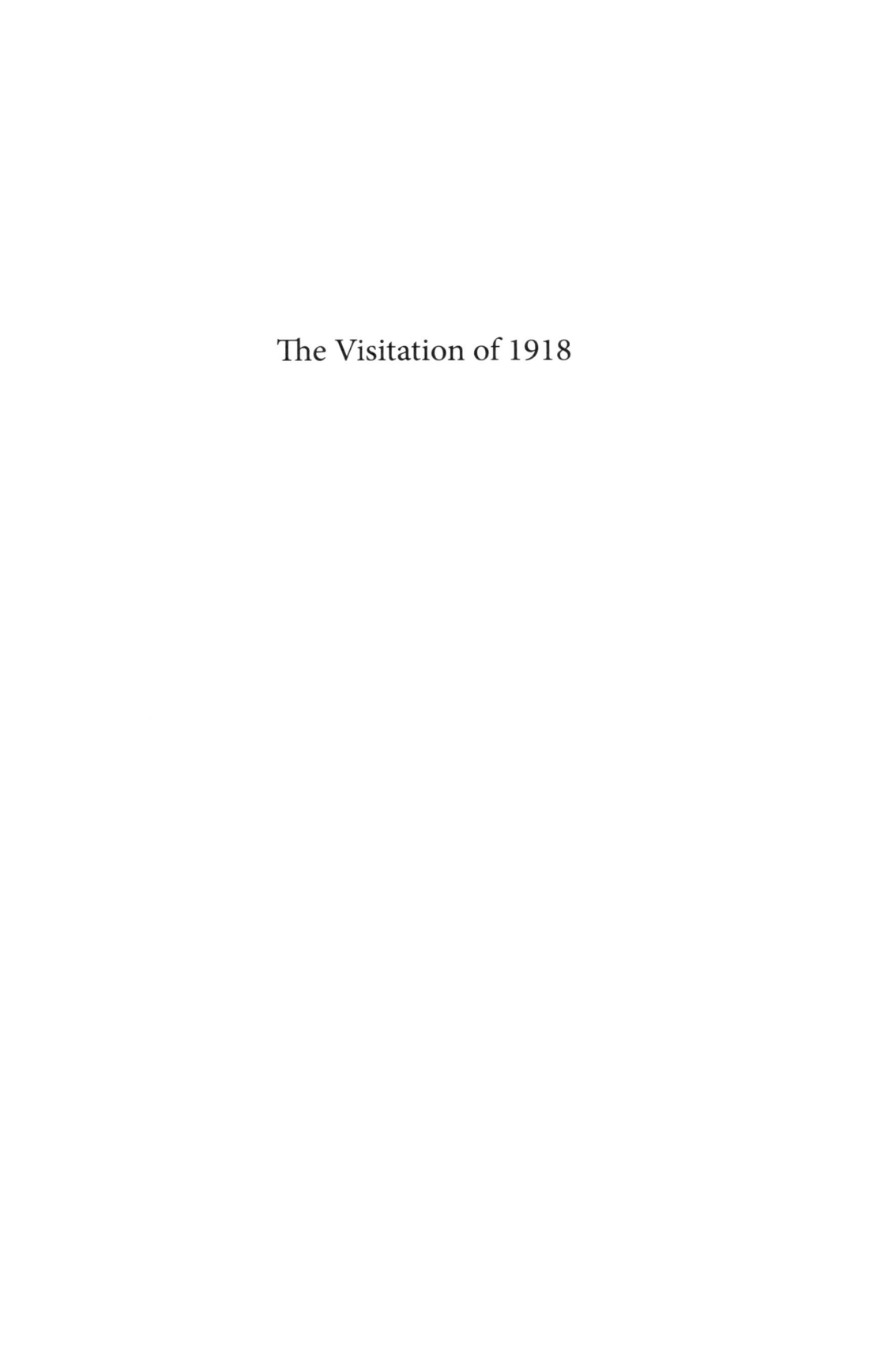

DIOCESE OF OXFORD
VISITATION, 1918

CUDDESDON,
March 1st, 1918.

MY DEAR BROTHER,

You know that I am to conduct a Visitation of the Diocese in May and June. The list of centres and dates is in this month's Diocesan Magazine. The Summons will be issued in April to all beneficed and licensed Clergy and to the Churchwardens.

Full enquiries have been made through the Rural Deans on a number of matters concerning the churches and churchyards; but there are certain enquiries which I desire to make directly of the Incumbents; and I beg you to let me have the answers to the following questions by March 25th.

Believe me to be
Yours very truly in our Lord
C. OXON:

Name of Parish: ………………………….

QUESTIONS TO BE ANSWERED BY THE INCUMBENT OR BY THE OFFICIATING CLERGYMAN

1. Give me the number of boys and girls and infants on the books of the day-schools of your parish (whether in church schools or no): -
    (a) this last year,
    (b) forty years ago (or thirty or twenty years ago, according as you have trustworthy information).

2. How many (a) men, (b) women, in your parish last year had signed the declaration qualifying them under the rules of the Representative Church Council to vote in the Parochial Church Meeting?

3. What can you report as to the moral and spiritual effect on the different classes in your parish
   (a) of War time, (b) of the National Mission?

4. Have you any fairly clear view of the policy which the Church should pursue with regard to the status of Church Schools in single-school areas?

Must we seek by all means to retain these schools in their present status, or can we rightly make some compromise (especially in view of the insistent demands of the N.U.T. and of the Non-conformists) as regards (a) management, (b) appointment of head-teachers, (c) the character of the religious teaching?

Would you regard the offer of more satisfactory conditions of religious teaching in "Provided" or Council Schools as justifying such a compromise?

5. (a) What changes in methods or hours of public worship since your last return (1914) have you to report?
   (b) What effects do you attribute to such changes?

6. (*For Oxfordshire Incumbents only*).
How many Roman Catholics, men, women and children, have you in your parish?

(The purpose of this return is to compare the numbers with those of 100 and 200 years ago, which exist at Cuddesdon. The return need not be made for parishes in Oxford itself unless you have statistics).

───────────────────────────────

(Signed)

───────────────────────────────

Incumbent.

ADDERBURY Incumbent C. F. Cholmondeley[1]

1. Number of Boys Girls and Infants on books of day schools: a. Last year. b. 20 30 or 40 years ago.

1892: Infants 84; 1898: Infants 94, Boys 60, Girls 68; 1918: [Infants] 65, [Boys] 60, [Girls] 66.

2. a. Men and b. Women qualified to vote in Parochial Church meeting. (a) 26, (b) 30.

3. Moral and Spiritual effect of: a. Wartime b. National Mission.

(a) There is a good deal of activity in the way of working in various ways, providing for comforts for the troops, nursing etc and subscribing to war funds. Congregations are not much different, and it is not easy to keep numbers at the intercession services. Among those who have had bereavements there is a tendency to neglect public worship on the ground that they could not control their feelings. Of the soldiers back from the war the majority show little change in the matter of religious observances. (b) We were bidden not to look for open results from the National Mission, and it is as well, for one can take hold of practically nothing definite. I should imagine that a good deal of thinking goes on and sometimes one hears remarks as to the justice of God and to the love of God in connexion with the war. But I think there is very little if any unsettling of faith. I think that when the stress of the war is over we may look for an improvement in spiritual matters.

4. Status of Church Schools. Options for compromise on a. management, b. head teachers, c. character of religious teaching. Might compromise be justified by better arrangements for Church teaching in state schools?

I think that the Church should grant facilities for religious teaching of nonconformist children if asked, but I don't think they would be taken advantage of.

The difficulty to my mind is that I have never come across parents who were really interested in the matter of their children's religious education whether here or elsewhere. I have always found that church people were quite content to let their children go to nonconformist or council schools, and nonconformist parents to church schools. If the parents really demanded special treatment for their children I think they would get it. The Church Schools should be retained for definite church teaching without modifying it, as parents who objected could always remove their children from religious instruction. As regards management, that is practically all in the hands of the County Council. I don't think that in church schools any but church people should be head teachers.

I do not think that facilities in Provided Schools would justify a compromise in (a) (b) and (c).

5 a. Changes in Public worship since 1914. b. Effects of the changes. On the 5th Sunday in the month I have arranged a congregational choral Communion at 9.45

followed by Mattins at 11. It is attended by about 30 who much appreciate it. But those who I thought would really be pleased practically ignore it altogether.

6. Number of Roman Catholics in the Parish. [*No response*].

1. See 1914.

ALBURY   Incumbent R.W.C. Hunt[1]

1. Number of Boys Girls and Infants on books of day schools: a. Last year. b. 20 30 or 40 years ago.

No. on Books

Year	Boys	Girls	Infants	Total
1918	15	17	9	41
1878	16	19	12	47
1888	14	15	10	39
1898	17	15	11	43

2. a. Men and b. Women qualified to vote in Parochial Church meeting. Four, but I was very ill about that time and could Do nothing. I hope to get a larger register this year – but we are singularly lacking in intelligent folk who will come to meetings, especially nowadays with so many men away.

3. Moral and Spiritual effect of: a. Wartime b. National Mission.

I see very little difference. The greater absorption of the men remaining, in agricultural work has made church going for them rather more difficult. I think that the spiritual life of not a few of my people has been deepened but I cannot say that either the War or the National Mission has touched those who were careless and indifferent before.

4. Status of Church Schools. Options for compromise on a. management, b. head teachers, c. character of religious teaching. Might compromise be justified by better arrangements for Church teaching in state schools?

I have no Nonconformist children here. On general grounds I am a strong believer in giving freedom for Nonconformist teaching in our schools – and I should welcome the admission of Nonconformists as managers, but I should deem it essential if the school is to be regarded as a church school – that the Head Teacher should be a Churchman and that the majority of managers should be Church men. I think it to be all important that we should try to come to terms with the Nonconformists on this matter, both as to Church Schools in single-school areas and as to all other schools, whether Church Schools or Council.

5 a. Changes in Public worship since 1914. b. Effects of the changes. a. Ever since the war broke out I have had Mattins (said) with Eucharist (choral except Kyrie) at Sunday at 11 with no break. The people have had a good deal of teaching about it and have learned to love it. The effect on the children has been most marked. They come most regularly whether they belong to the Sunday School or not. b. I have had Daily Eucharist (whenever I have been well enough) for nearly three years. It is much appreciated. This is a tiny place and save for the members of my own household the people have to come from Tiddington to Albury. I have only twice had to give up the Celebration because no one came there. Usually there are from six to fourteen daily – seven or eight would be about the average.

6. Number of Roman Catholics in the Parish. None.

1. See 1914.

ALVESCOT   Incumbent E. J. Hewlett[1]

1. Number of Boys Girls and Infants on books of day schools: a. Last year. About 63, half of whom are infants. **b. 20 30 or 40 years ago.** I have no trustworthy information.

2. a. Men and b. Women qualified to vote in Parochial Church meeting. We have no Parochial Church Meeting.

3. Moral and Spiritual effect of: a. Wartime b. National Mission.

(a) I have found that the people here attend their church very well on Sunday evenings. The attendance at special intercession services is spasmodic. I think the spiritual effect of the war shews itself in a deepening of the spiritual lives of those to whom religion was already a reality but the careless are apparently still careless. People have become more sober minded on the whole. There is an increased lack of discipline amongst the elder children. (b) I cannot say what effect the National Mission has had on the people here, as my experience of the parish is too limited.

4. Status of Church Schools. Options for compromise on a. management, b. head teachers, c. character of religious teaching. Might compromise be justified by better arrangements for Church teaching in state schools?

(a) Would only compromise to the extent of admitting in proportion to the number of Nonconformist children attending the School, Nonconformists as Managers. (b) I think the appointment of a headteacher to a Church School should invariably be Churchman or Woman. (c) I would strongly oppose any alteration in the religious teaching in a Church School – Nonconformists have their remedy in their right to keep their children away from religious instruction. To the last question, I would reply "No".

5 a. Changes in Public worship since 1914. b. Effects of the changes. (a) A Choral Eucharist is now provided on alternate Sundays. (b) The attendance at the Sung Eucharist is distinctly better than on the Sundays when Morning Prayer is sung.

6. Number of Roman Catholics in the Parish. None, to my knowledge.

1. Edward James Hewlett graduated AKC in 1897 and was ordained priest in 1899. After an initial curacy 1898–1905 he was Vicar of Christ Church Clapton between 1905 and 1917, when he became Rector of Alvescot. He was 54 in 1918 and at the 1911 census he was sharing a household with a student boarder, a widowed housekeeper and one other unmarried female servant.

AMBROSEDEN   Incumbent C. Bayfield[1]

1. Number of Boys Girls and Infants on books of day schools: a. Last year. Provided School. 30 boys, 16 girls, 11 infants. **b. 20 30 or 40 years ago.** 40 years ago, total 53. There is no trustworthy information as to numbers of boys, girls and infants.

2. a Men and b Women qualified to vote in Parochial Church meeting. 11

3. Moral and Spiritual effect of: a. Wartime b. National Mission.

(a) I have to meet arguments "How can there be a good God with so much suffering permitted", and also, I fear, "Perhaps there is no truth revealed or no God at all." (b) A few were led to think, but many seem to have not been touched by the National Mission.

4. Status of Church Schools. Options for compromise on a. management, b. head teachers, c. character of religious teaching. Might compromise be justified by better arrangements for Church teaching in state schools?

[*No response*].

5 a. Changes in Public worship since 1914. b. Effects of the changes. (a) None, unless sometimes at Evening Prayer substituting Intercessions for the State Prayers, the latter having been used at Morning Prayer. (b) None.

6. Number of Roman Catholics in the Parish. 1, a man (Irish). He is nominally a Roman Catholic, but does not object to anything in the Church of England except that he must take care lest he offend his priest.

1. See 1914.

ARDLEY   Incumbent H. G. Wheeler[1]

1. Number of Boys Girls and Infants on books of day schools: a. Last year. b. 20 30 or 40 years ago. No day schools at Ardley.

2. a Men and b Women qualified to vote in Parochial Church meeting. None; I hope to get a combined council for Ardley and Fewcott formed as soon as I return from the army.

3. Moral and Spiritual effect of: a. Wartime b. National Mission.

I only had three weeks in this parish before joining the army as CF.

4. Status of Church Schools. Options for compromise on a. management, b. head teachers, c. character of religious teaching. Might compromise be justified by better arrangements for Church teaching in state schools?

I have no clear views on these subjects.

5 a. Changes in Public worship since 1914. b. Effects of the changes. No changes since 1914.

6. Number of Roman Catholics in the Parish. None.

1. Henry George Wheeler was ordained priest in Honduras in 1900 and held cures in South America until 1902 when he became Curate of Selborne in Hampshire. After a further curacy in London he was Chaplain of the Boys Home in Kingham Hill between 1906 and 1917, when he became Rector of Ardley. He was 47 years old in 1918 and at the 1911 census he shared a household with his wife, three children under 5, and one unmarried female servant.

ASCOT-UNDER-WYCHWOOD   Incumbent C. Walford[1]

1. Number of Boys Girls and Infants on books of day schools: a. Last year. Boys 12, Girls 14, Infants 21 Total 47. **b. 20 30 or 40 years ago.** 34 years ago: Boys 26, Girls 29 Infants 34 Total 89.

2. a. Men and b. Women qualified to vote in Parochial Church meeting. 4 men, 9 women.

3. Moral and Spiritual effect of: a. Wartime b. National Mission.

[*No response*].

4. Status of Church Schools. Options for compromise on a. management, b. head teachers, c. character of religious teaching. Might compromise be justified by better arrangements for Church teaching in state schools?

[*No response*].

5 a. Changes in Public worship since 1914. b. Effects of the changes. [*No response*].

6. Number of Roman Catholics in the Parish. One woman.

My husband is too ill to fill this paper in. I have given information as far as I possibly can. [*Signed*] Julia Walford.

1. See 1914.

ASTHALL   Incumbent W. H. K. Ward[1]

1. Number of Boys Girls and Infants on books of day schools: a. Last year. Boys 13 Girls 8 Infants 8 Total 29. **b. 20 30 or 40 years ago.** Boys 11 Girls 18 Infants 14 Total 43 in 1899 the only record I can find.

2. a Men and b. Women qualified to vote in Parochial Church meeting. (a) 11 (b) 22.

3. Moral and Spiritual effect of: a. Wartime b. National Mission.

(a) For the most part, the parishioners live as if there was no war, or at any rate as if it did not concern themselves. The young women and girls I am glad to be able to say have in this parish with hardly an exception behaved well. (b) It is difficult at present to say what effect the National Mission has had. We can only hope that the leaven is working unseen. There has been a decided improvement in the number of communicants which is a more hopeful sign, but apart from this there is little show of renewed spiritual life.

4. Status of Church Schools. Options for compromise on a. management, b. head teachers, c. character of religious teaching. Might compromise be justified by better arrangements for Church teaching in state schools?

I do not see what changes could be made in the status of Church Schools without their ceasing to be Church Schools in everything but name. In my school I am quite willing for Ministers of other denominations coming in during the hours for Religious Instruction and giving the instruction they wish to the children of their own denomination. In this Parish there has never been any desire on the part of Nonconformist parents to withdraw their children from the Religious Instruction as given in the School: the only objection ever made was by Baptist parents who objected to their children being made to say the answers to the first portion of the Church Catechism, which was only natural and their wishes were at once complied with. The Management of the School is as follows:

(1) the Vicar (2) the churchwardens (3) one Manager co-opted by (1) and (2) (4) one appointed by the County Council (5) one by the Parish Council. These last two have for many years been Non-conformists, but all the Managers have worked together in perfect harmony. I do not see what change could be made. (b) I think not [*sic*] change could be accepted. It is absolutely essential that the Headteacher

should be a Churchman or a Churchwoman. (c) I do not think any compromise should be made.

5 a. Changes in Public worship since 1914. b. Effects of the changes. (a) No change in hours, but in the Chapel of Ease of St John the Evangelist Asthalleigh, at the Eucharist after Matins on the first Sunday in the month, when it had been customary to make a pause after the Prayer for the Church Militant and for non-intending communicants to go out, the Sermon has been dropped in order to shorten the service and the service taken without any pause. (b) I find by this change which was made with the New Year that we have a much larger number of communicants.

6. Number of Roman Catholics in the Parish. None.

1. See 1914.

ASTON, NORTH   Incumbent P. Walde[1]

1. Number of Boys Girls and Infants on books of day schools: a. Last year. b. 20 30 or 40 years ago.

	Mixed		Infants	
	Boys	Girls	Boys	Girls
(a) 1917	5	8	3	6
(b) 1891	29	28	14	8

(earliest available record.)

2. a. Men and b. Women qualified to vote in Parochial Church meeting. (a) Men 34, (b) Women 57.

3. Moral and Spiritual effect of: a. Wartime b. National Mission.

(a) <u>Wartime</u> (i) <u>People of Education and Position</u> These are few in number in this parish. The spiritual effect of bereavement and anxiety, and the necessary curtailment of pleasure and amusement has, I should say, been markedly good. Sympathy and serious thought are the rule: attendance at church is not affected. (ii) <u>Labouring Classes</u> In this case I cannot see the same good result: "War-troubles" seem to have a depressing rather than an awakening effect: while "War-prosperity" seems to be in every way most unsettling, especially among the young people who are quite out of control. (b) <u>National Mission</u> The National Mission was over before my arrival in the Parish. Owing to the continued illness of my predecessor (the Rev H. R. A. Wilson), I understand that very little was attempted; and I cannot trace any definite results.

4. Status of Church Schools. Options for compromise on a. management, b. head teachers, c. character of religious teaching. Might compromise be justified by better arrangements for Church teaching in state schools?

This is my first experience of a single-school area: the school is very small; there is no Dissent in the place and no contentious questions have yet arisen. I do not feel qualified to give definite answers to points of detail; but should imagine that an offer of more satisfactory conditions in "Provided" schools would justify any reasonable concessions in Church single-school areas.

5 a. Changes in Public worship since 1914. b. Effects of the changes. No changes to report, the services are fairly-well attended on ordinary occasions; special services (held as in former years) are as a rule very-well attended.

6. Number of Roman Catholics in the Parish. 1 woman 1 child (Belgian refugees).

P.S. I must apologise for the delay in making this return due (as already stated) to serious illness.

1. Cornelius Paul Walde graduated from New College Oxford in 1896 and trained at Ridley Hall Cambridge in 1897, being ordained priest in 1900. He held three curacies in London between 1899 and 1915 and was appointed as Vicar of North Aston in 1917. He was 45 years of age in 1918 and at the 1911 census he was unmarried and shared a household with his unmarried sister.

ASTON, STEEPLE   Incumbent F. J. Brown[1]

1. Number of Boys Girls and Infants on books of day schools:

a. Last year.	Mixed School	62,	Infants	28
b. 20 30 or 40 years ago.	1898	101		66
	1878	77		60

2. a. Men and b. Women qualified to vote in Parochial Church meeting. (a) 24 (b) 43.

3. Moral and Spiritual effect of: a. Wartime b. National Mission.

(a) The strain of the war time has told on all classes. Those with fixed incomes are pinched; the rise of wages and the army allowances coming to so many houses do not keep down discontent. Though the local Education Committee keeps a strict look out our Boys taken from school for farm labour the services of children are in great request with consequences as to discipline which may easily be imagined. The aerodrome at Upper Heyford, two miles away, is making all labour questions more difficult already and I fear for what may happen with regard to young and flighty girls.

(b) I cannot report any great results. There was an effect in certain quarters which I hope may be maintained. But it is the day of small things in the way of holding on. I hope we are doing that. We have 20 candidates for Confirmation – a rather larger number than usual and we get about 25 people for a weeknight Lenten service in spite of the bad weather. That is not a falling off. Our Christmas communicants were as many as in 1916, though one house with at least 6 communicants in it was closed, and another with 3 communicants, had changed hands to nominal Presbyterians who go nowhere.

4. Status of Church Schools. Options for compromise on a. management, b. head teachers, c. character of religious teaching. Might compromise be justified by better arrangements for Church teaching in state schools?

I have known intimately only 2 schools since 1872 i.e. St Philip & St James Oxford and this and I do not wish to be the "Chimera bombinans in vacuo".[2] In neither of these schools was there any difficulty with Nonconformists as regards (a) (b) and (c). In this parish we have a Nonconformist Manager and we have had from time to time since 1904 a Nonconformist teacher on the staff.

If I may say so it is a begging of the question to speak of "Management", the Managers only carry out the requirements of the Education Authority after appointing Head Teachers and arranging the character of the religious teaching. Still I suppose some compromise is inevitable. But how, it is not for me with my narrow experience to say.

5 a. Changes in Public worship since 1914. b. Effects of the changes. I have not seen my way to make any changes since 1914. The Report of the Diocesan Mission Council I hope to speak of at the forthcoming Parochial Church Meeting.

6. Number of Roman Catholics in the Parish. None. In my incumbency from 1897, there has been one family of RCs and one domestic servant.

1. See 1914.
2. Literally a Chimera buzzing in a vacuum – implying, in this case, making a worthless comment.

ASTON ROWANT — Incumbent G. Dangerfield[1]

1. Number of Boys Girls and Infants on books of day schools: a. Last year. b. 20 30 or 40 years ago.

(a) 54. (b) In 1893 according to the Log Book there was an <u>average</u> attendance of about 65. No earlier record. In 1900 there were 90 children on the books.

2. a. Men and b. Women qualified to vote in Parochial Church meeting. a. 21. b. 41.

Circumstances (of which the Archdeacon is cognisant and about which I asked his advice) have prevented my forming a Parochial Church Council much as I wish to. Consequently there is no great interest in the Roll of Qualified Electors.

3. Moral and Spiritual effect of: a. Wartime b. National Mission.

(a) I came here soon after the war began so am not properly qualified to compare the condition of the Parish now with its pre-war condition. Two things I feel sure of 1. That the Spirit of Prayer is more fully realised in the parish. Parishioners come readily to any special services for prayer and <u>feel</u> what it means to be praying together. 2. That the Spirit of Self-sacrifice is growing. I have to judge by collections made in church and these have been steadily increasing whatever their object. In spite of the fact that we live at a lower ebb in these villages and are without most of our bellringers – Choirmen etc there is no falling off in the spiritual life as evidenced by attendance at Sacramental and other services. People's faith seems strengthened rather than weakened.

(b) No result whatever as far as the spiritual life of the parish is concerned. We had a very good and holy man to conduct special services but one altogether unfitted to stir people up or make them realise that a new movement was beginning. Consequently the attendance at the services tailed off (nearly every communicant made his or her communion at the time) and an impression was left but one of disappointment, for there had been a great deal of preparation.

4. Status of Church Schools. Options for compromise on a. management, b. head teachers, c. character of religious teaching. Might compromise be justified by better arrangements for Church teaching in state schools?

I feel very strongly that we should do everything possible to help forward the new scheme of education and to make it as uniform as possible that it may be the more easily worked.

For that object we should be prepared to give up our Church schools to be run on the same lines, with regard to management and the appointment of head-teachers, as "Provided" Schools. But we should insist with all the force at our disposal that there should be some guarantee of real religious teaching at the <u>beginning</u> of each school day. And further we should endeavour to secure the right of entry of qualified teachers into the school to give definite denominational teaching to children whose parents desire it. Such qualified teachers would naturally include the Clergy and Ministers of other denominations. It should thus become one of the <u>first</u> duties of the Parish Priest to instruct the children in the day school and to see that Church people claim their right to have their children thus instructed. I do not yet understand what the "more satisfactory conditions of religious teaching in "Provided" schools" may mean but I would support the surrender of a great deal that we have held in the past to further the new plans for education if only I could be sure that some real religious teaching would be given in the first hour of the school day.

5 a. Changes in Public worship since 1914. b. Effects of the changes. I have endeavoured to introduce a Choral Celebration of the Holy Eucharist as the service for Sunday. To this end I held such services at 9.30 am two Sundays in the month. I found that the old-fashioned and very regular parishioners simply could not understand the point of view though I did all I could to make it clear. Consequently I have given up one of the Sundays and have Choral Celebration on 2nd Sunday at 10 am (the half hour made a great deal of difference) with Sermon. Mattins and Litany are said plain at 11.30. (b) Many parishioners very greatly value the Choral Celebration though quite a new service to them and appreciate the object of the change. We have always a very nice service. The old-fashioned people have had a point conceded to them and are very little interfered with. The service as The Service is kept before people's minds and the Sunday School children come to it better than to morning Sunday School, and behave excellently without supervision.

6. Number of Roman Catholics in the Parish. None.

1. George Dangerfield (formerly Bubb) graduated from Worcester College Oxford in 1895 and trained at Wells Theological College in 1896, being ordained priest in 1898. He served four curacies between 1897 and 1914, when he was appointed as Vicar of Aston Rowant. He was 45 years of age in 1918 and at the 1911 census he shared a household with his wife, three children under 12, and two unmarried female servants.

BALDON, MARSH WITH TOOT   Incumbent H. A. Goodwin[1]

1. Number of Boys Girls and Infants on books of day schools:

a. Last year. Marsh Baldon 1917 = 39. Toot Baldon = 30.

b. 20 30 or 40 years ago. Marsh Baldon 1897 = 50 Toot Baldon 1899 = 70; 1880 = 41.

2. a. Men and b. Women qualified to vote in Parochial Church meeting. (a) 3 (b) 2.

3. Moral and Spiritual effect of: a. Wartime b. National Mission.

I cannot perceive any decided moral or spiritual effects. The congregations at Marsh Baldon are larger, those at Toot Baldon smaller.

4. Status of Church Schools. Options for compromise on a. management, b. head teachers, c. character of religious teaching. Might compromise be justified by better arrangements for Church teaching in state schools?

I have experienced no difficulties in the management of the Church Schools in these Villages. The religious difficulty does not exist. We have a non-conformist on the committee and the Teacher would allow a child to be withdrawn from the Religious Instruction if a parent desired it. But no such request has ever been made.

I do not think any non-churchman could reasonably wish for greater consideration or for more generous treatment than that already granted.

I have had to elect new Head Teachers for Marsh Baldon School during my stay here. My committee gave me a free hand in the appointment. I think it essential that all Church Schools should have members of the Church of England as Head Teachers.

The only nonconformists here are two farmers, both of whom attend Church with more or less regularity. My opinion is that if extreme teaching can be kept out of the Day Schools, a good deal of the opposition to Church Teaching will vanish after the War. Parents should be allowed to make a statement, if they wish that their children should not receive distinct church teaching.

5 a. Changes in Public worship since 1914. b. Effects of the changes. None.

6. Number of Roman Catholics in the Parish. None.

1. See 1914.

BAMPTON PROPER Incumbent G. E. C. Rodwell[1]

1. Number of Boys Girls and Infants on books of day schools: a. Last year. December 1917: Boys 53 Girls 55 Infants 54. **b. 20 30 or 40 years ago.** December 1877: Boys 61 Girls 72 Infants 85.

2. a. Men and b. Women qualified to vote in Parochial Church meeting. Men 22, Women 37.

3. Moral and Spiritual effect of: a. Wartime b. National Mission.

Amongst most a desire to work more than hitherto. A considerable growth of the spirit of enmity and faction and want of consideration: a blunting of finer feelings. A new element in the parish of almost open immorality in the case of soldiers wives and women who have come in from outside. A precocity and wilfulness among older boys and girls. A deep subcurrent of impatience at the war expressing itself in the senseless phrase "Let those who made it go and fight it, I say,"

(b) I can see no outward result of the mission: but I have reason to believe that private prayer is more real than formerly in many cases either as an effect of (a) or (b). People are certainly more ready to speak about their intercessory prayer: and ask for services of a mission type: and are ready to come together for such services. I believe that sung Mattins and Evensong are now not the best adapted services for the poor in country places except for those long habituated to them: or to those engaged in singing them. As the oldest people die off it happens in the country places I know that the church becomes void of agricultural labouring men. Communicants have not increased during the war: but this may be owing to the absence of many of the young who made up the bulk of our communicants.

4. Status of Church Schools. Options for compromise on a. management, b. head teachers, c. character of religious teaching. Might compromise be justified by better arrangements for Church teaching in state schools?

I can only speak from experience here. The present status is satisfactory to me and I believe to practically all the Parishioners. The Nonconformists appear to be quite satisfied practically, but have a theoretical grievance which they might possibly in a few cases emphasize in obedience to their leaders. Great consideration is paid to such of the Managers as are Nonconformists. The question of appointment of head-teachers has not come up in my experience and I do not know what attitude would be taken: but I do not think it would be against the present system. No children are withdrawn from religious instruction. There appears to be no objection here whatever to teaching that is strictly scriptural and on Prayer Book lines. If the clergy instead taught their personal fancies, there probably would be trouble. Dissent here, – as in a parish in which I took a Mission – is not so much a matter of doctrine as of vested interests in the one side and preference for a simpler kind of service on the other.

5 a. Changes in Public worship since 1914. b. Effects of the changes. I have made none, and after consulting the Church Parochial Council I do not see that any can satisfactorily be made. The hours of service depend on the hours of meals and (in the evening) the hours of work have some influence. I believe that in the mind of people the Holy Communion at 8 am is far and away now the Principal Service of the day although it is the least noisy, or perhaps because it is the least noisy.

6. Number of Roman Catholics in the Parish. None. There have only been two in the last twelve years.

1. See 1914.

BAMPTON ASTON AND COTE   Incumbent N. Germon[1]

1. Number of Boys Girls and Infants on books of day schools: a. Last year. December 31st 1917 Boys 37 Girls 48 Infants 36 Total 121. **b. 20 30 or 40 years ago.** December 31st 1897 Boys 53 Girls 34 Infants 48 Total 155.

2. a. Men and b. Women qualified to vote in Parochial Church meeting. 20 men, 30 Women.

3. Moral and Spiritual effect of: a. Wartime b. National Mission.

I cannot see that either the war or the National Mission have effected any appreciable change, moral or spiritual, in the life and habits of the people in the parish.

4. Status of Church Schools. Options for compromise on a. management, b. head teachers, c. character of religious teaching. Might compromise be justified by better arrangements for Church teaching in state schools?

I think that we should seek to maintain Church Schools in their present status, but I would give facilities to the children of Nonconformists for receiving the Religious teaching their parents desire. The appointment of head-teachers should certainly remain as it is.

5 a. Changes in Public worship since 1914. b. Effects of the changes. The only change I have made is that at Evensong after taking the Office to the 3rd Collect, and after a hymn and the Sermon, I have on many occasions conducted from the pulpit a short service of Intercession which I have reason to believe has been found helpful.

6. Number of Roman Catholics in the Parish. None.

1. See 1914.

BANBURY   Incumbent A. J. Jones[1]

1. Number of Boys Girls and Infants on books of day schools: a. Last year. b. 20 30 or 40 years ago.

(a) <u>Boys</u> 233 <u>Girls</u> 197 <u>Infants</u> 155 at S. Mary's C. of E. school – the only day-school in this Parish.

(b) <u>Boys</u> 159 (1889) <u>Girls</u> 194 (1904) <u>Infants</u> 201 (1906) These are the earliest available records.

2. a. Men and b. Women qualified to vote in Parochial Church meeting. (a) men 154 (b) women 234.

3. Moral and Spiritual effect of: a. Wartime b. National Mission.

<u>Wartime</u>. (i) <u>Moral effect.</u> A noticeable feature has been the slackening of discipline among children, owing principally to the absence of their fathers and elder brothers, and to the feeling of change and unrest which prevails, also to improved financial circumstances in many cases. There have been many sad cases of unfaithfulness among soldiers' wives, and the downfall of some of them is directly traceable to drinking habits. The atmosphere of war has conduced to a lowering of moral standards in some respects and an easier condonation of moral lapses. The greater freedom of intercourse between the sexes which the changed conditions of war work has brought about has inevitably led, but not so widely as was feared, to a loss of refinement and to a coarser tone. On the other hand, the war has provoked a very wonderful growth of the spirit of national service and there is an undeniable readiness of generosity which is evoked not only in response to war claims, but by almost any appeal of a charitable or religious nature. There are growing evidences too, as the war drags on, of a sterner and more resolute note in the national character, and of a more appreciable sense of the inevitableness of the revaluation of old values brought about by the war.

(ii) <u>Spiritual effect.</u> While it is impossible to say that this war has "brought the nation to its knees", or that there has been any apparent sort of correspondence between the call of the war and the increase of spirituality, yet I have certainly remarked in this Parish a very definite advance in the practice of corporate intercession and a very evident interest awakened in the truths which are bound up with belief in the Communion of Saints and the Resurrection of the Body, and while, no doubt, owing to the claims and strains of war work, week day services are scarcely so well attended as before the war, I am bound to say that I have never seen such large Sunday congregations in the twelve years I have been in Banbury as are now assembling.

(b) <u>The National Mission.</u> Being embedded in the great war, and in a great measure, springing out of it, it is extremely difficult to separate its results, even in thought, from those of the war itself. All that I am able to say at the present moment of the effects of the National Mission, so far as this Parish is concerned, is that they are not of a general but of a circumscribed character, except of course so far as the influence of a comparatively few is bound to be widely diffused. The National Mission certainly gave those whom its appeal reached, furiously to think, and that, as a preliminary step, is of inestimable value, and will in due time undoubtedly lead to the measures which follow the awakening of the conscience informed as to the way of passive acquiescence. But in this Parish, the effect, educative, moral and spiritual, upon a small band of about fifty men and women, was really quite striking, and while, in the main, the National Mission, was from the essential nature of things, disappointing in its measurable issues, the normal influence of this small band on an ever widening circle, is a result for which we must be profoundly thankful.

4. Status of Church Schools. Options for compromise on a. management, b. head teachers, c. character of religious teaching. Might compromise be justified by better arrangements for Church teaching in state schools?

I am inclined to suggest that the best working theory as a contribution towards the solution of a most thorny question lies in the direction of the nationalization of all public elementary schools. There should be representation of the parents of the children on the Committee of Management. In every school there should be definite and rigid provision made for religious instruction during the first hour by accredited teachers according to the faith of the parents. In every parish the head-teachers should confer with representatives of the various religious bodies with a view to enlisting their co-operation. No lesson of a religious character should be given by a teacher who does not believe what he is to teach, and no lesson shall be given by a teacher of one denomination to children of another. This would necessitate the re-grouping of staff in many schools. The children of secularist parents would be given some secular work during the first hour. The work of religious teaching in the elementary schools would in most cases devolve upon the clergy and the school staff; but every Parish Priest should be prepared to welcome, and make concessions for, and eagerly grasp, the opportunity of imparting daily instruction to the children of his faith in whatever elementary school they may happen to be.

5 a. Changes in Public worship since 1914. b. Effects of the changes. a) The only change in methods of public worship since the last Return relates to Sunday Evensong. The Sunday Evening Service Book compiled by Mr Iremonger has been in use for about two years. The only change in hours of public worship are (i) the alteration of time of the childrens' Sunday Catechism from 3 pm to 2:30; and (ii) an occasional choral Eucharist at 9:30 am i.e. four or five times a year, as an experiment which is still under observation. (b) (i) the nine Litanies in the Sunday Evening Service Book are much appreciated, and I think that they supply an evident need. (ii) The earlier hour for the Sunday afternoon catechism is popular with the teachers, as it enables them to take a longer walk afterwards. (iii) The 9:30 am Choral Eucharist is quite well attended: though many contend that household arrangements make the time an exceeding difficult one. Although earlier Eucharists are provided, the majority communicate at 9:30. Still I am satisfied that the only thing to do is to go on making experiments in this very difficult parish.

6. Number of Roman Catholics in the Parish. The resident Roman Catholic priest, Father Brabazon, tells me that he has lent his book containing the names of his flock so that at present he is not able to say what the number of men, women, and children, is respectively. But he states that the number of souls under his care in Banbury is 852.

1. See 1914.

BANBURY, SOUTH   Incumbent J. E. Smith-Masters[1]

1. Number of Boys Girls and Infants on books of day schools: a. Last year. b. 20 30 or 40 years ago.

Church Schools (a) Boys and Girls 264 Infants 104.

(b) 1884 Boys and Girls 216 Infants 102 (records go back only 11 years).

Council and R.C. (a) Boys, Girls and Infants about 1312 these schools have only been opened some ten years.

2. a. Men and b. Women qualified to vote in Parochial Church meeting. Men 38, Women 42.

3. Moral and Spiritual effect of: a. Wartime b. National Mission.

The effects of (a) and (b) seem to be largely interwoven. The general effect on the faithful has been to deepen their spiritual life, to make them more serious, and to draw them to more frequent and regular Communion. Others have been drawn in, and become more regular in worship and Communion. But a large number have been left almost untouched, especially amongst boys and girls, who have tended to become generally undisciplined, except those who come under the influence of the

C.L.B., Scouts, and G.F.S. The war has made the pressure of work so heavy, that for the most part only those people who had already some strength of character have been able to maintain their religious balance at all satisfactorily. So many weaker characters have made the strain of things an excuse for less observance of religion and so have missed the support which was ready for them. The Headmaster of the Church Day School reports that "with many of the scholars there is a decided improvement of disposition towards one another. The children are much more sympathetic and show a finer tone and are not nearly so superficial. They think more deeply."

4. Status of Church Schools. Options for compromise on a. management, b. head teachers, c. character of religious teaching. Might compromise be justified by better arrangements for Church teaching in state schools?

Church Schools in single-schools areas should retain their present status as regards (a), (b), and (c). But Non-conformists should be offered facilities for sending accredited teachers to give religious teaching to their children on (say) two days a week, or, failing that, the parents should be invited to say whether they wish their children to receive instruction in Bible, Prayer Book and Catechism, from the Clergy and Day School Teachers, or in Bible only from the Day School teachers. Church children in Council Schools should receive like privileges.

5 a. Changes in Public worship since 1914. b. Effects of the changes. Sung Eucharist made the chief Service of Sunday morning. The result – a congregation increasing in numbers and devotion in both the Parish Church and District Church. In both Churches Mission Services in Lent both last year and this on week-day afternoons and evenings have been largely appreciated. Mission Services with instructions at St Leonard's Church on Sunday evenings this Lent have attracted growing congregations.

6. Number of Roman Catholics in the Parish. This parish only having existed for 67 years, this question will be answered for the town by the Vicar of Banbury.

1. John Ernest Smith-Masters graduated from Keble College Oxford in 1880 and was ordained priest in 1881. After an initial curacy 1880–85, he was Vicar of Tylehurst 1885–89, Kidmore End 1889–1906 and then of Stewkley between 1906 and 1915, when he was appointed as Vicar of South Banbury. He was Rural Dean of Mursley between 1912 and 1915. He was 61 years of age in 1918 and at the 1911 census he was sharing a household with his wife, his 20-year-old son and two unmarried female servants.

BARFORD ST MICHAEL   Incumbent A. C. Highton[1]

1. Number of Boys Girls and Infants on books of day schools: a. Last year. b. 20 30 or 40 years ago.

1917 Av = 46, about 12 come from Kempton 20 infants, boys 22, girls 24 1875 Av = 35 1885 Av = 64 1898 Av =95 None of the children came from Kempton in those days.

2. a. Men and b. Women qualified to vote in Parochial Church meeting. Before the war I had a social evening for Communicants at Easter, when discussion was invited on church matters. I have no parochial council in its stricter meaning.

3. Moral and Spiritual effect of: a. Wartime b. National Mission.

I can find in our parish no instance of conversion as the effect of either the one or the other. Those that were holy are holy still, those who were unholy are unholy still. The men from the front who were communicants before they went, take their communion when on leave. The war seems to have made but little religious impression on the others, judging outwardly. Both at the national and the sisters mission the services were well attended. The former was more in the form of a parochial seven days retreat, though out of door services were held also. The spiritual life I hope was deepened of those that attended. 75 per cent of the men at the front are said to be churchmen. The officers speak highly on the whole of their character, which says something for our schools, though their highest spiritual life may lack development. The people have the Incarnation, the Church and the Bible and Christian teaching in the Church Schools at any rate, if they are not converted by these means, it is not likely that war, pestilence or famine should convert them, nor if one rose from the dead, as one has indeed risen.

4. Status of Church Schools. Options for compromise on a. management, b. head teachers, c. character of religious teaching. Might compromise be justified by better arrangements for Church teaching in state schools?

I think we must take in consideration (1) that church schools in single school areas have been built by Church-Funds, they are kept in repair by the same means, the state is allowed the use of them free of cost, though it neither built them nor pays anything towards the upkeep of the fabric. (2) that council schools are paid for not by dissenters only but by churchmen also. The teaching in them is along dissenting lines. All the teachers in a church school, in my opinion should be elected by the managers. It is fatal for a child's mind to be taught by teachers who differ in what they teach. At the same time, if the parents of 12 children at least wish for nonconformist teaching, and there is a separate classroom for the purpose, a nonconformist minister or teacher might be admitted say twice or three times a week, if the same privilege was granted to churchmen in council schools. The question remains whether the noncon. teachers should pay something for the privilege, as they pay nothing towards the upkeep as churchmen do in the case of council schools. There are two dissenters on our management of 5. The older children attend a communion service once a month on a weekday only one child is withdrawn out of 45 and none from the religious teaching.

5 a. Changes in Public worship since 1914. b. Effects of the changes. Twice a month I have a celebration at 11 o'clock on Sundays without matins, but with a short sermon. There is I know an increase of communicants. I have also a weekday celebration for children at 9 o'c once a month. The children like to come, and there are often some adults also. The teachers usually communicate at this service.

6. Number of Roman Catholics in the Parish. None.

1. See 1914.

BARTON, STEEPLE   Incumbent S. Stephen[1]

1. Number of Boys Girls and Infants on books of day schools: a. Last year. b. 20 30 or 40 years ago. [*No response*].

2. a. Men and b. Women qualified to vote in Parochial Church meeting. [*No response*].

3. Moral and Spiritual effect of: a. Wartime b. National Mission.

Spirit of self-sacrifice, brotherliness, docility, humility, discipline, interest in the life of the community.

4. Status of Church Schools. Options for compromise on a. management, b. head teachers, c. character of religious teaching. Might compromise be justified by better arrangements for Church teaching in state schools?

Retain in places where all the inhabitants belong to the Church. In other place[s], were it impossible to retain them, it depends on the nature of the rapid development and changes of events which point to vast improvement to the better in the relations of the Church and Nonconformity.

5 a. Changes in Public worship since 1914. b. Effects of the changes. Evening Communion Evangelical teaching. Considerable accessions to Holy Communion. Especially among the poor zeal kindled for Foreign Missions, reading of the Word of God; increase of devotion to the Person of Our Lord, personal religion; increase of faith, hope and charity, purity, temperance, strength of character, deeper spirituality, power of the Holy Spirit.

6. Number of Roman Catholics in the Parish. One married couple. One woman.

1. See 1914.

BARTON WESTCOT   Incumbent C. R. Tyrwhitt[1]

1. Number of Boys Girls and Infants on books of day schools: a. Last year. Twelve at Steeple Barton these go to Sandford St Martin. **b. 20 30 or 40 years ago.** No very exact information.

2. a. Men and b. Women qualified to vote in Parochial Church meeting. None.

3. Moral and Spiritual effect of: a. Wartime b. National Mission.

No very appreciable difference in church attendances can be reported as the result in either case. There is perhaps some sign of weariness in regard to attendance at Intercession Services. There is sign of greater independence of spirit in some cases of persons who have for various reasons returned to the parish after absence for considerable periods. This has not perhaps made them easier to deal with.

4. Status of Church Schools. Options for compromise on a. management, b. head teachers, c. character of religious teaching. Might compromise be justified by better arrangements for Church teaching in state schools?

[*No response*].

5 a. Changes in Public worship since 1914. b. Effects of the changes. As a result of the Mission effort some few of the leading parishioners were consulted as to change of hour of service on Sundays in part with a view to making H.C. more definitely the chief service. It has not seemed possible to advocate to change the present arrangement.

6. Number of Roman Catholics in the Parish. None.

1. See 1914.

BECKLEY Incumbent J. K. Smith[1]

1. Number of Boys Girls and Infants on books of day schools: a. Last year. 44. b. 20 30 or 40 years ago. Between 90 and 100: but 20 of those were children in Waifs and Strays Home then existing at Beckley.

2. a. Men and b. Women qualified to vote in Parochial Church meeting. Have not yet felt able to ask for such signatures at Beckley.

3. Moral and Spiritual effect of: a. Wartime b. National Mission.

It is impossible to say. At first I felt that the National Mission had left no impression on Beckley. As to the war, I am not in a position to say. I do not think much. But I am beginning to feel that there is going on a deepening of spiritual life in the really earnest and devout church people at Beckley, as evinced by more frequent communions: more regular and frequent attendance at the services: and an increasing heartiness and cooperation. It would be impossible to divide this between the above-mentioned causes and other cooperative causes. Perhaps all have their share.

In regard to some very few individual instances and these are of more wealthy class. I am afraid that the long war has had a hardening and repelling effect as to the religious spirit. This, however, may be only in a greater visibility rather than a greater degree of actual reality. It may have been there before, but less manifested.

4. Status of Church Schools. Options for compromise on a. management, b. head teachers, c. character of religious teaching. Might compromise be justified by better arrangements for Church teaching in state schools?

As regards (a) yes. Not as regards (b) or (c). The religious difficulty is not felt at all in this parish. No children are 'withdrawn'. This is largely due to the long tenure of office of the present Head teacher (30 years) perhaps also, in a measure, – though I am not inclined to think this – to the impossibility under present circumstances of a more active participation by the parish priest in the teaching. The whole of the children within fair reach, attend Sunday School. In a previous parish, the question on one occasion did come forward. I made an offer to the Wesleyan authorities at Witney, who had a Chapel at Minister Lovell, to allow a representative to take a class of Wesleyan children, who might wish to avail themselves of the opportunity. Nothing came of it: the question was dropped and did not recur. Such experience as I have is that in small country parishes the 'Religious difficulty' is not felt at all.

5 a. Changes in Public worship since 1914. b. Effects of the changes. Owing to the Vicar of Beckley being also Vicar of Horton-cum-Studley, some services have had to be dropped. There is a Sunday H.C. at 8 and after Matt. alternately. Evensong during the six winter months is at 3: the people so preferring. Services during the week and on Saints' Days have had to cease – except occasionally, and in Lent. I do not find any noticeable loss or decrease. The regular are very regular. The collections have, if anything, increased – especially if viewed proportionally to the number of services. The serving of the men in the Army have, of course, reduced the number of communicants – especially at the great Feasts. But not otherwise. During the winter the attendance of men is very difficult and scarce. It is better during the summer in the evenings, but not so much as to suggest a change. The lighting difficulty also comes in.

6. Number of Roman Catholics in the Parish. None.

1. See 1914 Minster Lovell.

BEGBROKE   Incumbent A. H. Gillmor[1]

1. Number of Boys Girls and Infants on books of day schools: a. Last year. b. 20 30 or 40 years ago.

There is no <u>Day</u> school in this parish, and there has not been one for over forty years.

2. a. Men and b. Women qualified to vote in Parochial Church meeting. Eleven men, fourteen women.

3. Moral and Spiritual effect of: a. Wartime b. National Mission.

I have not observed any marked difference as the result of wartime. As regards the National Mission there has been I think more regular attendance by some at the Holy Communion.

4. Status of Church Schools. Options for compromise on a. management, b. head teachers, c. character of religious teaching. Might compromise be justified by better arrangements for Church teaching in state schools?

If the schools could be retained in their present status it would I think be for the benefit of the Church. I am opposed to compromise.

5 a. Changes in Public worship since 1914. b. Effects of the changes. The Litany at 10.15 o'c is a separate service on the Sundays when Holy Eucharist is at 11 o'c: on the other Sundays, the Litany at the usual hours. Owing to difficulties in darkening windows Evensong on Sundays in winter at 3 o'c. On Easter Day Evensong will be resumed at 6.30 o'c. The attendance at the earlier hour much the same as at the later. I prefer the later Evensong, but the earlier hour is of course only temporary.

6. Number of Roman Catholics in the Parish. So far as I can ascertain there are about 34 Roman Catholics 4 men, 5 women and 25 children. Most of these children are pupils resident at the Priory, some additional ones came lately. All the Roman Catholics came from outside the Parish. In 1898 the old Manor House was bought by Roman Catholics and turned into a "Priory". Previous to 1898 there were never any Roman Catholics in this Parish. My predecessor found the Roman Catholics at the Priory very unpleasant and undesirable neighbours, which has been my experience also for the last 9 years.

1. See 1914.

BICESTER   Incumbent W. O'Reilly[1]

1. Number of Boys Girls and Infants on books of day schools: a. Last year. Boys 130, Girls 137, Infants 129. **b. 20 30 or 40 years ago.** I can find no record by which to answer. In the Log Book of the Girls' School in the year 1873 there are records of two separate examinations of the whole school, the numbers present being respectively 80 and 76.

2. a. Men and b. Women qualified to vote in Parochial Church meeting. 39 men, 63 women.

3. Moral and Spiritual effect of: a. Wartime b. National Mission.

The shortage of labour and at times the presence of troops billeted in this town have made a good deal of difference to the congregation; the alms have fallen off by about ⅙. On some few the effect has been to make them more regular at church. It has had a bad effect on the boys, they have got out of hand partly owing to want of control at home, and partly to the fact that so many of them are engaged in work.

b) The National Mission attracted a large number of people at the time, especially to war services on the Sunday: but so far as I can judge it had very little effect on the majority. The number of communicants increased slightly: some coming who had lapsed for some years.

4. Status of Church Schools. Options for compromise on a. management, b. head teachers, c. character of religious teaching. Might compromise be justified by better arrangements for Church teaching in state schools?

If we can have the entry into all "Provided" Schools for teaching the <u>faith of the Church</u>, I think that a compromise might be justified. But the appointment of Head Teachers should be retained and restricted to a church man. An Assistant Teacher who was a Nonconformist might be permitted: and I should give Nonconformist Ministers the right of entry, if we had it in "Provided" Schools. I do not know exactly what the demands of the N.U.T. are; but so far as this parish is concerned there seems to be no religious difficulty. Hardly any of the Dissenting children are withdrawn from the Religious Teaching.

5 a. Changes in Public worship since 1914. b. Effects of the changes. There have been no changes.

6. Number of Roman Catholics in the Parish. The Roman Priest tells me that there are 72.

1. See 1914.

BINSEY   Incumbent C. A. Heurtley[1]

1. Number of Boys Girls and Infants on books of day schools: a. Last year. b. 20 30 or 40 years ago. The Parish has no school.

2. a. Men and b. Women qualified to vote in Parochial Church meeting. The parish is so small – at the present time not more than 32 adults (14 houses) – that we were content last year to appoint at the Easter vestry our Churchwarden as the lay Representative for the Parish – he being almost the only person available – and we propose to adopt the same procedure this year.

3. Moral and Spiritual effect of: a. Wartime b. National Mission.

I cannot report any change.

4. Status of Church Schools. Options for compromise on a. management, b. head teachers, c. character of religious teaching. Might compromise be justified by better arrangements for Church teaching in state schools?

[*No response*].

5 a. Changes in Public worship since 1914. b. Effects of the changes. No change.

6. Number of Roman Catholics in the Parish. One family of 4 persons.

1. See 1914.

BIX   Incumbent C. W. Formby[1]

1. Number of Boys Girls and Infants on books of day schools: a. Last year. 23 Boys, 20 girls, 18 Infants. **b. 20 30 or 40 years ago.** No records existing.

2. a. Men and b. Women qualified to vote in Parochial Church meeting. None. I tried to arouse some interest in the matter 3 years ago but it proved very difficult. Since then the subject has been in abeyance. Another attempt will be made this year.

3. Moral and Spiritual effect of: a. Wartime b. National Mission.

It is extremely difficult to find definite evidence of any lasting effect. Parents of those on active service seem to be aroused for a time but do not appear able to continue to sustain their efforts. The general pressure of work is against more regular attendance at church just now. No doubt some good effect has been produced by (a) and (b) but it has not produced marked outward results. The war has affected the young men eligible or becoming eligible for service more than any others.

4. Status of Church Schools. Options for compromise on a. management, b. head teachers, c. character of religious teaching. Might compromise be justified by better arrangements for Church teaching in state schools?

Any change in the present status however small might prove the edge of the wedge for other changes for which the present is a bad time. After the war the whole question could be dealt with. A better light would be available then for seeing the way things ought to move. At the same time no moment is too early for any safe step towards co-operation with Non-conformists. Probably any changes now would arouse again the old points of contention.

5 a. Changes in Public worship since 1914. b. Effects of the changes. Afternoon Service and Evening Service in Parish Room was tried but found to be a failure. The omission of State Prayers in the evening in favour of War Prayers appears to be an acceptable change.

6. Number of Roman Catholics in the Parish. 4 men 4 women 1 child.

1. See 1914.

BLACKBOURTON   Incumbent H. O. Shore[1]

1. Number of Boys Girls and Infants on books of day schools: a. Last year. 45. **b. 20 30 or 40 years ago.** 53.

2. a. Men and b. Women qualified to vote in Parochial Church meeting. [*No response*].

3. Moral and Spiritual effect of: a. Wartime b. National Mission.

Not very much to report. Those who have relations at the front come regularly to the intercession services – others very irregularly. All are most willing to work for Red Cross and come on Special Intercession Sundays. (b) Grieve to state that though attendance at mission services were good the permanent result is practically nil.

4. Status of Church Schools. Options for compromise on a. management, b. head teachers, c. character of religious teaching. Might compromise be justified by better arrangements for Church teaching in state schools?

I maintain that by every means we should retain the schools in their present status. I have no faith in the "scraps of paper" of the N.U.T. Socialistic and nonconformist ideas are too prevalent for us to give an inch which would mean in the end the N.U.T. taking the ell.

5 a. Changes in Public worship since 1914. b. Effects of the changes. No changes.

6. Number of Roman Catholics in the Parish. [*No response*].

1. See 1914.

BLETCHINGDON   Incumbent C. J. Ball[1]

1. Number of Boys Girls and Infants on books of day schools: a. Last year. 72 at present on the Registers. **b. 20 30 or 40 years ago.** About 132 eighteen years ago.

2. a. Men and b. Women qualified to vote in Parochial Church meeting. None. In these old and rapidly decaying villages, subject to one-man rule, there is no scope for independent opinion or action. Μή κινεῖν Καμαρίναν[2] is a good rule for the present. But changes are on the way.

3. Moral and Spiritual effect of: a. Wartime b. National Mission.

(a) At first an increased seriousness was perceptible, with a good attendance at the Services of Intercession. This effect, however, was transitory and gradually disappeared as the war dragged on. I fear also that the rapid rise in the scale of wages, and the employment of lads and girls at unprecedented rates, have tended to demoralisation; a tendency aggravated by the presence of bodies of troops in the neighbourhood and soldiers billeted in the village.

(b) Nothing of a permanent nature. Missions are no remedy for bad housing (bedrooms, without doors, opening into each other; no gardens, and no proper sanitary arrangements).

4. Status of Church Schools. Options for compromise on a. management, b. head teachers, c. character of religious teaching. Might compromise be justified by better arrangements for Church teaching in state schools?

No difficulties have arisen here. There are only two or three Dissenting families among the indigenous population and I have never heard of any objection to learning the Catechism. The Religious Knowledge prizes have often gone to children of Methodist parents. No doubt the case may be very different in more populous places and may require special arrangements. I have baptised several adult Dissenters and the infants of others. They usually prefer to be married in church. In 18 years there has been only one case of a Dissenting parishioner being buried "under the Act".[3]

5 a. Changes in Public worship since 1914. b. Effects of the changes. None.

6. Number of Roman Catholics in the Parish. One (a married woman).

1. See 1914.
2. 'Don't disturb Kamarina.' A proverb (roughly equivalent to 'let sleeping dogs lie'), derived from a story about a Greek city in Sicily which, defying the advice of their own oracle, drained a marsh in order to end a plague only to find that the dry ground outside their walls allowed Carthaginian invaders to assault and capture the city.
3. A reference to the legislation passed in 1880 and 1900 which allowed nonconformist burial services to be held in Anglican churchyards and abolished the distinction between consecrated and unconsecrated ground in public burial grounds.

BLOXHAM Incumbent W. Fothergill Robinson[1]

1. Number of Boys Girls and Infants on books of day schools: a. Last year. 73 boys, 83 girls, 78 infants, 234 total. **b. 20 30 or 40 years ago.** In 1877 (40 years ago) the numbers were: Mixed school, (boys and girls unspecified) 104, Infants 84 Total 188.

2. a. Men and b. Women qualified to vote in Parochial Church meeting. I understand that no men or women have signed the declaration and I much regret, that in spite of frequent discussion of the subject with the Churchwardens and the sidesmen, I can find no real interest in the subject. I hope however, that this interest may be created, and I undertake to try to get signatures as stated.

3. Moral and Spiritual effect of: a. Wartime b. National Mission.

(a) Owing to the shortness of my incumbency at Bloxham I cannot report satisfactorily. Any estimate is haphazard; but I am inclined to think 1) the moral condition of the parish is what one would expect in a country parish of this kind, save that, as I hear elsewhere, there are difficulties with the children of men serving, and these might become a very serious distress. 2) Of the 14 well-to-do houses there are only 4 from whom I can count on at all for regular Communicants, or any real interest in Church (as opposed to Parish) matters. The Church does not seem to be so full as it should be of the poorer people either for ordinary or intercessory services. The numbers of communicants at Christmas were if anything on the good side.

(b) It would be useless for me to try to estimate the result of the National Mission. I hear of one or two cases where it was really helpful, but they seem to be few.

4. Status of Church Schools. Options for compromise on a. management, b. head teachers, c. character of religious teaching. Might compromise be justified by better arrangements for Church teaching in state schools?

So far as I can estimate, we are very free in this parish of school troubles in connection with single-school difficulties. If the Church can say with a really clear conscience that there is no cause of injustice in the present system, then I should much regret any compromise, but I cannot make my own mind quite easy on this point, though I do not find that the question is a matter of moment to-day in this parish. Speaking from past experience, both my own, and what I have seen, I realise how much I have needed instruction in the art of teaching; without such method, I do not believe that the children are likely to gain much by an extension of facilities in provided Schools. But I say this with the greatest hesitation, as in most of the many schools in which I have had to teach, (many owing to the nature of St Andrews Society work in the Diocese of Salisbury) I have felt that the religious teaching was not satisfactory. Where (as in Bloxham) the school master is a good Churchman, I feel that the children are well helped by his teaching. It would be a great loss were compromise in other directions to lose this positive gain.

5 a. Changes in Public worship since 1914. b. Effects of the changes. I can report nothing on this point, save that during the last month, owing to the Sunday at Milcombe (one Sunday in the month) preventing a Morning Service at Bloxham, the Head Master of All Saints has given us his High Celebration of the Holy Communion in the Parish Church. This he has done, after consulting with the Wardens, and in spite of the fact that this parish had no recent experience of vestments etc, and was rather in opposition. So far as I can judge (and I was at the first service and preached) the reverence and beauty of the service cleared away many misconceptions, and every casual person of that big congregation whom I have seen tells me that they liked it thoroughly, and were much impressed. From this I think that the experiment has done real good, and I hope that it will be the normal service one Sunday in the month in term time.

6. Number of Roman Catholics in the Parish. Men nil. Women 1. Children 2. I believe that this is all, but there is no record.

[*Appended letter*]. March, 5. My Lord, I return you herewith my replies to your Visitation Questions.

I fear that in the nature of things, as I have been here so short a time, they will be of little value. The extraordinarily kindly acceptance of the monthly Choral

Eucharist, mentioned under sec. 5. is due I think to the facts, (1) that popular rumour has led them to anticipate something very unintelligible, and (2) the people are fond of Grier, and as it was not a parish service, but the school service provided for the parish, they had no wish to object. I have marvelled at the ease with which it came about. [*Signed*] Yours very dutifully and sincerely, W. Fothergill Robinson.

1. William Fothergill Robinson graduated from New College Oxford in 1900 and trained at the Leeds Clergy School, being ordained priest in 1902. He served two curacies 1901–06 and then as a St Andrew's Missionary in the diocese of Salisbury 1906–09. He was Vicar of South Newton between 1909 and 1911 and was appointed as Vicar of Bloxham and of Milcombe in 1917. Fothergill Robinson was 41 in 1918.

BODICOTE   Incumbent H. N. Fowler[1]

1. Number of Boys Girls and Infants on books of day schools: a. Last year. 120. **b. 20 30 or 40 years ago.** 20 years ago: 160.

2. a. Men and b. Women qualified to vote in Parochial Church meeting. About 10 men.

3. Moral and Spiritual effect of: a. Wartime b. National Mission.

This is a difficult question to answer: as we have to judge from outward signs which are not always reliable. (a) As to wartime: the moral and spiritual effects are more noticeable, with regard to the so-called better class people: among whom there has been shown much self-denial and self-sacrifice. As to religious worship among all classes I cannot say that there has been improvement in church attendance since the war began: but it should be remembered that the necessities of the war make it harder for some to come to church on Sundays. (b) The National Mission had at the time a good moral and spiritual effect on the parish: as far as I could judge.

4. Status of Church Schools. Options for compromise on a. management, b. head teachers, c. character of religious teaching. Might compromise be justified by better arrangements for Church teaching in state schools?

I think the Church should see that a Church School in a single-school area should hold as good a position as a Council School: eg Salaries of teachers should be as good; the Correspondent should receive payment as in a Council School and more financial support should be given to the maintenance of the School building etc. I have often thought that it would be a good thing if feasible for all elementary schools to be worked on the same lines: the difference between Provided and Non-Provided being done away with, but as things are now I would answer your 3rd question in the affirmative as far as regards (a) Management: dissenters should have representative [*sic*] among the School-Managers in proportion to the number of children of dissenters in the school. (c) the character of the religious teaching – as to (b) the head-teacher in a church School should of course always be a Churchman.

5 a. Changes in Public worship since 1914. b. Effects of the changes. I would only mention the change from evening to afternoon Service on Sundays during the last two winters, owing to lighting difficulty. Congregations in the afternoon have been fair but not so good as in the evening. This parish is so near Banbury, that those who prefer an evening service are able to go there.

6. Number of Roman Catholics in the Parish. I know of only one man.

1. See 1914.

BOURTON, GREAT   Incumbent S. R. Standage

1. Number of Boys Girls and Infants on books of day schools: a. Last year. 25 (This is only an Infants' School now.) **b. 20 30 or 40 years ago.** 40 But then the children were allowed to stay longer.

2. a. Men and b. Women qualified to vote in Parochial Church meeting. None.

3. Moral and Spiritual effect of: a. Wartime b. National Mission.

I can't say that there is any spiritual advance looking at it from this point of time. Certainly both at the beginning of the war and also after Mr Peake's mission there seemed to be a larger attendance both at Holy Communion and at Mattins and Evensong but the effort was not sustained and now we are about as we were before. Our numbers, at Evensong at least, are always fairly high.

4. Status of Church Schools. Options for compromise on a. management, b. head teachers, c. character of religious teaching. Might compromise be justified by better arrangements for Church teaching in state schools?

I have not come across any difficulties since I have been Incumbent at either Claydon or Great Bourton at the Schools – and I have no clear opinion to express on the subject.

5 a. Changes in Public worship since 1914. b. Effects of the changes. No changes and therefore no differences to record.

6. Number of Roman Catholics in the Parish. 3 men, 2 women. There are 7 children where one parent is a Roman Catholic and the other is either Church or Chapel but I cannot say in what way they are being brought up. But none of them, so far, come to Church and all are quite young.

1. See 1914.

BRADWELL WITH KELMSCOT   Incumbent H. T. Adams[1]

1. Number of Boys Girls and Infants on books of day schools: a. Last year. 42. **b. 20 30 or 40 years ago.** Number on books in March 1888, 20; in March 1898, 21. Kelmscot School was closed in 1901 and the children admitted to Broadwell school.

2. a. Men and b. Women qualified to vote in Parochial Church meeting. No members of the Congregations signed afresh last year. The Parochial Church Meeting is to be held in the Parishes in Easter week or the week after.

3. Moral and Spiritual effect of: a. Wartime b. National Mission.

I think the war has made church goers more earnest in their devotion. The National Mission certainly had an effect on the more spiritually minded of the congregations, but not on the whole of those congregations.

4. Status of Church Schools. Options for compromise on a. management, b. head teachers, c. character of religious teaching. Might compromise be justified by better arrangements for Church teaching in state schools?

The Church Schools should be maintained as at present. No thought of Compromise should be maintained, unless the Terms of a Compromise be far more favourable to Denominational Schools, than any that have yet been put forward.

5 a. Changes in Public worship since 1914. b. Effects of the changes. No change.

6. Number of Roman Catholics in the Parish. No Roman Catholics in the Two Parishes.

1. See 1914.

BRIGHTWELL BALDWIN[1] Incumbent T. Hainsworth[2]

1. Number of Boys Girls and Infants on books of day schools: a. Last year. b. 20 30 or 40 years ago.

Council School serves Britwell and Brightwell Baldwin. Britwell Boys 12, Girls 10, Infants 7. Brightwell Baldwin Boys 10, Girls 12, Infants 1. 1879: Brightwell Baldwin 30 Children. 1879: Britwell 24 children.

2. a. Men and b. Women qualified to vote in Parochial Church meeting. [*No response*].

3. Moral and Spiritual effect of: a. Wartime b. National Mission.

Neither the war nor National Mission had any noticeable effect. While both perhaps have led to a deeper realisation of the meaning of life.

4. Status of Church Schools. Options for compromise on a. management, b. head teachers, c. character of religious teaching. Might compromise be justified by better arrangements for Church teaching in state schools?

Not able to express an opinion. I take a class each Friday morning at the Council School for religious instruction and meet with no difficulty.

5 a. Changes in Public worship since 1914. b. Effects of the changes. Because of lighting restrictions Evening service held at 3.0 pm. This was not found convenient. After third collect instead of State Prayers a form of Intercession used. This has be [*sic*] greatly appreciated by congregation.

6. Number of Roman Catholics in the Parish. None.

1. See 1914.

BRITWELL SALOME WITH BRITWELL PRIOR Incumbent J. C. Mansfield[1]

1. Number of Boys Girls and Infants on books of day schools: a. Last year. b. 20 30 or 40 years ago.

There are no schools in this parish. The children attend Brightwell Baldwin School or Watlington. I believe there were two Dame schools held in cottages here at one time. The population has shrunk in 60 years to one fourth.

2. a. Men and b. Women qualified to vote in Parochial Church meeting. None. My congregation consists of poor labourers' families. The farmer is a dissenter and there is no one else. The landowners live in London and give no help!!!

3. Moral and Spiritual effect of: a. Wartime b. National Mission.

I can see very little difference.

4. Status of Church Schools. Options for compromise on a. management, b. head teachers, c. character of religious teaching. Might compromise be justified by better arrangements for Church teaching in state schools?

[*No response*].

5 a. Changes in Public worship since 1914. b. Effects of the changes. We made few changes. I had to cut down number of Services and all the parish room classes owing to lack of funds and difficulties of heating and lighting.

6. Number of Roman Catholics in the Parish. There are no Roman Catholics in this parish.

1. See 1914.

BRIZENORTON Incumbent T. W. Sturgiss[1]

1. Number of Boys Girls and Infants on books of day schools: a. Last year. 103 Council School **b. 20 30 or 40 years ago.** 40 years 86, 30 years 120, 20 years 116. Sorry not to have items of sexes, but they [are] about equal. Out of 103 not six over 12 years of age.

2. a. Men and b. Women qualified to vote in Parochial Church meeting. Parish Council to be formed April 8th next. I don't anticipate above 60 to sign.

3. Moral and Spiritual effect of: a. Wartime b. National Mission.

(a) The parish is much depleted in numbers both in men at war and women at munitions, especially of church folk which makes judgement difficult. At home everybody physically fit is hard at work, some overworked. Result smaller attendance at church especially on Sunday mornings and week days. Contributions to Red Cross and war charities is spontaneous, generous and general but to church and church work less generous, except in Foreign Missions which has increased. Those who have lost members of the family are more devout others not altered. The farmers and others who make most out of the war are not a scrap more generous in any way. The worship of Mammon has increased more than the worship of God. There is a further decline in the discipline of the young, absence of parents at war or work partly accounts for this.

(b) The National Mission has apparently had no effect, unless it be that those already devout are more so in some few cases.

4. Status of Church Schools. Options for compromise on a. management, b. head teachers, c. character of religious teaching. Might compromise be justified by better arrangements for Church teaching in state schools?

I have been a school manager for over 30 years till I came here and found a Council School built in 1870. There has <u>never</u> been a Church School in this ancient parish, but only a Dame School held by uneducated persons in a cottage. In one case the village cobbler did it in his spare time. I think it would be good policy to give Nonconformists a larger share of management in Church Schools in Single School areas. I have always found them friendly and helpful and that they had no objection to sound scriptural teaching by Church Teachers though a few object to the Sacramental teaching of the Catechism and Prayer Book. In these cases their conscientious scruples ought to be cordially respected and arrangements made accordingly. We ought to make a compromise. I am convinced that only a very small minority of Nonconformist parents object even to Church teaching and that we should gain and not lose by being just and generous. Yes. It would be a great gain to obtain admission to the Council schools. I regard the bare reading of Holy Scripture as in this school beginning at Genesis and reading through without explanation or note or comment as almost worthless. Our Children are absolutely heathen and ignorant of the simplest facts even of the Patriarchs, or of our Lord's Life. In many cases, as here, if the clergy have no voice in the teaching the Bible is a dead letter.

5 a. Changes in Public worship since 1914. b. Effects of the changes. a) No change except more frequent weekday meetings for intercession. They attended well in 1914 and 1915. Since then a gradual falling away. (b) No effect.

6. Number of Roman Catholics in the Parish. Two families, husband, wife and 4 children in each case. 12 in all.

1. See 1914.

BROUGHTON
Incumbent B. W. Bradford[1]

1. Number of Boys Girls and Infants on books of day schools: a. Last year. (a) Boys 29, Girls 23, Infants 26. **b. 20 30 or 40 years ago.** In 1878. The average attendance was 95. Mixed 56, Infants 39.

2. a. Men and b. Women qualified to vote in Parochial Church meeting. Nil.

3. Moral and Spiritual effect of: a. Wartime b. National Mission.

I cannot perceive much spiritual effect. I do not find that the means of grace are more used. Morally I think there is a noticeable improvement – people are more sympathetic, and are more willing to give their time, their work and their money to worthy objects, than they were before.

(b) Altho' our mission service was very well attended, by many who seldom or never attend church, I cannot say that there has been any permanent effect.

4. Status of Church Schools. Options for compromise on a. management, b. head teachers, c. character of religious teaching. Might compromise be justified by better arrangements for Church teaching in state schools?

In this Parish, a single school area, and a Church School, we have never had a child withdrawn from religious teaching, and there has never been any difficulty with the parents during the 18 years I have been here, so I do not feel competent to express an opinion.

5 a. Changes in Public worship since 1914. b. Effects of the changes. Owing to lighting restrictions in the winter we have had to have Evensong at 3 pm instead of at 6 pm. It is not so well attended as the later service, which we recommence as soon as possible. We now have a Celebration of the Holy Communion at 8 am every Sunday except the 1st of the month when it is at midday, instead of only on the 3rd Sunday of the month. I find that a few who practically never missed coming on the 3rd Sunday now do not always come once a month.

6. Number of Roman Catholics in the Parish. <u>None</u>.

1. See 1914.

BROGHTON POGIS
Incumbent W. P. Roberts[1]

1. Number of Boys Girls and Infants on books of day schools: a. Last year. 10 Church School of Filkins 5 boys, 4 girls, 1 Infant (boy). **b. 20 30 or 40 years ago.** I cannot say as the children of Broughton and Filkins are mixed.

2. a. Men and b. Women qualified to vote in Parochial Church meeting. (a) 5 men, (b) 16 women. This calculation was taken at Easter Meeting 3 years ago.

3. Moral and Spiritual effect of: a. Wartime b. National Mission.

The war drags on and the people feel very tired just now with extra work especially female labour and they seem to be inclined to be slack in church attendance.

(b) The National Mission seems to have done much good in some cases, in others to be but a mere 'flash in the pan'. I think generally speaking just lately there is a hopeful outlook as the National crisis created though the fall of Russia seems to make people look more to live in their Refuge, Christ.

4. Status of Church Schools. Options for compromise on a. management, b. head teachers, c. character of religious teaching. Might compromise be justified by better arrangements for Church teaching in state schools?

(a) The Church School is at Filkins – called Broughton-cum-Filkins School. I am one of the managers. I can only say generally that it seems a pity that in this time of national crisis that there should be any changes with regard to the Education Act in view. With regard to N.U.T. as this seems to savour of Teachers Unionism I hardly contemplate it with much favour. This is a very small parish and I teach at Filkins School once a week. The management is chiefly in the hands of the Chairman of the School Managers and the Vicar of Filkins. It is most difficult to know how far the Nonconformists should have a free hand in Education – especially in single school areas.

5 a. Changes in Public worship since 1914. b. Effects of the changes. (a) The War Intercessions are kept up since the beginning of the War in 1914. 1 Extra celebration of H.C. a week. (b) It is not very easy to get the people to attend the services. But on the whole things are satisfactory. There are so many other parishes round which tends to make the parishioners like variety.

6. Number of Roman Catholics in the Parish. One young war widow is a Roman Catholic (no children).

[P.S.] 22nd March 1918 I am afraid that these questions are not very definitely answered – but this being a small parish it is [*indeciph.*] difficult to exactly define matters as would be the case in a larger one.

1. See 1914.

BUCKNELL   Incumbent E. C. E. Owen[1]

1. Number of Boys Girls and Infants on books of day schools: a. Last year. 34? **b. 20 30 or 40 years ago.** [*No response*].

2. a. Men and b. Women qualified to vote in Parochial Church meeting. None.

3. Moral and Spiritual effect of: a. Wartime b. National Mission.

No appreciable effect in either case.

4. Status of Church Schools. Options for compromise on a. management, b. head teachers, c. character of religious teaching. Might compromise be justified by better arrangements for Church teaching in state schools?

In Bucknell there is no Dissent and I do not think any change or compromise need be made.

5 a. Changes in Public worship since 1914. b. Effects of the changes. (a) The only changes being in regard to the Sunday Evening Service during the Winter. There was a difficulty in complying with the Lighting Regulations and consequently Evensong of a Mission character has been sung in the Schoolroom. A shortened form has been used. (b) The result has been satisfactory. The School was much warmer than the Church could be made and the congregations have been quite good and the services very hearty.

6. Number of Roman Catholics in the Parish. None during Dr Harris' incumbency.[2]

NB. As I have just come into residence, the above answers have been made by Dr Harris.

1. Edward Charles Everard Owen graduated from Balliol College Oxford in 1883 and was ordained priest in 1888. He held a Fellowship at New College 1884–91 and was an Assistant Master at Harrow School between 1886 and 1918, when he was appointed as Rector of Bucknell. He published a range of literary works including *Latin Syntax for Upper Forms* (1888) and an edition of Byron's *Childe Harold* (1897). He was aged 57 in 1918 and at the 1911 census he shared a household with his wife, two 19-year-old sons (both unmarried and in employment), two younger children, and his elderly widowed mother, together with two unmarried female servants.
2. See 1914.

BURFORD WITH FULBROOK   Incumbent W. C. Emeris[1]

1. Number of Boys Girls and Infants on books of day schools: a. Last year. b. 20 30 or 40 years ago.

		Boys	Girls	Infants	Total
Burford Council Schools	1899	88	96	78	262
	1917	54	60	47	161
Fulbrook C E School	1885	27	38		65
	1917	17	14		31

2. a. Men and b. Women qualified to vote in Parochial Church meeting. None signed last year. About 85 names appear on our Roll some of which belong to persons who have died or left the Parish. Up till now about 20 fresh names have been added this year and others are coming in.

3. Moral and Spiritual effect of: a. Wartime b. National Mission.

The effect of the war upon this parish has been to diminish greatly the population. Everything tends to take people away, nothing to bring them here except visitors in the summer. The result is depression. We are just able to carry on and that is all. There is some sign of insubordination among older children but not to a serious degree. There is no increase of intemperance and no trace of moral trouble. There has been a distinct increase of earnestness among those in close touch with the church. The Intercession Services have been well attended and maintained and the number of communicants has perhaps somewhat increased, allowance being made for those regular communicants who are absent owing to the war. On the other hand, there is little sign of any wide or marked religious effect upon the general life of the place owing to the war, except the attendance at church on certain special days of intercession, notably on the first Sunday in this year.

(b) The one mark that the National Mission has left is seen in a greater sense of corporate feeling among regulars and devout church people.

4. Status of Church Schools. Options for compromise on a. management, b. head teachers, c. character of religious teaching. Might compromise be justified by better arrangements for Church teaching in state schools?

The Position of religious teaching in the Provided School in this Parish is not unsatisfactory under the circumstances. The teachers are all Church people and the Creed the Lord's Prayer and the Ten Commandments are taught but of course not their interpretation as given in the Catechism. Still there is no security for the present condition of things, and other parishes in the neighbourhood are not so fortunate. It would seem right and wise to maintain the present position until if possible an agreement could be reached whereby children should be instructed in the religion of their parents.

With regard to Burford Grammar School the Governors have been forced to give up the provision whereby all pupils were taught the Catechism unless the Parents expressed a desire that they should not. Now no pupil may be so taught unless the Parent or Guardian expresses in writing a desire that he should be instructed in the Catechism. Forms are sent to the Parents of all boys entering the School and these are for the most part filled up. We find that as a result rather more boys are being taught the Catechism than before.

5 a. Changes in Public worship since 1914. b. Effects of the changes. No changes have been made.

6. Number of Roman Catholics in the Parish. None.

1. See 1914.

[*Appended Statistics*]
Burford Council School No. of Children on the Roll

	Boys	Girls	Total
Christmas 1899	88	96	184
1900	84	96	180
1901	85	100	185
1902	81	100	181
1903	68	90	158
1904	72	85	157
1905	75	88	163
1906	83	85	168
1907	74	75	149
1908	69	74	143
1909	68	71	139
1910	68	68	136
1911	55	72	127
1912	50	72	122
1913	56	67	123
1914	62	73	135
1915			118
1916			116
1917	54	60	114

Burford Council Infant School

Number on registers	
1894	87
1895	85
1896	85
1897	71
1898	77
1899	78
1900	71

1901	66
1902	62
1903	55
1904	60
1905	53
1906	63
1907	69
1908	70
1909	64
1910	65
1911	46
1912	55
1913	56
1914	58
1915	48
1916	50
1917	47
to March 1918	46

The records of the Girls' Dept. previous to 1899 seem to have been wholly destroyed. I could give figures for the Boys for earlier years if desired.

CASSINGTON   Incumbent C. G. Paget[1]

1. Number of Boys Girls and Infants on books of day schools: a. Last year. 59. b. 20 30 or 40 years ago. There are no records of the school attendance a generation ago, but I gather that there were at least a dozen more cottages than there are now, though possibly the school attendance was no higher than now.

2. a. Men and b. Women qualified to vote in Parochial Church meeting. I don't think any steps were taken last year to form a register of Parochial Church Electors.

3. Moral and Spiritual effect of: a. Wartime b. National Mission.

We are all one class here and I have been here such a short time that I am not able to give any certain opinion of value. But I am inclined to think that the effect of the war has been to draw all families together in neighbourliness and helpfulness to each other. There has also been a readiness to take up little jobs of war work such as are practicable in a country place such as a war savings association, gathering blackberries, chesnuts etc. And generally speaking most of us have learned to take a wider look out on life. On the other hand war conditions have been disastrous to their children – both at home and in school. All the boys leave school as soon as they reach 12, and some are employed on work before school hours and after. There is a great lack of discipline owing to the lack of home discipline, and the premature sense of independence which has grown up.

I can say nothing about the National Mission, as I know nothing as to the previous condition of the Parish. All I can venture to say is that there seems to have been a great lack of definite church teaching.

4. Status of Church Schools. Options for compromise on a. management, b. head teachers, c. character of religious teaching. Might compromise be justified by better arrangements for Church teaching in state schools?

We must hold on to our Church Schools but give a right of entry to nonconformist teachers who teach the children of their own persuasion, and claim the same right for Church teachers in provided schools. To give way on (a) or (b) would endanger little (c).

5 a. Changes in Public worship since 1914. b. Effects of the changes. [*No response*].

6. Number of Roman Catholics in the Parish. None.

1. Cecil George Paget graduated from Christ Church Oxford in 1877 and was ordained priest in 1878. He occupied three curacies from 1877 to 1905 and was Rector of Stock Gaylard between 1905 and 1917, when he became Vicar of Cassington. He was 64 years of age in 1918 and at the 1911 census he shared a large household with his wife (whose occupation was described as 'Suffragist'), two sons described as students, and two younger children, together with six servants: a widowed female cook, four unmarried female servants and one unmarried male servant.

CAVERSFIELD[1]   Incumbent W. O'Reilly (Priest in Charge)[2]

1. Number of Boys Girls and Infants on books of day schools: a. Last year. b. 20 30 or 40 years ago.

There are no schools.

2. a. Men and b. Women qualified to vote in Parochial Church meeting. 3 men, 5 women.

3. Moral and Spiritual effect of: a. Wartime b. National Mission.

The war has made it more difficult for the people to come to church owing to the shortage of labour. It is very difficult to see any moral or spiritual effect of The War or of the National Mission. The people seem just about as they were.

4. Status of Church Schools. Options for compromise on a. management, b. head teachers, c. character of religious teaching. Might compromise be justified by better arrangements for Church teaching in state schools?

See reply for Bicester.

5 a. Changes in Public worship since 1914. b. Effects of the changes. The only change has been that of time, owing to being singlehanded Matins is said at 10.0 instead of 11.0. It makes no difference.

6. Number of Roman Catholics in the Parish. None.

1. Population 70.
2. See 1914 Bicester. O'Reilly seems to have been incumbent of a joint benefice combining Caversfield with Bicester.

CHALGROVE WITH BERRICK SALOME   Incumbent T. O. Floyd[1]

1. Number of Boys Girls and Infants on books of day schools: a. Last year. b. 20 30 or 40 years ago.

In <u>1918</u>: B. 25, G. 26, I. 23 = 74. In <u>1878</u>: B. 41, G. 37, I. 52 = 130.

These figures are only for Chalgrove. Berrick Salome children go to Benson school.

2. a. Men and b. Women qualified to vote in Parochial Church meeting. About 25 I think, but being away from home I cannot say exactly.

3. Moral and Spiritual effect of: a. Wartime b. National Mission.

(a) A considerable decrease in congregations owing to there being more work for the people who are left at home. Before I joined the army I had gathered a few people for a mid-week communion on behalf of those engaged in the war: but the people who came were not those who had members of their households at the front for the most part. I think there is some war-weariness, and no very clear idea of the principles for which we are fighting: but in a certain minority some considerable deepening of the spiritual life. (b) I have not been able to detect any spiritual results from the National Mission.

4. Status of Church Schools. Options for compromise on a. management, b. head teachers, c. character of religious teaching. Might compromise be justified by better arrangements for Church teaching in state schools?

In my opinion it is only in a minority of the church schools that the teaching given on religious subjects is any other than that which can be given in council schools. And most of this minority are in towns and not in single school areas. The religious tone of the village school depends chiefly on the character and sympathy of the headteacher and no amount of church teaching given by a H.T. who calls himself a churchman will be of much value if he does not go to church or only goes very seldom. It is only in a very small number of cases that difficulties arise in regard to management: and then generally when there is some quarrel already existing in the village between Church and dissent, of which the village education committee is made one of the battle grounds. I should like to see simple bible teaching given by the ordinary teachers in the school provided they believe it: with right of entry for C. of E. clergy and nonconformist ministers to give denominational teaching on (say) 2 days a week. The difficulties in regard to this are that in many cases clergy and in most cases noncon. ministers do not want to give the teaching. But I do not think that any compromise is likely to be accepted – as I feel that the tendency to remove all religious teaching from the schools is becoming more and more definite.

5 a. Changes in Public worship since 1914. b. Effects of the changes. None.

6. Number of Roman Catholics in the Parish. None.

1. See 1914.

CHARLBURY WITH CHADLINGTON   Incumbent J. D. Payne[1]

1. Number of Boys Girls and Infants on books of day schools: a. Last year. b. 20 30 or 40 years ago.

Charlbury 25 years ago: 61 boys, 75 girls 64 infants = 200. But as the population was 3 per cent more, the attendance regulations must have been less strict.

Charlbury 1917: Boys 89, Girls 83 = 172 Infants boys 28 infants girls 50 = 78 [Total] 250.

Owing to Glove factories our population is fairly constant: a drop of 3 per cent in 10 years. The number of children has been about 250 for past 15 years.

Chadlington 1917: Boys 27, Girls 28 = 55 Infants boys 18, Infants girls 16 = 34 [Total] 89.

Chadlington purely farming. Number of children has dropped from 135 to 90 in the past 20 years.

Chilson[2] though purely agricultural hamlet, has maintained its population in most years and average number of 35 children. 1918: boys 11, girls 13, infants 8 [Total] 32. 20 years ago 1898 on books 35.

2. a. Men and b. Women qualified to vote in Parochial Church meeting. At Charlbury at Easter 1916 we asked that communicants should put their names for the Roll in a box in the Church: and we received 242 names (men and women) this number includes a number of men now absent on service. At Easter 1917 at meeting of Parochial Church Council at Charlbury, 11 men, 1 woman; at Chadlington, 9 men Total 20 men, 1 woman, signed declaration. Owing to war conditions, our number of men, who can be present, is less than half what it used to be.

3. Moral and Spiritual effect of: a. Wartime b. National Mission.

I am not aware of any bad moral effects of war conditions in Charlbury. We have a Guild of Help (of 5 men and 7 women) who meet fortnightly (for social betterment of the parish). I always attend and we should probably be able to judge. As to the religious effect of the war the men who come home on leave are most regular in attending church and in coming to Holy Communion before they return to the front. The best demonstrable advance is in the regular number of communicants monthly: owing to an opportunity of the whole morning congregation remaining for the complete service of Holy Communion on the 1st Sunday in the month. Our average morning congregation has always been about 200. Now (if the weather is not very bad) we have 50 communicants at 8 am and 40 at 11 am on that Sunday. Some of our communicants have two miles to come, and attend church both at 8 am and 11.

The National Mission emphasised and helped the above habit: but it began with the war and the need of intercession. There has been a steady attendance at daily service during the war. A few people say that the War has made them give up attendance at church. Really it appears to be a want of foundation of belief. I have seen them, and given them useful books on the points at issue. They have not themselves responded. Other members of their household 'come *for* them'.

As Charlbury had a long Quaker tradition (since 1660) the fact of War has been a great puzzle to many of our people.

Generally our church people have responded nobly to the losses of the war. 10 of our Church Lads' Brigade have been killed in action: and in Charlbury above 27 men killed. At the outlining hamlet of Chilson, out of a former Confirmation Class of 6 lads, 3 killed. Most of the relations have answered 'Such troubles draw us nearer to God.' These troubles and sympathy have stilled sectarian bitterness and united classes. I have tried to estimate by households who have sons or husbands serving. I think ⅔ of the whole population take part in public and private prayer ⅓ are indifferent: but the children of the latter attend for the most part.

4. Status of Church Schools. Options for compromise on a. management, b. head teachers, c. character of religious teaching. Might compromise be justified by better arrangements for Church teaching in state schools?

Chadlington is a Church School. Out of our 6 managers we have 4 Churchmen 1 Wesleyan 1 Baptist. I think this gives confidence, and a sense of fair play. As it is quite understood that it is a Church School, they do not oppose the religious instruction. For considerable time no child withdrawn from Prayer Book Lesson at present 1 child withdrawn. We ask the Managers to be present at the Diocesan Inspection. They never come, but the invitation gives a sense of confidence. Similarly at Chilson a Council School inspected by Diocesan Inspector, the Managers are invited: and only allow that inspection, because they are invited. They also never come. The school always does well. Where Managers and parents see that what we are anxious for is definite personal religion, and not controversy, there appears to be no opposition or grievance. In each village it would be quite easy to put a match, and cause an explosion.

In Charlbury our school is a Council School. Of our whole people about one half are effective Church people, of the remaining half, a large number are active and good Wesleyans. I do not think a Church School, as the only School, would be possible in Charlbury: nor did it ever exist. But our Teachers for the most part, during the past 14 years, have been Church people and communicants: and of our present body of 6 (democratically elected) Managers 5 are Church people. I think we could not here have the Diocesan Inspector. But a better syllabus might well be provided.

The same distinction applies. Religion, definite personal religion and definite truth, is welcome: controversy is fatal. The main danger in Council Schools is the possibility of having a Head Teacher devoid of any religious belief. Our <u>Head Teacher</u> (for the War) now is one of my best helpers. I think it is largely a question of whether the people have confidence in their Clergy and in the teachers: and whether we can be chivalrous in difficult circumstances. Having 3 different types of schools, each in a single school area and 3 miles apart, I feel that there is room for a variety of types.

5 a. Changes in Public worship since 1914. b. Effects of the changes. (Already partly answered under question 3) (a) 1st Sunday in the month 8 am Holy Communion (said) 11 am Holy Communion (sung). The whole ordinary Sunday morning congregation of about 200 being present at the latter. On a good Sunday 50 communicants at 8; 40 communicants at 11 am. (b) The effect has been to double the number of communicants on that Sunday and generally to bring our congregation to value the opportunity. It is welcomed by all our people. I think it has the best effect, devotionally, of any change since I have been here, viz. for 14 ¾ years.

6. Number of Roman Catholics in the Parish. There was a small Roman Catholic Chapel at Chadlington in use with 2 families in Chadlington. Now the Chapel has been unused for say 10 years, except in the case of one funeral. Not a single R.C. remains in Chadlington. Our only R.C. family in Charlbury left a few months ago.

1. See 1914.
2. Also known as Shorthampton.

CHARLTON-ON-OTMOOR Incumbent C. E. Prior[1]

1. Number of Boys Girls and Infants on books of day schools: a. Last year. Boys 19 Girls 24 Infants 19. Total 62. **b. 20 30 or 40 years ago.** In 1877: number of children on the books 84; 1883: 105; 1898: (about) 110.

2. a. Men and b. Women qualified to vote in Parochial Church meeting. None signed last year; a few signed some years ago.

3. Moral and Spiritual effect of: a. Wartime b. National Mission.

War time has made the farmers very busy: they do not come to church except in the evening. The attendance in the evening has not increased. I do not think so much of intoxicants is consumed as formerly, but high prices may have a good deal to do with that. The young lads, now that many of their fathers and elder brothers are away, consider themselves rather as independent, and the increased value of their services encourages this feeling. Eight of them, however, were confirmed the other day, and will I hope be communicants. There is no particular effect to be noticed in the women: some of them and of the children come to War Intercessions.

National Mission The services were well attended chiefly by women and children. I have not seen any manifest effects, except insofar as the introduction of new types of service has made people more ready to come to such services.

4. Status of Church Schools. Options for compromise on a. management, b. head teachers, c. character of religious teaching. Might compromise be justified by better arrangements for Church teaching in state schools?

(a) I think that as the Schools generally are in the hands of Churchmen, they should remain so. The trustees (or possibly the managers) undertake to keep them up, and the Inspectors see that they do their duty in this respect. (b) I think the appointment of the Head Teacher should be in the hands of the managers subject to the approval of the County Council. (c) I do not know enough about Council Schools to be able to estimate the value of a compromise, but wherever desired Nonconformists should be allowed to have separate instruction in the hours of Prayer Book Instruction.

5 a. Changes in Public worship since 1914. b. Effects of the changes. On Wednesday evenings when there was always a church service here, I have now a Service at the School, consisting of Prayers, hymns, and an address, and there are 30 or more present instead of only 6 or 8. Sometimes we use National Mission Prayers, sometimes a shortened Evensong, and sometimes Prayers and addresses relating to Foreign Missions. Since Xmas Day I have had a Celebration of the Holy Communion at 11 o'clock, ending about 12.15. I invite everyone to stay, which they do. Two men who never communicated before (in 22 years) came on Xmas Day, and I think the change suits people's hours better than 8 am or "after Morning Prayer". I have this service on the first Sunday of the month.

6. Number of Roman Catholics in the Parish. None.

1. See 1914.

CHASTLETON Incumbent J. A. Burnley[1]

1. Number of Boys Girls and Infants on books of day schools: a. Last year. 20 children. **b. 20 30 or 40 years ago.** March 5th 1878: 26 children.

2. a. Men and b. Women qualified to vote in Parochial Church meeting. With one or two exceptions all are church people and regular communicants of the C. of E. The Annual Parochial Church Meeting is held after the Vestry Meeting.

3. Moral and Spiritual effect of: a. Wartime b. National Mission.

The people are doing their best.

4. Status of Church Schools. Options for compromise on a. management, b. head teachers, c. character of religious teaching. Might compromise be justified by better arrangements for Church teaching in state schools?

Retain these Schools in their present Status.

5 a. Changes in Public worship since 1914. b. Effects of the changes. No change.

6. Number of Roman Catholics in the Parish. None.

1. See 1914.

CHECKENDON
Incumbent J. T. Munn[1]

1. Number of Boys Girls and Infants on books of day schools: a. Last year. 10 boys, 14 girls, 18 infants = 42 **b. 20 30 or 40 years ago.** The school was only used as a Sunday School till about 1865 and in the early days the attendance was only about 20. Another school was opened at Wyfold in the Parish for some years taking a part of the children, it was closed about 8 years ago.

2. a. Men and b. Women qualified to vote in Parochial Church meeting. 8 males, 7 females.

3. Moral and Spiritual effect of: a. Wartime b. National Mission.

I do not see much effect of either.

4. Status of Church Schools. Options for compromise on a. management, b. head teachers, c. character of religious teaching. Might compromise be justified by better arrangements for Church teaching in state schools?

In this Village there is no Chapel and very few Dissenters and no religious difficulty of any kind has arisen at the School. I should prefer to retain our Church Schools in their present status, though if duly safeguarded I should not be adverse to the admission of non conformists to a voice, but not a controlling one, on the management and on the teaching staff though not as head teachers. I should be sorry to see any change in the definite teaching of at any rate the Church children. I am very doubtful if the offer of more satisfactory religious teaching in Council Schools would justify a compromise.

5 a. Changes in Public worship since 1914. b. Effects of the changes. None.

6. Number of Roman Catholics in the Parish. None.

1. See 1914.

CHESTERTON   Incumbent S. H. Baker[1]

1. Number of Boys Girls and Infants on books of day schools: a. Last year. b. 20 30 or 40 years ago.

	Boys	Girls	Infants	Total
1917–1918	17	13	14	44
Oldest registers 1903	18	29	27	74

A teacher who has been in the School 21 years informs me that 20 years ago the total number was 85 but can give no exact figures as to Boys Girls and Infants.

2. a. Men and b. Women qualified to vote in Parochial Church meeting. None.

3. Moral and Spiritual effect of: a. Wartime b. National Mission.

(a) Employers: the curtailment of their ordinary pleasures, reduction in establishments, efforts to extend their war savings and in utilizing the land to the best advantage the many war work services undertaken tend to simplicity of living and this self denial and spirit of service which should augur well for the future. Tenant farmers have shown great diligence and in face of great difficulties have risen to a high sense of their responsibility.

Employed: It is generally felt that there is a growing spirit of independence and that workers generally are less trustworthy and reliable than they were. There are, as no doubt elsewhere, evidences of a desire to exploit the war to their advantage: e.g., continual efforts for raising of wages, marriage with a view to secure separation allowances, great readiness to allow children to be withdrawn from school for farm work at the earliest possible moment.

Children: Especially boys tend to [be] somewhat out of hand owing partly to the absence of fathers.

General: There are evidences of a desire to be of use in war time: the War Savings Association has been supported even by some of the poorest; not only charitable funds for the war such as Red Cross, King George's Fund for Sailors etc, but all special collections for church and charitable purposes have been very generously supported. There appears to be little direct evidence here of any general lowering of the moral standard owing to war conditions.

(b) The National Mission was received with interest here and nearly all the parishioners attended some of the services and must have derived benefit from doing so. I think some people have been more regular at Church and Holy Communion since the Mission was held. There has been a slight increase in the number of communions made. The attendance at Church on Sunday mornings and on weekdays has shown no increase, but the attendance on Sunday evenings has been good.

4. Status of Church Schools. Options for compromise on a. management, b. head teachers, c. character of religious teaching. Might compromise be justified by better arrangements for Church teaching in state schools?

1 yes 2 the Schools should be maintained in their present status 3 no.

5 a. Changes in Public worship since 1914. b. Effects of the changes. Daily services have been introduced. Celebrations of Holy Communion have been increased in number from 2 to 3 on Great Festivals. On the 1st Sunday in the month there is a Celebration at 8.30 am in addition to the one at mid-day which had been customary for many years. On the 3rd Sunday in the month the Holy Communion is celebrated at 7.30 instead of 8.30. Holy Communion is now celebrated on Holy Days when the attendance of communicants can be secured. Special Services of Intercession for the War are held weekly. (b) An increase in the number of communicants in a parish of which the population has decreased.

6. Number of Roman Catholics in the Parish. None.

1. Samuel Howard Baker graduated from New College Oxford in 1883 and trained at Cuddesdon College, being ordained priest in 1885. He served five curacies 1884–1908 and was Chaplain of the Warneford and South Warwickshire Hospital between 1909 and 1914, when he became Vicar of Chesterton. He was aged 57 in 1918 and at the 1911 census he shared a household with his wife, two young daughters and their governess, together with three unmarried female servants.

CHINNOR   Incumbent L. Baldwyn[1]

1. Number of Boys Girls and Infants on books of day schools: a. Last year. b. 20 30 or 40 years ago.

	Boys	Girls	Infants			[Total]
			(Boys	Girls	[Total])	
Feb 1898	73	76	(46	53	99)	248
Feb 1918	63	56	(26	25	51)	170

2. a. Men and b. Women qualified to vote in Parochial Church meeting. None so far. At each Easter Vestry we elect from the body of Church Officers (all being communicants) a Church Council. For over 10 years we have found this method to work very well and on special occasions such as the churchyard enlargement, rehanging of bells etc, I have derived much useful help and good advice from the Church Council so called.

3. Moral and Spiritual effect of: a. Wartime b. National Mission.

I cannot say that the war has had any very marked effect on this parish. A few have undoubtedly been led to more regular worship and have attended our weekly intercession regularly. Of the young men who have gone to the front and who were communicants before they left, I find that they still come to communion when on leave. Most of those who were indifferent to religion before the war seem to remain the same in spite of their experience. I have about three cases of men who have taken a more thoughtful view of things and these I am in touch with and if they are not able to be presented for confirmation at the front, I shall hope to secure them on their return.

The National Mission was helpful although we have not experienced the full results I could have wished for. However it enabled us to start a men's class last winter, but this year most of the members have been called away from the parish.

4. Status of Church Schools. Options for compromise on a. management, b. head teachers, c. character of religious teaching. Might compromise be justified by better arrangements for Church teaching in state schools?

I certainly think we should retain the appointment of Head Teachers in our schools. As regards religious teaching in these Schools (Church Schools) we have had no trouble. Our school staff are all good Church people and although there is a large body of Dissent in the Parish I can only remember three instances in 16 years where a child has been withdrawn from Church Teaching. I am quite ready to support any reasonable scheme for the future which would make the matter of religious teaching absolutely fair to all.

5 a. Changes in Public worship since 1914. b. Effects of the changes.

We have not found it necessary to change the hours of worship since 1914. We have a fairly full complement of services for a country parish. But we have instituted a regular weekly intercession service on Wednesday nights since 1914 and the attendance has been most satisfactory and does not fall off at all.

6. Number of Roman Catholics in the Parish. None.

1. See 1914.

CHIPPING NORTON   Incumbent H. H. Arkell[1]

1. Number of Boys Girls and Infants on books of day schools: a. Last year. b. 20 30 or 40 years ago.

Boys 1917: 82, 1891: 99; Girls 1917: 107, 1898: 119; Infants 1917: 81; 1898: 123.

We also have [a] Council School in the parish. The approximate number on the books at the present time is: Boys 120, Girls 97, Infants 79.

2. a. Men and b. Women qualified to vote in Parochial Church meeting. On inquiring I find that apart from calling a Parochial Church Meeting for the election of lay representatives to Ruridecanal Conference they have had no regular (annual) Parochial Church Meeting – and only the few who attended the meeting for this purpose signed the declaration. But I am now asking that this "declaration" may be extensively signed and we are looking forward to a well attended Parochial Church Meeting after Easter. Already 70 have signed the declaration 48 women 22 men. We hope of course many more will do so – the district visitors will shortly report I hope a large return.

3. Moral and Spiritual effect of: a. Wartime b. National Mission.

There can be no doubt that on (and for a short period after) the first shock of war there was promise of a high moral and spiritual effect. Men and women of all classes were touched and drawn to each other and towards God and to God. Our ordinary services were better attended, our special intercession services well attended. There was a "soberness and watching unto prayer". But now looking back to the first six months of the war and comparing them to the last six a great change is noticeable. It came gradually at first but soon after the entrance of the second year of the war it became definite. The wonderful God-consciousness and dependence on God, which the first shock of war brought – with the list of killed and the appearance of the wounded amongst us, gradually (as we got used to the daily list of casualties) gave place to reliance on mere man-power. This had set in definitely when in October 1915 I left my last parish – and I noticed the same thing on my arrival in this parish. In our first dire need we depended on God but gradually as a nation we came to lean only on men. First it was Russia – all would be well when Russia came up. Then when Russia delayed – it was our own man-power with a plentiful supply of munitions and shells. Then it was America – now it is our impregnable position in the west with Japan in the background of the east. In short the nation recovered from the shock of war then settled down to "the war" as inevitable – and as our own parish itself has experienced no real war-horror we have got a great deal too much accustomed to the present state of things and I notice the following effects – on (1) Men – for most part indifferent to the great world crisis – short handed and therefore some excuse and with great temptation to make money when, as they openly say, "money is so plentiful it will grow scarce after the war". (2) Lads unruly and out of hand through absence of their fathers and guardians – great increase of petty theft. (3) Girls many of them seriously affected by the presence of soldiers in the place. I came across evidence of this in my confirmation work. (4) Women as a whole affected more for good than any class. Bereavement and constant anxiety for sons and husbands has brought things home to them. In visiting them and from attendance at our intercession services I have noticed a real soberness and prayerfulness of mind.

The National Mission coming upon this state of things did not (with of course exceptions) reach the men as a whole – and was disappointing as regards the lads and girls, but it, I believe to a great extent, reached the women and helped the children. Our children's services were specially well attended and the children are not forgetting their resolutions. Of course the 'faithful few' who before were "on the way" received a great blessing from the National Mission. Their spiritual life was I believe deepened and the way they 'witnessed' by coming in "procession" after Sunday Evensong to our outdoor services before and after the Mission was encouraging. I hope through them the effect of the National Mission is still going on. We are still having outdoor services which are largely attended by Nonconformists as well as our own people.

4. Status of Church Schools. Options for compromise on a. management, b. head teachers, c. character of religious teaching. Might compromise be justified by better arrangements for Church teaching in state schools?

I think we should seek by all means to retain our Church Schools in single-school areas. Neither the management, appointment of head teachers or the character of religious teaching should be altered lest it should interfere with the <u>"atmosphere"</u> of the school. It is this "atmosphere" that is so tremendously important. So many children have no real homes and a school under proper management and loyal Church Teachers with no vagueness of undenominationalism can be made a real home and "mother" to teach them <u>devotion</u> and in addition one has to remember there is such a thing as teaching secular things religiously. The sense of Church membership too can only be fostered by attendance at such a school. I venture to think that the sad lack of sense of membership, and ignorance generally of their own Church, revealed by so many soldiers at the front (we are told) is owing to attendance at Council Schools or Church Schools <u>compromised out of all character</u>. Sunday Schools however efficient cannot make up for this "atmosphere". That is why in my opinion "facilities" in Council Schools should not be obtained at the cost of endangering this atmosphere in our Church Schools. My experience has been that very seldom indeed is there any objection made by <u>parents</u> of Nonconformists to the teaching in our Church Schools – the difficulty is largely manufactured by leading political Nonconformists – many Nonconformists send their children to our Church Schools though <u>here</u> they have the choice of a Council School should they prefer it.

5 a. Changes in Public worship since 1914. b. Effects of the changes. I was not instituted here until October 1915, but understand no changes were made between the last return (1914) and that time. Early this year I have started a Choral Celebration at 9am on the <u>third Sunday in the month – with sermon</u> – so that there is no sermon on that Sunday at 11 o'clock Matins. The result has so far been a very great increase in Communicants on that particular Sunday. Many have come who say it is impossible to attend at the ordinary 7am or 8am or 11 o'clock celebration (first Sunday in month) on account of home duties. So far this increased attendance at the 9 o'clock Celebration has made little difference in numbers attending Matins on that particular Sunday, so that it would seem a real need has been met.

6. Number of Roman Catholics in the Parish. The Roman Catholic authorities give the number as 200 (men, women and children) in Chipping Norton and Over-Norton. My own visiting book and that of my curate record 45 families of Roman Catholics so that the above estimate of 200 seems correct. There appear to be (out of this 200) 45 or about 45 children of school age. I understand that the Priest in charge here claims a little over 300 in the R.C. Mission as a whole which stretches from Barford.

1. Henry Herbert Arkell graduated from Jesus College Oxford in 1891 and trained at Wycliffe Hall, being ordained priest in 1893. He served two curacies 1892–1901 and was Vicar of Tytherington between 1901 and 1915, when he became Vicar of Chipping Norton. He was 49 years old in 1918 and at the 1911 census he shared a household with his wife, two young children, three unmarried female servants and an unmarried male gardener.

CLANFIELD   Incumbent W. Bryant[1]

1. Number of Boys Girls and Infants on books of day schools: a. Last year. b. 20 30 or 40 years ago.

	Boys	Girls	Infants
1917	28	31	36
1907	18	34	34
1897	22	24	40

1887, 1877 Records not trustworthy.

2. a. Men and b. Women qualified to vote in Parochial Church meeting. None.

3. Moral and Spiritual effect of: a. Wartime b. National Mission.

(a) Less parental control noticeable in cases w[h]ere the father is on military service. In many cases children please themselves about attending school and Sunday School, the mothers do not attend church so regularly, perhaps in part accounted for by field work during greater part of week. I fear bad language is more common among the children probably accounted for by absence of the fathers. I do not think private prayers have been neglected if the public worship has been.

(b) No noticeable effect.

4. Status of Church Schools. Options for compromise on a. management, b. head teachers, c. character of religious teaching. Might compromise be justified by better arrangements for Church teaching in state schools?

I think we ought by all means retain our Schools in their present status until there is a reasonable likelihood that the right of parents will be recognised and full equality of treatment given in all Public Elementary Schools. From the religious point of view I would put no confidence in N.U.T. as officially continued opposition seems to be offered to all suggestions of equality of treatment. The Union seems so strongly to favour universal undenominational teaching.

5 a. Changes in Public worship since 1914. b. Effects of the changes. Winter 1916–1917 Afternoon Service instead of Evening. <u>Slight</u> diminution of numbers though a few preferred the change. Since then we have continued Evensong at 6pm. So there would be no alterations since last return.

6. Number of Roman Catholics in the Parish. None.

1. See 1914.

CLAYDON   Incumbent A. C. Hoggins[1]

1. Number of Boys Girls and Infants on books of day schools: a. Last year. 27. **b. 20 30 or 40 years ago.** I am unable to get trustworthy information on this point – but the numbers were over 40–42, I think – six years ago and large enough to employ two teachers (apart from infants) ten years before that – the proportion of older people continually increasing in a largely diminishing population.

2. a. Men and b. Women qualified to vote in Parochial Church meeting. No men, no women.

3. Moral and Spiritual effect of: a. Wartime b. National Mission.

(a) Direct effect of the war nil – but that may be because of the smallness and isolation of the place. And probably there will be marked effects when those who have gone from the village begin to return. Indirectly the increase of wages has led to increased consumption of food in spite of prices and to indolent habits – women especially rising much later than they did. There is diminished keenness in work on allotments. But the number of tramps has very notably decreased. Spiritually the war has produced no effects so far. There is no sign of even a dawning perception of the fact that the war has any connection with national or individual shortcomings.

(b) The National Mission has produced either no effect or in the direction of greater laxity. The effects here have been discounted by previous mission work which has had the effect of making the people see that the old idea that religion consists in merely attending convenient services (in the Evening, chiefly) and gaining what temporal advantages generally belonging to a religious body cannot longer be maintained. The one or two who practice 'the duties of religion' are very much more real but the majority appear to feel that as 'religion' no longer offers commercial advantages it may be more or less entirely dispensed with. It is probable that this condition while seeming to be disastrous in the present contains good hope for the future. The idea that you can make the future safe by a minimum and cold hearted adherence to some of the outward forms of religion seems passing away. And it is I think clear that devotion when it does come will clothe itself in a garb to which we have been hitherto unaccustomed.

4. Status of Church Schools. Options for compromise on a. management, b. head teachers, c. character of religious teaching. Might compromise be justified by better arrangements for Church teaching in state schools?

I should want to write at too great length on this subject and I should hardly be justified in doing this since I cannot derive my "view" from the experience of my own parish. As far as that (this parish) is concerned I can only repeat more emphatically what I said after six months' experience of it – that in a tiny village like this a Council School (which is so small that high-class teachers cannot be expected to apply for teacherships) humanly speaking renders it impossible to hope for the spread of any religious feeling among the people – it practically kills religion. The religious influence of a School depends not only on the teaching but much more I think on the "atmosphere". To give up Church Schools in return for very doubtful concessions in the Provided Schools would be more than disastrous. The supposed difficulties of Church Schools in single School areas are surely over-rated. It is always possible to deal tactfully with those very few who will not wish to attend the religious instructions – and the religious atmosphere of the School will be more and more valued as religion itself is more and more valued in the area. Possibly some of the difficulties are due to the vagueness of much of the teaching which has been given in Church School – a great educationalist – the President of Columbia University N.Y. – has rightly said that an "emasculated" religious teaching is of no or at most very little value. If concessions are made I imagine that the most valuable would be to transfer the weekly holiday to <u>Thursday</u> (instead of Saturday) with the understanding that that would allow the religious bodies to arrange for the teaching of religion (perhaps in the school rooms) on that day.

5 a. Changes in Public worship since 1914. b. Effects of the changes. The arrangement Sung Eucharist at 10 Matins at 11 on Sundays has been changed to Matins at 10 Sung Eucharist at 11. Matins at 11 was said in deference to two men in the village who got tired of coming alone and for some time no one came. The children came at 10. Now the children and one or two adults come at 11, no one at 10. I think it would have been better had the Eucharist been retained at 10 and Matins thrown back to 9 – or if even the Eucharist has been fixed for 9 but this more doubtfully – but the difficulty in this is that the one or two adults who come at 11 say they could not come on 10.

6. Number of Roman Catholics in the Parish. There are <u>no</u> R.C.'s in the parish.

1. See 1914.

CLIFTON HAMPDEN   Incumbent R. Gibbs[1]

1. Number of Boys Girls and Infants on books of day schools: a. Last year. 60. **b. 20 30 or 40 years ago.** 20 years ago 50.

2. a. Men and b. Women qualified to vote in Parochial Church meeting. (a) Men 16, (b) Women 26. These enrolled 2 years ago.

3. Moral and Spiritual effect of: a. Wartime b. National Mission.

(a) Of the educated class those who had time on their hands have taken up war work of one kind and another splendidly but it is difficult to judge of the effect of the war on others. Wives with husbands at the war have taken up the extra burden of home work most bravely. There has been no increase of immorality that one knows of. On the other hand, there has been no apparent spiritual awakening of those who before the war neglected worship and the sacraments.

(b) The effort made in the autumn of 1916 was appreciated by some regular church goers.

4. Status of Church Schools. Options for compromise on a. management, b. head teachers, c. character of religious teaching. Might compromise be justified by better arrangements for Church teaching in state schools?

Our own parish is favoured and there is no need for any change here for there is no hardship to dissenters. I think the teachers in Church School in Single School areas should always be sound Church Teachers. I mean teachers who hold the Faith and teach it lovingly. But where there is the demand I should say that Dissenting Ministers should be allowed to teach their own flock in the school if there should be room or at their own houses and chapels during the Religious Hour and that the same liberty should be given to us in Provided Schools.

5 a. Changes in Public worship since 1914. b. Effects of the changes. Since Jan?/15 (i) we have had on the 2nd Sunday in each month a Celebration at 9 o'c with simple music. I have come to the conclusion that it is not a good hour. (ii) And on the last Sunday of each month a Choral Celebration (Merbecke) at 11 o'c, Mattins at 10.30 (singing only the Gloria Benediction and one hymn attendance not compulsory for the choir boys). Those who used before to communicate late communicate and much more regularly. There is always a very fair congregation. It is appreciated by the village folk. "The Gentry" do not like it much but some of them come. These changes are helping to give the Eucharist greater prominence. Since the war the Litany except on the last Sunday in the month is said after the Sermon. Mattins Sermon Litany. There is no special object in this – a few go out before the Litany instead of before the Sermon.

6. Number of Roman Catholics in the Parish. None.

1. See 1914.

COGGS   Incumbent R. W. Hudgell[1]

1. Number of Boys Girls and Infants on books of day schools: a. Last year. 110. b. 20 30 or 40 years ago.

Upon enquiry I find that early School Registers have been destroyed. In 1877 the number on the Register was 74.

2. a. Men and b. Women qualified to vote in Parochial Church meeting. None.

3. Moral and Spiritual effect of: a. Wartime b. National Mission.

(a) I cannot discern much moral and spiritual improvement in the lives of my parishioners as the result of the war. People are depressed and dwell on their miseries and privations. A few only attend the weekly War Intercessions or the daily services. There is much worldliness, selfishness and indifference to vital religion, to say nothing of Catholic belief and practice.

(b) The National Mission in this parish bore spiritual fruit in many ways. There has been a spirit of earnestness amongst the faithful ever since, and there has been a larger attendance at Divine Worship ever since, especially at the Holy Eucharist. The house-to-house visits of the Missioners were of great value and carried out with very much tact and adaptability. It is my opinion that the National Mission was of great and permanent spiritual value.

4. Status of Church Schools. Options for compromise on a. management, b. head teachers, c. character of religious teaching. Might compromise be justified by better arrangements for Church teaching in state schools?

I should deprecate any further compromise in our Church Schools. Every consideration is made for Nonconformists – whether Roman Catholics or dissenters – by Existing arrangements. We must by all means teach the Faith and the necessity of True Religion in order to acquire a proper and complete education unless we become Recreant to our spiritual trusteeship.

5 a. Changes in Public worship since 1914. b. Effects of the changes. a. The Holy Eucharist has taken the place of Matins at the 11 o'clock service on the first Sunday in the month Evensong on Sundays is said at 6pm instead of 6.30pm. b. Larger and more reverent congregations. Opportunity for Out-door Services after Evensong in the Summer months.

6. Number of Roman Catholics in the Parish. None, as far as I know, and I think I know every parishioner. Two R.C. children came to the Day School but they were Visitors.

1. Robert William Hudgell graduated L.Th. from King's College, Windsor, Nova Scotia in 1887 and was ordained priest in the same year. After a brief period as a travelling missionary he served a number of cures in Canada and the USA before coming to a curacy in England in 1904. He was Chaplain of St Mary's Hospital Paddington between 1908 and 1914 and became

Vicar of Coggs in 1915. He was aged 58 in 1918 and at the 1911 census he was sharing a household with his wife and their 19-year-old daughter who was a medical student.

COMBE   Incumbent S. S. Pearce[1]

1. Number of Boys Girls and Infants on books of day schools: a. Last year. b. 20 30 or 40 years ago.

The number of children on the Books of Combe (C of E) school 27 years ago was 122 viz in 1891.

This year (1918) the number is 72.

2. a. Men and b. Women qualified to vote in Parochial Church meeting. None.

3. Moral and Spiritual effect of: a. Wartime b. National Mission.

(a) The effect of the war on the parishioners of Coombe has not born as far as one can see any appreciable result in increasing the number of those attending the services of the parish church or the numbers of the communicants (of these latter, I do not notice any decrease since the national mission). The weekly Wednesday evening service of intercession (when the names of all those serving from this parish are read out) started in August 1914 and carried on to the present time has maintained its interest and the numbers attending have not fallen off – and may be said to be satisfactory and I hope may have created amongst some of us a habit of weekday worship once each week – which was certainly not existent before the war. I propose to continue the weekday service after the war. The Sunday scholars are less regular in attendance especially the elder boys and this irregularity is reflected in church attendance – even among the choir boys. Partly this due to the ease with which the boys at day school can go to work at a much earlier age and now do work and earn wages more largely both on week days and Sundays – as they fill up the gaps left by the absent men. Doubtless the absence of teas and treats has something to do with the less regularity of S. school scholars, though I should not feel inclined to place much stress on the absence of treats as the cause of slackness of S. school attendance.

(b) As regards the national mission – it does not seem to have touched the careless and indifferent: but as regards the more devout and serious minded, it has I think tended to make them more regular and attentive to the ordinances of religion. A good many of nonconformists came to the earlier addresses of the missioners but they dropped off before the end. Some things said perhaps were hardly tactful or likely to have proved attractive to the ordinary uneducated Wesleyan. The lady pilgrims were well received and thoroughly appreciated, but their stay was too short even to visit half the parishioners.

4. Status of Church Schools. Options for compromise on a. management, b. head teachers, c. character of religious teaching. Might compromise be justified by better arrangements for Church teaching in state schools?

In our church schools I do not advocate any changes nor do I hear any expression from Nonconformists complaining of our methods. I have taught the upper students for many years and a good many are not scholars of our Church Sunday School. They have the same Prayer Book lessons as the Church children – a chapel child often wins the Bishop's prize – of course the Diocesan Inspector is not informed which are church children or who are Chapel children. The parents are, I believe, pleased to have me teaching their children and the Teachers are grateful. I am not aware that I have ever watered down any Church Teaching – though at the beginning of 1st lesson each year I tell them I know their parents wishing them to attend chapel I have no wish to draw them away from their usual place of worship – while they are young they must obey their parents. I know little or nothing about the difficulties which occur in other parishes that I do not feel I can add any further suggestions or proposals of any worth.

5 a. Changes in Public worship since 1914. b. Effects of the changes. There have been no changes initiated in the services at Combe Parish Church since 1914 – except the War service of Prayer and Intercession on Wednesday evenings and that seems to be not only of spiritual advantage to this parish but likely to be educative; teaching the minds of the people to realize the need of our turning to God about the present day things that are taking place around us and which touch us all closely – it teaches the place also of intercession for others etc. The intercession services would hardly have been maintained unless some such feeling was at work in the minds of the people who come to them. Though the novelty of intercession and war services must long ago worn off, the interest in them has not evaporated – so far as I can judge.

6. Number of Roman Catholics in the Parish. There are no Roman Catholics in this parish.

1. See 1914.

CORNWELL Incumbent R. P. Burnett[1]

1. Number of Boys Girls and Infants on books of day schools: a. Last year. b. 20 30 or 40 years ago.

We have no "day-school". The Children attend Churchill School. (Our Sunday-Schools number about 17).

2. a. Men and b. Women qualified to vote in Parochial Church meeting. (a) 15. (b) 22.

3. Moral and Spiritual effect of: a. Wartime b. National Mission.

(a) Owing to shortage of labour, our intercessory services on a Sunday have suffered but the evening have been decidedly better attended. (b) Great interest was shown at the time of the mission and I think it has had a good effect on the parish generally.

4. Status of Church Schools. Options for compromise on a. management, b. head teachers, c. character of religious teaching. Might compromise be justified by better arrangements for Church teaching in state schools?

I think Church Schools should be under the management of Church people, as also the appointment of the teachers. For all <u>Church</u> Schools there should be <u>distinct Church</u> teaching.

5 a. Changes in Public worship since 1914. b. Effects of the changes. In addition to our <u>ordinary</u> Services, we have had "a Service of Intercession", once a week, for a blessing on our Soldiers and Allies in the war. It has, I think, been useful in keeping up interest in the matter.

6. Number of Roman Catholics in the Parish. None.

1. See 1914.

COTTISFORD, HARDWICK AND FINMERE

Incumbent S. M. Statham[1]

1. Number of Boys Girls and Infants on books of day schools: a. Last year. 14 boys, 10 girls, 11 infants. **b. 20 30 or 40 years ago.** Twenty years ago about the same average 35.8.

2. a. Men and b. Women qualified to vote in Parochial Church meeting. I do not remember any.

3. Moral and Spiritual effect of: a. Wartime b. National Mission.

(a) Practically no difference. (b) The attendance was satisfactory but I cannot say I think much difference in other respects.

4. Status of Church Schools. Options for compromise on a. management, b. head teachers, c. character of religious teaching. Might compromise be justified by better arrangements for Church teaching in state schools?

Religious principle to be kept at all costs.

5 a. Changes in Public worship since 1914. b. Effects of the changes. No changes.

6. Number of Roman Catholics in the Parish. One family Rothery – left last month February.

1. See 1914.

COWLEY Incumbent G. Moore[1]

1. Number of Boys Girls and Infants on books of day schools: a. Last year. Boys 120, Girls 144, Infants 155. **b. 20 30 or 40 years ago.** A mixed school of 80 children.

2. a. Men and b. Women qualified to vote in Parochial Church meeting. We were unable to get them together for this purpose.

3. Moral and Spiritual effect of: a. Wartime b. National Mission.

(a) The war has injured this parish, a real advance has been made in wages, boys who before the war earned 8/- a week on the land 16 years of age are now receiving 35/- a week. There is no out-look in the older ones for good. The people who profess to look after them encourage <u>by example</u> habits which have always been considered from a church point of view, detrimental to spiritual good such as girls <u>smoking</u> from 15 years of age, during the dinner hour allowed in the munitions works <u>openly</u> in the street walking to and from their work. Six mothers have complained to me and have come to this house to do so. Night is turned into day no respect for Sunday although many of them only work 4 days in the week.

(b) No respect or regard for Public Worship in fact religion is ignored.

4. Status of Church Schools. Options for compromise on a. management, b. head teachers, c. character of religious teaching. Might compromise be justified by better arrangements for Church teaching in state schools?

I consider and believe that Church should hold her Schools and that Parents should decide the point about the religion of their children. Every other class do in this Country, why deprive the worker of this privilege? I have been closely involved with Parish Schools for 45 years, we have now just under 500 in daily attendance. I have never had a single case of withdrawal from the teaching of the Church. If I had one I should certainly meet the case of the <u>Parent if</u> possible. We ought in my opinion to retain Church Schools in their present status. The N.U.T. in my opinion wishes to diminish the influence of the Church of England in the Schools. a. The management under the Act of 1904 is a compromise but a very fair one. b. The managers <u>must, as at present, appoint</u> the Head Teachers if there are to be Church Schools. c. I have always followed the Diocesan Syllabus a real help in every way. In my opinion the real danger is that my brethren the Clergy do <u>not</u> visit the Schools enough and that they do not look upon them as one of the most important branches of their work.

5 a. Changes in Public worship since 1914. b. Effects of the changes. No changes.

6. Number of Roman Catholics in the Parish. The school built by Mr. Cruikshank and afterwards sold to the Roman Catholics has some influence here now. They have a congregation of about 20. We have about 10 families Roman Catholics, mostly Irish. Their Chapel is nearly a mile away from the Parish Church and this is an advantage to them. They are not unfriendly and have given me £10 for the School in 7 years.

1. See 1914.

COWLEY ST JOHN Incumbent A. C. Scott[1]

1. Number of Boys Girls and Infants on books of day schools: a. Last year. S.S. Mary and John 1027. Cowley S. John 700 **b. 20 30 or 40 years ago.** ? S.S. Mary and John schools were not built.

2. a. Men and b. Women qualified to vote in Parochial Church meeting. None – they are doing it now.

3. Moral and Spiritual effect of: a. Wartime b. National Mission.

(a) I don't see much difference – at first people came together for prayer and intercession. Now it has dropped back almost to where it was before.

(b) The National Mission was chiefly noted for getting back the relapsed and for deepening of those who had attended church.

4. Status of Church Schools. Options for compromise on a. management, b. head teachers, c. character of religious teaching. Might compromise be justified by better arrangements for Church teaching in state schools?

With regard to the 3rd point – I don't consider "the offer of more ..." worth having. It means introducing special teachers into schools just at the time when Public Schools have given them up. In older days the French Master, the Singing Master, the Drawing Master came in from outside and the discipline etc was bad. Judging by the attempts at Birmingham 15–20 years ago it is just the same with 'religious' teachers going into Council Schools. Generally the Head Teachers hate it, and many of the clergy do too and the classes are far too big and beyond the people who can be found to go. Unless they can count on being helped by Head Teachers and Class Teachers this is practically useless.

5 a. Changes in Public worship since 1914. b. Effects of the changes. Sunday Evensong altered from 7 to 6.30. Sung Mass at St Albans Mission Service at 9.30.

6. Number of Roman Catholics in the Parish. ? not many.

1. See 1914.

CROPREDY Incumbent G. Barr[1]

1. Number of Boys Girls and Infants on books of day schools: a. Last year. Boys 38, Girls 26, Infants 27, Total 91 **b. 20 30 or 40 years ago.** Total in year 1868 = 147. Sectional details, re Boys, Girls and Infants, not obtainable beyond the past Ten years.

2. a. Men and b. Women qualified to vote in Parochial Church meeting. Not any that I am aware of. I have no knowledge of any such organisation having been set up in the parish – prior to my incumbency, which commenced last year.

3. Moral and Spiritual effect of: a. Wartime b. National Mission.

Not having lived in Cropredy before the time of the war or that of the National Mission, I can make no comparison as between before and after. But, examining one's common sense and power of observation, I should say that the "moral and spiritual effects" of (a) and (b) "on the different classes in this parish" has been as nearly as possible Nil.

4. Status of Church Schools. Options for compromise on a. management, b. head teachers, c. character of religious teaching. Might compromise be justified by better arrangements for Church teaching in state schools?

I am not sufficiently expert in these matters to offer an opinion. My experience of over thirty years has been that most of the so-called "difficulties" in regard to "(a)", "(b)" and "(c)" are unreal.

5 a. Changes in Public worship since 1914. b. Effects of the changes. I can only speak in regard to the past thirteen months during which period there have been no such changes.

6. Number of Roman Catholics in the Parish. 1 man 1 woman 2 children total 4 all one family.

1. George Barr graduated from St John's College Cambridge in 1876 and was ordained priest in 1879. After serving two curacies 1877–83 he was Vicar of Holy Trinity Milton-next-Gravesend 1883–97 and then Rector of Longhope between 1897 and 1917, when he became Vicar of Cropredy. He was 66 in 1918 and at the 1911 census he was sharing a household with his wife, two unmarried daughters aged 31 and 32, and two unmarried female servants.

CROWELL   Incumbent F. N. Davis[1]

1. Number of Boys Girls and Infants on books of day schools: a. Last year. b. 20 30 or 40 years ago.

Children attend school at Chinnor.

2. a. Men and b. Women qualified to vote in Parochial Church meeting. None, population about 80 all poor and ignorant.

3. Moral and Spiritual effect of: a. Wartime b. National Mission.

I think the church-goers have become more serious in their view of life and in their devotions. Those not touched by religion previously to the war remain untouched.

4. Status of Church Schools. Options for compromise on a. management, b. head teachers, c. character of religious teaching. Might compromise be justified by better arrangements for Church teaching in state schools?

I think the Church should insist on retaining the right of appointing the head teacher, but chiefly with a view to keeping out undesirables. I am afraid that I do not think that Church Schools have been of very much direct service to the Church. Where the incumbent and the staff of a <u>Board</u> School work together much good work is done – where the incumbent is not in the confidence of teachers or of the parents of the children, a <u>church</u> school is not very useful. I know many schools of both types in this diocese. I do not express this opinion freely or publicly; I am prepared to join in the general effort to retain our own schools. I should be prepared for any compromise provided we appoint the head teacher.

5 a. Changes in Public worship since 1914. b. Effects of the changes. The only change is that the 11 o'clock morning service is now The Holy Communion. I cannot report any direct effects, but I hope that the idea of worship is being developed.

6. Number of Roman Catholics in the Parish. None.

1. See 1914.

CUDDESDON   Incumbent J. B. Seaton[1]

1. Number of Boys Girls and Infants on books of day schools: a. Last year. 53. **b. 20 30 or 40 years ago.** Thirty years ago – 130.

2. a. Men and b. Women qualified to vote in Parochial Church meeting. I am not able to put my hands on the register at this moment. It is amongst the books of my curate which are packed in a case. But a considerable number of men and women have signed the declaration.

3. Moral and Spiritual effect of: a. Wartime b. National Mission.

I could not say that there has been any increase in attendance at public worship as a consequence of war-time or the National Mission. The lives of the regular church people have been undoubtedly deepened. There is a general willingness on their part to undertake work and a spirit of readiness and receptiveness amongst them. Even amongst those who do not attend church I am persuaded that there is greater seriousness and thoughtfulness, a real quickening of mental activity and a widening of outlook and a spirit of kindliness. They are much more alive and ready to talk and less reserved. I do not think that there is any slackening of discipline amongst the young. In fact I should say that the general tone is less rough than it was. I have a greater sense of the growth of community spirit which no doubt can be traced to our community of burdens and need.

4. Status of Church Schools. Options for compromise on a. management, b. head teachers, c. character of religious teaching. Might compromise be justified by better arrangements for Church teaching in state schools?

I have never worked in a single-school area except here, where there is no difficulty. I should, however, be glad to see some compromise. In regard to management and the appointment of teachers, I feel that the current system would work the best, but I should be prepared for some compromise in regard to (c). In the Cape Provinces, the Dutch Church and the Church of the Province were able to induce the Govt to accept the Heidelburg Catechism as the basis of religious teaching in Govt schools. I should certainly regard the offer of more satisfactory conditions of religious teaching in "Provided" or "Council" Schools as justifying such a compromise.

5 a. Changes in Public worship since 1914. b. Effects of the changes. a. None, save the short service of intercession for the War after Evensong on Sundays, which is appreciated.

6. Number of Roman Catholics in the Parish. None.

1. See 1914.

CUXHAM   Incumbent Thomas Hainsworth[1] (Officiating Clergyman)

1. Number of Boys Girls and Infants on books of day schools: Church school: **a. Last year.** 27 on books: 13 girls and 14 boys. **b. 20 30 or 40 years ago.** 20 years ago, 22 on books: 10 girls, 12 boys.

All infants. Elder children going to Watlington.

2. a. Men and b. Women qualified to vote in Parochial Church meeting. [*No response*].

3. Moral and Spiritual effect of: a. Wartime b. National Mission.

[*No response*].

4. Status of Church Schools. Options for compromise on a. management, b. head teachers, c. character of religious teaching. Might compromise be justified by better arrangements for Church teaching in state schools?

[*No response*].

5 a. Changes in Public worship since 1914. b. Effects of the changes. [*No response*].

6. Number of Roman Catholics in the Parish. [*No response*].

1. See 1914 Brightwell Baldwin. Hainsworth came to Cuxham in 1918.

DEDDINGTON   Incumbent T. Boniface[1]

1. Number of Boys Girls and Infants on books of day schools: a. Last year. b. 20 30 or 40 years ago.

	Boys and Girls	Infants	Total
(a)	118	55	173
(b) <u>1907</u>	174	89	263

No earlier records.

2. a. Men and b. Women qualified to vote in Parochial Church meeting. a. 16 men. b. 17 women.

3. Moral and Spiritual effect of: a. Wartime b. National Mission.

I much regret to state that I see no direct moral and spiritual effect on the different classes in my parish arising from a) the war b) the national mission. Some I fear are more reckless, thoughtless and indifferent than before.

4. Status of Church Schools. Options for compromise on a. management, b. head teachers, c. character of religious teaching. Might compromise be justified by better arrangements for Church teaching in state schools?

I think it is only fair to the founders of Church Schools in single school areas – that the Schools should retain as far as possible their present state in (a) management, (b) appointment of head-teachers, and (c) the character of the religious teaching, – but in places where there is a conscientious objection to the Church Teaching: some provision should be made, if possible, for the children of the Parents, objecting, to be taught in accordance with their views.

5 a. Changes in Public worship since 1914. b. Effects of the changes. There have been no material changes in the <u>methods</u> or <u>hours</u> of public worship since 1914 except those caused by the lighting restrictions.

6. Number of Roman Catholics in the Parish. 1 man 2 women.

1. See 1914.

DORCHESTER WITH BURCOT   Incumbent N. C. S. Poyntz[1]

1. Number of Boys Girls and Infants on books of day schools: a. Last year. Boys 38; Girls and Infants 111. **b. 20 30 or 40 years ago.** 1899: Boys 58, Girls and Infants 144. 1917: Boys 38; Girls and Infants 111.

2. a. Men and b. Women qualified to vote in Parochial Church meeting. None.

3. Moral and Spiritual effect of: a. Wartime b. National Mission.

(a) In some cases a demoralising effect: in many a lessening of spiritual effort.

(b) In some cases a closer drawing towards the Church.

4. Status of Church Schools. Options for compromise on a. management, b. head teachers, c. character of religious teaching. Might compromise be justified by better arrangements for Church teaching in state schools?

If the Church believes in Herself she cannot recognise other forms of religion, or make any compromise with them. In Baptism She becomes the Spiritual Mother of the Baptized and cannot rightly hand them over to another form of religion. Hence She must try to retain (a) (b) and (c) in Her own hands.

5 a. Changes in Public worship since 1914. b. Effects of the changes. None.

6. Number of Roman Catholics in the Parish. One Priest and housekeeper. Six laity adults three laity children. There is a church here for the District.

1. See 1914.

DRAYTON Incumbent W. Spendlove[1]

1. Number of Boys Girls and Infants on books of day schools: a. Last year. b. 20 30 or 40 years ago.

a. Last year: Infants 10, Boys 14, Girls 8 = 32. b. Twenty years ago: 36.

2. a. Men and b. Women qualified to vote in Parochial Church meeting. None. The Churchwardens objected and threatened to resign if I persevered with effort. There is no one else suitable to act in their stead.

3. Moral and Spiritual effect of: a. Wartime b. National Mission.

(a) The war has stirred up a patriotic spirit among the farmers and their men who are about the only class in this small village. Young men and women have responded to the call for service very well, consequently there has been decreased attendances at Divine Worship, but more regularity and liberality is observable among those able to attend.

(b) The National Mission aroused some lapsed Christians but did not affect the non church-goers very much. Intercession services have been well attended.

4. Status of Church Schools. Options for compromise on a. management, b. head teachers, c. character of religious teaching. Might compromise be justified by better arrangements for Church teaching in state schools?

In small villages such as this we might make a slight compromise as regards:-
(a) Allow Nonconformists to be represented in the management for purposes of

representation of these people for reason of conciliation. (b) Male teachers are necessary among rough and ignorant folk.

(c) We must not sacrifice any principle, but the County Council syllabus meets the situation in a small village. I think the religious character of the teachers must be demanded and teaching given on Missions and generally of a broader character including a knowledge of the religion in our own Empire and Empire Day should be established. We observe it here with good effect on the people.

5 a. Changes in Public worship since 1914. b. Effects of the changes. a. Afternoon service on Sunday instead of evening had to be adopted, but with ill affect. b. Villagers near the town went there on Sunday night – not to their best interests. The church goers here have appreciated slight alterations in the second part of evening services – more use of authorised Litanies, Prayers and Hymns.

6. Number of Roman Catholics in the Parish. There is only one Roman Catholic (male) in this parish and no Non Con place of worship.

1. See 1914.

DRAYTON ST LEONARD Incumbent W. Williams[1]

1. Number of Boys Girls and Infants on books of day schools: a. Last year. b. 20 30 or 40 years ago.

(a) 31 children. (b) 1878: 57 children; 1888: 54 children; 1898: 48 children. Figures from School Register.

2. a. Men and b. Women qualified to vote in Parochial Church meeting. None, so far I can tell. I feel that the communal sense is as yet, so undeveloped in the peasantry (who are the vast majority of the parishioners) that we are not ready for this. It would be impossible to work it on sound democratic lines; we should get the old oligarchical tradition reaffirmed afresh, and so far put the clock back. Little can be done until the peasantry can be got to realize that they ought to exercise their ecclesiastical franchise. As a strong Socialist I am against formal action in the matter yet a while – whatever may apply elsewhere, what I have stated applies here.

3. Moral and Spiritual effect of: a. Wartime b. National Mission.

The only class of which I can speak is that of the peasants. (a) It appears to me that (i) The great rise in wages, right and fair as it is, has been and still is a danger. It emphasises the importance of material things out of all proportion; it tends to encourage extravagance; the rudes, suddenly handling so much money, only too readily lose their heads. As one instance, I heard say that, whatever the price of beer they will have as much as they can get. (ii) The general impression prevails that the issues of the war are with brute force directed by "slimness".[2] There is little sense of the fact that "God is in his heaven"; where religion comes in at all it partly comes in to give "Dutch courage" and not to confirm faith in the moral government of God. (iii) The advent as workers on the land of women from the towns, eg shop girls from Harrods stores and Whiteley's, is a dangerous element. I have not come across any women at this work who lift the standard of thought and practice.

Per contra (i) The attention drawn to the prevalence of sexual vice and venereal disease has been good; it gives an opportunity of plain speaking and the facts revealed are certainly in the direction of a deterrent and punishment appears as the other half of crime. (ii) A very small proportion of people are shocked into seriousness; the events of the war do, of course, sift people, and there is the opportunity of forming a nucleus of those who are really in earnest. (iii) Also are home on the land some of the soldiers; eg those who are socialists from the towns; these stir up the muddy water and give the people courage to protest against eg bad housing conditions. But there are practically no definite church folk amongst them.

(b) I am afraid that in my experience the National Mission did not touch the careless; with a few who are already pious, it proved a fresh starting point, and it gave the opportunity of establishing the Lord's Service as the Sunday act of worship with really encouraging results in a few instances.

4. Status of Church Schools. Options for compromise on a. management, b. head teachers, c. character of religious teaching. Might compromise be justified by better arrangements for Church teaching in state schools?

(i) I think that the right of entry to all schools, 'Provided' or not, should be granted to the Roman Catholics and the denominations for purposes of religious instruction – so far as the instruction in religion given to Anglican children is concerned, I think that is seriously hampered by the examination system, which facilitates opportunities of "cramming" and tends to foster the notion that religion is a "subject" equally with geography and history etc. I do not think that anything really satisfactory can be achieved until inspection is substituted for examination by notice. I have depended for the religious instruction of the children entirely on the Sunday Catechism and that can be taught at informal – or more or less informal – meetings at my house in the winter evenings. A singing class gives excellent opportunities – I find the children distressingly ignorant of the foundation verities of religion – My wife (who is herself a certificated teacher) got an answer lately to the question addressed to a newcomer "Who was Jesus Christ" – "a wonderful man". On all this I feel very strongly. The reason why there is so much leakage is not the children cannot be impressed and held but rather that they are not impressed and held.

(ii) Without some reforms of a drastic nature I greatly doubt whether the schools are worth retaining in the present status.

(iii) If the schools are to be retained, I do not quite see how the head-teachers or the infant teachers are to be other than Anglicans. I should welcome head-teachers as members of the Managers' Body, and also some educational expert appointed by the County Council, but he or she must be an expert.

(iv) I think a great deal is to be said for making all schools "Provided", and giving Anglicans and others the right of entry. But – the clergy, if they teach must learn to teach scientifically.

5 a. Changes in Public worship since 1914. b. Effects of the changes. (a) Mattins and Litany said at 9.15 and Sung Communion Service at 10 has been substituted for Mattins and Litany at 11. (b) Several lapsed peasant communicants have been brought back and generally the duty of Communion has been emphasised, and the obligation of attending the Lord's Service on Sunday is beginning to be realized. The number of children attending church has greatly increased, perhaps trebled, and several other lads who never attended except in the evening now come in the mornings. The Catechism which follows at 11 am is always related to the Gospel for the day which is expounded at the 10 o'clock service.

6. Number of Roman Catholics in the Parish. There were several Roman Catholics last year; now there is only one. A man, an Irishman and an Officer on Active Service.

With apologies for my prolixity.

1. Watkin Wynn Williams graduated from Christ Church Oxford in 1882 and was ordained priest in 1884. After an initial curacy he was Vice-Principal of the Dorchester Missionary College 1888–91, Fellow and Tutor of St Augustine's College Canterbury 1891–1904 and then Vicar of Monkton between 1904 and 1915, when he became Rector of Drayton St Leonard. He published widely in theological subjects including *An Introduction to the Articles of the Church of England* (1895) and *Maxims of the Mystics* (1909). He was 58 in 1918 and at the 1911 census he was sharing a household with his wife, their 4-year-old son, two unmarried female servants, and a 13-year-old male servant, described as a page.
2. Slimness: a colloquial word for slyness or cunning, especially in English-speaking South Africa.

DUCKLINGTON WITH HARDWICK   Incumbent C. Tristram[1]

1. Number of Boys Girls and Infants on books of day schools: a. Last year. 94. **b. 20 30 or 40 years ago.** Twenty years ago there were 88.

2. a. Men and b. Women qualified to vote in Parochial Church meeting. 14 men, 4 women.

3. Moral and Spiritual effect of: a. Wartime b. National Mission.

In this parish the War has made us more Christian in thought and less contented with ourselves and with our National Life. We have realised the devotion and comradeship of the men at the front, and how little that has appeared in our own lives. The war has also deepened the ties of home life, and caused a great deal of real sacrifice. I hope that we are beginning to see how these qualities ought to appear in our own religious life, and help us to live more for each other and less for self. My 18 confirmation candidates were more attentive than any I have had before, and they were always interested by any reference to the War and its bearing upon religious faith and practice. The attendance at Church has got better and there is a hope of more Communicants. I have encouraged the boys of 14 to 17 to learn bell ringing this year; they now ring us to church and help to arouse the people.

(b) The National Mission helped us to see our faults and to realise that we needed change, which is what country folk most dislike. The visit of the Pilgrims did real good because they visited in the homes. It is friendliness with the People in their homes and at their work, and with the children, which has most effect in country villages. As one result of the Mission I hope that the people do realise that the Church is interested in their lives and social condition, and desires to help effect changes for the better in the coming years.

4. Status of Church Schools. Options for compromise on a. management, b. head teachers, c. character of religious teaching. Might compromise be justified by better arrangements for Church teaching in state schools?

Some compromise might be made in the matter of management and character of religious teaching. The Sacraments are often better taught in Church at Children's services or Guilds where there is more feeling of devotion or reality than in a stuffy classroom. The offer of more satisfactory conditions in Provided schools would be well worth a compromise, but if the Clergy are to teach in Council schools some will have to be more tactful towards the teachers than they have been. It is the very extreme views and teaching of some which have alarmed even moderate nonconformists. In the Farnham Council schools besides a syllabus the Apostles Creed was taught, and the Head Master thought it a great addition, as giving a definite foundation on which to teach. This was perhaps an exceptional arrangement, but it was found to work smoothly. The schools were examined alternately by the Diocesan Inspector and by a Nonconformist Minister. The Teachers hated both examinations alike.

5 a. Changes in Public worship since 1914. b. Effects of the changes. There are no changes to report, though I am very willing to make any changes that would suit the convenience of the People.

6. Number of Roman Catholics in the Parish. There are none. A Roman Catholic priest came in the summer of 1917 to ascertain if there were any here. He admired the church and after luncheon departed to Chipping Camden.

1. See 1914.

DUNSDEN[1]   Incumbent H. Wigan[2]

1. Number of Boys Girls and Infants on books of day schools: a. Last year. b. 20 30 or 40 years ago.

Last year: Boys 26, Girls 37, Infants 25. 1891: Boys 62, Girls 59 (Infants included).

2. a. Men and b. Women qualified to vote in Parochial Church meeting. None to my knowledge.

3. Moral and Spiritual effect of: a. Wartime b. National Mission.

(a) I cannot see that the chastisement of the war has, as yet, any real effect upon the people spiritually. The difficulty in obtaining the necessaries of life absorbs an increasing amount of time and attention.

(b) The National Mission was, thank God, a time of real Blessing in this place. There were only about a dozen actual Conversions as far as I can see, but these included an elderly farmer and another elderly man with a past and made a real stir in the place; There was however a real reviving of many whose love had grown cold and at the close of the last meeting over 20 stood up and publically testified to having received blessing, and after this lapse of time I have no reason to doubt that it was in every case genuine.

4. Status of Church Schools. Options for compromise on a. management, b. head teachers, c. character of religious teaching. Might compromise be justified by better arrangements for Church teaching in state schools?

In my own experience, I have never found the 'Religious difficulty' to exist in small country Parishes unless the teaching is of an ultra Catholic type, and I am strongly in favour of a reasonable compromise as being the only way in which the opportunity for giving Religious Instruction in Day Schools is likely to be preserved for long. The distinctive Church of England teaching of Catechism and Prayer book are, in my opinion, much more suited to the Sunday School and to the Bible Class than to the Day School where the short time available should be devoted to Scripture only.

5 a. Changes in Public worship since 1914. b. Effects of the changes. No change.

6. Number of Roman Catholics in the Parish. None.

1. Population 531.
2. Herbert Wigan graduated from Oriel College Oxford in 1887 and trained at Cuddesdon College, being ordained priest in 1889. He served two curacies and a period as Chaplain of All Saints School Bloxham between 1888 and 1904, when he became Vicar of Dunsden. He was 55 in 1918 and at the 1911 census he was unmarried, sharing a household with a male groom-gardener, his wife the cook-housekeeper, and one unmarried female servant.

DUNS TEW   Incumbent A. Smith[1]

1. Number of Boys Girls and Infants on books of day schools: a. Last year. b. 20 30 or 40 years ago.

	1918	1898	1893
Boys	20	15	14

Girls   7   13   11

Infants 11   20   22

No information for earlier years.

2. a. Men and b. Women qualified to vote in Parochial Church meeting. None last year.

3. Moral and Spiritual effect of: a. Wartime b. National Mission.

I cannot report any apparent effect.

4. Status of Church Schools. Options for compromise on a. management, b. head teachers, c. character of religious teaching. Might compromise be justified by better arrangements for Church teaching in state schools?

In small village schools where there is Head Mistress (or Master) and only one probably Junior assistant – I think the Head should be Ch. of England. In larger schools where there is the duly qualified assistant, the Head (b) might be Non Conformist, provided the assistant were Church of England.

(a) I think Nonconformists might be appointed to share the duties of Managers. We had a nonconformist for several years on our Board of Managers and no unpleasantness arose. (c) I think the character of the Religious Teaching should be what it is now i.e. of course with exemption for those wishing it. I should be in favour of some compromise if greater facilities etc were given in Provided schools.

5 a. Changes in Public worship since 1914. b. Effects of the changes. I have no changes to report.

6. Number of Roman Catholics in the Parish. No Roman Catholics in this Parish.

1. See 1914.

ELSFIELD   Incumbent W. H. Elkington[1]

1. Number of Boys Girls and Infants on books of day schools: a. Last year. 40. **b. 20 30 or 40 years ago.** 20 years ago: about 15–20.

2. a. Men and b. Women qualified to vote in Parochial Church meeting. None.

3. Moral and Spiritual effect of: a. Wartime b. National Mission.

Some turn to Almighty God in prayer and feel the seriousness of the times – others seem unmoved to any great extent. (b) For a time a slight influence seemed to have been made upon a few.

4. Status of Church Schools. Options for compromise on a. management, b. head teachers, c. character of religious teaching. Might compromise be justified by better arrangements for Church teaching in state schools?

Religious Teaching should be upheld.

5 a. Changes in Public worship since 1914. b. Effects of the changes. No changes.

6. Number of Roman Catholics in the Parish. No R.Cs.

1. See 1914.

EMMINGTON[1]   Incumbent L. Baldwyn[2]

1. Number of Boys Girls and Infants on books of day schools: a. Last year. b. 20 30 or 40 years ago.

No school. Children attend Chinnor or Sydenham school. At present time only one child of school age in Parish.

2. a. Men and b. Women qualified to vote in Parochial Church meeting. Population is 36 and mostly ignorant people.

3. Moral and Spiritual effect of: a. Wartime b. National Mission.

The population is too small to be able to make any statement under these heads. There is no dissent in the place and the little community is remarkably good in its attendance at worship.

4. Status of Church Schools. Options for compromise on a. management, b. head teachers, c. character of religious teaching. Might compromise be justified by better arrangements for Church teaching in state schools?

[*No response*].

5 a. Changes in Public worship since 1914. b. Effects of the changes. a. None needed.

6. Number of Roman Catholics in the Parish. None.

1. Population 38. A combined benefice with Chinnor, with Baldwyn as incumbent from 1908.
2. See 1914 Chinnor.

ENSTONE   Incumbent W. J. Palmer[1]

1. Number of Boys Girls and Infants on books of day schools: a. Last year. b. 20 30 or 40 years ago.

(a) Mixed school – average for year ending Feb. 28th 1918 was 84, the highest number on books being 92. Infant school – average 40 (28 of 5 and over, 12 under 5 years), on books 46.

(b) 60 in Infant School 20 years ago.

Mixed School May 13 1878: 100 present in morning and 103 in afternoon. Average year ending Feb 28 1888 was 85, 1898 it was 99 (with 118 on books). Average for year 1878 was 81.8. The highest number on books was 142 and the highest average for any one week was 123.

N.B. Registers are not expected to be kept more than 10 years.

2. a. Men and b. Women qualified to vote in Parochial Church meeting. 3 men and 5 women, who attended the meeting called to elect representatives for the R.D. Conference. This is my own fault for not having made further effort to obtain signatures. I have been content to work loyally with church officers and workers who are all communicants. None but communicants attend the Vestry; but I should be thankful for the Vestry to be superseded by a Parish Church Council.

3. Moral and Spiritual effect of: a. Wartime b. National Mission.

Before the Military Service Act this parish was conspicuous for the number of men and lads in the Navy and Army – no recruiting meeting having to be held. Those whom the Military Service Act embraced have gone willingly. I did the greater part of the canvassing under the Derby Scheme. I have been in this parish now just over 20 years (the first 6 as curate) and I cannot but come to the conclusion that on the whole we have suffered nearly as much as we have gained morally and spiritually of the war. This is an agricultural parish comprising two villages and seven hamlets. With few exceptions, we are only farmers and labourers. It has been demoralizingly easy for those "partially" dependent upon men and lads taken for the army to obtain government allowances. One wonders how some could have managed to qualify. As representative of the Sailors and Soldiers Families Association I have had documents and evidence that have grieved me. Real mutual satisfaction between farmers and labourers is not as extensive as one would wish. Labour in this parish, as elsewhere, can now look back and see that it has not had a fair share and opportunity and that we have been contented to acquiesce in the conditions we found. The charity of the church or great houses near are not a substitute for a living wage. Men and lads converse freely with one as an old friend as to what belongs to their daily work and outlook. I am not down-hearted as long as we aim at the realization of our membership in Christ and his Church in the life of the new England that one can see is rising out of the war. The war only emphasises here the question of "work and wages" and what I see and hear makes me anxious for better education and housing and the daily remembrance that members of Christ are members one of another. I am sure that people here have greater sympathy with one another through their common anxiety for those belonging to them who are serving their country.

We were very thankful for the National Mission which strengthened those who cared for God's House and His means of grace. The missioner (Rev. G. Dangerfield) said that it was evident to him that preparation had been made. He was heard gladly and has preached at our Harvest Thanksgiving since. Many have come to church more regularly than before.

4. Status of Church Schools. Options for compromise on a. management, b. head teachers, c. character of religious teaching. Might compromise be justified by better arrangements for Church teaching in state schools?

Yes. Insist upon facilities being given in all Public Elementary schools for children being instructed according to the religious belief of the Parents. Insist upon all teachers in Church schools giving proof that they believe in what they are required to teach.

Do not compel teachers in any other school to give religious instruction unless they whole-heartedly desire to do so. Let the management be as representative as possible so long as you can get people who are in sympathy with education. 'Undenominational' teaching ought not to be inflicted upon the children of the Church. The character of the teachers and its influence upon the children – ought to be more regarded. N.B. This Parish has not had its church Schools since about 1870.

5 a. Changes in Public worship since 1914. b. Effects of the changes. I have said the Litany after the 3rd Collect at Evensong on Sundays when there has been a celebration of H.C. after Morning Prayer in addition to the early celebration. Many come to church in the Evening who do not ordinarily attend in the forenoon, and have thus been helped by the Litany to take their part in intercessions. In response to your Lordship's letter in the Magazine at the first anniversary of the war I have tried to follow your example in bidding the prayers of the people after the sermon from the pulpit (being much helped by the Cuddesdon Manual of Intercession, for instance), after 3rd Collect at Evensong. I did this regularly for some months, except when I said Litany after 3rd Collect at Evensong. During this last winter I have not omitted the prayers of the Prayer Book after 3rd Collect, but have had war prayers and intercession just before the "Blessing". Sunday evening is a great opportunity and I am sure the above method and variety have helped people anxious about their men and lads in navy and army. It has helped bring many to Communion.

6. Number of Roman Catholics in the Parish. 5 men, 11 women, 5 children. These are found in 7 cottages and at Enstone House lately taken by a Roman Catholic lady. Also at Radford (in this parish) a Roman Catholic resident Priest (of German nationality); and a Convent with Mother Superior and two sisters, who have an orphanage or boarding school. I do not know the numbers of their children, who come from Birmingham and neighbourhood. The R.C. colony at Radford used to belong to Kiddington formerly owned by a R.C. nobleman. When the property changed hands they were provided for close by in our hamlet of Radford.

1. See 1914.

EWELME   Incumbent J. A. Dodd[1]

1. Number of Boys Girls and Infants on books of day schools: a. Last year. b. 20 30 or 40 years ago.

(a) B. 17, G. 26, Inf. 17. (b) No information earlier than 1901 when the number was: B. 25, G. 29, Inf. 42.

2. a. Men and b. Women qualified to vote in Parochial Church meeting. 3 men, 7 women.

3. Moral and Spiritual effect of: a. Wartime b. National Mission.

(a) War time. The war has made all classes more serious and thoughtful and has greatly widened the interests of the working people. They have attended very readily on the occasions when special services have been ordered, eg the anniversary of the beginning of the war, or the 1st Sunday in the New Year. They were ready to hear what the church had to say with reference to the events and conditions of the time. I think they are greatly puzzled and perplexed by what is happening and how it is to be reconciled with the Divine Government of the world? If God is on the side of right, why doesn't right win speedily and decisively? Can the Christian view of the world maintain itself against material force? I do not think the effect of the war has been generally favourable to religion – at least, not to organised religion.

(b) National Mission. I do not think that the effects of the mission have been very noticeable. It did not seem to bring anything new – it was only saying 'a little louder' what the clergy had been saying all along. It would have done better if it had dealt more with the intellectual side of religion and the difficulties which people feel in that respect, and above all with the need for a more Christian social order.

4. Status of Church Schools. Options for compromise on a. management, b. head teachers, c. character of religious teaching. Might compromise be justified by better arrangements for Church teaching in state schools?

I do not think that Church schools in single-school areas are likely to be permanent, and I do not think the Church would lose very much by their being incorporated in a national system. Whatever system was ultimately adopted, a clergyman who was really able to teach, would easily arrange for the instruction of the children of the Church. For this, it would be essential that the clergy should be trained in the art of teaching and if this were done, the difficulty would be solved. The details of the compromise would matter little.

5 a. Changes in Public worship since 1914. b. Effects of the changes. The only change which I have made was to have an afternoon service in the place of an evening, during the winter of 1916–17, and the experiment was fairly successful. Congregations certainly did not diminish and people from outlying houses, who had not been able to come morning or evening, came regularly in the afternoon. I was not able to continue this during the late winter, having taken on a second parish in addition to my own.

6. Number of Roman Catholics in the Parish. 2 families, each composed of husband, wife and two children, 8 in all.

1. See 1914.

EYNSHAM   Incumbent W. N. Bricknell[1]

1. Number of Boys Girls and Infants on books of day schools: a. Last year. b. 20 30 or 40 years ago.

140 Boys, 142 Girls, 150 Infants 25 years ago. Now: 102 Boys, 105 Girls, 106 Infants. Many children go to Witney or Oxford Schools who previously attended Eynsham schools.

2. a. Men and b. Women qualified to vote in Parochial Church meeting. None. The People here are not in favour of a Parochial Church Council. We have a good number of people who are always ready and willing to work for the Church without being elected on a Church Council.

3. Moral and Spiritual effect of: a. Wartime b. National Mission.

There has been a more devout spirit among the different classes in the parish since the war commenced: and this I feel sure overshadowed the national mission. The new intercession services held here from the very commencement of the war and the fact of so very many of those of military age going to the front has brought home to all here the need of real worship.

4. Status of Church Schools. Options for compromise on a. management, b. head teachers, c. character of religious teaching. Might compromise be justified by better arrangements for Church teaching in state schools?

The Schools here are Provided Schools. I have been Chairman and Correspondent for many years and all my Co-managers are Church people and Communicants. All our Teachers with one exception are members of my Congregation and no friction has arisen as regards the religious instruction given.

5 a. Changes in Public worship since 1914. b. Effects of the changes. Hold Intercession Services weekly and on Sundays. Same hours. Several people come to these Services who previously went nowhere.

6. Number of Roman Catholics in the Parish. Only one Woman.

1. See 1914.

FARRINGDON, LITTLE Incumbent J. H. Kirkby[1]

1. Number of Boys Girls and Infants on books of day schools: a. Last year. 20 (so reduced by boys taken to farming). **b. 20 30 or 40 years ago.** Thirty years ago between 30 and 40 – (larger families then, not mere householders).

2. a. Men and b. Women qualified to vote in Parochial Church meeting. (a) 11, (b) 15.

3. Moral and Spiritual effect of: a. Wartime b. National Mission.

(a) There is an observable spirit of patience and submission to the restrictions imposed by the conditions of wartime, with recognition that all must contribute in service and sacrifice (as of son-soldiers) for the sake of the country.

(b) Readiness to sympathise with suffering, and generosity in contributions made in response to appeals for soldiers and sufferers by the war. The National Mission was welcomed, the services well attended, and I feel that that [sic] its effect was real and lasting.

4. Status of Church Schools. Options for compromise on a. management, b. head teachers, c. character of religious teaching. Might compromise be justified by better arrangements for Church teaching in state schools?

My experience in this small Parish, untroubled by sectarian disputes, does not give me grounds for contributing matter of any value on the subject. My personal feeling would lead me to side with those who would study methods and policy of conciliation and compromise: so long as the importance of truly religious Gospel teaching in education is insisted upon for children.

5 a. Changes in Public worship since 1914. b. Effects of the changes. (a) Modified finish to Evensong, with Mirfield Mission Hymns added to Hymns Ancient and Modern. (b) Services better attended and heartily joined in.

6. Number of Roman Catholics in the Parish. 1 only – (lady farm worker).

1. See 1914.

FEWCOTT Incumbent W. A. Penyston[1]

1. Number of Boys Girls and Infants on books of day schools: a. Last year. b. 20 30 or 40 years ago.

No Day Schools.

2. a. Men and b. Women qualified to vote in Parochial Church meeting. None.

3. Moral and Spiritual effect of: a. Wartime b. National Mission.

(a) The People realise about the war but come to church rather irregularly.

(b) The Nat. Mission has left little or no effect on the Parish.

4. Status of Church Schools. Options for compromise on a. management, b. head teachers, c. character of religious teaching. Might compromise be justified by better arrangements for Church teaching in state schools?

[*No response*].

5 a. Changes in Public worship since 1914. b. Effects of the changes. a. No changes. b. Attendance irregular as to church going.

6. Number of Roman Catholics in the Parish. None.

1. William Adolphus Penyston (formerly Partridge) graduated from Brasenose College Oxford in 1903 and was ordained priest in 1907. He occupied a series of three curacies between 1906 and 1915, when he became Perpetual Curate of Fewcott. He was 39 in 1918 and at the 1911 census he was unmarried and living in a single-person household.

FIFIELD AND IDBURY   Incumbent G. E. Mann[1]

1. Number of Boys Girls and Infants on books of day schools: a. Last year. 43. b. 20 30 or 40 years ago.

No records kept, but numbers considerably decreased both through decreasing population and the attendance of the children of Foscott Village at Bledington School Glos.

2. a. Men and b. Women qualified to vote in Parochial Church meeting. None.

3. Moral and Spiritual effect of: a. Wartime b. National Mission.

Both here have the same effect, a <u>decrease</u> of interest in spiritual things though for several months the attendance of church at Fifield on Sundays has markedly increased.

4. Status of Church Schools. Options for compromise on a. management, b. head teachers, c. character of religious teaching. Might compromise be justified by better arrangements for Church teaching in state schools?

In this parish the loss of the Church School would be great. Almost all the children nominally belong to the church and attend our services, though the parents are indifferent and discourage the interest of the children in the church and in religion. This influence would be considerably stronger if the school were removed from the control of the Church, and a dissenting or indifferent head teacher appointed. <u>If</u> definite dogmatic teaching could be <u>assured</u> in all Provided and Council Schools, it might, of course, be right to <u>sacrifice</u> our little parish schools for the good of others
…

5 a. Changes in Public worship since 1914. b. Effects of the changes. The fortnightly Sung Eucharist was started in March 1914. The attendance, though not satisfactory, is greater than that at Matins in previous years. More especially when the decrease of population is taken into consideration.

6. Number of Roman Catholics in the Parish. No Roman Catholics.

1. See 1914.

FINMERE   Incumbent H. W. Trower[1]

1. Number of Boys Girls and Infants on books of day schools: a. Last year. Boys 8, Girls 8, Infants 9 = 25. **b. 20 30 or 40 years ago.** I have no reliable information so far back. 40 years ago our population was 400. Before the War it was 220 – today not more than 170.

2. a. Men and b. Women qualified to vote in Parochial Church meeting. None.

3. Moral and Spiritual effect of: a. Wartime b. National Mission.

The people generally are bearing the strain and hardships due to war cheerfully. There is no grumbling about hard times, but I cannot say there is any sign of spiritual effect in better church attendance or in the number of Communicants.

The National Mission – except in the case of a few faithful men – is quite overshadowed by the War and by the cottage classes is regarded as a thing over and done with.

4. Status of Church Schools. Options for compromise on a. management, b. head teachers, c. character of religious teaching. Might compromise be justified by better arrangements for Church teaching in state schools?

I think we should do all we can to retain our Church Schools in their present status and make no compromise in Management, appointment of Head Teachers or the character of the religious teaching.

5 a. Changes in Public worship since 1914. b. Effects of the changes. We have made no change in methods or hours of Public Worship since last return.

6. Number of Roman Catholics in the Parish. None.

1. See 1914.

FINSTOCK AND FAWLER   Incumbent T. P. Field[1]

1. Number of Boys Girls and Infants on books of day schools: a. Last year. b. 20 30 or 40 years ago.

	Boys	Girls	Infants	Total
1918	39	40	30	109
1888	45	41	41	127

2. a. Men and b. Women qualified to vote in Parochial Church meeting. No record of any.

3. Moral and Spiritual effect of: a. Wartime b. National Mission.

As I have been at Finstock only for a few months I am hardly in a position to be able to answer this question. Since I came I have begun – at Sunday Evensong – to pray for those on active service <u>by name</u> – which had not previously been done – and I find the people appreciate it and, on the whole, there is a better attendance. The cold weather has hindered many, as the heating apparatus is completely out of order: but I hope to make that good before next winter.

4. Status of Church Schools. Options for compromise on a. management, b. head teachers, c. character of religious teaching. Might compromise be justified by better arrangements for Church teaching in state schools?

The Schools here are Church schools. The leading Nonconformist is one of the managers. During the short time I have been here the Managers' meetings have been held without friction. The children of Nonconformists have the opportunity of withdrawal from definitive religious instruction, but none have availed themselves of the opportunity.

5 a. Changes in Public worship since 1914. b. Effects of the changes. There have been no changes since 1914.

6. Number of Roman Catholics in the Parish. I only know of one man who is by way of being Roman Catholic, his wife and children are Church.

1. Thomas Perrott Field graduated from Worcester College Oxford in 1900 and trained at Cuddesdon College, being ordained priest in 1902. He served three curacies 1901–12 and was Curate in Charge at Chadlington between 1912 and 1917, when he became Vicar of Finstock. He was 42 in 1918 and at the 1911 census he was unmarried and living in a single-person household.

FREELAND   Incumbent C. J. Penrice[1]

1. Number of Boys Girls and Infants on books of day schools: a. Last year. 40. b. 20 30 or 40 years ago.

I have no information.

2. a. Men and b. Women qualified to vote in Parochial Church meeting. None.

3. Moral and Spiritual effect of: a. Wartime b. National Mission.

I do not think (a) or (b) has made any difference either way.

4. Status of Church Schools. Options for compromise on a. management, b. head teachers, c. character of religious teaching. Might compromise be justified by better arrangements for Church teaching in state schools?

I regret I have hardly any view and certainly none which could honestly be called "fairly clear" especially as in this parish the necessity for clear thought or action on these matters has not arisen in my Vicariate.

5 a. Changes in Public worship since 1914. b. Effects of the changes. With the exception of very minor details I carry on the hours and methods of my predecessor. I say Compline daily at 9 pm in the Church in the presence of a faithful few.

6. Number of Roman Catholics in the Parish. Three.

Forgive my Lord my not having sent this before.

1. Charles John Penrice graduated from Trinity College Cambridge in 1887 and was ordained priest in 1890. He served four curacies between 1889 and 1897, interspersed with chaplaincies in Venice and Nice, and was then Chaplain to the Devon House of Mercy between 1897 and 1915, when he became Vicar of Freeland. He was 53 years old in 1918. At the 1911 census he was a widower and shared a household with two unmarried female servants.

FRINGFORD   Incumbent S. Meredith Brown[1]

1. Number of Boys Girls and Infants on books of day schools: a. Last year. 65.

b. 20 30 or 40 years ago. 20 years ago: 1898 – 66; 30: 1888 – 58; 38: 1879 – 86; 46: 1871 – 82.

2. a. Men and b. Women qualified to vote in Parochial Church meeting. Nil.

3. Moral and Spiritual effect of: a. Wartime b. National Mission.

Taking them generally, I believe all parishioners are impressed by the war in a right direction. It has roused and strengthened their faith and called forth many a prayer which would not have been uttered. The possibility of invasion with all its horrors has awakened serious thoughts. As we have some 43 men serving there are few families uninterested in the welfare and success of our troops. I am unaware of any moral trouble in connection with troops nor do I anticipate any.

The National Mission, seems to have been a great failure, as I expected it would be. It was wrongly and untimely initiated and organised. Much better plod on in touch with the people. The[y] attend services here very well on Sundays and they fail on Thursdays H.C. 9.30 and Intercession at 3 pm.

4. Status of Church Schools. Options for compromise on a. management, b. head teachers, c. character of religious teaching. Might compromise be justified by better arrangements for Church teaching in state schools?

I have never had any difficulty with schools and I know little of the "Policy" needed, but I should certainly advocate their retention in their present status. I don't believe in compromise, and there is plenty of money with church people if rightly approached.

5 a. Changes in Public worship since 1914. b. Effects of the changes. a. Nil and do not desire, nor is it desired to make any.

6. Number of Roman Catholics in the Parish. Two.

1. See 1914.

FRITWELL   Incumbent J. L. Meredith[1]

1. Number of Boys Girls and Infants on books of day schools: a. Last year. boys 24, girls 35, Infants 13. These numbers include the children from Fewcott. **b. 20 30 or 40 years ago.** In 1888: Boys 21, Girls 25, Infants 33.

2. a. Men and b. Women qualified to vote in Parochial Church meeting. (a) 19, (b) 19.

3. Moral and Spiritual effect of: a. Wartime b. National Mission.

(a) We practically have only one class in this parish ie the labouring class – consisting of small farmers, carpenters etc etc small artisans working on their own, and farm labourers.

A greater practical belief and use of Intercessory Prayer. A more liberal spirit in almsgiving not only to "war objects" but to parochial and missionary eg the church expenses fund is now out of debt in spite of increased cost a thing which it has never been before, for 22 years. The communicants are perhaps more regular than before the war and the majority (all with one or two exceptions) of the men away on active service take the opportunity to make their communions when home on leave.

(b) No effect either one way or the other.

4. Status of Church Schools. Options for compromise on a. management, b. head teachers, c. character of religious teaching. Might compromise be justified by better arrangements for Church teaching in state schools?

From my own experience in this parish, as well as from that as a Diocesan Inspector, I am led to the following conclusions: (1) We must strain every effort to retain our schools as Church schools.

(2) The Head teacher must be a consistent Churchman or Church woman, believing and living the Catholic Faith (a) because the whole atmosphere of the school is affected by the personality and character of the Headteacher at all times. (b) because

he or she will in most cases have to take the Upper Groups in Religious Knowledge etc and they cannot teach what they do not believe and practice themselves.

(3) The character of the teaching should be even more definite from the <u>Church</u> point of view than it is now, e.g. there should be more teaching of the Faith, the Prayer Book, and Church History.

(4) Facilities should be granted to Dissenters to enter and teach their own children by means of an appointed delegate during the hours of religious instruction. In schools where the teaching staff is large enough (in country schools it is not) a teacher (not the head) might be asked to take the children of Dissenters as a separate class to be taught according to some such syllabus as that of the O.E.C. for "provided" schools, if a sufficient number of the parents of the said children expressed <u>in writing</u> their desire for such teaching to justify this This class would only be held on mornings when the Church children were being taught the Catechism etc or were taken to Church. This would be a fair exchange for the facility of right of entry to "provided" schools for the Parish Priest or his delegate to teach the Catholic Faith during the hours of religious instruction.

N.B. As regards management our own place works excellently viz 4 Foundation Managers (Churchmen), 1 Manager elected by the Parish Council viz our leading Dissenter, 1 O.E.C. Manager – who is merely a nominal Churchman as it happens but might be a Dissenter.

P.S. "Compromise may act in politics but concentration is needed in wars." and this is war to the knife against the hideous monster of "undenominationalism".

5 a. Changes in Public worship since 1914. b. Effects of the changes. None.

6. Number of Roman Catholics in the Parish. None.

1. See 1914.

GARSINGTON   Incumbent E. H. Horne[1]

1. Number of Boys Girls and Infants on books of day schools: a. Last year. 90. **b. 20 30 or 40 years ago.** <u>124</u>, in 1878.

2. a. Men and b. Women qualified to vote in Parochial Church meeting. None. I am one of the many clergy who object to limiting the membership of the Church of England to communicants. The idea of the "status" of a communicant is quite beyond my parishioners, and only arouses suspicion.

3. Moral and Spiritual effect of: a. Wartime b. National Mission.

(b) In such a parish as this, it is impossible to do more than arrange a few special services. These were well attended by our usual church people: the addresses were good: and there was, I believe, some increase of interest as a result.

(a) The war has increased Sunday garden-work, and given more excuse to men for neglecting church. It has excited the boys, and given them high wages, so that though I get as many at Sunday School, I find it almost impossible to hold their interest. In some cases people attended the intercessions at first but gave up when a son was killed.

4. Status of Church Schools. Options for compromise on a. management, b. head teachers, c. character of religious teaching. Might compromise be justified by better arrangements for Church teaching in state schools?

The single-school area difficulty has not arisen in my last or present parish: and I have no other experience of school management. The difficulty appears to be entirely connected with teaching not sanctioned by the Church of England formularies.

5 a. Changes in Public worship since 1914. b. Effects of the changes. No changes, except special intercession after the third Collect once a month: and a Bible reading in Church each week.

6. Number of Roman Catholics in the Parish. None now. One family, till recently (F. M. and 3 ch.)

1. See 1914.

GLYMPTON   Incumbent H. W. Sawyer[1]

1. Number of Boys Girls and Infants on books of day schools: a. Last year. b. 20 30 or 40 years ago.

a. Five boys, five girls, four infants. b. 1897: Eighteen boys, twenty-four girls (including infants).

2. a. Men and b. Women qualified to vote in Parochial Church meeting. Nine men. Twenty-one women.

3. Moral and Spiritual effect of: a. Wartime b. National Mission.

(a) A small number have made a real effort to attend intercession services. The attendance at Sunday services is adversely affected by the hard work men and women are doing during the week. I am inclined to think that the labour of girls and women on the land tends to coarsen them and that there must be much neglect of the homes.

(b) It is difficult to notice any effect.

4. Status of Church Schools. Options for compromise on a. management, b. head teachers, c. character of religious teaching. Might compromise be justified by better arrangements for Church teaching in state schools?

[*No response*].

5 a. Changes in Public worship since 1914. b. Effects of the changes. a. Once a month and on Great Festivals Morning Prayer is said at 10.15 and there is a Sung Celebration at 11. b. That the children grow up with some knowledge of the Communion Service and its meaning and cease to look upon it as something strange and abnormal.

6. Number of Roman Catholics in the Parish. None.

1. See 1914.

GODINGTON[1]   Incumbent T. I. Pocock[2]

1. Number of Boys Girls and Infants on books of day schools: a. Last year. b. 20 30 or 40 years ago.

There are no schools in this parish.

2. a. Men and b. Women qualified to vote in Parochial Church meeting. None.

3. Moral and Spiritual effect of: a. Wartime b. National Mission.

(a) The grasping disposition of some of the people has been brought out clearly, and their independence of restraint. I have observed no spiritual effect.

(b) I have observed no effect.

4. Status of Church Schools. Options for compromise on a. management, b. head teachers, c. character of religious teaching. Might compromise be justified by better arrangements for Church teaching in state schools?

I am not qualified to give an opinion on these points. Religious teaching in schools is a doubtful benefit, so far as my experience goes, because it is divorced from practice, as well as for other reasons.

5 a. Changes in Public worship since 1914. b. Effects of the changes. Instead of Antecommunion Service at 11 on Sundays I now have a sung Celebration. There is more reverence at the Church Services than there was, and in some cases an improvement in Communions, which may perhaps be attributed to the change. N.B. There are from 22 – 25 confirmed persons in the parish. Baptism is now administered at Mattins or Evensong on Sunday according to the rubric.

6. Number of Roman Catholics in the Parish. None.

1. Theodore Innes Pocock graduated from Corpus Christi College Oxford in 1891 and was ordained priest in 1909. He served two curacies between 1909 and 1915, when he was appointed as Rector of Godington. He was 49 in 1918. His household was not found in the 1911 census.

GORING Incumbent A. E. Dams[1]

1. Number of Boys Girls and Infants on books of day schools: a. Last year. b. 20 30 or 40 years ago.

	1892		1918	
Goring	Boys	67	Boys	63
	Girls	52	Girls	52
(No separate register of Infants)			Infants	38
Goring Heath	Boys	40		65
	Girls	35		52
	Preparatory (Under 9)	45	Infants	31

2. a. Men and b. Women qualified to vote in Parochial Church meeting. Men 36, Women 65.

3. Moral and Spiritual effect of: a. Wartime b. National Mission.

The parish is partly residential and partly agricultural, the two elements being fairly sharply separated, in that the former is on the whole collected in and near the village, the latter distributed over a great area mainly in the hill country behind. The parish church is conveniently situated for those living in the village, much less so for those in the large adjacent district of Cleeve, and entirely out of touch with the upper part of the Parish, which is served by the Mission Room at Crays Pond, the Chapel at Alnut's Hospital, Goring Heath, and the neighbouring Churches at Woodcote and Whitchurch Gate. The war has not brought about either economic distress or prosperity. Its moral effects, such as they are, are not the result of any extremes of that kind. There is no military camp in the neighbourhood nor any munition centre nearer than Didcot on the one hand and Reading on the other. Therefore our people have not been affected to any extent by these conditions.

On the moral side, there has been no increase of illegitimacy or of crime. But there is no visible diminution of the materialism and worldliness which were so noticeable everywhere before the war. The pursuit of pleasure, however, has wholly ceased, and people of all classes are gravely and earnestly industrious. There is a deep sense of a great wrong done to humanity by Germany, and a firm will to resist it, much patience in bearing privation, anxiety and sorrow. Amongst the men of the upper classes there is an almost savage feeling of resentment against the enemy, and no response at all to the Gospel spirit in that regard. There is no desire to see anything but evil befall the enemy, little or no sense of national or personal sin, and therefore no general readiness for a message calling to repentance.

For these reasons the National Mission was coldly received by many, especially of the upper classes, and resented by some. At first it had no visible effect, either in the attendance at church, or in the general attitude of the people to religion. The poor were indifferent, the richer people (some of them) criticised "the Church" in the fashionable way, but did not criticise themselves as members of the Church. They were out for "the parsons", but they were not unfriendly, only repeating the catch words. But there was a solid core of earnest people, representing all classes, who sought to catch the message of the Mission, and to hear the call of God. These were mostly the faithful of old days and at first the Mission did not seem to go beyond them. But the last year or so has seen a slow change. More of the poor are seen at Church than used to be, and some have become regular. The intercession services are still poorly attended, but little private meetings for prayer are increasing. There is little increase, if any, in the number of communicants. There is little evidence of the missionary spirit, in the wider sense. Sermons are listened to with great attention. The relations between clergy and people are wholly friendly. The young people, especially the boys, are more difficult to hold than before the war.

4. Status of Church Schools. Options for compromise on a. management, b. head teachers, c. character of religious teaching. Might compromise be justified by better arrangements for Church teaching in state schools?

I think that we ought to try to retain our Church Schools in all areas, but not at all costs of hindering a settlement in national education. If we can gain our end by other means, we ought to be ready to do so, and that end is the bringing up of children in a right relation to God and man. The principle for which I conceive that Church Schools stand is that Education is an integral thing, and not two parallel processes, one secular and the other religious, going on independently though at the same time. But I do not think our Church Schools have stood to their ideal. The sacred and the secular are almost as sharply separated in them as in Council Schools. What we really have is not Religious Education, but the right to teach certain religious subjects in certain schools. Therefore I think that our main aim should be to gain a full recognition of the true nature of Education.

As to details of Management, Appointment of Teacher, and the rest, these would depend on the fullness of the recognition that we gained. I should like to see the cooperation of all religious bodies fully and freely sought, and a readiness on their part to throw all their resources into the general work of Education. I should like to see, not only Religious Teaching _in_ the school, but also teaching and worship _of_ the school _in_ the Church, the children being brought there as a matter of course, regularly and frequently, and not occasionally as a concession to the claims of parents and others, but not, of course, against the wish of parents. Worship is an essential part of Education, and the Church is the natural place for it, and some kinds of instruction can best be given there. Cooperation to these ends ought not to be impossible. Given this, the details we have fought for in the past lose much of their importance; but if it is denied, I think we ought to stand out for what we have.

The above supplies the answer I should give to the last question. This view of the matter is tentative, and represents the stage I have come to in trying to think out afresh the question of Education. I am very much impressed by the effort now being made to reconstruct our Educational ideals.

5 a. Changes in Public worship since 1914. b. Effects of the changes. None, except the use of special Intercessions after the sermon at Evensong on Sundays, instead of before.

6. Number of Roman Catholics in the Parish. As near as I can tell 6 men, 7 women, 2 children.

1. See 1914.

HAILEY CUM CRAWLEY   Incumbent F. C. Nash[1]

1. Number of Boys Girls and Infants on books of day schools: a. Last year. b. 20 30 or 40 years ago.

(a) Boys 34 Girls 43 = 76 Infants. Boys 33 Girls 23 = 56 Total 133. (b) 1878: 63 Boys 66 Girls Total 129.

2. a. Men and b. Women qualified to vote in Parochial Church meeting. (a) 26 (b) 42.

3. Moral and Spiritual effect of: a. Wartime b. National Mission.

(a) I have not found that wartime has produced any evil moral effect on our people. A few have valued the Intercession Services. Many have been obliged, through the absence of labour, to live more strenuous lives, and it has somewhat affected the attendance at the Church's services. I foresee difficulties in the future on the part of those who have earned very high wages in government work.

(b) I think the National Mission helped many of our people to regard life more seriously. It certainly helped to increase interest in the work of the church overseas.

4. Status of Church Schools. Options for compromise on a. management, b. head teachers, c. character of religious teaching. Might compromise be justified by better arrangements for Church teaching in state schools?

In this single-school area, with good Church teaching in the School, matters have worked smoothly for many years, although we have a good many Nonconformists in the Parish.

We have a Wesleyan among our Managers, but we have always worked harmoniously.

As long as the inhabitants have a considerable majority on the Church side I think it would be a great misfortune to have a Nonconformist Head-teacher, nor do I think it would be advisable to alter the character of the Religious teaching in the School. I do not recall a single case during the past 13 years in which a child has been withdrawn from the Religious instruction in the school.

In making any compromise as regards Religious teaching in Provided Schools I fear the gain would not be commensurate with the loss we would sustain.

5 a. Changes in Public worship since 1914. b. Effects of the changes. a. No important changes. I have held during the Summer months occasional Open-Air Services at Crawley. b These have been well-attended, but I do not think they have had any appreciable effect.

6. Number of Roman Catholics in the Parish. None.

1. See 1914.

HAMPTON POYLE   Incumbent S.T. Gwilliam[1]

1. Number of Boys Girls and Infants on books of day schools: a. Last year. b. 20 30 or 40 years ago.

There are no day-schools in the parish. The children (about 15) go to Bletchingdon or to Kidlington, and are probably included in those returns.

2. a. Men and b. Women qualified to vote in Parochial Church meeting. There is no parochial church council here.

3. Moral and Spiritual effect of: a. Wartime b. National Mission.

I have had intercession services in this parish and services connected with the National Mission, but I do not feel justified in reporting any change in the people, all seem, good and bad alike, to be quite unmoved.

4. Status of Church Schools. Options for compromise on a. management, b. head teachers, c. character of religious teaching. Might compromise be justified by better arrangements for Church teaching in state schools?

During the last 27 years I have had no practical experience of the education question, therefore I feel I cannot say anything that would be of any value, accordingly I should be glad to be excused answering these questions. Personally I am of course all in favour of definite religious teaching, and I am glad to say I agree with what your lordship has said about it.

5 a. Changes in Public worship since 1914. b. Effects of the changes. None at all.

6. Number of Roman Catholics in the Parish. None in the parish.

1. See 1914.

HANWELL   Incumbent J. P. Morgan[1]

1. Number of Boys Girls and Infants on books of day schools: a. Last year. 30. b. 20 30 or 40 years ago. Forty years ago: 50.

2. a. Men and b. Women qualified to vote in Parochial Church meeting. None: being absent from my Parish, by permission, from May to November, 1917, and serving as a Clergyman Superintendent (unpaid) of a C.A. Hut with the B.E.F. France, after consultation with my parishioners, it was decided to postpone the establishment of a Parochial Church Council till after the War.

3. Moral and Spiritual effect of: a. Wartime b. National Mission.

(a) The Parishioners of this small country Parish are, with the exception of one household, exclusively agricultural labourers or farmers (tenant). On the former who are hardly ever without religious convictions, the effect has been to deepen their belief in things spiritual and enhance their estimate of the Christian faith. So many of their sons have been called to fight for their country. There has been more thrift due to higher wages and the work of the war savings committees. Our branch has been successful. On the latter, the effect has not been so good, perhaps increased prosperity seems, in some places, though not here in this Parish, to have led to a not very seemly gaiety. The common method of raising a contribution for the Red Cross and so forth, is the Whist-drive! Farmers have not been called on to join the army in great numbers.

(b) On the whole the Mission had as good results as could be expected of it, reasonably. In proportion to the population the attendance was good: all the non-conformists, I think, were present at some one or other of the Services. 'Revival Services' are much indulged in by nonconformists at all times: they are held at least once a year in the chapel in this Parish: so that here as elsewhere the Mission was not a 'novelty'. But from the fact that there has been found reason to drop one of the two Services held till recently in our local chapel on the Sunday, it would seem that people generally do not respond very freely to emotional appeals. It is beneficial in the Church of England for the people to have an opportunity to hear a fresh presentation of the truth: tho' Parishes in these days change hands more often than is usually recognised.

4. Status of Church Schools. Options for compromise on a. management, b. head teachers, c. character of religious teaching. Might compromise be justified by better arrangements for Church teaching in state schools?

The School in this Parish is a C.C. one: and was so long before I came here.

I have not sufficient knowledge of the subject in all its manifold bearings to justify me in expressing an opinion when others are so much better fitted to do so.

5 a. Changes in Public worship since 1914. b. Effects of the changes. a. In the depth of the Winter we had to hold an afternoon instead of an Evening Service, in order to comply with the lighting regulations. Otherwise there has been no change either in our Sunday or Week-day Services since 1914. b. It was found that an Evening Service is preferred.

6. Number of Roman Catholics in the Parish. One woman.

1. See 1914.

HARDWICK WITH TUSMORE[1]   Incumbent S. M. Statham[2]

1. Number of Boys Girls and Infants on books of day schools: a. Last year. b. 20 30 or 40 years ago.

No schools.

2. a. Men and b. Women qualified to vote in Parochial Church meeting. I do not remember any.

3. Moral and Spiritual effect of: a. Wartime b. National Mission.

See Cottisford.

4. Status of Church Schools. Options for compromise on a. management, b. head teachers, c. character of religious teaching. Might compromise be justified by better arrangements for Church teaching in state schools?

[*No response*].

5 a. Changes in Public worship since 1914. b. Effects of the changes. No changes.

6. Number of Roman Catholics in the Parish. One family Harris in Hardwick.

1. Population 141.
2. See 1914 Cottisford. Statham was incumbent of both Cottisford and Hardwick from 1911.

HARPSDEN   Incumbent C. E. de Coetlogon[1]

1. Number of Boys Girls and Infants on books of day schools: a. Last year. 13. 8. 2. **b. 20 30 or 40 years ago.** In 1894 the Total was 31.

2. a. Men and b. Women qualified to vote in Parochial Church meeting. I do not know. I only took over on Sept the 6th, 1917. Mr Willy who was in charge may know. I do not know his address; he has left Henley.

3. Moral and Spiritual effect of: a. Wartime b. National Mission.

(a) So far as I can judge, having been here so short a time, all appreciate the gravity of the situation: great attention is given to the War Prayers in Church: the people ask for certain hymns ie hymns such as 595.[2] I have heard of no one who has lost faith through the war, or whose faith in Christianity has been weakened. But of course there may be some. But I don't think it. There has been a slight increase in the number of Communicants. This was especially noticeable at Christmas, although a good many are Serving and therefore not in residence.

(b) I haven't heard the National Mission mentioned by anyone.

4. Status of Church Schools. Options for compromise on a. management, b. head teachers, c. character of religious teaching. Might compromise be justified by better arrangements for Church teaching in state schools?

No. I have only recently returned from serving 25 years in India. We have a Church School here which suits this parish very well. All the children are Church children. There is no reason at all for a change here.

5 a. Changes in Public worship since 1914. b. Effects of the changes. a. The only change I have made is that I stopped the exit of the Choir after the Church militant prayer. We now have Morning Ser. complete, and then a Celebration after as an entirely separate Service.

6. Number of Roman Catholics in the Parish. None that I know of.

1. Charles Evelyn de Coetlogon graduated from Selwyn College Cambridge in 1885 and was ordained priest in 1886. He served two curacies 1885–91 and then a series of chaplaincies in India 1892–1914. He served as a Lieutenant in the Recruiting Staff in 1916–17, and was listed as retired but was appointed as Rector of Harpsden in 1917.
2 Probably the hymn 'For Absent Friends' in *Hymns Ancient and Modern*.

HASELEY, GREAT　　　　　　　　　　　Incumbent W. G. Edwards[1]

1. Number of Boys Girls and Infants on books of day schools: a. Last year. b. 20 30 or 40 years ago.

(a) Boys and Girls: 50 Infants: 24. (b) I have looked at the Log Books and Summaries and find that they have not been continuously preserved for the years mentioned above and no trustworthy statistics are therefore at hand so far back.

2. a. Men and b. Women qualified to vote in Parochial Church meeting. a. 24, b. 24.

3. Moral and Spiritual effect of: a. Wartime b. National Mission.

(a) The most marked effect of War time appears among the younger members of the community. The children taking advantage of the absence of their fathers seem to be out of their mothers' – and indeed out of general – control. The elder lads, who have prematurely come into the position of those above them in age now at the front, show their independence. As regards the general public, the war at last seems to be really stirring their minds – but at present little or no spiritual advance can be noted.

(b) The National Mission, without creating any immediate or startling change has certainly had a good effect on many individuals and has increased our Church attendance slightly.

4. Status of Church Schools. Options for compromise on a. management, b. head teachers, c. character of religious teaching. Might compromise be justified by better arrangements for Church teaching in state schools?

My opinion, as regards this village is that there is practically no discontent, on the part of Nonconformists, with the management, appointment of head-teachers or the character of the religious teaching; and therefore would suggest no change. Though willing to remedy any Nonconformist grievance, I believe it would be better to press for the right of parents to settle what form of religion their children should be taught in all schools: and this would involve no need for compromise such as contemplated in paragraph 2. Above.

I believe that there is a feeling among head-teachers that, if anyone is deputed to teach religious knowledge, they will object to be present at the time merely as maintainers of discipline.

5 a. Changes in Public worship since 1914. b. Effects of the changes. I have availed myself of all the opportunities of more 'elasticity' in the character of the services, and to this, as well as to the National Mission I attribute better congregations. During the winter months we have had Evening Prayer on Sundays at 3pm and this has proved successful in a village with several hamlets: but the mass of people prefer the evening service later in the day.

6. Number of Roman Catholics in the Parish. None.

1. See 1914.

HEADINGTON

Incumbent A. N. Armstrong[1]

1. Number of Boys Girls and Infants on books of day schools: a. Last year. b. 20 30 or 40 years ago.

	Boys	Girls	Infants	Total
(a)	84	75	73	232
(b) in 1902	145	127	104	376

(Prior to Council School being started in Highfield Parish.)

2. a. Men and b. Women qualified to vote in Parochial Church meeting. None.

3. Moral and Spiritual effect of: a. Wartime b. National Mission.

(a) No apparent effect beyond a greater disregard of the young for Parental authority.
(b) None.

4. Status of Church Schools. Options for compromise on a. management, b. head teachers, c. character of religious teaching. Might compromise be justified by better arrangements for Church teaching in state schools?

This question does not affect me personally in this parish as there are both Church and Council schools but I should favour a compromise provided that the religious teaching is safeguarded so that church children are instructed in Church teaching by teachers that are Church men or women.

5 a. Changes in Public worship since 1914. b. Effects of the changes. No changes in methods or hours of public worship. The ritual has been simplified especially at the Evening Service and while it has apparently caused some secessions it has attracted others, especially of the poorer class, to the evening service.

6. Number of Roman Catholics in the Parish. I am not aware of any Roman Catholics in this parish: any [*indeciph.*] but their number is very small.

1. Alexander Nenon Armstrong graduated from St Mary Hall Oxford in 1884 and was ordained priest in 1887. He served five curacies 1885–1908 and was Vicar of St Michael's Beckenham between 1908 and 1915. He became Vicar of Headington in 1916. He was 56 in 1918 and at the 1911 census he shared a household with his wife and 10-year-old son and an unmarried female servant.

HEADINGTON QUARRY   Incumbent P. V. Doyne[1]

1. Number of Boys Girls and Infants on books of day schools: a. Last year. 260. b. 20 30 or 40 years ago.

30 years ago: 205 children on Books. A Council School has been built in the Parish during the last 10 years which draws a good many children.

2. a. Men and b. Women qualified to vote in Parochial Church meeting. The Church Wardens tell me that some 30 or 40 had signed but I can find no record or roll of these figures. A Roll is being made out at the present time and signatures being sought.

3. Moral and Spiritual effect of: a. Wartime b. National Mission.

(a) <u>Of Wartime</u>. Having come to the Parish since the War broke out and consequently having little or no knowledge of the Parish in pre-war days, it is not possible to make comparisons or arrive at any definite conclusions. That its effect morally and spiritually has not been what might have been expected must be reluctantly allowed.

(b) Of the National Mission. This too has been disappointing – coinciding within two or three months of my arriving it was not possible without knowing the people to organize proper preparation for it. The spiritual life of the faithful was no doubt deepened – but apparently the careless indifferent were but very slightly touched by it at the time though since there are some signs of the shaking of the dry bones.

4. Status of Church Schools. Options for compromise on a. management, b. head teachers, c. character of religious teaching. Might compromise be justified by better arrangements for Church teaching in state schools?

In my humble opinion the Church Schools in the country – where the single school areas exist – should not be sacrificed to the town schools and larger areas – at the same time facilities might be offered to Nonconformists to give religious instruction to the children belonging to their Sects. The National Societies Clause in the Trust Deed should be safeguarded and kept inviolate.

I view with some misgivings the offer of more satisfactory conditions of religious teaching in Provided Schools on the grounds that it would appear unlikely to be availed generally of owing to pressure of Parochial work and shortage of persons capable of undertaking it.

5 a. Changes in Public worship since 1914. b. Effects of the changes. On alternate Sundays generally the Holy Eucharist at 11 o'clock takes the place of Mattins, which is said at 10 o'clock and followed by the Litany. This was done after consultation with several of the Parishioners with the full concurrence of the Church Wardens and the effect is certainly favourable as regards the Sundays when there is the Eucharist in the larger congregation – and greater reverence in worship.

6. Number of Roman Catholics in the Parish. Some eight all told.

1. See 1914 Beckley. Doyne moved to Headington Quarry in 1916.

HENLEY-ON-THAMES   Incumbent S. C. Saunders[1]

1. Number of Boys Girls and Infants on books of day schools: a. Last year. b. 20 30 or 40 years ago.

Boys	Girls	Infants
1918	1918	1918
On the Books 215	On the Books 215	No. on Books 144
Average 200	Average 191	Average 100
1868	1870	1880
On the Books 164	Probable on the Books 120	Probable no. on Books 120
Average 108	Average 77	Average 85

In the <u>old</u> Log Books only the average attendance seems to have been given so the number given is only 'Probable'.

2. a. Men and b. Women qualified to vote in Parochial Church meeting. The roll in this Parish is only fragmentary – it contains not more than 90 names out of a population 3500. In my late parish every qualified person had the opportunity to sign and a complete roll was made up. This does not seem to have been done here. It would be impossible to do this now. (1) I have not the time to superintend the work (2) all the men are away – at least most of them. (3) the usual Church workers are all engaged in war work. It will have to wait happier times I am afraid.

3. Moral and Spiritual effect of: a. Wartime b. National Mission.

War As I came here 14 months after the war began I am unable to compare the parish in pre-wartime to now. Speaking generally, although there has been no general return to God I think the hearts of men and women have been moved in a way they never have been before. There is much less selfishness – more brotherly love and the fault found with the Church shows that men are thinking more about sacred things than they can openly to show. Our congregations are much larger and the communicants more. Perhaps this is not a true guide, as Henley is very full just now. The morality of the people is real, I think, more than before the war, although there has been much more freedom among people.

National Mission The National Mission was disappointing outwardly. After months of preparation the people did not respond – the congregations were not larger than normal nor the communicants above the average during the Mission. The weather and the time of year may, somewhat, account for these things. It would however be a want of faith to say it was a failure – the result can only be known to God.

4. Status of Church Schools. Options for compromise on a. management, b. head teachers, c. character of religious teaching. Might compromise be justified by better arrangements for Church teaching in state schools?

I do not think I have thought sufficiently about it to have anything like a clear view of the policy which the Church should pursue at this time re our schools. But I do not think that the present state of things can continue and I think we must be prepared to give up much which we have hitherto held dear. I think every grievance should be removed so that Churchmen and Nonconformists may join together in meeting the evil which threatens our schools viz in having teachers, in our schools, who believe in nothing and who say to the children "I have taught you this but I do not believe a word of it". I think in any bill, 1st Managers should have the right to inquire not only into teachers qualifications in secular things but also as to what he believes. 2 that all teachers should be appointed for a certain number of years (they should [sic] eligible for reappointment.) At the present time it is most difficult to remove a teacher so long as the school is fairly efficient. Now, once appointed, teachers look upon the school almost as their freehold. 3 that in every school, one or more women should be on the board of management. 4 that in single school areas, the Nonconformist minister should be allowed to enter and teach in the school. That he is not allowed to do this is a grievance. If he was allowed his entry the grievance would be removed and then he would not come to teach in the school. My experience is that Nonconformist ministers never teach in the school if they allowed [*sic*] to do so. 5 that the privileges granted to Nonconformist ministers should also be granted to the clergy in Provided Schools. I think that Mr Fisher's bill should be passed even if the religious question is, pro tem, laid on one side.

5 a. Changes in Public worship since 1914. b. Effects of the changes. The hours of the Services are the same with the following addition (1) we have now a daily Celebration in the place of one on weekday and Saints days. This is much appreciated and has generally had from 40 to 50 Communicants during the day. (2) we have now a Choral Celebration on Sunday once a month at 10. A few like it but it is not well attended.

6. Number of Roman Catholics in the Parish. I cannot answer this question but if it is important I will try to find out so far as I am able to do so. I am afraid I could only see in number of families.

1. See 1914 Watlington. Saunders came to Henley in 1915.

HENLEY, HOLY TRINITY (ROTHERFIELD GREYS)
Incumbent R. M. Willis[1]

1. Number of Boys Girls and Infants on books of day schools: a. Last year. b. 20 30 or 40 years ago.

(a) Boys 125, Girls 128, Infants 84. (b) Year 1884: Boys, 60, Girls 60 Infants included not being separate department. Year 1899: Boys, 115, Girls 118, Infants 103.

2. a. Men and b. Women qualified to vote in Parochial Church meeting. Only a few men signed 'the declaration' some time back; with some hundreds of men gone from this Parish on military service the formation of the Electoral Roll has been deferred.

3. Moral and Spiritual effect of: a. Wartime b. National Mission.

(a) This Parish consists in the main of weekly wage-earners, the remainder being chiefly people belonging to the lower middle class, tradesmen and the like. I am not aware that the War has had any specially marked effect on the morals of the people. Certainly the deterioration anticipated from the presence of large numbers of soldiers, who were for a considerable period in billets in the Parish, has not been apparent: e.g. very few illegitimate births have come to my knowledge. There is, I believe, less drinking than in pre-war days, but this may be due simply to the restrictions.

The spiritual effect of the War on the people generally has not been encouraging. It has not touched and turned the hearts of the men to God, as I have hoped and prayed for: I mean that, so far as outward observation goes, the War has not got the mass out of the rut. Indeed they come less to Church Services. On the other hand our faithful church members have been quickened to greater spiritual activity.

(b) I set out and sent to your Lordship in the Autumn of 1916 a full and detailed statement of the many steps which I and my band of parish workers took to pave the way and prepare for the National Mission. We tried to leave nothing undone which could be done to make it serviceable. The spiritual results however of the National Mission have not been conspicuous on the surface, but I trust that some good seed was sown which will eventually bear fruit.

4. Status of Church Schools. Options for compromise on a. management, b. head teachers, c. character of religious teaching. Might compromise be justified by better arrangements for Church teaching in state schools?

Holy Trinity Parish is not a single-school area, it contains a large British School. As one who has given religious instruction in Church day-schools for twenty-five years regularly once or twice a week, and continues to do so, I am profoundly convinced of the necessity of doing our utmost to maintain their definite status as far as possible. I find the School to be the invaluable nursery of the Church. It is through teaching and knowing the children that I find doors open to me in houses which would be otherwise, in a sense, closed. (a) When I became Incumbent of this Parish, some six years ago, I found two Nonconformist managers of our Schools under the 1902 Act, (one appointed by the Oxford Education Committee and the other by the Education Committee of the Borough Council). As Chairman I have experienced no difficulty in consequence, and see no reason why a Nonconformist element should not form part of the management of Church Schools. (b) I think it essential that the appointment of Head-Teachers should be so safe-guarded that they are always members of the Church. (c) I think the character of the religious teaching given to the children of Church parents can admit of no compromise. It must be in accordance with the principles of the Church. At the same time I am in favour of full facilities being accorded to Nonconformists to give instruction in Church Schools to the children of Nonconformist parents: but I consider that this should carry with it as a corollary full facilities for the clergy or accredited church teachers, to give instruction to the children of church parents in Council Schools.

5 a. Changes in Public worship since 1914. b. Effects of the changes. The hour of Evensong on Sunday has been changed, from 6.30 to 6pm. After the Third Collect at Evensong on Sunday, War prayers, preceded with appropriate biddings, are said, not intoned, in lieu of those provided in the Book of Common Prayer. War prayers are used at all the Services on Sundays and Week-days. These changes have proved acceptable, and I think the people fully appreciate the larger latitude of the allowable prayers which have been issued by authority from time to time during the War.

6. Number of Roman Catholics in the Parish. I have made enquiries, but have not succeeded in arriving at the numbers. In my house-to-house visiting in this Parish (population 3,778) I have found few Roman Catholics.

1. See 1914.

HETHE Incumbent W. Pendavis[1]

1. Number of Boys Girls and Infants on books of day schools: a. Last year. b. 20 30 or 40 years ago.

(a) 67 (b) 28 years ago (1890) there were apparently 90. We have 2 schools in the Parish. The C of E School for the Standard for all denominations (including R.C.) and St Philip's R.C. School for all infants. It is, I believe, the only parish in England in which this arrangement exists. There has been no difficulty or friction – it has worked smoothly enough. At the hour for Religious Teaching the R.C. children go to St Philip's and our infants come to our school.

2. a. Men and b. Women qualified to vote in Parochial Church meeting. [*No response*].

3. Moral and Spiritual effect of: a. Wartime b. National Mission.

(a) As to any moral effect produced by War time I can see no evidence one way or the other: as to spiritual effect – I feel sure that the religious life of the deeper natures has been deepened:- and though few (in an agricultural parish such as this) have leisure to attend Intercessory Services for the Troops – many do pray, and pray earnestly too – as they have never done before. More than one man has told me so.

(b) As to moral and spiritual effects of the National Mission the only difference I could see was that in a few cases religious life was deepened. But otherwise no effect was produced – as far as one can say.

4. Status of Church Schools. Options for compromise on a. management, b. head teachers, c. character of religious teaching. Might compromise be justified by better arrangements for Church teaching in state schools?

[*No response*].

5 a. Changes in Public worship since 1914. b. Effects of the changes. (a) change of hours – during the dark months – under the Lighting Act impossible (or at least most difficult) to darken the Clerestory windows – Evensong held at 3pm; reverting to 6pm during the Summer. The change of hour has also solved the oil difficulty, and as we have 18 large duplex lamps this was a real difficulty as oil became scarce and expensive. (b) the old people prefer the Service in the afternoon – it is a better time for failing sight and failing limbs. The young prefer the service at 6pm. There is no doubt that the later hour is more popular – and the later service better attended. (c) Evensong at 6pm from Easter Day (31 Mar.) until St. Michael and all Angels – 29 Sep.

6. Number of Roman Catholics in the Parish. In this parish there is a R.C. Church and Priest Resident in the Presbytery. There are 60 R.Catholics in the parish. This includes several who are at present away from their homes – on service etc.

1. See 1914.

HEYFORD, LOWER Incumbent V. R. Lennard[1]

1. Number of Boys Girls and Infants on books of day schools: a. Last year. b. 20 30 or 40 years ago.

(a) Boys 14, Girls 20, Infants 27, Total 61 Dec 1917. Caulcott Boys and Girls 6.

(b) March 31st 1877   Boys   Girls   Infants

No. on register   27   27   33 (Boys 19 Girls 14)

N.B. a number of children go to Middleton Stoney school and one family to Upper Heyford.

2. a. Men and b. Women qualified to vote in Parochial Church meeting. None.

3. Moral and Spiritual effect of: a. Wartime b. National Mission.

(a) Not gravely injurious but not favourable. The large Aerodrome in process of construction at Upper Heyford, flooding the Village with lodgers is a great hindrance to Church-going, even to good people, and a serious temptation in other ways to weak or vicious people. The Villagers generally are abnormally busy and preoccupied, and somewhat elated by the sudden increase in earnings. Labourers, and Boys in their teens, accustomed to a wage of 15/- [are] earning at the Aerodrome from £2–£3 pounds per week. Congregations seriously depleted not only by the withdrawal of 63 men out of a population of 450, to serve in Army and Navy, but by the above causes, also by the necessary change to afternoon for Evening service during the winter months.

(b) The above causes more than counteract any added seriousness induced by the National Mission.

4. Status of Church Schools. Options for compromise on a. management, b. head teachers, c. character of religious teaching. Might compromise be justified by better arrangements for Church teaching in state schools?

I do not feel able to offer an opinion on this most difficult question in small village schools.

5 a. Changes in Public worship since 1914. b. Effects of the changes. a. War Prayers after 3rd Collect at Evening Prayer. Certainly appreciated during war time. Short Intercession Services held Tu and Thursday and Saturday each wk at 5 (winter) and 6 (summer). Attendance 6 to 18 average about 12. Confined rather to the devout. Not attended generally by Parents and Relatives of those serving in the war.

6. Number of Roman Catholics in the Parish. None.

1. See 1914.

HEYFORD, UPPER Incumbent S. Cooper[1]

1. Number of Boys Girls and Infants on books of day schools: a. Last year. b. 20 30 or 40 years ago.

(a) boys 26, girls 24, infants 15, total 65. (b) 1880: boys 11, girls 16, infants 19, total 46.

2. a. Men and b. Women qualified to vote in Parochial Church meeting. (a) 10, (b) 16.

3. Moral and Spiritual effect of: a. Wartime b. National Mission.

(a) The war has called our charitable instincts, as shown chiefly in a generous and widespread contribution of eggs for military hospitals; but it has diminished attendance at church and except in the already devout in no way stimulated devotion.

(b) The National Mission has seemingly had no result whatever.

4. Status of Church Schools. Options for compromise on a. management, b. head teachers, c. character of religious teaching. Might compromise be justified by better arrangements for Church teaching in state schools?

The present 'dual' system, unsatisfactory and illogical as it is, has at least two advantages. (1) The retention of denominational schools probably secures a higher standard of religious education in provided schools lest they should suffer by comparison. (This was certainly the case in Frome.) (2) They are an asset for the Church in view of a final (?) settlement. It would be questionable policy to abandon them for a paper agreement liable to be reversed at a change of government as unworkable in practice. This denominational character could not but be seriously impaired if dissenters could be appointed Head teachers: but I can see no serious objection, if the building allowed, and a dissenting teacher were forthcoming, to the separation of such children as had asked through their parents for 'undenominational' teaching from the other children in the hour of religious instruction, as is already done on the mornings when the church children go to church. An assistant teacher might be a dissenter. The Boards of Statutory Managers might well be increased by the addition of at least two parents elected by the parents. In country places the farmer element is much too strong on the board. 'One man management' was probably much better.

5 a. Changes in Public worship since 1914. b. Effects of the changes. No alteration in hours. More latitude with regard to intercessions on Sundays. I have observed no effects, and heard no criticisms.

6. Number of Roman Catholics in the Parish. 1 woman.

1. See 1914.

HEYTHROP   Incumbent H. J. Gulley[1]

1. Number of Boys Girls and Infants on books of day schools: a. Last year. 66. **b. 20 30 or 40 years ago.** 40 years ago: 100; 20 years ago: 130.

2. a. Men and b. Women qualified to vote in Parochial Church meeting. The peculiar conditions of this Parish made such an attempt impossible. All the parish (with exception of 2 tenant farmers) are private Servants of the Squire. Labouring as they do under the blessings of a benevolent despotism, they conform to and accept whatever is suggested and would regard the expression of their private wishes and views as an act of disloyalty to or disrespect to their master.

3. Moral and Spiritual effect of: a. Wartime b. National Mission.

In a small Parish of about 170, no great or evident changes are easy to detect. Both the War and the Mission has had a steadying and sobering effect on all. An earnest desire to prove themselves worthy of the sacrifices being made for them, has made all classes eager to offer their services for their country, the women and girls particularly coming out well in their work on the land and gardens etc. They gratefully responded to the Intercessary Services, between 70 and 80 coming to the weekly services. The number of communicants increased to considerably over a hundred and there was the largest number of candidates for confirmation that have ever presented themselves, all the young men who have hung back for some years offered themselves in a body.

4. Status of Church Schools. Options for compromise on a. management, b. head teachers, c. character of religious teaching. Might compromise be justified by better arrangements for Church teaching in state schools?

We do not know anything of difficulties, nor is there any discord or discontent in school matters in this Parish. There are no dissenters here, a religious teaching and training is given regularly both by the teachers and myself. The condition of things is too satisfactory to make us fruitful of suggestions for change.

5 a. Changes in Public worship since 1914. b. Effects of the changes. (None.)

6. Number of Roman Catholics in the Parish. <u>one woman R.C.</u>, with 8 children, also R.C., but who are all at the front or in Service.

1. Henry James Gulley graduated from Keble College Oxford in 1893 and was ordained priest in 1895. He was Curate of Deddington 1893–99, Precentor of the collegiate church at Stratford-upon-Avon 1899–1901, and then served in clerical posts in Argentina, returning to England in 1909 as Curate of Shipton Moyne 1909–10. He then served as Curate of Fylingdales between 1911 and 1914, when he became Rector of Heythrop. He was 46 years old in 1918 and at the 1911 census he was unmarried and living in a single-person household.

HIGHFIELD   Incumbent F. T. Colson[1]

1. Number of Boys Girls and Infants on books of day schools: a. Last year. b. 20 30 or 40 years ago.

There are no day schools in the Parish.

2. a. Men and b. Women qualified to vote in Parochial Church meeting. (a) 20 (b) 9.

3. Moral and Spiritual effect of: a. Wartime b. National Mission.

It is exceedingly difficult to state what has been the effect, but roughly speaking

(a) War time has sobered all classes and made them more thoughtful, but its effects are wearing off as they have grown accustomed to it. Most people seem to want to do something to help their country, but I doubt if the majority desire to help the Church.

(b) The National Mission gave a distinct impetus to our workers and regular Church goers and to some extent it touched outsiders, who came in large numbers to our Mission Services in the Parish Room after the first part of the Mission was over. There has been an increase in the number of Communicants and acts of Communion, and fresh workers have been obtained. But the careless and indifferent are much the same as before.

4. Status of Church Schools. Options for compromise on a. management, b. head teachers, c. character of religious teaching. Might compromise be justified by better arrangements for Church teaching in state schools?

Judging from my experience of two sets of Church schools in Reading, I think it would be wise to make a compromise and allow nonconformists a larger share in the management in the Schools and even in the teaching. I should certainly regard that in return for this, Church teaching should be allowed in Council Schools to children whose parents desired it for them.

5 a. Changes in Public worship since 1914. b. Effects of the changes. (a) There are weekly celebrations on Thursdays at 8, and Intercession Services on Wednesdays at 3, also a Celebration at 7 a.m. on the 2nd Sunday in each month. We avail ourselves of the opportunity of having intercessions after the 3rd Collect at Evensong. (b) The effect of substituting intercessions for the State prayers is to make the services more real, and less monotonous. We try to give as great variety as is permissible.

6. Number of Roman Catholics in the Parish. 1 Man 2 Women 3 Children.

1. See 1914.

HIGHMORE   Incumbent J. Hughes[1]

1. Number of Boys Girls and Infants on books of day schools: a. Last year. b. 20 30 or 40 years ago.

a. 18 Boys, 15 girls, 18 infants. b. No record found before 17 years ago. 17 Boys, 18 girls, 28 infants.

2. a. Men and b. Women qualified to vote in Parochial Church meeting. [*No response*].

3. Moral and Spiritual effect of: a. Wartime b. National Mission.

Highmore Parish is small and hence one hesitates to give an opinion for general guidance. The signs are encouraging and as far as one can judge the moral character of the people has improved. The women have borne their part nobly and faithfully and since the war began there has been no case which has caused regret. The conduct of the young men has been most encouraging. The spirit of willingness to support the spiritual work of the Parish is always evident when an appeal is made. The effort on behalf of missions last summer, war time, produced good results when most of the work was done by the working people of the parish.

(b) Again in a small parish it is difficult to record the moral and spiritual effect of the National Mission. The Pilgrims during their visit to the Parish expressed their appreciation of the spiritual efforts witnessed in the Parish. Mrs Illingworth, Misses Stevenson and West can testify to their several experiences. It is still the normal life of the Parish.

4. Status of Church Schools. Options for compromise on a. management, b. head teachers, c. character of religious teaching. Might compromise be justified by better arrangements for Church teaching in state schools?

[*No response*].

5 a. Changes in Public worship since 1914. b. Effects of the changes. No change.

6. Number of Roman Catholics in the Parish. 1 woman 3 children.

1. See 1914.

HINKSEY, SOUTH AND NEW   Incumbent W. W. G. Lloyd[1]

1. Number of Boys Girls and Infants on books of day schools: a. Last year. 165, 153, 126. **b. 20 30 or 40 years ago.** In the year 1897, average boys 135 girls 145.

2. a. Men and b. Women qualified to vote in Parochial Church meeting. None, because after repeated efforts to form a Church Council they refused to attend meetings called to explain their nature. There is a feeling that it means responsibility which they are afraid of.

3. Moral and Spiritual effect of: a. Wartime b. National Mission.

A. The War has of necessity called many men and women into different kinds of employment with the result that when the fathers are absent there has been a large increase of lack of discipline and dislike for any sort of control. This is especially noticeable amongst those who have shortly left school. It is a very great pity that here in Oxford the Education Committee are willing to grant labour certificates to boys and girls in spite of the protests which Head Teachers have made. In many cases young people find unsuitable employment. In other cases employers have told us that they are afraid to say anything as the young people take themselves off without a moment's notice. We have in this parish had two cases of boys who have been sent to Industrial homes who, under ordinary conditions would have been quite well behaved boys. Then again the increase in money in some homes has not been a blessing as there has been a tendency to neglect children and home and to spend the money without forethought and in some cases in amusements and in the public houses. On the other hand there are homes in which the wife is doing her best to look after her children, and many of these cases are those for whom the National Mission has been helpful. (The Head Teachers notice a state of restlessness and the need of greater discipline in school hours.)

B. In this parish we had the National Mission as a preparation for a Parochial Mission which was held last Lent and which reached a considerable number of people. Speaking generally the impression which I have of this parish is that it was helpful to a certain number of the faithful. (A certain number of our faithful did not attend the mission) and further resulted in gaining a few others who were confirmed some of whom have continued, but many have fallen back again. There are many in this parish who occasionally go to Church while others wander about and go to various churches in Oxford. The majority of parishioners was not touched by it. To sum up – there has been an increase in weekly communions but a decided falling off in attendance at Evening Service which is most attended by the people of this parish.

4. Status of Church Schools. Options for compromise on a. management, b. head teachers, c. character of religious teaching. Might compromise be justified by better arrangements for Church teaching in state schools?

It is difficult for me to write on this subject as so many of the children which attend our schools come from other parishes, while a certain number of our[s] attend Council Schools or the Wesleyan School. If the Schools in this parish were condemned as they would have been but for the War it would have been impossible to have raised sufficient funds to have built others.

It has been my experience that where facilities for religious teaching have been offered to nonconformists they have not availed themselves of it.

5 a. Changes in Public worship since 1914. b. Effects of the changes. I have had a Mission Service on Wednesday Evenings in the place of a Choral Evensong which

I found when I came. And there is now a daily celebration of Holy Communion which is on the whole fairly well attended. (b) A certain increase in numbers, but after the novelty has worn off they are anxious for something new.

6. Number of Roman Catholics in the Parish. Four males four females three children.

1. William Wellesley Gordon Lloyd graduated from St John's College Oxford in 1893 and trained at Cuddesdon College in 1894, being ordained priest in 1896. He served two Berkshire curacies between 1895 and 1909, when he became Vicar of South and New Hinksey. He was 49 in 1918 and at the 1911 census he shared a household with his wife and three female servants.

HINKSEY, NORTH[1]   Incumbent J. G. Dale[2]

1. Number of Boys Girls and Infants on books of day schools: a. Last year. b. 20 30 or 40 years ago.

1918: 17 boys, 21 girls, 16 infants – total 54. 1893: 56 total 1888: 43 [total].

2. a. Men and b. Women qualified to vote in Parochial Church meeting. I understand from the churchwarden that no one had signed the declaration. It is being signed this year.

3. Moral and Spiritual effect of: a. Wartime b. National Mission.

(a) I have not been here long enough to judge. The attendance at Church is not very good on Sundays and not at all good on weekdays: no one comes to a weekday Eucharist as a rule and the two weekday evening Intercession Services are very poorly attended.

(b) I have no means of judging. I have not heard of any apparent results, and no one appears to regard it now as having been a time of any special revival.

4. Status of Church Schools. Options for compromise on a. management, b. head teachers, c. character of religious teaching. Might compromise be justified by better arrangements for Church teaching in state schools?

In answer to (i) I should not be in favour of altering the present arrangement of managers by which two out of the six may be Nonconformists, and I am clear that we ought to keep the right to appoint the Head teacher in Church Schools, to preserve the religious atmosphere. In answer to (ii) I should think that the right of entry to teach Church teaching in Council Schools would justify us in offering facilities for Dissenting teaching in Church Schools.

5 a. Changes in Public worship since 1914. b. Effects of the changes. The only direct change of which I am aware is that the midday Eucharist on the 1st Sunday in the month is now sung and no one goes out after the Prayer for the Church Militant.

Morning Prayer and Eucharist form one service, with a very brief sermon, lasting not more than 1½ hours. The congregation, including the children, stay throughout, and a few people communicate. This arrangement appears to be agreeable to some and not aggressively distasteful to any so far as I have heard.

6. Number of Roman Catholics in the Parish. [*No response*].

1. John Greenshields Dale graduated from Wadham College Oxford in 1901 and trained at Cuddesdon College in 1902, being ordained priest in 1903. He served three curacies between 1902 and 1917, when he was appointed as Vicar of North Hinksey. He was 39 in 1918 and at the 1911 census he was unmarried and sharing a household with his widowed stepmother.

HOLTON   Incumbent A. Langdale-Smith[1]

1. Number of Boys Girls and Infants on books of day schools: a. Last year. b. 20 30 or 40 years ago.

Our School is closed as in 1915 there were only 13 Scholars and the Ox. Ed. Committee represented to the managers of our school that the cost of educating so few was unwarrantable in war time. The School therefore was closed and the children go to Wheatley School. In 1899 there were 40 Scholars. I never remember more than 43. I cannot give the proportion of B. G. and Inft. There has usually been a predominance of Boys over Girls.

2. a. Men and b. Women qualified to vote in Parochial Church meeting. [*No response*].

3. Moral and Spiritual effect of: a. Wartime b. National Mission.

I cannot honestly say that I can report any particular visible effect – either moral or spiritual – of wartime or of the National Mission. At the same time I feel that the Nat Mission did create an atmosphere which has not yet been dissipated. We had a week's visit from one Missioner.

4. Status of Church Schools. Options for compromise on a. management, b. head teachers, c. character of religious teaching. Might compromise be justified by better arrangements for Church teaching in state schools?

I think that Free churchmen should not be penalized for living in any particular area. I think that for the most part they do not desire to interfere in (a) management or (b) in the appointment of head teachers but they resent the religious teaching which in many cases approximates to Roman teaching. In schools where the religious teaching is not made the means of inculcating what is generally described as "very High Church" doctrines (I hate that unsatisfactory designation as much as I do "Low Church") in my experience the Free church parents make no objection and are glad that their children should be taught the plain ungarbled truth from the Bible.

5 a. Changes in Public worship since 1914. b. Effects of the changes. a. None, except that in winter time, owing to the Darkness, we have had Evensong at 3. Instead of at 6.30. b. The Afternoon Service seems to meet the requirements of the parish quite as well as the Evening. The older people much preferred it and the younger ones were quite pleased to come in the afternoon instead of the evening. I think it is a salutary arrangement though when light permits we will probably go back to the evening which suits some of the men better. If there should be in this question a reference to the unwarrantable disorganisation of Sunday Morning services which is taking place in so many churches at the present time, and which is alienating so many church people from their parish Church, I have to say that it does not obtain here. The order of the administration of the LORD's Supper is not, and never was intended, for general or universal use: and the present movement is a false error, and will do harm instead of good.

6. Number of Roman Catholics in the Parish. None.

1. See 1914.

HOLWELL   Incumbent J. B. Rainey[1]

1. Number of Boys Girls and Infants on books of day schools: a. Last year. Boys 6, Girls 10, Infants 8. **b. 20 30 or 40 years ago.** In 1898, Boys 17, Girls 18, Infants 13.

2. a. Men and b. Women qualified to vote in Parochial Church meeting. Men 27, Women 35.

3. Moral and Spiritual effect of: a. Wartime b. National Mission.

There has been much bereavement and sorrow in this small parish during the war. One hesitates to speak too definitely of the moral and spiritual effect; but upon the whole I think the condition is hopeful. There has been an increase of regular communicants since the time of the National Mission.

4. Status of Church Schools. Options for compromise on a. management, b. head teachers, c. character of religious teaching. Might compromise be justified by better arrangements for Church teaching in state schools?

It seems to be our duty to maintain as far as possible the status of our Church Schools. I can only speak from my experience of a small Church School in a single-school area. Here, two out of six Managers could be Dissenters. The one, appointed by the County Council is a Dissenter; the other, elected by the Parish Meeting, is a Churchman. So far there has been no friction in the Management. I should consider it to be of the utmost importance that the head-teacher should be a Churchman. There has been definite Church teaching in this School, as is evidenced by the Reports of Diocesan Inspectors. No children have been withdrawn from the religious teaching or Inspection.

5 a. Changes in Public worship since 1914. b. Effects of the changes. (a) An 8 o'clock celebration on the 3rd Sunday in the month. (b) An increase in the number of Communicants and in some cases more frequent Communions.

6. Number of Roman Catholics in the Parish. There are no Roman Catholics in this parish.

1. See 1914.

HORLEY WITH HORNTON[1] Incumbent H. J. Buxton[2]

1. Number of Boys Girls and Infants on books of day schools: a. Last year. b. 20 30 or 40 years ago.

Horley Church (Endowed) School (a) 38, (b) no records. Hornton Council School (a) 64, (b) no records.

2. a. Men and b. Women qualified to vote in Parochial Church meeting.

	Men	Women
Horley	5	7
Hornton	8	16

3. Moral and Spiritual effect of: a. Wartime b. National Mission.

(a) The effect of wartime (fourth year) is apparently deadening for the outward religious life of the agricultural labourer. In spite of the minimum wage, the war has not brought him any vision or new hopes – only a growing discontent with his present portion, and with the Church which has acquiesced in it. In this district, there is no movement towards the formation of Labourers' Unions so far as I am aware; nor any rally to the Church.

The war is dimly felt to be an exposure of the hollowness of our Christianity. Farmers and Labourers alike are full of questions as to the value and utility of the Church. The old message of "personal salvation" does not apparently grip. No one can hold a congregation, or at any rate win the younger generation with that gospel, alone. However, people are more ready to see through shams, and more anxious to be rid of "bunkum" than before. All this is good as far as it goes. We are clearing the ground. The heart of the country people is sound. There is so much kindness and goodness – ever ready to break out, and plenty of response to what is called 'practical Christianity'.

(b) The National Mission here seemed to us to be an attempt to justify the church. At any rate, it shewed a life and energy in the church, which the non-conformist bodies do not possess.

1. It brought a few <u>lapsed</u> Church people back to church. 2. It gave a new idea to some of our people, namely, that the Christian religion has something to do with <u>national</u> affairs. 3. It emphasised the shame of our schisms, and the need for unity.

4. Status of Church Schools. Options for compromise on a. management, b. head teachers c. character of religious teaching. Might compromise be justified by better arrangements for Church teaching in state schools?

Retaining our Church Schools in single-school areas.

<u>Pro.</u> The religious 'atmosphere' is enormously valuable when clergy and teachers are both keen and work together. Formality and unreality of the religious 'hour' in Council Schools. Withdrawal of children from Catechism teaching is almost unknown in this area.

<u>Contra.</u> The County Authorities give favour and preference to their own schools. Church schools are not given quite the same treatment, as regards equipment and so on. The majority of teachers favour a unified system.

I have not sufficient experience to venture a decided opinion; but my inclination is to think that we might make some compromise as regards (a) management and (b) appointment of head teachers – in place of further facilities for denominational teaching in Council Schools.

5 a. Changes in Public worship since 1914. b. Effects of the changes. Rendered <u>very</u> simply:

(a) 1. The Lord's Service, chief service on alternate Sunday mornings (since 1914). Mattins 10 a.m: Lord's Service and Sermon 10.30 am. 2. The "English Hymnal" introduced (at Horley only). 3. All seats have been made free and unappropriated. 4. Rogation open-air services revived – 1917.

(b) These changes (1, 2, and 3) were much criticised during the first six months – less so in this parish than might have been expected in other villages, owing to previous neglect. Careful and constantly repeated explanations of every change were made, both in church and outside. The changes have now been accepted and welcomed by the majority of each congregation, Horley and Horton.) I feel convinced that the spirit of worship is aroused by such changes – if they are carried out with careful preparation and explanation.

6. Number of Roman Catholics in the Parish. None.

1. Population 601.
2. Harold Jocelyn Buxton graduated from Trinity College Cambridge in 1903 and was ordained priest in 1906. After an initial curacy he served chaplaincies in Burma 1907–10 and was then Curate of Thaxted between 1911 and 1914, when he became Vicar of Horley with Hornton. He was 38 in 1918. He served as Chaplain to the Forces in France in 1915 and was attached to the Russian Red Cross in Erzerum in 1916.

HORSPATH[1]   Incumbent G. H. Haines[2]

1. Number of Boys Girls and Infants on books of day schools: a. Last year. b. 20 30 or 40 years ago.

(a) Boys 25; Girls 30; Infants 18 – total 73. (b) No. on books in the year 1873 was 68. In the last 10 years the number on the books has been 90 and in the last 5 years over 80.

2. a. Men and b. Women qualified to vote in Parochial Church meeting. (a) None. (b) None. Note: In 1915 a list of "qualified electors" was made up – no fresh names have been added – the number of names has been greatly reduced owing to the war.

3. Moral and Spiritual effect of: a. Wartime b. National Mission.

(a) It is not easy to give any information of value in answer to these questions. One way by which one could get a kind of answer would be to take the effect caused by the death of a son (killed in action) upon a mother and father. If that is done one gets an indefinite answer – for whereas there are cases in which such a loss has helped the soul it has hindered another. "Inequality in sacrifice" – viz "that one should be taken and another left" has been a hard burden to very many. On the other hand it is a pleasure to record the hearty response that has been made to appeals for war charities such as Red Cross, Lord Roberts' Memorial, Prisoners of War Fund etc.

(b) I find it impossible to separate (a) and (b). Had there been no war it would have been perhaps possible to give a clear answer to (b). The main effect of the National Mission (in Horspath) was to deepen the spiritual life of the people. Outwardly there was little to shew = viz the congregation here not better nor the number of regular communicants larger. For a time people came to Intercession Services and extra services (week-day) readily, but they are weary of the War, and the special appeal has lost its effect, or they are too busy with war work.

4. Status of Church Schools. Options for compromise on a. management, b. head teachers, c. character of religious teaching. Might compromise be justified by better arrangements for Church teaching in state schools?

(a) Yes. (b) Yes. (c) No. I do not consider the conditions of religious teaching in Council Schools satisfactory but "such a compromise" is not the way to settle the question. In Horspath the Nonconformists are quite satisfied with the present condition (CofE School) – at least since July 1914 I have heard nothing which would lead me to think otherwise.

5 a. Changes in Public worship since 1914. b. Effects of the changes. (a) None except that Evening Prayer ends with the 3rd Collect and the Sermon is followed by intercession conducted from the Pulpit. (b) People like the change – no effects.

6. Number of Roman Catholics in the Parish. None.

1. Population 350.
2. George Henry Haines graduated from Magdalen College Oxford in 1892 and trained at Cuddesdon College in 1903, being ordained priest in 1905. He served as Chaplain and Assistant Master at Trinity College Glenalmond 1903–10 and then as Curate of Bradninch between 1911 and 1914, when he became Vicar of Horspath. He was not found in the 1911 census.

HORTON-CUM-STUDLEY   Incumbent J. K. Smith[1]

1. Number of Boys Girls and Infants on books of day schools: a. Last year. 26. b. 20 30 or 40 years ago. Between 50 and 60. Population has decreased from 420 to about 230.

2. a. Men and b. Women qualified to vote in Parochial Church meeting. (a) 14, (b) 30.

3. Moral and Spiritual effect of: a. Wartime b. National Mission.

I think that in this parish, through all classes, the effects both of the War and the National Mission have been deep, and enduring. Also, though this is not so certain, there has been an increase of congregations, – and also of more frequent communicants, especially at 11.30. But it can only be a matter of opinion, concerning the causes this progress is to be assigned to. We have lost severely in the war: as many as 9. In no one does the bereavement seem to have hardened, or lessened, the religious spirit: on the contrary. The people have loyally shared the public troubles: and the food and other difficulties.

No "moral" difficulty has occurred here during the war, or as arising out of the war. A number of lads verging on military age remain, and there are also several girls at home. But I have no reason to be anxious about the graver issues. These slow lads seem untouched religiously: but in the same degree as in pre-War times. Their problem is made more difficult by the uncertainty of their continued stay at home.

4. Status of Church Schools. Options for compromise on a. management, b. head teachers, c. character of religious teaching. Might compromise be justified by better arrangements for Church teaching in state schools?

See answers as regards "Beckley". Same applies to Horton cum Studley.

5 a. Changes in Public worship since 1914. b. Effects of the changes. On appointment of present Incumbent the Services were arranged: 8. H.C.: 10.45 Matt. with Sermon: 11.30 H.C. Choral, 2.30 C.S.: 6.30 Evensong. After a short interval, this arrangement was working excellently. The attendance at 11.30 increased: until it was unusual for anyone to leave after Matt. This arrangement was somewhat disturbed by the necessary disuse of some services consequent on the Vicar's presence at Beckley. Since Sept. 1916 the 8. H.C. and the 10.45 Matt. and 11.30 H.C. have alternated on successive Sundays: and Evensong in summer is alternately at 3 and 6.30: in winter at 6.30. This arrangement has worked and is working exceedingly well. The congregation seem to have accepted, and to appreciate, the 11.30 Eucharist as the Principle Service. The congregations at both the Morning and Evening Services are, under the circumstances, regularly good: collections have increased. There is an excellent readiness for cooperation. I do not, after 1½ years, think that a better arrangement could have been devised – or a congregation responded better.

The alternate Sunday afternoon service is not successful, but the contrary. On the other hand, the defect seems made up by increased congregations at 6.30 pm.

6. Number of Roman Catholics in the Parish. None.

1. See 1914 Minster Lovell. Smith came to Horton-cum -Studley in 1915.

IFFLEY   Incumbent O. S. E. Clarendon[1]

1. Number of Boys Girls and Infants on books of day schools: a. Last year. Boys 18, Girls 26, Infants 29. **b. 20 30 or 40 years ago.** Forty years ago: Boys 30, Girls 38, Infants 32.

2. a. Men and b. Women qualified to vote in Parochial Church meeting. Men 4, Women 11.

3. Moral and Spiritual effect of: a. Wartime b. National Mission.

(a) The War has stirred up the Communicants to increased earnestness – and others here availed themselves of the Week-day Intercession Service for the War – but taking the Parish as a whole I regret that I cannot notice much increase in spiritual earnestness, as regards public Worship – although I am sure that these anxious years are telling for good in the private lives of many. But the young people show a marked tendency to get out of hand – now that so many fathers are away.

(b) I fear that the National Mission has not produced any marked effect here – save that in the poorer part of the Parish: a few have come back to their Communions – and my little Mission Service held in a cottage has been better attended. But I am thankful to say that the number of communicants has kept up well; and decided improvements have taken place at the Great Festivals.

4. Status of Church Schools. Options for compromise on a. management, b. head teachers, c. character of religious teaching. Might compromise be justified by better arrangements for Church teaching in state schools?

From my personal experience as a Parish Priest and a Diocesan Inspector, I feel strongly that our Church Schools should maintain their present status. I have never come across either here or in the Lincoln Diocese, any really expressed desire on behalf of Nonconformists to seek for special treatment as regards religious teaching in our Schools. In a very few cases have children been withdrawn from religious instruction in the Schools which I inspect and this has usually been on personal rather than religious grounds. I hail it with great pleasure, when I am able to award the Bishop's Prize to a Non-Conformist. I rejoice that the Council Schools in Oxfordshire have been thrown open for us to inspect and examine them on their own syllabus. This I take as a very cheering sign. But no reason why we should be justified with tampering with our present status.

5 a. Changes in Public worship since 1914. b. Effects of the changes. I have Intercessions for the War each Sunday Ev after 3rd collect; and these are much appreciated and in the Winter when Evensong on Sunday is at 6 ocl: rest of the year 6.30 (as before). Congregations in the Evenings in the Winter on the whole have been smaller.

6. Number of Roman Catholics in the Parish. Iffley Village – 1 man, 5 women, and 5 children.

1. See 1914.

IPSDEN WITH NORTH STOKE   Incumbent H. J. Warner[1]

1. Number of Boys Girls and Infants on books of day schools: a. Last year. 41 (Ipsden), 35 (North Stoke with Mongewell). **b. 20 30 or 40 years ago.** No records.

2. a. Men and b. Women qualified to vote in Parochial Church meeting. None, as far as I know.

3. Moral and Spiritual effect of: a. Wartime b. National Mission.

I cannot speak for the National Mission, for I was not here when it was held. The War, however, has produced a better understanding between class and class. Doles are being displaced by co-operation and thoughtlessness among the poor and selfish luxury among the rich are practically things of the past. The scarcity of food is borne with great cheerfulness. There is no intemperance and greater attention is being paid to the value of child life. On the other hand Sunday drills and parades and agricultural work are given as reasons for absence from Church. Also owing to the father being "called up", the mother cannot in many instances leave home to attend church; but I do not think that in this parish the home discipline of the children has been adversely affected.

4. Status of Church Schools. Options for compromise on a. management, b. head teachers, c. character of religious teaching. Might compromise be justified by better arrangements for Church teaching in state schools?

(a) If the Church School is private property, and the owner receives a rent for it, the Trust deed should not contain any provision whereby he has a controlling voice in its management. I have not found any difficulty in admitting Nonconformists amongst Managers. They become more reasonable because better informed. (b) The appointment of Head Teachers of Church Schools might be exercised by the County authorities, provided that such Teacher is always a Churchman. In our larger schools I think the appointment of a non-churchman would be less mischievous than in the smaller schools, inasmuch as there is now so much clerical work for a headmaster to do that he is less a teacher than ever. (c) The admission of non-conformist religious teaching into the School would create a better spirit between Church and Dissent. It would shew the weakness of the latter, and the slight difference in the fundamentals, such as children are capable of grasping. I believe very soon the teacher, if he came only for religious instruction, would cease to attend, and the Church would have the credit of having offer[ed] facilities which were accepted as satisfactory and then let drop through lack of enthusiasm.

5 a. Changes in Public worship since 1914. b. Effects of the changes. (a) Special week day Intercession Service for the War. (b) Instead of Service in Church on week-day (Wed), a Mission Service with extempore prayer and set forms of prayer in the Schoolroom at North Stoke on week-day (Wednesday) evening. The attendance is much better, and the people have expressed their preference for it. In Lent we reverted to the Church. I do not know what return was made for this parish in 1914.

6. Number of Roman Catholics in the Parish. None.

1. Henry James Warner graduated from St John's College Cambridge in 1885 and was ordained priest in 1888. After an initial curacy 1887–89 he was Vicar of Brixton 1889–97 and then of Yealmpton between 1897 and 1917, when he became Vicar of North Stoke with Ipsden. He published a *History of Yealmpton* (1907). He was 55 years old in 1918 and at the 1911 census he was sharing a household with his wife, two sons aged 18 and 20, two unmarried female boarders from Germany, both aged 17, and two unmarried female servants.

ISLIP   Incumbent J. H. Carter[1]

1. Number of Boys Girls and Infants on books of day schools: a. Last year. 98. **b. 20 30 or 40 years ago.** I have no trustworthy information.

2. a. Men and b. Women qualified to vote in Parochial Church meeting. (a) 17. No women.

3. Moral and Spiritual effect of: a. Wartime b. National Mission.

The war has taken away most of our energetic and public-spirited men and some of the women. Those left behind do not seem greatly affected by the national crisis through which we are passing. All are very war-weary. A strong patriotic feeling was observable at the beginning and most of the young men volunteered for service. It was considered disgraceful to wait to be fetched. We shall have to wait for the return of these men before we can gauge the spiritual effect of the War on the parish. Attendance at Intercession Services has fallen off.

(b) Our National Mission produced no permanent effect. The attendance at Sunday evening services is good but few come in the morning.

4. Status of Church Schools. Options for compromise on a. management, b. head teachers, c. character of religious teaching. Might compromise be justified by better arrangements for Church teaching in state schools?

I see no signs of dissatisfaction in the parents with the present arrangement of the Church School in this single-school area. Personally I think that right of entry into all schools would be worth purchasing at the cost of surrendering some of our privileges with regard to Church Schools in single-area districts.

5 a. Changes in Public worship since 1914. b. Effects of the changes. Since 1914 we have made The Sung Eucharist at 11 o'clock the chief service of the day. We have lost a few of the older parishioners tho the attendance as a whole is about the same. We have Mattins at 10.15 as a separate service and always a plain Eucharist at 7 or 8.

6. Number of Roman Catholics in the Parish. One.

1. See 1914.

KENCOT   Incumbent H. E. Cooper[1]

1. Number of Boys Girls and Infants on books of day schools: a. Last year. b. 20 30 or 40 years ago.

No day school in the parish: children attend Bradwell school. (Sunday School – Boys 20, Girls 18).

2. a. Men and b. Women qualified to vote in Parochial Church meeting. (a) 6, (b) 7.

3. Moral and Spiritual effect of: a. Wartime b. National Mission.

(a) On the leisured class the effect has been decided though perhaps moral rather than spiritual work, in one or two cases very hard work, has been taken up. On the farmer class the effect appears to have been nil. On the working class the effect has been decidedly sobering, especially in the last 12 months.

(b) The effect of the National Mission seems to have been disappointingly small: I am inclined to think that in a parish such as this the effect would have been greater and more lasting if it had been more on the lines of a parochial mission.

4. Status of Church Schools. Options for compromise on a. management, b. head teachers, c. character of religious teaching. Might compromise be justified by better arrangements for Church teaching in state schools?

I think a really satisfactory offer of improved religious teaching in Provided Schools might justify a compromise as to Church Schools in single school areas; though in any case there ought to be opportunities of definite Church teaching for the children of Church people.

5 a. Changes in Public worship since 1914. b. Effects of the changes. The only change is the introduction of a War Intercession Service on Wednesday evenings and after Evensong on the First Sunday in the month.

6. Number of Roman Catholics in the Parish. None.

1. See 1914.

KIDDINGTON   Incumbent A. F. Bellman[1]

1. Number of Boys Girls and Infants on books of day schools: a. Last year. Mixed boys and girls 30, Infants 13 = 43. **b. 20 30 or 40 years ago.** 1885 Mixed boys and girls = 60.

2. a. Men and b. Women qualified to vote in Parochial Church meeting. [*No response*].

3. Moral and Spiritual effect of: a. Wartime b. National Mission.

Sunday labour etc are deadening – no remedy.

4. Status of Church Schools. Options for compromise on a. management, b. head teachers, c. character of religious teaching. Might compromise be justified by better arrangements for Church teaching in state schools?

The school is financed and managed by the Squire. Private property.

5 a. Changes in Public worship since 1914. b. Effects of the changes. None.

6. Number of Roman Catholics in the Parish. None.

1. See 1914.

KIDLINGTON   Incumbent A. C. R. Freeborn[1]

1. Number of Boys Girls and Infants on books of day schools: a. Last year. Boys 76, Girls 66, Infants 97. **b. 20 30 or 40 years ago.** Infants 1882: 86. In the year 1893: Boys 61, Girls 66. In the year 1880: Boys 70 (Girls Register lost). In the year 1872: Boys 58 (Girls Register lost).

2. a. Men and b. Women qualified to vote in Parochial Church meeting. None.

3. Moral and Spiritual effect of: a. Wartime b. National Mission.

(a) The labouring classes are somewhat discontented by the rise in the price of commodities and by the scarcity of food. About 30 men from this parish have fallen in battle – and on the whole their loss has been borne with remarkable fortitude. The people are becoming more anxious and depressed than they have been previously. They come well to Church, and I think they are more earnest, but there is a feeling of deep resentment at the men being obliged to go – and they are loath to accept the necessity of fighting the war to the finish. The upper classes readily accept the situation – and are most loyal and patriotic: they take an optimistic view and practice considerable self denial with regard to food and general expenditure. I am inclined to think that there is an improved religious spirit among them.

(b) The National Mission had a marked effect at the time on all classes – but it would be hard to say how far its influence is lasting; or how far the awakened spirit of devotion is due to the War.

4. Status of Church Schools. Options for compromise on a. management, b. head teachers, c. character of religious teaching. Might compromise be justified by better arrangements for Church teaching in state schools?

My general impression is that in single school areas no difficulty arises unless there happens to be (1) an exceptionally antagonistic opponent of the Church, or (2) a lamentable want of tact and common sense on the part of Churchmen. Very few children are withdrawn from religious instruction in the schools of the Woodstock Deanery which I have inspected for upwards of 20 years. In my own school no child has been so withdrawn for many years past. Some time ago I purposely secured the election of two non-conformist managers for our own school – but they raised no difficulties and eventually retired voluntarily. I am opposed in principle to compromise – but I can easily imagine that a time may come when it must be better to accept such conditions than to sacrifice religious teaching altogether. Whether the "more satisfactory conditions" offered in "Provided" or Council Schools really justify a change, I do not feel competent to judge, not knowing the circumstances of schools outside my Deanery: but I feel bound to add that I believe what are called religious objections of parents with regard to the teaching their children receive at School arise far more from political or social bias, than from serious spiritual conviction.

5 a. Changes in Public worship since 1914. b. Effects of the changes. (a) I use all prayers connected with war – as ordered. I use some of the Intercessions at Evensong on every Sunday after the 3rd Collect. I have a special Intercession Service for women on every Wednesday afternoon at 2.30 – so as to enable the mothers and wives of sailors and soldiers to attend while the children are at school. The other services in Kidlington Church are as usual – but Intercessions are used at all of them. (b) I think undoubtedly that people are growing more earnest and devotional: at the same time the change has mainly arisen from temporal anxieties rather than spiritual fervour.

6. Number of Roman Catholics in the Parish. There is one family which has recently come to Kidlington – consisting of a mother and a few children. She is the wife of a soldier at the front: she professes to be a Roman Catholic, but she sends her children to the Religious Teaching in our Schools. There are no other Roman Catholics in Kidlington.

1. See 1914.

KIDMORE END Incumbent B. H. Bird[1]

1. Number of Boys Girls and Infants on books of day schools: a. Last year. b. 20 30 or 40 years ago.

1917 <u>Kidmore End</u> (C.E.): Boys 36, Girls 27, Infants 29 = 92. <u>Sonning Common</u>: Boys 63, Girls 55, Infants 55 = 173. (This was the highest figure and includes children from other parishes. The average attendance was 140). 1886 <u>Kidmore End</u>: Boys 45, Girls 43, Infants 40 = 128. (Sonning Common school was opened January 1913).

2. a. Men and b. Women qualified to vote in Parochial Church meeting. Men 34, Women 38 = 72. (Of these about 16 have died, left the Parish, or are non-parishioners who no longer attend this Church.)

3. Moral and Spiritual effect of: a. Wartime b. National Mission.

As I came here in the middle of the war, and at the time of the National Mission, I am unable to compare things now with things before. But my impression here is much the same as elsewhere –

That those who were serious are more so: Those who thought – think more: Those who were religious are more so: Those who practised their religion do so rather more: The good are better.

But those who didn't think, and those who didn't appear religious, and who didn't practice their religion – seem much the same.

And yet – there <u>does</u> seem much more seriousness: and I am told the services are as well attended, in spite of numbers of regular attendants having gone! Here as elsewhere, the absence of the fathers and the increased (labour) value of the boys, tends to make the latter troublesome.

4. Status of Church Schools. Options for compromise on a. management, b. head teachers, c. character of religious teaching. Might compromise be justified by better arrangements for Church teaching in state schools?

Again – I feel most unqualified to express an opinion. But – as regards retaining them in their present status I should say, yes. The Conscience Clause seems to me to meet the case fairly.

I should not regard more satisfactory conditions of religious teaching in "Provided" Schools as justifying such a compromise. This seems to me what we have the right to demand. I feel – we should <u>gradually</u> lose everything and <u>eventually</u> gain nothing.

5 a. Changes in Public worship since 1914. b. Effects of the changes. (a) Since 1914, previous to my arrival here, I don't know of any particular changes beyond <u>War Intercessions</u>. This we now have on 3 Sunday evenings each month after 3rd collect (Missionary Intercessions on 4th); and on one weekday evening – which is fairly well attended. Since my arrival, there have been no striking changes worth reporting, but the following may be worth mentioning.

Children – I have service on all Saints Days etc at 9.10 H. Baptism – is normally at Children's Service on Sun, 3 instead of [*indeciph.*]; cards – particulars and godparents required to be filled in beforehand. Holy Communion – rather fewer (1 Sun for 2, and 1 Fri each month 10.30 for 11.30 each week) late celebrations. Same ceremonial at all celebrations – instead of differences between early and late. 11 Choral at Festivals – Mat said – instead of 12. Dedication – 1st Sun in Oct. Athanasian Creed said when ordered. Benedicite – as provided – in Lent and Advent. Litany – as printed. Number of communicants this year is a good deal higher than last. (b) No particular effects. But all have been taken to kindly; and some explanation given where required.

6. Number of Roman Catholics in the Parish. I do not think that there are any Roman Catholics in the Parish.

1. Bertram Hugh Bird graduated from Jesus College Cambridge in 1902 and trained at Cuddesdon College, being ordained priest in 1903. He served two curacies between 1903 and 1916, when he became Vicar of Kidmore End. He was 37 years old in 1918 and at the 1911 census he was unmarried and living in a single-person household.

KINGHAM   Incumbent W. Fisher[1]

1. Number of Boys Girls and Infants on books of day schools: a. Last year. b. 20 30 or 40 years ago.

(a) 1916–17: Mixed boys and Girls 60, Infants 37. (b) There is no previous record but the Headmaster thinks the numbers would be much the same for a long period.

2. a. Men and b. Women qualified to vote in Parochial Church meeting. About 8 altogether.

3. Moral and Spiritual effect of: a. Wartime b. National Mission.

(a) Changed conditions have compulsorily affected pre-War habits and the continued thought and sense of the war have toned the ordinary mind but there are no very visible signs of any moral or spiritual transformation or of any undercurrent that promises to emerge into definite and permanent improvement.

(b) Apparently there have been no results that can still be recognised.

4. Status of Church Schools. Options for compromise on a. management, b. head teachers, c. character of religious teaching. Might compromise be justified by better arrangements for Church teaching in state schools?

I think a sound Religious Education – in matters of faith and morals – is nationally imperative. Education purely or mainly for commercial necessity and advantage must materialize the object of it – and the rest inevitably follows even if all nations are leagued together.

The demand for it must extend to the "Provided" as well as the Church Schools and it must also be conceded conversely by those who demand it. If it could be <u>permanently</u> supplied in "Provided" schools the need for Church Schools would seem to be diminished if not dissipated.

I would advocate fair and open treatment in all Elementary Schools as far as possible of all religious beliefs. I am not competent to answer on (b) and (c). They are too complicated for my limited experience.

5 a. Changes in Public worship since 1914. b. Effects of the changes. (a) None. There is no need of any in this country parish.

6. Number of Roman Catholics in the Parish. There is one man, and one woman lately come to Kingham as Postmistress whose residence may be temporary.

1. See 1914.

LANGFORD   Incumbent F. B. Hearn[1]

1. Number of Boys Girls and Infants on books of day schools: a. Last year. b. 20 30 or 40 years ago.

(a) 50. (b) 30 years ago number averaged 50–60.

2. a. Men and b. Women qualified to vote in Parochial Church meeting. 12 men, 20 women.

3. Moral and Spiritual effect of: a. Wartime b. National Mission.

There is very little *visible* moral and spiritual effect of any kind. But the labouring class are exceedingly suspicious of being asked to do anything more in the way of worship or prayer than they have done.

The effect of the National Mission was strictly confined to the faithful. I think it did good in rousing within them some sense of corporate responsibility.

4. Status of Church Schools. Options for compromise on a. management, b. head teachers, c. character of religious teaching. Might compromise be justified by better arrangements for Church teaching in state schools?

My experience is that the present system works absolutely fairly, two nonconformists being on our council. I never hear any complaint. I fear it is vital to the character of a Church School that our Headmaster should be a Churchman. Provision should be made for non-conformists to teach their own children, if they wish to do so.

5 a. Changes in Public worship since 1914. b. Effects of the changes. None.

6. Number of Roman Catholics in the Parish. None.

1. Frank Basil Hearn graduated from New College Oxford in 1888, and trained at Wells Theological College and was ordained priest in 1890. He served five curacies 1889–1904 and was then Rector of Maids Moreton 1904–11 and Curate of High Wycombe between 1911 and 1914, when he became Vicar of Langford. He was 53 in 1918. At the 1911 census he was described as a widower and was visiting his sister. At his home in the rectory at Maids Moreton those family members listed are an unmarried sister and an 8-year-old son. The household also included an unmarried nursery governess and two unmarried female servants.

LAUNTON   Incumbent F. M. Burton[1]

1. Number of Boys Girls and Infants on books of day schools: a. Last year. Boys 23, Girls 25, Inf 33, Total 81. **b. 20 30 or 40 years ago.**

	Boys	Girls	Inf	Total
22 years ago	45	54	44	143
30 years ago	44	55	42	141

2. a. Men and b. Women qualified to vote in Parochial Church meeting. None.

3. Moral and Spiritual effect of: a. Wartime b. National Mission.

(a) Great want of thrift, many girls and married women running after soldiers, lawlessness and bad behaviour of young men.

(b) Better attendance at all church services.

4. Status of Church Schools. Options for compromise on a. management, b. head teachers, c. character of religious teaching. Might compromise be justified by better arrangements for Church teaching in state schools?

i. Facilities for religious education by the Minister or other person of nonconformist children.

(a) Put a dissenter on if desired. (b) The Head should be a churchman. (c) See answer i.

5 a. Changes in Public worship since 1914. b. Effects of the changes. None.

6. Number of Roman Catholics in the Parish. None.

1. See 1914 South Banbury. Burton became Rector of Launton in 1915.

LEAFIELD WITH WYCHWOOD   Incumbent T. W. Lee[1]

1. Number of Boys Girls and Infants on books of day schools: a. Last year. b. 20 30 or 40 years ago.

(a) Boys 53, Girls 49 Infants 65 (b) 1878: Boys 73, Girls 47 Infants no record; 1888: Boys 58, Girls 65 Infants 72; 1898: Boys 54, Girls 66 Infants 90 The total population has diminished by ⅕ within this period.

2. a. Men and b. Women qualified to vote in Parochial Church meeting. None. They were not asked and few other dissenters.

3. Moral and Spiritual effect of: a. Wartime b. National Mission.

(a) One obvious effect of the war on the moral life of the village has been the increase of unruliness and discourtesy among the children, which is generally ascribed to the absence of so many of the fathers and elder brothers.

The effect on the spiritual life of the village is very hard to estimate. Probably owing to the continued effect of the war and of the National Mission, the spiritual life of a good many seems to have been deepened and their attendance at Church (esp. at Intercession) services has been more regular. But the great majority are no more drawn to take their share in corporate religion than before. One feels that this is partly due, especially in the case of the men, to the prevalent sense of the horror and cruelty of war, combined with most natural ignorance of the real issues at stake, and the lack of any vision of a good end which will compensate for personal loss and suffering.

4. Status of Church Schools. Options for compromise on a. management, b. head teachers, c. character of religious teaching. Might compromise be justified by better arrangements for Church teaching in state schools?

I think that the Church of England should be as brave and faithful as the Roman Catholics, who refuse compromise. (a) In business matters indeed, a minority of Dissenting Managers might be useful in clearing away ignorant suspicions. (b) Headteachers must be Churchmen in Church Schools. (c) For religious teaching by some dissenters (e.g. anti-paedo-baptists and unitarians) would nullify the very raison d'etre of Church schools. "Satisfactory conditions", that is thorough teaching of the Church Catechism, could hardly be expected.

5 a. Changes in Public worship since 1914. b. Effects of the changes. On Whit Sunday 1916, we began to have Holy Communion with hymns and a little other music at 11 am on the first S of each month without any pause after the prayer for the Ch. Militant. The number of Communicants has been much increased, especially by the presence of younger and more recently confirmed persons. Mattins and Litany without music precede at 10 am, with an attendance very unsatisfactory. On the evening of the 1st S. in month, we now have the Sermon after the Third Collect, followed by reading the Roll of Honour of about 120 names and war intercessions, always well attended. At the Parish Room, at 2.45 a monthly prayer meeting is well-attended by about 12 women regularly.

6. Number of Roman Catholics in the Parish. No Roman Catholics.

1. See 1914.

LEWKNOR   Incumbent R. T. Espinasse (Curate in Charge of Lewknor pro tem)[1]

1. Number of Boys Girls and Infants on books of day schools: a. Last year. 73. **b. 20 30 or 40 years ago.** In 1895: 108; 1905: 89; 1915: 84; 1918: 73.

2. a. Men and b. Women qualified to vote in Parochial Church meeting. 39: 15 men, 24 women.

3. Moral and Spiritual effect of: a. Wartime b. National Mission.

I have only one year's experience of Lewknor, and therefore can give no decided opinion of any value, as I was very little acquainted with the condition before I took temporary charge. So far as I <u>can</u> judge I should say with regard to (a) – War time has not influenced those who were indifferent to spiritual affairs previously, to any great extent. I think there appears rather less restraint among the young and adolescent than in normal times though no doubt some of the adult population have been influenced for good. The saddest point is the fact that 'war weariness' had taken the form of neglect of united intercessions at the weekly intercession. On Sundays, however, good congregations attend and there is considerable interest taken to see that no names are omitted from the list of parishioners and friends which is read out each time.

(b) I am afraid I cannot find in my conversation with the people that the effect of the National Mission was very deep or very lasting. It was too short and not nearly thorough enough.

4. Status of Church Schools. Options for compromise on a. management, b. head teachers, c. character of religious teaching. Might compromise be justified by better arrangements for Church teaching in state schools?

(a) All schools to be kept up to date by church, as to buildings etc. (b) appointment of teachers independent of outside conditions. (c) Right of entry. Yes, I have extremely strong and may I say with all humility clear views on this first point. First it should be a matter of the <u>first importance</u> that the Incumbent should attend nearly every morning and give religious teaching himself and supervise it in every way throughout the school. If a priest cannot teach in school he should go at once and get taught the art.

    Amicable arrangements should be made whereby the children of non Church of England parents could be taught by any recognised representative of their denomination in our buildings. If they cannot provide such a teacher it is grossly unfair that children of church parents should be deprived of church teaching which is their right by virtue of the trusts of the Church Schools. If we are to retain our schools every effort must be made to keep the buildings and all that we are responsible for in a condition to compare favourably with provided schools which is not always the case owing probably to the disinclination of the laity to pay, as they consider, twice over, for Education now that they pay a share through the rates. I think it is a grievance which has a certain amount of justification that conditions such as playing the organ, undertaking Sunday School, are made when weighing the claims of candidates for head teacherships. I think we should be absolutely false to our trust to feed Christ's lambs if we agreed to any restraint on dogmatic church teaching though perhaps mistakes have been made through want of consideration for the religious beliefs of our brethren who are not of our fold. I write strongly as I feel strongly after nearly <u>forty</u> years teaching beginning as a boy teacher in my father's Sunday School.

5 a. Changes in Public worship since 1914. b. Effects of the changes. Owing to the Vicar's absence, I have had to alter the services as follows. 8.30 o'clock H Com monthly to 8.00 11 o'clock Mattins to 9.30 and 11.30 different Sundays. I have no record of the congregation but I fancy the difference is very small though some may make the excuse that 9.30 is inconvenient. Obviously this is wrong as the objection to 11 o'clock being too late to get back to cook Sunday dinner is removed by the earlier hour.

6. Number of Roman Catholics in the Parish. I only know of one who has lately come into the Parish a Belgian refugee married to a farmer. I think she is probably going to renounce and become Church of England.

1. See 1914 Adwell with South Weston. Espinasse added Lewknor to his existing charge in 1917.

LITTLEMORE Incumbent G. J. Champion[1]

1. Number of Boys Girls and Infants on books of day schools: a. Last year. b. 20 30 or 40 years ago.

There are about 250 children in the day schools at the present time, about 100 being Infants, and the Mixed School being almost equally divided between boys and girls. I do not know the number 40 years ago, but judging by the growth of population, I should say about 100.

2. a. Men and b. Women qualified to vote in Parochial Church meeting. About 20 men and 35 women.

3. Moral and Spiritual effect of: a. Wartime b. National Mission.

I think that the War has had the effect of drawing our people closer together and it has certainly brought out very deep and real sympathy for those in trouble. On the other hand it brought out, before Conscription, a good deal of bitter feeling towards those who were looked upon as shirkers and since then towards those who have obtained exemption, unfairly as they might consider. There has been a certain amount of unrest among the girls, and I am afraid that their seeking of munitions work has more often been owing to the high pay than to patriotism. Though we have had no cases of immorality with the men serving in the army, a good number of girls have got very much out of hand. I have found that a good many of the mothers, and some of the fathers, of the men abroad, have regularly availed themselves of opportunities of Intercession, but this has not been so to the same extent with the wives, who excuse themselves with the care of their children, not always a valid excuse, as they seem able to find time for secular amusement.

The National Mission certainly deepened our earnest people, and at the time made a great impression on practically everyone.

4. Status of Church Schools. Options for compromise on a. management, b. head teachers, c. character of religious teaching. Might compromise be justified by better arrangements for Church teaching in state schools?

If definite Church teaching were allowed to Church children in Provided Schools, I should be quite willing – if the Trust Deeds could be amended to allow it – that Non-conformist children should be taught, in Religious matters, by a Non-conformist. This would entail, in a Parish like Littlemore, there being a N.C. teacher on the staff, and I think it very unlikely that anyone could be found to come and give it from among the Non-conformists here. But I have not discovered on what lines Dissenters would wish such a teacher appointed. In Littlemore the Chapel is Baptist, and those who are not Church people, if they go anywhere, go there, but I cannot imagine that this really meets the wishes of serious minded members of other branches of Dissent.

5 a. Changes in Public worship since 1914. b. Effects of the changes. (a) A daily celebration of the Holy Eucharist. A sung Eucharist on Sundays at 11. (b) There has been a decided growth in the congregation at 11 compared with what we had for sung Mattins, and a much greater movement of devotion. The worship has become more congregational and the change has appealed greatly to the children.

6. Number of Roman Catholics in the Parish. 2 men 3 women.

1. See 1914.

MAPLEDURHAM   Incumbent F. St J. Thackeray[1]

1. Number of Boys Girls and Infants on books of day schools: a. Last year. b. 20 30 or 40 years ago.

(a) Boys 30, Girls 33, Infants: Boys 10, Girls 7, Total 80. (b) 40 years ago Total 45: Boys 13, Girls 17, Infants 15.

2. a. Men and b. Women qualified to vote in Parochial Church meeting. None. I consulted with the Churchwardens and we agreed that it was not practicable in a Parish like this, composed mainly of Farmer and Labourers.

3. Moral and Spiritual effect of: a. Wartime b. National Mission.

(a) The War has made the women much more thrifty and industrious. They work very hard on the Land. They do their best to manage well, they put their money into the War Saving Association and the Penny Bank. – They value Prayer for the War, at the Mothers' Union meeting and in Church. It has not increased the attendance in Church and at the Holy Communion.

(b) I believe that the National Mission touched a small number here, chiefly members of the Mothers' Union. – One effect has been a greater regularity in communicants ever since. It did not increase the attendance in Church.

4. Status of Church Schools. Options for compromise on a. management, b. head teachers, c. character of religious teaching. Might compromise be justified by better arrangements for Church teaching in state schools?

I am afraid that my acquaintance with other Church Schools is so slight that my opinion as to the first question would be of little weight, and I can only state what I feel about the Church School in this Parish. – I do not see that here any alteration or compromise is called for. There are very few Non-Conformists in the Parish, and I have never had any complaints from them about the religious education of their children.

There has always been a Colony of Roman Catholics here since the Reformation. They used to have a School and School-Mistress of their own kept up by the Squire the late Mr Darell Blount. In 1893, 25 years ago, I had – at a great expense – to build a new School-room for Infants. Mr Blount gave a small subscription and then it was arranged that the Roman Catholic children should attend at the Parish Church School and be visited for religious instruction by the Roman Catholic chaplain. – This arrangement has worked well and there has never been the slightest friction.

5 a. Changes in Public worship since 1914. b. Effects of the changes. (a) Early Celebration of the Holy Communion (8 am) is held on <u>every</u> Sunday. (b) The number of communicants has increased. They consist chiefly of women and servants and others who cannot come at midday. The distances are so great that often in bad weather, or in the depth of winter, the only communicants are the members of the Vicarage household.

6. Number of Roman Catholics in the Parish. The number of Roman Catholics at present, as far as I can ascertain it, is 8 men 20 women 12 children total 40.

1. See 1914.

MARSTON Incumbent J. H. Mortimer[1]

1. Number of Boys Girls and Infants on books of day schools: a. Last year. b. 20 30 or 40 years ago.

(a) 26 boys 28 girls, 24 infants. (b) The numbers given for 1890 in one Log Book (the earliest record we have) is boys and girls 68 (no details given) and infants 33.

2. a. Men and b. Women qualified to vote in Parochial Church meeting. All whom I asked to do so, but I cannot remember how many and I did not persevere with the matter. The business of the parish is carried out easily in a comparatively small parish such as mine by a meeting when necessary of Church workers and C.E.M.S. members.

3. Moral and Spiritual effect of: a. Wartime b. National Mission.

(a) A good effect on the whole. The spirit of the people as a whole has been admirable. There has been a cheerful acceptance of war conditions, much unselfishness, and real Christian courage in sorrow. There have been a few cases of misconduct with soldiers, but drunkenness has practically vanished. Church attendance has not increased, but those who come seem more earnest and I notice a great change for the better in many of our lads who have returned from the Front.

(b) None that I can see.

4. Status of Church Schools. Options for compromise on a. management, b. head teachers, c. character of religious teaching. Might compromise be justified by better arrangements for Church teaching in state schools?

I am quite convinced that we should strain every nerve to maintain our Church Schools in their present status with regard to all three points. There may be exceptional cases which call for exceptional treatment, but in the majority of Church Schools the present system seems to work with little or no friction. There has certainly been none in the schools I have known, and any sweeping change in the direction of compromise would I feel sure be as regrettable as it is unnecessary.

5 a. Changes in Public worship since 1914. b. Effects of the changes. None.

6. Number of Roman Catholics in the Parish. 5 men 9 women 10 children.

1. See 1914.

MERTON   Incumbent C. F. Girdlestone[1]

1. Number of Boys Girls and Infants on books of day schools: a. Last year. b. 20 30 or 40 years ago.

Nil. School closed.

2. a. Men and b. Women qualified to vote in Parochial Church meeting. None.

3. Moral and Spiritual effect of: a. Wartime b. National Mission.

Absolutely (a) none, (b) none. Farmers generally indifferent, now, too. Poor per[s]ons!

4. Status of Church Schools. Options for compromise on a. management, b. head teachers, c. character of religious teaching. Might compromise be justified by better arrangements for Church teaching in state schools?

In Merton there is no ground for development of these questions.

Apart from this – that which, to me, seems to stand first, is some sort of fraternal relationship to bodies of Christian disciples, brought up outside, and so religiously educated, (or not educated) outside the definite line of teaching held by those (called English Churchmen). Next there would appear naturally to follow a fraternal agreement together apart from the rigid species of Church (or Chapel) systems so as (as in case of our national feeling now let us get on with the war) to get on with a good heart teaching of the young. The obstacle, I believe, is based upon the antipathy existing between Church and Chapel, for which the ministration of the former may be largely to blame. Old bitterness dies hard: little of our love of God, of Christ, of Faith, of souls is about systems, habits, and red tape – and a new vision will of course give the Dissenting body a little official liberty, power, authority; I fear no results. He will (they will) do all you desire – I have seen this carried out. The questions thus answer themselves.

5 a. Changes in Public worship since 1914. b. Effects of the changes. a. None. b. None.

6. Number of Roman Catholics in the Parish. None.

1. See 1914.

MIDDLETON STONEY   Incumbent W. H. Draper[1]

1. Number of Boys Girls and Infants on books of day schools: a. Last year. b. 20 30 or 40 years ago.

	40 years ago	30	20	now
Boys	41 (by photograph)	33		29 (1917)
Girls and Infants	42	90	63	46

2. a. Men and b. Women qualified to vote in Parochial Church meeting. None last year. (My fault?) Very few the year before. But I had better state that the lines on which we are running are: That our Ch Council (started over 20 years ago) is now composed of all Communicants of Full Age in the "Parish". This seems most suitable for small Parishes and as I see signs of something like this being prepared for small Parishes I hesitate to make alteration.

3. Moral and Spiritual effect of: a. Wartime b. National Mission.

I hesitate to report but am not without hope – morally the more thoughtful are more thoughtful still – of the rest as in other missions the Day will declare. I should say that our Mission was much obscured with difficulties – Illness of Missioner. Mistakes re Witnesses time etc. so I don't think it is a case to quote.

4. Status of Church Schools. Options for compromise on a. management, b. head teachers, c. character of religious teaching. Might compromise be justified by better arrangements for Church teaching in state schools?

Church Schools should be maintained. Head Teachers – these should be "sound" Churchmen and Church Women qualified. They must give "sound" Church Teaching – allowing parents who object to withdraw their Children from it and be set to something else. A NC teacher should be allowed to come and teach NC Children Church Teachers being allowed to do the like in NC schools. Of course all duly regulated. Possibly (if staff admits) an NC Assistant might be engaged to take Religious Instruction of NC Children but not Church Children.

5 a. Changes in Public worship since 1914. b. Effects of the changes. The most marked change of hour was owing to my being obliged to service 2 afternoon services a week in place of evening services – attendance practically nil.

6. Number of Roman Catholics in the Parish. None to my knowledge, except a Belgian family of 3 lodged at the Stable Buildings in the Park (whom I commended to the care of the Roman Priest at Bicester).

1. See 1914.

MILCOMBE   Incumbent W. F. Robinson[1]

1. Number of Boys Girls and Infants on books of day schools: a. Last year. b. 20 30 or 40 years ago.

1917: 6 boys, 13 girls, 10 infants. Total 28. 1877: 28 boys and girls (numbers of each unstated), 10 infants. Total 38.

2. a. Men and b. Women qualified to vote in Parochial Church meeting. None, but this is being undertaken at the present moment.

3. Moral and Spiritual effect of: a. Wartime b. National Mission.

Owing to my very short incumbency, I cannot give any useful answer.

4. Status of Church Schools. Options for compromise on a. management, b. head teachers, c. character of religious teaching. Might compromise be justified by better arrangements for Church teaching in state schools?

I have tried to answer the question under the same heading in my returns for Bloxham.

5 a. Changes in Public worship since 1914. b. Effects of the changes. Owing to the combining of this benefice with that of Bloxham it has been found needful to reduce the services at Milcombe. I do not find that the people take full, or even nearly full advantage of the opportunities which they now enjoy, though I hear from the Church Wardens that the Church is better attended than has been the case for many years. If this be so – which I doubt – the attendance still remains very far from good. There is very little doubt that the change is unpopular in Milcombe, but this was to be expected. The Churchwardens, and the more solid people – and even the better Churchpeople among the poorer classes – are happily in favour of the change.

6. Number of Roman Catholics in the Parish. One widow woman.

1. See 1918 Bloxham.

MILTON, GREAT   Incumbent J. T. Fox[1]

1. Number of Boys Girls and Infants on books of day schools: a. Last year. b. 20 30 or 40 years ago.

	Boys	Girls	Infants		
(a) 1917	25	22	28	=	75

(b) 1874   (69 children present Sept 7th 1874, abnormal entry in log book).

In November 1891 the average full attendance was 94.4. No division made.

2. a. Men and b. Women qualified to vote in Parochial Church meeting. The lay representatives of the Ruridecanal Conference were elected after notice at a meeting of Communicants following the Easter Vestry.

3. Moral and Spiritual effect of: a. Wartime b. National Mission.

(a) The faithful have joined together in very regular public war Intercession; but among the irregular and non-churchgoing people I fear the spirit of indifference and self-sufficiency has increased.

(b) The National Mission caused a very momentary stir-up, but the lasting effects for good were not equal to the good lasting effect of a Parochial Confirmation. The permanent result is disappointing and scarcely noticeable.

4. Status of Church Schools. Options for compromise on a. management, b. head teachers, c. character of religious teaching. Might compromise be justified by better arrangements for Church teaching in state schools?

No. But I dread the effect of such "compromise". In Single School areas the Church would merely "give" and "get" nothing in return. In our Village Single School areas the urban authority and the Parish Council can leaven the management effectually, and any forthcoming leavening would inevitably mean that the Nonconformists could, and in many cases would, have a majority on the Board of Management. So unfair an arrangement would effectually in time squeeze out all Church Schools in Single School areas.

5 a. Changes in Public worship since 1914. b. Effects of the changes. None. Except at Sunday Evensong the Sermon follows the 3rd Collect and a war intercessory service follows led from the Pulpit. I think this has been a help and comfort to many of our poor people.

6. Number of Roman Catholics in the Parish. No professed Romans.

1. See 1914.

MILTON, LITTLE   Incumbent R. Townsend[1]

1. Number of Boys Girls and Infants on books of day schools: a. Last year. b. 20 30 or 40 years ago.

	1874	1877	1887	1897	1917
Boys	23	23	23	28	12
Girls	20	20	26	21	10
Infants	21	15	40	14	18

2. a. Men and b. Women qualified to vote in Parochial Church meeting. 31 men, 51 women.

3. Moral and Spiritual effect of: a. Wartime b. National Mission.

(a) I believe the person of devout mind has been driven to more earnest prayer and the loss by death, of a dear son has turned the parent to God. Yet in another case, there appears no evidence of having had any chastening effect. The mass, or generality of the people, seem as indifferent to religion as before the war. The war has manifested, by the absence of the father, what existed before, viz. lack of parental discipline in the home, especially in the case of the elder children.

(b) The spiritual effect of the National Mission has not been what was hoped for. Yet good was done, and it abides. The harvest was late and the cottagers were late therefore in harvesting their potatoes, hence the time of preparation was so broken: and the duration of the Mission was too brief.

(a) Very noticeable is the less amount of drinking and swearing, due perhaps to some young men having been "called up" but evidenced waywardness in older children and many middle aged and older people morally as before. (b) The Pilgrims of Prayer were very helpful to many, who afterwards so testified, more so among the women.

4. Status of Church Schools. Options for compromise on a. management, b. head teachers, c. character of religious teaching. Might compromise be justified by better arrangements for Church teaching in state schools?

I have heard of no complaint on the ground of religious teaching, nor has any demand been made for any child to be exempted from church teaching as given in the School – hence as far as this parish may be viewed – continue as hitherto. (a) Admit, say, ¼ or ⅓ according to circumstances, of number of Managers who are Nonconformists. (b) Should say the Head Teacher in Church Schools ought to be communicant of the Church of England in all cases. (c) Local conditions so much vary that it seems impossible to lay down any rule, or statement which could be acceptable.

5 a. Changes in Public worship since 1914. b. Effects of the changes. a. Omission of Mattins on 2nd and 4th Sundays in the month since August 1917 and 5 o'clock Evensong instead of 6 pm on 1st 3rd and 5th Sundays in the month. And absence of Vicar from Sunday School 2 Sundays in the month. These changes due to duty at Chalgrove. b. The 5 pm Evensong is not so well attended; the reason given is that men who have Sunday afternoon work with cattle etc have not time to return home change and have tea and get to Church by 5 o'clock, and also the housewife is so hindered. Also a diminution in the amount [of] the offertories on 2nd and 4th Sundays.

6. Number of Roman Catholics in the Parish. 1 only, a woman who professes to be a Roman Catholic.

1. Raymond Townsend was ordained priest in 1908 and was Curate of West Wycombe between 1907 and 1914, when he became Vicar of Little Milton. He was 52 in 1918 and at the 1911 census he shared a household with his wife and two children under 12.

MILTON-UNDER-WYCHWOOD   Incumbent A. Shildrick[1]

1. Number of Boys Girls and Infants on books of day schools: a. Last year. b. 20 30 or 40 years ago.

(a) Boys 46, Girls 49, Infants 41. (b) Forty years ago: No record. Thirty years ago: 113 in all. Twenty years ago: 140. Twelve years ago: 112.

2. a. Men and b. Women qualified to vote in Parochial Church meeting. There appeared to be little interest taken in the matter and although the matter was brought before the congregation at the Easter Vestry meeting and on other occasions there were only of men 4 who signed and of women 6.

3. Moral and Spiritual effect of: a. Wartime b. National Mission.

(a) There does not appear to be any marked difference. If we might take [i] Church attendance, [ii] Attendance at Holy Communion [iii] and personal interest in Church work as a basis upon which our opinion is formed I should say:

[i] Our attendance at Church services has always been for a country parish, quite up to, if not slightly above the average and this condition, considering the much

depleted number of young men, has been maintained. [ii] I regret that I cannot report any advance under this heading. [iii] There has always been a disposition to help in any way possible and during the war, this help has been more than maintained. I cannot say that I can observe any moral change in our people, on account of the war, either for the better or worse.

(b) I earnestly wish I could conscientiously answer this question by being able to report great progress but this I cannot do. I observe no change. I feel that the effects of the National Mission should be distinctly spiritual effects and I feel that it is a very difficult matter to tabulate these. It may be that our line of action, when the special services were being held, was not altogether the line calculated to produce the best results. I remember when in Retreat at Radley, at the meeting held specially in regard to the National Mission, one of the speakers referred to the fact that the discussion, until he spoke, had not embraced even the word <u>Repentance</u>, but was more concerned in speaking of a multiplicity of services, etc. Perhaps if we had had courage to proclaim with no uncertain voice, the need of Repentance and the benefit of Confession, we should have been able to report more favourably. I would not like it to be inferred, however, that no good has resulted. We are still hoping for, and striving to make the results beneficial.

4. Status of Church Schools. Options for compromise on a. management, b. head teachers, c. character of religious teaching. Might compromise be justified by better arrangements for Church teaching in state schools?

(a) I believe in denominational schools, first, last and all the time and anything which could carry forward this idea would in my humble opinion be on the right lines. (b) I abhor compromise generally and absolutely when a matter of principle is involved. (c) Answered in (b).

5 a. Changes in Public worship since 1914. b. Effects of the changes. (a) None. (b) Answered by (a).

6. Number of Roman Catholics in the Parish. To the best of my knowledge 1 man only.

1. See 1914.

MINSTER LOVELL   Incumbent C. Farr[1]

1. Number of Boys Girls and Infants on books of day schools: a. Last year. 75. **b. 20 30 or 40 years ago.** In 1878: 72; 1906: 75; 1913: 81; 1915: 86; 1916: 82.

2. a. Men and b. Women qualified to vote in Parochial Church meeting. No one has been asked to sign the aforementioned declaration since 1915, when 23 men and 35 women signed it.

3. Moral and Spiritual effect of: a. Wartime b. National Mission.

(a) The moral and spiritual effect of the War in this parish is most unsatisfactory. There is no marked increase of desire for spiritual things.

(b) I cannot trace the slightest result for good in the efforts made at the National Mission. An energetic and careful preparation was given the people, and they seemed to respond. Unfortunately the weather, during the days of the actual mission, was so bad that the congregations were exceptionally small.

4. Status of Church Schools. Options for compromise on a. management, b. head teachers, c. character of religious teaching. Might compromise be justified by better arrangements for Church teaching in state schools?

By all means let us retain our schools in their present status. Compromise means that sooner or later we shall be deprived entirely of the schools. Unless the trend of public opinion changes, the day is not far distant when religion will not be taught in the "Provided" schools at all. Then, too late, it will appear that all our sacrifice has been in vain.

5 a. Changes in Public worship since 1914. b. Effects of the changes. No changes in methods or hours of public worship have been made since 1914, except that on the second Sunday of the month Mattins is at 10.15 and the Holy Communion sung at 11 o'clock. I am endeavouring to get all Communicants to have a rule of, at least, monthly Communion. Many men and some women work in the early hours of Sunday, and except for an occasional Communion never Communicate. The service at 11 am evidently supplies a need, and some 12 people (on average) avail themselves of it – principally men. There is also a Celebration on Thursday at 9.30 for the women. I understand that it is generally impossible for the women to leave their homes on Sunday mornings in many cases – principally on account of the children. The week-day Celebrations afford a good opportunity to those who desire it. The congregations vary from seven to a dozen or even more.

6. Number of Roman Catholics in the Parish. There is not a Roman Catholic in the parish.

1. Charles Farr graduated AKC in 1898 and trained at St Stephen's House Oxford in 1899, being ordained priest in 1900. He served five curacies between 1899 and 1916, when he became Vicar of Minster Lovell. He was 44 in 1918 and at the 1911 census he was living in a household with his wife.

MIXBURY   Incumbent B. A. Patten[1]

1. Number of Boys Girls and Infants on books of day schools: a. Last year. 28. **b. 20 30 or 40 years ago.** 50.

2. a. Men and b. Women qualified to vote in Parochial Church meeting. None.

3. Moral and Spiritual effect of: a. Wartime b. National Mission.

(a) I think that the war has drawn people together and softened animosities. It has, I think, revealed the good qualities of many, who are displaying cheerfulness and courage in trying circumstances.

(b) The visit of the Missioners to Mixbury was much appreciated and I believe some of our best Church people were helped spiritually by the Mission. But I am afraid I cannot say that it had any real influence on the Farm Labourers.

4. Status of Church Schools. Options for compromise on a. management, b. head teachers, c. character of religious teaching. Might compromise be justified by better arrangements for Church teaching in state schools?

In my Parish of Mixbury there is really no desire for any change either in the management or the character of religious teaching. The very few Nonconformists are quite satisfied with the religious teaching as given. But my view is that while the Church should retain the <u>management</u> of her schools, facilities should be given for religious teaching according to the wishes of Dissenting Parents. This is, I believe, already done in some Schools in the Diocese, where there are sufficient Nonconformist Children to form a separate class.

5 a. Changes in Public worship since 1914. b. Effects of the changes. a. Evensong in the afternoon during the winter months to comply with the order to darken windows. War Intercessions after the 3rd Collect instead of the State Prayers (at Evensong). b. The afternoon service is fairly well attended by women but not by the men, chiefly on account of necessary farm work.

6. Number of Roman Catholics in the Parish. One.

1. See 1914.

MOLLINGTON   Incumbent J. R. Dummelow[1]

1. Number of Boys Girls and Infants on books of day schools: a. Last year. b. 20 30 or 40 years ago.

(a) Twenty-five; (b) At least double.

2. a. Men and b. Women qualified to vote in Parochial Church meeting. None.

3. Moral and Spiritual effect of: a. Wartime b. National Mission.

Owing to the War almost all our young men and women have left the Parish. Longer hours of labour among both sexes during the week seem to have made them less inclined for church going, but the weekly Intercession Service is fairly attended. Owing to difficulties in obtaining drink there is less excessive drinking. Afternoon Service, made necessary in winter by lighting difficulties, has proved less popular than Evening Service.

4. **Status of Church Schools. Options for compromise on a. management, b. head teachers, c. character of religious teaching. Might compromise be justified by better arrangements for Church teaching in state schools?**

[*No response*].

5 a. **Changes in Public worship since 1914. b. Effects of the changes.** See on Question 3.

6. **Number of Roman Catholics in the Parish.** One woman.

1. John Roberts Dummelow graduated from Queens College Cambridge in 1883 and was ordained priest in 1884. He served four curacies 1883–1901 and was Perpetual Curate of Pitcombe with Wyke Champflower between 1910 and 1914. He became Vicar of Mollington in 1916. He was the editor of *The One Volume Bible Commentary*, 8th edn (1917). He was 58 in 1918 and at the 1911 census he was sharing a household with his wife, 9-year-old son and one unmarried servant.

NETTLEBED   Incumbent P. Armitage[1]

1. **Number of Boys Girls and Infants on books of day schools: a. Last year. b. 20 30 or 40 years ago.**

[*No response*].

2. a. **Men and b. Women qualified to vote in Parochial Church meeting.** None.

3. **Moral and Spiritual effect of: a. Wartime b. National Mission.**

(a) We have been very little affected as there are no soldiers in this neighbourhood. The people have been busier and so it is more difficult for them to get to church.

(b) Although we had a particularly good man, I must own that I am not aware of any marked moral and spiritual effect of a lasting nature, due to the National Mission.

4. **Status of Church Schools. Options for compromise on a. management, b. head teachers, c. character of religious teaching. Might compromise be justified by better arrangements for Church teaching in state schools?**

[*No response*].

5 a. **Changes in Public worship since 1914. b. Effects of the changes.** None except a week night intercession service for those at the war.

6. **Number of Roman Catholics in the Parish.** I don't know of any.

1. See 1914.

NEWINGTON Incumbent J. R. Pendlebury[1]

1. Number of Boys Girls and Infants on books of day schools: a. Last year. b. 20 30 or 40 years ago.

There is no school of either kind. Our children will be included in the numbers returned from Stadhampton and (and in a few cases) from Benson.

2. a. Men and b. Women qualified to vote in Parochial Church meeting. 3 men and 1 woman. Hitherto the declaration has only been made by those actually attending the meeting. But now that the matter is no longer a novelty and is better understood – signatures can be asked for by visiting the houses, and with more success than would have been the case at the first. Those concerned are all of the humblest class.

3. Moral and Spiritual effect of: a. Wartime b. National Mission.

The evidence from this parish is of a special kind. (I). There are not "different classes" to be reported upon – for no parish in this Deanery consists so entirely of the one class of the Oxfordshire labourer of the humblest grade. There is a "Big House" – but at present it is unused, the lady being in France on war work. The farms are mostly in the hands of non-resident farmers. (II) The "geography" of the parish is peculiar and unfortunate – making any real unity of parish life impossible. In the centre is less than ⅓ of the population, – which alone we can call fully our own. At each extremity we have a portion of what would seem to a stranger to be the compact populations of 2 other parishes – Berrick Prior with Berrick Salome and Brookhampton with Stadhampton. At Brookhampton there are two residents of the farmer class – who recognise this as their church, but distance hinders them. It should be said that the distant cottagers being mostly newcomers do attend this church very well – better than those close by. (III). For, as regards this central hamlet and its older inhabitants, longer time is still required to overcome our past history. Until 23 years ago there was no church life whatever. Holy Communion was only celebrated twice in the year – and no one attended except from the Rectory. My immediate predecessor was here only a short time, but was able to rescue the church fabric from its terrible condition and set on foot the proper amount of Sunday services, reverently rendered. Of course it has been the younger people who have chiefly responded to the more recent church teaching and work. I hope that all this does not seem to wander too far from the Question. For (really) it gives the key to what we now find, when the younger men have all gone to the war and the younger women have also found occupation elsewhere. Those who are left belong to the old evil past – and tend to slip back into its indifference, now that the influence of those who never knew that past has been removed. This applies to the women more than the men. The older men and the big lads attend church and come to communion excellently – and even under present war conditions they form fully half our numbers – an average evening congregation of 35 – and always 4 or 5 communicants every Sunday. What pulls us together is the visit on leave of those serving in the War. One and all they are a joy – not only in their keenness about church (and communion) but in their extraordinary development of intelligence and wider outlook on general questions. If we can only get them settled again in the parish after the war (with all the improvement of social conditions and housing involved), all will be well. Meanwhile, the young wives are sometimes an anxiety. We have had 2 cases of misconduct. It was of the women that the "Pilgrims" who came to us in the National Mission volunteered to me the remark that of "all the parishes we have visited in this Deanery, you have the hardest job." The Priest who came here had a wonderful response from the men – and greatly helped our communicants – during 1917 – 396 communions were made.

4. Status of Church Schools. Options for compromise on a. management, b. head teachers, c. character of religious teaching. Might compromise be justified by better arrangements for Church teaching in state schools?

When I was in charge of a large district in the North, with 2 large schools, I should have been tenacious of the full privileges of the church. But that was because they were being fully used – with effective church teaching of very intelligent children. Here in the country I realise how much there is of the very first rudiments of religion which has constantly to be taught and which we do not seem to get beyond – elements which are common to all (broadly) orthodox Christians. And from my experience of our children attending the Council School at Stadhampton, I should put in a plea for more generous recognition and appreciation of the teaching given in the very great majority of such schools. If we safeguard against any anti-church teaching it is all to the good. Anything that can be additionally secured for definite church instruction in Council Schools is to be tried for to the uttermost. And conversely "church" teaching in church schools will be made more real than it often is by concessions in regard to non-church children. But I should try to keep the appointment of Head Teachers in Church Schools. On the whole I tend to accept some "compromise" – for it is possible that otherwise we shall lose everything – now that the state has all schools in its financial grip.

5 a. Changes in Public worship since 1914. b. Effects of the changes. None – the changes were made when the present Rector began.

6. Number of Roman Catholics in the Parish. At the present moment the "Big House" is closed. But before the war (and presumably after), the lady had a friend permanently living here – an American Roman Catholic. Also 2 ladies-maids (French) – and a kitchen maid (Austrian). The French "chef", wife and 3 children are away at present but keep on their house and occasionally come here. Presumably they will be permanent again after the war. (It may be interesting to add that these 3 children attended the Sunday afternoon catechising in church and were brought by the mother frequently to Evensong. Being foreigners, of course, made the difference).

1. See 1914.

NEWINGTON, SOUTH   Incumbent C. J. Whitehead[1]

1. Number of Boys Girls and Infants on books of day schools: a. Last year. 29. **b. 20 30 or 40 years ago.**

In 1899: 46, 1900: 49, 1901: 50. The average attendance (not numbers on the books) from 1867–1900 oscillates between 40 and 50.

2. a. Men and b. Women qualified to vote in Parochial Church meeting. None.

3. Moral and Spiritual effect of: a. Wartime b. National Mission.

(a) liberal giving to the church and other purposes.

(b) impossible to estimate.

4. Status of Church Schools. Options for compromise on a. management, b. head teachers, c. character of religious teaching. Might compromise be justified by better arrangements for Church teaching in state schools?

By all means retain the School; with sympathetic management there is little difficulty about the religious teaching; and I hope that growing friendliness between Churchmen and Nonconformists will in time eliminate such difficulties as do exist in some places. In Church Schools Head Teachers should be bona fide Church people – but in answer to any real demand Nonconformist Teachers should be gladly granted facilities to give religious teaching to the children of Nonconformists. Similarly in 'Provided' schools Church teaching should be allowed for the children of the Church.

Let each party pay for its own religious teaching: but with regard to Church Schools, the provision and maintenance of the School Buildings more than pay this. It is very important that all clergy should take their full share in religious teaching. Sometimes we feel that the regular teachers teach so much better than we can, that we have kept away but I sadly think that this is a great mistake. At the same time the religious training of intending teachers is of paramount importance.

As to the religious teaching itself, is it always remembered that the spiritual and moral aspects are vastly more precious than the historical side?

5 a. Changes in Public worship since 1914. b. Effects of the changes. The only change is that week-day Evening Services in Advent and Lent have not been possible.

6. Number of Roman Catholics in the Parish. None now.

1. See 1914.

NEWTON PURCELL AND SHELSWELL   Incumbent A. St Q. Armstrong[1]

1. Number of Boys Girls and Infants on books of day schools: a. Last year. 22. **b. 20 30 or 40 years ago.** 25 in 1874.

2. a. Men and b. Women qualified to vote in Parochial Church meeting. [*No response*].

3. Moral and Spiritual effect of: a. Wartime b. National Mission.

People seem to be more in earnest. Service attended better, and communicants more regular.

4. Status of Church Schools. Options for compromise on a. management, b. head teachers, c. character of religious teaching. Might compromise be justified by better arrangements for Church teaching in state schools?

Should be sorry to lose control of Religious teaching in the school.

5 a. Changes in Public worship since 1914. b. Effects of the changes. Since 1914, the following services have been added Fridays 7 pm. 1st Sunday in month, Children's Service at 3 pm. 3rd Sunday in month early celebration.

6. Number of Roman Catholics in the Parish. None.

1. See 1914.

NOKE   Incumbent J. H. Carter[1]

1. Number of Boys Girls and Infants on books of day schools: a. Last year. b. 20 30 or 40 years ago.

(a) 20. (b) No records preserved.

2. a. Men and b. Women qualified to vote in Parochial Church meeting. None.

3. Moral and Spiritual effect of: a. Wartime b. National Mission.

(a) This is a parish of about sixty people. The few men who are left are so busy that attendance at Church is very difficult for them, all being occupied in some way with cattle.

(b) No attempt was made to hold a Mission here – they were invited to join with Islip.

4. Status of Church Schools. Options for compromise on a. management, b. head teachers, c. character of religious teaching. Might compromise be justified by better arrangements for Church teaching in state schools?

There are no Nonconformists in this parish and consequently no grievance is felt in regard to the Church School.

5 a. Changes in Public worship since 1914. b. Effects of the changes. No changes since last return.

6. Number of Roman Catholics in the Parish. None.

1. See 1914 Islip. Carter added the charge of Noke to his existing benefice of Islip in 1915.

NORTHLEIGH   Incumbent W. J. H. Wright[1]

1. Number of Boys Girls and Infants on books of day schools: a. Last year. b. 20 30 or 40 years ago.

	Boys	Girls	Infants
(a)	26	35	36
(b) (1887)	53	62	65

2. a. Men and b. Women qualified to vote in Parochial Church meeting. None.

3. Moral and Spiritual effect of: a. Wartime b. National Mission.

(a) Morally I see no difference. (b) <u>Spiritually</u> – both on War and the National Mission, speaking truthfully I can see little difference. It may have made people think more – but outwardly it has been little shown, except just at the beginning and on special occasions.

4. Status of Church Schools. Options for compromise on a. management, b. head teachers, c. character of religious teaching. Might compromise be justified by better arrangements for Church teaching in state schools?

I think Church Schools should be retained. Although we rightly prefer our church children to have church teaching, if we are really striving after that unity of Christians which is always being talked about and so little ever done it seems that some compromise must be. We cannot as church people expect to take all and give nothing nor can we give all and take nothing. This does not mean that I do not uphold Religious teaching in schools for I regard education as useless and even dangerous if separated from a definite religious training and teaching.

5 a. Changes in Public worship since 1914. b. Effects of the changes. None.

6. Number of Roman Catholics in the Parish. None.

1. See 1914.

NORTHMOOR   Incumbent A. Griffiths[1]

1. Number of Boys Girls and Infants on books of day schools: a. Last year. 39. b. 20 30 or **40 years ago. 59.**

2. a. Men and b. Women qualified to vote in Parochial Church meeting. None.

3. Moral and Spiritual effect of: a. Wartime b. National Mission.

It seems to me that both the classes in this parish viz. farmers and labourers (there are no others) have been affected for the better morally and spiritually by the War. Drunkenness has disappeared from sight altogether. Three years ago it was the cause of great trouble. There is a better public feeling with regard to sexual impurity – and the few transgressors (viz those fallen during the war) are making a braver struggle in the way of repentance. There are no persons now living a scandalous life. Those formerly living in adultery are married – with the exception of one family which has lately removed to Ducklington and whose condition has been made known to the Rector.

The attendance at Services has steadily improved and the regular Communicants are increasing in number. There is a kinder and more helpful behaviour of richer to poorer. The sufferings of the war have certainly refined the character of the parishioners generally.

The National Mission was conducted earnestly for 6 days the week before Christmas 1916 – the only time suitable to the Missioner. Unfortunately the weather was most severe – and there was an epidemic of influenza. Three or four persons were well effected [*sic*]. There is no effect whatever noticeable on those who had hitherto seemed to keep themselves apart from ordinary Christian influences. Certain farmers and a larger number of labouring men never attend public worship of any kind. Nearly all the women and all the children are regular worshippers in Church. Very few labouring men are regular: but the most are occasional.

4. Status of Church Schools. Options for compromise on a. management, b. head teachers, c. character of religious teaching. Might compromise be justified by better arrangements for Church teaching in state schools?

We should seek to retain these schools in their present status – and not make the compromise proposed.

5 a. Changes in Public worship since 1914. b. Effects of the changes. I have not seen the 1914 return. The question of changes has several times been put to the parishioners. The answer always has been – no change desired. I think no changes have been made as to Sunday Services except the addition of Children's Service 10 am. Weekday Evensongs as early celebrations have been added.

6. Number of Roman Catholics in the Parish. None.

1. Alfred Griffiths graduated from St John's College Cambridge in 1877 and was ordained priest in 1879. He served five curacies 1878–1900, and then served in Scotland as Priest in Charge of the Holy Cross Mission Davidson's Mains 1900–13 and then as Assistant Priest of Holy Trinity Haddington between 1913 and 1915, when he was appointed as Vicar of Northmoor. He was married and aged 65 in 1918.

NORTON, HOOK   Incumbent E. C. Freeman[1]

1. Number of Boys Girls and Infants on books of day schools: a. Last year. 186. **b. 20 30 or 40 years ago.** 1878: 157; 1898: 225; 1908: 216; 1918: 186. There was an epidemic in 1917–18. Also many boys of late have been prematurely withdrawn and allowed to go to work on account of the war.

2. a. Men and b. Women qualified to vote in Parochial Church meeting. 2 men. I have attempted to hold three meetings on the subject, but cannot stir up any interest in it. To be quite frank the people at present seem to regard the movement simply as involving unnecessary machinery. They seem to have a great objection to signing declarations.

3. Moral and Spiritual effect of: a. Wartime b. National Mission.

(a) Those who were regular in the performance of their religious duties before the war seem to be more regular and earnest still, while those who were irregular and unsatisfactory seem to be growing more and more hardened.

(b) The same seems to be true with regard to the National Mission.

4. Status of Church Schools. Options for compromise on a. management, b. head teachers, c. character of religious teaching. Might compromise be justified by better arrangements for Church teaching in state schools?

(a) I think that the Church must maintain her hold over her Church Schools at all hazards. The Act of 1902 considerably weakened her influence. What little remains must be anxiously kept and safeguarded, in earnest hope of what good fruit may come of it in the future. (b) We must make no further compromises as to management. With regard to the appointment of head-teachers, the utmost care must be taken to secure men who are definitely Churchmen, and not merely so in name. The influence of the head-teacher throughout the school and parish is very great and real. For five hours five days in the week, the children are at the mercy of his views on religion and history. The character of the religious teaching must be of a definitely Church character. Joint syllabuses are greatly to be deprecated. They simply "water down" the Faith. The Non-conformists in most villages – certainly in this – are quite capable of looking after themselves. They are often in a better position financially and in social village life than the Church people. (c) No. I regard the right of the Church to teach her own children in Provided Schools as one which has been for many years unjustly withheld from her. N.B. The secular history books require a great deal of overhauling with regard to their presentation of the circumstances, origin and case of the church.

5 a. Changes in Public worship since 1914. b. Effects of the changes. None.

6. Number of Roman Catholics in the Parish. None.

1. See 1914.

NUFFIELD   Incumbent V. D. Browne[1]

1. Number of Boys Girls and Infants on books of day schools: a. Last year. 15 Boys, 9 Girls, 12 Infants. **b. 20 30 or 40 years ago.** 24 Boys, 19 Girls, 20 Infants.

2. a. Men and b. Women qualified to vote in Parochial Church meeting. None. I know no one in this small hamlet of 150 persons nearly all agricultural labourers and their families who has sufficient education or intelligence to make his or her vote of any real value. My Churchwarden is a business man in London and only comes down for the weekend occasionally. 42 young men and lads are serving their country as soldiers.

3. Moral and Spiritual effect of: a. Wartime b. National Mission.

[*No response*].

4. Status of Church Schools. Options for compromise on a. management, b. head teachers, c. character of religious teaching. Might compromise be justified by better arrangements for Church teaching in state schools?

Whatever ground the NUT and the Nonconformists have or think they have for demanding a change in (a) or (b) they have no real grievance as to the religious teaching in the Church Schools which in nine cases out of ten is of an entirely undenominational and nebulous character and could not affect the consciences of any really religious Nonconformist. Political Dissent may and does object to the influence which the Church exerts through the management and the appointment of Head Teachers but to raise a protest against the Ch. Catechism and the very mild questions on the Prayer Book usually asked in Religious Examinations is a parading of a quite senseless grievance from any point of view and one which by itself is probably not deeply felt. Therefore were these subjects omitted from the usual syllabus of our Religious Inspectors it would be unreasonable to hope that on this ground at any rate the Nonconformists' grievances would be appeased.

It is hard to see what possible advantages could be derived by the Church or the Children from any religious teaching which does not greatly differ from what is now given in Council Schools. Less satisfactory it could not be and a <u>slight</u> improvement would not be worth the suggested bargain.

A solution of the major part of our difficulties would, I believe, be found (a) in infusing greater definiteness into our Sunday School instruction and (b) in employing the short time appointed for so-called Religious instruction in the Day Schools in plain and simple <u>moral</u> duties. eg Truth telling, honour, honesty, modesty, unselfishness, and the like. A knowledge of certain parts of Bible history either of the old or N. Testament will not save children from lying and stealing and foul speech. To suppose the contrary is to try to build on an inverted pyramid. A plain, wisely drawn up moral catechism compiled by our Authorities, Clerical and Lay, and used daily in our schools would evoke no protest from any man whatever his religious creed and would be of immense spiritual as well as moral benefit to the rising generation of our land – especially in country districts.

5 a. Changes in Public worship since 1914. b. Effects of the changes. On account of the lighting order Evensong for the last 6 months has been said at 3.30 pm instead of at 6.30 pm. This change has not unnaturally reduced our small congregation. However, we shall shortly resume the Evening Service.

6. Number of Roman Catholics in the Parish. [*No response*].

1. See 1914.

NUNEHAM COURTENAY   Incumbent H. T. G. Alington[1]

1. Number of Boys Girls and Infants on books of day schools: a. Last year. 15 Boys, 15 Girls, 24 Infants. **b. 20 30 or 40 years ago.** In 1878: 24 Boys, 19 Girls includes Infants.

2. a. Men and b. Women qualified to vote in Parochial Church meeting. 6 M 3 W.

3. Moral and Spiritual effect of: a. Wartime b. National Mission.

(a) At first there was a distinct awakening. There has lately been a falling-off. This however is not necessarily from slackness as there is a great deal more outdoor work in the villages for those left behind.

(b) The Services during the Mission were well attended. It is hard to say whether the effect has been permanent. Undoubtedly those at present in the villages are working very hard during the week-days and have a certain amount of excuse for a slackness occasionally observable on Sundays.

4. Status of Church Schools. Options for compromise on a. management, b. head teachers, c. character of religious teaching. Might compromise be justified by better arrangements for Church teaching in state schools?

There are very few Nonconformists in the village and these for the most part come to Church. No children are withdrawn from religious instruction so the question has not arisen here.

5 a. Changes in Public worship since 1914. b. Effects of the changes. The church cannot be effectually darkened so we have Evensong 3 pm in the winter. Many of the elder folk have much appreciated this as they are unable to get to Church in the dark.

6. Number of Roman Catholics in the Parish. None.

1. See 1914.

ODDINGTON   Incumbent S. H. Scott[1]

1. Number of Boys Girls and Infants on books of day schools: a. Last year. b. 20 30 or 40 years ago.

No day schools. Children attend Charlton.

2. a. Men and b. Women qualified to vote in Parochial Church meeting. [*No response*].

3. Moral and Spiritual effect of: a. Wartime b. National Mission.

I never expected the National Mission to have any effect. How could it? There was no definite object, and unless the promoters are agreed as to the Faith how could it be otherwise? C.f. our B. Lord's words about the man going out to fight and first reckoning what he has to meet. Less talk and more prayer could have accomplished something. "In quietness and confidence shall be your strength." The Roman Catholics had no Mission of Repentance and Hope and to judge by what I saw of Westminster Cathedral in Holy Week and especially Good Friday I should imagine they did very well without it.

As for the War, the peoples minds are numbed.

4. Status of Church Schools. Options for compromise on a. management, b. head teachers, c. character of religious teaching. Might compromise be justified by better arrangements for Church teaching in state schools?

[*No response*].

5 a. Changes in Public worship since 1914. b. Effects of the changes. [*No response*].

6. Number of Roman Catholics in the Parish. None.

1. Sidney Herbert Scott graduated from Durham University in 1898 and was ordained priest in 1901. He served four curacies 1900–08 and then held chaplaincies at the Army School Maidenhead 1908–11, the Imperial Service College Windsor 1911–12, and King's College Taunton between 1913 and 1915, when he became Rector of Oddington. A leading Anglo-Catholic, he is remembered as introducing changes to the church which were not altogether acceptable to his parishioners.

OXFORD ALL SAINTS CUM ST MARTINS   Incumbent A. J. Carlyle[1]

1. Number of Boys Girls and Infants on books of day schools: a. Last year. b. 20 30 or 40 years ago.

There are no day schools in St Martin and All Saints Parish.

2. a. Men and b. Women qualified to vote in Parochial Church meeting. (a) 15, (b) 17.

3. Moral and Spiritual effect of: a. Wartime b. National Mission.

(a) I don't think that I can make any definite statement as to the effect of the war on the spiritual and moral condition of the parishioners. There was for the first few years of the war an attendance of from 10 to 20 at the Daily service of Intercession [*indeciph.*] the service has been attended much as usual.

(b) I can't say that I have seen any definite effects of the National Mission in the parish. In the City of Oxford the organisation of an Inter church Council for Social Reform was the direct outcome of the mission, and [*indeciph.*] the clergy get together their people for social work, this is already doing important work which is may we hope contribute materially to an improvement in the standard of life and living and to the better future of young people.

4. Status of Church Schools. Options for compromise on a. management, b. head teachers, c. character of religious teaching. Might compromise be justified by better arrangements for Church teaching in state schools?

Having no school I am not technically qualified to offer an opinion My opinion however is that the Church should come to some understanding with the Free Churches and the National Union of Teachers on all these points – and this not merely as part of a bargain but as being in truth reasonable concessions to reasonable demands. If our concern about elementary teaching in Provided Schools can be urged [*conj.*] it will I think be useful.

5 a. Changes in Public worship since 1914. b. Effects of the changes. a. None. b. [*No response*].

6. Number of Roman Catholics in the Parish. None I think.

1. See 1914.

OXFORD ST ALDATE   Incumbent T. W. Ketchlee[1]

1. Number of Boys Girls and Infants on books of day schools: a. Last year. b. 20 30 or 40 years ago.

The Schools originally had Boys, Girls and Infants Departments. In 1885 there were only Boys and Girls and the number on books was 172. (How long before 1885 the Infants Dept had been abandoned I do not know). In 1910 in the Scheme adopted for the 3 parishes – St Aldates became only a Boys School, Holy Trinity Girls, St Ebbe Infants. In 1910–11 there were 104 boys on the books at the present time there are 97 on the books.

2. a. Men and b. Women qualified to vote in Parochial Church meeting. 57 men, 116 women.

3. Moral and Spiritual effect of: a. Wartime b. National Mission.

The effect of War Time on the people in the Courts has been bad – there has been considerable immorality among the wives of soldiers: and a good deal among girls. There is too much money – the people have not felt the pinch of war, except lately, in the difficulty of obtaining supplies. The effect on the few people of rather higher social standing (tradespeople etc) has not been marked.

The effect of the National Mission was very small in the Courts: but on the Congregation it was greater. It certainly aroused more earnestness and greater readiness to take part in the work of the Church.

4. Status of Church Schools. Options for compromise on a. management, b. head teachers, c. character of religious teaching. Might compromise be justified by better arrangements for Church teaching in state schools?

1. The management should be as present constituted. 2. The Appointment of Head teachers should be in the hands of the Managers. 3. The religious teaching should be along the lines of the Church Catechism: but facilities given for Nonconformist children to be taught separately – perhaps one of the Assistant Teachers being a Nonconformist with this end in view. (I have had no personal experience of the Nonconformist difficulty in a single area school. One of the schools in my Lancashire parish was a single area school, with Nonconformist children in attendance. But, as far as I can remember, in the eight years I was Vicar there, no child was withdrawn from the religious Teaching: or was any wish expressed that any child should be withdrawn). 4. I cannot think that the just demand for Church Children to receive proper religious Teaching in provided schools should be made a matter of bargaining for impairing Trusts of Church Schools in single-school areas.

5 a. Changes in Public worship since 1914. b. Effects of the changes. No changes have been made since 1914 except the introduction of Daily Matins and Evensong.

6. Number of Roman Catholics in the Parish. [*No response*].

1. See 1914.

OXFORD ST ANDREW Incumbent J. A. Harriss[1]

1. Number of Boys Girls and Infants on books of day schools: a. Last year. b. 20 30 or 40 years ago.

There are no schools in the parish.

2. a. Men and b. Women qualified to vote in Parochial Church meeting. (a) Nine men residing in the parish (13 others from outside). (b) Seventeen women residing in the parish (6 others from outside).

3. Moral and Spiritual effect of: a. Wartime b. National Mission.

(a) There has been a marked difference since the war in the attitude especially of the well-to-do women and girls towards social and philanthropic efforts. I cannot add towards religious matters. Previous to the war many were apparently doing nothing but live for their own pleasure. That is now entirely changed. I do not know of a single young woman residing in the parish who is not now bearing her part in some work on behalf of others either in or away from Oxford. (b) I cannot say that I have observed any marked moral and spiritual effect among the people of the parish of the National Mission.

4. Status of Church Schools. Options for compromise on a. management, b. head teachers, c. character of religious teaching. Might compromise be justified by better arrangements for Church teaching in state schools?

Not having had to do directly with any Church Schools for many years, I do not feel competent to express any opinion on the above points.

5 a. Changes in Public worship since 1914. b. Effects of the changes. With the exception of using sometimes prayers in connexion with the War after the 3rd Collect at Evening prayer on Sundays, instead of the State prayers, there have been no changes in methods of public worship since the last return. A change on the hour of Evening Prayer on Sunday was made for a few weeks in order to meet the requirements of the Lighting Order, but this was soon rendered unnecessary by other arrangements. I cannot say that I have noticed any effects from the above changes.

6. Number of Roman Catholics in the Parish. I know of only one woman.

1. See 1914.

OXFORD ST BARNABAS Incumbent A. G. Bisdee[1]

1. Number of Boys Girls and Infants on books of day schools: a. Last year. b. 20 30 or 40 years ago.

(a) 1917–18: Boys 174, Girls 172, Infants 198. Total 544. (b) 1878: Boys 125, Girls 140, Infants 257. Total 522. (In 1892 there were boys 257, girls 265, infants 330: total 852, this was the highwater mark: since then a steady decline.)

2. a. Men and b. Women qualified to vote in Parochial Church meeting. I cannot discern that this has been done and in the past and this year as before our representatives were elected at the Vestry Meeting. It seems almost impossible to raise any great interest while there is practically nothing for parochial representatives to do except attend Ruri-decanal conferences.

3. Moral and Spiritual effect of: a. Wartime b. National Mission.

As I wasn't here before the war it is difficult to judge: but probably this parish is less affected than many. There are few if any munitions workers, and only such changes in wages, cost of living, general conditions, etc, as are general throughout the country. The presence of cadets etc in Oxford probably affects us less than some as we are to some extent secluded. The attendance of parishioners at church strikes me as a newcomer as above the average but I cannot tell how far this is due to war time. The absence of fathers is felt of course in dealing with children: and many excuses are found for absence from school. I think, however, that this is only partly due to the difficulties of the time and that there is great need for the local education authority to be far more thorough and strict in enforcing the attendance of children at elementary schools. The teachers work under a continual sense of discouragement in this respect. (b) Of the National Mission I can discover no permanent result whatever; – except a dislike of long sermons.

4. Status of Church Schools. Options for compromise on a. management, b. head teachers, c. character of religious teaching. Might compromise be justified by better arrangements for Church teaching in state schools?

I have no experience of single school areas strictly speaking: though in practice this is almost one. The influence of our schools from a religious point of view is very valuable: this is mainly due to the strong influence of very good Headteachers. I should venture to think that the appointment of Headteachers is the point of greatest importance for the Church to contend for in any legislation affecting Church schools: if this is secured the character of religious teaching would surely be mainly secured. I could not personally support any scheme for religious teaching which was "undenominational" in any way: but I should have thought that some compromise might be made about management if the appointment of headteachers is secured. In theory I have felt that the offer of facilities for denominational teaching in provided schools would more than compensate for any compromise or even for the loss of Church Schools. But in practise I am always assured that the practical difficulties of the scheme and the strong opposition of the N.U.T. and teachers generally, make it hopeless.

5 a. Changes in Public worship since 1914. b. Effects of the changes. (a) Two small alterations of hours – Daily Evensong moved from 7.30 – 8 pm and some music introduced: both are popular and a simple sung Mass on Sundays moved from 9 to 9.30 am: this has considerably increased the congregation attending who are mainly working class mothers and children. One constant effort is to combine a dignified and even elaborate ritual with good and simple congregational singing and this is much appreciated especially by the young men.

6. Number of Roman Catholics in the Parish. No statistics: very few R. Catholics here.

1. Alfred Gerald Bisdee graduated from Keble College Oxford in 1903 and trained at Cuddesdon College, being ordained priest in 1905. He held two curacies between 1904 and 1917, when he was appointed as Vicar of St Barnabas in Oxford. He was a married man and 37 years old in 1918 and seems to have been absent at the 1911 census – possibly travelling as he had strong interests in the Alps and the music of Wagner.

OXFORD ST CLEMENT　　　　　　　　　　Incumbent T. W. Gilbert[1]

1. Number of Boys Girls and Infants on books of day schools: a. Last year. b. 20 30 or 40 years ago.

(a) Boys 140, Girls 141, Infants 133. (b) An old Log Book shows that there were 97 Boys in 1874 and that this number had gone up to an average of 158 Boys in 1899. In the case of the Girls there is a record that 81 Girls were present in 1878, this increased to an average attendance of 110 in 1889 and rose to 215 present in 1895. In the case of the Infants there is a record of 104 Infants being present in 1863.

2. a. Men and b. Women qualified to vote in Parochial Church meeting. (a) 3. (b) 3.

3. Moral and Spiritual effect of: a. Wartime b. National Mission.

The war has acted differently on the different types of people in the parish. It has added a seriousness to those who were already spiritually inclined, this has deepened as the war has continued. In addition many who were not habitual church goers come regularly to the weekly Intercession Service but in many cases the habit has become less frequent and the restrictions on the street lighting further hampered the lukewarm. There is a further body for whom the war meant more regular money and increased freedom from restraint and in the early days of the war there was in consequence a certain licence in drinking. Increasing prices, however, and the sobering effect of continuing war have modified this attitude considerably. There is still cause for anxiety however in the somewhat looser attitude towards the conventions of social intercourse adopted by the young women.

One extraordinary and helpful feature may be chronicled. On Palm Sunday 1918 there was a noticeable feeling of tension at all the services and later in the evening after the evening service the suggestion was made that an all night service of prayer for our army and navy should be held. This took place on Monday night March 25th. In spite of the shortness of the notice about two hundred people assembled in church at 10 pm and the service of Prayer went on until after 4 am. (b) The National Mission was of a two-fold nature. It was directed first of all to the regular members of the Congregation and resulted in a more general readiness for Christian witness. One outcome of this was the readiness with which many of the congregation walked in procession through every street of the parish on several occasions, giving an invitation to an eight-days mission. This eight days mission was meant as an effort to use the regular churchgoers to bring in the non-churchgoers. Services were held every night and not less than three hundred were present at each service. Some careless and profligate people were definitely helped and uplifted and a more favourable attitude created towards the Church and towards that for which the Church stands.

4. Status of Church Schools. Options for compromise on a. management, b. head teachers, c. character of religious teaching. Might compromise be justified by better arrangements for Church teaching in state schools?

(a) I have not come face to face with the practical difficulty, as a Council school exists in the adjoining parish. (b) No demand has ever been made in my hearing for any alteration of the present status as to management of appointment of head-teacher or as to the character of the religious teaching. So far as the last mentioned point is concerned we have a number of children of Nonconformist parents in the schools who regularly attend Wesleyan Sunday Schools but no request has ever been made to withdraw any children from religious instruction. (c) Personally I should welcome any compromise which would allow an authorised clergyman or minister or other fit person to teach religious knowledge according to the tenets of his denomination in any Provided or non-Provided school, for any children belonging to his denomination in such schools. The opinion of our own Schoolmaster at St Clements inclines to the general restriction of religious teaching to 'Bible teaching' leaving all denominations to give denominational teaching in Sunday Schools.

5 a. Changes in Public worship since 1914. b. Effects of the changes. (a) I have regularly used War Prayers since the beginning of the war and on occasion have read such Prayers from the pulpit. I have also occasionally used a small collection 'War Hymns' edited by Lady Carberry and published by Novello.[2] After consultation with the Church Council we decided to make no alteration in the hours of service when the lighting restrictions came into force.

(b) The 'War Prayers' and 'War Hymns' have made the services much more real and there is a greater spirit of devotion and worship noticeable. As our church is somewhat out of the way we find a diminution in the congregation on very dark nights. The morning congregation however is larger and I feel confident that we have suffered less in our attendance than if we had made alterations of the hours of the Sunday evening service.

6. Number of Roman Catholics in the Parish. [*No response*].

1. See 1914.
2. Victoria Cecil Evans-Freke, Baroness Carberry (ed.), *A Selection of Hymns from the Church Hymnal For use during the war* (London, 1916).

OXFORD ST CROSS   Incumbent O. D. Watkins[1]

1. Number of Boys Girls and Infants on books of day schools: a. Last year. b. 20 30 or 40 years ago.

(a) Boys 18, Girls 16, Infants 17. Total 51.

(b) Annual Report of Inspectors for year 1877 shews 36 children (of whom 14 infants) present. They are described as <u>Mixed under Mistress</u>, without farther distinction. For the year 1887 the average attendance was 14 Boys, 33.7 Girls – Total given as 48. Of these 31 were presented for examination, the rest being presumably infants.

2. a. Men and b. Women qualified to vote in Parochial Church meeting. [*No response*].

3. Moral and Spiritual effect of: a. Wartime b. National Mission.

(a) <u>The war time morals</u> there are now no young men in the parish – except two or three invalids and some soldiers on duty. Of the young women resident*, I am thankful to report that I have not yet heard of one who has been morally led wrong under present opportunities. (b) <u>The National Mission</u> The Mission at S. Cross, conducted by Canon Coles, was not a Mission mainly addressed to the careless. It was a Parish Retreat intended to raise the spiritual level of the faithful. I believe it to have been attended by some real success.

(a) The <u>spiritual effect</u> on the different classes of the <u>war time</u> I do not assume to calculate. I note that in the first 9 Sundays of 1914 there were 179 communicants early, an average of 20: and in the first 9 Sundays of 1918 there have been 253 early communicants, making an average of 28.

There is a general contribution to the army of the sons of the households. The interest and concern are therefore keen and deep. The women of the various classes are for the most part trying to do something. A party of middle-class women meets weekly at the Vicarage for needle-work, and with what they take home turn out an extraordinary amount of work. With all this I believe there may be discerned a deeper spiritual earnestness. Certainly I have no reason to deplore any falling off of spiritual life.

* I mean of unmarried women. One married woman, about 35, whose husband went to the war took to loose courses. She is now in another parish and her conduct is reported good.

4. Status of Church Schools. Options for compromise on a. management, b. head teachers, c. character of religious teaching. Might compromise be justified by better arrangements for Church teaching in state schools?

My English experience of the last sixteen years has been only at Colchester and at Oxford – never in a single-school area. For 26 years before that I was in India.

I think it best to express no views.

5 a. Changes in Public worship since 1914. b. Effects of the changes. (a) From September 1915 (i) A sung Eucharist service has been added to the other Sunday Services at 9.45. It is fairly well attended. (ii) The Eucharist has been celebrated <u>daily</u>. (iii) The Eucharistic vestments (coloured) have been in use. (b) There are now more communicants at 8 on Sunday than formerly. There is a smaller attendance at sung Mattins at 11. The daily Eucharistic service is attended by a congregation varying from 5 or 6 to 10 or 12 – in place of the former attendance of perhaps 2 on days when only Mattins was said.

6. Number of Roman Catholics in the Parish. I estimate the inmates of the Ladies College under Sisters at Cherwell Edge as perhaps 35. The whole number of Roman Catholics in the parish will not exceed 40. I do not recall any <u>men</u>, or any <u>children</u>.

1. See 1914.

OXFORD ST EBBE   Incumbent J. S. Stansfield[1]

1. Number of Boys Girls and Infants on books of day schools: a. Last year. 210 Infants only. **b. 20 30 or 40 years ago.** Twenty-five years ago there was a mixed school of about 260 children. At present the boys go to St Aldates, the girls go to Holy Trinity and the infants to St Ebbes.

2. a. Men and b. Women qualified to vote in Parochial Church meeting. 32 men, 70 women.

3. Moral and Spiritual effect of: a. Wartime b. National Mission.

(a) Morally disastrous with a small section of the women. With a section there is a deeper reliance on God. (b) I fear only temporary effect on many but a few women have stood out bravely for God and some were confirmed this week.

4. Status of Church Schools. Options for compromise on a. management, b. head teachers, c. character of religious teaching. Might compromise be justified by better arrangements for Church teaching in state schools?

I think that we should compromise on "a" and "b" but we should have opportunity for doctrinal teaching.

5 a. Changes in Public worship since 1914. b. Effects of the changes. Next Sunday (Easter Day) Holy Communion – 9.30 am – will be substituted for Matins – by consent of the Bishop. This is to meet greater spiritual need of the people. Those who wish for Mattins can worship at St Peter le Bailey – 150 yards from St Ebbes Church.

6. Number of Roman Catholics in the Parish. I only know two families: 2 men, 3 women, 5 children.

1. See 1914.

OXFORD ST FRIDESWIDE   Incumbent G. H. Tremenheere[1]

1. Number of Boys Girls and Infants on books of day schools: a. Last year. b. 20 30 or 40 years ago.

Boys, 118 (1878); 182 (1917 Church); Girls, 50 (1873); 111 (1887 Church); 172 (1917: Council); Infants, 22 (1873 Church) 198 (1917: Council).

2. a. Men and b. Women qualified to vote in Parochial Church meeting. None except the Communicants, numbering 123 men and 291 women.

3. Moral and Spiritual effect of: a. Wartime b. National Mission.

(a) On the whole, a depressing effect, and a tendency to doubt and distrust. Intercession services (except on the Day of Intercession) have been very poorly attended. But on the soldiers, so far as I have seen them when home on leave, or they have written to me, I should say that the effect both morally and religiously, had been very much for good. (b) The National Mission, which here took the form of week's Teaching Mission, was well attended, mainly by regular and irregular Churchgoers. I think its main effect was one of <u>Encouragement</u> to the people. Its sequel, the Missionary Mission of last year, was very fairly well attended, and has resulted in a fair number taking regularly Missionary Magazines, and undertaking to pray and contribute regularly.

4. Status of Church Schools. Options for compromise on a. management, b. head teachers, c. character of religious teaching. Might compromise be justified by better arrangements for Church teaching in state schools?

I feel, more strongly than I can express, that no more satisfactory conditions of teaching in Council Schools would in the least degree compensate for the loss of our Church Schools. The really important problem I consider to be not the religious instruction, which, after all, can be given in other ways, but religious education: that the whole training and development of the child should be based on a religious ideal, and that the Catholic ideal, and should be religious in aim and in method. If this is to be the case, <u>everything</u> depends on the choice of Teachers, and practically on nothing else. Therefore, it is absolutely vital that the Management, and the choice of Teachers (not merely head-teachers) should remain in the Church's hands.

Moreover, this factor further affects the Training of the Teachers. Councils select Teachers on purely technical and professional grounds: no questions are asked about religious knowledge, or religious or moral influence. This tends to the crowding out of those elements from the Teachers' training, and has already largely had that result. Such elements will remain in the training of some Teachers only if there are still Managers who regard such qualifications as of real importance. In regard however to the religious teaching, I would have the fullest facilities and encouragement given for the instruction of Nonconformist children by their own authorized teachers in school-hours, either in the School-premises, or elsewhere, as may be preferred.

5 a. Changes in Public worship since 1914. b. Effects of the changes. (a) None, except the substitution of the Gregorian tones for Anglican chants, in May 1917. (b) Several persons have left the Choir and Church, some complain still of the change, a few say they find it has made the Psalms more real to them.

6. Number of Roman Catholics in the Parish. As far as I know, only 2 women and 2 children.

1. George Herbert Tremenheere graduate from Trinity College Oxford in 1882 and trained at Cuddesdon College in 1883, being ordained priest in 1884. He served three curacies 1883–98 and was Vicar of St Agatha Portsea 1898–1911 and Diocesan Chaplain and Licensed

Preacher in the diocese of Oxford between 1912 and 1914, when he became Vicar of Oxford St Frideswide. He was 58 in 1918 and at the 1911 census he was unmarried and living in a household with his curate, also single, a widowed cook and a male servant described as a gymnasium attendant. In addition, he had three unmarried male 'guests' who were in naval occupations and may possibly have been boarders, or part of his mobile Portsea flock.

OXFORD ST GILES   Incumbent C. C. Inge[1]

1. Number of Boys Girls and Infants on books of day schools: a. Last year. b. 20 30 or 40 years ago.

	This year	in 1874	in 1884	in 1886
St Giles Girls school	83 on books	56		86
St Giles Infant school	61 on books		67	

There is in the Parish the St Aloysius R.C. Boys School. Number on books about 75. I have no record of former years.

2. a. Men and b. Women qualified to vote in Parochial Church meeting. 32 men, 73 women.

3. Moral and Spiritual effect of: a. Wartime b. National Mission.

(a) The educated classes are giving themselves with great devotion to all kinds of war-work. Many of the domestic servants have left to work on the land or at munitions and so are removed from my observation. The other classes in the parish have not changed their mode of life much. There has been no appreciable increase of immorality and none of drunkenness so far as I can judge in this parish. The attendance at church is well maintained at the regular services, though, compared with the first few months of the war, the congregations at the intercession services are rather smaller. A few people are learning to use the church for silent prayer. I have not found that the war has shaken the faith of more than one or two among my friends here and on the other hand there are some who take a more spiritual view of life than they did formerly. (b) The effects of the National Mission are impossible to estimate. We aimed rather at deepening the spiritual life of the faithful, than at bringing in the careless. And the efforts we did make in the latter direction were not, so far as I can judge, successful. In so far as the great bulk of the population is concerned, the conditions are unchanged. Some of our Church people gladly undertook various kinds of religious work, which has been a great advantage.

4. Status of Church Schools. Options for compromise on a. management, b. head teachers, c. character of religious teaching. Might compromise be justified by better arrangements for Church teaching in state schools?

I should welcome the assimilation of all elementary schools in respect of management etc. But the prohibition of denominational teaching should be removed, before Church Schools can be handed over to the Councils.

5 a. Changes in Public worship since 1914. b. Effects of the changes. No changes, except the holding of Intercession Services for the War, on Sunday at Evensong – on Tuesday at the Holy Communion, and on Wednesday at Evensong. These have been fairly well attended.

6. Number of Roman Catholics in the Parish. [*No response*].

1. See 1914.

OXFORD ST MARGARET   Incumbent E. W. Pullan[1]

1. Number of Boys Girls and Infants on books of day schools: a. Last year. b. 20 30 or 40 years ago.

We have no Day Schools.

2. a. Men and b. Women qualified to vote in Parochial Church meeting. None. We took a great deal of trouble five years ago to get the forms delivered at every house to obtain signatures. About a dozen people attended the Parochial Church meeting, and we have not repeated the experiment.

3. Moral and Spiritual effect of: a. Wartime b. National Mission.

(a) There is less discipline than ever in the poorer homes, but having some definite work to do in connection with the War has been I think a blessing to many of the more leisured. (b) It has strengthened the faithful, but conversions have not been numerous among people who were hitherto indifferent. There has been a small increase in the number of confessions and a marked increased attendance at the Daily Eucharist.

4. Status of Church Schools. Options for compromise on a. management, b. head teachers, c. character of religious teaching. Might compromise be justified by better arrangements for Church teaching in state schools?

[*No response*].

5 a. Changes in Public worship since 1914. b. Effects of the changes. No changes.

6. Number of Roman Catholics in the Parish. About a dozen (including a few Belgian refugees).

1. See 1914.

OXFORD ST MARY MAGDALEN   Incumbent A. H. Gilkes[1]

1. Number of Boys Girls and Infants on books of day schools: a. Last year. 40 boys, 32 girls, 32 infants. **b. 20 30 or 40 years ago.** In 1897: 76 boys, 66 (girls and infants counted together then.)

2. a. Men and b. Women qualified to vote in Parochial Church meeting. None. I did not know of the matter. We are taking steps now in connection with it.

3. Moral and Spiritual effect of: a. Wartime b. National Mission.

(a) I believe that most people are less conventional in some degree and somewhat kinder: I expect this means something spiritually. (b) I believe it has not left any effect; I daresay that it was in the minds of many connected with formal religion, and the saving of their own souls.

4. Status of Church Schools. Options for compromise on a. management, b. head teachers, c. character of religious teaching. Might compromise be justified by better arrangements for Church teaching in state schools?

I believe that compromise is both possible and likely to be beneficial. I think the present position unsatisfactory. It makes unpleasant feelings between boys, and girls, and to some extent bad blood. It makes the Church disliked, and I believe that reverence for the sacraments is not likely to be the effect of the system. I do not mean only that boys are apt to dislike what they are taught in school; but that in itself a very particular view of any doctrine will never commend itself ultimately to more than ⅙ of those who hear it and when it leaves, it tears much away with it.

5 a. Changes in Public worship since 1914. b. Effects of the changes. I do not like to criticise, as in this case I should seem to be doing, (since I have been here only a year,) my excellent predecessor.

6. Number of Roman Catholics in the Parish. I believe none, excepting a Belgian child or two, and two religious houses for men, in which there seem to be about 4 men in each.

1. Arthur Herman Gilkes graduated from Christ Church Oxford in 1872 and was ordained priest in 1915. He was Curate of St James Bermondsey between 1915 and 1917, when he became Vicar of Oxford St Mary Magdalen. He was 68 in 1918 and at the 1911 census he was 'Master' (headmaster) of Dulwich College, living in a household with his wife, four sons ranging from 10 to 18 years old, an unmarried elder sister, and five unmarried domestic servants (a butler, nurse, cook and two maids).

OXFORD ST MARY THE VIRGIN — Incumbent C. A. Whittuck[1]

1. Number of Boys Girls and Infants on books of day schools: a. Last year. b. 20 30 or 40 years ago.

No schools of any kind at St Mary's.

2. a. Men and b. Women qualified to vote in Parochial Church meeting. Six men and nine women. (The outparishioners (communicants), who of course were vastly more numerous, could not be persuaded to exercise their privileges except in a few cases. I hope this time more of them will come, but many people communicate at St Mary's who do nothing else there.

3. Moral and Spiritual effect of: a. Wartime b. National Mission.

1) <u>Moral and Spiritual effects of the War</u>. The war produced amongst the parishioners and members of the congregation frequenting St Mary's much disturbance, but it also in a measure united them and in a measure also made them more devotionally inclined. It played havoc with the congregation especially with the large evening congregation which it deprived of the chief part of its manpower, previously abundant. And of course the undergraduate intercession services, corporate communion services and meetings in the parish Room by degrees ceased to exist. (This latter, however, is an academic and not parochial consideration.) On the other hand the number of the communicants has been maintained and during the last year has increased, this result being due partly to the attendance of many of the Somerville girls now lodged at Oriel, partly to a slight accession of university residents. I think I may say that the celebrations are more appreciated and I suppose one may attribute this fact at all events in part to the influence of the war. Nor do the services in general or the sermons delivered at them evoke less interest than they did before the war though it is hard to estimate the effects thus produced, the members of the congregation being scattered and only to a small extent in personal touch with myself. I have been obliged to speak of the parish and congregation together as forming one unit, with regard to the parishioners strictly so-called, I cannot say that they have been noticeably influenced. They number only one hundred and fifty, not approaching the number of communicants at the church. One section of them has a long-standing connection with the parish, excellently disposed people and full of esprit de corps if also somewhat old-fashioned and limited in their outlook. I think the war may be said to have intensified their keenness and their devotion to St Mary's; in the case of some of them the influence exerted may have gone further than this. The other section is composed of newcomers and persons who have little or nothing to do with the church. Amongst these I have found individuals whom the war has affected but there is not much to be said about them collectively.

2) <u>Moral and spiritual effects of the National Mission</u>. I should say that the effect had been more moral than spiritual. Thus, I cannot see that in consequence of the Mission people became more devout, still less that they became possessed of anything like inspiration. I have said that at St Mary's (and I doubt not also elsewhere) there appeared to be some, though not very strong, evidence of a spiritual advance in certain respects. But even if the advance is to this extent a fact, and even if it was more strongly marked and was not by reason of failure in certain other respects subject to qualification, I do not think that the National Mission can have much if anything to do with it. I do not urge this point by way of depreciating the Mission

which perhaps was not intended by its promoters to serve this purpose. For I believe that in so far as it was an effort "to cleanse" and by so doing "to defend" the church, the effect produced by the Mission was both real and valuable, and certainly both at St Mary's and at Oxford generally the Mission was accepted and welcomed in this sense and as having for its object the correction, revision, reform, reconstruction, and more generally the adaptation of the church to modern needs. After the Mission was over, Sermons and addresses on these subjects received a sympathetic hearing. In conversation, people often discussed the question as to how the Church had better set its house in order. When the report of the Archbishop's Committee was introduced here, the interest taken in it was undoubtedly in part due to its having been prepared for by the National Mission. I do not know how far the "Missionary effort" was also thus influenced (there is a good deal of interest in Foreign Missions here independently) but I am sure that people's minds were opened and enlarged as a result of their having taken part in the Mission. I could mention several practical undertakings which directly or indirectly owe their origin to its stimulus.

At the same time, I think one can go on too long crying "Great is Diana of the Ephesians". The movement having served its purpose should change its name and reappear under some other forum.

4. Status of Church Schools. Options for compromise on a. management, b. head teachers, c. character of religious teaching. Might compromise be justified by better arrangements for Church teaching in state schools?

I am not sure that I have any right to answer this question. For though I taught for long years in country schools, served as a Diocesan Inspector, and since coming here until the war was a member of the Oxford Education Committee, I am not now in a representative position, having no schools in my parish.

The present arrangement in Single-area (Church) Schools, though theoretically indefensible, works very fairly well, and both for that reason, as well as because a satisfactory substitute would be most difficult to find, I am in no hurry to change it. The opposition to it, however, (particularly that of the NUT which I think is more likely to be attended to than that of the Non-Conformists because both Parliament and the Education office are more sensitive to objections on the ground of real or supposed interference with Educational efficiency than they are to merely Sectarian objections) is unquestionably strong. I do not very much like the idea of making concessions in one class of schools in order to obtain a quid pro quo in another. But one must not be over-squeamish, and no doubt this is the method commonly adopted. The question then arises what sort of change would the Church be willing to accept in Country Schools? And what compensation would the Church expect to obtain in Town Schools.

This seems on the face of it a great concession. But would it really and in practice amount to anything very different from the present system? The church managers already, having regard to the extent to which the County authority and Government Inspectors regulate almost everything, are a negligible quantity and if they dropped out, it would mean very little. They have, it is true, the appointment of the head teacher, but even as to this they often consult, and always have to keep in view, the County Education Committee. Again, the clergy have now only by courtesy anything to do with the School Curriculum, indeed they have nothing to do with it in the strict sense. Similarly, the position of the School teacher would be the same as it is now, except that he or she would not be necessarily entrusted with the religious instruction (a great advantage surely).

The religious teaching itself would be in the hands of those who ought to be most fitted to impart it and by them too its character would exclusively be determined. As to the second part of the question – I notice that the most expert educational authorities (Sadler e.g. but others also. See Sadler's reports) hold strongly that in other than Single School areas – different types of schools are not a drawback but an advantage. And I do not think it at all impossible that at Whitehall the same view may be taken: Church Schools, not hampered and bullied, as they often are now, might be allowed to exist and might even flourish in Towns where there are also other schools, and therefore a choice of Schools. I mean real Church Schools. I much prefer this plan to the proposal that all denominations should have the right of entry into Council Schools, a proposal which is not at all likely to materialise. I am with the Romans in preferring unity of religious teaching in a school, and a common school atmosphere. No school ought to be divided into denominational pens.

Letter dated April 2nd 1918

The part cropped out in the answers to the question as to the Schools has reference to possible concessions in single school areas. Though I seem to myself to have a fairly clear opinion on this subject, I mistrust my statement in the absence of more time, space and thought to devote to it. In any case it is not the sort of thing wanted in an answer of this kind. For any such solution presupposes a government not maliciously disposed as regards Church Schools but I am quite aware that this is not a thing to be counted upon as a certainty. In the case of a government not even moderately thus amicable, one might have to take a different line altogether. I mean that the Church should make a greater effort to do the work out of school hours.

5 a. Changes in Public worship since 1914. b. Effects of the changes. [a] None except changes in times of intercession services; the war prayers after the 3rd Collect on Sunday Evenings and in 1915 (not since) change in the hour of the Sunday evening service due to the lighting order.

[b] Necessary and beneficial.

6. Number of Roman Catholics in the Parish. [*No response*].

1. See 1914.

OXFORD ST MATTHEW   **Incumbent W. A. Williamson**[1]

1. Number of Boys Girls and Infants on books of day schools: a. Last year. 107 (Infants). **b. 20 30 or 40 years ago.** 23 years ago when School was opened there were over 200 Infants, but there were then no South Oxford Schools, nor New Hinksey School.

2. a. Men and b. Women qualified to vote in Parochial Church meeting. About 25 men, no women.

3. Moral and Spiritual effect of: a. Wartime b. National Mission.

I think that war time has had a sobering effect upon a great number of people and certainly in families which have suffered loss, but with the exception of those who previously looked at things in the right way I cannot see that it has brought more people to intercession in church. I fear that the many who have more money than they formerly were accustomed to are now going in for pleasure and luxuries to a larger extent than known before. The National Mission has done good to Church Societies (such as C.E.M.S.) in making them more keen, but I am unable to see, so far, any beneficial effect upon outsiders.

4. Status of Church Schools. Options for compromise on a. management, b. head teachers, c. character of religious teaching. Might compromise be justified by better arrangements for Church teaching in state schools?

I do not feel competent to give an opinion worthy of consideration, especially as I only have an Infants' School in my parish. As regards Church teaching we are favourably situated, though one feels that more definite religious teaching might well be aimed at in all schools by a more careful selection of teachers.

5 a. Changes in Public worship since 1914. b. Effects of the changes. No change in hours of public worship, but in method we have introduced more Intercession in the use of National and War prayers, after the 3rd Collect at Morning and Evening prayer (except when Ante-Communion service is said) also at the weekly Men's Service, and almost entirely at the mid-week Special Intercession. The effect has been decidedly good in the way of the better attention and devotion of the people to something they have not always been accustomed to; and in showing that the Church can adapt herself to varying needs and emergency.

6. Number of Roman Catholics in the Parish. So far as I know, only two families, comprising not more than 2 women, one man and 3 children.

1. See 1914.

OXFORD ST MICHAEL   Incumbent A. C. Smith (Curate)[1]

1. Number of Boys Girls and Infants on books of day schools: a. Last year. b. 20 30 or 40 years ago.

No Schools.

2. a. Men and b. Women qualified to vote in Parochial Church meeting. I am sorry that I cannot find the list. I fancy the Vicar has it, but he is away as an Army Chaplain.

3. Moral and Spiritual effect of: a. Wartime b. National Mission.

It is difficult to say, as I do not want to give any possibly mistaken impressions of mine. We have had more regular communicants: our Services of Intercession are well attended: and our offertories for all war appeals are good. But I do not really think that, as a rule, the spiritual effect has been what I hoped. The parish is small and though, on Sundays, the church is always full, the congregation is not made up of our own people, our people come but the others we have difficulty in getting to know personally. If I judged by Sunday services, I should say that more people come regularly to church. Morally, I do not think the girls, who have had great, I feared, temptations have been influenced for evil. We have many shop girls from other parishes at our services. I advised them to make no friendships with officers or cadets, unless they took their friends to their own homes. Several of them I knew have done this and I know of no case in which even a flighty girl has fallen.

4. Status of Church Schools. Options for compromise on a. management, b. head teachers, c. character of religious teaching. Might compromise be justified by better arrangements for Church teaching in state schools?

Personally I have rather strong views about our Schools: but we have no Schools at St Michael's and I should not be justified in writing in my Vicar's name.

5 a. Changes in Public worship since 1914. b. Effects of the changes. We have only had extra Services of Intercession: and these are well attended.

6. Number of Roman Catholics in the Parish. No statistics.

1. Alfred Cecil Smith graduated from St John's College Oxford in 1878 and was ordained priest in 1880. He served three curacies 1879–83, was Vicar of Summertown 1883–97 and of Chadlington and Shorthampton 1897–1903. He became Curate of St Michael's in 1907. He was the author of *A Brief History of the English Church* (1889). He was aged 63 in 1918 and at the 1911 census he was living in a household with his wife, two adult unmarried daughters and two unmarried female servants.

OXFORD ST PAUL   Incumbent B. J. Kidd[1]

1. Number of Boys Girls and Infants on books of day schools: a. Last year. b. 20 30 or 40 years ago.

(a) In 1918, we have 59 boys on books (we have our girls' or infants' school).

(b) Records in an old log book only: very imperfect but, 1882, 86 presented for examination. 1887, 111 in average attendance; 1897: 74 presented for examination.

VISITATION 1918 505

2. a. Men and b. Women qualified to vote in Parochial Church meeting. 16 men, 32 women.

3. Moral and Spiritual effect of: a. Wartime b. National Mission.

(a) The war has depleted the congregation, as many men being away in the army and women on war-work. Of those that remain at home, there are many working longer hours: doing other people's work and so forth. They are all getting better wages: grown up people thinking more about work and money: boys and girls suffering from lack of discipline. I do not find any keener desire for spiritual things.

(b) The National Mission, as far as I have been able to judge by any outward results, made no difference and effected nothing.

4. Status of Church Schools. Options for compromise on a. management, b. head teachers, c. character of religious teaching. Might compromise be justified by better arrangements for Church teaching in state schools?

As I have never had to do with a single-school area I am afraid I have not thought the matter out.

5 a. Changes in Public worship since 1914. b. Effects of the changes. (a) None. (b) None.

6. Number of Roman Catholics in the Parish. No statistics.

1. See 1914.

OXFORD ST PETER LE BAILEY Incumbent J. S. Stansfield[1]

1. Number of Boys Girls and Infants on books of day schools: a. Last year. 310.

b. 20 30 or 40 years ago. I have no record.

2. a. Men and b. Women qualified to vote in Parochial Church meeting. 22 men, 46 women.

3. Moral and Spiritual effect of: a. Wartime b. National Mission.

(a) The more earnest people are praying more. The bulk of the people are unaffected.

(b) The people were stirred for a time but I am not sure of permanent results.

4. Status of Church Schools. Options for compromise on a. management, b. head teachers, c. character of religious teaching. Might compromise be justified by better arrangements for Church teaching in state schools?

I am sure that we ought to compromise with regard to (a) management and (b) appointment of head-teachers but we ought to have an opportunity for doctrinal teaching.

5 a. Changes in Public worship since 1914. b. Effects of the changes. No change.

6. Number of Roman Catholics in the Parish. I only know of one family 1 man and 1 woman.

1. See 1914 St Ebbe. Stansfield took charge of St Peter le Bailey in 1914.

OXFORD ST PETER IN THE EAST   Incumbent J. H. Skrine[1]

1. Number of Boys Girls and Infants on books of day schools: a. Last year. b. 20 30 or 40 years ago.

(a)   1918: Boys 22, Girls 78 (5 years of age and over; no 'infants')

(b)   In 1894: Boys 60, Girls 43. Total 103. Infants 21 Grand Total 124.

In 1900: Boys 49, Girls 39. Total 88 (No mention of Infants).

2. a. Men and b. Women qualified to vote in Parochial Church meeting. (a) 20 men. (b) 40 women.

3. Moral and Spiritual effect of: a. Wartime b. National Mission.

(a) War time. Moral effect What can be confidently certified is an increase of kindness, fellowship and service; greater sympathy, understanding and helpfulness between classes as between individuals. These are things which can be observed, and I find they are recognised by my parishioners as well as by myself.

Spiritual effect The above effect may be rightly classed under the head of 'spiritual', but of spiritual as distinct from moral effect it is less easy to speak with confidence. 'It cometh not with observation.' Religious observance and practice can be reported of and I do not note much change in this within our small circle. Early in the war churchgoing increased on Sundays and weekday services of intercession had a small congregation. The Sunday congregations are presently reduced by a third or more, by assignable causes (absences, hard work, lightless streets). A very small group only came to the weekday intercessions, and no exhortations brought any more. Under the circumstances of our people in the parish or outside this was to be expected. But a priest may usefully report impressions of which the correctness cannot be demonstrated. A sense of reality in life has come on people, can be felt in intercourse and sometimes does get expression. The subject of religious belief is met by an openness rare hitherto, and only with a shyness which is the reserve of reverence not of stiffness, disinclination, and timidity. A preacher's own feeling of παρρησία[2] in speaking to and dealing with the people may be put down in great part to the sympathy of the flock, to a 'mutual faith' both of him and them: this will be a 'spiritual effect'. And this interest aroused whenever attempt is made in sermons to associate the war-facts with the personal religious life is unmistakable and often acknowledged.

(b) The National Mission The area of observation in St Peter's is a narrow one. In the Mission Week the three grouped parishes of High Street were not, we thought, adequately attended. Darkness accounted for the small evening congregations. The Week was not, at St Peter's, followed by any marked increase of church-going. Spiritual and moral effects of a more general kind than church-going are not easy to estimate, especially in a small group of steady-going, middleclass persons with traditional habits of religious practice. But the preparation for the Mission had some nameable results. We had then numerous meetings of the women to hear addresses, from other than their own clergy, on church history and social duty, and something of really warm interest was evoked by these. Two very practical results were obtained. (1) The parish produced one highly enthusiastic worker in the Flying Squadron (a churchman who, unemployed by the church, had previously done evangelistic work in another communion, but is now a regular communicant with us), who went on many expeditions with the F. Sqdn and has been highly praised by the Incumbents to whose parishes he went. (2) A girl was stirred up by the meetings to gather a number of other girls for weekly meetings of prayer and instruction which have had a long run of a year and more. And she is now a Probationer for the Women Messengers, and highly approved of by the authorities of that body.

4. Status of Church Schools. Options for compromise on a. management, b. head teachers, c. character of religious teaching. Might compromise be justified by better arrangements for Church teaching in state schools?

It is my strong hope that England may use this portent of German conduct in the war as an object lesson in the necessity for religious teaching of the whole nation, and that a thorough-going Christian instruction will be given in all the schools. This will require some compromise, (a) in management. Some representation of Nonconformity would seem necessary, when Nonconformists are many. (b) The headteacher should in Church Schools be still a churchman. (c) The syllabus applied to the whole school should cover all Christian doctrine which is the necessary basis of life as a spiritual being: and the distinctive teaching of the several communions be provided with a due separate opportunity.

5 a. Changes in Public worship since 1914. b. Effects of the changes. (a) No change has been made except the introduction on greater festivals (on occasions) of a Choral Communion at 11 (with Mattins) at 10.30. The change was prepared for by explanation of the reasons and though a novelty was in no way resented. At first the congregation was smaller but those who communicated were in very good proportion to those present, and among them were some who previously had not been communicants in St Peter's, and perhaps not elsewhere.

6. Number of Roman Catholics in the Parish. I have no statistics. Three or four RCs are the most I have known of in St Peter's.

1. See 1914.
2. 'parresia' or boldness. Almost certainly a reference to Paul's discussion in 2 Cor. 4: 7.

OXFORD ST PHILIP AND ST JAMES   Incumbent C. R. Davey Biggs[1]

1. Number of Boys Girls and Infants on books of day schools: a. Last year. b. 20 30 or 40 years ago.

(a) Boys 110, Infants 130.

(b) The Schools are always as full as accommodation allows. It has, of course been reduced several times since they were built by changes in the Government standard of floor space etc.

2. a. Men and b. Women qualified to vote in Parochial Church meeting. Last Easter, 1917, communicants simply gave notice of the hours at which they wished to present themselves for Communion at the Great Festivals and we checked the roll made in 1916 by that means. The proportion of men to women on the roll, 1 to 5 is a fair index to the population of the parish. We have from 600 to 700 communicants at Easter, but only about 400 are 'registered'.

3. Moral and Spiritual effect of: a. Wartime b. National Mission.

(a) People are so overtaxed in their work that they are obliged to rest on Sunday and we rarely get our men who are in shops to church in the morning. They are resting, or working in their gardens, or drilling with the volunteers or doing any of the other countless varieties of war work. Women are engaged either in definite war work as V.A.D. etc or go to the hospitals on Sundays to play or sing to the soldiers, so that the number of possible worshippers is greatly diminished. They are not "slack", but the claims of the war have to be satisfied, and we who can be in church have to uphold them as Moses did Israel against Amalek. There is a steadily maintained increase of communicants and worshippers at the week day masses, and the special Lent services have been excellently attended.

The National Mission was preached here by the Rev. E.M. Walker of Queen's College and led to the arousing of a very definite interest in social responsibilities of Christians.

4. Status of Church Schools. Options for compromise on a. management, b. head teachers, c. character of religious teaching. Might compromise be justified by better arrangements for Church teaching in state schools?

[*No response*].

5 a. Changes in Public worship since 1914. b. Effects of the changes. Mattins on weekdays is now at 10.30 except Fridays at 11.30: and Holy Communion is at 7.45. Many more people can get to Holy Communion now they are out of Church in time to have breakfast comfortably before going to work at nine: and we always have a congregation at Mattins whereas at 7.30 nobody came. The reason for 11.30 on Friday is that we have War Prayers and Bible Study at noon and the morning is not broken up.

6. Number of Roman Catholics in the Parish. I am not able to answer this question: although some R.C. families are well known to me, and very friendly, there are houses in the parish into which neither I nor my curates obtain admission and we do not know what the religion of the occupants is.

1. See 1914.

OXFORD ST THOMAS   Incumbent B. S. Hack[1]

1. Number of Boys Girls and Infants on books of day schools: a. Last year. b. 20 30 or 40 years ago.

(a) Boys 106, Girls 124, Infants 128. (b) In 1908: Boys 112, Girls 100, Infants 155.

2. a. Men and b. Women qualified to vote in Parochial Church meeting. (a) 10. (b) 10.

3. Moral and Spiritual effect of: a. Wartime b. National Mission.

a. I do not see that the war has caused any appreciable change with outside people or with those who are nominally church people. But I think that many devout people have become more devout.

b. The same.

4. Status of Church Schools. Options for compromise on a. management, b. head teachers, c. character of religious teaching. Might compromise be justified by better arrangements for Church teaching in state schools?

There can be no compromise as regards the character of religious teaching or the appointment of head-teachers. The latter is as necessary to preserve the religious tone of the school as the Church Catechism – even more.

    As regards management, provided that the appointment of teachers and the religious teaching are in the hands of the church, I see no reason why there should not be more Non-conformists on the committee, but as the Act of 1902 has already reduced the powers of the Managers almost to vanishing point in some districts I do not think that the Non-conformists would gain any advantage.

    As for the N.U.T., I should not consider the society at all. There are cantankerous parsons here and there and teachers may suffer from them, but this does not justify the hostile attitude taken up by the N.U.T. In the matter of discharging teachers the Managers are very helpless. I have had two cases of incompetent teachers, both complained of by the Head Teacher and the Inspector. In neither case could we get a discharge. Fortunately one has improved and the other has got preferment in a country school.

    I have no clear view of the policy to be pursued in single-school areas. Opportunities ought to be given to Non-conformists to teach their own religion. They do not want this right of access and the battle would rage around the question of teachers and the demand for an undenominational religion. I do not believe that there would be so much trouble but for the political dissenters. It is a pity that the Act of 1902 was passed; church people did not like paying twice over for education but it would be better to suffer an injustice than to create the present state of things.

5 a. Changes in Public worship since 1914. b. Effects of the changes. (a) No changes in the hours of public worship. Intercessions at the time of the State Prayers on Sunday evenings. Day of prayer once each month. Holy Communion with special intention for sailors and soldiers once each week. Holy Communion with special intention for those fallen in the war once each week. Names of sailors and soldiers from the Parish and Congregation read out every Sunday morning. (b) I know of no effects except that the remembrance on Sunday mornings gives a good deal of pleasure.

6. Number of Roman Catholics in the Parish. [*No response*].

1. See 1914.

OXFORD HOLY TRINITY   Incumbent E. W. Cox[1]

1. Number of Boys Girls and Infants on books of day schools: a. Last year. b. 20 30 or 40 years ago.

The number of girls on our books is 192. We have only a Girls' (C. of E.) School.

As the whole of the South Oxford Schools were re-arranged eight years ago no figures which could be provided would form a basis of comparison.

2. a. Men and b. Women qualified to vote in Parochial Church meeting. None.

3. Moral and Spiritual effect of: a. Wartime b. National Mission.

This parish is entirely a poor one – the bulk of the people being of the labouring class, the others being employed mainly in the rougher work of shops or colleges. The prevailing attitude to spiritual things is one of indifference though they are quite willing for one to pray with them in their homes. Most of the men of the parish are away – either as soldiers or in munition works. A number of our younger unmarried women have also gone to munition works. A very large proportion of our remaining women work every day either at Didcot or as char- or kitchen-women in connection with the Base Hospital or the colleges which have cadets. The result of this is that they are away from their homes practically all the week except at night and on Sundays. The results of this are that (1) Sunday becomes largely a day of house work and (2) the children are allowed a very loose rein. This last is especially noticeable in connection with our Sunday Schools which are fallen away dreadfully (an additional cause of this being the absence of treats). Our Sunday Schools are also very adversely affected by our teachers having left for war work or service.

I believe that the moral tone of the parish is better than it was a year or so ago ie during the darkness of the winter of 1916–17. It was then very bad so far as some of our women were concerned. The increasing pressure of the war seems to have a somewhat sobering effect. The girls of from about fifteen years upwards seem to have it as their aim in life to impress the cadets stationed in Oxford. This shows itself largely in the manner of dress (short skirts and transparent stockings etc) and in their forcing themselves upon the attention of the cadets.

The effect of the National Mission was seen within our <u>Church</u> rather than in the <u>parish</u>. Although every house was visited and papers circulated I cannot say that there is the slightest sign of effect in the <u>Parish</u>. In the <u>Church</u> however there was a distinct increase in spirituality.

4. Status of Church Schools. Options for compromise on a. management, b. head teachers, c. character of religious teaching. Might compromise be justified by better arrangements for Church teaching in state schools?

As this is not a single school area the matter has not forced itself on my consideration. So far as we are locally concerned no changes seem desirable.

5 a. Changes in Public worship since 1914. b. Effects of the changes. In the winter of 1916–7 we had to advance the hour of our Sunday evening service as we were not able then to darken our church lighting. This led to a greatly decreased attendance. We then (with the Bishop's permission) had Evening Prayer at 3.0 and a lantern service in Church for eight Sunday nights at 6.30 pm. These were crowded and the behaviour was good. The expense however was very considerable and many of our regular congregation asked for a renewal of the ordinary service. We were by this time able to resume our ordinary service at the ordinary time (6.30), but as soon as the lantern services stopped the attendance <u>immediately</u> dropped to the old state. I cannot therefore feel that the lantern services had any lasting effect and I should hesitate to adopt them again. This 1917–18 winter we have been able to shade our lights and have had our ordinary service at 6.30 pm. Our congregations have been fairly good considering the fact that there is not a single street lamp alight in the Parish and consequently our older folk will not venture out.

6. Number of Roman Catholics in the Parish. [*No response*].

1. See 1914.

PIDDINGTON   Incumbent G. R. Tidmarsh[1]

1. Number of Boys Girls and Infants on books of day schools: a. Last year. 26.

b. 20 30 or 40 years ago. Twenty years ago: 35–40; Thirty years ago: 50–60; Forty years ago: 60–70.

2. a. Men and b. Women qualified to vote in Parochial Church meeting. None.

3. Moral and Spiritual effect of: a. Wartime b. National Mission.

(a) I regret to say that the desire to escape military service has in some cases led to much trickery and falsehood. One family has gained considerable notoriety in this way, the result of which has been much talk and excitement, which have largely counteracted any good spiritual effect the war might otherwise have had. (b) Very little effect, I am afraid. But these are difficult questions to answer: it is not easy, even if it is possible, to gauge spiritual effect. Unfortunately the National Mission raised controversy. One or two non-conformists attended the services and naturally heard things that they did not agree with: hence arose discussion of a rather heated character. In spite of all this I think I may fairly claim that the spiritual state of the Parish is slowly improving: the Services are better attended and the people are in earnest.

4. Status of Church Schools. Options for compromise on a. management, b. head teachers, c. character of religious teaching. Might compromise be justified by better arrangements for Church teaching in state schools?

There is in the Parish a Non-Conformist element of an ignorant and therefore narrow and bigoted type. My predecessor had not entered the school for ten years at least, and consequently my going in to give religious instruction raised a little storm which in course of time led to the withdrawal from all religious instruction of about a dozen children (nearly half). As there is only one room, these children cannot be compelled to come to school till 9.50 am, and this fact puts religious instruction at a great disadvantage and is bad for the discipline of the school. I have represented these facts to the Education Committee of the County, but have as yet had no reply to my letter written four months ago.

As regards the first part of the question above: The only solution would seem to me to be facilities in all schools for children to be instructed according to the religious tenets of their parents. But if nonconformists are admitted to Church Schools, they must be those qualified to teach, which the great majority of Local Preachers are not. Some compromise might perhaps be made, but the greatest care would have to be exercised, as what is sought is not so much a voice in the management of the Schools and the appointment of headteachers as the control of them. Interference with the character of religious teaching is an even more serious matter, as in all probability nothing short of the sacrifice of all definiteness would meet with approval.

5 a. Changes in Public worship since 1914. b. Effects of the changes. In the evening the Sermon after the Third Collect and Intercession after the Sermon. No change of hours. Very little effect.

6. Number of Roman Catholics in the Parish. None.

1. See 1914.

PISHILL   Incumbent G. M. J. Hall[1]

1. Number of Boys Girls and Infants on books of day schools: a. Last year. b. 20 30 or 40 years ago.

(a) Boys, 11 Girls 10 Infants 11. (b) 30 years ago: Boys 18, Girls 18, Inf. 5.

2. a. Men and b. Women qualified to vote in Parochial Church meeting. None.

3. Moral and Spiritual effect of: a. Wartime b. National Mission.

The National Mission was not found to be satisfactorily workable in this parish. I do not know of any marked moral and spiritual effect of war time. Considering the fact that the parish contains no well-to-do people but only farmers and farm labourers and the shortage of hands compared with the extra agriculture taken on hand, the people on the whole have shown themselves very generous in everything connected with the war and ready to render such service as was in their power, bearing cheerfully the self denial involved, satisfied if only our soldiers and sailors could be helped by it.

4. Status of Church Schools. Options for compromise on a. management, b. head teachers, c. character of religious teaching. Might compromise be justified by better arrangements for Church teaching in state schools?

As no demands of the kind indicated have been made here I have not had the opposition which tends to call forth clear views.

5 a. Changes in Public worship since 1914. b. Effects of the changes. (a) No change in hours. The introduction of special war prayers in the method. (b) An additional intensity in the worship.

6. Number of Roman Catholics in the Parish. Men 9, Women 17, Children 8.

1. See 1914.

PYRTON   Incumbent F. N. Crowther[1]

1. Number of Boys Girls and Infants on books of day schools: a. Last year. Boys 9, Girls 10, Infants 7.

b. 20 30 or 40 years ago. In 1882: Boys and Girls 6 Infants 12. In 1883: Boys 16, Girls 12, Infants 16.

In 1888: Boys 13, Girls 17 (Infants not given separately).

2. a. Men and b. Women qualified to vote in Parochial Church meeting. (a) 19. (b) 10.

3. Moral and Spiritual effect of: a. Wartime b. National Mission.

(a) I notice very little if any change in the ordinary agricultural labourer: he was not adverse to religion before the War: he is not adverse now: he remains unmoved: among the women especially those who have sons or husbands at the War there has been a fairly good response to the invitation to attend a weekday intercession service: it would be very difficult for the men to attend but among those (men and women) present at the Sunday evening service there has seemed to be hearty response to the special prayers from the pulpit at the close of the sermon.

(b) The services during the Mission were well attended: but I cannot say that I can trace any permanent effect: one hopes that good was done but it has not reflected itself in bringing the non Churchgoers to Church: or the more Communicants to Communion: we remain practically what we were before.

4. Status of Church Schools. Options for compromise on a. management, b. head teachers, c. character of religious teaching. Might compromise be justified by better arrangements for Church teaching in state schools?

I think that the one <u>absolutely essential</u> point is that <u>we retain the appointment of the head-teacher</u>: if this is secured I should be quite ready to give the Nonconformists facilities for teaching their children in our schools and in schools where there are several teachers and a number of Nonconformist children one of the under teachers might be a Nonconformist: but I feel very strongly that we <u>must never surrender the appointment of the Headteacher</u>, nothing will compensate us for such a loss. If we give facilities in our Schools to Nonconformists as I should be prepared to vote for under the above named condition it seems only reasonable and fair that equal facilities should be given us to teach in Provided Schools.

5 a. Changes in Public worship since 1914. b. Effects of the changes. No changes have been made.

6. Number of Roman Catholics in the Parish. 1 woman, 6 children (4 boys, 2 girls).

1. See 1914 Aston Rowant. Crowther moved to Pyrton in 1914.

RAMSDEN   Incumbent H. R. Hall[1]

1. Number of Boys Girls and Infants on books of day schools: a. Last year. b. 20 30 or 40 years ago.

(a) 58. (b) Average attendance on March 17 1893: 84.9.

2. a. Men and b. Women qualified to vote in Parochial Church meeting. None.

3. Moral and Spiritual effect of: a. Wartime b. National Mission.

(a) The moral effect of the war is likely to be great i) as teaching the results of extravagance and forgetfulness of God. ii) as helping to break some dangerous class barriers.

(b) We can testify to no apparent result of the National Mission, but we believe that, combined with the war, it will in the end prove to have been of great value.

4. Status of Church Schools. Options for compromise on a. management, b. head teachers, c. character of religious teaching. Might compromise be justified by better arrangements for Church teaching in state schools?

Yes: we must retain Religious teaching. The Creed must never be left out. The Commandments must be rightly interpreted. But the Catechism might with advantage be reconstructed as far as 'the Desire', and 'the Duties' are concerned. No compromise can be made apart from the above with the N.U.T. No more satisfactory conditions could be made than that the first portion of each day's instruction should be based upon the reading of God's Word in order to emphasize sound religious and moral teaching on the broad lines of Church Doctrine apart from Sectarianism.

5 a. Changes in Public worship since 1914. b. Effects of the changes. (a) None, except that during the war we have found a better attendance at Evening Service, apparently as a result of having the Sermon after the 3rd Collect and Intercessions afterwards.

6. Number of Roman Catholics in the Parish. None.

1. See 1914.

ROTHERFIELD GREYS   Incumbent W. Wood[1]

1. Number of Boys Girls and Infants on books of day schools: a. Last year. 38.

b. 20 30 or 40 years ago. 30 years ago: 55.

2. a. Men and b. Women qualified to vote in Parochial Church meeting. No declaration signed.

3. Moral and Spiritual effect of: a. Wartime b. National Mission.

The war has brought us nearer to each other by common interest in those serving as soldiers or workers: whose names are read out once a month in church and posted at the Church Door, and for whom special prayer is made every Sunday in the evening service. So also by the Parish sending food regularly to those in prison-camps whose cards acknowledging receipt are exhibited on the Board of Honour in the Porch. Still, outwardly, we are singularly apathetic and the fact of special prayers being offered does not draw many to join in them publickly. On the whole the effect of the war has been for good in drawing classes together and in general sobriety and seriousness of feeling.

I do not myself believe in the enormous moral or religious change which many anticipate when the War is over. There will be inevitably much disappointment and suffering from the general disorganisation; while the growing and dangerous tendency to force the government to comply with inordinate claims may lead to revolutionary changes and fresh disappointment.

(b) In so small and scattered a Parish as this, there is little to report. The National Mission here was chiefly represented by the "Pilgrims", who were kindly received. Their meetings both out of doors on the Green and in the School, as well as in the cottages, were much appreciated. We have no "Non Conformists" in the Parish.

4. Status of Church Schools. Options for compromise on a. management, b. head teachers, c. character of religious teaching. Might compromise be justified by better arrangements for Church teaching in state schools?

A. The Church and Non Conformist Bodies (as represented by the Free Church Council) must agree on a common scheme.

B. In Single School Areas and Country Schools generally, the Schools should be retained, as at present, with exception to allow Non-Con. Minister (or other authorised representative) to give Religious Teaching to a class specially exempted from Church Teaching, at arranged hours, when the rest of the School is occupied in secular work. In order to decide of whom such class should consist, the Parents should sign (on a child's name being entered) a form claiming such Teaching.

The Church School in Single School areas in other respects, as regards (a) management; (b) appointment of Head Teachers; (c) Religious Teaching to be carried out as present.

5 a. Changes in Public worship since 1914. b. Effects of the changes. (A) The only changes made (in <u>method</u>, none in <u>hours</u>) are: a) A little more freedom in use of Special Prayers, from Forms sent out by Authority, in all the Services. b) at Evening Service (after the 3rd Collect) the use of such Special Forms and Special Hymns. There have been no essential changes in hours of worship. I would earnestly request continued permission for such liberty as I have described.

6. Number of Roman Catholics in the Parish. No Roman Catholics.

1. See 1914.

ROTHERFIELD PEPPARD Incumbent M. Jones[1]

1. Number of Boys Girls and Infants on books of day schools: a. Last year. 57 all told.

b. 20 30 or 40 years ago. In 1881: 55 all told.

2. a. Men and b. Women qualified to vote in Parochial Church meeting. <u>None</u>. I have taken no steps to form an Electoral Roll during the absence of two-thirds of the men in the Parish. And further <u>the basis of the Church Franchise</u> has not yet been decided upon and I do not agree with the proposals to shut out a large proportion of baptized members from any participation in the government of the Church.[2]

3. Moral and Spiritual effect of: a. Wartime b. National Mission.

I cannot honestly profess to be able to report that either the war or the National Mission have had any substantial moral or spiritual effect on this parish. This does not imply that the parish only attains to a low standard in these respects but merely that the church life in the parish has not been stimulated to any considerable degree by either of these causes. The Sunday congregations are excellent, the number of communicants is up to the average but I cannot say that the general situation is due either to the War or to the Mission. The Mission was well prepared for by months of strenuous work. We had an excellent Mission – the Mission Services of all descriptions were very well attended and there, as far as any visible signs are forthcoming, the matter ended. I can point to only <u>two men</u> who seem to have been influenced by the Mission, neither of whom was previously in the habit of attending a place of worship. One has become an occasional communicant and the other a fairly regular attendant at the Sunday Evening Service.

The war does not seem to have had any marked effect upon the spiritual life of the parish as a whole. The intercessory services are not well attended and I do not consider that, taking the situation generally there has been any closer approach to God as the result of the War and its trials. It should not be forgotten however that every person in the parish is so engrossed in work of some kind that very little leisure is left available for attendance at church services and religious exercises and I imagine that this has much to do with the apparent indifference to the claims of religion.

The one tangible result of the National Mission has been the formation of a <u>Women's Bible Class</u> which is well attended by women of all classes and arouses real interest.

4. Status of Church Schools. Options for compromise on a. management, b. head teachers, c. character of religious teaching. Might compromise be justified by better arrangements for Church teaching in state schools?

As far as my experience has taught me and I have been an Incumbent only for three years, I am doubtful whether we are justified in retaining the Church Schools on their present basis if that retention is becoming a hindrance to the establishment of a National System of Education which shall commend itself to the community as a whole. There has been a Church School in this Parish for close upon 50 years, but I cannot find that it has been instrumental in building up convinced Churchmen. Practically all the men of the artisan and labouring classes in the Parish have been educated at the School, and yet it is a rare exception to find among them a Communicant. A Church School which produces a beggarly harvest of this kind is certainly not worth retaining, if in doing so we are standing in the way of a really efficient National System of Education which shall include religious instruction as an essential component. I am therefore in favour of a compromise that will bring together all the religious opinion and force in the country and so prevent the imposition of a purely secular form of Education, which can hardly be avoided, unless those in favour of one educational system that shall include the teaching of religion among its essential features, present a united front.

5 a. Changes in Public worship since 1914. b. Effects of the changes. On the 3rd Sunday in the month instead of Morning Prayer and Sermon followed by a separate Celebration of the H.C. I have substituted plain Matins and Litany at 10.15 followed by a Choral Celebration and Sermon at 11.0. The change has not commended itself to the older members of the congregation who generally absent themselves from the service and the congregation at the Choral Celebration is considerably below average. The non-communicants cannot be persuaded to stay until the end of the service, in spite of continued appeals and they all depart after the sermon. On the other hand, the number of communicants at this service is far in excess of the number that used to attend when the H.C. was held as a separate service after Morning Prayer. The average numbers are now in the proportion of 30 under the new system to 15 under the old so from this point of view the time change would seem to be justified.

6. Number of Roman Catholics in the Parish. So far as I am aware there are no Roman Catholics in this parish.

1. Maurice Jones graduated from Jesus College Oxford in 1884 and was ordained priest in 1887. He served two curacies 1886–90 and a year as Organising Secretary of the Additional Curates Society 1888–89. He then occupied chaplaincies between 1890 and 1915 including postings to Aldershot, Gosport, Malta and Jamaica. He was in South Africa 1900–01 where he won the Queen's medal with three clasps. He was the author of *St Paul the Orator* (1910) and *The New Testament in the Twentieth Century* (1914). He was described as retired in 1915 but was appointed later that year by his old college to the Rectory of Rotherfield Peppard. He was 54 in 1918 and at the time of the 1911 census he was recorded as a widower, living alone in Gosport and acting as Chaplain to His Majesty's Forces.
2. A reference to the contemporary debate about whether the right to register to vote in church elections should be open to all baptised Anglicans who had not since become members of another church or whether it should be restricted to Anglicans who had been confirmed – the expressed preference of bishop Gore.

ROUSHAM   Incumbent C. H. Faithfull[1]

1. Number of Boys Girls and Infants on books of day schools: a. Last year. b. 20 30 or 40 years ago.

(a) 16. (b) 35 in 1878: the year the School was opened.

2. a. Men and b. Women qualified to vote in Parochial Church meeting. None, as we have no Parochial Church Meeting.

3. Moral and Spiritual effect of: a. Wartime b. National Mission.

I cannot see any marked effect.

4. Status of Church Schools. Options for compromise on a. management, b. head teachers, c. character of religious teaching. Might compromise be justified by better arrangements for Church teaching in state schools?

I think we should do our utmost to retain our Church Schools in their present states.

5 a. Changes in Public worship since 1914. b. Effects of the changes. During the shorter days we were obliged to have our Afternoon Service at 3 o'clock during the last two winters as we could not darken the windows. The farmers and their families attended very badly as being so short of labour they had much Sunday work which was absolutely necessary.

6. Number of Roman Catholics in the Parish. None.

1. See 1914.

SALFORD   Incumbent A. W. Callis[1]

1. Number of Boys Girls and Infants on books of day schools: a. Last year. 12 boys, 15 girls, 20 infants. **b. 20 30 or 40 years ago.** 1903: 18 boys, 30 girls, 24 infants. (There is no School or Church Council at Little Rollright).

2. a. Men and b. Women qualified to vote in Parochial Church meeting. None.

3. Moral and Spiritual effect of: a. Wartime b. National Mission.

There is but one class in my parish and that the working class. I came here just when the war broke out, and I have not yet come across a case of immorality or drunkenness. I see little decrease in the indifference to religion either on account of the war or since the national mission. Things have gone on smoothly and quietly, some there are who call out about the high price of food, yet many there are who are far better off in a monetary point of view than they have ever been before in their lives, and they do not appear to be anxious that the war should come to an end.

Speaking generally, I think it a great mistake, that so much should be published in the public press by church people about what is called "the failure of the church" as it must be undermining the church's authority, and also be playing into the hands of our enemies. We must confess our failures and shortcomings but let it be amongst ourselves and our attitude to the nation be one of hopefulness and self confidence of the right kind, not of self depreciation.

4. Status of Church Schools. Options for compromise on a. management, b. head teachers, c. character of religious teaching. Might compromise be justified by better arrangements for Church teaching in state schools?

Ours is a Council School of which I am one of the Managers. All the children are those of church people with two exceptions and these children come to the Church Sunday School. I should greatly welcome an opportunity of being allowed to go into the school once a week, say for an hour, and give some religious teaching.

5 a. Changes in Public worship since 1914. b. Effects of the changes. (a) Of the four celebrations of Holy Communion, in the month, I have one at 9 a.m. instead of 8 a.m. and the (b) attendance is rather better at that hour than at 8 a.m.

6. Number of Roman Catholics in the Parish. I have no Roman Catholics in the parish with the exception of one of my domestic servants (a Belgian) who has been in my service for 5 years and comes to our Holy Communion.

1. Arthur Wright Callis graduated from St John's College Cambridge in 1876 and was ordained priest in 1883. He was Assistant Master, Surrey County School 1876–85, Headmaster of King Edward's School, Wymondham 1885–94 and of King Edward's School, Bury St Edmunds 1894–1907. He was Rector of Sproughton between 1907 and 1914, when he was appointed as Rector of Salford. He was 64 in 1918 and at the 1911 census he was living in a household with his wife, an unmarried female cousin, a 19-year-old unmarried son, three unmarried female servants (a cook and two maids) and an unmarried male under-groom/general servant.

SANDFORD ST MARTIN Incumbent B. M. Hawes[1]

1. Number of Boys Girls and Infants on books of day schools: a. Last year. b. 20 30 or 40 years ago.

(a) Boys 11, Girls 13, Infants 19. Total 43. (b) In the year 1867, the then Head Teacher wrote, "the number on Roll varies from 50–70". In January 1900, there were about 60 on the Books.

2. a. Men and b. Women qualified to vote in Parochial Church meeting. None. I propose to get them to do so at the next Easter Vestry.

3. Moral and Spiritual effect of: a. Wartime b. National Mission.

(a) I think the war has made nearly everybody more thoughtful and the evening service on Sundays is for the size of the population in my opinion unusually well attended. At this service prayers in connection with the needs of the war are always said. There has also throughout the war been a weeknight intercession service attended by a few, and on occasions by a good many. All classes have felt the moral obligation to contribute to the war in finance, and there has been very little grumbling with regard to the sacrifices which the war has brought, whether in suffering or economy of food. An excellent example in all these respects has been set by the Squire.

(b) There was no actual National Mission held in this Parish, owing to a vacancy in the Benefice at the time, but since I have been here, I have endeavoured to bring the war in one or others of its phases every Sunday before the people, and so to do what the National Mission might have done.

4. Status of Church Schools. Options for compromise on a. management, b. head teachers, c. character of religious teaching. Might compromise be justified by better arrangements for Church teaching in state schools?

This Parish is in the rather exceptional and satisfactory condition of having no Chapel (or Public House) in Sandford, and at the hamlet of Ledwell in the same Parish, both the above are closed. However, though there is perhaps no very deep or definite Church membership realized, it is peculiarly a parish of men and women of goodwill to the church. Therefore from the narrow parochial point of view here, one would be apt to wish that sleeping dogs might lie unmolested by controversy. On wider grounds, my own view is, that if the church could obtain an entry to teach in Council Schools, it would be worthwhile and fair to give Nonconformity the privilege of teaching their own children in Church Schools in single-school areas: that it would be better to teach a few church children definitely than a large number indefinitely or whose church teaching is counteracted at home – and that it would make for Christian fellowship and charity.

5 a. Changes in Public worship since 1914. b. Effects of the changes. I was not here in 1914 and so (b) does not arise.

6. Number of Roman Catholics in the Parish. Two R.C. women, neither of whom are very staunch to their faith, and in the case of the family of one of the two women, her children have lately joined our Sunday School and Catechizing. The husbands in both cases are C of E.

1. Bernard McNaughten Hawes graduated AKC in 1897 and from Keble College Oxford in 1900, being ordained priest in 1899. He served three curacies 1898–1907, his first being at Oxford St Margaret. He was then Vicar of Longcot 1907–14 and of South Baddesley between 1914 and 1916, when he became Vicar of Sandford St Martin. He was 44 in 1918 and at the 1911 census he was living in a household with his wife, two daughters under 7, and three unmarried female servants.

SANDFORD-ON-THAMES Incumbent W. I. D. S. Read[1]

1. Number of Boys Girls and Infants on books of day schools: a. Last year. b. ~~20 30 or~~ **40 years ago.**

(a) 84 viz. 27 boys, 28 girls, 29 infants. (b) about 60 children.

2. a. Men and b. Women qualified to vote in Parochial Church meeting. Not any.

3. Moral and Spiritual effect of: a. Wartime b. National Mission.

(a) There seems to be a more or less general sense of depression as the war drags on. In the early days there was a good attendance at the week-night service of intercession. But the attendance at this has for some long time very much fallen off.

(b) There is a slight increase in regular Communions since the Mission. Perhaps (if one can judge by externals) some spiritual good was done to the faithful by the National Mission, but the indifferent majority do not seem to have been influenced.

4. Status of Church Schools. Options for compromise on a. management, b. head teachers, c. character of religious teaching. Might compromise be justified by better arrangements for Church teaching in state schools?

I wonder if difficulties arise much in small country parishes. In Sandford there are very few Dissenters, and these have never objected to or protested against the religious teaching in the school, nor have they withdrawn their children from attendance at Church e.g. on Ascension Day.

Still, I am inclined to think that if facilities could be given in all schools for children to be instructed in the professed faith of their parents, we might get a less colourless teaching for our Church children than is often the case.

5 a. Changes in Public worship since 1914. b. Effects of the changes. Since 1915 War Intercessions have been used at Evensong on Sundays instead of the appointed prayers after the 3rd Collect – and then, and also at all Celebrations the names of those serving from the parish are read out.

For 5 months I have tried having Morning Service at 10.30 instead of the long-established 11, hoping that the longer time before Sunday dinner might lead to an increased congregation. But the attendance has been less, and I am reverting to 11. Also about the Great Festivals (generally in the Octave) I have had a Choral Eucharist (Matins being said earlier). The choir have been interested, and have shewn some keenness, and some of the people have attended congregational practices. The slackness in attendance at Public Worship is very distressing. The idea of obligation seems almost non-existent, and anything else is allowed as an excuse for not coming to Church.

6. Number of Roman Catholics in the Parish. 2 men, 1 boy, 1 woman.

1. See 1914.

SARSDEN CUM CHURCHILL   Incumbent E. J. F. Johnson[1]

1. Number of Boys Girls and Infants on books of day schools: a. Last year. b. 20 30 or 40 years ago.

(a) Boys 52, Girls 50, Infants 39. (b) 1877: Boys 39, Girls 83. 1881: Infants 36. 1863: Boys 53.

2. a. Men and b. Women qualified to vote in Parochial Church meeting. Sarsden: men 16, women 28. Churchill: men 67, women 85.

3. Moral and Spiritual effect of: a. Wartime b. National Mission.

(a) (i) On children. Children have been less happy than usual. In school one has noticed less alertness and brightness in manner. Some realisation of what war means has been very apparent, especially among the older children. Boys who left school for labour were especially sensible of their own importance, but when they returned to school seemed to appreciate very much the opportunity of resuming their lessons.

(ii) To Adults. One cannot help remarking the marked awakening of generosity in all classes not only for war purposes, but also for church missions overseas. The interest in this respect during the first year of the war was striking. There has been one offer for the foreign mission field by a young woman who has joined the Home Preparation Union of the CMS although the Parents are still unwilling to give consent to her being a Missionary.

(b) It is difficult to say what has been the effect generally – possibly the interest in Missions may have been stimulated by it.

4. Status of Church Schools. Options for compromise on a. management, b. head teachers, c. character of religious teaching. Might compromise be justified by better arrangements for Church teaching in state schools?

Church Schools in Single School areas. There should be no difficulty in maintaining the Church School in a Single School Area, when the Management act with wisdom. Should the question of Religious Instruction be met fairly, matters can very quickly be adjusted between Churchmen and Nonconformists and usually there are few parents who object to Church Teaching – The views of those who differ should be respected and freedom to withdraw their children from Church Teaching should be recognised. – This freedom is seldom exercised.

Thus a compromise is advisable, and if Nonconformists have representation on the Management, the appointment of teachers and the Religious Teaching question, can, with common sense, be agreed upon. The N.U.T. agitation is of course run on "business lines", but there are very many teachers who do not agree with their proposals. The offer of satisfactory conditions of Religious Teaching in Council Schools, is surely an acknowledgement that such teaching is valued, and the Church should see to it, that she takes her share of these opportunities with other Religious Bodies, and making a point of securing the best, clear, and definite instruction for these occasions.

5 a. Changes in Public worship since 1914. b. Effects of the changes. (a) Evening service. Sermon is preached after the 3rd Collect followed by War Intercessions. For the local invalids thanksgivings for recovery or any other event which comes to one's notice. The general Thanksgiving is said by the people in the litany. The Holy Communion on Saints Days is administered after due notice on the previous Sunday at the most convenient hours to the parishioners, between 7 am and 11.30

– the latter has been the one generally selected. A Box is placed in the Church for suggestions and for Prayers. The week night service for War Intercessions at which a regular reading is used is appreciated – and better attendances on Sunday are the result. At the suggestion of the Sarsden Parochial Church Council the Holy Communion is administered once a month at the Afternoon service, for the benefit of those who cannot attend earlier or who live at a distance with the result of a better attendance.

6. Number of Roman Catholics in the Parish. One woman.

1. See 1914.

SHENINGTON WITH ALKERTON   Incumbent A. Blytheman[1]

1. Number of Boys Girls and Infants on books of day schools: a. Last year. 43. **b. 20 30 or 40 years ago.** Shenington and Alkeston have now a joint school at S. I find an entry in the Shenington Log Book on July 4, 1879, "average for past week 72, the highest since the School has been opened". Then we took children over 3; now not until they are 5 years old. In the Alkeston Log Book I find, "Sep 16, 1872, number present 37".

2. a. Men and b. Women qualified to vote in Parochial Church meeting. No steps have yet been taken here 're' a Parochial Church Council.

3. Moral and Spiritual effect of: a. Wartime b. National Mission.

(a) I do not know that there is very much real difference. I have heard one or two who have lost sons in the war complain at first of God allowing it to take place. But I doubt if they meant it actually.

(b) Through a misunderstanding our Mission was held on only 3 weekdays. I think it did good at the time, but I also think that it would have been more effective, if a Sunday had been included.

4. Status of Church Schools. Options for compromise on a. management, b. head teachers, c. character of religious teaching. Might compromise be justified by better arrangements for Church teaching in state schools?

Here we have never had any trouble as regards the religious teaching in our National School. All Dissenters have thus far allowed their children to have the same teaching as the C. of E. children; and in due case [sic] a few years ago even a Roman Catholic parent allowed his children to have the same up to 10 years of age. Moreover, on Saints Days the Dissenting children all attend Service in the Parish Church at 11.15 am, no parent ever having objected to this. The chief Dissenter's boy at present on these occasions blows the Organ. As I have had no experience of awkwardness on the part of parents 're' religious teaching during nearly 50 years, I am a poor judge in the matter; but I think the wishes of a parent should be met as far as possible in all schools, C. of E. and "Provided".

5 a. Changes in Public worship since 1914. b. Effects of the changes. (a) We have not darkened our Church, and so have had no late Evensong in Autumn and Winter the last 2 years, when the days begin to draw in. (b) I think this has somewhat reduced our congregation.

6. Number of Roman Catholics in the Parish. One man and his daughter.

1. See 1914.

SHIPLAKE   Incumbent W. Elphick[1] (for C. A. W. Aylan,[2] temporary Chaplain in the Navy)

1. Number of Boys Girls and Infants on books of day schools: a. Last year. b. 20 30 or 40 years ago.

(a) 98. (b) In the year 1874: 65.

2. a. Men and b. Women qualified to vote in Parochial Church meeting. 182 altogether. (a) <u>Men</u>, 78; (b) <u>Women</u>, 104.

3. Moral and Spiritual effect of: a. Wartime b. National Mission.

(a) The war seems to have left the parish unchanged.

(b) The National Mission has had no lasting effect on the parish as a whole. But it has certainly made the keen church folk keener – the effect it was desired to have – making them more ready to work for the conversion of their brethren. It has also taught the clergy the value of Mission Sermon Services – e.g. during a course of evening sermons this Lent on "the Work and Influence of the Holy Spirit" – on the lines of the Bishop of London's "Mission of the Spirit" – the congregations have steadily increased and the people are constantly saying how much they are helped by that type of preaching. It has taught us new methods. Possibly the National Mission also accounts for the larger numbers now attending the 10 o'clock Sung Eucharist every Sunday and for the increasing supply of Church workers.

4. Status of Church Schools. Options for compromise on a. management, b. head teachers, c. character of religious teaching. Might compromise be justified by better arrangements for Church teaching in state schools?

[*No response*].

5 a. Changes in Public worship since 1914. b. Effects of the changes. None.

6. Number of Roman Catholics in the Parish. In a changing population it is not easy to discover exactly. But among permanent residents there are: 3 men, 9 women, 3 children.

1. William Elphick graduated from Keble College Oxford in 1913 and trained at Cuddesdon College, being ordained priest in 1915. Shiplake was his first curacy. He was 26 in 1918 and at the 1911 census he was living in the household of his father (a butcher). Also living in the household were his parents, an unmarried aunt, an unmarried boarder, his father's unmarried male clerk, and an unmarried female servant.
2. See 1914.

SHIPTON-ON-CHERWELL[1]   Incumbent G. Duncan[2]

1. Number of Boys Girls and Infants on books of day schools: a. Last year. 9. **b. 20 30 or 40 years ago.** Seven years ago: 26; twenty years ago: 11; a little more than twenty years ago: 18.

2. a. Men and b. Women qualified to vote in Parochial Church meeting. [*No response*].

3. Moral and Spiritual effect of: a. Wartime b. National Mission.

At first there was great searchings of heart and all seemed moved but as wages rose rapidly a more materialistic spirit arose in the people and the sudden prosperity began to lead to pleasure seeking. Later, however, the deeper meaning of the war appears to be making its appeal. All through a section – not a large one – has been earnest and steadfast and seems to increase in reverent devotion. Some of the women workers show their moral sense in the steady way they do work that cannot be altogether pleasant and needing great moral effort. As to the men, it is difficult to judge their moral position. The price of beer is almost prohibitive and one could hardly say what would have been their position had beer been cheap and wages at their present rate. The steady element is more solemnly impressed. It is difficult to say what the result of the National Mission was as there have been so very many other events moral and spiritual constantly bearing on the people.

4. Status of Church Schools. Options for compromise on a. management, b. head teachers, c. character of religious teaching. Might compromise be justified by better arrangements for Church teaching in state schools?

I have had to do with Church Schools in single school areas in three parishes in this Rural Deanery and I have never found any feeling worth speaking about the status of the schools. There have certainly been a very very few discontented ones but the vast majority have been glad to have their children educated in institutions with a definite religious character: very few indeed a negligible quantity were ever exempted from religious instruction: the status of the Church schools in question should be as present: the body of Managers might be enlarged provided the proportion of foundation managers is the same. The appointment of the headteacher should most certainly be retained by the Body of Managers. The character of the religious teaching has a tendency to be too "examinational" and needs more scope for the personality of the teacher, on the lines of the Bible and Prayer

Book (Catechism especially) exclusively. I do not consider the offer of teaching in provided schools would at all compensate for the disturbing influence for Church Schools. When the teacher does not give the religious instruction the Clergyman of the Parish is almost invariably recognised as the proper person to do it.

5 a. Changes in Public worship since 1914. b. Effects of the changes. None.

6. Number of Roman Catholics in the Parish. [*No response*].

1. Population 134.
2. George Duncan graduated from Wadham College Oxford in 1884 and was ordained priest in 1886. After an initial curacy 1885–95, he was Vicar of Steeple Barton between 1895 and 1898, when he became Rector of Shipton-on-Cherwell. He was aged 57 in 1918 and at the 1911 census he was sharing a household with his wife, a widowed cook and two other unmarried female servants.

SHIPTON-UNDER-WYCHWOOD   Incumbent W. J. Oldfield[1]

1. Number of Boys Girls and Infants on books of day schools: a. Last year. b. 20 30 or 40 years ago.

March 1918 No. on Books: Boys 25, Girls 25, Infants 24 b. and 18 g. Total 92.

1875 No. on Books: Boys 37, Girls 41, Infants 23 b. and 29 g. Total 130.

2. a. Men and b. Women qualified to vote in Parochial Church meeting. 10 men.

I hope to alter the above figures this year. [*Note added to the return*] 'He wrote later to say that he had got 17 men and 31 women this year'.

3. Moral and Spiritual effect of: a. Wartime b. National Mission.

I have consulted the churchwardens and the doctor and they are all agreed that they are unable to perceive any effect. This is also true of Culham. One cause of the failure of the National Mission I venture to attribute to the insufficiency (for the purpose) of Missioners. While we have many men who are able to conduct with spiritual profit retreats of piously disposed people, we have very few at the present time possessed of that personal magnetism, inspired by the conviction of a divine mission, that is necessary to set on fire the souls of the careless and indifferent. As Joubert says: "Why is even a bad preacher almost always heard by the pious with pleasure? Because he talks to them about what they love. But you who have to expound religion to the children of this world, you who have to speak to them of that which they once loved perhaps, or which they would be glad to flee – remember that they do not love it yet and to make them love it take heed to speak with power. You may do what you like, mankind will believe no one but God; and he only can persuade mankind who believes that God has spoken to him."[2]

But there is also a larger cause of the failure of both the war and the National Mission to stir the spiritual depths of the great mass of the people. The "general atmosphere" of human souldom (if I may coin a word) is, at the present time, nowhere in that state of tension which would enable it to respond to a 'spark' from without. The oxygen has usually been eliminated and only argon is left. This is a symptom of some deep lying causes in our social and ecclesiastical life, and it should be the business of the Church to devote earnest study to the question and try to seek out those causes. I can see things that might have produced the result but it is subject for much thought and comparison of the results of different thoughts.

4. Status of Church Schools. Options for compromise on a. management, b. head teachers, c. character of religious teaching. Might compromise be justified by better arrangements for Church teaching in state schools?

Nonconformists will always believe they have a grievance so long as the Church holds any sort of privileged position with regard to any schools. There will therefore always be some difficulty in coming to terms with them. I speak of them as a body, not of their more clear sighted leaders.

Our chief difficulties lie in two other directions: (1) the indifference of parents and (2) the resistance, active or passive, of the great body of the teachers. The first has its roots in the lack of brotherhood in the Church. The second is the result of leaving the teachers outside our councils and counsel. If we are not prepared to rouse ourselves to the task of dealing with these two causes the only course would seem to be to acknowledge defeat and accept the best terms we can get. But history will condemn us for our lack of courage and enterprise.

5 a. Changes in Public worship since 1914. b. Effects of the changes. I believe the only alteration has been the institution of a choral celebration of the Holy Communion at 11 on the first Sunday of the month preceded by Mattins at an earlier hour. The latter has never had any congregation. Complaint was made by those accustomed to late communion but unappreciative of the choral service that this arrangement deprived them of their communion altogether. I offered a choice of these alternatives (i) the choral celebration at 9 (ii) the choral celebration at 11 alternately with plain on the first Sunday (iii) additional celebration plain at 11 on third Sunday. The last has been adopted; but it gives me three celebrations on that Sunday as there is a 9.45 at the Mission Room.

6. Number of Roman Catholics in the Parish. Two men and two women no children.

1. See 1914 Culham. Oldfield came to Shipton in 1917.
2. Joseph Joubert, a French moralist – this statement was possibly more widely known in English because it was cited in a discussion of Joubert in Matthew Arnold, *Essays in Criticism* (1865), p. 235.

SHIRBURN   Incumbent F. J. Hall[1]

1. Number of Boys Girls and Infants on books of day schools: a. Last year. b. 20 30 or 40 years ago.

1878 Total on register 68: 30 boys, 38 girls of whom 35 were infants: 13 boys, 12 girls.

1917 Total on register 37: 23 boys, 14 girls of whom 14 are infants: 8 boys, 6 girls.

2. a. Men and b. Women qualified to vote in Parochial Church meeting. 1917: 19 men, 29 women = 48. 1918: 23 men, 36 women = 59. This is to some extent approximate as I have not had all the papers signed and returned.

3. Moral and Spiritual effect of: a. Wartime b. National Mission.

(a) The effect of wartime? I think the war has left its mark in my parish: there is a more serious tone a greater inclination to turn to the comforting strength of religion especially when the grief at the loss of a dear relation is on them; here and there there is a little discontent. War weariness, but little or no loss of faith, are exemplified by their words and actions: there is a slight improvement in attendance at church: at first there was quite a good attendance at my daily service of intercession, but that has gradually decreased.

(b) The effect of the National Mission? I can trace but little if any effect from it, though such little as I fancy I trace makes for good. I was unfortunate in the arrangements I made. We united the three parishes of Pyrton, Stoke Talmage and Shirburn, and the Missioner was particularly anxious to hold all his Services in one Church, we chose Pyrton as the most central and in spite of repeated exhortation to do so but few came from Shirburn. On the other hand I know of no vice in the parish, no drunkenness, no immorality, and perhaps the goodness in the parish may be, more than I think, due to the Mission and the preparation for it. The people are good, always glad to see me, always friendly, but there is a lack of religious earnestness, a casualness about coming to church, due I think partially to the irregularity of the Sunday services before I came. I have tried hard to overcome this by continual visiting and bright Services but with only partial success. My greatest success was in some open air Rogation Services last year which were attended by nearly everyone, but did not lead as I hoped to further attendance at church. There is no public house and no chapel in the parish, but a good many are what they call "chapel people" and the parish has decreased in number by nearly half in these last years. I know and recognise the difficulty mothers with small families have to come to church.

4. Status of Church Schools. Options for compromise on a. management, b. head teachers, c. character of religious teaching. Might compromise be justified by better arrangements for Church teaching in state schools?

After more than 43 years of school work, I naturally have followed with the greatest interest the awakening of the public conscience as to education – and the new bill is a long step in the right direction, but I cannot but view with great anxiety the future of religious education.

I feel very deeply that real religious education should be given in all elementary schools, and I cannot but think a scheme for such young children, i.e. to the age of 14 might be developed which would not be objectionable to any sect: after that in the continuation schools I think the parish clergy, and where there are such, nonconformist ministers must be appealed to, to carry on the religious teaching given in the elementary schools on more definite lines. Confirmation classes would, as now, help, but for, say two half hours a week, definite religious teaching in the tenets of the religion of the parents should be given to the age of 18 and in single school areas where in all probability nonconformist ministers are not to be had, the parents should be allowed the option of exempting their children: in actual fact I believe that very few would be exempted. As to the other points in the question, (a) management (b) appointment of head teachers, I do not think I have sufficient experience to give an opinion. I hold that the years of 14 to 18 is so tremendously important when young minds are developing that every possible effort that can be made should be made that their religion be not neglected. I do not like 'compromise', it always seems to me to be but a temporary settlement of a difficulty, and the time will come when the question must be fought out on its own merits.

5 a. Changes in Public worship since 1914. b. Effects of the changes. I have a daily service of intercessions, well attended at first, now poorly so. I have also had Celebrations of Holy Communion weekly. Before there were only two in the month without any special good result.

6. Number of Roman Catholics in the Parish. None.

1. See 1914.

SIBFORD GOWER AND EPWELL   Incumbent L. Moxon[1]

1. Number of Boys Girls and Infants on books of day schools: a. Last year. b. 20 30 or 40 years ago.

		Boys	Girls
Sibford	1898	46	51 = 97. 2 Dames Schools in the village.
	1918	46	34 = 80.
Epwell	1878	40 altogether.	
	1918	16	17 = 33.

2. a. Men and b. Women qualified to vote in Parochial Church meeting. 4 men, 3 women.

3. Moral and Spiritual effect of: a. Wartime b. National Mission.

(a) The Intercession Services were fairly well attended at first, but the last three years have fallen off to no more than before the war. Any special effort on the anniversaries has been well answered to especially the day last January when a United Service was held on the Sunday Evening. There is a quiet, restrained, demeanour, and I believe the Parents' prayers for the sons in the War are very real but there is little finding of that strength in the Holy Sacrament. There is a really splendid spirit of self sacrifice and little grumbling at the shortness of food.

(b) With regard to the National Mission I cannot see outwardly any result, but I believe the value of the Witness of the Mission in our country villages was real. The present shortage of labour and the push of the work made Church Attendance small but there was an objection by many to do Sunday work. The boys in the village have been encouraging they have attended a Voluntary Night School during the Winter and many gave their own names in for confirmation.

4. Status of Church Schools. Options for compromise on a. management, b. head teachers, c. character of religious teaching. Might compromise be justified by better arrangements for Church teaching in state schools?

I do not see that any change is necessary with regard to religious teaching. Dissenters are well represented on the Managers Board I should be perfectly willing to encourage their teaching their own faith to their own children but there is no desire for it neither are any children removed from the religious teaching which is of a definite Church tone We have a quaker on our School Managers Board and at Epwell 2 Dissenters.

5 a. Changes in Public worship since 1914. b. Effects of the changes. We have started a Choral Eucharist at 11 o'clock (Mattins said at 10.15) as the principal Service once in the 2 months. Some have not attended who come other Sundays but those who come have expressed a real liking for the Service and I have little doubt that it will eventually win its way.

6. Number of Roman Catholics in the Parish. 1 man and 1 woman only.

1. See 1914.

SOMERTON   Incumbent G. E. Barnes[1]

1. Number of Boys Girls and Infants on books of day schools: a. Last year. b. 20 30 or 40 years ago.

	Year	Boys	Girls	Infants	Total
Somerton C of E	1878	26	30	6	62
School. No. on the Books.	1888	21	19	10	50
Day School	1898	18	18	18	54
4th year of the Great War	1918	11	14	14	39

2. a. Men and b. Women qualified to vote in Parochial Church meeting. (a) none. (b) none.

3. Moral and Spiritual effect of: a. Wartime b. National Mission.

The effect of (a) war time does not seem, generally speaking, to result in making people more religious. Attendances on Church Services are not so good as in times of Peace, but there are certain reasons for this, such as the scarcity of hands for farm labour, which means <u>Sunday</u> labour as well as week day for Farmers, labourers and boys. On the other hand, all 'Appeals for assistance' for our own War Funds for those Abroad have been <u>generously</u> responded to by our small population and shews that there is a Christian spirit in this respect.

(b) As regards the National Mission: the result has been disappointing:- At the actual Mission week all the Special Services were well attended and the Children's Services, but the "Meeting" at the School Room specially for the <u>men</u> and <u>youths</u> was very sparsely attended:- Any special lasting effect from the Mission and preparatory teaching does not shew itself outwardly at any rate.

4. Status of Church Schools. Options for compromise on a. management, b. head teachers, c. character of religious teaching. Might compromise be justified by better arrangements for Church teaching in state schools?

Personally, I consider that these schools should by all means be retained in their present status, and every effort made to retain the teaching of the "Church Catechism". A few sentences which seem to cause <u>great offence</u>, such as to "order myself lowly and reverently to all my <u>betters</u>" might be <u>left out or differently worded</u> as not quite suitable in these democratic times, but the "Catechism" in its main teaching should be preserved intact at all costs if possible. "<u>Compromise</u>" is rarely satisfactory and as far as my opinion goes, would be a <u>mistake</u> in this case. I do not consider the offers of more satisfactory conditions of religious teaching in "Provided" or County Schools would justify such compromise.

5 a. Changes in Public worship since 1914. b. Effects of the changes. Since the declaration of war in 1914 we always have the "Litany" and "War Prayers" at 8.30am on Wednesdays. These services fairly well attended, but not so well lately as at an earlier period, still, these Intercession Services are much appreciated by some of the Parishioners at any rate.

6. Number of Roman Catholics in the Parish. None left now.

1. See 1914.

SOUTHLEIGH   Incumbent E. B. Rand[1]

1. Number of Boys Girls and Infants on books of day schools:

a. Last year. For year ending 30 June 1917: B 17, G 20, I 26. Total 63.

b. ~~20 30 or~~ **40 years ago.** For year ending 30 June 1877: B 16, G 20, I 29. Total 65.

2. a. Men and b. Women qualified to vote in Parochial Church meeting. No Parochial Church Meeting.

3. Moral and Spiritual effect of: a. Wartime b. National Mission.

(a) Moral effect: no special immorality to report. Spiritual effect: more callous and indifferent. (b) No effect whatever, morally or spiritually.

4. Status of Church Schools. Options for compromise on a. management, b. head teachers, c. character of religious teaching. Might compromise be justified by better arrangements for Church teaching in state schools?

The present policy should be pursued with regard to (a) (b) and (c) without any compromise.

5 a. Changes in Public worship since 1914. b. Effects of the changes. (a) Your Lordship allowed me to make the following change:- Sung Eucharist (at 11 o'clock) on 1st Sunday in month and Sung Matins on other Sundays instead of Sung Eucharist every Sunday.

(b) No increase in attendance but less grumbling in the Parish.

6. Number of Roman Catholics in the Parish. None.

1. Ebenezer Bacon Rand graduated from Caius College Cambridge in 1868 and was ordained priest in 1872. He served six curacies 1871–1915, with a brief period as Assistant Master at Reading Grammar School 1873–74. He was appointed Vicar of Southleigh in 1915. He was 73 in 1918 and at the 1911 census he was living with his wife and an unmarried female servant.

SPELSBURY   Incumbent T. C. Tanner[1]

1. Number of Boys Girls and Infants on books of day schools: a. Last year. b. 20 30 or 40 years ago.

(a) Boys 14, Girls 17, Infants 20. (b) (sixteen years ago 1902) Boys 26, Girls 25, Infants 19.

2. a. Men and b. Women qualified to vote in Parochial Church meeting. Men 4. Women 3.

3. Moral and Spiritual effect of: a. Wartime b. National Mission.

My knowledge of the Parish is confined entirely to the period of the war and dates but little before the National Mission – I am therefore unable to give any detailed report but generally

(1) The number of children attending Sunday School average 30 as against 4 or 5 in the latter years of my predecessor. (2) There is a very great improvement in Church attendance. (3) The Churchgoers generally I am sorry to say regard the 'Holy Communion' as an 'extra' and confine themselves to coming at the Great Festivals. (4) Little interest is taken by the older generation in Church matters – they expect everything to be done for them. The rising generation through the organisation of "King's Messengers" one is led to hope are learning to take a wider view.

4. Status of Church Schools. Options for compromise on a. management, b. head teachers, c. character of religious teaching. Might compromise be justified by better arrangements for Church teaching in state schools?

We may justly claim that children should receive definite religious instruction in the faith of their parents and that where this cannot be given by the Staff the right of entry should be granted to the Clergy to do so. Granted this may be secured all else is of small matter, though why a Headteacher should not be appointed in the case of Single Area Schools in which Church Children are in a majority passes my understanding. Surely schools are for the benefit of scholars and not mere post[s] of emolument for the Teachers. The compromises so far suggested with any hope of acceptance do not seem to me to justify a surrender of our Schools – When we can secure definite Church Teaching in Council School, I agree that the present dual system can be abolished.

5 a. Changes in Public worship since 1914. b. Effects of the changes. (a) The Evensong was formerly 3 pm and now is 6 pm. (b) Result, better congregations. The 3 o'clock service is stilled, [sic] retained as a Children's Service with catechizing.

6. Number of Roman Catholics in the Parish. Men 4, Women 6, Children 1.

1. Thomas Combe Tanner trained at Sarum College in 1891 and graduated from Durham University in 1896. He was ordained priest in 1897, served three curacies 1896–1907, was Rector of Sydenham Damarel between 1907 and 1914, and was appointed Vicar of Spelsbury in 1915. He was 46 in 1918 and at the 1911 census he was sharing a household with his wife and two unmarried female servants.

STADHAMPTON   Incumbent A. A. D. Harding[1]

1. Number of Boys Girls and Infants on books of day schools: a. Last year. b. 20 30 or 40 years ago.

(a) 1918: Boys 28, Girls 30 Infants 25. Total 83.

(b) 20 years ago, 1898: Boys 22, Girls 15, Infants 33. Total 70.

2. a. Men and b. Women qualified to vote in Parochial Church meeting. None. Although I drew up a scheme for a Parochial Church Council in which I myself took the place of Secretary and made a Churchwarden Chairman, no one here would have a Council. The reasons were (a) the Council had no real power (b) the business assigned to it was not enough to make it worthwhile.

3. Moral and Spiritual effect of: a. Wartime b. National Mission.

(a) In the words of one who is not a conspicuous Christian the effect of the War has been to make the good better and the bad worse. (b) On the whole I think there are signs of a deepening spiritual sense but there are still with us many discouraging features. The National Mission was most useful (a) in arousing the people from their mechanical habit of regarding religion (b) in helping myself as their minister to shake off the tyranny of worn out methods of expression and to seek new forms of expression for old and well-known truths.

4. Status of Church Schools. Options for compromise on a. management, b. head teachers, c. character of religious teaching. Might compromise be justified by better arrangements for Church teaching in state schools?

The present position which shuts the parish priest out of the village Council School is most unsatisfactory. It has a direct effect upon the discipline of the young: and especially so where the schoolmaster is a formal Christian or for any reason whatever is in direct antagonism or passive opposition to the parish priest. My experience of a Council School in a village is that the schoolmaster becomes in effect a second moral, if not a spiritual authority: and as he possesses direct authority as against the clergyman's influence, the resulting position is most difficult for the clergyman unless he and the schoolmaster are working hand in hand in the Church which cannot always be. Such a position may be neutralized to a certain extent if the clergyman has been appointed a manager: but if not, the farmers who are managers are practically swayed by the schoolmaster in their action as managers. Though I succeeded in claiming a holiday on Ascension Day two years ago in this parish (it was also given without further request on my part last year) I did it by the help of the secretary to the County Council Education Department, who directed a manager's meeting to be called. The attendance at Sunday School suffers from (a) want of teachers (b) want of adequate buildings (c) distance of teachers from necessary instruction in how to teach (d) difficulty of instructing in one school in church both older scholars and infants (e) the indifference of parents and the refusal of children to attend and if compelled the lack of behaviour which renders their absence desirable for the sake of those who come to learn. Hence satisfactory conditions of religious teaching on weekdays in Council Schools would be most valuable and in my judgement indispensable to the restoration of that active spiritual sense and moral uplift of which the young are the hope. Indeed that more effective secular education which is coming into force can only accentuate the spiritual trend downwards. The definite recognition of a system of national religious training alongside of the intellectual training and partaking of its compulsory character would be worth the surrender of the separate control of what we now call Church Schools. It ought to be established as a definite principle of educational life that every such institution, (elementary school, secondary school, college, etc) should have its Chaplain. In a village like this the parish priest would naturally be the Chaplain. He should have definite powers of instruction on a definite syllabus, right of entry to the school at all hours by right of his position an Hon. manager with a right of speech but not of voting, and capable of being elected to a full managership and the chairmanship. The same limitation proposed as regards the stay of a clergyman in any one parish should apply to the schoolmaster, 15 years is long enough without a change. Both the school and the man need the change.

5 a. Changes in Public worship since 1914. b. Effects of the changes. None.

6. Number of Roman Catholics in the Parish. None.

1. See 1914.

STANDLAKE   Incumbent T. Lovett[1]

1. Number of Boys Girls and Infants on books of day schools: a. Last year. b. 20 30 or 40 years ago.

1917: B. 31, G. 37, In. 31. 1895: B. 39, G. 31, In. 61.

2. a. Men and b. Women qualified to vote in Parochial Church meeting. None.

3. Moral and Spiritual effect of: a. Wartime b. National Mission.

(a) I think the moral effect is certainly shewn in the behaviour of all classes in this parish which consists entirely of farmers and their labourers. More kindness is evident and more charity towards each other's failings and more readiness to help each other. As regards temperance I think there is a slight improvement but only slight. On the other hand discipline at home by reason of the fathers absence is notably very slack and discipline in the school is very much deprecated by the mothers. The spiritual effect is not very marked here. There may be a little better attendance at general services and a little more desire for spiritual things but it is slight. The Intercession Services have lost much of their first enthusiasm. Most people take the war as a matter of course to which they have grown accustomed and it does not seem to any great extent an incentive to repentance and seeking God.

(b) The effects of the National Mission are practically nil.

4. Status of Church Schools. Options for compromise on a. management, b. head teachers, c. character of religious teaching. Might compromise be justified by better arrangements for Church teaching in state schools?

(1) No. (2) Yes to retain them but some compromise as regards (a) and (b). (3) Yes I should say so.

5 a. Changes in Public worship since 1914. b. Effects of the changes. No changes.

6. Number of Roman Catholics in the Parish. None.

1. See 1914.

STANTON HARCOURT   Incumbent F. W. J. Butler[1] (Curate in Charge)

1. Number of Boys Girls and Infants on books of day schools: a. Last year. 85.

b. 20 30 or 40 years ago. 22 years ago: 120 (high-water mark) Lowest 1912: 75.

2. a. Men and b. Women qualified to vote in Parochial Church meeting. No persons in this parish have signed, the declaration qualifying them under the rules of the Representative Church Council to vote in the Parochial Church meeting, so far as I can gain information.

3. Moral and Spiritual effect of: a. Wartime b. National Mission.

(a) Generally a deeper seriousness of mind and openness to religious influences in time of war. Distinctive Christian doctrines and facts have increased influence: the Incarnation, the Cross, Forgiveness, the Triumph of Love, the new life.

(b) The National Mission has had some influence here but it is mainly dependent on the constant influence of life and doctrine, Word and Sacrament. Nothing tells more than the regular quiet sustained parochial work, preferably of a ministry lasting many years or a lifetime: all the most potent influences are quiet. There is reason to believe that generally the influence of the war on moral and spiritual life will be good: it will emphasise those distinctive aspects of Christian belief. Historic entrance of God, the Cross as the concentration of the work of God into one historic deed of eternal and spiritual import etc. The great need of the time is emphasis upon <u>the positive movement</u>, the new life in the power of the Resurrection: the negative movement is all essential, but apostolic Christianity is full of the <u>positive</u> life towards God. The return <u>from</u> the Wilderness in the power of the Holy Spirit <u>into Galilee</u>. The "thou shalt not" is the indispensible preliminary to the "thou shalt" – in general perhaps the Christian religion requires more emphasising of its positive element.

4. Status of Church Schools. Options for compromise on a. management, b. head teachers, c. character of religious teaching. Might compromise be justified by better arrangements for Church teaching in state schools?

The Headteacher should be a Churchman in church schools. Management should be in the hands of Churchmen. If a type of religious teaching acceptable to Churchmen and agreed to by the others could be found, it might be made use of both in Church and "Provided" Schools. Distinctive Church doctrines should <u>also</u> be taught in school hours. It might be allowable to seek a compromise on these lines if more satisfactory conditions were given in Council or "Provided" Schools.

5 a. Changes in Public worship since 1914. b. Effects of the changes. There is no change to report.

6. Number of Roman Catholics in the Parish. No Roman Catholics in this parish.

N.B. The above answers were written on a separate sheet of paper and have been copied by me. W.L.C.

1. Frederick William James Butler graduated from London University in 1895 and was ordained priest in 1911. He held four curacies between 1910 and 1917, coming to Stanton Harcourt for his fifth in 1917. He was the author of *The Permanent Element in Christianity* (1910) and *Personality and Revelation* (1914). He was 42 in 1918 and at the 1911 census he was living in a two-person household with his wife.

STANTON ST JOHN   Incumbent E. B. Roberts[1]

1. Number of Boys Girls and Infants on books of day schools: a. Last year. b. 20 30 or 40 years ago.

(a) 100.

2. a. Men and b. Women qualified to vote in Parochial Church meeting. 1916: (a) 4, (b) 10.

3. Moral and Spiritual effect of: a. Wartime b. National Mission.

The parish is in a fluctuating condition, as the present population is largely families of men at the front living with their mothers having given up their own homes.

(a) The Tractor working all Easter Day has lowered the tone of Sunday with observance. The youth and children have needed asking hard as the more responsible members are at the front. Reverence and respect have both suffered. On the other hand there is a far better attendance now at Holy Communion.

4. Status of Church Schools. Options for compromise on a. management, b. head teachers, c. character of religious teaching. Might compromise be justified by better arrangements for Church teaching in state schools?

We have no difficulty in the school policy here, as the one School stands for the two parishes of Stanton St John and Forest Hill in perfect harmony.

5 a. Changes in Public worship since 1914. b. Effects of the changes. [*No response*].

6. Number of Roman Catholics in the Parish. One family of Belgian Refugees consisting man, wife, and six children. They attend Sunday School, Church and Guild.

1. Ernest Basil Roberts graduated from Worcester College Oxford in 1902 and was ordained priest in 1903. He served two curacies and a chaplaincy at the Oxford Medical Mission in Bermondsey 1902–07. He was Perpetual Curate of St Paul Hyson Green, Nottingham

1907–11, Vicar of St Katherine's Northampton 1911–14 and of All Saints Viney Hill between 1914 and 1916, when he was appointed Rector of Stanton St John. He was 38 in 1918 and at the 1911 census he was sharing a household with his wife and two female servants, one widowed and one unmarried.

STOKE LYNE[1] Incumbent G. A. Littledale[2]

1. Number of Boys Girls and Infants on books of day schools: a. Last year. 32.

b. ~~20 30 or~~ **40 years ago.** 60.

2. a. Men and b. Women qualified to vote in Parochial Church meeting. None.

3. Moral and Spiritual effect of: a. Wartime b. National Mission.

"As it was in the beginning, is now, and (I suppose) ever will be":

A small minority seem to have their heart touched and their will turned Godwards alike by the mission effort and the stress of the war; A larger proportion may or may not be touched; they do not show it; A large number never attend any special service, and some never enter church except on Harvest Festival, but each and all of such are no doubt very busily employed and let that employment be an excuse for not publically witnessing to the Christianity.

4. Status of Church Schools. Options for compromise on a. management, b. head teachers, c. character of religious teaching. Might compromise be justified by better arrangements for Church teaching in state schools?

(1) Parents should, under compulsory education, have the right to obtain for their children religious instruction according to their beliefs: with this as a general principle I would facilitate the entry of Nonconformist teachers for religious instruction into the Church School in a single-school area in return for the entry into rate provided schools of C of E Teachers during the Religious Instruction hour.

(2) As regards (a) <u>management</u> I would welcome a non-conformist element provided that (b) the appointment of Head-teacher remained in Church hands. (3) See reply to (1).

5 a. Changes in Public worship since 1914. b. Effects of the changes. [*No response*].

6. Number of Roman Catholics in the Parish. 1 family, consisting of man, wife and child who attends the Church at ¼ to 10, avoiding religious instruction.

1. Population 175.
2. See 1914 Chipping Norton. Littledale moved to Stoke Lyne in 1915.

STOKE ROW   Incumbent T. W. Hutchinson[1]

1. Number of Boys Girls and Infants on books of day schools: a. Last year. 83.

b. 20 30 or 40 years ago. No information.

2. a. Men and b. Women qualified to vote in Parochial Church meeting. None. The Parish practically consists of 3 Hamlets, the central one is strongly nonconformist and contains the Chapel. The other 2 for many years past have attached themselves to Checkendon and Highmore and do not attend Stoke Row church or take any interest therein.

3. Moral and Spiritual effect of: a. Wartime b. National Mission.

The effect of the War has been to raise wages to an unprecedented figure. The result is that the greatest difficulty is experienced in digging a grave the relatives wishing to pay the usual charges and no man being willing to work at ½ or less than the present wage. The same difficulty occurs in church cleaning, care of lamps and stoves and keeping graveyard in proper order.

4. Status of Church Schools. Options for compromise on a. management, b. head teachers, c. character of religious teaching. Might compromise be justified by better arrangements for Church teaching in state schools?

I think the best policy would be to let the schools at say 5% on the capital value of buildings and pay itinerant teachers decent salaries to take the religious instruction and nothing else. The rent received would amply remunerate selected teachers who would go from one school to another at different times. The Church Training Colleges ought also to be more careful to receive only bona fide members of the Church of England. Apparently many pass through these places without being definite Churchmen. A Diocesan Committee would manage the religious instruction and R.D. Committees would report to them. An inefficient religious teacher would then be easily eliminated and the bad example set by Headteachers of Church Schools in many Country Parishes of non-attendance at Public Worship put a stop to. The Head Teacher then representing the L.E.A. and not the church.

5 a. Changes in Public worship since 1914. b. Effects of the changes. The Lighting Order obliges us to hold Sunday Afternoon Services in place of Evening through part of the year. This diminishes the Congregation. Until this year I have held Sunday Evening Services in the Church Institute; but it has been entirely at my own expense: I doubt whether I am justified in carrying on what a successor may not be in a position to pay for, and this year I have discontinued such services, the experience of some years showing that there is no real demand for the services and they must be <u>perfectly free</u> if attendance is desired.

6. Number of Roman Catholics in the Parish. None.

1. See 1914.

STOKE, SOUTH WITH WOODCOTE[1] Incumbent H. G. Nind[2]

1. Number of Boys Girls and Infants on books of day schools: a. Last year. 82 at S. Stoke: Mixed 59, Infants 23; 71 at Woodcote: Mixed 51, Infants 20. Total 153. **b. 20 30 or 40 years ago.** S. Stoke: mixed 36, Infants 24 = 60; Woodcote: mixed 46, Infants 23 = 69 [Total] 129.

2. a. Men and b. Women qualified to vote in Parochial Church meeting. Only one that I am aware of.

3. Moral and Spiritual effect of: a. Wartime b. National Mission.

I think that all are more thoughtful and sober minded than they were, there is also a greater amount of courtesy and thought for others, and an increasing tendency to thrift, but whether it is due more to war, or the effects of the National Mission, I cannot pretend to say. There is also a better attendance of the women and the younger members of the Parish at the services of the church.

4. Status of Church Schools. Options for compromise on a. management, b. head teachers, c. character of religious teaching. Might compromise be justified by better arrangements for Church teaching in state schools?

The schools throughout the parish have been under a Board for about 46 or 47 years, and have worked harmoniously under various teachers: our Managers consist of Churchmen and Non-Conformists, and we have hitherto had no interference from the N.U.T. so that I have not formed any clear view of the policy the Church should pursue, though it seems to me that it must ever be a policy of forbearance, of live and let live. At the present moment it seems idle to suggest anything, till we know clearly how we are going to stand in the future, as regards the Church and Education.

5 a. Changes in Public worship since 1914. b. Effects of the changes. The only changes have been weekly intercessory services and the insertion of Intercessor Prayers and Litanies, in our regular Services, since the war began. I think the effect of these is good.

6. Number of Roman Catholics in the Parish. I cannot say that there are any, except one woman who has lately come into the Parish, and is said to be a R.C.

1. See 1914.

STOKE TALMAGE Incumbent W. Lambert-Baker[1]

1. Number of Boys Girls and Infants on books of day schools: a. Last year. 25.

b. 20 30 or 40 years ago. From the Log Book: present Nov. 1884: 41; present Nov 1 1898: 35.

2. a. Men and b. Women qualified to vote in Parochial Church meeting. None.

3. Moral and Spiritual effect of: a. Wartime b. National Mission.

(a) War conditions have produced quite encouraging results to our church life. It is remarkable that although many of our young people have been called away, there has been no falling back of church things in any direction but a tangible progress with the attendance and support.

(b) In this small place, I feel that the National Mission has been followed by encouraging signs of deepening religious life. There has been more prayer and more readiness to repair to Church for definite prayer and intercession and certain[l]y a deeper sense and experience of Sacramental Grace. More frequent attendance at the Blessed Sacrament has been marked amongst us.

4. Status of Church Schools. Options for compromise on a. management, b. head teachers, c. character of religious teaching. Might compromise be justified by better arrangements for Church teaching in state schools?

For the sake of Education generally, and so as not to hinder the passing into law of what certainly will be, when it comes, a great step forward in the national Education, I feel that the time is come for us to be willing to make compromises as to agree to the same basis for all schools (under the same type of management), to agree to no special religious qualifications for Head Teachers, but to demand as a minimum that religious teaching shall be given in all schools during the first hour of each day. And in return for our compromise to press for the acknowledgement of a claim that our clergy and Ministers of Religion and other qualified religious teachers should have a right of entry into all schools for definite denominational teaching.

5 a. Changes in Public worship since 1914. b. Effects of the changes. None.

6. Number of Roman Catholics in the Parish. None.

1. William Lambert-Baker graduated from St John's College Cambridge in 1897 and trained at Wycliffe Hall Oxford in 1898, being ordained priest in 1900. He served three curacies 1899–1906 and then was Vicar of St Matthew Duddleston between 1906 and 1915, when he became Rector of Stoke Talmage. He was 43 in 1918. William was absent from home at the 1911 census but was described as married.

STOKENCHURCH   Incumbent F. C. Load[1]

1. Number of Boys Girls and Infants on books of day schools: a. Last year. Council Schools: 82, 86, 90 (258) [age] between 5 and 14.

b. 20 30 or 40 years ago. In 1875, between ages of 3 yrs and 13: 397. (No separate numbers can be obtained.)

2. a. Men and b. Women qualified to vote in Parochial Church meeting. (a) 9 men only have signed: since it was always decided not to hold elections in war-time, owing to absence of men (260) from Parish. This year another effort is to be made and already those who can qualify have been advised and declaration to be signed will be carried to each. (I may as well say that the opinion has been that as there had been no re-election of Secular bodies, there was no need for these elections, Parochial and Diocesan.)

3. Moral and Spiritual effect of: a. Wartime b. National Mission.

It is more than difficult to answer these questions particularly the first, since it is probably only the long after effects that will be permanent. It is difficult, too, to judge anything apart from the influence of the war.

(a) To me it seems that the sudden and unwarranted increase in wages (boys of 15 in the chair trade being paid 25/- a week; log carters £2–5 and so on) seems to have unbalanced most of the working class. In the same way traders and chair masters finding they make large profits spend more lavishly just as their employees do – only they apologise for their extra efforts and increase by protesting they do all as war-work. However it may be it appears to me as if they find something not quite right in their extra money or even in the way they were [working], something that does not square with their religion. I cannot find that any sect can claim much spiritual awakening if any from the war. On Sunday evenings there are good congregations in church but fewer <u>communions </u>have been made in the last two years, and the weekday intercessions for our sailors and soldiers have never been attended by more than a dozen and latterly by one or two. I have never seen any Good Friday so given up to work as this one. Men and even women frequent public houses more than in peace-times – The women work like men and seem to suffer morally and spiritually. Returned soldiers continue the same life as before serving i.e. the man who came to church or chapel does the same again; the man who went nowhere does not attend now; the man who drank drinks as before; and so on. One of the worst sights to me is that increased wages has brought no idea of betterment. These people still demand the same charity, the same relief, medical and otherwise, as needed by their smaller wage – these amounts are greater every day. It is invidious to speak of the better class when the parish holds but 3 or 4 such, tho I can say that the chief family has given the greatest support not only in religious matters but a good lead in every way. I wish I could say the same of the others.

4. Status of Church Schools. Options for compromise on a. management, b. head teachers, c. character of religious teaching. Might compromise be justified by better arrangements for Church teaching in state schools?

(1) Were I in such an area, I would hold on to the Church School at all costs. (2) (a) might be met by compromise but (b) and (c) represent to my mind all the differences that Church Schools make.

(3) One could not be certain that the conditions would be carried out any better than they are at present. Some ways of teaching religious truth kill some more easily than no religion. As I am now in a parish that has always had its state school I am able every minute to compare the children and people with those of other parishes I know and have known. The Church School in these seems to make all the difference in courtesy, refinement and morality quite apart from the religious hold of the Church in such parishes. I am speaking of Country Parishes and I would say that in the Parish with its Church School you find more real self-respect, more understanding and more content amongst all classes than in the others. The Church Schoolmaster is most often a Religious man and it affects every part of his work.

5 a. Changes in Public worship since 1914. b. Effects of the changes. (a) Have used after the third Collect at Evensong on Sundays Intercession and Prayers in Time of War. Latterly have used the sung Metrical Litany of Intercession followed by two or three of the usual prayers. This Litany has been sung by all, kneeling. (b) Much more interest has been displayed by the people since the singing of this Litany in which they all make the petition. N.B. I have noticed that on Saints Days which fall on Sundays and Great Festivals the people as a whole always express their pleasure at there being a Procession at Evensong.

6. Number of Roman Catholics in the Parish. [*No response*].

1. See 1914.

STONESFIELD   Incumbent T. Kane[1]

1. Number of Boys Girls and Infants on books of day schools: a. Last year. b. 20 30 or 40 years ago.

Council School		Mixed	Infant	Total
(a) Number on books year ending Feb 28th	1918	64	34	98
(b) Number on books year ending Feb 28th	1885	78	49	127

2. a. Men and b. Women qualified to vote in Parochial Church meeting. None.

3. Moral and Spiritual effect of: a. Wartime b. National Mission.

(a) If anything there is a greater tendency for men to think more about religion. (b) Only having been appointed to this parish in October 1917 I am not in a position to express an opinion.

4. Status of Church Schools. Options for compromise on a. management, b. head teachers, c. character of religious teaching. Might compromise be justified by better arrangements for Church teaching in state schools?

I am absolutely convinced from the general conduct of children taught in Church Schools compared with the conduct of those taught in Council Schools, that we should strive to retain our Church Schools in their present status.

5 a. Changes in Public worship since 1914. b. Effects of the changes. (a) None. (b) None.

6. Number of Roman Catholics in the Parish. None.

1. Thomas Kane graduated from the Royal University of Ireland in 1891 and was ordained priest in 1893. After an initial curacy 1892–94 he became a naval chaplain, serving in a total of ten ships between 1904 and 1914 and ending at the Royal Naval Hospital, Haulbowline 1914–17. He was listed as retired in 1917 but was appointed as Rector of Stonesfield that year. He was 53 in 1918 and at the 1911 census he was listed as married but was serving as a chaplain on board HMS *Queen*.

STRATTON AUDLEY[1]   Incumbent W. E. Sawyer[2]

1. Number of Boys Girls and Infants on books of day schools: a. Last year. b. 20 30 or 40 years ago.

(a) Boys 16, Girls 19, Infants 18.

(b) In 1901 there were 36 boys and 34 girls, But I cannot say how many of these were infants.

2. a. Men and b. Women qualified to vote in Parochial Church meeting. 9 men. 5 women.

3. Moral and Spiritual effect of: a. Wartime b. National Mission.

(a) Judging from attendance at Intercession Services, I do not think the War has had any spiritual effect on the richer people in this Parish. Neither at Special War Celebrations of the Holy Communion nor at Intercessions at Evensong have any of them attended during the whole course of the War. With regard to the poorer class, I think there has been a decided deepening of the spiritual life, with more regard to the importance of the Holy Communion, and far more attendance at weekday evensong. The moral tone of the Parish is good, with one exception.

(b) It is more difficult to write of the effect of the National Mission, as I feel that any failure is my fault, as I undertook the conduct of it myself though I had no experience of Missions. The richer class practically ignored it all through. The poorer people attended the special services fairly well. The number of communicants in the Parish is high.

4. Status of Church Schools. Options for compromise on a. management, b. head teachers, c. character of religious teaching. Might compromise be justified by better arrangements for Church teaching in state schools?

I do not feel myself qualified in answering the above questions.

5 a. Changes in Public worship since 1914. b. Effects of the changes. (a) There are more frequent Celebrations at an early hour. On the first Sunday in each month and on all the great Festivals there is a choral Celebration at 11, Mattins being said at 10. (b) The effect of more frequent and earlier Celebrations is distinctly encouraging. I strongly believe that if we are going to get the country popula[tion] to the Holy Communion we must have services sometimes at 5 and 6. The attendance at the monthly Choral Celebration is about the same as we get at the 11 am mattins.

6. Number of Roman Catholics in the Parish. One man. No women or children.

1. Population 305.
2. William Ellis Sawyer graduated from Trinity College Cambridge in 1900 and trained at Wells Theological College, being ordained priest in 1902. He served three curacies between 1901 and 1914, when he became Vicar of Stratton Audley. He was 39 in 1918 and at the 1911 census he shared a household with his wife, his young son and daughter, their nurse and two unmarried female servants.

SUMMERTOWN   Incumbent R. M. Hay[1]

1. Number of Boys Girls and Infants on books of day schools: a. Last year. b. 20 30 or 40 years ago.

Church Schools		Boys	Girls	Infants
Numbers on books in	1918	125	147	149
	1878	57	45	90 (approximately)

2. a. Men and b. Women qualified to vote in Parochial Church meeting. 32 men, 87 women.

3. Moral and Spiritual effect of: a. Wartime b. National Mission.

(a) I notice a considerable change brought about towards the idea of death especially among the middle class whose attitude hitherto has been neither the ready familiarity of the poor, nor the semi-stoic reserve of the patricians. The previously narrow outlook has become widened and the subject of death and a future life is more readily discussed in all its bearings.

Arising partly out of this and other common problems of War time, one has noticed an increase of sympathy and mutual understanding between different classes. One outstanding moral effect has been the reduction of snobbishness arising from common privations and measures of universal application, food rationing etc. Very marked is the increased generosity of all classes in all directions. It looks as though a habit of giving and indeed of service generally has arisen, probably as a result of the willing response to national calls. The man who pays income tax cheerfully will submit to other exactions of a less compulsory nature with something akin to pleasure. On the other side I have noticed a marked declension in the discipline and tone of the elder children of school age. In many cases this is set off by a rapid assumption of responsibility on leaving school and finding themselves put to adult's work at high wages. In other cases it continues (especially with the girls) and has disastrous results.

(b) I find it extremely difficult to put anything down to the account of the National Mission exclusively. Probably the greatest benefit came from the period of preparation when the spirit of serving and the sense of the need for spiritual progress was very marked among the faithful. The mission itself had extremely little effect on those less closely attached to the Church.

4. Status of Church Schools. Options for compromise on a. management, b. head teachers, c. character of religious teaching. Might compromise be justified by better arrangements for Church teaching in state schools?

I have never had any experience of single school areas, and do not know the details of the problem, but from my experience with School Management in London and Oxford I should say as regards (a) compromise in the question of management might readily be conceded, but after the first onset would probably result in a return to the existing state of affairs, because I do not believe that in the majority of instances Nonconformists would take the trouble to accept their share (if offered) in the management. (b) I should be very strongly against any surrender of the rights of Church School Managers under this head. (c) I should favour permission being granted to Nonconformists and others to teach their own children in our schools. I think the competition thus created would be healthy for both parties. But I should oppose any modification of Church teaching to suit the views of outsiders.

5 a. Changes in Public worship since 1914. b. Effects of the changes. The only differences introduced during my incumbency have been (a) to put Choral Eucharist at a fixed hour of 11.30 every Sunday morning, preceded by Choral Mattins. This has resulted practically in a largely increased attendance at the Eucharist, without affecting attendance at Mattins – thus giving a double congregation on Sunday mornings. (b) Daily Eucharist, has led to more frequent communions and an increased sense of corporate Church life.

6. Number of Roman Catholics in the Parish. No certain statistics but I should say about 10 or 12 families actually in the parish.

1. Robert Milton Hay graduated from St John's College Oxford in 1908 and trained at Wells Theological College, being ordained priest in 1910. He was Curate of St Pancras between 1909 and 1915, when he became Vicar of Summertown. He was 33 in 1918 and at the 1911 census he shared a household with his wife, their infant son, his nurse and one other unmarried female servant.

SWALCLIFFE WITH SHUTFORD   Incumbent V. W. Peake[1]

1. Number of Boys Girls and Infants on books of day schools: a. Last year. b. 20 30 or 40 years ago.

Swalcliffe Day School (Church)

	Mixed school	Infants	Total
(a)	10 boys 15 girls	6 boys 8 girls	39

(b) In the year 1876: 23 boys, 27 girls = 50 in schools; further details cannot be found.

Shutford Church School (Day)

	Mixed School	Infants	Total
(a)	18 Boys 16 Girls	14 boys 4 girls	52

(b) In the year 1878,: <u>average attendance</u> 55.6 further details cannot be found.

2. a. Men and b. Women qualified to vote in Parochial Church meeting. (a and b) None. I intended to get a Parochial Church Council started here if possible and have mentioned it to some of the parishioners. But now I am leaving it to the next man.

3. Moral and Spiritual effect of: a. Wartime b. National Mission.

Judging from the outward observance of the duties of Religion, neither the war nor the National Mission seem to have made any difference at all. With regard to morals there is no difference, one way or the other. With regard to spiritual things there seems to be no improvement. In Swalcliffe and Shutford there has been a slight improvement in the attendance at Matins and Evensong, specially the latter, and more communions have been made. I attribute this to visiting preaching and teaching. I was talking to a young man, who is a communicant, and has worked on a farm all his life, and was home here, and I asked him whether he thought the war had had a good effect on the men of the parish and his answer was – "they are worse than they were." This answer only refers to the men who have been working all the time of the war on the farms about here.

4. Status of Church Schools. Options for compromise on a. management, b. head teachers, c. character of religious teaching. Might compromise be justified by better arrangements for Church teaching in state schools?

(a) I cannot say I have any clear view of the policy which the Church ought to pursue with regard to the status of Church Schools in single school areas. But from my experience since 1884 during which time I have had to do with 4 village schools (not including Swalcliffe and Shutford) I have never had any trouble about the Church teaching given in Church Schools. One of those 4 schools was a "board school" and I was elected one of the managers, in that school the Bible was allowed to be read but not explained, and I could not get anything done to improve matters. There we invited the school children to come to church at 4-30 pm once a week for service and instruction, and the majority of the children came. This custom still continues in that parish. In the 3 Church Schools the non-conformists were quite willing the children should receive the full teaching given in those schools. Tact is the great thing needed. With regard to (b) it seems very unfair to allow a nonconformist or a non Christian to be headteacher in a Church School, unless provision is made for the religious teaching to be given by a churchman or woman. There is not too much <u>definite</u> teaching in Church Schools, but still too little. With respect to (c), if the authorities will allow the clergy to give definite Church Teaching to Church Children, in Provided or Council Schools, then I would be prepared to allow nonconformists to give their particular teaching to their children in Church Schools. But I doubt very much whether they would avail themselves of the privilege. The nonconformists very much wanted to be allowed to take Burial Services in our consecrated church yards. The Bill was passed allowing them to do so. But very seldom do they use this privilege, in the country at least generally the nonconformists prefer the Vicar to bury their dead, so I have found.

5 a. Changes in Public worship since 1914. b. Effects of the changes. I have a Sung Eucharist on one Sunday in each lunar month at Swalcliffe and likewise at Shutford. Weekly Eucharist at 8 am on Sundays. Saints Days 7.30 am. Evensong on Saturdays at 5 pm. Wednesday service at Shutford at 4.30 with address in Lent, without at other times. Daily Matins. Wednesday Eucharist at 7.30 am. I have often addressed the people both at Evensong on Sundays and on other special occasions on Weekdays, standing in the Nave and walking about and talking to them. It seemed to be appreciated. (b) The people are beginning to see that the Eucharist is <u>the</u> Christian service. But country people move very slowly, it takes <u>several years</u> to move them!

6. Number of Roman Catholics in the Parish. In Shutford, 4 men (R.C.) 2 women (R.C.). The children of these R.C.'s attend the Church Day School and the Sunday School and the Services in Church. None of the grown up R.C.'s ever go to the RC Church at Wroxton which is about 3 miles off, nor to Banbury RC Church. They never go to Confession nor to Mass.

1. Vincent William Peake graduated from St Edmund Hall Oxford in 1883 and was ordained priest in 1885. He served three curacies 1884–1907, was then Vicar of Hoveton 1907–16 and of Swalcliffe with Shutford 1916–18, and then became Vicar of Horley with Hornton. He was 57 in 1918 and at the 1911 census he was sharing a household with his wife, two daughters and their governess together with two unmarried female servants.

SWERFORD

Incumbent C. J. Shebbeare[1]

1. Number of Boys Girls and Infants on books of day schools: a. Last year. b. 20 30 or 40 years ago.

(a) just under 40. (b) 20 years ago: about 60.

2. a. Men and b. Women qualified to vote in Parochial Church meeting. None.

3. Moral and Spiritual effect of: a. Wartime b. National Mission.

(a) The people, as a whole, have taken very reasonable views of the war. There has been considerable liberality, in relation to the general poverty of the parish, towards War Charities; the Food Economy question has been taken up with a good deal of enthusiasm, especially by a Committee selected by the Parish Council and consisting of men and women both of the farming and labouring classes. On the other hand, the Intercession Services (except some of the services in the earliest days of the War) have not been well attended, and attended curiously little by those whose sons and brothers are fighting. Several of the people here, chiefly women have said pretty freely that the War has destroyed, or shaken, their belief in God.

(b) The services at the opening of the National Mission, while Mr Emmet was staying here, were well attended, and one of the meetings held preparatory to those services before he came was very encouraging. The very bad weather, and my illness, which followed very close upon the conclusion of Mr Emmet's visit, made it difficult to trace visible results and prevented me from following up the work in the way that I had planned. This winter an outcome of the Mission has taken the form of a Study Circle. The meetings have been attended with good regularity and have resulted in some real Bible study and some genuine discussion. I had hoped to revive the weekly Prayer Meeting which continued for many years till some 5 or 6 years ago, and were for years very well attended both winter and summer. After years of regular attendances the Meeting very rapidly declined. I had almost taken for granted that those who were the mainstay of the Prayer Meeting would attend the Study Circle meetings. But so far this has not happened. The Mothers' Union have done good work in the last year or so, and I hope during the summer to have services for mothers etc while the children are at school.

4. Status of Church Schools. Options for compromise on a. management, b. head teachers, c. character of religious teaching. Might compromise be justified by better arrangements for Church teaching in state schools?

I am afraid that my views on this subject are that of a very small minority of the Clergy. What I feel most strongly is that the present system tends to make each teacher present to the children a <u>minimum</u> of his or her personal religious convictions. They say to themselves "I must not say <u>this</u>, or I shall not be dealing fairly with the children of dissenters: I must not say <u>that</u>, or I shall not be dealing fairly with the children of strong Churchmen." So far as I have had opportunity of observation, the teaching in Church Schools hardly differs from that in Council Schools. The Church teachers do not usually give the teaching which the clergy wish, and perhaps suppose, them to give. I, therefore, should welcome almost any compromise that put an end to the sense of grievance. I think that the present system sets up the backs of some teachers and of many nonconformists and that in many schools the Church gets little or nothing in return for this disadvantage. If such a thing were possible, I should like to see a system under which (with safeguards against bitterly controversial teaching such as would justly be offensive to consciences on the one side or the other) we could all agree to encourage the individual teachers, High, Low or Broad, to teach what they themselves really feel most strongly and believe with most conviction. This does not seem to me impossible. But I am afraid that your Lordship will regard me as an enthusiastic dreamer.

5 a. Changes in Public worship since 1914. b. Effects of the changes. (a) We have occasionally had Weekday service of Holy Communion at 7.30 and on the whole these have been well attended. Between the 3rd Collect and the Grace I habitually substitute War Intercessions for the State Prayers. The form of these Intercessions varies from Sunday to Sunday. Sometimes I have led the Intercessions in extempore prayer from the Pulpit. Some of the members of the Congregation like and approve this latter method. Some of them, I am pretty sure, find it uncongenial. (b) On the whole, as compared with the days of from 1900 onwards, when there was a movement of very remarkable religious earnestness in the village which touched Church and Chapel alike, there is now a much feebler interest in spiritual things and the National Mission has not changed things for the better as much as I had hoped. There is no <u>hostility</u> to religion, but a disconcerting deadness: though there are still a 'little flock' who keep up steady religious ways.

6. Number of Roman Catholics in the Parish. None.

I am afraid that my answer to 5 (b) does not answer your question directly: but I do not know how better to describe the state of affairs.

1. See 1914.

SWINBROOK AND WIDFORD   Incumbent F. E. Foster C.F.[1] (3rd Bedford Regiment Land Guard, Felixstowe)

1. Number of Boys Girls and Infants on books of day schools: a. Last year. b. 20 30 or 40 years ago.

(a) 1917: 14 infants, 6 boys, 18 girls. Total 38. (b) 1887: 14 infants, 12 boys, 24 girls. Total 50.

2. a. Men and b. Women qualified to vote in Parochial Church meeting. None. The parish has only about 200 inhabitants.

3. Moral and Spiritual effect of: a. Wartime b. National Mission.

(a) The moral condition of the parish during war time has been unchanged, generally good, there have been marriages with young girls in consequence of the war conditions, that way an improvement has been made as those young girls were such as would perhaps cause trouble.

(b) The National Mission certainly did good, fortunately we had two excellent women messengers (I forget the name they were called by) and the Church army did some good. Country people always rally round any one coming to help them in "a mission way" – our communicants perhaps wanted a little stiffening which they got by the Mission and we had an extra communicant or two.

4. Status of Church Schools. Options for compromise on a. management, b. head teachers, c. character of religious teaching. Might compromise be justified by better arrangements for Church teaching in state schools?

I think we should make a compromise, in fairly large church-schools in single areas, a nonconformist teacher should be appointed to take the nonconformist children and in council schools the same facility should be allowed for C of E children. I should be sorry to see and should think it very unfair to have a nonconformist head teacher in a church school. As regards my parish no complaint has ever been made during the last 20 years by a non-conformist and at the present time every child in the village comes to the Sunday catechising in church and in school. I should very much object to delineate any particular kind of Church Teaching from the Diocesan Syllabus because of a few nonconformist children in the class, if parents objected the children could be withdrawn for that lesson, or in a larger school they could be put into one class and taught by a nonconformist teacher.

5 a. Changes in Public worship since 1914. b. Effects of the changes. The only change is that we have a celebration every Sunday whereas before the war we had two a month. We had extra on Saints Days and Festivals of course. We have introduced now and again choral communion.

6. Number of Roman Catholics in the Parish. None.

1. See 1914.

SWYNCOMBE   Incumbent C. A. K. Irwin[1]

1. Number of Boys Girls and Infants on books of day schools: a. Last year. b. 20 30 or 40 years ago.

(a) Boys 19, Girls 17, Infants 25. Total 61. (b) 40 to 25 years ago: varied from 55 to 70.

20 years ago: temporarily up to 120, owing to extra paroch. children – dropping to 100 and 90 and present figure.

2. a. Men and b. Women qualified to vote in Parochial Church meeting. Records missing.

3. Moral and Spiritual effect of: a. Wartime b. National Mission.

(a) General unsettlement leading to discontinuance of traditional habits, but a fine readiness to accept the inevitable, and bear the extra burdens of labour in both sexes and all ages, testifying the existence of a moral conscience. The unashamed lasciviousness of many of the younger women is indisputable, but is not in evidence in the area of this particular parish. Generally speaking there seems to be in sexual matters an unstable condition, and no sufficiently definite standard – a temporary wave of unsettlement. Spiritually – an uneasy lethargy and almost paralysis of religious feeling, prejudicial to previous habits and Church attendance. Even in the case of Communicants, but the external pressure of anxiety and overwork must be taken into account. Indications of a reawakening begin to manifest themselves.

(b) Apparently without any result, but I am convinced that such a statement does not conclude the matter. It may be impossible to point to definite result as yet, but impression was made, and fruit will follow. At any rate a second effort will profit by experience of the many mistakes of the first. The talk of Reunion seems frequently to be interpreted to mean that it does not matter much what we believe, and so to prejudice sound doctrine and definite faith.

4. Status of Church Schools. Options for compromise on a. management, b. head teachers, c. character of religious teaching. Might compromise be justified by better arrangements for Church teaching in state schools?

The alleged difficulty of single-school areas was at the best a manufactured grievance and the problem, such as it was, has been a steadily vanishing one. Any compromise as to (c) would be fatal to our whole position, especially in view of the possibility of disestablishment, in which case we should be able to take the same stand as the Roman Church. Any compromise now would prejudice fatally our case. And <u>anything less</u> than equal freedom for all in Provided Schools would be just such a prejudicial compromise. (a) is already nominal only, and (b) is becoming so.

5 a. Changes in Public worship since 1914. b. Effects of the changes. (a) Holy Communion from 8.0 am to 7.30 am. (b) None.

6. Number of Roman Catholics in the Parish. One woman.

1. See 1914.

SYDENHAM

Incumbent W. Morris[1]

1. Number of Boys Girls and Infants on books of day schools: a. Last year. b. 20 30 or 40 years ago.

a. 51: Boys 19, Girls 16, Inf. 16. b. 93.

2. a. Men and b. Women qualified to vote in Parochial Church meeting. [*No response*].

3. Moral and Spiritual effect of: a. Wartime b. National Mission.

(a) I do not note that the war has produced any marked effect, but the results of (b) the National Mission is shown specially in a more ready response to appeals for prayer.

4. Status of Church Schools. Options for compromise on a. management, b. head teachers, c. character of religious teaching. Might compromise be justified by better arrangements for Church teaching in state schools?

This being a Single School Area, I feel very strongly that the school should be retained at all costs, as the influence over the children and through them over the parish generally is very great. We do not meet with any difficulties regarding management, or the question of religious teaching.

5 a. Changes in Public worship since 1914. b. Effects of the changes. I have made very small changes in the services as they are on the whole well attended and seem to meet the needs of the parish. In some cases I have introduced greater freedom in the use of the prayers after the 3rd collect in the evening service.

6. Number of Roman Catholics in the Parish. 1 woman.

1. See 1914.

TACKLEY   Incumbent G. Perry Gore[1]

1. Number of Boys Girls and Infants on books of day schools: a. Last year. Boys 13, Girls 20, Infants 24. **b. 20 30 or 40 years ago.** Ten years ago: 77. Twenty years ago: 67. Thirty years ago: 63. Only the totals have been preserved.

2. a. Men and b. Women qualified to vote in Parochial Church meeting. I have only quite recently been able to take the first steps towards creating the Qualified Electors Roll and so far only a very few have responded. Note: The Church Wardens of 44 years and 20 years standing are not exactly progressively inclined.

3. Moral and Spiritual effect of: a. Wartime b. National Mission.

(a) It has certainly sobered and solemnized life with most of the people, and has enlarged their sense of fellowship and sympathy.

(b) One of the chief gains has been I think to increase the disposition to witness for God on the part of some of the Church people. It has certainly increased the volume and intensity of Prayer both (1) In the Church and (2) In the Home. It is I think a present leaven and not merely a past event.

4. Status of Church Schools. Options for compromise on a. management, b. head teachers, c. character of religious teaching. Might compromise be justified by better arrangements for Church teaching in state schools?

I increasingly incline to the conviction that it would be wise to admit a larger share of public interest and control in the (a) Management (b) Appointment of Head Teachers (c) Religious teaching.

Note: Both my experience by teaching in the old Board Schools in Nottingham in the eighties and my observation of the working out of the method in Queensland the year before last confirms me in this conviction. In Nottingham the results were invariably encouraging with Managers, Teachers and Children. In Queensland It seemed to me to inspire a much larger interest in our own clergy with the whole matter of Education and particularly of the Religious responsibility.

In Tackley I found a certain soreness existing owing to the Wesleyans being denied the use of the Schools for any social purpose and some of the children were withdrawn from Church attendance for Religious Instruction. On the second Sunday after my institution I visited the Wesleyan S. School and subsequently made it known they could have access for Religious Instruction if desired. I consented a few months since to our own S. School children uniting in a Home reading association of the Scriptures. Result – not a single child is now withdrawn from church attendance. A few weeks ago I was asked to give an address on the Bible at the Wesleyan chapel to the members and parents of the Association which I was glad to do.

5 a. Changes in Public worship since 1914. b. Effects of the changes. (a) 1. Have increased gradually the said portions of the Sunday Offices. 2. Have adopted with considerable edification the Bidding method at all extra-liturgical prayer from the pulpit. 3. Have ordered and used the chancel as a choir-chapel and instituted a Saturday Evening Service of preparation for the Sunday. This is the 5th parish in which I have established this Service and have always found it met a want. The chapel helps here to break down shyness and to enlarge the sense of fellowship.

6. Number of Roman Catholics in the Parish. None.

1. See 1914.

TADMARTON   Incumbent A. E. Riddle[1]

1. Number of Boys Girls and Infants on books of day schools: a. Last year. 15 boys, 16 girls, 12 infants – total 43. **b. 20 30 or 40 years ago.** 11 boys, 19 girls (9 under 5, 11 under 6) 20* under 7 Total 50 for yr. ending 31/12/1876.

*in proportion of 3 girls to 2 boys.

2. a. Men and b. Women qualified to vote in Parochial Church meeting. None.

3. Moral and Spiritual effect of: a. Wartime b. National Mission.

It appears unavoidable that the answers to the two sections of this question should overlap. Being directed to conserve energy as much as possible in the conducting of the N. M., I acted as my own Missioner in this small village, chiefly concentrating on the women and children as the men were absorbed in their work. For the children I held, with the sanction of the Managers and L.E.A., a simple service of intercession from 9–9.45 am every Monday morning for 8 weeks from Oct 9th – Nov 27th with short addresses on humility, obedience, sympathy, unselfishness, purity, truthfulness, patience and love (culminating in self-sacrifice); for adults, special services in School with addresses <u>ad hoc</u> at 7 pm from Nov 1st – 29th. At this there was fair attendance at first, but a falling away towards the end. To one it was a matter of some surprise that the Mission was not set on foot until the war had been in progress for two years an element of weakness ab initio. As regards effect on character and spiritual growth subtle influences may be making themselves felt, but any result is for the most part hidden from observation, though in a few instances one is inclined to notice a more serious outlook on life and a more conscious dependence upon God though this may be attributable more to the general impression made by the war than to the incidence of the National Mission. As the war progressed the imagination of a people so remote as the villages of Mid-England is gradually being awakened by such things as restriction in food and the irregularity of the post, intelligence of great importance being sometimes delayed; such things make people think and trace them to their source. When by an accumulation of such comparative trifles, the situation has been fully grasped, then the creature may be ready to acknowledge his own comparative helplessness and seek back to the Creator. But this in general. In detail, I should lean towards a more hopeful and encouraging conclusion, though the premises are confused. Regarding the population of Tadmarton sectionally we have (a) "Gentry", (b) Farmers and others, (c) i. Labourers and ii. small tradesmen.

Out of 5 of (a) I should say the effect on 3 is practically nil while 2 are deeply impressed, diligent in work and regular in intercession. On (b) I fear I must again report "Nil", except so far as personal inconvenience is felt. There is no retrogression from former standards, but neither is there any levelling up. Owing to increased demand on personal industry they are to a considerable extent hindered from attendance to outward religious observances. In "others" I am chiefly thinking of the ex-schoolmaster, who, though far above the general average, yet seems entirely unable to visualize the situation religiously, and never once has attended special Intercessory Services between Sundays; if this is to be regarded as an index.

Of (c) I should say, again taking the weekly Intercession Service as test, that the men are entirely preoccupied with their work on farm or allotment, and therefore can hardly be expected to attend, but some of their wives and of the women of ii together with 2 of (a) and the present School teachers form a little knot of suppliants some coming at one time some at another, who continuously week by week plead with GOD that He may see fit to deliver us from battle and murder by virtue of His own Agony, Cross, and Passion; and that it would please Him to succour, help and comfort all who are in danger, to preserve travellers by land or water, to shew pity upon prisoners and captives, to comfort the bereaved and oppressed to have mercy upon all, to forgive our enemies, to give us the fruits of the earth and finally to give us true repentance. Of course this pleading is not everything, but it points to a certain steadfastness of purpose and seriousness of spirit which obtains with some and may influence others.

4. Status of Church Schools. Options for compromise on a. management, b. head teachers, c. character of religious teaching. Might compromise be justified by better arrangements for Church teaching in state schools?

<u>Prima facie</u> it would appear that, as the Church was the pioneer of "Elementary Education" in this country, so far as its extension to <u>all</u> classes is concerned such that without her efforts such Education would be in a very elementary state indeed, she ought to be allowed to conduct the education she provides according to her own religious principles, and, if a School conducted by her is the only School in a given area the parents of children attending it should rest content that their children should be instructed in accordance with its syllabus in <u>all</u> respects. But, insomuch as the El. "Ed." Act of 1870 was but the sequel to and outcome of the Church's early movement, she herself is to be regarded in a sense to have been the instigator of that Act. She was in a secondary manner its creator. Therefore she, in her turn, should be content to waive her doctrinal religious tenets in the case of Nonconformists, as far as such tenets are contained in her set formulae, in consideration of the genesis of the Act, as above stated, and of the immense gain of universal education secured by her own early efforts in that direction. Moreover, as Education is now compulsory, it would seem unjust to compel parents to send their children to a School where religious instruction is given on lines of which they honestly disapprove. It is true that such children may be withdrawn or rather excluded from such instruction, but in that case they, for the most part, get no religious instruction at all. There is no difficulty made about the matter here (Tadmarton). In the course of 32 years, I do not remember a single case of withdrawal from such teaching which includes P.B. Catechism, nor even of complaint. And it is no doubt the same in many another parish. Still, looking at the matter as a whole, I should be inclined to favour a compromise as regards (c), which would apparently involve (a) and (b), especially if more satisfactory conditions of religious teaching in Council Schools would be thereby secured. Much, however, would depend upon the nature of the compromise it would seem impossible in many cases to over-ride the terms of the Trust Deeds.

This cutting is from the "Banbury Guardian" of March 20th in an account of a meeting of the local branch of the N.U.T.

'THE NEW EDUCATION BILL – "THE RIGHT OF ENTRY" ONCE MORE

The Chairman then made some observations on the new Education Bill, in which he said there was nothing new, for the teachers had been asking for what the bill proposed to do for thirty or forty years. The N.U.T. had been asking for this measure ever since it was started, so there was nothing new in it as far as the teaching profession was concerned. Asking what education was, he said his idea of education was the growth and development and culture of child life, so as to enable the child to start on an honourable and worthy career – (applause) – and to instil into its mind happier, brighter and ampler views of life here and hereafter. He thought that Mr. Fisher had somehow got the right conception of the problem of the education of the child, and he (Mr. Dommett) should like to know who put him up to it – (a laugh). The Bill, the speaker said, was the *habeas corpus* of the child, and Mr. Fisher had said that the Bill was for the child's physical, mental, moral and spiritual benefit, and on each of these things the speaker enlarged, showing their advantage not only to the child but to the State. One good point in the bill was that it differentiated as to the abilities of the children, which was an important matter. He deprecated Mr. Fisher's speaking of "the children of the poor," which he characterised as unbecoming for a man in Mr. Fisher's position*, and vigorously condemned the attitude of a number of Lancashire mill owners in the matter of child labour. He went on to remark that certain people spoke somewhat patronisingly of "elementary schools," and loftily of public schools, which were not public – (a laugh) – and secondary schools, some of which he knew were very secondary. He quoted the *Church Times* as saying they must come to some agreement on the religious question, but they must not give up any principle, and the speaker said that he did not see how they could come to an agreement under those circumstances. In towns such as Banbury he could see that the schools were going to be "mixed up," and what was wanted by some was the old idea of "the right of entry," and unless the teachers were alive and active they would find people coming to their schools to see whether the Lord's Prayer and the Ten Commandments were properly said.'

*Why? [*Added in manuscript.*]

5 a. Changes in Public worship since 1914. b. Effects of the changes. The Holy Communion is now celebrated every 1st Sunday in the month at 11 am, with Sermon in appointed place, Matins having been said previously and the Litany being recited at Evensong. On all other Sundays there is a Celebration at 8 am. The 11 o'c Celebration seems to be appreciated. At the 8 am I don't think that there are ever so many Communicants as there used to be at the 3rd Sunday in the month Service, but the increased frequency of opportunity afforded fully makes up for this.

6. Number of Roman Catholics in the Parish. One family of the small farmer class, consisting of man and wife, one son at the front, and one daughter.

1. See 1914.

TAYNTON　　　　　　　　　　　　　　　　　　　　Incumbent J. L. Sloane[1]

1. Number of Boys Girls and Infants on books of day schools: a. Last year. b. 20 30 or 40 years ago.

(a) Boys 6, Girls 8, Infants 10. (b) Boys 0, Girls 12, Infants 19.

All elder boys went to Barrington School in 1878.

2. a. Men and b. Women qualified to vote in Parochial Church meeting. 30 men, 48 women.

3. Moral and Spiritual effect of: a. Wartime b. National Mission.

I was not here before the war but the only change I have noticed 1915–1918 is the decreased attendance at week day services especially and to a certain extent at Sunday services of women owing to work in the fields. Otherwise I cannot say I notice any change in any class.

The National Mission left us much as it found us.

4. Status of Church Schools. Options for compromise on a. management, b. head teachers, c. character of religious teaching. Might compromise be justified by better arrangements for Church teaching in state schools?

The difficulty does not arise here, we have only two nonconformist families and their children leave at Catechism. We never have any objection. There is no demand for change here and I cannot imagine how any change in theory of management would cause an actual alteration in personal [*sic*]. Certainly I am of the opinion that owing to the influence of headteacher and the importance of his character such proposals as made above would not be desirable. The difficulties in the way of getting rid of an unsatisfactory person in a country parish have been increased by 1902 Act. As we cannot expect these small schools to go on the secular work being so poor in consequence of numbers I think a compromise might be made. I certainly would prefer it to the retaining of Village School with less authority over the teacher.

5 a. Changes in Public worship since 1914. b. Effects of the changes. None.

6. Number of Roman Catholics in the Parish. None.

1. James Ledlie Sloane graduated from Trinity College Dublin in 1894 and was ordained priest in 1897. He served six curacies 1896–1914, was appointed Vicar of Great Barrington, Gloucs. in 1915 and Vicar of Taynton in the same year. He was 45 in 1918 and at the 1911 census he shared a household with his wife and one married female servant.

TETSWORTH   Incumbent P. O. Potter[1]

1. Number of Boys Girls and Infants on books of day schools: a. Last year. b. 20 30 or 40 years ago.

Present Year: 56, Last year: 56, Year 1901: 121.

2. a. Men and b. Women qualified to vote in Parochial Church meeting. Men 12, Women 20.

3. Moral and Spiritual effect of: a. Wartime b. National Mission.

We are gratefully conscious of a larger and deeper spiritual life. God is nearer to us.

Throughout the parish generally one feels that the spirit of worship is more marked: religious indifference is less pronounced.

4. Status of Church Schools. Options for compromise on a. management, b. head teachers, c. character of religious teaching. Might compromise be justified by better arrangements for Church teaching in state schools?

My own feeling is that the offer of more satisfactory conditions of religious teaching would justify some compromise.

5 a. Changes in Public worship since 1914. b. Effects of the changes. Our methods and hours of public worship remain the same.

6. Number of Roman Catholics in the Parish. One man, one woman, two children.

1. See 1914.

TEW, GREAT   Incumbent J. P. Malleson[1]

1. Number of Boys Girls and Infants on books of day schools: a. Last year. Boys 13, Girls 25, Infants 24. **b. 20 30 or 40 years ago.** 1879 (av. Attendance for whole school 79, – on roll say) 84.

2. a. Men and b. Women qualified to vote in Parochial Church meeting. None.

3. Moral and Spiritual effect of: a. Wartime b. National Mission.

(a) A willingness to give. This applies not only to War Funds, but to such a purpose as Foreign Missions. Our contribution to the latter has risen far beyond any former amount.

(b) I cannot point to anything definite.

4. Status of Church Schools. Options for compromise on a. management, b. head teachers, c. character of religious teaching. Might compromise be justified by better arrangements for Church teaching in state schools?

I would make no compromise in regard to management or appointment of head-teachers. I think facilities for nonconformists to give certain lessons to their children in our schools in single-school areas might be granted in return for similar facilities given to the Church in Council Schools.

5 a. Changes in Public worship since 1914. b. Effects of the changes. No changes of importance. In winter 1916–17 we had afternoon service in church on Sundays, owing to the lighting difficulty. In winter 1917–18, we had instead Evensong at the school at 6.0 pm. The latter was well attended and liked.

6. Number of Roman Catholics in the Parish. None.

1. See 1914.

TEW, LITTLE   Incumbent J. P. Malleson[1]

1. Number of Boys Girls and Infants on books of day schools: a. Last year. b. 20 30 or 40 years ago.

(a) Boys 5, Girls 15, Infants 7. (b) 1878: Boys 19, Girls 23, Infants 15.

2. a. Men and b. Women qualified to vote in Parochial Church meeting. None.

3. Moral and Spiritual effect of: a. Wartime b. National Mission.

I have nothing to report of Little Tew under these heads.

4. Status of Church Schools. Options for compromise on a. management, b. head teachers, c. character of religious teaching. Might compromise be justified by better arrangements for Church teaching in state schools?

See my answer on G. Tew paper.

5 a. Changes in Public worship since 1914. b. Effects of the changes. Only temporary changes due to the illness of my colleague Rev G. G. Tombe.

6. Number of Roman Catholics in the Parish. None.

1. See 1914 Great Tew. Malleson was given charge of Little Tew in addition to Great Tew in 1916.

THAME   Incumbent G. C. Bowring[1]

1. Number of Boys Girls and Infants on books of day schools: a. Last year. Mixed Sch. 101, Infants 50. **b. 20 30 or 40 years ago.** Mixed Sch: (1878) 127; Infants (1885) 54.

2. a. Men and b. Women qualified to vote in Parochial Church meeting. (a) 37. (b) 62.

3. Moral and Spiritual effect of: a. Wartime b. National Mission.

(a) Among the better classes the special demands of the war, due largely to the loss of servants, male and female, has thrown such burdens on many that their attendance at Divine Worship has been made really difficult. The Sunday morning drills of the V. T. C. have not been conducive to attendance at Divine Worship. I am assured by the O.C. that it is impossible to allow it on weekdays or the Sunday afternoon. The Sunday labour in the fields and now gardens [and] allotments has been another hindrance, in all classes, to attendance at church. It is difficult to say how far this last has come to stay but we trust not as not a few persons are making a definite stand against it. Among the lower classes there is less drunkenness but among the married women there have been not a few cases of marital infidelity. This has had a bad effect on the younger women. In this particular there is this specially sad feature, namely the early age at which girls go out with soldiers.

(b) The National Mission in this town laboured with much graver disabilities (a) The absence at the war of some of the very best men (b) the heavy strain placed on those left behind and (c) the strictness of the lighting order which plunged our town into utter darkness. These things made it very difficult to follow up the Mission as such an effort should be. It is admitted at every and all sides that the permanently beneficial result of a Mission depends very largely on the afterwork. Nevertheless there has been one very definite result viz. the greater impetus given to Bible Study so that the Sunday School Institute Bible Reading Union of this Parish has over 200 men very soon one hundred and twenty of whom are [sic] adults or have left school. Another definite result has been the greater care, spiritually and physically, that has been and is being devoted to young people of both sexes from 14–18.

4. Status of Church Schools. Options for compromise on a. management, b. head teachers, c. character of religious teaching. Might compromise be justified by better arrangements for Church teaching in state schools?

I should consider more satisfactory conditions of religious instruction in "Provided" Schools as justifying some very real compromises in (a), (b) and (c), provided always that the teaching of Church Doctrine to Church Children was adequately safeguarded.

5 a. Changes in Public worship since 1914. b. Effects of the changes. (a) <u>Methods</u>: we have slightly shortened the services as we found that the increasing strain of the war was not conducive to sustained attendance. We have made no alteration in the hours of public [worship] except in hours [of] services to meet the wants of the people.

(b) <u>Effects</u>: I think the above has helped a little to keep our young people together.

6. Number of Roman Catholics in the Parish. Men 4 Women 12 Children 12. The above numbers do not include the few Belgians still in Parish who are – 1 man, 3 women and 1 child.

1. See 1914.

WARDINGTON   Incumbent M. Kirkby[1]

1. Number of Boys Girls and Infants on books of day schools: a. Last year. b. 20 30 or 40 years ago.

This year 80. Forty years ago: about 90 to 100. NB as near as Mr Walton our old School master can tell 60 years ago: about 40. <u>Then</u> the Railway line being made raise[d] number to 100–150.

2. a. Men and b. Women qualified to vote in Parochial Church meeting. I have asked none to sign yet. My Communicants' roll is about at present 120. Of these possibly over 100 would be <u>asked</u> to sign. Our difficulty here, is the "Authority of the Old Vestry". No representative Church Council will be acceptable until the authority of the old vestry is taken away, and given to the new Parochial C. Council. I speak not for myself but as the majority here give me to understand to be their views.

3. Moral and Spiritual effect of: a. Wartime b. National Mission.

With the exception of one family which is absolutely without morals (each daughter as she grows up has illegitimate children) the state of the parish is distinctly good. There is very little drinking, very little uncleanness. The people are honest, and on the whole straightforward. All our young men has [sic] gone, without being fetched to the army. There is no grumbling. The people are saving and paying in about £4 weekly into the parish clubs (shoes, coal, clothing and saving). The number of communions made during the year is exceedingly good. In 1916 1900 were made – last year 1660. This year up to now 1540. At Easter the number will be over 1700. This is in spite of our lads away. A splendid sign is the fact that, as each lad comes home on Leave, we are sure of him (if a Communicant) making his Communion. The Sunday School has increased from 35 in 1914 to 75 this year. The principal services for children are the Catechism at 3 pm and the fortnightly Missa Cantata at 10 am.

We do not thank the National Mission so much as valuable help given by Father Cruran S.S.J.B.[2] (who held a short mission) also help by Father Frith S.B. Oxford now in London (also) The <u>Rev Fynes Clinton</u> of St Mary's Banbury. I speak for all classes.

4. Status of Church Schools. Options for compromise on a. management, b. head teachers, c. character of religious teaching. Might compromise be justified by better arrangements for Church teaching in state schools?

Yes. I think she should boldly teach the faith (The Catechism and Sacraments). My experience is the majority of parents look for it. The children hate a difference being made: some even think an insult is meant if you make a difference. Very few children in the Deanery are withdrawn – none here – from religious instruction. The parents even encourage their children if the chapel is closed to come to church and look to the church for much. We <u>must retain our Church Schools at all cost</u>. The N.U.T. is not altogether honest. It is sectarian and mostly in the hands of political Dissenters. No Compromise can be made without fatal results. (a) <u>The Management</u> is not ideal, but at present the Vicar picks out the most capable men to help him. Those <u>who at least know something about education</u>. If you look at the election of the parish council you will have some idea of what we should have to expect. "Turn and turn about" is what is considered <u>fairness</u> of election, without any regard to the fitness of office – and <u>the child suffers</u>. (b) The appointment of

Head teachers should be absolutely in the hands of the Vicar perhaps in consultation with the Church Council and Wardens. NB with the sanction of course of the Education Committee who are the best judges of a teacher's teaching prowess. A well known School Head teacher only last week, said the Vicar and Headmaster must work together to help on <u>the real good</u> of the parish. (c) The Character of the religious teaching should be loyal to Church Doctrine. Simple as you like, but absolutely <u>loyal to our Faith</u>. (a) Where Council Schools are – I say God help the parish!!! A Council School at present spells strife in a parish, and destroys the very ground work of religion.

5 a. Changes in Public worship since 1914. b. Effects of the changes. I have a daily celebration at 8 am. On great festivals Holy Com: at 6, 7, 8, 10 Sung Mass besides Matins, Catechising and Evensong. I have now got Missa Cantata twice a month at 10 instead of once a month. Many I find who can never come to Holy Communion before 9 (owing to Cattle) take advantage of the 10 Missa Cantata and like it. Some also who used to come at 12 much prefer to come at 10. I am hoping 10 will soon take the place of 11 as the principal hour of Service – then Missa Cantata will be the weekly service for worship.

6. Number of Roman Catholics in the Parish. None – I am sorry to say.

1. See 1914.
2. Possibly associated as a chaplain with the Community of St John the Baptist, an Anglican sisterhood. More likely a mistake for S.S.J.E. – the Cowley Fathers.

WATERPERRY   Incumbent B. L. Carr[1] (Officiating)

1. Number of Boys Girls and Infants on books of day schools: a. Last year. b. 20 30 or 40 years ago.

(a) 8 Boys, 10 Girls, 9 Infants: Total 27. (b) 1884 On Books: 23 Boys, 18 Girls: Total 41.

2. a. Men and b. Women qualified to vote in Parochial Church meeting. (a) 23. (b) 42.

3. Moral and Spiritual effect of: a. Wartime b. National Mission.

[*No response*].

4. Status of Church Schools. Options for compromise on a. management, b. head teachers, c. character of religious teaching. Might compromise be justified by better arrangements for Church teaching in state schools?

[*No response*].

5 a. Changes in Public worship since 1914. b. Effects of the changes.

[*No response*].

6. Number of Roman Catholics in the Parish. None.

1. See 1914 Waterstock.

WATERSTOCK   Incumbent B. L. Carr[1]

1. Number of Boys Girls and Infants on books of day schools: a. Last year. b. 20 30 or 40 years ago.

(a) The School has been closed temporarily for about 2 years but 6 children attend Piddington School. (b) Children in School 1894: 14 Boys, 18 Girls. Total 32.

2. a. Men and b. Women qualified to vote in Parochial Church meeting. (a) 21. (b) 24.

3. Moral and Spiritual effect of: a. Wartime b. National Mission.

(a) People seem more serious and especially the young men who return from the Front, they mostly attend the Church services and Holy Communion.

(b) There is no perceptible difference. The church services were well attended and a very high proportion of communicants which is still maintained.

4. Status of Church Schools. Options for compromise on a. management, b. head teachers, c. character of religious teaching. Might compromise be justified by better arrangements for Church teaching in state schools?

[*No response*].

5 a. Changes in Public worship since 1914. b. Effects of the changes. No changes.

6. Number of Roman Catholics in the Parish. None.

1. See 1914.

WATLINGTON   Incumbent C. W. E. Cleaver[1]

1. Number of Boys Girls and Infants on books of day schools: a. Last year. b. 20 30 or 40 years ago.

	1918	1893	1898	1888
Boys	50	167		89
Girls	54		115	81
Infants	46		80	74

2. a. Men and b. Women qualified to vote in Parochial Church meeting. Men 182, Women 296.

3. Moral and Spiritual effect of: a. Wartime b. National Mission.

For a considerable time a distinct downward tendency both morally and spiritually and a wildness among the children particularly the girls. The National Mission affected only a very few; but such as did come under its influence have certainly progressed. Latterly I have noticed a slight swing of the pendulum in the opposite direction among all sections.

4. Status of Church Schools. Options for compromise on a. management, b. head teachers, c. character of religious teaching. Might compromise be justified by better arrangements for Church teaching in state schools?

I have had no personal experience of Single School areas. In my opinion no compromise would be advisable as it would only be interpreted by the other side as a confession of weakness and used as a pretext for further demands. I would like to examine "the more satisfactory conditions" before giving an opinion.

5 a. Changes in Public worship since 1914. b. Effects of the changes. (a) 1. A daily Celebration of Holy Communion. 2. A Sung Eucharist at 9.30 on Sundays. (b) A greater reverence for the Blessed Sacrament, I trust. Many of the Communicants appear to me to be getting a better grasp of Its significance.

6. Number of Roman Catholics in the Parish. Men 0 Women 4 Children 4.

1. See 1914 Caversham. Cleaver moved from Caversham to Watlington in 1915.

WENDLEBURY   Incumbent H. W. Gresswell[1]

1. Number of Boys Girls and Infants on books of day schools: a. Last year. 4 Boys and 11 Girls (Upper School); Infants: 6 boys and 9 girls = 30 Total. **b. 20** ~~30 or 40~~ **years ago.** 13 boys and 16 girls Upper School; Infants: 10 boys and 12 girls = 51 Total.

2. a. Men and b. Women qualified to vote in Parochial Church meeting. 2 men and 1 woman.

3. Moral and Spiritual effect of: a. Wartime b. National Mission.

(a) It is difficult in a small parish like this which has shrunk in population considerably in last 2 years, owing to deaths of parishioners, those killed in the war, those out at the war, removals of other parishioners to other parishes, to state the effect of the war. With regard to Infants and Children it has had no visible effect. They accept the situation and so do the old people who are numerous here, but a time of war had a sobering effect on some of the young people. Those say from 20–30 it has had visibly a depressing effect and may lead into a certain leaning towards Superstition. On the whole however the people have got used to the war and are not materially affected by it.

(b) The N.M. has had the effect of awakening an interest in spiritual matters among the people and there has been a tendency to deepen their spiritual life and make them think of the life to come.

I think on the whole that the effect may not die away or lessen. The people want reminding by prayer and Sermons on the Subject.

4. Status of Church Schools. Options for compromise on a. management, b. head teachers, c. character of religious teaching. Might compromise be justified by better arrangements for Church teaching in state schools?

On the whole I think it would be best to stay and retain the schools in their present status.

5 a. Changes in Public worship since 1914. b. Effects of the changes. <u>Evening Service at 3pm</u> during the summer months and during the <u>winter months – 6pm</u>. It practically makes no difference whether the 2nd Sunday Service be at <u>3</u> or <u>6</u>. No other changes in methods or hours.

6. Number of Roman Catholics in the Parish. None.

1. See 1914.

WESTON-ON-THE-GREEN[1]   Incumbent P. C. Bevan[2]

1. Number of Boys Girls and Infants on books of day schools: a. Last year. 29.

b. 20 30 or 40 years ago. [*No response*].

2. a. Men and b. Women qualified to vote in Parochial Church meeting. None have signed it.

3. Moral and Spiritual effect of: a. Wartime b. National Mission.

(a) On the whole I do not think that the War has had any marked effect on the moral and spiritual condition of the Parishioners. Perhaps there is less revival of religious interest now than at first.

(b) The National Mission has not left any great results.

4. Status of Church Schools. Options for compromise on a. management, b. head teachers, c. character of religious teaching. Might compromise be justified by better arrangements for Church teaching in state schools?

No. a and b should be maintained, as at present. Before accepting a compromise, any proposed alterations in religious teaching should be very clearly defined. If the 'offer' provided some distinct Church teaching for the children of those parents who desired it, a compromise might be justified.

5 a. Changes in Public worship since 1914. b. Effects of the changes. None.

6. Number of Roman Catholics in the Parish. None.

1. Population 271.
2. Philip Charles Bevan graduated from Pembroke College Cambridge in 1880, having been ordained priest in 1872. He served four curacies 1871–85 and was Rector of Marsh Baldon between 1885 and 1912. He became Vicar of Weston on the Green in 1914 and served as Hon. Diocesan Inspector of Schools for the Oxford diocese 1887–1910. He was 72 in 1918 and at the 1911 census he was a widower, living in a household with three unmarried female servants.

WESTON, SOUTH WITH ADWELL   Incumbent R. T. Espinasse[1]

1. Number of Boys Girls and Infants on books of day schools: a. Last year. b. 20 30 or 40 years ago.

Our children go to Lewknor.

2. a. Men and b. Women qualified to vote in Parochial Church meeting. 10 Men. 10 Women. This number will be increased I think.

3. Moral and Spiritual effect of: a. Wartime b. National Mission.

(a) At the beginning of the war the moral and spiritual effect was distinctly good. A working man suggested a special service in church for the dismissal of our young men who joined up in September 1914 and I think hardly a man woman or child was absent from that service. The daily intercession was well attended. As time went on the attendance gradually diminished until now it is very small indeed. It is difficult to gauge the real feelings of the people but I am afraid it has not increased their religious faith or fervour.

(b) I am afraid that I cannot say the National Mission has effected any permanent improvement. It was not long enough though I had done all I could to prepare for it. The pilgrims of prayer were much too young and had no knowledge of public speaking. I think that part was a distinct failure. They also seemed most disinclined to accept help or otherwise from myself.

4. Status of Church Schools. Options for compromise on a. management, b. head teachers, c. character of religious teaching. Might compromise be justified by better arrangements for Church teaching in state schools?

[*No response*].

5 a. Changes in Public worship since 1914. b. Effects of the changes. None, except that I held very informal services of a missionary character in my own Hall this Lent on weeknights. I think it might be developed usefully. I invited questions but got none. I have an idea I might even get to that point another year. I did the same at Lewknor.

6. Number of Roman Catholics in the Parish. None.

1. See 1914.

WESTWELL   Incumbent W. R. Sharpe[1]

1. Number of Boys Girls and Infants on books of day schools: a. Last year. 10.

b. 20 30 or 40 years ago. 13, thirty years ago.

2. a. Men and b. Women qualified to vote in Parochial Church meeting. None.

3. Moral and Spiritual effect of: a. Wartime b. National Mission.

Outwardly the people of each Class are altogether unaffected by the War, there has been no increased observance of Sunday or of religious duties generally and no sustained interest in Special Services or Intercessions. Curiously this parish has contributed one only to the Army this fact may in part explain the above. As regards the National Mission some were I believe influenced at the time. I fear there is not much of the effect of the mission remaining so far as may be judged by practice.

4. Status of Church Schools. Options for compromise on a. management, b. head teachers, c. character of religious teaching. Might compromise be justified by better arrangements for Church teaching in state schools?

My opinion in regard to this inquiry is worth little. I have had an experience of some 38 years but only with a very small school. During that period I have never had any complaint as to the Religious Teaching nor has any child been withdrawn from that teaching. Personally I think there is not much fault to find with the present system: any compromise or concession made is certain to be used as a pretext for further claims and demands.

5 a. Changes in Public worship since 1914. b. Effects of the changes. There has been no material change in methods or hours. I notice a decreasing interest on the part of those above the labouring class in what is commonly designated "morning service" (ie the usual 11 o'clock Sunday Service).

6. Number of Roman Catholics in the Parish. None.

1. See 1914.

WHEATFIELD   Incumbent D. H. Davys[1]

1. Number of Boys Girls and Infants on books of day schools: a. Last year. Three.

b. 20 30 or 40 years ago. 20 years ago: about 17.

2. a. Men and b. Women qualified to vote in Parochial Church meeting. None – no Parochial Church Meeting held in the Parish to present date.

3. Moral and Spiritual effect of: a. Wartime b. National Mission.

A steadier and more serious tone and more inclination to help one another in trouble and difficulties.

4. Status of Church Schools. Options for compromise on a. management, b. head teachers, c. character of religious teaching. Might compromise be justified by better arrangements for Church teaching in state schools?

I have always been of opinion that some compromise should be made with nonconformists as regards management, appointment of head teachers, and the character of the religious teaching. At Tetsworth County School, where our few children attend, we arranged for the religious teaching to be taken on alternate weeks by Church Clergy and the resident Nonconformist minister. We found this plan to work smoothly and well.

5 a. Changes in Public worship since 1914. b. Effects of the changes. An extra weekly Celebration of the Holy Communion – War Prayers Services – otherwise no changes either in methods or hours

6. Number of Roman Catholics in the Parish. Two.

1. See 1914.

WHEATLEY   Incumbent W. D. B. Curry[1]

1. Number of Boys Girls and Infants on books of day schools: a. Last year. 190. **b.** 20 30 or 40 **years ago.** 120. This must not be taken that population has increased but that during the last 15 years attendances have been more carefully looked into.

2. a. Men and b. Women qualified to vote in Parochial Church meeting. Ten.

3. Moral and Spiritual effect of: a. Wartime b. National Mission.

I find that the War has made very little difference to those who were unaccustomed to go to any place of religion before the War. When their men come home they stay at home and nothing will bring them to Church as their wives or mothers do not come. It is most disheartening but there it is.

With regard to the National Mission – I had early each year a fortnight's regular mission and the results have been most marked. I had the same mission again this year for another ten days for the purpose of consolidation. It is astonishing what an amount of devotion there is in country people but it takes years of acquaintance before they open their hearts to you. Apathy is the great difficulty I am doubtful if the great questions evoked by the National Mission have been much thought of here.

4. Status of Church Schools. Options for compromise on a. management, b. head teachers, c. character of religious teaching. Might compromise be justified by better arrangements for Church teaching in state schools?

Headteachers must be appointed by the Managers. If that was given up endless difficulties would be constantly cropping up. Otherwise my opinion is that we ought to compromise. Definite religious teaching might well be given for 1½ hours on Saturday mornings more especially as children will shortly have to remain at school until they are 14. There might be one paid teacher and the others could be voluntary. The children or at any rate a great number of them would come if it was made attractive to them.

5 a. Changes in Public worship since 1914. b. Effects of the changes. Matins since 1917 Jan. has been said at 10.15. At 11 oc there is a Choral Celebration with quite plain music in which the congregation can join and in fact which they sing as for the present I have very little choir. A certain number of the old people object but some of them are coming round to the alteration and certainly the number of communicants have been increased. The effect on the young is very marked as it is accustoming them to the service and by having suitable hymns they are able to take their part. I am not convinced that 11 oc is the best time but it is difficult to know what is the most suitable hour. I preach a very short sermon so that the whole service may be over by 12 oc. or shortly after.

6. Number of Roman Catholics in the Parish. Five.

1. See 1914.

WHITCHURCH   Incumbent E. P. Baverstock[1]

1. Number of Boys Girls and Infants on books of day schools: a. Last year. b. 20 30 or 40 years ago.

This last year: 51. In 1870: 67.

2. a. Men and b. Women qualified to vote in Parochial Church meeting. (a) 32. (b) 104.

3. Moral and Spiritual effect of: a. Wartime b. National Mission.

(a) War Time Beyond the departure of men, for the naval and military service, and the employment of women in gardens and on the land this parish has not been affected by the war. We have no munition factories or training camps in the neighbourhood and therefore the difficulties connected with the social life in such areas have not been felt here. As to the general moral and spiritual effect of war time here, it cannot be said that the effect either way has been very marked. The strain of the war and its effect upon the faith of some has not been very noticeable here: on the other hand it cannot be said that the common trial and sorrow has meant an increase in the number of those who worship in church. Special days of Intercession have been fairly well observed.

(b) The National Mission The preliminary teaching and the special week of the mission were not without effect upon the regular worshippers. Undoubtedly there has been an improvement in the religious tone of our worshippers but again no accession of strength in the way of fresh worshippers.

General remarks

1. As regards the residents in larger houses in this parish, there is a fair proportion of worshippers at Mattins on Sunday morning and there are many communicants; chiefly monthly. 2. As regards the poorer inhabitants, there are few male communicants and the attendance at church is chiefly confined to Evensong; at that service there is a slight improvement in attendance of late.

4. Status of Church Schools. Options for compromise on a. management, b. head teachers, c. character of religious teaching. Might compromise be justified by better arrangements for Church teaching in state schools?

I have never come across any difficulty in my experience; but I recognise <u>that it does exist</u> in certain places. I certainly think if possible the church day schools should be maintained as part of the parochial church life. I recognize the difficulty of ensuring even under present conditions that the headteachers although classified as Ch. of England are religious persons and earnest about the religious influence upon the children; but still, I do think that in a parish it is the greatest help to have a distinctly religious tone about the day school on the lines of the Church. The visit of a parish priest to a provided school, even if he is to be permitted to teach his own subject to his own children, is not the same in effect as a visit to a school which is part of his parochial organisation.

 I recognise the hardship which nonconformists feel about the appointment of headteachers. As there are so many church schools in country districts it rather limits the number of appointments to headteacherships open to them: but I think it would be rather difficult for a nonconformist to be responsible for the religious teaching of a school part of which teaching he could not assent to. In spite of my conviction expressed in paragraph 2 above: in the interests of Christian fellowship I would willingly surrender the teaching of the Church Catechism in a school in a single school area and leave that for Sunday catechising: provided that the gain would be the recognition of the <u>religious as distinct from mere moral training</u> of children in <u>all</u> schools. The religious conviction of the teacher is after all of more importance than the excellence of a syllabus.

5 a. Changes in Public worship since 1914. b. Effects of the changes. I have added one or two more celebrations of Holy Communion at 7 am: which appear to meet the needs of certain people. On great festivals the Holy Eucharist is sung at 9.45 am. I have not yet seen my way to have this service at the usual hour 11 am. The school children attend the Holy Eucharist on Ascension Day and on the other great festivals. I look forward to seeing some results from this in the devotional life of the parish in the future.

6. Number of Roman Catholics in the Parish. 3: 1 man 2 women (one of whom left the Anglican communion a few years since). The other two are husband and wife who have been Roman Catholics from childhood.

1. Edward Perry Baverstock graduated AKC in 1888 and was ordained priest in 1889. He served two curacies 1888–1906, was Vicar of Yarnton 1906–10, and was then Organising Secretary of the Bishop of Oxford Fund between 1910 and 1914, when he became Rector of Whitchurch. He was 52 in 1918 and at the 1911 census he shared a household with his wife, their 8-year-old daughter, an 11-year-old female boarder and one unmarried female servant.

WIGGINGTON Incumbent H. J. Riddelsdell[1]

1. Number of Boys Girls and Infants on books of day schools: a. Last year. b. 20 30 or 40 years ago.

(a) B 13, G 17, I 10. (b) 1893: average all over: 30.4. 1894: average all over 31.047. 1895: average all over 26. 1903: on books: B 21, G 20, under 5: 7.

2. a. Men and b. Women qualified to vote in Parochial Church meeting. (a) 12. (b) 19.

3. Moral and Spiritual effect of: a. Wartime b. National Mission.

Neither very marked.

The congregations except at Holy Communion, do not increase: the Sunday evening congregation fluctuates considerably, but is decidedly smaller than a few years ago. This last fact is not to be attributed to any change made in the evening services. The desire to pray together in public is at a very low ebb and is easily conquered by any chance happening. The sense of self-sacrifice is still abnormally under-developed in the church people of Wigginton, except in the one respect of giving money: there they are decidedly generous. This quality appears as a result of the war, though it would be going beyond the evidence to say that the war created it. I do not think that the war has caused (a) Any greater wildness or lawlessness among the young. (b) Any growth of a desire to do fair work for a fair wage. (c) Any desire to get rid of the rather slight discomforts and difficulties of war time, by a premature peace. As a fact, no one in the parish is in serious want and many are a good bit better off than in 1914.

On the whole, I think that the war has perhaps brought the "corporate" sense a little bit into prominence. The moral and spiritual effect of the war on the people of the parish is thus slight. Of the National Mission I am unable to trace any effect: though I hope and believe that much may remain beneath the surface. We are slow moving people. One good lesson learnt in the course of a long ministry would stick, and would be worth more than many less lasting efforts to teach.

4. Status of Church Schools. Options for compromise on a. management, b. head teachers, c. character of religious teaching. Might compromise be justified by better arrangements for Church teaching in state schools?

Any opinion I could offer on these points would lack the valuable background of present experience: none of the usual difficulties appear to occur here at all.

5 a. Changes in Public worship since 1914. b. Effects of the changes. a. Holy Communion celebrated at varying hours:- eg 2nd Sunday of month at 7 last Sunday of month at 11 with music and sermon etc. Several days (1 Jan, Ascension Day etc) at 9.5 with children present. b. Sunday evening service goes down to 3rd Collect: then comes sermon: and biddings to prayer (chiefly in connexion with war but not exclusively.) c. New Lectionary used as an experiment.

Results a. More communions made; and more regularity secured in monthly communions. A greater readiness on the part of both priest and people to make and seize spiritual opportunities. b. Complaints from confirmed grumblers, especially those who never go to church. Other effects none, except (I think) increased heartiness of response: sometimes very marked. Also, I believe, more alertness on my own part. c. A certain appreciation of the shortness and pointedness of the picked Sunday psalms; and of the appropriateness of the lessons. The latter point is of great importance to the reader and the preacher.*

6. Number of Roman Catholics in the Parish. None, as far as I am aware.

*I am at present preaching on O.T. lessons, on Sundays.

1. See 1914.

WILCOTE[1]   Incumbent H. R. Hall[2]

1. Number of Boys Girls and Infants on books of day schools: a. Last year. b. 20 30 or 40 years ago.

None.

2. a. Men and b. Women qualified to vote in Parochial Church meeting. None.

3. Moral and Spiritual effect of: a. Wartime b. National Mission.

Same as Ramsden.

4. Status of Church Schools. Options for compromise on a. management, b. head teachers, c. character of religious teaching. Might compromise be justified by better arrangements for Church teaching in state schools?

We have no school in the parish.

5 a. Changes in Public worship since 1914. b. Effects of the changes. None.

6. Number of Roman Catholics in the Parish. None.

1. Population 8.
2. See 1914 Ramsden. Hall was incumbent of both Ramsden and Wilcote from 1904.

WITNEY   Incumbent R. Unsworth[1]

1. Number of Boys Girls and Infants on books of day schools: a. Last year. b. 20 30 or 40 years ago.

Church Schools on green Holy Trinity 118 Mixed and Infants. Wesleyans: 131 Boys, 144 Girls, 112 Infants [Total] 320. Forty years ago: Church Schools the only Schools: 85 boys, 73 girls, 30 infants.

2. a. Men and b. Women qualified to vote in Parochial Church meeting. a) 30. (b) 15*

*As far as I can make out from the Roll.

3. Moral and Spiritual effect of: a. Wartime b. National Mission.

(a) The war has left the adult members of the parish pretty much where it found them. It has not led to any visible increase or decrease in the attendance at services. The arrival here of (i) about three hundred men of the A.S.C. (ii) an equal number of Portuguese and (iii) the pressing in at present moment of a number of men engaged in work at the large aerodrome has had a bad effect upon the girls especially those between 14 and 16. It seems to have carried them away and the younger the girl the more noticeable is the way in which she flings herself upon the men. The Portuguese foreman of workers tells me that such sights as he has seen in Witney would be unknown in his country: the mothers wouldn't have allowed their daughters the license permitted here.

(b) After being here for less than six months, I am hardly qualified to express an opinion but from inquiries made in different quarters I should say that the visible and measurable result was nil.

4. Status of Church Schools. Options for compromise on a. management, b. head teachers, c. character of religious teaching. Might compromise be justified by better arrangements for Church teaching in state schools?

My views on the religious question are, I am afraid, quite unorthodox. In theory, of course, reason and common sense demand that the children should be brought up in the faith of their parents: in practice the principle counts for little or nothing compared with other considerations e.g. the proximity of the school to the home, the superiority or inferiority of school buildings the class of children attending the schools. Here in Witney we have two types of School – Church of England and Wesleyan, the latter with the better buildings. The Wesleyan Schools are attended by large numbers of Church children and vice versa. The situation of the home in relation to the school is a determining factor in a great many cases; in many more the status of the children who attend the school. In the Church School we have the children of the poorer and rougher strata of society: the Wesleyan school is recruited from the better class homes. Wesleyan children have the Church teaching and our children have the Wesleyan teaching and nobody minds in the least. Neither teaching has any permanent effect upon the children so it seems to me: the lessons are a pure intellectual matter like geography and history and are forgotten like the latter as soon as school days are over.

As regards (a) Management. The present arrangement seems satisfactory as regards representation. The difficulty is to get Managers to take any interest in the Schools. As regards (b) – The head teacher makes the whole difference to the School and I should greatly regret his appointment being taken out of local hands. He or she should certainly belong to the denomination which controls the school as long as denominational schools exist. This guarantees in some measure religious belief. (c) As regards this:- there is too much of it. I am sure the children are fed up with religious lessons – five days every week and twice on Sundays. I take great care that my own children are not surfeited as the elementary school children are. Religion is to them knowing facts not living a life.

I could write much more about religious education if there were room for it and if I thought my views were worth consideration. From my experience in London, Worcester, Woodburn and here I should say that the chief difference between provided and unprovided schools is in the matter of tone or atmosphere. It is certainly better in denominational schools. But it only counts during school days. After they have left school it is impossible to distinguish between the product of the two types.

5 a. Changes in Public worship since 1914. b. Effects of the changes. (a) There is now a children's Eucharist at 9.30 once a month. No other changes have been made as far as I know. (b) It is far too early yet to measure the effects.

6. Number of Roman Catholics in the Parish. To the best of my knowledge, 2 who live here altogether and 2 who spend their holidays here with their people.

1. Reece Unsworth graduated from University College Oxford in 1893 and was ordained priest in 1896. He held three curacies 1895–1904 and then was Vicar of Wooburn between 1904 and 1917, when he was appointed Rector of Witney. Unsworth was 47 in 1918 and at the 1911 census he was sharing a household with his wife, three young children, their nurse and one other unmarried female servant.

WOLVERCOTE Incumbent E. A. Sydenham[1]

1. Number of Boys Girls and Infants on books of day schools: a. Last year. 247.

b. 20 30 or 40 years ago. In 1875: 71.

2. a. Men and b. Women qualified to vote in Parochial Church meeting. None.

3. Moral and Spiritual effect of: a. Wartime b. National Mission.

(a) Amongst Church people there has been a more regular attendance at public worship, especially at the Holy Eucharist. In the parish, amongst nominal or non-church people there is a decided tendency towards frivolity and loose morality. The number of illegitimate births has been greater during the war than is usual.

(b) Possibly the National Mission may have stimulated greater regularity in the matter of church going but it is difficult to say. Certainly a greater effort towards assisting the Missionary work of the Church has been made.

4. Status of Church Schools. Options for compromise on a. management, b. head teachers, c. character of religious teaching. Might compromise be justified by better arrangements for Church teaching in state schools?

Personally I have small hope of any good being gained by the suggestion made in the second paragraph. The existing system is an anomaly and also an anachronism. I should welcome greater facilities for teaching definite Religion in Council Schools if possible, but the trend of modern Educational ideals seems entirely opposed to anything of the kind. I know of many Churchmen, holding definitely Catholic views, who advocate purely secular education in elementary schools. I feel personally that the only intelligible system is that all schools should be on the same footing and should be entirely under State control.

5 a. Changes in Public worship since 1914. b. Effects of the changes. Evensong on Sundays is at 6 o'clock instead of 6.30. The change has certainly met with the approval of our people.

6. Number of Roman Catholics in the Parish. 31.

1. See 1914.

WOOD EATON   Incumbent R. Hutchison[1]

1. Number of Boys Girls and Infants on books of day schools: a. Last year. b. 20 30 or 40 years ago.

The Rector of Noke cum Islip will supply this information.

2. a. Men and b. Women qualified to vote in Parochial Church meeting. [*No response*].

3. Moral and Spiritual effect of: a. Wartime b. National Mission.

Nothing makes any visible impression on small rural parishes of this type.

4. Status of Church Schools. Options for compromise on a. management, b. head teachers, c. character of religious teaching. Might compromise be justified by better arrangements for Church teaching in state schools?

Our school is at Noke and under an excellent mistress our children have done very well. The status of single area Church schools (judging by this case) should continue as at present.

5 a. Changes in Public worship since 1914. b. Effects of the changes. Holy Communion on alternate Sundays after Benedictus. The congregation is almost the same hardly any communicants except on First Sunday in the month. Evening services in winter at 5 pm owing to lighting regulations. Congregation much smaller.

6. Number of Roman Catholics in the Parish. None.

1. See 1914.

WOODSTOCK   Incumbent H. W. L. O'Rorke[1]

1. Number of Boys Girls and Infants on books of day schools: a. Last year. b. 20 30 or 40 years ago.

Boys 64, Girls 129, Infants 50 Woodstock. Bladon B.G.I. 103. 34 years ago: 86.

2. a. Men and b. Women qualified to vote in Parochial Church meeting. 16.

3. Moral and Spiritual effect of: a. Wartime b. National Mission.

(a) A growing value of Intercession – but as I only came here 14 months after the war began, I cannot compare the previous and present state of the parish. The weekly Intercession service is _very_ well attended.

(b) The National Mission has apparently not made much impression.

4. Status of Church Schools. Options for compromise on a. management, b. head teachers, c. character of religious teaching. Might compromise be justified by better arrangements for Church teaching in state schools?

Retain the schools at all costs – whilst making concessions as to "right of entry".

5 a. Changes in Public worship since 1914. b. Effects of the changes. [*No response*].

6. Number of Roman Catholics in the Parish. 7 Roman Catholics 2 Belgian one French.

1. Henry William Leycester O'Rorke graduated from Trinity College Cambridge in 1892 and trained at Wycliffe Hall in 1893, being ordained priest in 1894. He served a series of chaplaincies to Missions to Seamen in Liverpool and San Francisco 1893–1901, was Vicar of Send 1901–04 and of Farnham 1904–08, and then Perpetual Curate of Edensor and Domestic Chaplain to the Duke of Devonshire between 1908 and 1915, when he became Rector of Woodstock and Domestic Chaplain to the Duke of Marlborough. He was 48 in 1918 and at the 1911 census he shared a household with his wife, six children aged between 5 months and 8 years, their two nurses and five other unmarried female servants.

WOOTTON   Incumbent F. R. Marriot[1]

1. Number of Boys Girls and Infants on books of day schools: a. Last year. 90.

b. 20 30 or 40 years ago. 140.

2. a. Men and b. Women qualified to vote in Parochial Church meeting. In 1916: 10 women, 6 men.

The matter seemed to be hardly ripe then. But by Easter this year, I hope that over 50 will have signed the declaration.

3. Moral and Spiritual effect of: a. Wartime b. National Mission.

This is a purely agricultural Parish, with a few "Gentry" in the main – 3 classes – (1) "Gentry" (2) Farmers and (3) Villagers (with their 'grades' clearly marked and strictly observed among themselves).

The <u>moral</u> effect, whether of the War or the National Mission, is not noticeably apparent among Gentry or Farmers. As to the Villagers, I see no change (I have no reason to think that there has been any increase in immorality in its usual meaning) <u>except</u> among the <u>lads</u> – owing probably to the departure of the elder young-men there is a general want of discipline among the younger lads and boys and a good deal of <u>malicious</u> annoyance of neighbours. Also there has been a marked stiffening and emphasising of class bitterness, <u>where there was bitterness before</u>. The war has made the bitter folk more bitter.

On the <u>spiritual</u> side I believe that the <u>National Mission</u> did real good. I believe this, despite the fact that so far the actual fruit has not been great, or the <u>positive</u> results apparent. It deepened the spiritual life of many – though it did not <u>gain</u> many "outsiders". It came at a moment when there <u>might</u> have been a great falling away of the more or less careless and I believe that it saved many from 'falling away', even though it did not result in actual gain. But even among the less-faithful, it will not be forgotten – it shewed to them that the National Church was awake and keen, and they recognised that the effort was a faithful one, though they would not go so far as to be affected or moved by it.

As to the war, and its "spiritual" effect. At the beginning of the war, people were eager to come together for 'Prayer' – now, but few come. They doubt about the power or the use of Prayer – and I think the chief effect of the war has been seen among the faithful to diminish their faith in the efficacy of intercession. Only the <u>few</u>, who realize that Sacrifice is necessary if the really great is to be attained, retain the spirit of Prayer. Apart from this, there is no marked effect.

4. Status of Church Schools. Options for compromise on a. management, b. head teachers, c. character of religious teaching. Might compromise be justified by better arrangements for Church teaching in state schools?

I think that Church Schools ought to be kept as Church Schools – As far as I can judge, there is <u>no</u> desire to change the status. I have been 17 years in this parish, with a large Nonconformist element in it, and I have <u>never</u> heard one word of dissatisfaction as to the management or the religious teaching. The people generally wish to have their children taught the <u>Christian Faith</u> and they want that teaching to be given by teachers who are <u>Christians</u>. I sincerely believe that (apart from politics) the bulk of the people would dislike the demand of the N.U.T. being conceded. They may not like 'Tests' – but they do not want teachers who may be atheists to look after their children.

As to Nonconformists – Christians – <u>we</u> ought to meet them – and to arrange a Schedule of Religious Teaching in the Schools satisfactory to them and to Church People. I attach no importance whatsoever to what is called definite church teaching in the elementary schools. If the church authorities and the authorities of the Free Churches could meet together and arrange a Schedule of Religious Teaching suitable for the children, it would be a grand thing. It could be done in a day. It could not harm the Church – and would be an immense gain to the Christian religion.

5 a. Changes in Public worship since 1914. b. Effects of the changes. The only change is that once a month on Sunday evening we use the 'Sunday Evening Service' (Iremonger) allowed by the Bishop. No choir. I think the people like it <u>as a change</u>.

6. Number of Roman Catholics in the Parish. No R.C.s.

1. See 1914.

WORTON, NETHER[1]   Incumbent H. A. W. Buss[2]

1. Number of Boys Girls and Infants on books of day schools: a. Last year. 15.

b. 20 30 or 40 years ago. 1897: 22.

2. a. Men and b. Women qualified to vote in Parochial Church meeting. None.

3. Moral and Spiritual effect of: a. Wartime b. National Mission.

Very little difference from Pre-War and Pre-National Mission time.

4. Status of Church Schools. Options for compromise on a. management, b. head teachers, c. character of religious teaching. Might compromise be justified by better arrangements for Church teaching in state schools?

I think the Schools should be retained in their present status.

5 a. Changes in Public worship since 1914. b. Effects of the changes. None.

6. Number of Roman Catholics in the Parish. None.

1. Population 51.
2. See 1914 Over Worton. Buss was incumbent of both Over Worton and Nether Worton from 1913.

WORTON, OVER   Incumbent H. A. W. Buss[1]

1. Number of Boys Girls and Infants on books of day schools: a. Last year. b. 20 30 or 40 years ago.

No schools.

2. a. Men and b. Women qualified to vote in Parochial Church meeting. None.

3. Moral and Spiritual effect of: a. Wartime b. National Mission.

Very little difference from Pre-War and Pre-National Mission time.

4. Status of Church Schools. Options for compromise on a. management, b. head teachers, c. character of religious teaching. Might compromise be justified by better arrangements for Church teaching in state schools?

[*No response*].

5 a. Changes in Public worship since 1914. b. Effects of the changes. None.

6. Number of Roman Catholics in the Parish. None.

1. See 1914.

WROXTON WITH BALSCOTE   Incumbent J. S. Pettifor[1]

1. Number of Boys Girls and Infants on books of day schools: a. Last year. Wroxton 41; Balscote 25. Average attendance for 1917. **b. 20 30 or 40 years ago.** I much regret that I am unable to give this information.

2. a. Men and b. Women qualified to vote in Parochial Church meeting. Wroxton: 28 Males, 50 Females, total 78. Balscote: 4 Males, 18 Females, total 22.

3. Moral and Spiritual effect of: a. Wartime b. National Mission.

As I have been here less than a year, I am somewhat in a disadvantageous position to answer these questions. My impression, however, is first as regards the war, that it has been the means, judging from the satisfactory attendance at our week-day Intercession Services, of arousing and sustaining spiritual effort among the various classes in our parish and accordingly its moral and spiritual effect has been good. The same applies in respect of the National Mission, only that it is very difficult to get hold of the men, our Services being somewhat sparsely attended by the adult male population, but possibly this may in some measure, be accounted for by the present shortage of labour, owing to so many men of military age being away serving in His Majesty's Forces, and also from the fact that this being an agricultural parish the needs of agriculture have to be attended to and the question of feeding the stock, although with more effort, one cannot but think that the religious duties might be more adequately fulfilled.

4. Status of Church Schools. Options for compromise on a. management, b. head teachers, c. character of religious teaching. Might compromise be justified by better arrangements for Church teaching in state schools?

I think they should by all means be retained as Church Schools, on account of the all importance of giving Religious Instruction in accordance with the Trust

Deeds, which specify that they shall be used as and for Schools for the education of the children of the poor in the principles of the Established Church, but, possibly, we should do well to appoint on the Board of Management one Non-Conformist representative, in order that the Non-Conformists in the parish might not feel to be entirely excluded from the Management of such Schools, while we are not unmindful of the fact that, in most at least of our Parishes, a not inconsiderable number of the children attending our Church Schools are the children of Non-Conformist parents. I think this course, if adopted, would create and foster a better feeling amongst the Non-Conformists towards the Church. In a Church School, I think, the Head Teacher should be either a Churchman or a Churchwoman, as the case might be, and that such teacher should be well qualified to give Church teaching. The compromise indicated would, I think, be justified so long as we have and retain the Diocesan Syllabus for Religious Instruction, and this I consider we ought not by any means to surrender or hand over.

5 a. Changes in Public worship since 1914. b. Effects of the changes. (a) During the winter months, on account of the War we have had to hold our usual Evening Service in the afternoon. (b) I find the men do not attend so well.

6. Number of Roman Catholics in the Parish. Possibly a dozen or so.

1. John Shipley Pettifor trained at the Chancellors School Lincoln in 1891 and was ordained priest in 1894. After an initial curacy 1893–96 he was Vicar of Baston, Lincs. 1896–1900 and then of Thurlby between 1900 and 1917, when he became Vicar of Wroxton. He was 48 in 1918 and at the 1911 census he shared a household with his wife, two daughters and two unmarried female servants.

WYTHAM[1]   Incumbent C. H. Meyrick[2]

1. Number of Boys Girls and Infants on books of day schools: a. Last year. b. 20 30 or 40 years ago.

(a) Boys 7, Girls 7, Infants 9 [total] 23.

(b) In 1878, the total on Register was 46, but there are no details as to how many boys and girls.

2. a. Men and b. Women qualified to vote in Parochial Church meeting. (a) 5 men. (b) No women.

3. Moral and Spiritual effect of: a. Wartime b. National Mission.

(a) There is practically only one class in this parish, as the one big house is too uncertain in its tenancy to be reckoned definitely. Amongst the people of the working class, the moral effect of the war has been very slight. There has been no deterioration, if anything, a slight uplift, due probably more to the difficulty and expense of obtaining alcoholic drinks than to any more serious cause. But this parish has been, so far as my knowledge goes, remarkably free from either immorality or drunkenness both before or during the war. I do not know of more than one case of immorality, which occurred before the war, nor are there any habitual hard drinkers here. As regards the spiritual effects of war-time, they are not very noticeable. The number of communicants has remained practically stationary (allowing for the absentees in the Army), the morning congregations of late have shown a considerable decrease, the evening ones are practically stationary, though, naturally, there are fewer men present.

(b) I do not know that I can report any definite effect of the National Mission; I was absent in France during the year of the National Mission, and I have not noticed any real change which I could attribute to the Mission.

The population of the parish is 170: average attendance at morning service about 30; at evening service about 70. Numbers of communicants on the roll, 60. Average attendance of communicants per celebration, 7 or 8.

4. Status of Church Schools. Options for compromise on a. management, b. head teachers, c. character of religious teaching. Might compromise be justified by better arrangements for Church teaching in state schools?

There are no Nonconformists in this parish: there has never been, to my knowledge, any objection to the full Church teaching being given to the children. Practically all the day-school children attend the Sunday School also. It would be a great pity if small schools of this sort were not able to continue this work of teaching the faith. But as my experience is limited to so peaceful a sphere as regards religious education, I am afraid that my views can carry but small weight.

I might mention that this school has a small endowment of about £22 per annum, which is conditional upon the teaching of the Church of England being given.

5 a. Changes in Public worship since 1914. b. Effects of the changes. (a) No changes on Sunday. The weekly Intercession Service has been changed from Friday to Thursday night, at the request of some members of the congregation, who found the latter night more suitable. (b) A slight increase in the attendance has resulted.

6. Number of Roman Catholics in the Parish. [*No response*].

1. Population 170.
2. Cyril Henry Meyrick graduated from St John's College Oxford in 1902, trained at Cuddesdon College in 1905 and was ordained priest in 1907. After an initial curacy 1906–11 he was Priest in Charge of Okanagan MS between 1911 and 1913, when he returned to England as Rector of Wytham. He was 39 and a married man in 1918.

YARNTON   Incumbent B. Parsons[1]

1. Number of Boys Girls and Infants on books of day schools: a. Last year. boys 31 girls 25 Inf 8. <u>Total 64.</u> **b. 20 30 or 40 years ago.** 1878: Boys 11, girls 17, infants 15. <u>Total 43.</u>

2. a. Men and b. Women qualified to vote in Parochial Church meeting. Men 14, Women 21.

3. Moral and Spiritual effect of: a. Wartime b. National Mission.

For quite a long time both the War and the National Mission had the effect of bringing many more people to public worship. A few who before the War very rarely came to church are now fairly regular worshippers, but several others have drifted back to their old ways. In some cases the drifting away seems to be due to the pressure of agricultural work rather than any other cause. There seems to be an improvement as regards the question of 'Drink'.

4. Status of Church Schools. Options for compromise on a. management, b. head teachers, c. character of religious teaching. Might compromise be justified by better arrangements for Church teaching in state schools?

No single difficulty had occurred as regards the religious education in this school during the 8 years that I have been here, and no child has been withdrawn from any portion of the teaching. I think it would be well to give facilities to Nonconformists if they so desired to give religious instruction to nonconformist children in single-school areas.

The Parish Council has the appointment of one Manager in our school. They have appointed a Nonconformist but no question has ever arisen as regards the religious education, and I therefore do not see that any change is necessary as regards "management". I do not think that any change is desirable as regards the appointment of "head-teachers", nor any compromise necessary as regards the character of the religious teaching. I think that facilities should be given in <u>all</u> schools for religious teaching in accordance with the views of the parents.

5 a. Changes in Public worship since 1914. b. Effects of the changes. Evensong on Sundays at 6 pm instead of 6.30. "War Prayers" instead of Prayers for Royal Family at Evensong. There is a sense of much deeper earnestness and devotion when the War Prayers are used.

6. Number of Roman Catholics in the Parish. Men 1, women 2, children 0.

1. See 1914.

YELFORD[1]   Incumbent T. Lovett[2]

1. Number of Boys Girls and Infants on books of day schools: a. Last year. b. 20 30 or 40 years ago.

No schools.

2. a. Men and b. Women qualified to vote in Parochial Church meeting. None.

3. Moral and Spiritual effect of: a. Wartime b. National Mission.

The parish only at present containing 9 people, it is quite impossible to report on any moral or spiritual effect from either a or b.

4. Status of Church Schools. Options for compromise on a. management, b. head teachers, c. character of religious teaching. Might compromise be justified by better arrangements for Church teaching in state schools?

[*No response*].

5 a. Changes in Public worship since 1914. b. Effects of the changes. None.

6. Number of Roman Catholics in the Parish. None.

1. Population 14.
2. See 1914 Standlake. Lovett was incumbent of Yelford in addition to Standlake from 1912.

Glossary

Associate of King's College (AKC) A theology qualification offered by King's College London, from 1848, to Anglican ordinands on the basis of three years of study equivalent to an undergraduate degree.

Band of Hope A temperance organisation aimed particularly to attract working-class children, the Band of Hope began in 1847 and had a membership of over three million by the turn of the century.

British and Foreign Bible Society (BFBS) Founded in 1804, to promote the translation and distribution of Bibles, the BFBS was the largest of the Evangelical inter-denominational societies.

Church Army Founded in the 1880s, the Church Army trained Anglican lay evangelists who operated in parishes at the invitation of incumbents and also undertook a range of social work. Its teams were sometimes known as 'Flying Squadrons'.

Church of England Men's Society (CEMS) Formed in 1899 from an amalgamation of predecessor organisations with support from the archbishop of Canterbury, the CEMS, operating through parish branches, provided a range of social and educational activities for adult men.

Church Lads' Brigade (CLB) Founded in 1891 as an amalgamation of a range of predecessor organisations, the CLB was the main Anglican youth organisation for boys before the first world war, with over 70,000 members in 1908. It developed close links with the territorial army from 1911 and was a major source of recruits in the early years of the war.

Church Missionary Society (CMS) Founded in 1799, the CMS was the most significant of the Anglican Evangelical missionary societies, with major missions in Africa, India and Australasia. It had a well-developed supporters organisation including at parish level local branches of the 'Gleaners Union' for adult supporters and 'Sowers Bands' for junior ones.

Colonial and Continental Church Society An Evangelical missionary society ministering to British colonists overseas especially in Canada and Australia.

Evangelical Alliance An international organisation founded in 1846 to promote cooperation between Evangelicals across denominational barriers. It promoted inter-denominational prayer meetings during the first world war.

Girls Friendly Society (GFS) Founded in 1875, the Girls Friendly Society aimed to help single working-class girls by providing a range of support, from opportunities for respectable social activity, to safe accommodation. It was divided into working-class members and middle-class associates and had a total strength of almost 200,000 in the decade before the first world war.

King's Messengers (KM) A junior branch of the SPG.

Marden System A Sunday school teaching system based around visual props including coloured stamps and pictures.

Mothers' Union (MU) Founded by Mary Sumner in 1876 as a local organisation in her husband's parish aimed to promote mutual support between social classes in motherhood, the MU became a national organisation in the 1880s and 1890s with a membership of over 150,000 in the years before the first world war.

National Union of Teachers (NUT) Founded in 1870, the NUT was the main trade union representing teachers in elementary schools.

Ragged Schools Ragged Schools supported by philanthropic donations and volunteers aimed to provide free education and often material support for the poorest children.

Scripture Union Beginning in 1867 as the Children's Special Service Mission, Scripture Union was an inter-denominational organisation which developed both a range of activities for children and resources including plans and notes for daily Bible reading.

Society for the Propagation of the Gospel (SPG) Founded in 1701, the SPG was the oldest of the Anglican missionary organisations. In the early twentieth century it was supported by a wide cross-section of Anglicans and not dominated by any particular group.

Universities Mission to Central Africa (UMCA) An Anglican missionary society founded in 1857 and representative of the Anglo-Catholic tradition within the church.

Select Bibliography

Austin, M. (ed.), *Under the Heavy Clouds: The Church of England in Derbyshire and Nottinghamshire 1911–1915: the parochial visitation of Edwyn Hoskyns Bishop of Southwell* (Whitchurch, 2004)
Austin, M., *'Like A Swift Hurricane.' People, Clergy and Class in a Midlands Diocese, 1914–1919* (Chesterfield, 2014)
Beaken, R., *The Church of England and the Home Front 1914–1918: Civilians, Soldiers and Religion in Wartime Colchester* (Woodbridge, 2015)
Bebbington, D. W., *The Nonconformist Conscience: Chapel and Politics, 1870–1914* (London, 1982)
Bell, S., *Faith in Conflict: The Impact of the Great War on the Faith of the People of Britain* (Solihull, 2017)
Brown, C. G., *Religion and Society in Twentieth-Century Britain* (Harlow, 2006)
Carey, H. M., *God's Empire: Religion and Colonialism in the British World, c.1801–1908* (Cambridge, 2011)
Chapman, M. D., *God's Holy Hill: A History of Christianity in Cuddesdon* (Charlbury, 2004)
Cotter, J., *Oxfordshire: Remembering 1914–1918* (Stroud, 2014)
Daunton, M., *Wealth and Welfare: An Economic and Social History of Britain 1851–1951* (Oxford, 2007)
Field, C. D., 'A Godly People? Aspects of Religious Practice in the Diocese of Oxford, 1738–1936', *Southern History*, 14 (1992), pp. 46–73
Field, C. D., 'Keeping the Spiritual Home Fires Burning: Religious Belonging in Britain during the First World War', in *War and Society*, 33 (2014), pp. 244–68
Graham, M., *Oxford in the Great War* (Barnsley, 2014)
Green, S., *The Passing of Protestant England: Secularisation and Social Change c.1920–1960* (Cambridge, 2010)
Gregory, A., *The Last Great War: British Society and the First World War* (Cambridge, 2008)
Gregory, A., 'Beliefs and Religion', in J. Winter (ed.) *The Cambridge History of the First World War* vol. III (2014)
Grimley, M., *Citizenship, Community, and the Church of England: Liberal Anglican Theories of the State Between the Wars* (Oxford, 2004)
Haig, A., *The Victorian Clergy* (Beckenham, 1984)

Harrison, B., 'For Church, Queen and Family: The Girls' Friendly Society 1874–1920', *Past and Present*, 61 (1973), pp. 107–38

Herring, G., *The Oxford Movement in Practice: The Tractarian Parochial World from the 1830s to the 1870s* (Oxford, 2016),

Horn, P., *Rural life in England in the First World War* (Dublin, 1984)

Knight, F., *The Nineteenth-Century Church and English Society* (Cambridge, 1995)

Louden, L., *Distinctive and Inclusive: The National Society and Church of England Schools 1811–2011* (London, 2012)

Masom, G., 'Parishes under Pressure – The Church of England in South Buckinghamshire 1913–1939', *Journal of Religious History*, 42 (2018), pp. 317–42

Moyse, C., *A History of the Mothers' Union: Women, Anglicanism and Globalisation, 1876-2008* (Woodbridge, 2009)

Obelkevich, J., *Religion and Rural Society: South Lindsey, 1825–1875* (Oxford, 1976)

Porter, A., *Religion versus Empire? British Protestant Missionaries and Overseas Expansion, 1700–1914* (Manchester, 2004)

Russell, A., *The Clerical Profession* (London, 1980)

Smith, M., '"War to the Knife"? The Anglican Clergy and Education at the End of the First World War', *Churches and Education, Studies in Church History*, 55 (2019) doi:10.1017/stc.2018.22

Snape, M., *God and the British Soldier. Religion and the British Army in the First and Second World Wars* (London, 2005)

Snape, M., 'The Great War' in H. McLeod (ed.), *The Cambridge History of Christianity, Volume 9: World Christianities c.1914–c.2000* (Cambridge, 2006) pp. 131–150

Stanley, B., *The World Missionary Conference, Edinburgh 1910* (Grand Rapids Mi., 2009)

Strong, R., 'The Oxford Movement and Missions' in S. J. Brown, P. Nockles and J. Pereiro (eds), *The Oxford Handbook of the Oxford Movement* (Oxford, 2017), pp. 485–99

Simmonds, A. G. V., *Britain and World War One* (London, 2012)

Thompson, D. M., 'War, the Nation, and the Kingdom of God: The Origins of the National Mission of Repentance and Hope 1915–16' in W. J. Sheils (ed.), *The Church and War: Studies in Church History, 20 (1983)*, pp. 337–50

Tiller, K. and Darkes G. (eds), *An Historical Atlas of Oxfordshire* (Oxford, 2010)

Wolffe, J., *God and Greater Britain: Religion and National Life in Britain and Ireland, 1843–1945* (London, 1994)

Yamaguchi, M., *Daughters of the Anglican Clergy: Religion, Gender and Identity in Victorian England* (Basingstoke, 2014)

Yates, N., *Anglican Ritualism in Victorian Britain 1830–1910* (Oxford, 1999)

Index

Adams, Charles, 267
Adams, Henry, 103, 104 n.2, 369
Adderbury, 12, 15, 20 n.104, 54 n.251, 69, 341
Additional Curates Society, 39, 518 n.1
Adwell, 22 n.119, 24 n.132, 55, 206, 320–1, 465 n.1, 568
Albury, 12, 13, 14 n.62, 18 n.89, 23 n.128, 30 n.181, 42, 45 n.283, 58 n.385, 70–1, 342–3
Alice, Sister, 178
Alington, Hildebrand, 232, 233 n.2, 486
Alkerton, 17 n.85, 18 n.93, 22 n.119, 54 n.353, 273–4, 524–5
Alkeston *see* Alkerton
Alvescot, 18 n.90, 71–2, 343–4
Ambroseden, 6, 24 n.137, 54, 60 n.408, 72–3, 344
Anson, Mr W., 272
Ardley, 16, 74 n.2, 156, 345
Arkell, Henry, 388, 391 n.2
Armitage, Philip, 43, 222, 223 n.2, 477
Armstrong, Alexander, 433, 434 n.2
Armstrong, Arthur, 226, 227 n.2, 480
Ascot-under-Wychwood, 7 n.25, 44 n.278, 74–5, 216 n.2, 345–6
Asthall, 23, 43 n.267, 45, 76–7, 346–7
Asthall Leigh, 76–7, 347
Aston, North, 19, 44 n.274, 60 n.411, 77–8, 347–8
Aston, Steeple, 46 n.293, 48 n.304 49 n.313, 75 n.2, 78–9, 103 n.2, 348–9
Aston, Rowant, 12 n.51, 14, 40 n.251, 44 n.276, 50 n.321, 56, 79–81, 349–51, 514 n.1
Aylen, Charles, 40, 275, 277 n.2

Bailey, Robert, 171, 172 n.2
Baker, Samuel, 386, 387 n.2
Baldon, Marsh, 81–2, 351–2, 568 n.2
Baldon, Toot, 81–2, 351–2
Baldwyn, Leonard, 124, 125 n.2, 387, 412
Ball, Charles, 99, 100 n.2, 365
Balscote, 333–4, 581–2
Bampton, Proper, 25 n.2, 46, 58 n.383, 82–3, 352–3
Bampton, Aston, 21, 83–4, 353–4
Bampton, Lew, 33 n.211, 43 n.265, 84–5, 263 n.2
Banbury, 1, 4, 6, 8, 12, 19, 21 n.111, 26, 32 n.204, 41, 46, 49 n.313, n. 318, 50, 56, 59 n.390, 60, 86–7, 147, 173, 354–6, 369, 558, 563
Banbury, South, 6, 13, 23, 58 n.384, 87–8, 356–7, 462 n.1, 549
Band of Hope, 27, 44, 74, 140, 194 258, 306, 587
Barford, John, 294, 296 n.2
Barford, St Michael, 9, 23, 53, 88–9, 357–9, 391
Barnes, George, 280, 281 n.2, 531
Barnes, Mrs, 280
Barr, George, 400, 401 n.1
Barrington, 112 n.2, 559
Barton, Steeple, 23, 33 n.211 35, 50 n.321, 60 n.400, 89–90, 359, 527 n.2
Barton, Westcot, 14, 25 n.146, 51, 90–1, 359–60
Baverstock, Edward, 571, 573 n.1
Bayfield, Charles, 54, 72, 73 n.2, 344 check
Bayliff, Norah, 155
Beaken, Robert, 13
Beckley, 9 n.39, 37 n.228, 54, 58 n.382, 91–2, 329 n.2, 360–1, 435 n.1, 452,

Begbroke, 6 n.16, 9 n.36, 29, 35 n.220, 38, 43 n.266, 60, 92–3, 361–2
Bell, John, 262, 263 n.2
Bell, Stuart, 45 n.279, 50 n.322, 51, 54 n.350
Bellman, Arthur, 196, 197 n.2 457
Benson, 6 n.18, 24, 58 n.388, 93–4, 95 n.2, 380, 478
Berrick Salome, 43 n.266, 117–18, 224, 380–1, 478
Bevan, Philip, 567, 568 n.2
Bible Reading League, 26, 147
Bible Reading Union, 211, 300, 562
Bicester, 1, 6, 24 n.136, 41, 42, 49 n.314, 58 n.387, 60 n.402, 95–6, 204, 214 n.2, 362–3, 380, 470
Binsey, 8, 23, 61, 96–7, 267 n.2, 363–4
Birch Reynardson, Mrs, 320
Bird, Bertram, 459, 460 n.1
Birley, Archdeacon, 258
Bisdee, Alfred, 49, 490, 491 n.1
Bix, 17 n.87, 18 n.90, 55 n.363, 97–8, 364
Blackbourton, 98–9, 364–5
Bladon, 330, 578
Bletchingdon, 46, 99–100, 365–6, 429
Blount, Darrell, 467
Bloxham, 13, 14 n.62, 21 n.112, 28, 100–1, 366–8, 410 n.2, 470–1
Blytheman, Arthur, 273, 274 n.2, 524
Bodicote, 6 n.21, 19, 101–2, 368–9
Boniface, Thomas, 144, 145 n.2, 404
Borneo Association, 288
Bourton, Great, 102–3, 369
Bowring, Godfray, 312, 313 n.2, 561
Boy Scouts, 27, 211, 262, 357
Brabazon, Fr, 356
Bradford, Basil, 107, 108 n.2, 373
Bradwell, 18 n.95, 103–4, 196, 369–70, 456
Brancker, Rev., 116
Bricknell, William, 153, 154 n.2, 416
Brightwell Baldwin, 23 n.124, 104–5, 106, 370–1, 403 n.1,
Brine, James, 39, 191, 192 n.2
British and Foreign Bible Society, 30, 39, 172, 201, 273, 282, 301, 587
British and Foreign Schools Society, 20, 180, 181, 313, 438

British Colombia Church Aid Association, 32, 296
Britwell, 370
Britwell Salome, 9, 105–6, 371
Britwell Prior, 9 n.38, 105–6, 371
Brizenorton, 9, 12 n.52, 36 n.226, 55 n.364, 57 n.377, 60 n.401, 106–7, 371–3
Broadwell *see* Bradwell
Brookhampton, 224, 478
Broughton, 19, 25, 107–8, 158, 373
Broughton Pogis, 28, 31 n.199, 55 n.364, 108–9, 373–4
Brown, Callum, 51, 52 n.337
Brown, Frederick, 78, 79 n.2, 348
Browne, Valentine, 231, 232 n.2, 484
Bryant, William, 126, 127 n.2, 391
Bucknell, 7 n.25, 10, 37 n.230, 38 n.235, 39 n.242, 45 n.282, 110, 111 n.2, 374–5
Burcot, 20 n.101, 40 n.252, 42 n.262, 145–6, 404–5
Burford, 18, 24 n.138, 57 n.377, 111–12, 172 n.2, 225 n.2, 375–378
Burnett, Richard, 133, 134 n.2, 397
Burnley, James, 121, 384
Burrough, Charles, 297, 298 n.2
Burton, Frederick, 86, 87, 88 n.2, 462
Buss, Harold, 332, 333 n.2, 580
Butler, Frederick, 54, 537, 538 n.2
Butler, Mrs, 270
Buxton, Harold, 449, 450 n.2

Cadmore End, 23, 24 n.131, 26, 29 n.182, 112–14, 192 n.2, 319 n.2
Caldicott, Arthur, 314
Callis, Arthur, 519, 520 n.2
Carberry, Lady, 493
Carlyle, Alexander, 234, 235 n.2, 487
Carr, Benjamin, 317, 318 n.2, 564, 565
Carter, James, 194, 195 n.2
Carter, William, 277, 278 n.2
Cassington, 17 n.86, 25 n.146, 29 n.184, 38 n.234,
Cave, Mr, 246
Caversfield, 163 n.2, 379–80
Caversham, 4, 8, 21 n.112, 26 n.154, 28 n.175, 29 n.183, 115–17, 566 n.1

Chadlington, 12 n.56, 27 n.159, 29 n.179, n.180, 42 n.261, 54 n.352, 56 n.368, 59 n.397, 118–19, 381–3, 420 n.1, 504 n.1
Chalgrove, 43 n.266, 117–18, 224, 380–1, 473
Champion, George, 207, 465
Charlbury, 12, 27 n.159, 29, 42 n.261, 54 n.352, 56, 59 n.397, 118–19, 381–3
Charlton-on-Otmoor, 25 n.141, 26 n.151, 37 n.229, 58 n.383, 119–121, 383–4, 486
Charterville, 219 n.3
Chastleton, 32 n.202, 43 n.266, 121, 384–5
Checkendon, 30 n.188, 33 n.211, 122–3, 385–6, 540
Chesterton, 28 n.168, 32, 44, 48 n.302, 51 n.330, 123–4, 386–7
Chilson, 118, 381–3
Chinnery, Mr, 164
Chinnor, 7 n.25, 11, 13, 25 n.139, 57, 58 n.387, 124–5, 139, 387–8, 401, 412
Chipping Norton, 4, 14, 20 n.105, 21, 27 n.159, n. 161, 43 n.269, 55, 58 n.384, 59 n.396, 60 n.402, 125–6, 388–91, 539 n.2
Cholmondeley, Charles, 69, 341
Church Army, 430, 552, 587
Church Association, 146
Church of England Friendly Society, 102, 133
Church of England Men's Society, 28–9, 52 n.341, 80, 86, 88, 98, 101, 116, 119, 130, 131, 141, 155, 169, 172, 178, 181, 189, 211, 213, 219, 228, 248, 249, 254, 262, 263, 264, 265, 288, 291, 294, 298, 302, 313, 330, 331, 333, 468, 503, 587
Church of England Temperance Society, 27, 170 n.2
Church Lads' Brigade, 27, 119, 126, 202, 213, 357, 382, 587
Church Missionary Society, 30–2, 36, 39, 40, 148 n.2, 161, 162, 172, 176, 182, 187, 201, 205, 211, 223, 233, 235, 237 n.2, 239, 253 n.2, 256, 259, 260 n.2, 273, 275 n.2, 282, 301, 309, 317, 523, 587
Churchill, 6 n.18, 28 n.169, 32 n.205, 44 n.271, 134, 272–3, 397, 522
Clanfield, 32 n.201, 40 n.250, 126–7, 391–2
Clarendon, Owen, 192, 193 n.2, 453
Clark, Mrs, 155
Claydon, 6 n.18, 16, 17 n.78, 19 n.97, 20 n.105, 22 n.114, 25, 29 n.185, 103 n.2, 127–9, 231 n.2, 288 n.2, 369, 392–3
Clayton, Horace, 246, 247 n.2
Cleaver, Charles, 115, 116 n.2, 565, 566 n.2
Cleeve, 426
Clifton, 144, 145
Clifton Hampden, 6 n.18, 12 n.55, 129–30, 394
Clinton, Fynes, 563
Coggs, 26 n.154, 35 n.219, 57, 130–1, 395–6
Coles, Canon, 494
Colonial and Continental Church Society, 30, 223, 587
Colson, Francis, 186, 188 n.2, 443
Combe, 12 n.51, 49, 52 n.341, 56 n.365, 131–3, 396–7
Coombes, Herbert, 40, 193, 194 n.2, 222
Cooper, Herbert, 195, 19 6 n.2, 456
Cooper, Sydney, 184, 185 n.2, 441
Cornwell, 22 n.119, 40 n.247, 133–4, 278 n.2, 397–8
Cote, 21 n.111, 83–4, 353–4
Cottisford, 7, 134–5, 398, 431
Cowley, 4, 22, 41, 47 n.296, 48, 60 n.406, n.408, 91 n.2, 135–6, 399–400
Cowley St John, 8, 21 n.112, 26 n.150, 136–7, 163 n.2, 207 n.2, 400
Cox, Ernest, 10, 39, 258, 260 n.2, 510
Crawley, 37 n.228, 39 n.240, 169–70, 428–9
Crays Pond, 426
Cropredy, 36 n.223, 45, 137–8, 266 n.2, 400–1
Crowell, 58 n.386, 59 n.394, 138–9, 401–2
Crowther, Francis, 79, 81 n.2, 513, 514 n.1
Crowmarsh Gifford, 33 n.210, 139–41, 168 n.2
Cruran, Fr, 563

Cuddesdon, 28 n.166, 29 n.178, 51 n.331, 60, 142 n.2, 225 n.2, 402–3
   College, 34–6, 87 n.2, 101 n.2, 130 n.2, 163 n.2, 180 n.2, 185 n.2, 186 n.2, 192 n.2, 199 n.2, 221 n.2, 255, 277 n.2, 288 n.2, 387 n.1, 410 n.2, 420 n.1, 446 n.1, 447 n.1, 452 n.1, 460 n.1, 491 n.1, 496 n.1, 526 n.1, 583 n.2
Culham, 24 n.135, 58 n.386, 142–3, 216 n.2, 527, 528 n.1
Curry, William, 323, 324 n.2, 570
Cuxham, 143–4, 403

Dale, John, 446, 447 n.1
Dams, Allen, 167, 168 n.2, 426
Dangerfield, George, 349, 351 n.1, 413
Davenport, Edward, 292, 293 n.2
Davenport, Mrs, 292
Davey Biggs, Charles, 31 n.191, 254, 256 n.2, 508
Davidson, Lionel, 289, 290 n.2
Davidson, Mrs, 289
Davis, Francis, 138, 139 n.2, 401
Davson, Herman, 112, 114 n.2
Davys, Douglas, 322, 323 n.2, 569
De Coetlogon, Charles, 431, 432 n.1
Deddington, 44 n.274, 87 n.2, 103 n.2, 127 n.2, 144–5, 266 n.2, 404, 442
Devonshire, Duke of, 38, 578 n.1
Didcot, 426, 510
Dodd, Joseph, 152, 153 n.2, 415
Dorchester, 20 n.101, 40 n.252, 42 n.262, 145–6, 404–5
Dorchester Missionary College, 24, 39, 94, 105 n.2, 408 n.1
Doyne, Philip, 91, 92 n.2, 434, 435 n.1
Draper, William, 212, 214 n.2, 469
Drayton, 24 n.135, 26 n.157, 31 n.196, 40, 146–8, 405–6
Drayton St Leonard, 39, 46, 48, 49 n.312, 51, 60 n.400, 406–8
Ducklington, 20 n.102, 23 n.129, 26 n.154, 40 n.250, 50 n.321, 56 n.367, 148–9, 408–9, 483
Dummelow, John, 476, 477 n.1
Duncan, George, 48, 526, 527 n.2

Duns Tew, 20 n.103, 40 n.254, 42 n.257, 43 n.268, 149–50, 410–11
Dunsden, 56, 409, 410 n.2

Edwards, William, 175, 176 n.2, 432
Edwards, Mrs, 176
Elizabeth, Sister, 251
Elkington, William, 150, 151 n.2, 411
Elphick, William, 56, 525, 526 n.1,
Elsfield, 34 n.214, 150–1, 411
Elwes, Albert, 160, 161 n.2
Ewles, Mrs, 161
Emeris, William, 111, 112 n.2, 375
Emmet, Mr, 550
Emmington, 45 n.284, 56 n.365, 59 n.394, 412
Enstone, 11, 25, 26 n.156, 32 n.204, 45 n.279, 51 n.331, 59, 60 n.404, 151–2, 412–4
Epwell, 14 n.66, 43 n.267, 55 n.363, 279–80, 530–1
Espinasse, Richard, 320, 321 n.2, 464, 465 n.1, 568
Espinasse, Mrs, 24, 320
Evangelical Alliance, 30, 301, 588
Evans-Pritchard, Thomas, 316, 317 n.2
Every, Bishop Edward, 32, 123
Ewelme, 7 n.25, 10, 28 n.172, 32 n.204, 54, 60 n.401, 152–3, 415–16
Eynsham, 153–4, 416

Faithfull, Charles, 42, 268, 518
Farr, Charles, 53, 474, 475 n.1
Farringdon, Little, 18 n.96, 22 n.114, 38 n.235, 49, 50 n.321, 59 n.391, 154–5, 417
Fathers, George, 216
Fawler, 23 n.124, 26 n.151, 30 n.189, 36 n.224, 44 n.275, 45 n.284, 56 n.357, 160–1, 419–20
Fedden, Lorenzo, 143, 144 n.2
Fewcott, 16, 26 n.151, 37 n.230, 38, 41 n.256, 155–6, 345, 417–18, 422
Field, Clive, 3, 52 n.336, n.337, 54 n.358
Field, John, 93, 95 n.2
Field, Thomas, 118, 419, 420 n.2
Fifield, 18 n.91, 157–8, 418–19

Filkins, 25 n.142, 32 n.202, 109, 158–9, 373–4
Finmere, 7 n.28, 38 n.234, 134–5, 159–60, 398, 419
Finstock, 23 n.124, 26 n.151, 30 n.189, 36 n.224, 44 n.275, 45 n.284, 56 n.367, 160–1, 419–20
Fisher, William, 200, 201 n.2, 460
Fitzjohn, Thomas, 233, 234 n.2
Floyd, Thomas, 117, 118 n.2, 380
Forest Hill, 161–2, 538
Formby, Charles, 97, 98 n.2, 364
Foscott, 418
Foster, Francis, 301, 302 n.2, 551
Fothergill Robinson, William, 366, 368, 470
Fowler, Hugh, 101, 102 n.2, 368
Fox, John, 215, 216 n.2, 471
Freeborn, Albert, 197, 199 n.2, 457
Freeland, 8, 39 n.243, 43 n.265, 45 n.282, 162–3, 420–1
Freeman, Earnest, 230, 231 n.2, 483
Fringford, 56 n.370, 59 n.389, 163–4, 421–2
Fritwell, 31, 50, 156, 164–5, 422–3
Fulbrook, 18, 24 n.138, 57 n.377, 111–12, 375–6
Fulford, Henry, 139, 140 n.2

Garsington, 25 n.144, 44 n.275, 165–6, 423–4
Germon, Nicholas, 83, 84 n.2, 353
Gibbs, Reginald, 129, 130 n.2, 394
Gibson, Bishop Edmund, 1
Gilbert, Thomas, 42, 238, 240 n.2, 491
Gilkes, Arthur, 498, 499 n.1
Gillmor, Andrew, 37, 92, 93 n.2, 361
Girdlestone, Charles, 38, 211, 212 n.2, 468
Girls Friendly Society, 27–8, 44, 70, 73, 75, 80, 97, 104, 109, 119, 123, 131, 134, 140, 141, 148, 150, 157, 161, 172, 173, 176, 178, 181, 193, 196, 197, 202, 207, 211, 234, 244, 246, 248, 262, 271, 273, 285, 294, 302, 306, 308, 328, 330, 357, 588
Glympton, 12 n.55, 14 n.67, 47, 55 n.364, 59 n.396, 62, 158 n.2, 166–7, 424–5
Godington, 46 n.289, 425
Goldingham, Philip, 326, 327 n.2

Goldring, Arthur, 214, 215 n.2
Goodwin, Harry, 81, 82 n.2, 351
Gore, Bishop Charles, 1, 2, 10, 12, 13 n.60, 20, 21 n.107, 27 n.163, 30, 45, 52, 58, 59, 61, 63, 518 n.2
Goring, 26 n.156, 54, 56 n.366, 167–9, 426–8
Gregory, Adrian, 4 n.13, 48 n.305, n.307, 49, 52, 54 n.358, 55 n.362
Gresswell, Henry, 319, 320 n.2, 566
Griffiths, Alfred, 482, 483 n.1
Grimley, Matthew, 63
Gulley, Henry, 442
Gutch, A., 111
Gwilliam, Samuel, 170, 171 n.2, 429
Gwillim Rev G., 246

Hack, Bartle, 257, 258 n.2, 509
Haig, Arthur, 333, 334 n.2
Haig, Mrs, 333
Hailey, 37 n.228, 39 n.240, 169–170, 428
Haines, George, 451, 452 n.1
Hainsworth, Thomas, 104, 105 n.2, 370, 403
Hall, Frederic, 38, 56, 278, 279 n.2, 528
Hall, George, 261, 262 n.2, 513
Hall, Rev H. R., 246, 263, 264 n.2, 514, 574
Hamilton, Benjamin, 38, 41, 155, 156 n.2
Hamilton, Mrs, 156
Hampton Poyle, 9 n.35, 39 n.244, 45, 170–1, 199 n.2, 429
Hanborough, 28 n.169, 29 n.178, 31 n.191, 75 n.2, 171–2
Hanbourgh, Church, 171
Hanborough, Long, 171
Hanwell, 17, 31 n.194, 48 n.311, 56 n.374, 172–4, 430–1
Harding, Alfred, 284, 286 n.2, 534
Hardwick, 7 n.28, 20 n.102, 23 n.129, 26 n.154, 40 n.250, 50 n.321, 56 n.367, 134–5, 148–9, 398, 408–9, 431
Harper, Archdeacon, 209
Harpsden, 37 n.230, 38 n.236, 40 n.247, 174–5, 431–2
Harris, William, 39, 110, 375
Harriss, James, 236, 237 n.2, 489
Haseley, Great, 23 n.129, 175–6, 432–3
Hawes, Bernard, 520, 521 n.1

Hay, Robert, 546, 547 n.1
Headington, 8, 13 n.58, 22 n.118, 42 n.262, 176–7, 187, 188 n.1, 433–4
Headington. Quarry, 19 n.98, 28 n.169, n.175, 42, 177–9, 434–5
Hearn, Frank, 461, 462 n.2
Henley-on-Thames, 4, 8 n.32, 9, 17 n.85, 18 n.93, 21 n.113, 22, 26 n.149, n.152, 32, 50 n.234, 56 n.366, 179–80, 189, 267, 277, 325, 435–7
Henley Holy Trinity, 21, 23 n.130, 24 n.138, 29, 50 n.326, 53 n.346, 181–2, 437–8
Hensley, Henry, 307, 308 n.2
Herring, George, 7
Hethe, 11 n.47, 22, 39, 60 n.405, 182–3, 439
Heurtley, Charles, 96, 97 n.2, 363
Hewlett, Edward, 343, 344 n.1
Heyford, Lower, 25 n.143, 48 n.306, 55, 153 n.2, 183–4, 440
Heyford, Upper, 16, 55, 184–5, 348, 440, 441
Heythrop, 22 n.116, 37 n.229, 85–6, 442
Highfield, 11, 24 n.136, 32, 59, 186–8, 433, 443
Highmore, 22 n.117, 26 n.151, 32, 182, 188–9, 444, 540
Highton, Alfred, 53, 88, 89 n.2, 357
Hinksey, New, 7 n.24, 43 n.268, 48 n.304, 324 n.2, 444–6, 503
Hinksey, North, 20 n.105, 36 n.224, 37 n.228, 446–7
Hinksey, South, 7 n.24, 43 n.268, 48 n.304, 324 n.2, 444–6
Hoggins, Albany, 127, 129 n.2, 392
Holbrooke, Sydney, 264, 265 n.2
Holton, 8 n.29, 10 n.40, 15, 20 n.102, 24, 32, 189–90, 447–8
Holwell, 8 n.29, 59, 190–1, 448–9
Holywell, 240, 241, 253, 254
Holy Trinity Convent, 251, 256
Horley, 54 n.352, 449–50, 549 n.1
Horne, Edward, 165, 166 n.2, 423
Hornton, 54 n.352, 449–50, 549 n.1
Horspath, 12 n.52, 55 n.363, 451–2
Horton-cum-Studley, 14 n.64, 39 n.244, 191–2, 361, 452–3
Hudgell, Robert, 35, 395

Hughes, John, 188, 189 n.2, 444
Hughes, Thomas, 221, 222 n.2
Hulme, Walter, 311, 312 n.2
Hunt, Mary, 42,
Hunt, Robert, 29, 43, 70–1, 342
Hutchinson, Thomas, 290, 291 n.2, 540
Hutchinson, Mrs, 290,
Hutchison, Robert, 329, 577

Idbury, 18 n.91, 157–8, 418–9
Iffley, 11 n.47, 192–3, 453–4
Illingworth, Mrs, 444
Inge, Charles, 243–4, 497
Ipsden, 40 n.245, 50 n.323, 193–4, 454–5
Irwin, Charles, 302, 303 n.2, 552
Islip, 18 n.90, 24 n.136, 121 n.2, 194–5, 455–6, 481, 577

Jackson, Joseph, 84, 85 n.2
Jamaica Church Diocesan Association, 248
Jerram, Arnold, 202, 203 n.2
Jersey, Lady, 23, 213
Johnson, Edmund, 44, 272, 273 n.2, 522
Johnston, Charles, 177, 179 n.2
Johnston, Mrs, 178
Jones, Arthur, 56, 86, 87 n.2, 354
Jones, Maurice, 53, 516, 518 n.1

Kane, Thomas, 544, 545 n.1
Kelmscot, 18 n.95, 103–4, 369
Kencot, 25, 26 n.148, 31 n.194, 36 n.227, 104, 195–6, 456–7
Ketchlee, Thomas, 235, 236 n.2, 488
Kidd, Beresford, 250, 252 n.2, 504
Kiddington, 196–7, 414, 457
Kidlington, 26 n.154, 29 n.182, 33 n.212, 93, 127 n.2, 179 n.2, 197–9, 429, 457–8
Kidmore End, 32 n.202, 36 n.224, 42 n.261, 57, 199–200, 357 n.1, 459–60
Kilburn, St Peter, 116, 131
King, Bishop Edward, 151
Kingham, 18 n.92, 30 n.190, 39 n.243, 40 n.251, 200–1, 460–1
Kingham Hill, 269, 345 n.1
King's Messengers, 30, 32, 79, 86, 88, 101, 104, 116, 119, 145, 153, 168, 169, 179, 180, 185, 193, 225, 226, 256,

265, 274, 279, 295, 296, 307, 310, 334, 534, 588
Kirkby, John, 154, 155 n.2, 417
Kirkby, Marion, 155
Kirkby, Marsh, 315, 316 n.2, 562
Kirtlington, 16 n.74, 201–2
Knight, Frances, 5 n.15, 6 n.23, 15, 26 n.156
Knowles, Maurice, 298, 299 n.2

Lambert-Baker, William, 541, 542 n.1
Langdale-Smith, Arthur, 189, 190 n.2, 447
Langdale-Smith, Miss E., 190
Langdale-Smith, Rev E., 190
Langford, 27 n.159, 202–3, 461–2
Launton, 31 n.193, 46 n.288, 58 n.382, 203–4, 462
Leafield, 11, 18 n.89, 42 n.257, 49 n.314, 204–5, 462–3
Lebombo Mission, 214, 243
Lee, Thomas, 204, 205 n.2, 462
Lennard, Vivian, 183, 184 n.2, 440
Leathley, Mr, 281
Lewknor, 9 n.39, 24 n.132, 25, 33, 55, 60, 205–6, 320, 464–5, 568
Littledale, Godfrey, 125, 126 n.2, 539
Littlemore, 28 n.172, 43 n.268, 47 n.295, 58 n.58, 71 n.2, 207–8, 465–6
Lloyd, William, 444, 446 n.2
Load, Frederic, 293, 294 n.2, 542
Lovett, Thomas, 286, 287 n.2, 536, 584, 585 n.2
Lyan, Miss V. E., 240
Lyneham, 217

Malleson, John, 309, 311 n.2, 560, 561
Maltby, Maurice, 137, 138 n.2
Mann, Gother, 157, 418,
Mansfield, Joseph, 105, 106 n.2, 371
Mapledurham, 24, 28, 31, 38, 42, 44, 50 n.326, 57 n.375, 60 n.403, 208–10, 466–7
Maritzburg Mission, 263
Marlborough, Duke of, 38, 50, 88 n.2, 578 n.1
Marriot, Frank, 331, 332 n.2, 578
Marston, 24, 27 n.160, 29, 32, 57 n.377, 58 n.383, 107 n.2, 210–11, 467–8

New, 210–11
Old, 210–11
Maul, John, 179, 180 n.2
May, George, 201, 202 n.2
Meredith, John, 164, 165 n.2, 422
Meredith Brown, Stafford, 58, 163, 164 n.2, 421,
Merry, Walter, 249, 250 n.2,
Merton, 7, 32 n.201, 38, 211–12, 468–9
Meyrick, Cyril, 582, 583 n.2
Middleton Stoney, 18, 23, 27 n.159, 28, 29 n.176, n.178, 40 n.254, 42 n.257, 44 n.275, 58 n.387, 60 n.411, 212–14, 440, 469–70
Middleton Park, 23, 213
Milcombe, 9 n.39, 25 n.144, 32 n.200, 214–15, 367, 368 n.1, 470–1
Miller, Thomas, 268, 269 n.2
Miller, William, 203, 204 n.2
Mills, Mr, 209
Milton, Great, 215–16, 471–2
Milton, Little, 18 n.89, 20 n.103, 49 n.313, 57 n.378, 216, 472–3
Milton-under-Wychwood, 17, 26 n.153, 40 n.246, 52 n.340, 53 n.347, 217–18, 473
Minchin, Charles, 329, 331 n.2
Minster Lovell, 25 n.139, 36 n.226, 53, 218–19, 361 n.1, 453, 474–5
Missions to Seamen, 38, 40, 194 n.2, 578 n.2
Mixbury, 219–20, 475–6
Mollington, 17 n.82, 26 n.156, 33 n.210, 37 n.230, 58 n.388, 220–1, 476–7
Mongewell, 221–2, 454
Moon, Cecil, 185, 186 n.2
Moore, George, 135, 136 n.2, 399
Morgan, John, 172, 174 n.2, 430
Morris, Margaret, 44
Morris, William, 303, 304 n.2, 553
Mortimer, John, 210, 211 n.2, 467
Mothers' Union, 27–8, 44, 73, 80, 86, 98, 102, 109, 115, 153, 157, 172, 173, 176, 181, 197, 207, 209, 225, 233, 265, 266, 303, 313, 316, 467, 550, 588
Moxon, Leonard, 279, 280 n.2, 530
Munn, John, 122, 123 n.2, 385
Murcott, 120

Nash, Frederick, 39, 169, 170 n.2, 428
National Society, 16, 23, 80, 87, 117, 178, 180, 435, 524
Neate, Walter, 71, 72 n.2,
Negus, Albert, 161, 162 n.2, 289
Nettlebed, 30 n.190, 43 n.270, 222–3, 477
Newington, 9 n.37, 24, 56, 223–5, 478–9
    House, 60
Newington, North, 108
Newington, South, 17 n.82, n.86, 225–6, 480
Newton Purcell, 226–7, 480–1
Nind, Hubert, 291, 292 n.2, 541
Nixon, Mr, 255, 289
Noke, 227, 329, 481, 577
Norris, Charles, 44, 123, 124 n.2
Northleigh, 25, 36, 228–9, 482
Northmoor, 14, 21 n.110, 229–30, 271, 482–3
North Stoke, 40 n.245, 50 n.323, 193–4, 222, 454–5
Norton, Hook, 7, 9 n.36, 17, 31, 35 n.220, 57 n.378, 230–1, 483–4
Norton, Over, 391
Nuffield, 6 n.21, 10 n.41, 23 n.127, 36 n.223, 59 n.394, 231–2, 290, 484–6
Nuneham Courtnay, 10 n.40, 26 n.153, 43 n.270, 232–3, 486
Nutt, John, 174, 175 n.2

Obelkevich, James, 5, 26 n.156,
Oddington, 37 n.228, 39, 233–4, 486–7
Oldfield, William, 142, 143 n.2, 295, 527, 528 n.1
O'Reilly, Walter, 95, 96 n.2, 362, 379, 380 n.2
O'Rorke, Henry, 38, 578
Owen, Edward, 374, 375 n.1
Oxford, 1, 2, 4, 6, 7, 8, 9, 10, 21, 22, 36, 41, 46, 60, 137, 156, 193, 241, 244, 251, 264n.2, 416, 445, 487, 489, 490, 494, 501, 503, 510–11, 547,
    Holy Trinity, 10, 23 n.122, 29 n.184, 39, 43 n.267, 46, 49, 258–60, 313 n.2, 510–11
    All Saints cum St Martins, 16, 22 n.116, 179 n.2, 234–5, 262 n.2, 487–8

St Aldate, 8, 57 n.378, 235–6, 488–9
St Andrew, 10, 16, 31 n.199, 40 n.247, 58 n.387, 236–7, 489–90
St Barnabas, 8 n.31, 22, 35 n.219, 49, 88 n.3, 237–8, 490–1
St Clement, 12, 18 n.93, 26 n.150, 29 n.184, 42 n.262, 211 n.2, 238–40, 491–3
St Cross, 12, 19, 50 n.329, 53 n.344, 60 n.404, 240–1, 493–5
St Ebbe, 22, 46, 241–2, 495
St Frideswide, 6 n.19, 9 n.34, 14, 26 n.150, 29 n.181, 30 n.190, 53 n.344, 54 n.351, 242–3, 495–7
St Giles, 19 n.98, 43 n.270, 55 n.359, 243–4, 497–8
St Margaret, 9 n.34, 31 n.199, 60 n.410, 245–6, 498, 521 n.2
St Mary Magdalen, 21 n.112, 36 n.227, 42 n.261, 58 n.385, 60 n.410, 118 n.2, 136 n.2, 246–7, 498–9
St Mary the Virgin, 22 n.116, 29 n.176, 38, 247–8, 499–502
St Matthew, 7 n.28, 11, 48 n.307, n.311, 248–9, 502–3
St Michael, 22 n.116, 29 n.183, 47, 48, 249–50, 503–4
St Paul, 8 n.31, 16, 55 n.364, 250–2, 504–5
St Peter le Bailey, 7 n.28, 252–3, 264 n.2, 505–6
St Peter in the East, 28–9, 42, 50, 52 n.338, 56 n.373, 253–4, 506–7
St Philip and St James, 8, 17, 21 n.111, 25 n.144, 28, 29 n.182, 31, 50, 53 n.348, 79 n.2, 189 n.2, 254–6, 298 n.2, 349, 508–9
St Thomas, 6 n.19, 8 n.31, 10, 11, 24 n.138, 26 n.155, 30, 32 n.205, 192 n.2, 257–8, 509–10
Oxford Mission to Calcutta, 30, 163, 172, 215

Paget, Bishop Francis, 323
Paget, Cecil, 378, 379 n.1
Paget, Innes, 42
Palmer, William, 45, 151, 152 n.2, 412
Parr, Willoughby, 158, 159 n.2
Parsons, Bertram, 334, 335 n.2, 583

Patten, Basil, 219, 220 n.2
Payne, Edward, 130, 131 n.2
Payne, Julius, 118, 119 n.2, 381
Payne, Mrs, 131
Peake, Vincent, 369, 547, 549 n.1
Pearce, Stephen, 131, 133 n.2, 396
Pendavis, Whylock, 39, 182, 183 n.2, 439
Pendlebury, John, 24, 223, 225, 478
Pendlebury, Mrs, 24
Pengelly, Rev C., 178
Penrice, Charles, 420, 421 n.1
Penyston, William, 417, 418
Perry Gore, George, 304, 305 n.2, 554
Pettifor, John, 581, 582 n.2
Piddington, 58 n.388, 260-1, 511-12, 565
Pishill, 261-2, 513
Pocock, Theodore, 425
Potter, Pearson, 308, 309 n.2, 559
Poyntz, Nathaniel, 42, 145, 146 n.2-4, 404
Prior, Charles, 119, 121 n.2, 383
Protestant Reform Society, 39, 74 n.2
Pullan, Edward, 245, 498
Purdue, George, 220, 221 n.2
Pyrton, 27 n.160-1, 29 n.177, 32 n.200, 53, 58 n.386, 262, 263 n.2, 513-14, 529

Radford, 414
Radley, 52, 155 n.2, 266 n.2, 474
Rainey, James, 190, 191 n.2, 448
Ramsden, 16 n.76, 29 n.176, 50 n.323, 263-4, 514-15, 574
Rand, Ebenezer, 532, 533 n.2
Read, William, 271, 272 n.2, 452
Reading, 4, 188 n.2, 199, 426, 443, 533 n.1
Red Cross, 365, 372, 386, 430, 450 n.2, 451
Richards, William, 40, 274, 275 n.2
Riddelsdell, Harry, 325, 326 n.2, 573
Riddle, Arthur, 306, 307 n.2, 555
Roberts, Ernest, 538
Roberts, Lawrence, 34, 73, 74 n.2,
Roberts, William, 108, 109 n.2, 158, 373
Robson, Herbert, 199, 200 n.2
Rodwell, George, 46, 82, 83 n.2, 352
Rollright, Great, 29 n.177, 264, 265 n.2
Rotherfield Greys, 11, 29 n.183, 39 n.239, 42, 52 n.341, 181-2, 265-6, 437-8, 515-16

Rotherfield Peppard, 12, 15, 21 n.106, 39 n.243, 40 n.252, 43 n.265, 45 n.283, 53 n.348, 59 n.393, 267, 516-18
Rousham, 7, 10, 42, 268, 518-19
Rowley, James, 283, 284 n.2
Rudd, Eric, 281, 282 n.2
Russell, Mrs, 158

Salford, 6 n.17, 26 n.157, 44, 48, 62 n.416, 268-9, 519-20
Sandford-on-Thames, 15, 21 n.110, 271-2, 521-2
Sandford St Martin, 34 n.214, 49, 56 n.365, 270-1, 359, 520-1,
Sarsden, 6 n.18, 28, 32, 44, 272-3, 522-4
Saunders, Sidney, 318, 319 n.2, 435, 437 n.1
Sawyer, Herbert, 166, 167 n.2, 424,
Sawyer, William, 545, 546 n.2
Scott, Alfred, 136, 137 n.2, 400
Scott, Sidney, 39, 486, 487 n.1
Scripture Union, 26, 269, 588
Seaton, James, 141, 142 n.2, 402
Secker, Bishop Thomas, 1, 2 n.3, n.6
Sharpe, William, 321, 322 n.2, 569
Shebbeare, Charles, 299, 301 n.2, 549
Shelswell, 226-7, 480-1
Shenington, 17 n.85, 18 n.93, 22, 54, 273-4, 524,
Shifford, 83
Shildrick, Alfred, 217, 218 n.2, 473
Shilton, 36 n.226, 40, 85 n.2, 274-5
Shiplake, 19, 40 n.250, 56, 275-7, 525-6
Shipton-on-Cherwell, 48, 49 n.318, 50, 526-7
Shipton-under-Wychwood, 45, 56 n.370, 209, 277-8, 527-8
Shirburn, 39, 56, 278-9, 528-30
Shore, Harrington, 98, 99 n.2, 364
Shorthampton, 118, 383, 504 n.1
Shutford, 14 n.66, 20 n.104, 33 n.210, 43 n.269, 124 n.2, 298-9, 547-9
Sibford Gower, 14, 43 n.267, 55 n.263, 279-80, 530-1
Skrine, John, 52, 253, 254 n.2, 306, 506
Skrine, Mary, 42
Sloane, James, 558, 559 n.1
Smith, Albert, 40 n.254, 149, 150 n.2, 410

Smith, Alfred, 47, 503, 504 n.1
Smith, John, 218, 219 n.2, 360, 452, 453 n.1
Smith-Masters, John, 356, 357 n.1
Society for Promoting Christian Knowledge, 93, 134, 170, 173, 235 n.2, 295, 296, 317
Society for the Propagation of the Gospel, 30–2, 73, 79, 88, 93, 96, 98, 109, 116, 122, 125, 131, 134, 146, 157, 161, 162, 168, 170, 176, 180, 182, 187, 189, 198, 204 n.2, 205, 205, 209, 215, 218 n.2, 219 n.2, 220, 233, 252, 256, 258, 263, 265, 266, 271, 274, 276, 281, 282, 287, 288, 296, 301, 309, 310, 311 n.2, 312, 317, 320, 325, 330, 333, 334 n.2, 588
Somerton, 18 n.89, 31 n.198, 50 n.325, 280–1, 531–2
Sonning Common, 459
Souldern, 6 n.21, 281–2
Southleigh, 13 n.58, 20 n.104, 282–3, 532–3
Spelsbury, 14, 22 n.115, 23, 25 n.147, 31, 56, 283–4, 533–4
Spendlove, William, 40, 146, 148 n.2, 405
Stadhampton, 28 n.171, 224, 284–6, 478, 479, 534–6
Standage, Samuel, 102, 103 n.2, 369
Standlake, 49 n.315, 55 n.359, 56 n.370, 233 n.2, 286–7, 536–7, 585
Stansfield, John, 46, 241, 242 n.2, 495, 505, 506 n.1
Stanton Harcourt, 32 n.200, 35 n.220, 54, 143 n.2, 287–8, 537–8
Stanton St John, 44 n.275, 60 n.411, 162, 289–90, 538–9
Statham, Sherard, 134, 135 n.2, 398, 431
Stephen, Simon, 35, 89, 90 n.2, 359
Sterling, Kelsey, 34
Stevenson, Miss, 444
Stoke Lyne, 539
Stoke Row, 9, 10 n.42, 31 n.198, 48, 290–1, 540
Stoke, South, 16 n.77, 21 n.110, 33 n.211, 50 n.326, 291–2, 541
Stoke Talmage, 24 n.132, 31, 59 n.390, 292–3, 529, 541–2
Stokenchurch, 20 n.103, 31 n.198, 48 n.307, 59 n.392, 293–4, 542–4

Stonesfield, 17, 19, 24 n.137, 32, 39 n.242, 294–7, 544–5
Stratton Audley, 60 n.400, 545–6
Sturgiss, Thomas, 106, 107 n.2, 371
Summertown, 26, 41, 58 n.387, 60 n.402, 245 n.2, 297–8, 329 n.2, 504 n.1, 546–7
Swalcliffe, 14, 20 n.104, 33 n.210, 43 n.269, 124 n.2, 298–9, 547–9
Swerford, 30, 54, 299–301, 549–551
Swinbrook, 301–2, 551–2
Swyncombe, 17 n.86, 47 n.294, 302–3, 552–3
Sydenham, 29 n.183, 33 n.210, 44, 303–4, 412, 553–4
Sydenham, Edward, 328, 576–7
Symes-Thompson, Francis, 287, 288 n.2

Tackley, 25 n.140, n.147, 32 n.200, 40 n.248, 50 n.324, 304–5, 554–5
Tadmarton, 6, 11 n.49, 24 n.132, 25, 27 n.162, 44 n.276, 60 n.401, 306–7, 555–8
Tanner, Thomas, 56, 533, 534 n.1
Taynton, 33, 112 n.2, 307–8, 558–9
Tetsworth, 30 n.189, 58 n.382, 308–9, 559–60, 570
Tew, Great, 16 n.77, 309–11, 560–1
Tew, Little, 9 n.36, 10 n.42, 17, 36 n.226, 278 n.2, 311–12, 561
Thackeray, Francis, 38, 42, 208, 210 n.2
Thackeray, Miss E. K., 208–9
Thame, 21, 24 n.136, 26, 46 n.288, 60 n.211, 312–13, 561–2
Thorp, Henry, 227,
Tiddington, 343
Tidmarsh, George, 260, 261 n.2, 511
Tombe, Rev G., 561
Townsend, Raymond, 472, 473 n.1
Townson, Robert, 8, 42, 176, 177 n.2
Tremenheere, George, 495, 497 n.1
Tristram, Christopher, 148, 149 n.2, 408
Trotter, Henry, 324, 325 n.2
Trower, Henry, 159, 160 n.2, 419
Turner, Joseph, 229, 230 n.2
Tusmore, 431
Tyndale, Rev C. E., 190
Tyrwhitt, Cecil, 51, 90, 91 n.2, 359

Universities Mission to Central Africa, 30, 53, 89, 91, 122, 144, 172, 180, 198, 243, 247, 252, 258, 272, 283, 298, 328, 588
Unsworth, Reece, 575, 576 n.1

Verey, Cecil, 100, 101 n.2

Wake, Bishop William, 1
Walde, Cornelius, 347, 348 n.1
Walford, Charles, 74, 75 n.2, 345
Walford, Julia, 44, 346
Walker, Rev E., 508
Wallingford, 140
Walton, Mr, 562
Wantage, 1, 127
Warborough, 40 n.251, 58 n.384, 314
Ward, George, 114, 115 n.2
Ward, Miss, 289
Ward, William, 76, 77 n.2, 346
Wardington, 18 n.92, 32 n.201, 56 n.367, 315–16, 562–4
Warner, Henry, 454, 455 n.2
Waterperry, 174, 316–17, 564–5
Waterstock, 6 n.16, 7 n.27, 317–18, 565
Watkins, Oscar, 240, 241 n.2, 493
Watlington, 14 n.64, 36 n.223, 49 n.314, 58 n.387, 318–19, 371, 403, 437 n.1, 565, 566 n.1
Watson, James, 252, 253 n.2
Wendlebury, 23 n.127, 319–20, 566–7
West, Miss, 444
Weston-on-the-Green, 567–8,
Weston, South, 22 n.119, 24, 55, 320–1, 465, 568
Westwell, 22, 45, 321–2, 569
Wheatfield, 34 n.215, 322–3, 569–70
Wheatley, 45, 323–4, 447, 570–1
Wheeler, Henry, 345
Whitchurch, 7 n.24, 31 n.192, 35 n.219, 59 n.396, 324–5, 426, 571–3
Whitehead, Christopher, 225, 226 n.2, 480
Whittuck, Charles, 38, 247, 248 n.2, 499
Widford, 301–2, 551–2
Wigan, Herbert, 409, 410 n.2

Wiggington, 8, 48 n.307, 325–6, 573–4
Wilberforce, Bishop Samuel, 2
Wilcote, 574
Williams, John, 270, 271 n.2
Williams, Watkin, 39, 46, 406, 408 n.1
Williamson, Wilfred, 248, 249 n.2, 502
Willis, Rawdon, 53, 181, 182 n.2, 437
Willy, Rev, 431
Wilson, Ernest, 8, 162, 163 n.2
Wilson, Henry, 77, 78 n.2, 347
Wimberley, John, 205, 206 n.2
Witney, 1, 4, 6, 8 n.32, 19 n.98, 32 n.202, 47, 131, 159, 169, 204 n.2, 258 n.2, 326–7, 361, 416, 575–6
Wolvercote, 8, 328, 576–7
Wood, William, 42, 265, 266 n.2, 515
Wood Eaton, 39 n.239, 329, 577–8
Woodcote, 16 n.77, 21 n.110, 33 n.211, 50 n.326, 291–2, 426, 541
Woodstock, 22 n.120, 25 n.141, 38, 44 n.271, 56 n.365, 60 n.411, 329–331, 458, 578
Woolgrove, Kate, 311, 312 n.2
Wootton, 28, 331–2, 578–80
Worton, Nether, 332–3, 580
Worton, Over, 332–3, 580–1
Wright, Walter, 228, 229 n.2, 482
Wroxton, 333–4, 549, 581–2
Wychwood, 11 n.46, 18 n.89, 42, 49 n.314, 204–5, 462–3
Wyfold, 385
Wynter, Reginald, 282, 283 n.2
Wytham, 50 n.326, 582–3

Yarnton, 11 n.47, 56 n.367, 59 n.395, 334–5, 573 n.1, 583–4
Yates, Nigel, 7
Yelford, 49 n.315, 55 n.359, 286–7, 584–5
Young, Frank, 242, 243 n.2
Young Men's Christian Association, 244
Young Women's Christian Association, 223

Zanzibar Mission, 30, 89 n.2, 91 n.2, 258
Zenana Society, 289